Beautiful Souls

Beautiful Souls

by

Hal Eisenberg

Cover Illustration Copyright © 2020 by Jeslee Martinez

The author may be contacted at Hal@wooinc.org

ISBN: 978-0-9970143-3-4

Library of Congress Control Number: 2020945015

Published with the help of Peaceful Daily Publishing.
peacefuldailypublishing.com

Printed in the United States of America

First Edition

10 9 8 7 6 5 4 3 2 1

100% of the proceeds of Beautiful Souls will go to the mission, vision, and programs of Windows of Opportunity, Inc. (www. wooinc.org) and The Passion Centre, Inc. (www.thepassioncentre. com)

Windows of Opportunity has built and implemented the world's first and most comprehensive education system for raising 21st Century leaders and engineering a society that is going to support them.

Windows of Opportunity's vision is that the world becomes one healthy community through higher consciousness education. The systemic approach promotes healthy communication to encourage trust-based relationships, which supports acceptance of each other and reduces fear to create an expressive, open society. This leads to people connecting to and expanding their souls through a higher love consciousness, which helps people live optimal lives and supports others to do so as well.

The Passion Centre is a collective of amazing people finding and activating people's passions, building dreams, and creating optimized humans. **The Passion Centre** acts like a Passion Incubator; we help people from all walks and stages in life understand their PASSION and turn it into ACTION to move the world forward in a positive way.

Each of us has a dream in our heart that the world needs. There are gifts that lay dormant, and passions that are unexplored. At **The Passion Centre**, we believe people's dreams, gifts, and passions are the world's greatest hidden economic and social resource. To that end we have made it our mission to help you find your gifts, activate your passion, and build that dream that you have inside of you. It's only when we focus on that place do we truly service the world.

Dedication

Dedicated to those who bend, but do not break... and never back down....

To my "younger brother," Scott, who I always wanted to leave a legacy for... and a story that matters...

To all the beautiful souls who have taught me deep spiritual lessons, who have shared their energy and mutual experiences with me, and created the grateful man I am today.

Namaste.

Contents

Dedication vii

Acknowledgements.. xi

Prologue 5

Part I: The Becoming 7

Chapter 1: Ride the Wind................................... 9

Chapter 2: When the Children Cry...................... 19

Chapter 3: Inevitable Illusions............................. 31

Chapter 4: Goodbye to Romance 39

Chapter 5: The International Beer Club 49

Chapter 6: The Ghosts of Shattered Glass........... 69

Chapter 7: The Story Behind the Story............... 85

Chapter 8: November Rain 117

Chapter 9: On the Borrowed Sands of Time 143

Chapter 10: Midnight Confessions..................... 159

Chapter 11: Born to Be My Baby 185

Part II: The Reckoning................................... 201

Chapter 12: What a Wonderful World 203

Chapter 13: Southern Hospitality......................215

Chapter 14: Bottom's Up................................... 229

Chapter 15: 99 in the Shade.............................. 255

Chapter 16: Until Her Veins Run Dry............... 265

Chapter 17: I Finally Found Someone 277

Chapter 18: Are You a Tree? 293

Chapter 19: A Thin Line.................................... 303

Chapter 20: The Lights Went Out On Broadway 315

Chapter 21: Building Bridges 325

Chapter 22: Bridge Over Troubled Water.......... 339

Part III: The Rebirth **351**

Chapter 23: Too Late For Love 353

Chapter 24: Every Child Deserves a
Window of Opportunity 369

Chapter 25: Breaking the Habit 381

Chapter 26: Shine 391

Chapter 27: Red Tape and Sacrifice 407

Chapter 28: God Bless This Mess 427

Chapter 29: Alegría Espiritual 449

Chapter 30: Espera Un Poco 473

Chapter 31: Amen 499

Chapter 32: For Youth By Youth 519

Chapter 33: Adiós y vaya con dios 557

Part IV: The Awakening **621**

Chapter 34: The One that Got Away 622

Chapter 35: Higher Consciousness 634

Chapter 36: Refuse to Sink 664

Chapter 37: Keep the Faith 728

Chapter 38: Always Just Another Day 746

Chapter 39: This House is Not For Sale 830

Chapter 40: Carpe Diem 860

Chapter 41: You Gave Me Her 892

Chapter 42: Home 936

Chapter 43: Beautiful Souls 1052

Chapter 44: Epilogue 1080

About the Author 1090

About Windows of Opportunity 1092

About The Passion Centre 1094

Jeslee Martinez – Illustrator bio 1096

Acknowledgements

~

I think the most difficult part of writing this book, especially as a first time author, has to be sitting down and truly writing heartfelt acknowledgements. There are so many people I love and I am grateful for, that an entire book in itself could be written about the many souls who have graced my life. I love to write, and truth be told, I always felt I was pretty good at expressing myself in words. However, I have never attempted to write something of this magnitude or in this style before.

I have been journaling since I was a kid to try and work through my feelings and my confusion. This subsequently became the gift of awareness and growth to myself, as returning to these writings during later crossroads I faced, proved to be enlightening. Some evenings I would come home from a long day, and clearing my mind would consist of taking up to four hours just to write a social media post. Something in my day would inspire me, or teach me a lesson, and I wanted to share that with the world.

My hope has always been to come across as inspirational, impacting, and straight from my soul. Songs, poetry, posts, journaling, articles, and blogs… you name it, I have tried to write it all, EXCEPT a book! I always wanted to tackle the idea of writing a book, but never had the courage, confidence, comfort, nor the right mix of creativity and stories to write something that I felt would be worth releasing, as well as having something of substance to say. With some major changes in my life, combined with the decision to expand my personal mission and vision, I decided to take that leap, and finally stand in the light and be seen as I am.

This was a decision that did not come easy, as pulling back the veil of vulnerability so society can take a peek into my thoughts, my soul, my flaws, my hopes, my dreams, my struggles, my craziness, and my pain, is a scary place to be. The biggest fear I had to tackle was that of being judged as weak by the many who have often seen me as strong.

With that said, after much processing and prayer, it was clear to me on so many levels that it was time to lift the veil, see what lies beyond my limited vision of fear, and let my truth be expressed within this story. Fast forward from that revelation in my life a mere 2 years ago, it is very surreal that I am actually here, and actually completed this lifelong dream. It has been a cathartic journey that I am excited to share with all of you.

Before I get to the actual acknowledgments, I feel like I need to provide some clarification and a disclaimer. As I am sure you are aware of, often we see legal language provided in creative works such as: "Some names and identifying details have been changed to protect the privacy of individuals." Well, a statement like that must be inserted here, however, I feel the additional need to explain this with a little more detail and in my own thoughtful words. It does not make it easy that the flow of this book is in complete alignment with how I live my life… anything but normal! There is so much going on, and so much NOT going on in this book. From the start of this adventure, I have promoted Beautiful Souls as a "reality fiction," designed to tell "my story" through "my eyes" and "my opinions," and not necessarily reflecting the opinions of others. There are ALWAYS THREE sides to a story: my side, your side, and the truth.

Storytelling is a matter of perception.

It is very important, based on my own personal values and compassion for others, to consciously and intentionally leave lots of room to protect the innocent. I have never once wanted to tell **other people's stories**, especially when there are so many souls who have confided in me, trust me, and shared with me some of their deepest darkest secrets. That was never the purpose of my soul's journey through this process. However, there are so many "beautiful souls" that have impacted me profoundly, from whom I learned life-altering lessons from, that it would be quite impossible to pen a reality fiction without the philosophical representation of these relationships.

Some of the characters created in this book were inspired by beautiful souls that have graced my life, and many times I took some literary freedom and morphed the personalities of these inspirational souls into one powerful and dynamic character to grace these pages with poise, purpose, and an intended message. I may have taken a trait or something specific I liked about one person in reality, and made it the quality of a character within this book. So, yes! *Please keep in mind that any likeness is purely coincidental and often manipulated to share my own soul's truth in a way that I hope teaches a lesson and raises the vibration of hope for humanity.* Please keep in mind that even though names, characters, some businesses, places, and incidents are the products of my imagination and used in a fictitious manner, this is still a "reality fiction."

This is my personal journey of stories that have actually occurred in believable settings. This journey, and the experience faced in these chapters of my life, has been intensely real. In addition, the creation of fictional characters serves the purpose to react and interact similar with real people. This led to some freedom in creating plots that allowed me to explore the depths of my soul, my view on social events, my vision of the world or society around me, and the personal events that occurred along my journey.

The vision I had when I started writing Beautiful Souls was to express the experiences of my life through the stories and relationships that led me on a journey to the deeper parts of my soul and my spirituality. It was meant to be a search for a higher love consciousness and what that actually means from our human experience. After many painstaking days and evenings that led me to exhilarating and uplifting revelations, it is in my professional and personal opinion that I have achieved my goal. It is also my deep desire and prayer that the lessons laced throughout these pages impacts the readers' soul as well. If someone picks up this book 20 years from now and his or her life is transformed through its words, messages, and challenges, then my job is complete.

One thing I became very clear about within this journey is how blessed I am for the many relationships that inspired my reflections throughout these pages, and whom I share a true bond and a connection with. They are extremely rare and lovely relationships, ones that definitely shaped the man I have become today. Without sounding like a broken record, this was never meant to be a "tell all" book, but rather an opportunity for myself to "go as deep within as possible." I knew that I would discover so much about my own soul through writing Beautiful Souls, and that those lessons would help my life to become healthier, more optimal, and hopefully prepare me to experience that higher love consciousness I have been searching for.

I have the additional hope that sharing my perspectives with the world would also be inspiring enough that each reader would use these lessons to do their own self exploration. I challenge each of you to take that opportunity: to peel back the layers that make up the stories in your life. What is behind your tears, your smiles, your prayers, and your dreams? Who are you in terms of your values? What do you stand for? How are you showing up in this world from this day forward? These were the grappling questions that often swirled around my soul through the years, always leading me to pick up a pen in order to capture the insightful, intense and often overpowering energy behind the emotions going on in my own life.

In researching the backbone of this book, I sifted through miles and miles of written memories that were often laced with moments I had even forgotten about. It is my hope that I successfully captured an ebb and flow that did the lessons and blessings I desire to share with the world justice, showing an ounce of humility and a ton of gratitude, without offending anyone at all.

With all that said, there are many REAL people in my life that have my endless gratitude and need to be acknowledged properly. I truly want to get these "thank you's" 100% right! I do not want to forget anyone in my life, and there are simply so many people that I am indebted to eternally for their role during my journey, that I am sure it is inevitable that someone truly important to me will be mistakenly forgotten. Writing acknowledgements is honestly quite a nerve-wracking process that has kept me awake several evenings and has led to several edits.

Life would be incomplete without the occurrences in our day-to-day lives that drive our memories and our moments. With that being said I want to take this opportunity to mention from my heart and soul, with my deepest and best intentions, my gratitude for the countless souls that have graced my life. These precious souls know what they mean to me, and truth be told, after working with close to 300,000 families at the time this book was printed, and having so many incredible interactions with people on this planet, it would take volumes to thank everyone. As it is, I am pretty sure standard acknowledgements in a book are not supposed to be as long as I have written, but in an effort to stay in alignment with how I have always lived my life, I am going to "rewrite" that standard as well!

All I can say is that each and every one of you has my greatest and utmost respect from the depths of my heart. You are all beautiful souls in your own right, and I thank you for the gifts you bestowed upon my existence. There is simply no way to repay the love you have given to me. It is my universal wish that all of your dreams come true for yourself and your loved ones. The world is changing out there. Make each moment count, continuing to rise to your greatest potential. With that said, let's see if we can journey the sands of time and meet some of the beautiful souls that have graced my life:

As you will soon learn from some of the earlier chapters written, my childhood was not easy at all. Those early years felt like torture, but they also had a great share of smiles... and of laughs. ***Timmy, Paul "Pablo," and Jeffrey*** were the three buddies that shaped my younger years. Paul's older cousin holds a special place in my heart because he gave us the quintessential 80's dream of wanting to be deejays in order to follow in his successful footsteps, and I for one would spend hours in Paul's basement making mixed tapes. Rocker Hal on the turntables… talk about your juxtapositions! To this day, Paul was the funniest guy I ever met, and his humor brought light in the darkest moments. I never thanked him ever for the countless afternoons he saved me, and I am not sure he knows what he means to me to this day. Then, of course, if he didn't have me in stitches laughing, or we weren't mixing music, then we were tearing it up on the handball courts (with his friend Robin) and killing it…. My friendship with Timmy and Jeffrey led to an amalgamation of insanity that still makes me laugh at my innocence and ignorance to this day. Then high school came. With cars came girls, rock n' roll, and pretending we knew what the hell we were doing! There are a lot of these stories in the book, but **Dave and Diane** are my Bon Jovi buddies for life, and we created our own little mischief, time and time again without fail! Timmy was still there through my high school years, and very active in my life daily. Honestly, Tim never left. Neither did Dave. Dave and Tim are the quintessential best friends. Dave makes sure to this day to check in consistently, even when I am horrible at returning calls that are non-work related. He never gets reciprocated the right way but his friendship is valued deeply. Recently, when I was in the hospital for 3 weeks, diagnosed with COVID-19, I felt like I was on my deathbed. Dave went to the ends of the Earth to get Jon Bon Jovi to send me a personal video, in which Jon stated for me to get well and keep the faith. Priceless. That is real friendship. You can count on him and Diane in "the dead of night," and they have proved that over and over again. High school brought my first rock band together called Fase (the 'S" was a lightning bolt because we actually thought that was badass). I formed the band with my buddy **Louie**, who I remain close with to this day. Louie is doing great things in this world and it is an honor to be anywhere close to his circle of visionaries. The book mentions The International Beer Club and though many of those characters were morphed into only a few essential stories that had to be told, the hours of shenanigans were off the charts. I think Mötley Crüe did become our role models and we did the best we could make our "rock Gods" proud. God, we were stupid, and crazy… and lucky to be alive. These were my best friends before I derailed myself off the tracks, and I can honestly say I would not have gotten through the first 20 years of my life without them… that is for sure. The fact that Diane and these long life brothers of mine put up with what they did for years just simply shows where the depths of true friendship will go. I love them all and thank them deeply for their support and cherished memories.

Life takes on so many twists and turns when you least expect it… The rollercoaster will surely make you scream at times, but it will also give you the biggest thrills. **Scott (the main influence behind the character Bryan in this book)** was the next chapter in my life, and in all honesty, one of two stories that matters the most in this entire book to me. He is my greatest miracle and blessing any man can ask for. Scott saved me. There is single handedly no doubt behind that statement. The day he was born, the world changed colors, and my eyes opened up. It was a quintessential piece of my awakening. Seeing your son born provides a transformation within your soul. It is purely inexplicable how bringing life into the expansion of this universe impacts your perception. The two greatest phenomenons to the soul's existence is providing life, and having a true rare higher love consciousness relationship. I am blessed to have experienced both. This book is for Scott. I would not be alive today if the universe did not sanctify me with fatherhood. He is my greatest blessing, my best friend, my miracle, and I could not be more proud of him. I only hope I impacted his life half as much as he impacted mine. I love him like no other (even though everyone still thinks you are my younger brother!) See, what I did there? It rhymes!

I do not know how to thank the **SPARK family, the WOO family, and the thousands of names** that put my vision, my dreams, and myself on the map. There are close to 300,000 souls that have found, and built their dreams within this vision, and provide me with the feeling of fireworks within my heart. There is nothing I love more than seeing people spread their wings, become leaders in their own right, and follow their passion into action, creation, and impact despite the odds. There are simply too many people who fall under this umbrella to thank, and too many stories to tell properly. I think it would be a great exercise one day to put many of the souls that make up the SPARK family through a project to tell their stories and collaborate on a book together, because this was a special time in which the word "magic" does not even cover what truly happened. The "SPARKies" were the start of it all. That original crew made me believe and desire that I was going to work out of Room 339 in that school building for the rest of my career. They were true trendsetters and showed me the epic power of youth. Those kids told me and screamed a loud that they wanted more! They wrote curriculums, presented workshops, took it to the streets, created advocacy, built clubs, wrote books, created their own programs and their own work stations, gave up lunch hours and after school hours… all to just have a safe space and a voice. Long hours until midnight every night not goofing around, but making a difference. Then at 7 am they conjugated at Dunkin Donuts 3 blocks from the school, for a coffee powwow and a morning agenda meeting about the next steps for the day. Were these students or corporate stakeholders? They had a voice and they found a platform to express it. Heck, they created the platform to express it! They were the roots of the new American Educational Reform Program and Policy that our country has been crying for, and they were not even aware at the time this is what they were creating. They were the roots of Windows of Opportunity, which became the vehicle for thousands of more people to carry that initial "spark!" The SPARKies and Windows of Opportunity (they used to call themselves WOOsters) created the roots for an optimal approach to education reform. They were the ones who planted the seeds of inspiration that sprouted into my expanded vision of shifting systems. The SPARKies were all these things before these things existed. They knew what they wanted in order to better our planet, and they went after it. They truly blew me away day after day. I often could not believe I was even in this role and always coloring outside the lines in order for our youth to express fully and be empowered. They got me excited to wake up in the morning and take on the world. They were my teachers. They were my leaders. They were the SPARKies – a program that got defunded and destroyed. The education system never realized the magic they had in these youth and never knew how to cultivate bright minds for a bright tomorrow, but we did, and we still have the formula that began with their passion. They were the real deal… and real deals never die. Sparks can begin fires, and their fire is going to spread for generations to come.

Regina Rossi-Lamothe was there the day Windows of Opportunity was born. She is a rock star (literally and metaphorically) and a strong supporter of my dreams becoming a reality. Regina was the first person to probably plant the seeds inside of me of what it meant to have a dream. She is truly the reason I became a social worker… and a damn good one thanks to her example. The first time I saw her in a room with 300 teens, I knew for sure this was what I wanted to do! We have a crazy story, and one day we will collaborate on our own book, that is for sure. Regina's beautiful soul spent hours, night after night, on a cold kitchen floor when we didn't have 2 nickels to rub together, to teach me hope, faith, and how to take that first step. During that chapter in my life, she is the reason I got my ass off the ground and began to make something of myself. She supported me every step of the way. Her commitment to my soul's work is a blessing. It is extremely evident by the fact that her support did not end when we maturely recognized our paths had to take different routes in order for us to be true to both of our souls. Our book will surely be about breaking that particular social stereotype and discussing how we created that dynamic in a sometimes difficult, but very healthy manner. Regina teaches me and continues to teach me by her example of "being" and her endless unconditional acceptance and support. She will always be "family." Regina embodies hope, personal development, and a constant drive to better us all as individuals. She looks for the positive in all and my life is surely enhanced by her existence. Her friendships were fiery that became my friendships. She gave me change and grounding when I needed it most. She provided the music in my life for years and gave so many souls the platform to reach their dreams. She continues to do so daily and I am not so sure we caught up to her yet. There is no way to thank Regina, without mentioning our band Outlet. After begging her for a year to leave the karaoke circuit, and take the lead microphone for a rock band, she finally obliged by gifting me with the start of **Outlet**… a band that became and still remains family 22 years later at the release of this book. If I had to list the top 5 grateful things in my life, the hundreds of shows and thousands of Outlet memories would be on that list for sure. The band has raised over $100g for various charities and is still at it. I love playing drums for them and always look forward to the next performance. With Regina at the helm, God knows what will happen! That's a great thing!

The Mignone Family… I really need to write a book in itself to express the love, endless stories, memories, and gratitude I have for this incredible and beautiful family. The truth is there is simply no way to do this family justice, no matter what I write here. This family means the world to me and will have my gratitude eternally for not only what they have done for my company, but for me personally as well. What they produced within the fabric of Windows of Opportunity supported me in seeing that this company had much greater potential and reach than the earlier years of our vision. In many ways, this family put Windows of Opportunity on the map and showed me that expansion meant the sky is the limit. Anything is possible! When I met Tracy and Olivia, the company was a mere three years old, running part time with not much of a pulse, and with only one curriculum under our belt. We were coordinating workshops and conferences sporadically, and I thought that was pretty cool. I could do that jam for years to come and think I was making a difference... The Mignones had a work ethic that taught me differently! They embraced my dreams and made it their own in a way that lovingly brought my soul many lessons. Olivia, and her mom Tracy, took this company to an entirely different level that pushed the boundaries of what is possible in the non-profit sector, especially on zero funding. We took practically zero funding and impacted hundreds of thousands of lives – Shortstack, Hurricane Sandy, community work, photo shoots, workshops, curriculum, and a ridiculous work ethic of hours upon hours. When I say hours, I am talking 18 hours per day, 7 days per week! For years this family helped me work on building programs, writing letters, searching for funding, running groups, providing counseling, and so much more. They taught me to embody "where there is a will, there is a way." When the agency faced heartbreak and broken promises from major leads, or when we did not have enough funding, and it seemed we should pack it in, the Mignone family made sure I never stopped! I should say THEY never stopped! Their house and backyard often became home to WOO projects, and all hands were on deck to get whatever we needed to get done completed! The Mignone stories are endless and precious to my soul, as is their love, commitment and passion to a set of higher ideals. My thankfulness for the Mignone family simply cannot be put into the proper words to express "gratitude." They deserve words that have a much more powerful expression than "thank you." They are the epitome of family and they have the hearts of lions. Even today as I take Windows of Opportunity to new heights, into new endeavors, and into additional global systems, which I never imagined, its evolution is because that family showed me how to push outside the box. They showed me to not accept the norm, work hard, and "break the rules and set new standards;" the motto of the Shortstack program that Olivia founded, which historically was one of WOO's most impacting. Breaking the rules and setting new standards is literally a mantra I carry with me everywhere to this day.

I know I mentioned the Windows of Opportunity family earlier, and some of those incredible souls cross over into this acknowledgment. First and foremost I must give a quick shout out to **Katerina Theophanous**. Katerina works tirelessly daily to make sure our programs continue and there is hope brought to the students she connects with. She wears too many hats to mention, and we all at WOO love her dearly! Next: There are so many aspects to running a company, and it often feels like a million things are coming at me all at once. Being in a leadership role means you have to be able to multitask, trust your intuition, prioritize, and think of both the short term and long term vision as you are in action. Your skills have to include how to negotiate, disseminate, educate, navigate, coordinate, and facilitate; often at the same time. There are hours of planning, thinking, soul searching, and strategizing. You create a philosophy, and decide about alignment and positive energy as you carry out your goals. You have to build genuine relationships that are aligned to all you believe in, while thinking about all these factors continuously. It can be tremendously difficult and overwhelming at times. One major aspect of this whole wheel in motion is the simple fact that none of your vision is possible without funding. It takes **friends and your team** shopping the hell out of your vision, and **sponsors** to buy in to your vision in order to keep you afloat financially year after year. I used to get frustrated because I had to spend so much time on the back end cultivating the finances so I can keep the organization running, when all I wanted was to connect to my creativity, build programs, and put them into action. Being at the helm of carrying out programs I created is what gets me excited about life. That is always where my true heart and inspiration lies. I thank God for all the sponsors who came forth and believed in us, and made all our efforts possible. We have had many sponsors through the years, which I am tremendously grateful for. Thank you to every single one of you who have invested in this vision and dream, whether it was coming to an event, handing us product, or giving us your time. I wish I could mention you all here but please know my gratitude is extremely heartfelt. In addition to all those beautiful souls, I do wish to acknowledge, some additional dear friends who have gone above and beyond to sponsor me and make sure our vision continues to move forward: **Alex Garfield** is a 67 year old teenager that stands for bringing back the peace, love, and happiness of the 60's. His love for humanity and life is infectious. His compassion and friendship is timeless. He has guided me, advised me, supported me, and has passed his lifetime of success lessons to me. The education I have received from him is priceless and I hope Windows of Opportunity has half the reach that his charity work has accomplished. *Joe Rock* is one of my dearest friends of over 20 years. By day he is a deejay on a top New York Radio Station, he has been the host of our Annual Shortstack fundraiser for many years, the recipient of our Barbara Harmon Unsung Hero Award, and a solid supporter of all my dreams. He has always had my back. I am so grateful to have him in my life. *Tommy Hilfiger* has supported countless charities through the years, and is such a down to earth and nice person. The fact that I have made the list of charities he continues to support not only fills me with gratitude, but it also assures me that our vision of education reform has impact, and is on the right track. There are over a thousand more people I could thank and that I appreciate deeply. I am truly blessed. I wish I could list every sponsor, every program, and every program director that ever did something for Windows of Opportunity, but this is already running so long. My love and appreciation goes out to everyone that has touched this vision in one way or another, and made this all possible.

To my *Divine Love Community* that taught me the deep meaning of prayer and that a centre of light truly shines from inside our souls: *Al, Jeanne, Judy, Geoff, Jane, Kasia, Helge, Arie, Marion, Betty, Terry, Jolene, Eva, Susan, Catherine, Maureen, the entire Mercker family, and Kevin.* Thank God this community is so large, so loving, and so forgiving as I am sure I forgot someone! I thank you all for your loving support through my darkest challenges. Your prayers, and your connection helped more than you even realize!

As the next chapter of my professional career evolved, my journey started its expansion into coming full circle. Having the blessing to work with a visionary Principal for 7 years that believed in my dreams and allowed me the room to explore, build, create, test, and manifest real education reform has a priceless tone to it. Meeting *Cheryl Quatrano* changed my life. Having her invest in my life's work to the point that not only put me BACK on the map, but reinvented my career, is nothing less than a calculated move from the universe. It is professionally a blessing that saved my career and gave me a sense of strength and purpose beyond none. Her hours of guidance along with the spiritual coaching of her business partner and best friend **Melinda Spataro** will be the reason behind national education reform happening in this country. Those long nights of coffee, office talks, dinners, and so on, that were all around the evolution of social emotional learning and holistic education reform, will be the catalyst for what changes our country tomorrow. Within that world, Cheryl and Melinda allowed us to cultivate a dream team of believers, builders, and creators. I would be remiss to not thank the dream team of **Antonio Bausone** (seriously this man could run the country), **Kathy Garzon** (a work horse that gets the job done no matter what it takes), **Tara Crossman** (a mental health genius that will get the answers needed no matter what hoops she has to jump through), **Jamie Corrodus** (a man who I have worked with for 12 years now, that I have no idea how he has not been discovered yet. He has a full heart that has always been about developing the best youth development programs), **Veronica Rodas** (a parent and very dear friend of mine for over a decade now, who is taking spirituality to the next level for youth and families in the community), and last, but definitely not least, **Allison Fahrbach** (a rock star that everyone in this world should really get to know better because she has a heart of gold and is a programmatic / systemic genius... Allison, your friendship goes beyond the boundaries of "COSTUSA" – thank you will never capture how I feel.) Allison has to get an additional shout out here because her friendship is not only priceless, but she has also never said no to any project that is connected to this vision or that supports youth. Sometimes I may come up with a crazy ridiculous idea, and she will pause, cock her head, and look at me strangely because she knows it is a crazy ridiculous idea, and reply, "Okay, let's do it!" She puts her all into everything and for everyone! I am impressed on how she can edit documents and get to the soul of what we are trying to represent or present that is nothing less than a gift from the universe. She writes brilliant curriculum, and aggregates all of our data to help support the evolution of impacting programs. She put up with my insanity so many times over the past few years as I often called and said, "What do you think of this idea for Beautiful Souls?!" She again always replied, "That sounds great!" Your expertise Allison is so greatly appreciated! Allison is an author in her own right with her inspirational book on Amazon called Be Your Own Hero, which is a beautiful journey that connects to other souls. I suspect her book is going to be used as an elective curriculum for high schools in the near future. She is an inspiration that is going places in her career. I feel blessed she has gifted her talents to our team and mission. A mutual international partner of ours says it best: "I want an Allison! We all need an Allison in our life!" This entire dream team has provided me with a different level of friendship and professional growth that cannot be purchased in a textbook, or learned at a training. God bless you and I love you all.

Ms. Vittoria Venuti... There are no words I can find that will give justice towards the way my soul wants to thank your soul. How do I honestly and respectfully say thank you for the years of quiet encouragement, deep spiritual kinship, love, friendship, sustenance, and lifelines that you have provided my existence, as I explored the days in and the days out of building curriculum, trying to figure out the next steps of this monstrosity, and my life in general? Your tireless support, including picking me off the floor in those rare moments I needed picking up, will never be forgotten. You rose to the occasion and had my back endless times! You are absolutely hands down one of the most brilliant professionals in the teaching industry, an industry that is designed and structured to not recognize real rare talent such as yours. Your passion for your students is a beautiful thing to experience that surely does not get noticed enough. It has always deeply bothered me that you do not receive the credit you deserve for the good soul you are, the friendship and guidance you provide so many, and how you have such a creative pulse on improving programs. I know you do not want nor need the credit, but in my opinion you deserve it. You have tenacity, a dedication, and a commitment to your students that truly makes a very deep difference. You are an incredible teacher that connects amazingly with youth, and to be honest, the best co-teacher I ever had the pleasure of creating curriculum and running classes with. We make a great team! You have a canny way of coming up with simple solutions to challenges that seem difficult to me initially. If there was a real title of "Director of Common Sense" it should belong to you! I wish the world knew you the way I know you, so that they can see what a beautiful human being you truly are. Thank you for the laughs, the support, and the consistent encouragement daily! I will always be grateful for what you have provided my life, as there are no words. Your impact will never be forgotten and you will always have my deepest "gratitude" for who you are and what you bring to the table. Never give up and always embrace your power within!

Kira Ayisha Day... Knowing me, this will be rewritten 1,000 times because your friendship came at a time that was surely gifted by the universe. This is another thank you I know I will not be able to express well enough. If the universe is pulling the puppet strings, I thank the day it dangled your strings right in front of me. Personally, professionally, vision-wise, inspirationally, expansively, collectively, consciously, and spiritually, my entire existence shifted the day we met. You brought an entirely new level of professional awareness to my universe, and as I quickly learned, this is what you bring to every soul you encounter, and in every program you coordinate. I remember the first day we met and I told you I was writing this book. You were so supportive of my dreams, and had an articulate and genuine energy to how you carried yourself. The instant bond we had changed my entire world because I knew I had found the professional partnership to bring the vision I have long prayed for to the next level – one that would truly transform society the way I always dreamed of. There was a shift in the universe that day and it opened some sort of spiritual portal that said 'It is time." With your support and investment in my development, you showed me that idealistic could be, and will be reality. Kira, your friendship is so uplifting, your energy contagious, and you are surely one of the most beautiful souls I have ever met. Your programs, your vision for the planet, your intellect, and your work ethic is like nothing I have ever experienced collectively in another human being. All of your clients have echoed the same sentiments, so I know I'm not crazy! You have a light and energy that naturally connects to and transforms souls in a way that is your gift to the planet. Thank you so much for your guidance and for helping the expansion of Windows of Opportunity when you have so much on your own plate. You make time for everyone, and I truly do not know how you balance it all. Working with your level of intellectual expertise, allowing me to swim in your world, and letting me be a part of your incredible Torontonian tribe has been my greatest blessing and is truly humbling. Thank you for seeing the positivity in all challenges and being a stand for my health in the darkest moments of my life. Thank you for all the teamwork, the hours upon hours of building programs, vamping out ideas, and our deep dives about shifting systems. Deep diving and being in action around all our thoughts is still my absolutely favorite thing in the universe to do. We always said, give us four hours, and we will fix the world's problems! Thank you for all you are, all the inner light you bring to this team, (I think the New York tribe loves you more than me!), for developing this vision for our planet, all you bring to the table, and allowing me to partner in your vision and mission. Keep the path! Great things come to souls who give as much as you!

Sandy Corso from Peaceful Daily Publishing. Thank you to you and your team for making sure this book happened, as well as all your patience in navigating me through this step-by-step process. This book would not be a success without all your wisdom and guidance! Thank you especially to **Mindy,** who I knew the moment we spoke that your good vibes were divinely guided to me and this vision! Thank you for your guidance and drive to give me presence and a stage for this message!

I want to especially thank ALL the doctors and nurses who have provided me the utmost compassion and care during my bout with cancer the past 2 years, as well as my 2-month battle with COVID-19, that included a 3-week hospitalization. It was the scariest time of my life. Going through that experience awakened my soul on a level that was unexpected. The love within that experience, that I became conscious to, led me to one simple realization: I choose life.

There is no doubt that writing this book has brought me through a spiritual catharsis, which has been a journey into the depths of my soul that I never imagined possible. There has been tremendous loss in my life that shook me to my bones, including the too brief of a time span that my **Aunt Barbara** found me. My Aunt instilled a heartbeat and a set of values into my existence that can never be replaced. The miracle of her existence came at a time in my journey that would have left me for dead had she not shown up. Her sudden appearance and demise strategically propelled me into the man I am today. It is my daily wish that I have made her, and my circle of angels that surround me daily, as proud as can be. I spend every day trying to spread divine love throughout our planet, hoping to bring light to as many souls as possible. My love for her and the angels travels throughout all of eternity.

A quick shout out and thank you to *my sisters* who have supported me for years, and my beautiful niece *Marybeth* and incredible nephew *Jeremy*. Thank you all for teaching me what true strength is all about. I could not be more proud of you! I love you very much!

Last, but not least... and surely the most important that I want to make VERY CLEAR to the reader. My biggest fear as you dive into this journey is the reflection that society will have on *my parents*. I do not think that my parents got a fair representation in this story, nor did the time allotment really allow me to dig in and express more about how our relationship repaired through the years, and went through tremendous healing. It would be very unfair of me not to say that I did mend things with my family on an extremely deep, loving, and expansive level. My parents are very good people, and like in all walks of life, we are not given that road map on how to travel this existence day to day. We must be patient. We are all learning as we go along and they did the best they knew how with the tools they had. I hold no grudges against my parents; we have all worked on forgiveness and comprehension as a family, and I love them deeply. I thank them for raising me the best they could. I think the most beautiful gift that came out of the journey with my parents is the realization that so many souls of so many ages are hurting, and need programs to help them see their power within and discover their dreams. That is really the heartbeat behind all I am trying to do for our universe.

If I forgot anyone, I am sorry! But I love you all! You are all beautiful souls!

If you enjoy this book, I am currently working on 2 more releases that are very different than this once in a lifetime type of writing, and also very different from one another. The first is an inspirational, abstract, quote-filled, thought provoking book called *"KPT"* and the second book comes out of my professional experience for the educational world, and is called *"Social Emotional Learning is NOT Just a Color Chart."*

This is not a story of rags to riches, but rather from lost to found.

"My heart's like an open book
For the whole world to read
Sometimes nothing keeps me together
At the seams
I'm on my way
Home sweet home"

- Mötley Crüe

Prologue

~

"Scott, Scott, are you still with me," she shouted in my face.

I had never seen eyes so emerald and pure before, but then again, I had never seen these eyes before.

"Scott," she boomed once again. I tried with all my might to open my mouth, but something was stopping me.

I focused for what seemed like hours on prying my lips apart, but all I could feel was… actually, I couldn't feel. Why couldn't I feel anything? Why are my fingers numb? Why are my eyes so heavy?

Blue and red flashes of light flickered in the corner of my eyes.

The taste of metal lingered on my tongue as the woman with the emerald eyes hovered over me as I sat on the taupe sofa. Finally, I concentrated all of my energy on splitting my lips apart. A breathy yet exhausted, "Where" escaped my bloodstained mouth.

"Scott," the woman whispered. She placed a steaming cup of coffee in my hand; the porcelain clung to my fingertips tenderly.

With spots dancing across my line of sight, I realized where I was: the faint lights flashing in the windows, a silhouetted figure perched next to me, the defined lines from a gentle face contrasted with the dimly lit room. Sirens wailed as I felt my body jerk and spasm.

What did I do?

What did I do?

'Oh, yeah,' I realized, attempting to chuckle silently to myself... not like the woman sitting next to me could hear my internal monologue.

The beeping, the sirens, the panic grew louder. They echoed in my head as if they were trying to rearrange a melody. It was a delectable sound I had never heard before, but this would be the last time I would have the pleasure of conjuring sweet music ever again. I felt my chest rising and slamming with every crisp word that formed from within me.

For a moment I clung to the chirping of the sirens, but the woman's voice cut through the noise. Muffled noises circulated within the room. Her compassion burst through the chaos as the sounds grew into a roar.

Then a yell.

Then silence.

All of the laughter, the joy, the tears, and the memories slowly danced into the darkness.

Everything I knew was over, and everything that would have been escaped with the rise and fall of my bloodied tongue against the top of my mouth. One life was over and a new life had begun. Crunching metal echoed in my head as the woman before me pressed against my flesh with her hand.

"It will all be okay, Scott," sang from her soul.

The darkness swallowed me wholeheartedly and wrapped its arms around me, softly rocking me to a deafening lullaby reserved only for those on the cusp of death.

They always talk about an afterlife, but do they ever talk about an after near-life ending experience? I guess that's what this state of mind is: a blissful feeling that tomorrow isn't guaranteed, so we have to make today count.

The kindness from this absolute stranger was the embodiment of a juxtaposition: as life itself seemed to come to a screeching halt, I was warming up to the idea that second chances and new beginnings are at the edge of every single circumstance.

Our experiences are a manifestation of who we are and what we will become... from being a stranger in the night opening her door to a confused young man, or to being on the receiving end of a compassionate opportunity to live again.

An important concept is so crucial to grasp:

Death is certain, life is not.

Part I:

The Becoming

CHAPTER 1

Ride the Wind

*"They say only the bravest try where eagles
and angels dare to fly."*

- Poison, American Rock Band,
Mechanicsburg, Pennsylvania

"Keep it down," my father shouted. "You'll wake up Scott!"

"I don't care," my mother screeched. "Let him hear me! Let the whole neighborhood hear me!"

As my eyes crept open in the midsummer heat wave, I could feel my fingers sticking to the plastic sheets on my bed. The soft light that shot into the room bent around the slightly ajar door.

"We don't have enough money to stay here, Judy, it's just not possible," my father was desperately trying to whisper, but my mother was indifferent to his pleas.

"Where are we going to go?" Her voice appeared to grow louder. "Your family is here, our lives are here, this is home!"

My father's voice grew closer and closer. "The Bronx is no place to raise our family, Judy." I caught a glimpse of my father's fingers wrapping around the doorknob as he pulled the door shut. Their muffled voices continued their conversation as the night dwindled down.

This was a regular occurrence at my house: my parents always seemed to be fighting over money, though at two-years-old I could barely comprehend the fiscal distress our family was in.

I recall sitting against the wooden door, contemplating what could be so bad that my father wanted my mother to whisper about.

The stars twinkled far above my bedroom window as a reminder that life was happening just outside my window. There was a whole world out there waiting for me to explore.

I crawled back towards my bed and picked at the peeling white paint on the ledge. My eyes glimmered in the reflections from the metal air conditioning unit above the window. As the condensation dripped melodically, I lost track of time.

Life as I knew it was flickering before me like a candle in the wind, and I was barely able to form coherent thoughts at that point.

The next morning, I found myself playing with the fabric tablecloth on the wobbly dining room table.

"Scott," my mother bent down so she was at eye-level with me. "Don't do that, mommy ironed this just now."

I glanced up at her with last night's loud argument on my mind. To deter myself from asking her any questions, I pulled the newspaper closer and began to flip through the pages.

Growing up in the Bronx appeared to be a rather exciting adventure. I did not understand why my father was so keen on having us move away. Besides, where else would we go?

Having my grandparents and uncle living in the apartment directly above us was an absolute treat. In hindsight I realize the apartment complex we were living in was old and slightly run down, but it was a grand and exciting place for a young boy to experience.

Our extended family was even near us and everything seemed so perfect.

Seeming and actually being, however, were two different perspectives. We were in the midst of turmoil and the epicenter of violence, but our family was so comfortable being in the place where their childhood memories were manifested. No one seemed to mind the changes happening around us.

The Bronx was an extension of Manhattan's concrete jungle. Towering apartment complexes lined each block, but the hustle and bustle of glistening businesses were being replaced with cardboard boxes and the stench of overflowing sewers. My mind would often populate the streets with visions of grandeur, for after all, we were living on the Grand Concourse.

I would let my mind wander for hours while looking out the window.

"What are you doing, Scott?" My mother's voice cut through my imaginative state.

'Reading,' I continued flipping the pages of the paper.

I often got in trouble for doing things that were not up to my mother's standards, but I tried not to think about it too much at the time. As a child, I am sure I was preoccupied with other nonsense happening in my life, though those memories escape me now.

The unforgiving streets were lined with men in distinctive colors, though my youthful mind could not comprehend that each shade was indicative of the division lingering in our streets. Gangs were moving into the Bronx slowly but surely, and my parents were trying to hide that from my innocent little mind.

Even though I was inquisitive and curious at that age, I didn't really pick up on the sheer divisiveness growing in our neighborhood. All that I cared about was my family, for I was years and years away from noticing just how harsh the world could be.

Realistically speaking, my rose-colored lens of the world would extend until my teen years, though I would end up seeing far worse conditions over my lifetime than what my childhood was morphing into at those very moments.

My mother scooped me up from the table and brought me back into the bedroom. I had to get dressed, for I was going out with my grandparents in a little while.

As she tugged my white undershirt over my wispy blonde hairs, I sensed that her hostility was overflowing from the conversation she had with my father the night before.

She seemed partially panicked as she pulled my blue jeans over my tiny legs, but I was trying to focus on what my grandparents would be doing with me that day.

The bell rang and she dashed out of the room towards the front door. I teetered out into the living room with sheer happiness radiating across my cheeks.

I darted over to my grandfather and embraced his leg, 'Grandpa!'

"Hey sport," he hoisted me up. "Are you ready for the baseball game?"

I nodded excitedly.

This would be my first time going to a baseball game at the big stadium down the block. After blowing a kiss goodbye to my mother, my grandparents, uncle, and I made our way down the steps and onto the streets.

Fire hydrants were shooting water out every which way, but no one seemed to care on that scorching summer day.

The bright sun was a welcomed and pleasant view, considering the tattered green wallpaper only provided so much intrigue to a young boy.

As we made our way down the block, I watched the sun reflect off of the large buildings. People were dancing and running under the fire hydrants' spraying water with delight. Children were giggling as they leapt in the puddles forming in the street.

Again, life seemed good.

We made our way to the baseball stadium, where my grandfather held me in his arms as we walked through crowds of fans and merchants.

"Hot dogs," a man screamed. "Get your hot dogs!"

I giggled and reached out for one, but my uncle stood in front of me and smiled.

"They're for big kids, Scott," my uncle grinned and took me from my grandfather's grasp.

The two of us moved closer to the giant sign hanging precariously above us. The bold blue and white letters were difficult to sound out, but my uncle happily read the sign to me:

"It says 'Yankee Stadium.'"

'Yankee,' I replied. 'Scadium.'

"Oh, close enough kiddo."

The two of us laughed and found our seats.

As we watched the players run across the field, I was thrilled by the cheering, camaraderie, and vivid colors all around me. The four of us, my grandfather, grandmother, uncle, and I, were making beautiful memories that afternoon, though none of us were in tune with what that moment meant for our respective lives.

The sunset guided us home, where my parents would be fighting once again.

"Scotty," my uncle glanced over me as my grandparents rushed to quell my parents' argument. "Do you want an ice cream pop?"

'Ice cream pop!' I was so excited. It was a wonderful day and now I was about to eat ice cream. In my eyes, it was the best day ever!

My uncle carried me up the stairs as we recounted the day's activities.

The entire day was such a beautiful contrast to the fighting happening in my house, and my uncle's jovial demeanor clouded any sort of worry that could manifest in my little mind.

As the two of us sat on my grandparents' couch and ate the frozen treats, we watched the sunset dip below the other apartment complexes in our neighborhood.

Everything was perfect.

Life was beautiful.

My first memories seemed to be a picturesque progression to my budding life. The best was yet to come.

∞ ∞ ∞ ∞ ∞ ∞ ∞ ∞

To say that I was an outcast as a child was an understatement. The inner workings of my brain consisted of questions and innate curiosities, though I was just embarking on my inquisitive journey through life.

Time was fleeting and my memories were slowly forming.

Much of my early childhood was consistent of my flawless image of the Bronx, though like I said, life was far from what it seemed.

Around the time I was three-years-old, my mother and I were out for a midmorning stroll in the neighborhood. The brisk daylight was just what we needed to contrast the drab apartment we lived in.

"Ay lady," a man crept up behind my mother. "Where you goin'?"

My mother turned her head slightly to see what was happening behind her, but she continued to push my carriage forward.

Another man leapt in front of her, "What's a cutie like you doin' out here with a baby?"

She was silent. My mother tried to push me and the carriage away from the men, but one of them placed his hand over hers.

Another guy walked over and snickered, "You scared?"

At this point multiple men were circling my mother and the carriage, though I was joyfully clapping in the stroller.

"Give us your money, hun, we won't hurt the baby," the men laughed. One of them pulled out a knife that glistened in the harsh New York sunlight.

My mother started to cry a bit, but she would not let go of me.

"Here," she wiggled off her purse and threw it at one of the men. "Take it."

She rushed past the men and started to run with the stroller. I thought it was a relaxing ride through the neighborhood, but the trepidation in my mother's soft cries should have told me otherwise.

The two of us made our way up the three-stories of metallic stairs. As we dashed into the apartment, my mother collapsed into my father's arms.

Upon telling him what had happened, he held her tightly and their arguments seemed to melt away.

I found myself waddling into the bedroom to look out at the people below. My window was keeping me safe from the perils of the outside world, though I did not realize the unease slowly seeping through my family's veins.

The rest of my time in the Bronx was a blur, though I do remember having to say goodbye to my grandparents and uncle at dinner one night.

My grandmother was crying and refused to let go of me, but I did not comprehend that we would be leaving our home and our family behind.

As my father picked me up from my grandparents' couch and muttered, "Let's go Judy. Mom, dad, we'll see you guys soon," I drifted in my state of subtle consciousness.

∞ ∞ ∞ ∞ ∞ ∞ ∞ ∞

My eyelids fluttered open as the wheels of our rusted station wagon buckled under the potholes on the entrance ramp to the Whitestone Bridge. The cardboard boxes surrounding my tiny frame shifted their weight and toppled onto me, alerting my mother who was visibly upset in the passenger seat.

"Robert," she whispered, "the boxes just fell on top of Scott."

My father, still gripping the steering wheel, scoffed at her comment: "Judy, he's sleeping, he doesn't know the difference. We are almost home."

My mother twisted in the seat and looked uncomfortably at the boxes surrounding me. We locked eyes for just a moment. As a four-year-old, I thought she was merely exhausted. After everything, I discovered that deep down inside my mother was suffering far more than any of us could imagine.

Her deep-rooted pain was caught between sighs of, "I'm fine."

But I knew the truth.

Well, now I do.

As the path to the bridge became more narrower, and our car lurched forward onto the actual bridge, my eyes blurred in the reflection of something bright outside the car windows. The bridge itself was illuminated with gleams of blue, red, and yellow speckles. Tears streamed down my face, partially due to subconsciously feeling my mother's intense pain emulating from the passenger seat, and partially because I was in awe of the glimmer and glow from the bridge's lights.

At that very moment, it seemed to me that the lights were stars filled with the wishes of young boys like me hoping for a better life.

It wasn't that I had a terrible life. It was just that I spent so much time being misunderstood for my quizzical nature that life itself seemed like a never-ending puzzle. As soon as I would find another piece to solve something that was missing, another four pieces would present themselves before my very eyes.

However, on that very night, as my parents and I crossed the bridge from the Bronx to Queens, I had a feeling that my life was about to take a turn for the better.

It had to.

I was four years old and my life was just beginning at the edge of the Whitestone Bridge: my old life and my new one were combining and flourishing with the intent of living for a higher purpose.

Yet as a four-year-old, I don't think I put my life's intent towards a higher purpose in the back of a station wagon, while doused in cardboard boxes filled with my parents' materialistic hopes and dreams.

As we lurched off of the bridge and through winding streets and down darkened alleyways, we pulled up to a dark house. My mother and father spent over an hour moving boxes out of the car and into what I assumed would be our new home.

I sat gazing out at the stars and the silhouette of shadows escapading along the walls of other houses. It was quieter... it was... it just was. It was nothing like the Bronx or being in the arms of family. I had hoped that despite being apart from my grandparents and uncle, some things would be better.

Still, shouting cut through the somewhat peaceful night sky in what my parents called, "College Point." College Point... I guessed that was where our home was now.

I stirred a bit too much in the backseat and alerted my parents that I was, indeed, awake.

My father paused for a moment from screaming at my mother and glared right through me.

"Scott," he boomed, "get out of the car and get inside."

How naive of me to think that just because we were moving boroughs, we would be different people and a stronger family.

Well, in hindsight, I know that we were really a family.

Except this place that we just moved to was not a home...

It was just another house to build upon the catastrophic love story manifesting two more children to join the tale.

And even though our family grew from three to five seemingly overnight, my sisters, though adorable and sweet in their respective ways, merely perpetuated the notion that four walls and a roof cannot conceal the most abrasive comments: for when they are flung about, words can shatter glass windows just as sharply as fists can.

So as a family of five, we moved to another house in College Point.

And the cycle of being wedged under boxes and caught between my parents' violent verbal outbursts repeated again and again...

CHAPTER 2

When the Children Cry

~

"When the children cry, let them know we tried. 'Cause when the children fight, let them know it ain't right. When the children pray, let them know the way. 'Cause when the children sing, then the new world begins."

- White Lion, American Rock Band, New York City

Years of the same mundane arguments seeped into my elementary school experiences. Day after day it was the same thing: I was constantly reminded of how different and strange I was compared to the rest of the kids in my class.

My initial experiences with love prolonged the inevitable understanding that I would need to find a partner who would see me for who I am. This partner would need to accept me for the soul connection we could develop together. The odds of me using those words at the time were incredibly minimal, but the mindset was still festering from deep within me.

Hours upon hours would pass as I would putter about in my room: imagining a life that existed beyond the borders of Queens and beyond the minds of those who saw me as less than what I could ever become.

Love and my innate differences became intertwined upon starting the second grade. I can remember it as if it were yesterday: it was the typical schoolboy crush story with a hint of hopefulness that my heart would finally beat in tune with another human being's. After all, my pursuit of love and caring for others stemmed from something that burned within me: what it is, I yearned to find out.

My mother would pick Laurie up just as the sun danced along our rickety station wagon's hood. She would drop both of us off at school as a favor to Laurie's mom, for my mother had to upkeep her duty to be the community's beacon of hope: after all, mothers during that time period had to be the prim and proper matriarchs of their families. I sense some did it to offset how harshly they beat their children behind closed doors.

No matter how far my mind would stray from its path, Laurie's golden blonde hair swaying in the wind would make everything much clearer. As she held my hand in the back seat of the car day after day, I was lost in images of us being together forever. The innocence of second grade made me believe that we were married.

Our ritualistic morning handholding was everything and anything I could ask for, and at the time it made me feel that love would always be this simple and concise.

On the fateful day when Laurie was struck with a nasty case of the chicken pox, I was deeply saddened that I had to ride alone in the backseat, our backseat, in my mother's car.

I occupied my day by hatching a beautiful plan that would show Laurie just how much I cared for her and missed her. I gathered all of her homework and trotted out of the school with a huge stack of papers in my hands. I was awestruck by the wonder that would grow on her face upon her seeing me at her doorstep: her cute yellow house with ornate white shutters would be the backdrop of many timeless stories about how genuinely sweet I was to come to her rescue. Over the years she would recount the tale of how endearing I was, even in our youth.

When she answered the door behind her mother, my heart filled with glee. I pushed past her mother eagerly so that I could show her the papers I carried straight to her door. I grinned from ear to ear as she stood before me doused in red dots and a small smile. I was on top of the world until she single-handedly pushed me off of my pedestal a week later.

Seven days after carrying her homework to her, she did not do the same for me although I ended up contracting the disease from her. As I sat passively by my front window, peering out the sheer curtains to eagerly watch her gallop up my steps, I slowly realized that she was not coming to be by my side.

To add even more salt to my tears, my friend Billy was arm and arm with Laurie on my first day back to school. See, Billy had been getting a ride from my mom along with Laurie every morning, but since he was my best friend, I didn't think anything of it. Billy was my best and only friend at the time, for I was considered the school loser and everyone hated me. To this day, I never really understood why.

When I came back to school and saw him being so kind to her, I was enraged.

The next morning, when my mom picked Billy up to bring him to school, I just knew I had to make my move on Laurie.

I had to protect my precious crush, despite the fact that Billy seemed to have a crush on her as well.

He was my best friend, I figured, so he would have to understand.

When my Mom pulled up to Laurie's house, we both jumped out of the car to open the door for her. In retrospect, we should have turned to each other and laughed at how ridiculous the scene was: two best friends were longing for the same "love." (As if we knew what love was in the second grade.)

Billy glared at me with an evil stare that cut through me like a knife. "What are you doing," he barked at me, "Laurie is my girlfriend."

I chuckled slightly and said, 'No, she is my girlfriend.'

However, once he clocked me in the face, I had a sense that our friendship was over. While lying on the ground and succumbing to the throbbing pain on my face, I could see Laurie's eyes looking shamefully at me. It was more embarrassing than being beaten up at school.

My mother launched her body out of the car, screaming and shouting with such rage in her eyes. My voice fell into the pit of my stomach.

It was odd: my mother could pummel me into submission behind closed doors at home, yet if kids were picking on me, she would heroically dash to my side like the "Mother of the Year" she yearned to be. Mommy dearest's punches were no match for what my imagination would do to me after this embarrassing situation.

I distinctly remember not wanting to go to school anymore, refusing to do schoolwork, and panicking at the sheer thought that I would lose another fight.

My mind would often wander to images of Billy ferociously pouncing on me in the schoolyard, just yearning to paint his fist with my blood and skin. Life was slowly becoming a series of dodged punches and tear-soaked pillowcases.

It seemed that no matter what I tried to do, I was not what my parents had hoped for.

∞ ∞ ∞ ∞ ∞ ∞ ∞ ∞

Every single night became an internal battle between living up to my parents' standards and trying to survive. Thought after thought was consumed with the notion that I could be the perfect son, that I would find a love that felt the same way about me, and that I would not have to hide who I was behind a mask of smiles and perpetuated bruises.

On the night of my eighth birthday, I gazed out into the distant stars, begging to be seen. I wanted to be heard for who I was and not for the voices that my mother and father conjured up for me.

Week after week, we would sit in temple like the good religious family everyone hoped we were. Yet behind closed doors, our family story was flooded with black and blue dashes, sullied exclamation points sparking from the hearts of three young children, and, of course, the countless questions that always seemed to ring from somewhere deep inside me.

The members of our temple would flock to my parents: praising them for the three beautiful children they had, for my mother's continual radiance, and for my father's unwavering dedication to his family and to his community. After all, being part of New York City's bravest heroes, the fire department, came with its fair share of accolades and jovial praises.

I will never forget experiencing one of his most prestigious honors in what seemed like a scene from an action film. My father had been driving around the Bronx with me in the car. He was always taking me to the drastic scenes of major fires in the borough. I think it was his way of bonding with his only son. While growing up, despite the mixed messages I was getting from the way my parents treated me, he was my hero. I remember going to these fires, seeing his bravery, and thinking I want to grow up and save lives. I wanted to be a fireman and save lives.

I wasn't sure, but I knew saving lives had to be in my future.

Once, my dad was not scheduled to work and came across a burning building. A lady was hanging out of the window and screaming that she was trapped. My dad stopped the car, ran into the building, and saved her. Despite the flames shooting from the windows in their fit of rage, he got her out unharmed.

It was a big deal: there was an article in the paper and the community knew his name. Our family was invited to a ceremony. Many officers and firemen were there along with their families. My dad and my family were called up to the podium as the Mayor of New York City presented my dad with an award for his bravery.

I was in awe of being near the Mayor too, and thought about how cool it was to be in a position to commend someone for their heroic feats. I figured it must be exciting to run events that helped the community. Being the mayor is cool. Being a fireman is cool.

I wanted to be cool.

That award sat on a shelf and collected dust in our living room, but every time I walked around the house in pain, doused in bruises from my parents' latest beating, I saw that award and it would bring a smile to my face. Somehow, I knew everything would turn out okay.

∞ ∞ ∞ ∞ ∞ ∞ ∞ ∞

Before and after temple, elderly women would gather around us pinching my cheeks and telling my mother that she had a big brave young son.

"My son," my mother would squeal proudly, "he will be a doctor, a lawyer, a professional man." Women would enviously applaud my mother for her stunning family.

'Mom,' I would bellow, tugging on her skirt with childlike curiosity, 'Why do we have to go to temple?"

"Scott," she would sigh, "Stop asking questions."

We would walk in silence back to the station wagon parked at the far end of the block as a family of five with schools of thought that just never made the grade together.

My parents and teachers grew tired of me constantly badgering them with questions like, 'Why do people fight so much?' 'Why does the moon change shape every night?' and a plethora of other well thought-out ideas that I genuinely wanted to know.

"Scott," my father's anger was incredibly clear.

We got into the car with my solemn glare dripping down my face.

The cherry red station wagon before us clanked shut.

"Scott," my mother muttered, "Why do you have to ask so many questions?"

With a perplexed look on my face, I turned to her and said, "But mom, I can't help it." She looked right through me as if I told her I murdered someone. I was the epitome of everything she did not hold in high regard.

By that following Wednesday, I was staring down the hollowed eyes of three doctors with clipboards and lab coats that mimicked the sheer essence of what it felt like to be trapped. I was placed in a cage adorned with labels and false prophecies. The doctors draped questions about my brain: convincing me that I was less than the young, inquisitive boy that I was growing into.

I was deafened by my mother's chilling screams as the doctors said I was just a curious, insightful young boy who yearned to help others.

"My son," she shouted at the doctors, "My son will be a doctor, a lawyer, an extraordinary professional. He is not the boy you tell me he is. He is going to stop with the questions whether he likes it or not."

She snatched my hand and dragged me from the office: pieces of my heart smashing to the floor behind me as my fingers were caught in my mother's clutches.

"Scott," she shrilled, "you have to stop with the questions!"

But why? Was I hurting someone by asking so many questions? Was I acting like a disease, infecting someone with curiosity?

Was I the disgrace my mother made me out to be?

"Scott," my mother's eyes filled with tears as we rushed through the streets of College Point and back into our house. "Scott, you are too much."

'But mom,' tears rushed to the front of my eyes, 'It's not my fault.'

She stopped dead in her tracks and smashed her hand across my face.

All of the innocence I had brewing within me whittled down to two words and a question that would cling to my core for what felt like eternity:

Why me?

This can't be my life. My life is different.

I felt a voice from deep within itching at my core. Murmurs of "You are meant to be more," "Your life matters," and "You are here for a reason" sang from within me almost like an angelic prayer you would hear in those family Christmas movies.

It was a creeping sensation that I could not fully fathom back then.

It was a pulsating urge to burst at the seams of society and break into something.

Anything…

Something.

What? I just don't know…

Maybe I just wasn't ready to understand then.

I would tuck those thoughts away in my head for another introspective moment that would creep throughout my veins, never to be heard outside of the four walls that encased my mind from the harshness that was the sickening reality my mother forced me into: I was dangerously different and it was a bad thing.

My silence was a sinister act, not one of curiosity, but of the hostility growing from within me.

"Stop asking questions:" the only three words that my mother said to prove her *undying* love for her only son... the doctor, the lawyer, the... whatever she wanted.

The one who could never live up to her whining and crying.

But that wouldn't matter anyway.

The fights still continued.

In my mother's defense, she was not always beating me into submission. She had her moments where I did feel a tinge of comfort. She tried, she truly did, for it was clear that there was a part of her past that was just as obscure as she was. My parents had a difficult time making ends meet some weeks, but that did not mean they did not try everything in their power to ensure the well being of their children.

In hindsight, I sense that a lot of my mother's frustrations and actions were a direct result of something she endured when she was my age.

As a child, I just sat pensively and awaited my mother or my father's wishes. After all, they were my parents and I love them dearly.

Month after month, we were not able to afford some of the luxuries that other families in our neighborhood could have. Whenever I needed a haircut, we could not afford to go to a barbershop or one of those fancy salons on College Point Boulevard, so our salvation was the kitchen table. My mother would plop my sisters and I on the table, one by one, and cut our hair as best as she could. When it was my turn for a trim, I would dread what my mother would do to me. Each time, she plopped a bowl directly onto my head and took the shears to my locks, as if they were what she channeled her impulsive energy towards. I was trapped as she snipped bits of my hair from my head, using the bowl to guide the scissors in only a manner she could define as graceful. I was in awe of how happy she was to cut my hair for me. Still, I mourned my identity as it drifted to the floor; when she took the bowl off of my head, I shook the loose pieces of hair from my shoulders and held back my tears.

I wanted to make her happy. I wanted to please her. I wanted her to see how overjoyed despite being an unwilling participant in her makeshift barbershop in our humble kitchen. Though, as I looked into the metallic mirror she held up to my face, all sense of glee melted from my eyes as I muttered, 'That's great mom, thanks.'

Her happiness would dissipate throughout the night, and by the time I went to bed my bowl cut was the only thing truly untouched by her fists.

In school my head would be met with a stone wall, literally, as if the bullies at school could just smell the stench of abuse lingering on my breath. Chants of "stupid Jew, stupid Jew" were reverberating around my swollen brain. The blood dripping from my head was a quaint reminder that I was genuinely hated. I was seemingly despised by everyone for just being who I was, for being born into the skin I was in, and being an outcast in the grand scheme of childhood. One was not like the others, and that one just always seemed to be me.

With blurred vision and a trail of blood trailing behind my staggered walk back home, my mother's normally nasty demeanor shifted the moment she shouted, "Who did this to you, Scott!?"

The next day as we trotted up to the principal's office, my mother laced into the boys who tossed me about as if she were finally protecting her young. It seemed that her mommy dearest act dropped the second the maternal instincts kicked in.

"Stay away from my boy," she pierced the minds of the bullies before her and let genuine, unfiltered rage settle into their skulls. As we walked away and she clenched my fingers in her unwavering fit of anger, it dawned on me: she was my mother, but she was more prone to violence. Only she could have control over her son. Only she could push her child around and beat him senseless.

My cries for mercy felt meaningless at home and at school. Nothing seemed to stop the ever-sinking feeling deep within that represented my intense pain: like I probably mentioned, or you probably inferred by now, I had very little friends.

Walking the streets of College Point did give me some solace, but the moment that the neighborhood kids would find me, my peaceful minutes felt like painstaking hours. As I approached the candy store, one of my usual spots to get away from *it all*, I saw the bullies rounding the corner and eagerly stepping off of their bicycles.

As I turned to run in the other direction, Kevin, the biggest bully of them all, stood towering before me.

"Whatsa matter, Matheson? You goin' somewhere," his eyes morphed into narrow black dots of hatred and impending violence, "You a-fraid, ya big baby?" The other kids laughed and looked on in astonishment at the scene they were about to commit. I was waiting for one of them to pull out a knife and stab me in the back… but no… they had to make my punishment for existing much more painful.

Taunts of "Matheson, Matheson" echoed around my head as they sashayed and scampered around my quivering body. All it took was one slight shove and the kids were enthusiastically launching me about like a hacky-sack. I feared death, but I feared their perpetual ridicule even more.

My eyes were welling up with tears as I shrunk to the floor, when the most miraculous situation of instant karma appeared before me: Kevin lost his balance and flew face first into the candy store window. The other kids screamed and scattered: their loyalty was dissipating into the sunset as their minds fluttered to a state of fear, for they did not want their parents to berate them with words just as harshly as they beat me with their fists.

Kevin hung there, shattered glass strewn about like marbles on a child's bedroom floor, crying and screaming for help. The shop owner raced forward and began to inspect the damage from the incident, unknowingly yelling at a child of circumstance: he just tripped. It was an accident. It was as if someone was looking out for me and wanted to ensure my safety.

It was an abrupt miracle, and my chance to run into the sunset to seek out the one being that would never believe what just happened: Pokey.

Pokey was the most playful and vivacious golden retriever in all of College Point. He was the most stunningly loyal dog, always ready for an adventure and to simply listen to what I had to say. Once I darted up the stairs and held him tightly in my arms, my fears that the boys could come after me melted away.

The two of us dashed to the breadstick factory blocks away from our house, the fresh aroma of the bakery filling the air with a pleasantly delicious smell. Pokey tugged on the leash and met the workers at Angora's Breadstick Factory with the utmost innocence. The men would laugh and pat Pokey on the head, passing me compliments and a bag of freshly made breadsticks along the way.

Pokey's barks and jovial leaps could make absolutely anyone giddy and filled with glee: even the adults at Angora's, which was an enlightening experience for me. It felt good to be appreciated. The two of us rushed to College Point Park, sitting pensively on the rocks in the midst of the calm, patient nightfall.

Looking out into the distance, a bit of bread placed effervescently in my prepubescent fingers, I felt an inner peace. A voice spoke from somewhere within me again, echoing the same ideas I had tucked away time and time again: "You are meant to be more," "Your life matters," and "You are here for a reason."

I was here, with my best friend in the entire world, Pokey, and we were together. It was all that mattered, despite the beatings and the pain…

Yeah… that was all that mattered.

The sunset cascaded over the skyline and we began our journey back to reality, back to where we called home. Though in hindsight, was it ever really home?

Going to middle school became the only antidote to the bully-drenched illness my body was accustomed to each day. High school gave me the false hope that someone like me could find a love so pure and so genuine.

Again, it was just a matter of time before I let myself down believing that love was an open door. Instead, love began to seem like a series of stained-glass windows: you could admire them from afar and spend hours upon hours glaring at the beauty before you, but if you dare touch the precious elements, you would get cut by what you could never truly experience.

CHAPTER 3

Inevitable Illusions

~

"Why has there never been a holiday, where peace is celebrated all throughout the world? The time is overdue for people like me and you, who know the way to truth is love and unity to all God's children."

\- Stevie Wonder, American singer-songwriter, Saginaw, Michigan

Life as I knew it was dwindling before me.

If I was not being bullied at school, my mother was pushing me around at home to the point where I felt my body succumbing to each of her arduous remarks.

My skin was seething with the bruises she adorned on my abdomen.

I desperately needed to break free from the life I was following. I would have said leading, but I knew that I was not in control of my destiny at that point... or at least that is what I thought.

After school, my grandparents and uncle would often come visit me from the Bronx. If I was really lucky, my father would drop me off at their house for the evening on his way into the city.

It was a refreshing escape from the consuming borough of Queens and all that my parents pressured me with.

"Hey kid," my uncle was glad to see me as I crept into his room.

'Hey,' I plopped on his bed as he stood off to the corner.

"What's goin' on? Why do you look so sad?" He placed down what he was holding and moved towards me.

'Oh,' I swallowed hard. 'It's nothing.'

Every fiber of my being wanted to scream out. I wanted to rip my hair out and scrape at my skin until there was nothing left. I yearned to get the scent of the bullies' sweat from my body. I needed to rid myself of my mother's beatings, and I figured the only way to do so would be to shed my skin.

I had hoped that my silent, yet subtle scratching would alert my uncle that something was happening, though I was not brave enough to open my mouth just yet.

My uncle caught a glimpse of my teary eyes and assumed I was just dealing with drama I could not articulate.

"Here," he walked back over to the corner and placed the needle on the vinyl sitting on the player.

'What's that?'

The music started to play.

I could hear the subtle scratching of the vinyl as the lyrics sprung forth:

"You know it doesn't make much sense
There ought to be a law against

> *Anyone who takes offense*
> *At a day in your celebration*
> *'Cause we all know in our minds*
> *That there ought to be a time*
> *That we can set aside*
> *To show just how much we love you*
> *And I'm sure you would agree*
> *It couldn't fit more perfectly*
> *Than to have a world party*
> *On the day you came to be"*

"Have you ever heard of this album," my uncle began to shift his shoulders and shimmy across the room. "It's *Hotter than July*."

'But it's November.'

He laughed, "It's the name of the album."

'Oh,' I smiled. 'Okay.' I began moving to the rhythm.

"It's about harmony and peace and Martin Luther King, Jr."

The lyrics continued after a series of "Happy Birthdays" chirped over the speakers:

> *"I just never understood*
> *How a man who died for good*
> *Could not have a day that would*
> *Be set aside for his recognition*
> *'Cause it should never be*
> *Just because some cannot see*
> *The dream as clear as he*
> *That they should make it become an illusion*
> *And we all know everything*
> *That he stood for time will bring*
> *For in peace our hearts will sing*
> *Thanks to Martin Luther King."*

I later learned that Martin Luther King, Jr. was a civil rights activist who died fighting for truth and justice. The man was a leader among those who needed a voice.

My mind raced with questions and insightful thoughts.

I was devastated that he seemed to lose his life during his empowerment-laced prime, though I wondered if one day I could carry the torch he ignited.

A flame only remains bright if someone is willing to kindle the flame.

I wanted to be the one to rise up and do that, though at that age, I was drowning in a lack of self-confidence.

How could someone who could barely speak advocate for millions like Martin Luther King, Jr. did?

"There are lots of musicians you need to know about," my uncle continued moving around the room. "Elvis, The Beatles, The Bee Gees."

As we continued to talk about music, my mind floated through everything my uncle was saying. He spoke of music as if it were gospel; any sort of music seemed to be of interest to him, and he rambled on about harmonies with such passion.

I wanted that.

I wanted to be so passionate about something that I could enlighten and inspire people.

However, my mind was filled with questions and very few answers.

When the song finished, my uncle stood up and reset the needle. The song played over and over again, until both of us seemed to want to move on to another record.

This afternoon transpired into something much greater: in the months to come, my uncle took me to my first concerts: we saw an Elvis impersonator at a major amusement park in the area and got a chance to see Air Supply perform at Radio City Music Hall.

There was a certain thrill being in the presence of, as my uncle portrayed them, musical geniuses.

Still, nothing compared to that one day when my uncle sat down and introduced me to music. Hearing Stevie Wonder's song "Happy Birthday" over and over again filled me with a sliver of hope.

Between the lyrics and his advice, I felt that there was a chance I could find the strength to keep moving forward. After all, I knew that at some point I would not be living with my parents anymore.

My uncle's words that afternoon stuck with me throughout my entire life:

"You see, Scott, what I am trying to get at is that adversity can be overcome."

The two of us looked at each other.

My uncle put his hand on my shoulder, "Do you understand?"

I nodded.

I did, but at the time I did not know the solution to overcoming everything going on at home.

Life continued to drift away as his advice radiated through my head. The questions filling my mind were of an existential nature, though I did not know precisely what that term truly meant until I was way into my twenties.

As far as I knew then, life consisted of bullying, trauma, and questions that just never seemed to have answers.

∞ ∞ ∞ ∞ ∞ ∞ ∞ ∞

Just at the cusp of middle school, I found even more of a reason to question every fiber of my existence within the breathy pangs of question after lucid question.

Each Tuesday, Wednesday, and Sunday, I was glued to a chair at Hebrew school: I was sanctioned by my parents and the community around me to become the upstanding religious family man that I was *destined* to be.

Why were so many people eager to put someone into a box: why did we have to be limited to one set of thoughts or one religion?

My mind would rattle on with questions as I sat scratching at the edge of my marble notebook. The Rabbi would raise his voice and pump his hands towards the sky. He would remark about sacrifices and how we needed to be accepting of all cultures and creeds. He would wave his hands in honor of Abraham, Moses, and David: the stories he would tell painted the picture of a perfect world where peace was paramount. However, there were so many ideologies and religions in the world, I personally had a difficult time comprehending just why we were all separate.

If every human being is supposed to be cut from the same cloth, then why tear at the universal fabric of society?

The Rabbi caught my glazed look and assumed that the words festering within me were of a hallowed ground. His demeanor grew more impatient with each thought that circumnavigated my conscious.

"Scott Zachariah!" cut through me with such a rampant force.

The Rabbi stood diagonal to my desk and gleamed at me with disdain. Every young set of eyes was cast downward at my physical depiction.

"Scott, my boy, what say you," The Rabbi motioned to the board where a collection of characters melted into the desolation of the chalkboard. The lines and marks before me emulated the sense that something was wrong. There was a missing element of our universal coexistence between our planet and our inherent selves.

I felt it. I knew it.

I sensed it... somehow.

There was a longing to purse my lips together and push the questions forth from within me. On a wing and a silent prayer, I spoke:

'Rabbi, what is the meaning of life?'

"What," he was perplexed.

'Rabbi, if we are all supposed to be one and together, why do we have so many religions?'

The children in class giggled. Their eyes filled with tears as they assumed I was about to juxtapose everything the Rabbi spoke of for countless years.

"Scott, what are you rambling about?" The Rabbi seemed to chuckle and try to give me a chance: be it a chance to correct my questions or silence my curiosity, I will never fully understand.

'Rabbi, if the religions of the world also believe in God, then why are so many wars fought because of him?'

The room erupted in laughter as my list of questions went on and on. The Rabbi, clearly frustrated, began to screech and turn beet red with anger.

"Scott my boy, we cannot ask so many questions," he smiled in an attempt to hide his fury.

'Why can't I ask questions, Rabbi? What is wrong with being curious?'

"Stop," his command boomed throughout the room, "Stop asking all of these stupid questions!"

The silence distilled among the voices in the room. Everyone looked on in astonishment that I made such a brazen move. I did not think what I did was bold or crass. I thought this was something that everyone should do. I thought it was a natural way of life: to question, to implore, to inquire… for if we did not question everything, then how could we grow?

What sort of adventures exist beyond our view?

What could we truly create in this world if we all took a look at our beliefs?

It may seem that we are all so inherently different, though so much of who we inherently are is the same deep within us.

The conversation and my questions grew more rampant when I sat down for a family dinner with my parents and sisters.

My father's obsession with CBS-FM radio carried over into our suppertime, for his love of music cut through the chatter of clicking silverware and our awkward silence.

The Five Satins serenaded us with a melody as we ate:

"In the still of the night
I held you
Held you tight
'Cause I love
Love you so
Promise I'll never
Let you go
In the still of the night."

My mother's voice leapt over the melodic lyrics.

"Sarah, can you pass the mashed potatoes," my mother reached for my sister.

"Here mom," Sarah's little hands extended to the bowl.

My father was slurping down his water and bickering with my other sister, Rebecca, who was sheepishly pushing her fork against the peas on her plate.

Over the conversation between the four of them, I sat quietly glaring at my reflection in the dining room window. My next question was just on the tip of my tongue.

'Dad,' I perked up when the room fell silent and all eyes turned to me, 'Why are we reform?'

"Reform, as in," he retorted.

'Reform Jewish people.'

My family looked on in utter confusion.

"Because that is what we are son," he chuckled.

I sat in silence for a moment to collect my thoughts.

'Dad, but why are *we* reform? Why aren't we Orthodox or Conservative?'

"Because we just aren't, okay?"

'But Rabbi always says we need peace in the world, right?'

"Okay."

'And we are supposed to bring peace to the world, right?'

"Yes, son."

'But how can we be peaceful people if there isn't even peace between the Orthodox people, the Reform people, and the Conservative people? Aren't we all Jewish, so why don't we all get along?'

My mother bowed her head in disgrace as my sisters giggled. My father wiped his face with a napkin and tenderly set it on the table before unleashing yet another traumatic blow to my inquisitive conscience.

"Scott, again," he boomed, "Stop with all of these stupid questions!"

'But dad, they aren't stupid questions, these are real problems we are facing in the world and-'

"Go to your room. Don't eat, just go." His face hardened and I felt utterly unwanted.

I dragged my body from the table and meandered to my dreary bedroom. Pokey followed me, realizing that I was tormented by my curiosity almost as much as I was blessed by it. My mind drifted off as I cried myself to sleep that night.

How would we be able to heal the planet if we can't even heal ourselves?

How can we become more peaceful if we are fighting a war building within us?

How can we define our existence when we could spend a lifetime searching for so many answers?

How... just... how... just...

My mind faded to black and the last thing I could remember was Pokey sitting at my feet, nestling into my warmth as we settled in for another long and inquisitive night, just as we always had.

CHAPTER 4

Goodbye to Romance

~

"Yesterday has been and gone. Tomorrow will I find the sun or will it rain? Everybody's having fun except me. I'm the lonely one. I live in shame."

-Ozzy Osbourne, British singer, songwriter, actor and reality television star, Birmingham, United Kingdom

Once school let out for the year, I was preparing myself for a few months of hard work and well-deserved sunshine.

I stumbled upon the friendship of a beautiful young girl, Audrey, whose eyes were gentle and heart seemed pure. I figured that I could really get used to putting my arms around such a kind person and feel such sweet emotions from the two of us simply holding hands. I was sad that just as my life was beginning to look up, I had to wait for a few more weeks to tell her about my love for her.

The Boy Scouts Summer Camp program was separating us, but just for a few weeks. Then I could finally begin my relationship with Audrey. I am sure she could not wait for me to return, for she was just as giddy to see me, and I was just as smitten with her and her luscious black hair.

The summer heat pushed steadily against my forehead, oppressing my body in a way that only one-hundred-degree heat could cause. I was drenched in sweat by the time my father dashed out of the house and summoned me to his cherry red station wagon.

"Son," he boomed, motioning for me to hurry up, "we are going to be late."

I hopped into the car and grabbed my uniform from the backseat.

'Thanks for driving me dad, I appreciate it.' I was happy that we could spend some time together, since he was always off at work and too busy to have some genuine father-son bonding time together.

We rode around for a bit with silence between us while I tapped against the armrest. My father's radio blared Harry Chapin's "Cat's in the Cradle," which was a tender reflection of the time we were spending together:

> *"And the cat's in the cradle and the silver spoon*
> *Little boy blue and the man in the moon*
> *"When you coming home, dad?" "I don't know when"*
> *But we'll get together then*
> *You know we'll have a good time then"*

I looked at him with a sense of nostalgia deep within. We were part of the same family, but divided in so many ways. It was uncanny, honestly. How could two men who had the same DNA be wired so differently?

We were driving through the trees and up dirt roads. It was a stark contrast to the urban skyline that decorated the casual streets of the city limits.

My father glanced over at me with a hint of disdain. He softened his glances a bit and spoke quite solemnly, "What goes through your head, boy?"

'Huh?'

"Why do you always ask so many questions," he asked softly.

A long pause hung in the air. I did not know if this was a trick question.

'I-' I looked at his reaction to see whether or not I should continue. He seemed to want to hear what I was about to say as he hung on that 'I' so contently.

'I am just curious, dad.' He accepted that answer as the truth, for his smile became much clearer.

"Son, I just want you to know that although you are *different* from the other boys, that doesn't make you less of a man."

'I know, dad.'

"Son, my boy," he placed his hand on my shoulder, "be true to yourself and just believe in yourself."

Tears started to stream down my face. I was in utter disbelief that my father was showing a sign of compassion.

"Scott, why are you crying?" The song changed on the radio to something powerful. I could not hear what it was over the distraction my father was creating: his concern for me was a tad unsettling. I had to think of something.

I had to think of an excuse as to why I was crying, other than the sheer fact that my father was being sweet.

'It's just the boys at school,' I spoke softly, ' The boys at school call me Math man.'

"Just stand up for yourself, kid. It's a cruel world out there and if you let every single little thing hurt you, then this world will ruin you. Fight back," he boomed. "Knock 'em out."

'But dad,' I peeped. 'Fighting isn't right.'

"It's right if you make it that way."

I looked at him and realized that his view of the world would always be drastically different from mine.

We grinned at each other and turned the radio up to hear the song playing on 103.5 FM: a melody I hadn't heard before, but was drawn into the second I heard the piano and guitar combine to create a magical sound.

'Dad,' I gasped, 'What is that?'

"What is what?"

'The song,' I pointed at the radio eagerly.

"On the street where you live girls talk about their social lives
They're made of lipstick, plastic and paint
A touch of sable in their eyes
All your life all you asked
When is your Daddy gonna talk to you
But we're living in another world
Tryin' to get your message through"

The song played through and the DJ came back on the radio.

Emerging from some growing static, he said the words that struck me deeply: *"This was a new band, Bon Jovi, with their song 'Runaway,' hope you enjoyed it."*

'Bon' I paused, knowing my life was about to change forever, 'Jovi.'

Bon Jovi. The two words that would redefine my life... and eventually help define my absolute adoration for music that could touch the core of my body...

And eventually my soul.

As the car rounded the corner, I could see the dusk start to embrace the grotesque green buildings that were perched at the edge of the water. My father hit the brakes and we stepped out of the car almost in unison. The two of us would be working at the camp for the next two weeks. My father would be one of the adult supervisors while I was there so we could *try* to build a bridge in our relationship.

Night fell upon the lake and we circled around the adults who were starting to kindle our campfire. Like fireflies yearning to get closer and closer to the light, all of the boys and I darted to a place in the dirt. Once the fire was finally started, the real experience began.

Crackling embers shot forth from the fire, a dangerous reminder that even the most beautiful things in life require a cautious approach.

We talked until the stars encroached upon our twinkling eyes. The adults scurried back into the buildings while the boys and I remained outside in our natural habitat. About ten of us rested with our heads against various logs at the campsite. The shapes and lines that combined to form a beautiful picture pleasantly thrilled us.

"That constipation looks like a centaur," one of the boys exclaimed.

"You idiot," another spoke, "It's conservation, not constipation."

"No, no, no, you are both wrong," another yelled, "They are just stars."

'They are stars,' I said, 'But they are also constellations.'

The boys looked at me and in unison shouted, "NERD."

I didn't care. I was just so thrilled to be out in nature where I felt most at peace.

The boys took turns saying what they thought they saw, until one of the boys said that we all needed to make wishes on the stars up above.

"I wish for a big car when I grow up," one said.

"I wish that I could eat all the chocolate in the world," another said.

'I wish for true love,' I spoke with a tinge of wishful thinking in my voice.

The boys all started laughing again.

"Okay Scott," one of the boys said, "But that's a crazy wish."

We sat for a while and talked about a bunch of different things. I felt my eyelids get heavier and heavier as their voices drifted past the point of recognition.

The next morning, I woke to something wet dripping on my face. The fire had gone out and all of the boys had disappeared. It was just me.

It was always just me.

But at least this time I had someone waiting for me at home. And she was smart, funny, and everything and anything I could ask for. I had to spend another few weeks apart from her, but at least one thing was for certain:

Wishes and dreams are only crazy until they come true.

∞ ∞ ∞ ∞ ∞ ∞ ∞ ∞

Those two weeks flew by. My father and I barely spoke on the way back, for I was so entranced by the music blaring from the radio. He didn't really want to talk anyway, and he just seemed exhausted.

It was still early enough to get to the park by the time we got back, so I hopped on my bike and raced to where I knew Audrey would be. Unfortunately, as the wheels of my bicycle graced Fort Totten Park, the events that unfolded were akin to a bad movie scene. It kept replaying in my mind over and over again for years upon years.

I can't remember his name, but I could never forget his face. He was tall and skinny, leather jacket, black hair, a wallet with a chain that attached to his belt buckle, black boots, and a brush shoved in his rear pocket. He was the epitome of cool.

As I rode across the field I realized he had another accessory, but this one was attached to his lips: it was Audrey. At his feet was a boom box, and as I came closer, it came to my realization that their kiss was staged with the goal to have a good laugh at my expense. Blaring from the radio was "Goodbye to Romance," by Ozzy Osbourne.

Mr. Cool looked up and shouted, "Hey asshole, she's mine now, go away!" As he smirked and gloated, I turned and drearily rode away with my tail between my legs. I was hurt. I really liked her. I guess that what we had was not love.

The search for love was only just beginning. It had to be.

Clutching my shoulders and shivering almost felt second nature to me at that moment. His words stung through my heart like a pungent arrow. The stench of my fear made me sick, but nothing could escape the petulant moments he left me with: the taunting, the teasing, and the hope that Audrey would have been a dear friend, a girlfriend. A first love shattered. Why me? Why do I have to be bullied? Why do they have to tease me, taunt me, and push me into submission?

Why?

To this day, "Goodbye to Romance" is a song that I still can't listen to without it anchoring me to that quintessential moment in my life. Especially since music is a major part of my life. In actuality, it is my life. When I look at my life I can tell much of its story or parallel it to a soundtrack. "Goodbye to Romance" would make that soundtrack, along with anthems like "Jack n Diane" by John Cougar and "Living on a Prayer" by Bon Jovi. I love those two songs because they talk about the ideal relationships that can beat the odds. I wonder if that is a component of true love: a relationship that has odds to beat.

Audrey and I eventually became friends and we spoke later that summer. We sat on the rocks near Francis Lewis Park that we found by climbing through a hole in the fence. We talked about relationships, love, and life: much of the same things that I thought about sitting under the Whitestone Bridge by myself for hours upon hours.

As Audrey and I spoke, I stared out into the clear blue sky and got lost in the partial image of the Throgs Neck Bridge towering in the distance. Audrey's words made sense and I started to form some ideas about what love may actually be.

I realized something early on in life that day: I realized that Francis Lewis Park was where I will go to search for answers, and down by the Whitestone Bridge would be where I would find them.

I had only wished that I could speak to both Mr. Cool and Audrey more about the whole situation. I saw Audrey once before we lost touch for good. Still, if I could tell Mr. Cool and Audrey some advice about that day, I would love to tell them this:

For Audrey, I would ask her if we could still be friends and tell her that despite how hurt I was in that moment, I forgive her for being who she needed to be.

As for Mr. Cool, I would tell him that he obviously liked Audrey a lot, but he did not have to approach me in that manner. I do respect him as a human being and hope that he would treat her with the utmost respect. If you want to treat me badly, that is your prerogative, but I hope you did or do communicate very well with her. For now, if you would ever want to talk, I would be here for either one of you.

Until that moment comes, if it ever actually does, goodbye to romance.

∞ ∞ ∞ ∞ ∞ ∞ ∞ ∞

Later that evening, I found myself riding my bicycle nonchalantly through the streets of Queens. I was more in tune with how the waves underneath the Throgs Neck Bridge ebbed and flowed with my heartbeat than the thoughts ruminating in my head. My relationship with the Throgs Neck Bridge has always been interesting. Although the Whitestone Bridge and I had an intimate relationship, for it played a major role in my journey from the Bronx to College Point, the Throgs Neck had a pervasive role in my life.

In my youth and throughout my life, I have consistently been in awe of how bridges exist and stand as a testament to who I am and all that I yearn to be: a man of integrity whose unwavering commitment to love, liberty, and strength exist in everything I do. After all, bridges are meant to create connections between two worlds. Somehow in my youthful state, I was able to comprehend their eternal importance and the impact bridges would have on both me and the literal and figurative situations people would find themselves in.

As I gripped the handles on my jet-black bicycle, I looked down at the larger-than-normal wheels and realized that my purpose, somehow and in some way, was also larger-than-normal... as a teenager I just didn't realize how large my purpose would be.

To combat the imbalance I was feeling deep within me, I remained steadfast when it came to the community traditions my parents immersed me in.

Everything inside of me wanted to please my parents so much, yet I always felt that I was never enough.

My parents desperately yearned to be prominent community members who dedicated their lives to service and sincerity. Naturally, they wanted their children to echo their sentiments. Behind closed doors I was accustomed to torturous words being spewed from my mother's lips, however I was too fearful to tell the world what was truly going on.

I went along with my parents' wishes to be the best they wanted me to be, and I knew that no matter what, I had to keep forging forward.

Regardless of the bruises crawling along my skin, I always had to complete more projects than anyone else. Over the summers, I would be entangled in the local library's Reading is Fundamental Program to show off, as my mother always proclaimed, my literary prowess.

Every year, I had to be the one to read the most books. I zipped through the entire *Hardy Boys* and *Nancy Drew* series, but that was not good enough.

My mother would rush off to the library and turn in the book as I finished each and every one, just so she could show off her son, the avid reader and the *smartest* boy on the block.

The pressure she applied upon me would eat away at every aspect of my being, though I did not realize I was in the process of growing at the time.

Just as I was finishing up the *Little House on the Prarie* series, it was time to begin my community service project for the Boy Scouts, which I was still a part of.

I remained in the Boy Scouts program through the years, where both my parents would oversee my progress as troop leaders.

My father pushed me to have more merit badges than anyone else in the neighborhood. It was necessary that I show up and represent the Matheson family name.

Being an Eagle Scout is the highest honor in the entire scouting world, and back then, being a Scout meant that you were respected within the community.

After years of sexual predators' actions and lawsuits coming to light, the positive image of the Scouting program diminished. It is a sad reality, though my time with the Scouts was enlightening.

As part of being an Eagle Scout, it was mandatory that a certain number of merit badges were completed and a variety of qualifications be met. Two of the most intense and toughest badges in the entire program were the Wilderness Survival Badge and Mile Swim Badge.

The swim provided quite an adrenaline rush for me, though it was nothing compared to the Wilderness Survival Badge. For that specific badge, I was blindfolded and dumped in the middle of the woods with no supplies whatsoever. Though it may seem terrifying for most people, nature was where I felt the most peace.

It would be a day away from my mother's torment and my father's disapproval. I built a small hut using sticks, fed myself using nearby berries, and found droplets of clean water by a stream.

In hindsight, those badges, along with the Emergency Preparedness Badge, helped me survive in life.

However, I digress. In order to be an Eagle Scout, it was mandatory that an approved service project take place. Upon looking at my local community, I chose to restore a city park that was an utter eyesore. For days upon days I was sweating in the blistering sun, stripping paint from the old fences that lined the shrubs and making the area appear presentable.

Mayor Koch, the same man who gave my father his award, approved my project and helped me become the second youngest Eagle Scout in the entire nation to complete his community service plan.

Though there was plenty of pomp and circumstance surrounding my award, had I been approved earlier and the red tape from bureaucracy loosened its grip, I would have been the youngest Eagle Scout in the entire country.

As I stood on the stage and accepted my award, Mayor Koch patted me on the shoulder and shook my hand. Glancing over to my parents made me realize that they harbored a sense of pride in knowing their one-and-only son became the second youngest Eagle Scout in the country.

Second.

Second place would become a comfortable space to exist, for the appropriate moniker followed me throughout all but one situation in my entire life.

At least the one time I came in first was a revolutionary situation that symbolized my willingness to never give up… but more on that later.

CHAPTER 5

The International Beer Club

~

"Remember days of skipping school, racing cars and being cool...

With a six pack and the radio, we didn't need no place to go."

- **Bon Jovi, American Rock Band, Sayreville, New Jersey**

Although I was caught between my mother's merciless baseball bat at home and the bullies' fists in middle school, I never felt the overwhelming pressure to stop being the inquisitive young man I was developing into. Through music and through the lyrics that clung between the melodies, I continued to blossom and grow into someone far beyond the grasp of my mother's dismay.

While coming back from recess one brisk fall day, I let the tender crunching of leaves below my feet keep me company while I held the door open for my classmates to come inside. As the door monitor, I took on the exquisite responsibility of ensuring everyone's safety and security from recess: even as a teenager I was sacrificing energy to help others with their lives, no matter how large or small the task was, I wanted to make sure I was useful to some capacity.

Also, I would do practically anything to get out of class. Although I was trying to be productive by doing something helpful or service-based, I was usually doing myself a disservice. In hindsight though, being service-oriented was just something that ran through my veins: I worked with the color guard, I was the door monitor, I worked in the audio-visual room with the projector, and I helped where I could.

As I mentioned before, the Boy Scouts program was also incredibly important to me.

I tend to think I was constantly trying to help people because I was never at the receiving end of any sort of salvation at home.

I did however have great respect for Mrs. R, a phenomenal teacher and woman who went above and beyond to help me get through middle school while trying to be a moral and upstanding man. I am forever in her gratitude for all of the values and lessons she instilled within my soul. Two instances that really exemplify the kind of humanitarian she was stand out in my mind to this very day.

Her husband had died on a business trip and instead of pulling her from the classroom, the Assistant Principal told her in front of our class. Right then and there, Mrs. R broke down and cried. She was stoic and proud, yet in the moments when she broke, you could feel the energy in the room shift. In the days before social emotional learning, Mrs. R allowed herself to be vulnerable enough to show her emotions in front of students, to the extent where I went home and cried for her deceased husband.

Another profound moment also stands out in my mind, which took place due to Mrs. R's compassion. I consistently tried to mask my pain and agony at home and from the bullies through being a somewhat rambunctious teenager. I didn't think anyone really noticed me or my abuse, for no one had ever asked me about it. One day, Mrs. R asked my girlfriend at the time, Tina, and I to meet her at 6:00 P.M. in front of the school. Since she was my favorite teacher, I really did not think anything of it.

Tina and I met her in the evening at 6:00 P.M. Mrs. R brought another teacher with her to talk with both of us. The four of us sat on the steps for a moment, until Mrs. R said, "Mrs. G and I would like to take both of you out to dinner, would you join us?"

The two of us were ecstatic and complied happily. Mrs. R had a black Cadillac with tinted windows and leather seats. At that point, it was the nicest car I had ever been in.

In the car ride on the way to the restaurant I could not help but think that Mrs. R was the coolest teacher in the world. She took us to this really nice, fancy Chinese Restaurant just off of Little Neck Parkway and Union Turnpike in Queens. It is no longer there, but because of the experience I had that night, over the years I ended up taking many different girls to that restaurant on dates.

We walked into the restaurant and the Maître D had called her by her first name. They knew her and welcomed her with open arms. She slipped the man a $100 bill in front of us, and said, "Please make sure you take care of us."

I was in awe.

Who was this lady and why was I truly here?

Mrs. R said order anything on the menu, and in retrospect I realize that she saw I was skinny, knew I was probably very hungry, and that I must have been getting no attention at home.

Her kindness and compassion gave me more insight and education into my future career and livelihood in one night, as opposed to the many years of schooling I would eventually endure as an adult... but more on that later. In reality, if you could pinpoint a moment in my life that sparked my path to helping close to one million kids, this experience was it.

In a room with red velvet carpet floors, a giant fish tank in the center with massive fish, and oak tables that stretched clear across the restaurant, I experienced the epicenter of my own humanitarian existence.

I ordered spare ribs and fried rice, and devoured it in moments.

Mrs. R asked me if we knew why she brought us there, and through spoonfuls of food, Tina and I responded that we actually did not understand.

She wanted to know what was going on in my life. Mrs. R got the sense that something bad, very bad was going on and that no one was helping me. She wanted me to acknowledge that there were adults in the world who would be there if I needed it. She wanted me to see that I was not alone and that I did not have to face things on my own.

Mrs. R told me something that I had not heard before: "Scott, I don't know what it is, but I know, and I sense that you are going to do something really big in this world. You are different, you are smart, you are compassionate, and your life matters; you are way more important and special to this world than what is happening to you. You are more than whatever is going on around you."

At the time, I did not know how to verbalize my thoughts at that moment. Everything that was going on in my life was such a chaotic mystery to me, and I was in such a blurred state of misunderstanding. She proceeded to talk to me all night about good values, healthy choices, and rising above what I was going through to accomplish anything I set my mind to.

She explained that I had all this light and power within, and I was not sure if I comprehended what she was saying in the moment, but I just knew that this woman went out of her way. She went above and beyond to give me this message. I thanked her sincerely.

Mrs. R said that if I needed help, if anything was going on at home that I was concerned about, or that if something did not seem right, I should feel free and comfortable to speak to her.

I knew in those moments that her words were speaking to the voices deep inside of me. She was communicating with me in a way that was a sort of soul connection.

That night forever lingers in my mind, and although I never did speak to her about my turmoil at home, I clung to two valuable lessons that she instilled in me, which I carry to this day: the words she said would make sense and I would learn from these moments and the fact that I wanted to be just like her when I grew up. I knew that I wanted to be in a position that when I grew up, if I was given the chance to save or help someone, it was my duty to be there.

Even then, I knew somewhere deep down she circumvented the system for the greater good of humanity. She gave me hope in human beings. She gave me hope in humanity. I knew that if I could get into a position where I could make a difference in someone's life, I would pay that moment forward a million times over.

And to this day I do.

∞ ∞ ∞ ∞ ∞ ∞ ∞ ∞

In between allowing the few friends I had to tie my waist with an extension cord and shimmy down the small hole from the audio-visual room to the auditorium (so I can sneak past the security guard and get food, of course) and all of the service work I was doing, I tried to stay busy during the day. As the days passed and I was holding the door open once again at the end of recess, a kid with a bad haircut rushed up to me. He looked disheveled and appeared to be curious about my presence by the door.

"Hey Scott," he said in a friendly tone.

'Hey,' I didn't really know his name.

"You listen to Van Halen?"

'Of course!' Realistically, I didn't know who the kid was, nor what Van Halen was.

He gave me a high five and shouted, "I knew you were cool!" as he scampered back into the building. Hall and Oates was what my father listened to each and every night, but I still intended to find out who the Van Halen were. Like I said, music really spoke to me and had a special part in my life. After all, I had just heard one of Bon Jovi's songs and felt some sort of kindred connection with his lyrics and music.

My middle school adventures continued once I started going through puberty and realizing that this boy was developing into a man. In my youth, I must admit that I did not know how to "be" with a girl, nor did I understand what getting hot and heavy was, but in our teenage years I am certain my girlfriend Tina and I got close to it.

Eventually, her mother walked in on the two of us making out and practically naked in her room. We kept in touch for years after that, but

I felt that the moment was rather quintessential to piecing together my life as a growing teenage boy.

Like I have said, when it came to girls and relationships so far, I was not rather lucky. Still, I was able to find a few female friends that were loyal pals and fun to be around. I would ride my bike to the Whitestone Bridge and wait for Taryn and Lana to make their appearance in Francis Lewis Park. Both Taryn and Lana were crazy, but crazy in such a good way that brought a smile to my face. They taught me a lot about life and were a huge emotional support system when it came to my parents.

Taryn had exquisite fire-engine red hair and Lana resembled a centerfold model: they were truly a force to be reckoned with. All three of us were dealing with pretty major things and questioning life in our own ways. Taryn was going through a family divorce and possibly moving far away, which was practically like the end of the world to a thirteen-year-old. Lana was battling cancer and the whole school made fun of her because she wore a wig. Taryn and I were the only two who didn't tease her or judge her.

Due to her emotional burden and the stress she was dealing with, Lana became suicidal. Taryn and I talked her through every painful emotion, and the three of us created a kinship over growing up through bouts of teenage innocence and daily traumatic turmoil.

My life was becoming pretty great: I finally had friends I could converse with on a deeper level and I was not feeling too alone anymore.

∞ ∞ ∞ ∞ ∞ ∞ ∞ ∞

In the summer leading up to my first year of high school, Lana, Taryn, and I got into our fair share of mishaps and misadventures.

On my first day of high school, a part of me was petrified to potentially face bullies that would knock me down from the natural high I was feeling over the summer. I sat on the back of the Q65 bus feeling holistically alone, despite being surrounded by other kids who were making their way through Queens.

I felt a tingle creep down my spine almost as if I was about to experience something equally exciting and inspirational. A big guy got onto the bus and made a beeline for the seat next to mine. He was an incredibly handsome man, but as he approached me, I realized that he could not be much older than I was. He had that stoic, captain-of-the-football team demeanor that would be sure to make every teenage boy stand taller and every schoolgirl swoon.

As he plopped down next to me, I was feeling a little nervous and was on the verge of exploding. I heard him take a deep breath and he twisted his head in my direction.

"Are you going to Jamaica High School, too?" His voice sounded a lot friendlier than I thought it would be.

I looked at his chocolate brown eyes that were far smoother than the clunky movements he made walking towards the back of the bus.

'Yeah,' I said. Unsure what to say next, I smirked and re-adjusted myself in the seat. Lush trees reflected in the dirt-speckled windows of the bus. I glared off into the distance and silently wished that I were back in my lukewarm bed.

As our bus stop neared, I caught the glimpse of a young girl glaring back at me every so often. Each time I would catch her looking at me, she would rub her right shoulder against her face, almost as if she were trying to rub the look of curiosity off of her expression.

∞ ∞ ∞ ∞ ∞ ∞ ∞ ∞

The two of us hopped off of the bus and began strolling down the street to the tune of a friendly conversation. We passed a pond on our right side and a diner on the left. The scenery seemed so familiar and it emulated a picturesque scene from a movie. It appeared as if I knew this guy all my life. Tommy's kindness continued to permeate the lonely and anxiety-ridden parts of me.

The young girl from the bus was following not too far behind us, but she kept an awkward pace, almost as if she were working up the courage to address us.

We approached the building and were met with an illustrious sight: the high school was adorned with beautiful, ornate architecture. It was a pleasant sight between the middle of an urban jungle. The school itself was about to become a quintessential setting of my youthful life. Everything leading up to this moment was painted in the landscape of a run-down city juxtaposed with the alluring lights from the Throgs Neck and Whitestone Bridges.

As my new friend, Tommy, and I looked up at the school, the girl behind us was standing closer now. A breathy chuckle came from Tommy's lips.

"I wonder if I am ever going to graduate from here," he said stoically.

'Tommy, that's nonsense,' I muttered.

The girl behind us stepped next to us and officially made her presence known.

"You can graduate if you put your mind to it," she remarked.

We stood in silence for a moment to soak in all of the excitement life had to offer.

"I'm Wendy, by the way," the girl said.

The two of us responded with our names before fixing our eyes north. Our emerging trio gazed at that school with mixed feelings of trepidation and admiration: Jamaica High School was about to be our home in place of home for the next four years.

∞ ∞ ∞ ∞ ∞ ∞ ∞ ∞

I swaggered through the hallway with a stimulating sense of pride. It was true through and through: I was the school nerd and I was prone to my quirks and quips, but I was about to do my best to try to be the cool guy on campus.

All of my inhibitions melted away, for as Tommy and Wendy spoke it seemed like we knew each other for years. Wendy provided plenty of thought-provoking conversation, and Tommy and I were eager to learn more about this previously mysterious being who tottered behind us on our journey here.

A striking blonde, who was virtually perfect in every essence of the word, approached us with a classic smile. Her eyes were beckoning to some special part of my core and I was secretly hoping she was coming to speak to me.

Tommy kissed the girl on the lips and pulled her closer into his waist. Wendy and I looked on with sheer curiosity beaming from our eyes.

"Danielle, say hello," Tommy grumbled.

"Hi guys, I'm Danielle." She extended her hand to Wendy first and grinned from ear to ear. Danielle was the spitting image of a man's unwavering fantasy: her personality and looks made her seem like the perfect candidate for Miss America.

She was everything and anything I could have asked for, and she was Tommy's girl.

As part of typical guy code, or at least from what I gathered based on watching Western films with my dad, a true man never steals another man's girl.

And Tommy was *the* man.

We all rushed off to class after speaking for a few moments, but I had the overwhelming feeling that my life was about to become a whirlwind of excitement. I met a group of people who seemed genuinely unique and just like me.

What more could I really ask for at the moment?

∞ ∞ ∞ ∞ ∞ ∞ ∞ ∞

I adjusted my denim jacket and strolled into History class. Another stunning girl was sitting not too far from me, so it was only natural that I create some sort of trouble on the first day of school. I usually attracted trouble anyway, so why not try my hand at it?

I wrote a love letter, or a letter that at least professed some sort of emotion, to the young girl with auburn hair. The moment I heard someone say that her name was Anastasia; I was intrigued by her beauty and her utterly appealing name.

As people nudged one another to pass her the note, I grew anxious. As the note crinkled in her fingertips and she turned to meet my gaze, it was almost as if the entire room was moving in slow motion.

"Scott Matheson," the teacher squawked.

'Here,' I chirped. Momentarily taking my eyes off of her intrigued gaze. When I turned back however, I was greeted with the eyes of a rather distasteful glance: her boyfriend's. George was another one of those rather large though handsome fellows, and I just made his shit list.

Great.

More new friends.

George took his right finger and dragged it horizontally across his neck: it was a subtle threat that he was going to make an attempt on my life.

Great, again.

Scott Zachariah Matheson goofed again… another guy already took another stunning girl. I just had all the luck.

George mouthed something to me, but I squinted to make out his message. Then it hit me: Meet me outside at 3.

And so my first day was already shaping up to be my worst day.

∞ ∞ ∞ ∞ ∞ ∞ ∞ ∞

The rest of the day was rather uneventful. I had a few classes with Wendy and got a chance to eat lunch with her, Tommy, Danielle, and a few other people we met throughout the day. The group of friends I had made seemed incredibly nice and rather warm.

We became an instant family.

Wendy slurped her milk through a plastic straw, which clattered against the carton. She squinted and closed her eyes, almost to savor the sweet sensation of both the milk and our conversations.

Danielle was speaking about some rather profound things as she ran her fingers up and down the side of Tommy's head. She would giggle and rock her forehead against his hardened demeanor as we all continued to talk.

Tommy kept the stern look on his face: glaring about the cafeteria as if he were looking around the confines of a jungle, seeking out his prey.

I went to the rest of my classes and met the group outside of the school. The sunlight was a welcomed juxtaposition to the dreary walls of our school building.

As we walked, Tommy and Danielle were ahead of us and Wendy and I were engaging in a gentle conversation. I felt my shoulder pull backwards and my backpack caught my fall.

George stood over me on the sidewalk screaming in my face: "Stay away from Anastasia!"

Tommy pivoted, pushing Danielle and Wendy aside, and rushed George in a fit of rage. We were just paces away from the bus stop. We were almost safe.

George raised his right fist with my t-shirt clenched in his fingertips just as Tommy knocked him off of me and onto a nearby car. As George's head thudded against the old Honda, Tommy held George in the exact same position he had me in just moments ago.

"Do *not* touch Scott!" The capillaries in Tommy's eyes reached right to his irises. His face burned red with the excitement of getting to pulverize someone.

"Tommy, get off of him," Danielle shouted from close by. I could see her rushing to grab him as Wendy crossed her forearms and boosted me off of the floor.

George looked absolutely petrified as Danielle reached Tommy's right fist. She pressed her body against his back as she wrapped her fingers around his hand. Tommy turned to meet Danielle's gaze and softened his glance.

It is truly amazing what the calming gaze of a woman can do to a man.

Our group walked back over to the bus, leaving George and Anastasia by the car almost as if we were trying to forget what had just happened. Tommy wrapped his huge arm around my shoulder and drew me close in such a brotherly way. I was taken aback by what had just happened: it seemed like Tommy just adopted me.

"You don't know how to fight, brother?"

He called me brother!

'No, I mean,' I stuttered, 'No, not really.'

"We will change that," Tommy spoke confidently, "We will."

The four of us wandered onto the school bus and chatted all the way until I got off of the bus and sauntered back to my parents' house.

When I walked in, my mother was home by herself with my sisters because my father was on a business trip for work. No one asked me how my first day of high school was. No one bothered even glancing at me over the steaming mashed potatoes at dinner. It was silent, it was uncomfortable, and for once, I still knew that even though my house was not considerate, my home and family at Jamaica High School were.

∞ ∞ ∞ ∞ ∞ ∞ ∞ ∞

My next few days of school were rather uneventful: I went to classes, I met more new people, and had some more conversations with Tommy, Danielle, and Wendy. I was quickly realizing that Tommy was a hot-headed, heavy-tempered man. I sure was glad he was on my side.

That weekend, the group and I found ourselves at Cunningham Park. We threw a football around for a bit and sat on a picnic bench watching the fall foliage spread across the park.

Most of our weekends were spent like that: rummaging around our parents' basement or fridge to find some six-packs of beer to pound down at the park. The leaves would turn brown and float to the floor, but our hearts would burn red with love. We were growing a common bond built around our distaste for our biological families or we would create an escape from our trying or mundane lives. All of our individual reasons for getting closer and closer were different, but our unwavering care and consideration with one another was prevalent.

∞ ∞ ∞ ∞ ∞ ∞ ∞ ∞

One evening, Wendy and I went out to walk around College Point. She was trying to escape some of the mysterious occurrences going on at home and I was trying to hide from the thudding sound that my mother's baseball bat would make when it would follow her up the stairs.

We ended up getting lost for a little bit, our minds were too busy reminiscing about the puzzles that surrounded our lives instead of the maze that consisted of our urban Queens streets. Wendy's nose sniffled a bit in the tender frost that rested on her face. She tugged the pockets of her jacket forward with her hands still resting inside of them. Wendy was hiding something about what was going on at home, but at the time I was too ignorant or too naive to realize that deep within she was probably crying out for help as much as I was.

Our weeknights would consist of the kindling of a strong friendship and our weekends would be for the group's ritualistic shenanigans.

∞ ∞ ∞ ∞ ∞ ∞ ∞ ∞

High school had its fair share of memorable moments and fun experiences. A few friends that I made that year, Alec and Leslie, would hang with us on the weekends too and get involved in our unofficial group: The International Beer Club. No one ever knew why we truly named our group that, but most of us figured it was because we would constantly hang out at the park and drink beers. We thought it was a pretty funny name, The International Beer Club just had a nice ring to it, so we continued to call ourselves that and pound a few back at the park each week. Even in the wintertime, you would see all of us hanging out, freezing our asses off, and spending time together as a family.

Alec and I would always fight over Wendy's friendship. We would bicker about who was Wendy's best friend and why either one of us would even have that title. It was a common comical occurrence that our group would just succumb to over the coming months. The International Beer Club was just a group of people who enjoyed each other's company and always knew how to have our fair share of fun.

∞ ∞ ∞ ∞ ∞ ∞ ∞ ∞

The International Beer Club continued its weekly rituals all the way into the summer. Tommy and Danielle treated me as if I were a part of their respective lives since the beginning of time. Wendy and I continued our walks and truly enjoyed each other's company.

My life was flying by before my eyes, and being the young, somewhat naive boy I was, I never stopped to savor each moment or breath as it passed. If only I had, I wonder if I would still have evolved into the man I am today.

One could only speculate, I guess.

The thing about moments is that we rarely live in them or discover their full potential until we look back on our years and try to make sense of it all. Everything and anything we experience is just a series of fleeting memories that lay dormant in our minds. Who knows what opportunities pass us by as we wait for the next thing? Who knows what experiences we detach from while we cling to what does not serve our soul?

Tommy cared for me like I was his younger brother. In those memories however, I can't recall exactly why I ever started to judge him and his demeanor, other than pinpointing my superficial way of interpreting people at the time. From the moment I met Tommy, I saw him as somewhat of a macho man: to me, he was someone who was intelligent, strong, and hot-tempered, and to me that meant that he was very rough around the edges. Still, he did not hesitate to care for me and look out for me as I navigated through high school.

"You can't let these guys push you around, Scott," Tommy sat with me on the curb at Cunningham Park, a beer in hand, essentially having a brother-to-brother or father-son conversation.

'It's tough, you know.' I slurped my beer as the two of us looked out at Danielle, Wendy, Alec, Leslie, as the group chatted about something trivial.

"You have to learn to stick up for yourself, because ain't nobody in this world is going to treat you with respect unless you earn it." He crushed the beer can on the concrete and put his arm around me.

'I'll be okay.'

"Okay," Tommy scoffed, "I see you get your ass handed to you regularly. I'm surprised your brain isn't like scrambled eggs or something yet."

'Tommy, I'm okay." A slight whine came from my throat.

"Stand up." He jumped up with such vibrant intensity. "I am teaching you how to fight." He put his fists up in front of his face and began jumping from side to side. Danielle and Wendy rushed over to see what was going on, and the group was sure to follow.

"What's happening?" Danielle looked very concerned.

"I'm teaching Scott how to defend himself. Get up bud." Tommy continued to bounce back and forth. I got up and accidentally knocked my beer off of the curb. Wendy folded her arms and rolled her eyes. A clear disappointing sigh escaped her lips.

"Be careful, you knuckleheads," she muttered. In hindsight I realize that Wendy was always the voice of reason and someone whose gut feeling was always right.

Tommy began showing me how to make a fist, how to dodge a punch, and how to swing at someone without losing my balance. Everything was going well until I started getting a bit too cocky. Tommy extended his hand forward and I rushed right into his fist. I felt my nose crack and the blood begin dripping from my face as I hit the floor. Tommy fell to the ground with me as my head lurched backwards and towards the pavement.

"What did you do?" Wendy rushed forth and sat by my side.

Danielle grabbed Tommy in a panic and began to scold him. My vision blurred and I was at a loss for words.

"Oh fuck, oh my God, oh my God, Scott, I am so sorry." The fear and anxiety spread through Tommy's core. "You weren't supposed to step into the punch, ah shit."

The rest of the afternoon was spent in the Emergency Room, where my mother was playing the role of a concerned parent. The doctors saw my deviated septum and wanted to re-break my nose in order to properly fix it. Due to my mother's objection, my nose remained in the perpetually bent state it was in, for she didn't want her precious boy's nose getting worse. This, and another series of poor decisions later on in my life, would render my sense of smell virtually non-existent.

Tommy always felt guilty for hitting me even though he did not show it, but the fun continued that summer and I grew thicker skin. In a sense, I became more and more rebellious as a result of this incident. Come September, I was ready to be the seemingly dangerous cool guy who everyone wanted a piece of.

Whether it was smart of me to continue on this rebellious path or not I will always question, for my choices in high school apparently branded me for life. You could say that I was just a victim of circumstance, but it is hard to call yourself a victim when you have to do practically anything you can to survive.

∞ ∞ ∞ ∞ ∞ ∞ ∞ ∞

During my Sophomore year, I was *the* definition of a badass... that is if that word even existed at the time. A lot of girls would flock to me after seeing how kind puberty was to me over the summer. I was larger, I was smarter, and I was joining sports teams to show off just how this intelligent, athletic guy was making a name for himself.

At lunch during the first week of school, a perky brunette darted over to me, Tommy, Danielle, Wendy, and the group we formed. She dropped her lunch tray next to mine, and upon first glance it seemed that she was gearing up to ricochet around our group like a violent bolt of lightning.

We looked at her in a state of shock while she snatched an apple from her tray, bit into it hard, and cheerily, though nonchalantly, said, "Hi, I'm Stacey."

Stacey was a punk kid and a proud pyromaniac. She once said that if she was not lighting something on fire, she was not complacent. Stacey was the epitome of someone who had a heart of gold and we all adopted her into the group with open arms. She was younger than all of us, but although she was two years younger, she had an old soul. Her smile and vibrancy lit up a room and Stacey quickly became "one of us."

At first, Alec and I argued about which one of us would date her, but her spontaneous nature cut through both of us instantly.

"Neither of you could keep up with me, so don't bother," Stacey shouted to us as she continued to move down the hallway. I noticed the Guns n' Roses sticker on one of her binders, and I knew that she was just like me. She spoke the language of music, which was rather exciting to me because I was just beginning to explore the role music would have in my life. I was Mr. Rock n' Roll and Stacey provided me with the opportunity to further my passion for music.

Alec and I were incredibly enamored by Stacey and all that she did, but we truly were not "in love" with her. We appreciated Stacey's friendship for who she was and how she positively impacted our group in such a short period of time.

She was family. We were all one big happy family.

It turned out that Stacey and I hung out almost every day after school just listening to records or rockin' out to whatever was on the radio. With each passing day our conversations got deeper and deeper, and that part of my high school experience was truly thrilling.

Alec became a really good friend as well. Actually, he became my best friend who would stick by me for years and years to come. Him and Stacey were by my side through the trials and tribulations I had with my high school sweetheart... well, actually... sweethearts.

∞ ∞ ∞ ∞ ∞ ∞ ∞ ∞

After the drama I dealt with when it came to Audrey, I felt a lot of trepidation when it came to Nancy. She was a beauty unlike anyone I had ever seen in the halls of Jamaica High School. Though I had been known as a flirt and someone who was far from being a monogamous kisser, Nancy was about to change all of that. The two of us would have a rather passionate and exciting make-out session in the bathroom during the school day, and if we hadn't been caught by a teacher, I am sure the kissing session would have gone on a lot longer.

Our weeklong romance seemed like a picturesque Romeo and Juliet situation that only came crashing down when Nancy saw me talking to Alisha.

While standing in the hallway talking to Wendy and Alec, Nancy came up to me and began screaming.

"I trusted you, Scott Matheson, and you played me!" Nancy started crying.

Bewildered and caught in a state of utter confusion, I just responded, 'What?'

"I saw you," she whimpered through tears, "I saw you talking to Alisha."

Alec and Wendy looked visibly concerned.

'Nancy, we were just talking. Nothing happened.'

"Talking! Talking? Yeah, we were just *talking*, too."

A small crowd started to form around us. Nancy looked at Wendy and Alec for some support, but they both diverted their eyes to a distant spot down the hall. Nancy's rage grew and her eyes burst with merciless tears. I tried to reason with her, but it was too late.

As Nancy's hand slammed into my face, the only thing I could feel was the pangs of misunderstanding simmer across my skin. Alisha was just a friend at the time; she was from Guyana and was wonderful in every aspect of the word. I hadn't shown interest in anyone else but Nancy, yet she mistook my kindness towards Alisha as a blatant interest or longing.

When she walked away, I got the sense that my life would just be one misunderstanding after another... and another... and another.

Yet a week or so later when Alisha and I looked like we were shaping up to be high school sweethearts, it seemed as if Nancy was right all along. That is just how life works out sometimes: our greatest stories lay dormant in the pages that flutter by.

∞ ∞ ∞ ∞ ∞ ∞ ∞ ∞

Sophomore year proved to be rather uneventful... well, I mean I did get into my fair share of bathroom make-out sessions and steamy moments of skin-to-skin contact, but I was a rebellious teenager finding his way. Life was still pretty hectic at home, so in June I got a job at the local ice cream shop.

Alisha and I had been dating for quite some time at this point, but I continuously felt the urge to sweep her off her feet. I knew Alisha's favorite ice cream was Pralines and Cream, so I decided to take home a huge tub for her. I just had to go over the top and be her hopeless romantic.

In the process of stealing a giant tub for her, I didn't stop to think about anything. I figured, who would miss it? I mean, there were plenty of giant tubs.

But there was also a camera...

And after riding 45 minutes on the bus with it, Alisha was not pleased, for that large of a tub didn't even fit in her freezer.

Also, my boss was not pleased when he fired me the next day.

I learned quickly that theft and criminal activity were not the way to a girl's heart. It is so much easier to do the right thing, for the right person will love you unconditionally.

Still, no matter what I did to love Alisha, it was not enough.

∞ ∞ ∞ ∞ ∞ ∞ ∞ ∞

The International Beer Club met at its usual space in Cunningham Park the night I was fired. Much to my surprise, Alisha wandered off to somewhere else while we were all hanging out.

I went searching for her to find a green Peugeot parked in the reflection of a solitary light. Two silhouettes were pressed against the hood of the car, twisting in a tumultuous fashion while rapidly kissing one another. The hot and heavy scene became etched in my mind without remorse, for as I moved closer, I realized the shadows belonged to Alisha and a senior from the high school.

Days later Alisha admitted that she had sex with him on the baseball field atop those paint-chipped benches.

Still, I loved her.

So I stayed with her.

I didn't truly value myself, or the love inside of me...

And so my summer with Alisha began. Each painstaking act of malice I made against myself was a sign of times to come...

Thus began my journey to find a home in the hearts of souls who tried to see me for my value, without acknowledging my true worth.

CHAPTER 6

The Ghosts of
Shattered Glass

~

*"We've gotta hold on ready or not. You live
for the fight when it's all that you've got."*

**- Bon Jovi, American Rock Band, Sayreville,
New Jersey**

Desperation and opportunity were knocking on my bedroom door. I felt the summer haze dripping from my eyes as my father packed his bags and shuffled off on "business" for what felt like the eighth time this month. Each week, my ego would burst at its seams when my father would mutter, "take care of mom" as he trampled down the front steps and I transformed into the man of the house.

It was ironic. I was the "Man of the House" even though I was barely fifteen and between a tender collapse of being a hormonal teenager and a busting emergence of unrequited love. Being the man of the house meant understanding what it meant to be more than a boy and more than a man, for I was on the edge of yesterday and the peak of falling into the clutches of my misunderstood future.

As soon as my father would leave town, my mother was itching to place me atop a papier-mâché pedestal concocted from her elaborate stories and woven tapestry of blasphemous lies. It was not until years and years later that I realized she developed these stories because she could not help herself. She yearned to bury me in a coffin of her own deceit and misunderstanding. Someone had buried her long before she truly grasped the future; she could have built a castle from her tears and a lifelong journey of opportunities, though instead she lived a tale of vapid heartbreak.

In other words, I was becoming what she could not fathom, but there is much more to that story than what could be said right now: the reality that we create from our own perspective could be the death of someone else's fantasy.

Regardless, my friends and I continued on our journey of innocent debauchery. Our summer was inundated with memories of riding our bicycles to the rocks beneath the Whitestone Bridge, digging our feet in the sand at Francis Lewis Park, and watching the ice cream truck sail through the neighborhood at Astoria Park. As a matter of fact, most of my summer was spent pursuing bridges and getting closer to the water.

Nature always had a way of calming the stress and anxiety that occurred as a result of my mother and the intricacies of being a teenager. I was along for the ride of being beaten and bruised at home, yet rapidly driving through moments that would become distant memories.

The summer of my sixteenth birthday would be a quintessential part of who I would become and where I would be going in life.

∞ ∞ ∞ ∞ ∞ ∞ ∞ ∞

Dried drool glued my head on the pillow as I tried to pry myself from the bed. It felt as if my mind was mush, on the account of the remnants of alcohol from last night's binge strongly lingering on my breath.

Today would be one the last days I was fifteen years old, and today the finish line to my childhood was drawn in black and white boxes. The world would become my oyster, for I was its gleaming pearl just waiting to emerge from his shell.

Life itself was on the verge of teeming with so many windows of opportunity, and I was yearning to live.

As I finally crawled out of bed and into the closest pair of tattered jeans I could find, I was face to face with the reflection of a stunning young man. I was a compassionate gentleman wrapped in streaks of long blonde hair and a sharp grin that could cut down anyone in his path.

Well, who was I really kidding? The man I was in the mirror was far different than the one who was bullied and beaten in middle school.

Still, I lived vicariously unbalanced in a perpetual state of fear: my mother's abuse was growing more vulgar and incapacitating by the minute.

When my father would return home from a business trip, my mother would fill his head with lies about my behavior and fallacies beyond my wildest dreams. My father would sigh heavily, shrug his shoulders, and unleash his love through his merciless belt.

It grew tiresome being accustomed to hiding my painstaking agony. Not a single soul noticed my parents' rage being deposited on my skin: I would have thought the abuse were just a figment of my imagination, though the blood and mounting scars were a perturbing reminder that this was indeed my life.

The cycle of abuse would repeat behind closed doors day after day. This was not just a norm in my own home, for rather I always had the sense that a majority of my friends were being mistreated in their own homes as well.

Part of me thinks that their mothers were not being manipulative and diabolical behind the scenes though. My mother would appear to conjure up lies for hours upon hours, only so that she could sneer and snicker behind my father when the capillaries in his eyes would deepen and his rage would be acted upon. Out of all of the abuse, out of all of the wrath, ruin, and destruction, none of the physical pain inflicted upon me could compare to the sharp knife of my mother's laughter and excitement as she watched my punishment from behind my father.

We are all inflicted by the ills and ails of experiences and histories that come our way, but some of us who walk this planet have a mindset that is trapped in the imbalance that is surviving deep strife. As for my mother, understanding the root of her pain became more apparent as my lifetime progressed.

∞ ∞ ∞ ∞ ∞ ∞ ∞ ∞

My summer with my high school friends was just as great as the recent years that passed. I was on the cusp of sixteen and ready to enjoy life. However, my mother's baseball bat and father's persistent work out of town were part of the perfect storm that would mark my downfall.

On a hazy night in July, my mother caught me kissing one of my female friends, Taryn, in my room. Her rage and anger grew rapidly and I feared that upon my friend's sudden departure, my mother's rage would force my skull to bounce against the wooden panels in my room.

As she rushed Taryn from the house in a flurry of screaming and shouting, I crumpled up into a ball in the corner of my room. My fetal position between my dresser and the wooden panels would prove no match for my mother, who returned to the room with a firm baseball bat and a penchant for violence brewing behind her eyes.

It was bad enough that she had been physically and verbally abusing me, but she was chipping away at my soul.

On top of that, despite the fact that my mother knew I loved baseball and adored every single thing it stood for, when she stumbled across my baseball cards days prior, she launched an attack on who I was. Since the moment I saw my first baseball game at Yankee Stadium, I collected and saved every single baseball card I could get my hands on.

My collection was my pride and joy, though she diminished my decks to "utter crap" as she called them.

Despite my begging and pleading, she ended up throwing thousands of my cards out.

Not a single one was left for me to cherish.

She was diluting my love for baseball so much, that as each swing came from her baseball bat, my bruises grew wider and wider and I was too numb to flinch.

How I made it out alive after that incident became an eternal mystery to me.

When I finally stood, hoping that her anger dissipated, she gleaned into my core and dropped the bat. This was, however, not her final blow.

In our deadlocked state of mind, I was panicked that she would kill me. The look in her eyes was only reserved for those who were ready to kill or cause irreparable damage.

My sisters, who no doubt heard the commotion, appeared in the doorway and saw me attempt to push my mother away. In the process, I punched the glass window and dropped to the floor, begging for mercy. My mother berated me with comments that I was worthless, that I thought I was high above the law, and that I was a vile excuse for a son. Her beatings were consistently interwoven with emotional attacks, so that once the bruises faded and the blood dried up, I would still feel the scars that were unseen to the human eye.

My mother snatched the glass, bleeding due to her grasp on the shard, and cut my right hand and knuckles past any recognition that there was skin still clinging to me. The bloodshed made a permanent mark on the carpeted floor of our home, and I am pretty sure the stain was there even when my family moved again.

The cuts on my hand still remain to this day. When I look at them, I am reminded of the pervasive fragility that comes with being human: sometimes we do not know or realize what scars we give to one another, be it of a literal or figurative nature.

The next time I saw Taryn, she did not know of the fate that had been inflicted on my hand. The blood dried, the scars began forming, and all were too eager to turn a blind eye to the abuse that manifested behind closed doors.

∞ ∞ ∞ ∞ ∞ ∞ ∞ ∞

Weeks later, I thought I would finally have a tinge of good luck and celebration to keep me positive and hopeful for a bright future. In years past, my birthdays had been lackluster or filled with dread, such as when Pokey died, but this time... this time would be different.

At least I hoped.

My friends told me to come over to our buddy Steve's house for the night. My girlfriend Alisha insinuated that she prepared a few surprises for me. Life seemed good.

As I left for the night, my mother went on one of her dramatic, rage-fueled rampages. We got into yet another argument about me going out for a few hours at night, which was a mere hour before my father was due home from yet another business trip.

"You know, you don't deserve to have a birthday." My mother started to push over items around the house, barreling right towards me with her horrifying demeanor. "Get the hell out of my house. You don't have a home now."

I left.

I knew she was not kicking me out of the house necessarily, but I did not feel comfortable being in her presence. It felt as if she cast me aside without remorse despite being my own flesh and blood.

∞ ∞ ∞ ∞ ∞ ∞ ∞ ∞

I went down this long, narrow stairwell and I laughed. I was still with Alisha, who was my high school sweetheart. Our relationship was great while it lasted.

When we made it over to Steve's, Wendy was there along with a ton of my other friends. They made me a fantastic dinner and gave me an incredibly special birthday cake. To top it all off, they gave me $100 as a present. They explained that they wanted me to have something just for me. Getting $100 from your high school best friends was the coolest gift in the world, and I was so overwhelmed. After our festivities, we decided to go over to Cunningham Park to guzzle down wine coolers for the night.

As the night started to wind down, I realized that the sunset's glow was hours behind us. I walked Alisha to the bus stop and just as we stepped in, I frantically started to grab at my pockets.

"What's wrong, Scott?" Alisha's look of concern made me feel slightly panicked.

'My wallet,' I kept feeling my pockets, 'The money, my wallet… it's gone!'

Alisha and I dashed off of the bus and to the closest payphone I could find. My father's voice on the other end of the phone was clearly exhausted and worn out. After another one of his business trips, he did not need to pick up the pieces of his precious son's mistakes.

"Get your ass home. Your mother told me what you have been doing and I am honestly sick and tired of your shit. Get home now." My father slammed the phone down and I could feel his anger radiating down my spine.

Alisha looked at me and laced her fingers between mine. I could not resist her innocent eyes.

"Scott, let's go back to find your wallet," her tinge of hopefulness gave me the strength I needed to keep going that night.

And so, we kept going.

∞ ∞ ∞ ∞ ∞ ∞ ∞ ∞

We found my wallet, and the $100 gift from my friends, seemingly right where I left it. It was getting darker and being the true gentleman I was, the continuous pattern of sacrificing myself for love was in full bloom. Alisha lived far from where we were and I couldn't let her go home alone. We jumped on another bus and rode through three incredibly bad neighborhoods until she was safe in her house.

After her front door shut complacently in my face, I realized it was so late at night that the buses had stopped running. I had no way of getting home and I was overfilled with gratitude: Alisha was home safe, I had found my wallet, and life was all-around good.

I began walking. I began thinking about my life so far and everything that was happening at home. The sun started coming up and I realized I had made my way back home… about five hours after my father said I should be home.

I snatched the newspaper from the floor and gingerly snuck into the house. As I opened the front door, I didn't suspect anything was wrong. However, after walking into our small entryway and through the second door, my mother's fit of anger was the only warm greeting I received.

"Scott," she shrieked, grabbing the newspaper from my hand, "get your things and get the hell out of my house."

My father left for another trip already. He did not want to be bothered with me. Happy Birthday to me.

I called Alisha's house and she picked up utterly confused. She assured me that my mother was not throwing me out, prompted me to grab some of my things, and come over. I still felt that this was the end. I still felt that my mother was either going to demolish me, berate me, or end my life. I picked up the only paper I could find and began writing.

I finished my letter and walked downstairs to see my mother coldly sitting and reading the newspaper.

'Mom, I-' she cut me off and flicked her wrist.

"I don't have a son. Get out."

She didn't look up from the paper; she didn't pause to see if I had food or clothes with me. She just wanted me out.

I looked up to see the embroidered, 1970s-looking pattern hanging above our kitchen table. It was doused in rainbows, butterflies, and a small picture of a house. It read: "Today is the first day of the rest of your life."

How ironic.

My mother still did not move as I began my passage across the kitchen.

Outside the window collapsing pieces of ash fluttered through the air, almost as if they were beckoning me to look up at the sky. I cautiously complied with their demands and gazed into the clouds.

A solitary cardinal spread its wings and perched upon a nearby tree branch: a distant reminder that I, too, had to spread my wings and ascend into my next chapter.

The seconds were flickering by like the taper from one of the candles that perched itself upon the windowsill in the house. I was stunned by the analogies I would make on a regular basis, considering my world was always flooded with such inequalities.

I never wanted to feel the pain that burned within me day by day.

Looking down at my knuckles, I saw the ghosts of the shattered glass that were once embedded in my skin. Flashes of pain shrieked through my body and I was restless. I needed to leave; I just had to build up the courage to do so.

And do so before it was too late.

I needed a sign, a signal from a higher power... a feeling, a sensation.

Then it happened.

She finally did it.

My mother dragged her fist through my skull.

As the saliva shot out of my mouth and the pain radiated through my system, I looked out the window into the real world. This house was no longer my home, and this was the final penning of my chapter as a beloved member of this family.

I placed my letter on the table for my baby sisters to read and dragged my small suitcase to the door. My mother beamed her fatal glance into my core. A mixture of tears and dried blood hung on my lips as she boomed the last words I could coherently make out:

"Get out of my house."

So I did.

∞ ∞ ∞ ∞ ∞ ∞ ∞ ∞

I was too ashamed to go to Alisha's so I walked and walked until my feet collapsed beneath me. The sky was as jet black as the soul of the woman who cast me out onto the street.

I stumbled around until my head slammed into a pile of garbage that cascaded along an abandoned building.

The alcohol splashed around in my stomach, causing waves of vomit to spew from the inner depths of my soul. My head shattered against a metal garbage can as the stench seeped from every pore on my body.

The last moment I remembered was the fleeting memory of closing my eyes and drooping into the darkness that awaited me.

Something is wrong. Something dark is brewing inside of me... taking over every last inch of my existence and fueling some sort of unbridled energy within me.

What is happening?

My fist crashed through the glass pane and I finally felt no pain whatsoever. As the blood pooled around the window and a shrill filled the air, I could hear her dropping to the floor and crying.

My fist through the window and a smirk crawling up the edges of my cheeks, I felt the darkness consume the last bit of light I had within me.

'Time's up,' a burst of confidence sprung from my dry lips. 'Save yourself while you can.'

Shards of glass crackled and dripped to the floor almost as fluidly as the blood oozing from my peeled flesh.

Echoes of "there's no turning back" encircled me in a chant, as she lay stunned on the floor, glaring up at the visible darkness floating above.

It's coming, and it is merciless, violent, abhorrent... and there is no way to stop it.

"Stand your ground," hung in the air. Another chill burst up my arms and into my heart.

Falling into a cavernous pit felt almost peaceful at this point.

'Where am I?' I demanded to the shadowy figure in the corner.

A sole beam of light beckoned down upon the dusty floor.

'Where' breathy pauses clung to each word: 'Am I?'

The shadow moved deeper into the thick black mask from day.

Words dripped with the taste of crimson hanging impatiently from the corners of my mouth. More blood. My arm, my hand, my lips - all covered. Spitting out the remnants of the smashed window incident came to no avail.

An angelic beacon shone its warmth around me: "Stand your ground. Please, stand your ground."

We disappeared into the shadows and I found myself jolting awake on the kitchen floor, the ceiling fan spinning overhead mocking where I once lay months ago, and where I lay today.

"It's coming. Be ready."

'What's coming?'

"The darkness. Stand your ground, Scott."

I woke up to a trembling existence. It had been days since I last walked the floors of my parents' house. They were not coming for me. They were not coming to save me.

No one was, because no one cared.

Sunrise, sunset, sunrise, sunset, sunrise, sunset...

Sunrise...

A stark glow encompassed the limp body on the streets of Jamaica that night. The whispers of passers-by remind me that I was not a ghost. I was not invisible. Despite being the target of some hushed shock and awe, I was alive.

The fresh chunks of stale bread and moldy cheese smell just as pungent as they did going down as they do coming up.

Not a single person seemed to want to stop and help this exhausted soul emerge from its vomit-covered cocoon and step into the better side of what life could be.

The lonely streets show no mercy to a young boy lost in his own youth. The scars from a mixture of "I love you," "Scott, what is wrong with you," and broken glass woefully adorned my right hand: the reminder as to why I could not go back to my parents.

Upon further investigation into the garbage can in the alleyway, I find that the bottom of the barrel smells just as rancid as the top.

Still silence hung in the early morning air. Nightfall was rising and I could see a hint of the sun pretending to creep over the hill. We were hours from seeing any reminder of sunlight, yet I still saw a light popping between the buildings.

Maybe it was just my imagination.

Maybe.

Or I was just losing my mind once and for all, yeah... that could be it.

It had been a month since everything happened: the glances, the stares, the feeling of responsibility mounting on my shoulders. Yet, it all came crashing down.

Now a shell and a shadow stood where there once was a person. Glances fell hard and heavy with each passing moment.

"Don't water a dead plant," echoes around my brain. Dead plants. Wilted leaves that flop effortlessly off the side of a terra-cotta pot. Limp, lifeless, and without a trace of the vibrancy that once hung in the balance.

It's okay though. Death isn't the end. With the death of that poor plant, new seeds are planted.

Often, I have dreamt so fondly of the dead plant, that I sense a belonging to it. That is, because the plant and I share the same values: we both didn't get enough water. We both dried up, yet became planted...

Again.

To gain refreshed soil is somewhat of a mystery, yet there it is.

There it was, should I say.

The colors spring forth from the clouds with divine saturation: a reminder that light is needed for any plant to grow: dead or alive, or clinging to existence.

"Don't water a dead plant. Don't water a dead plant. Don't..."

The words trailed off into the night with more tenacity than you could ever know.

A beautiful mind is a terrible thing to waste, but so is a dead plant: for life exists even in the most exhausted of beings. My mother would have wanted me to remember that... or at least the hopeful version of my mother that I conjured in my head to save me from myself.

Faint whispers kept floating past: reminding me that a life exists. A life remains. Hardships and desolation do not symbolize the beginning of the end: this was just the end of a chapter.

As the sun crept over heaping piles of garbage, the makeshift plastic bags I used as a pleasant shelter slid down my sickly body.

A woman, petite and gentle in stature and in appearance, stood in front of me. Her pristine and soft composure was a true blessing, for all night I was greeted by hungry raccoons and violent screams from beyond the alleyway.

"Hello Scott," flowed from the woman's mouth with an angelic sigh trailing behind each word.

Scott. She knew my name. How?

"You don't know me," she appeared to be beckoning angels from the sky with each sentiment that sprung from her lips.

"I've been watching you sit here for quite some time." The woman's pristine emerald eyes fluttered in the sunlight. "May I take you out for some breakfast, my sweet?"

Tired, cold, sick, and starving, I followed, for it seemed like my first blessing had just sauntered into my life.

"Come," her extended hand showed immense compassion, "I'll give you a hand."

The stranger picked me up and ushered me to the closest shelter.

∞ ∞ ∞ ∞ ∞ ∞ ∞ ∞

The kindness of strangers is often a massive juxtaposition to how your family and closest friends could treat you. I mean, after all, I did not outwardly tell anyone about my homelessness, but it was a very kind gesture for a stranger to make. How many people would stop to help someone who seemed down on their luck? How many people would offer a hand to someone who clearly looked disheveled?

Humanity lurks around every corner. Sometimes we just need a reminder to display it outwardly.

As the stranger and I sat in the diner, she refused vehemently to give me her name. I could not understand why. It was a random act of kindness that seemed to prolong itself between mystery and conversation, but my inquisitive nature wanted to know more about the person sipping quite pleasantly from her cup of tea.

She was kind enough to allow me to order what I wanted from the breakfast menu, and though I was bashful at first, I ensured her that I was just going to eat some scrambled eggs, toast, and a few pieces of shredded hash browns.

As we sat in somewhat silence, I finally had some time to just think and clear my mind as my strange breakfast companion sat peering over a daily newspaper.

Even at that early age, I came to the revelation that I wear agony so well; it is almost like a birthmark. The pain has been there for so long, it has blended into every fiber of my being.

The best part? It is a mask. A shadow far in the dark present. Constantly there, but almost unrecognizable because I wear it so well.

The ropes anchoring my wrists are tearing. My grip sliding in slow motion from the sheer weight of the dreaded birthmark.

With each slight twitch, the ropes twist into shreds. With each writhe, they unravel. With each passing second, the ropes assist me as I droop into the abyss: like a raindrop, but with such fervor that it seems like, for one second, the pendulum will swing back... but still, the ropes lurch forward.

And with each glance at the birthmark, as do I.

My thoughts were interrupted when the woman finally decided to speak: "The weather is getting a bit cooler at night. You may want to get home to your family soon."

I peered up at her and shrugged: 'My family doesn't want me.'

"Are you sure," she said quizzically, "you look a bit young to be out here."

'I will survive, thank you.' I looked out the window into the alleyway where I was just moments before.

"Your family is waiting for you."

'Not my mom or dad.'

"Exactly," she said confidently. "Someone else is waiting for you. Another family. A new family."

She spoke as if she knew what my future would hold, but I knew she was just a stranger who just so happened to extend a helping hand… but then again, my curiosity peaked.

'Another family?' I sipped the water in front of me. The condensation from the cup dripped over my fingers.

"You will meet one or you will find the power to create one. You will have a home. A grand home. Don't you worry."

I was intrigued by her and her demeanor.

My stomach felt queasy and I stood to run to the bathroom. Questions flurried through my head and I was trying to figure out what I would ask her upon my return.

∞ ∞ ∞ ∞ ∞ ∞ ∞ ∞

After what felt like twenty minutes in the bathroom, I emerged to find some more food on the table and a solitary note:

There is faith in fortitude. Don't give up.

The waitress told me that the mystery woman paid the bill and left without even saying goodbye. It was a weird situation, I will admit, but something about the interaction stuck with me… it may have been her eyes or her innate kindness, but regardless it was a pleasant moment in time: maybe she is living proof that there is hope, we just need to believe in ourselves and believe in what we can create regardless of the circumstances.

∞ ∞ ∞ ∞ ∞ ∞ ∞ ∞

Back on the street, I became more in tune with my surroundings. I searched the crowds for the stranger, but did not see her again. I was waiting for days to tick by just so I can return to school after this miserable end to the summer.

There was a man who passed me everyday and muttered a bible verse. He carried a leather-bound case with what I determined to be his sacred bible. He carried it around to remind him of his dear mother's passing. He misses her dearly, you can tell from the sunken creases around his eyes. He wept for so long, clutching that leather-bound bible praying for a sign as to why she left him so soon. He misses the way she made her special lemon meringue pie. No matter how he tries tirelessly to duplicate her cherished family recipe passed down for generations, he can't understand why her meringues tasted better.

I often wanted to stop him on the street and explain that her love was the secret ingredient, but he never broke his stride, not even for a second, to glance in my direction. I hoped one day he would notice me and sit beside me. Until then, I will keep his mother's secret ingredient safe.

There was a woman with long silky legs who brought me a bottle of water each morning on her way to the bus stop. I perked up whenever I hear the clacking of her heels striking the pavement. Her shoes provided me with some of the most beautiful music to blossom in my ears. Her alabaster skin reflected the morning sun so beautifully; it is as if the sun needed her to survive. I imagine she was a big-name executive somewhere in Manhattan who knew what it felt like to live in a cardboard case as I did each day. She was probably kicked out of her home at age sixteen just as I had been, but she began working as a waitress in a fancy restaurant until she saved enough money to go for a degree in business.

She clawed her way up the ladder until she made it to CEO. Yet, she still rode the bus from Queens each day to remind herself of her roots and her past life.

Then there was Paulette, the bagel lady. She brought me the leftovers from the bagel shop each day. Surprisingly, people in Jamaica did not like to eat onion bagels. I got armfuls of bagels from Paulette, because she originally caught me digging through the shop's dumpster for food. I appreciated her feeding me more than she could ever realize.

I thought she worked two jobs to support her family, for when she left the shop at 4:00 P.M., Paulette always had a grease-stained apron dangling from underneath her coat. She had to be a diner waitress or something, because I imagined her carrying warm porcelain coffee pots to ceramic tables in the bleak hours of the night.

Faces pass us every single day. I always remember the faces that fill up the pages of my life. What faces do you remember?

While resting my head in the alleyway one night, a cardboard box nestled gently against my head, I could see a sea of red brake lights cascading along the walls. The radio from an open car window blared a familiar voice shrouded by a melody I had never heard before.

While barely clinging to a thread of hope, I heard the words and music that would seal my destiny for the rest of my life:

She says, we've got to hold on to what we've got
It doesn't make a difference if we make it or not
We've got each other and that's a lot for love
We'll give it a shot
Whoa, we're halfway there
Whoa, livin' on a prayer
Take my hand, we'll make it I swear
Whoa, livin' on a prayer

Around the same time I thought I was doomed to live a life on the streets, Bon Jovi released an entire album that sang to my soul. Suddenly, I realized there was a soundtrack to my life. Suddenly, music gave me the strength I needed to move forward.

My family is waiting for me: the family I would create and the people I would choose to surround myself with. I had to reach out to my friends. I had to let the music flow through me. There is faith in fortitude and I really couldn't give up.

After all, I was living on a prayer.

CHAPTER 7

The Story Behind the Story

~

"I'm the patron saint of the denial with an angel face and a taste for suicidal. Cigarettes and Ramen and a little bag of dope. I am the son of a bitch and Edgar Allan Poe. Raised in the city under a halo of lights"

- Green Day, American Punk Rock Band, East Bay, California

The moment I came clean to my friends about my living situation, they embraced me lovingly. They did not judge me. They did not scold me. They showed how much they loved me. Oftentimes, I think this is what is missing from the world: love. We have the capacity to show compassion towards one another, but do we choose to do so?

Do we make the conscious decision to love and make room for love? Do we give our friends, family, and even strangers enough credit to exercise the capacity to love? How do we love and what do we know about love? If I took all of the love-fueled experiences from my lifetime and all of the experiences from another person, would we be able to compare them to each other and comprehend their similarities and differences? Should we dare compare the love from one person to another?

We could sit and ruminate on what love is or our respective capacities to love, but we must live in each moment. Above all, our moments cannot be experienced again once they slip through the sands of time.

I connected with my friends, despite my fear that I would be judged for getting kicked out of my house. Alec, Alisha, and Wendy allowed me to rotate every night and stay at a different person's house each day. As school started up, seeking salvation by couch surfing began to look like the new norm. At first, their parents were a bit apprehensive about having me stay over somewhat often, but my presence turned out to be a rather beneficial one for all of us: I was quiet, I cleaned up after myself, and I wasn't a bother.

My carousel of couches served as home for quite some time.

By October, many of my friends' parents just accepted me as the guy that would appear and disappear with a humble "thank you" hanging from his lips. Alec's family was partial towards sitting on the sofa and watching television most nights, so when I stayed at his house, we would hang around outside for hours before I made my way back to the cushions for the night.

One night, Alec had this crazy idea that we would go watch the Mets play the sixth game of the World Series.

'Are you crazy, man? How are we getting in?' I looked at him over the roast chicken and pasta his mom made for us and was partially bewildered by his suggestion. The other part of me was worried that this was an actual, factual situation we were going to attempt.

"We can do it, who is going to stop us?" Alec shoveled steaming pieces of spaghetti into his mouth.

As bits of food sprinkled from his mouth, he continued on and on about how we could see the game and still get back home before anyone would realize we were gone. It was a brilliant plan, and it wasn't like we were doing anything else on that Saturday night, so we scarfed down our food and hurried out the side door. The rubber soles from our shoes kissed the sidewalk as we practically ran all the way to Shea Stadium.

The moon was closing in on us as we made our way to a dark alleyway near the stadium. Though we were rather in shape, both Alec and I were huffing and puffing due to our sudden run that brought us less than three miles from his house. Flushing was a stone's throw away from College Point, but this adventure would bring us to a national scale. After all, the Red Sox were doing pretty well for themselves and everyone wanted to watch a piece of baseball history unfold on their screens.

We were hoping we could get a glimpse of history before our very eyes.

The two of us snuck into the stadium after getting a friend who worked at Shea to throw us some spare uniforms. Alec and I changed clothes in the bus depot across the street before sneaking in through the Press Entrance. Not a single person realized that we were not vendors, and somehow, they believed that we ran out of souvenirs to sell so early in the game.

We made our way through the crowd and ditched the uniforms somewhere near the bathrooms. Our plan to see the World Series in person was a success... well, it was Alec's plan, but both of us were able to experience it.

∞ ∞ ∞ ∞ ∞ ∞ ∞ ∞

Though it was incredibly cool to see the game live, Alec was growing incredibly impatient minute by minute. By the ninth inning, it seemed that the Mets were about to lose to the Red Sox and our night out was just going to be about the experience. Though Alec was trying everything in his power to get me to agree to leave, something deep within told me that there was still a chance.

The bottom of the tenth inning rolled around.

'Alec, it isn't over until it's over,' I shouted at him over the banter of the cheering fans.

Mookie Wilson took the plate. Though he was my second favorite player next to College Point's own Lee Mazilli, something in the way he moved made it seem like he was about to step into the role of a champion.

With the first pitch came a foul ball…

Then a fastball…

Then another high pitch meant ball two…

With another foul ball, the Red Sox were just one strike shy of winning the 1986 World Series. Alec turned to leave and I grabbed the back of his shirt. He swatted at me and stood next to me again.

Wilson fouled the next pitch into the dirt and another foul pitch flew behind the plate. Alec became so impatient, almost as if he were in immense agony.

The pitcher tried to launch the ball close enough to push that final strike into place, but as the ball ricocheted past and the catcher went to grab it, Kevin Mitchell dashed towards home to tie the game.

The entire stadium rose to its feet. The noise was deafening and a stark contrast to the attitudes of many people just moments ago. Alec grabbed my shoulders and rocked into my body.

"Dude, holy crap, dude!" Nearly drowned out over the rest of the noise in Shea Stadium.

Wilson hit two more fouls and the tenth pitch at bat roared towards the plate.

Everything happened so fast and I was praying so hard that I forgot I was an Atheist at that moment. The greatest moment in baseball history, or at least the Mets' history, was just at the edge of each particle of sand in the hourglass.

Buckner, the first baseman from the Red Sox bent down to grab Wilson's hit, and should have been a sure out, but the ball rolled past him and the rest was, well, literally history.

A Mets player leapt onto the plate with the winning run as his teammates collided with him to celebrate.

They were still in the series.

∞ ∞ ∞ ∞ ∞ ∞ ∞ ∞

Growing up in College Point, being a Yankees fan was almost a crime. Shea Stadium was practically in our backyard and the fireworks show would, year in and year out, illuminate the skies above our houses with such a glorious sight. As I grew older and truly learned about both leadership and running a championship team, I was still drawn to the Yankees. Still, I have great respect for the Mets and all that they accomplished on the field that day.

As we walked down the exit ramp, still teeming with excitement over our adventure, two large guys jumped us. We were mugged, for lack of elaborate terms. Though as the guy ripped the chain from my neck and the larger guy tore Alec's money from his wallet, both of us discretely knew that we would return in a few nights for the seventh game of the World Series.

Two days later, we snuck into the stadium again by sliding some money to the security guys by the door. It was pure mayhem, but both of us thrived on the chaos, and the Mets won the 1986 World Series on Monday, October 27th.

The elated feeling of being immersed in historic prosperity would be something I treasured for years and years to come.

It was a stark contrast to the tragic history I would become a part of in the near future... but more on that later.

∞ ∞ ∞ ∞ ∞ ∞ ∞ ∞

As I evolved and continued my journey through homelessness, Alisha and I began to grow further apart. My high school memories were quickly filling up with tales of handball championships and lacrosse tournaments. Through bouts of chugging alcohol and the growing drug use, I still managed to get decent grades and survive Jamaica High School... barely.

After school one day, Wendy and Stacey caught me trying my hand at mixing Jack Daniel's whiskey and Coke. They didn't say much as I gulped the elixir down real fast, however I could tell from Wendy's cautious look that she recognized I was digging myself into a pretty steep hole. How steep, I just didn't realize, yet.

How could some harmless fun be anything more? How could drinking whiskey lead to anything else? I mean, I could stop any time I wanted to. I knew that. Wendy knew that. Still, I felt much better when I was drinking.

My junior year seemed to be filled with moments where I was drinking and functioning perfectly fine. Everything was okay. Everything was great. I didn't really have to worry at all.

I had enough responsibilities on my plate between staying afloat at school and being homeless. Although I was moving from couch to couch at my friends' houses, I didn't have a solitary place to call home. I was a lost boy. I was a kid thrust into manhood. Could you really blame me for drinking and having some fun? My life was a mess; I owed it to myself to enjoy what I could... right?

As winter rolled around, I was drinking Jack in my coffee to stay warm and stay awake. It helped get me through the day and, I guess as my father would have said, "Put hair on my chest." My drinking didn't really harm anyone, and I continued to sip coffee in the comfort of my denim jacket in the back of my English class in high school.

After school, Stacey and I would walk around the block to a little tree budding in a fenced-off pile of dirt. The streets of Queens were often lined with gentle shrubs or fresh flowerbeds, but this tree was different.

It was our tree.

The two of us would wander down from her apartment to the tree and perch atop some of the branches. It did not reach too far past the first few floors of the typical Queens apartment complexes, but it allowed us to climb high enough to feel that we were above all of the typical turmoil in our respective lives.

As the hours ticked by us, we would talk about practically anything.

Stacey sat there, picking away at the bark on the tree with a fractured twig, contemplating what life truly meant.

I wish I could have written down everything we spoke about, but I came to realize that our memories were what mattered most.

The little moments where we come to cherish the people who add color to our bleak and dismal lives matter most.

Between my friends' support and shenanigans, I felt my life was worth something.

Junior year seemed, well, pretty okay in my book.

∞ ∞ ∞ ∞ ∞ ∞ ∞ ∞

As the spring rolled around, The International Beer Club continued its weekly meetings. Wendy would often try leading me away from the alcohol long enough to talk some sense into me. You could just naturally tell that she was firmly rooted in family values and had a stern moral compass. I am sure that back then we did not call it that, but in hindsight those words just seem to fit Wendy so well.

After our brief conversations, Wendy would always offer me a chance to stay at her place, which I would *always* happily accept.

Wendy's aunt and mother would often be the ones taking me in for the night. They were the family that I didn't have and tried to keep me from straying too far into some troublesome situations. Still "boys will be boys," as people say. That phrase is so worn out: why do we try to justify behavior by saying "boys will be boys" and "girls will be girls," for it seems like those words are just a lame excuse for not understanding why someone chooses to do what they do.

Wendy's mother was the one that taught me how to drive, and with no questions asked. She knew that my family was absent from my life, but that did not stop her from practically raising me as her own.

One particular night after Wendy and I had a long talk about life and high school, she trotted into her room and shut the door with a resounding thud. It seemed like Wendy and her mom were done for the night.

Her aunt would usually stay up and pace for a while until she sensed that Wendy and her mom were sound asleep. I guess that is what caring family members do for each other.

The moment I heard the floorboards stop creaking, I knew Wendy's aunt was asleep for the night. Wendy had shut her bedroom door, leaving my mind wandering and hopeful on her living room couch. I flipped onto my back and gazed out into the illustrious night sky.

It was calling me to go.

It was calling me to explore.

There was more to life than just fermenting on your best friend's couch at 11 o'clock at night. I did what any teenage boy with a penchant for adventure would do: I crept into the dimly lit kitchen, its aroma wrapped in hints of fresh blueberry and leftover meatballs. The keys were just sitting there, desperately waiting to be snatched, doused in the spotlight from the solitary hanging light over the wooden table.

So I took the keys.

And I left.

∞ ∞ ∞ ∞ ∞ ∞ ∞ ∞

I peered around the yard and street before leaping into the dirt-drenched Plymouth Scamp. It wasn't like Wendy's aunt drove it around much anyway. Honestly, I was doing her aunt a favor. That car deserved to feel pavement brush against its tires. The car yearned to be so much more than an abrupt barrier for leaves that danced through the rain-soaked gutters of buckling Flushing streets.

As my hands stroked the steering wheel, I could feel my heart rising deep in my chest. The keys rattled in my hands and penetrated the ignition, with a single twist the engine roared and I was about to change the course of history.

This night would be my first night driving.

Alone.

Without a care in the world and with nothing to stop me.

No one would stop me.

Nothing would stop me.

I was free to roam the streets as long as the wheels were eager to take me where I wanted to go.

'Where,' that's the question, 'where to go?'

The star-speckled night sky was my map and my heart my compass.

The open roads of Queens were veins that brought life to the city.

I put the car in drive, removed my foot from the pedal, and let the exhaust dust where I had been: my soul grazed upon the adrenaline festering in my body and the future I had before me.

The headlights beamed bright: the future of this night would only grow to become an exquisite memory as my life carried on.

Each turn and twist of the wheel brought me closer to…

Nature.

Earth.

Water.

Something beautiful and breathtaking.

For what felt like hours, I blended into the city streets and found my way into Brooklyn. Driving faster and further into the depths of the borough, the Plymouth Scamp ushered me into a lush green landscape with paving stones spreading as far as I could see in that dark night. I parked on Willow Street and walked through the shrubbery.

Gazing out at the city, the famed New York City, I could not help but glimpse at the Brooklyn Bridge on the far right. Its lights and structure were perfectly balanced in my mind: a fusion of wires, iron, and steel shapes connecting Brooklyn and Manhattan together. The world's heart was beating before me, and I had the pleasure of seeing its pulse up close and personal. The water dividing Brooklyn and Manhattan was swaying oh so gently in the moonlight. Brooklyn Bridge Park's benches provided me with a front row seat to my future: one day the city would feel my presence. In some form or way, I would be perpetually connected to the life and strength that Manhattan had to offer.

Whether it be by bridge or by music, we would be linked. We would become a cohesive whole.

A tall tan building stuck out on the skyline, its vast windows and pointed structure were so beautiful even in the moonlight. The Twin Towers stood firm and glistening in the lights, sounds, and energy the city had to offer. It was truly a picture-perfect scene that would have never become such a remarkable part of my memory had I not ventured out.

Life has so much to offer, as long as we intend to live it.

Every breath and every movement we make draws us closer to nights like these, where peace and harmony come as they are.

And they never fade away…

Never.

∞ ∞ ∞ ∞ ∞ ∞ ∞ ∞

As I said before, Alisha and I were growing apart. In a sense, I would like to think that we were just two different branches growing on the same tree. The two of us were teenagers: living our lives in the confines of society and finding our way in the world.

After one of the International Beer Club's Saturday meetings, Alisha sat me down on the curb and held my hand gently. I sensed that something was off. I sensed that she was upset with me or ready to take our relationship to another level. I was pretty bad at reading her signals, although we were dating for about two years. Like I said, we were changing.

"I'm moving," were the only words I really remember her saying from the conversation.

'When?' I began crying. 'Why are you leaving me?'

Our chat dissipated into a long sigh and a few murmured words. I really loved her. She was one of the only people who I truly felt was close to being my real, true family.

And she was leaving…

To move to Florida.

Just my luck.

The next day when she was flying out of New York and to her new home in Florida, I took two buses in the pouring rain to say goodbye. There was a torrential rainstorm that seemed to appropriately mask my tears, but while waiting in the archway of a bank with tears cascading down my face, I felt that I was living in some sort of dramatic movie scene. That was how my mind was processing the situation at least.

When she finally left her home, hugged me goodbye, and got in the car to leave forever, I felt as if a piece of me was rotting away.

In a matter of days, Wendy and I pooled together the money we had for me to buy a '71 Oldsmobile. The car was $1,000, but the guy we were buying it from let me have it for $500 and the guarantee that I would pay him the rest. I hate to spoil the fun, but I never did pay him back.

I took the car and tried to make a daring and romantic attempt to win Alisha back. On my way down I-95 heading to Florida, I must have rehearsed my speech to her over a thousand times.

The police officer who pulled me over, however, seemed to make all of the words inside my head melt away. I got pulled over in Virginia without a driver's license and without the car's registration. I can't really remember the conversation I had with him because I was incredibly nervous, but by some miracle I ended up getting away with my escapade.

As I continued driving to Florida, I could not help but think that the cop truly felt bad for me. Regardless, I counted what blessings I had and mustered up the courage to make my way to Alisha's house.

∞ ∞ ∞ ∞ ∞ ∞ ∞ ∞

When I made my way up the concrete steps to Alisha's house, I could not help but admire the home. It was on the corner of two beautiful suburban streets, the picturesque palm trees bent towards the roof in an effort to see what was about to happen on these very steps.

Alisha was surprised to see me. When she saw my face in the window, she looked like she saw a ghost. She brought me into the house and her mother was even happy to see that I made it hundreds of miles away to Florida.

As her mother prepared us dinner, Alisha walked me down to the handball courts that she would be hanging out on with her new friends. The handball courts had three intersecting walls and were quite different from New York, but I really liked it in Florida. I really thought that she would welcome me into her home and that we could start a family together in the Sunshine State.

Then I met Chris.

At least he was a nice guy. Alisha explained that the two of them were dating and she was really happy in Florida.

As we walked back towards her house, it hit me: she didn't just leave New York... she left me, too. Another love of mine was lost somewhere in the world, and there was nothing I could really do about it.

I got back into the car that night to leave with the dignity I still had, but nothing during that trip was working out for me. As I started the car, I heard it stall along with any hope that I would be able to leave quietly. Alisha's mother was an incredibly good sport about it though, because she ended up allowing me to keep the car in her driveway until I could come back to Florida and fix it.

By nightfall the next day, I was on a plane heading back to New York. Wendy's words rung throughout my head as I watched the lights from Tampa fade into the distance: "You have all the luck, lover boy."

The clouds closed in on the plane and I felt a sudden sense of peace, knowing that at least I found out about Chris and this was not going to be another Audrey and "Goodbye to Romance" scenario.

Hours later when I landed in New York, seeing Wendy's face reminded me that I still had family in the world, even though Alisha was seemingly out of my life in the romantic sense.

∞ ∞ ∞ ∞ ∞ ∞ ∞ ∞

Weeks later I was back to hanging out with the International Beer Club and preoccupied with hunting down my next drink. My lacrosse jersey adorned with the number 88 on the back was my calling card: the 88 symbol spoke to me in ways that made me proud to wear that sports jersey. The uniform was a quintessential sign that our little group was filled with high school kids, but no one who passed by us seemed to even care.

It was Memorial Day weekend and Alec's parents were away on vacation for a few days. Naturally, being the good and wholesome teenagers we were, we threw a party.

It was all in innocent fun. We were listening to rock n' roll, loving life, escaping the daily pressures of being a teenager... fifteen kids in one car and holding the trunk down so we could all get to Alec's place to drink our Calvin Coolers and participate in innocent debauchery.

When we got to Alec's house, we all dashed out of the car as if it were on fire. We were all eager to get the night started and drink beyond any comprehension of the term, "intoxicated."

Lana had spent time with the International Beer Club before, but her appearance at this party was quite a surprise.

"Hey Scott," she shouted from across the room.

'Lana, hey!'

We moved towards each other as Motley Crüe's "Home Sweet Home" played and skipped at the same moment each time it played. Wendy used to say that you could set your watch to the second it would skip and have your watch be completely accurate. She could have just been over exaggerating, but anytime we would listen to the record it would skip without fail.

Lana and I made our way towards the stairs and sat for a moment. We laughed and reminisced about our middle school days and our shenanigans. Lana was wearing a faux-leather dress that hugged every curve on her body. Every guy at the party was glaring right at us and seemed to wish that they were me; I didn't understand why. Lana was down to earth and one of the most genuine women in my life, but I did not see her as anything more.

"Come on, let's go upstairs," she grabbed my hand and our footsteps receded from the crowd. We made our way into Alec's parents' bedroom and sat on the bed for a few moments. The door shut behind us and she seemed to cozy up to me quite naturally on the bed.

We talked some more as the noises from downstairs were slowly drowning in our amicable conversation. I realized that I had been so used to seeing Lana with wigs on. However, I never truly looked at her natural hair. It was blonde and wrapped around her shoulders with such poise.

She shot me a smile and touched my hand gingerly.

We sat in a still silence for a moment with just the muffled noises from downstairs filling the air.

"You know, I never did really say thank you for being there for me in middle school," she whipped her hair over her shoulder and fluttered her eyelashes. I grinned shyly and said, 'No problem, it was what anyone would do.'

"But it was not just *anyone* who was kind to me Scott," she leaned towards my body and softened her voice. "It was you, Scott. You were kind to me."

I giggled coyly and placed my hand on top of hers.

She leaned in and kissed me gently.

"You know," she started, "I always wanted to tell you…"

Another pause hung in the air.

"I had the biggest crush on you." Lana moved in closer to me and rested her hand on my face.

I cautiously placed my hand on her face and admitted, 'Me too.'

The two of us smiled and glanced at each other for a moment. Lana reached up and placed her hand over mine. She turned her lips towards my hand and began to plant sweet kisses on my fingertips.

As she pressed her body firmly against me, her nose brushed against mine. The sensation of her skin grazing my face excited me. I swallowed hard and closed my eyelids.

"I promise I will be kind," Lana whispered.

When I opened my eyes, she was already twisting her shirt off over her head. Her vibrant red bra was covered in intricate black lace, which provided a fantastical series of images that crossed my mind each time I closed my eyes.

Unsure of precisely what to do, I pulled my shirt off and undid my pants. I could hear my leather belt slap against the floor as Lana pulled my jeans from my waist. My hands landed on the luxurious silky sheets as she ran her hands up my chest.

As we engaged in our romantic encounter I was still in utter disbelief. After all of those years of innocent friendship, we manifested a beautiful experience that would be a reminder of who we meant to each other for years to come.

She leaned in to kiss me again and stood up while leading me towards the closet.

"Get in," she said.

Lana tugged on the small chord that hung below the solitary light bulb in the closet and pushed my back into a shelf. She began kissing me and I panicked.

'I-' I stuttered and gulped really loud. 'I don't know what to do.'

"Like I said," she whispered, placing her finger over my mouth, "I will be kind."

And she was.

Lana was my first and she took care of me.

You could tell she was experienced and being very gentle with me, and well, let's just say that Alec's mother must have been pretty furious when she came home and found some sort of sticky substance in her white patent leather heels.

∞ ∞ ∞ ∞ ∞ ∞ ∞ ∞

The house was so trashed from the party that Alec couldn't come hang out with the International Beer Club for weeks. That spring was rather quiet without him, but we knew that he would eventually return from being punished for our wild house party.

We were kids and, well, *boys will be boys.*

I continued to speak to Lana, but we both knew we were just really good, really close friends.

Back in the world that we created in high school, the International Beer Club and I would sit in our teacher's classroom at seven-something in the morning and learn the most valuable lessons known to man: 1) U2 songs such as "Sunday Bloody Sunday" were practically angelic and 2) There was a locker in the building where we could hide our Jack Daniel's.

As a group, the International Beer Club was a coat of many colors.

We were Jewish, we were African American, we were Indian. We did not see color and we did not see borders. We were from Queens, the Bronx, and Brooklyn.

We saw oneness.

We saw what I heard all those years ago when my uncle introduced me to Stevie Wonder's "Happy Birthday" song.

This was the world we were supposed to be living in; we needed a state of undeniable acceptance and we created it.

Again, life was good.

I was back to drinking in school again and the end of my junior year seemed that much more manageable. June was upon us and we were gearing up for another summer of thorough entertainment and innocent debauchery.

At some points during the month I was taking Vivarin, which was a nearly guaranteed way to stay focused and keep going. As a homeless kid without much parental guidance, I figured I really needed that extra caffeine boost to keep going.

My unfortunate incident of vomiting in the water fountain, however, was a clear sign that maybe I had to cut back on Vivarin. At least I had my trusty whiskey to help me through the day; though sometimes I forgot which locker I put the good stuff in.

∞ ∞ ∞ ∞ ∞ ∞ ∞ ∞

Some days I felt that I was on top of the world. Other days I felt that I was lower than the depths of hell. I guess that's what alcohol will do to you though, right?

The day of my super important college admissions exam, I showed up beyond intoxicated and reeking of vomit. I fell asleep between the lull of Jack and Coke and Vivarin, but I still managed to get a decent grade on the exam. I guess the world was showing me that being a punk teenager meant that you were still untouchable... at least to an extent.

On weekends, the International Beer Club and I would meander down bars in Manhattan to see our friend Dylan's father's band play. It was an exciting feeling: none of us were legally allowed to be there, but The Bitter End seemed like a rather cool place to be. We never got stopped and we never caused problems, so we were able to blend right in without anyone saying a word.

It was actually Dylan's father's band who inspired us to attempt to create a band of our own. We had an original song and we didn't really go anywhere, but I was thankful for the experiences we created.

To this day, I am sure that The Bitter End is still there, but with stricter security and different bands sharing their music with the city.

Speaking of music, when Alec finally made his parents see that he wasn't such a bad kid for throwing a party, we were able to get back to our regularly scheduled shenanigans.

Lana actually met us at the concert we were going to: another one of Bon Jovi's musical masterpieces at Madison Square Garden.

Alec and I had 8th row floor seats and the concert was beyond our wildest dreams. I mean, after all, it is Bon Jovi we are talking about.

Lana had seats in the 300 section of Madison Square Garden, but managed to charm her way down to the floor where we were sitting. As the three of us jumped around and sang to Bon Jovi's classics, I looked over at Lana and she smiled back at me.

She never said it, but I know she saw the world differently at such a young age considering it was almost ripped away from her. With each beat that sprung from the drums, we all moved as if we were genuinely living our best lives. It was crazy, it was fun, and we lived in every single moment.

Nights like those live in infamy in my mind and defined my life as a die-hard Bon Jovi fan.

∞ ∞ ∞ ∞ ∞ ∞ ∞ ∞

Back at school I was starting to struggle. I wanted to give up and just, for lack of better terms, become another statistic in the world of kids who just didn't make the cut. I was hopeless, yet hopeful that I was going to do something or be someone. I just really didn't know who yet.

I distinctly remember my guidance counselor pulling me aside one day and verbally beating some sense into me.

"Scott, what on earth are you trying to do?" He looked at me with a partially disapproving, partially paternal look in his eye.

I shrugged and told him that I wanted to leave school. I told him that I was done and that I couldn't see myself coming back for senior year.

He told me to get a job at the local supermarket and that he would help me figure out how to graduate from high school a few months earlier. It was not much, but there was some hope.

So being the punk teenager I was, I pulled the collar of my denim jacket up to my ears and agreed to stay in school long enough to graduate.

After school, I spoke to Wendy about the conversation I had with the guidance counselor and she agreed with him.

"What do you really have to lose if you are getting an education?" Wendy spoke sharply. She was curt, but I know it was out of compassion and love for the scared little boy that lived behind the eyes of a confused teenager.

To thank her, I drove her aunt's car all the way to New Jersey so I could show her a scenic outlook I had heard about from someone at school. It was one of the last weekends of our junior year and you could just tell Wendy needed some time away from her house.

As we drove the Plymouth Scamp back on the Palisades Parkway, our laughter drowned out any sense of teenage drama or reality we were dealing with. The two of us were just living in that moment. We existed in the idealistic sense that everything was truly okay. The two of us were able to just be ourselves and shed the masks that we were. In the car somewhere in the depths of New Jersey, we were merely the kids that we were destined to be.

In our jovial state, I must have forgotten where to turn and cut the wheel a bit too fast for Wendy's liking.

"Scott, be careful!" Wendy gripped the edge of the passenger seat.

'It's okay, it's okay,' I wanted to assure her that my driving habits were perfectly fine and that she just had to calm down a bit.

In hindsight maybe she was right to be cautious, for I guess the next move I made was not so smart.

I realized we missed where we were supposed to turn and cut the wheel just a bit too fast at 80 miles per hour. Let's just say Wendy's shrill when I drove the car through grass and debris on the side of the highway was quite appropriate.

The driver's side tire was flat and the two of us stood on the Palisades Parkway wondering just how we would get out of this predicament *I* managed to get us into.

"Nice going," Wendy said in a slightly condescending, yet sisterly tone.

Wendy moved towards the front of the car mimicking the line from our favorite movie, St. Elmo's Fire: "Blinding white light... Skid... Tree... Impact!... It was out of hand! It was a metaphysical precision collision."

∞ ∞ ∞ ∞ ∞ ∞ ∞ ∞

In Wendy's defense, I was prone to driving her nuts both literally and figuratively. The amalgamation of chaos she put up with showed just how patient and understanding she was, and how she never truly judged someone for their actions. Rather, Wendy was non-judgmental and in tune with the fact that sometimes people just need a little extra help getting by in life.

As the two of us stood in the damp grass between the northbound and southbound lanes of the parkway, two headlights beamed towards Wendy's car. The lights came to an abrupt stop close to where we were standing, but the lights prevented us from seeing who was behind the contrasted glow moving forward from the darkness.

"Need a hand?" The man spoke in a kind, yet stern voice.

I had heard the voice before, but I didn't realize from where until he moved into the light. You know how every family has an uncle that isn't really related to you? Well it just so happened that a good family friend of my father's was standing before me.

We hadn't seen each other in years, nor did he recognize me with my long, flowing blonde hair that long-marked the end of my less-than-perfect childhood.

Wendy and I were receptive to his kindness and he placed his knees in the mud to help us change the tire. To him, we were strangers in the night that needed some help. He did not recognize me, nor did he ask for payment or my name. He was just a good guy helping two kids who got into quite the predicament on the side of the road.

We need more people like that in the world. We need more individuals who recognize struggling souls and are willing to extend even an ounce of hope towards those in need. We never truly know what someone is going through, and it is so crucial that we consistently make an effort to be understanding. These ideas were not always obvious to me, but I learned them rather fast and from an unexpected moment.

In just two days time, I would realize all of this. However, in the moments that led up to the car being nearly demolished by a branch on the Palisades Parkway, I knew I was still learning.

My "uncle" changed the tire and we were on our way to Queens once again. I thanked him for his help, as did Wendy, but I never told him who I was or that I knew him. For him, it was an act of being a good samaritan just trying to make a slight difference in someone's life. Well, then again, I am not sure just what was going through his head at the moment.

I guess we never truly know what is happening in someone's life at any given time, even if they tell us what is going on... there is always... well, let me talk about that story now. Back before she said anything, I must admit that I was too judgmental for my own good at times.

∞ ∞ ∞ ∞ ∞ ∞ ∞ ∞

The International Beer Club, Wendy, and I met as we usually did on Saturday nights. We were all too eager to try out our latest stash of Calvin Coolers, and the humidity was not too oppressive outside for a change.

Wendy, Stacey, and I sat on the curb and watched our group's nightly rituals take place. Danielle would sit somewhat close to us and nurse her cup all night. She would sit pensively watching over the commotion the others would create as they scampered around. She never got involved in Tommy's antics, but she would always be there to stop him from doing something too stupid.

Tommy was brutish and unwavering in his commitment to being the tough, cool guy at school. Even in front of his friends, he did just about everything and anything to show how strong and furious he could be. Tommy and Alec were play fighting as the girls and I sat idly by.

I can't recall what we were talking about that night, probably something music related, for the lesson of a lifetime seemed to overshadow everything I was dealing with in those very moments.

Tommy swung at Alec a little too harshly, knocking him to the floor with a resounding thud.

"What the fuck, man?" Alec brushed himself off and got up wearily.

Danielle rushed over and grabbed Tommy's arm.

She whispered something in his ear, and his demeanor softened instantly.

Tommy didn't seem so irate anymore.

Danielle's grasp loosened and all I could think about was a gentle woman like her holding my shoulder. I was enamored by her ability to soothe him with a look and a single grasp.

I wanted that.

I was looking for a genuine love to see me for who I am, and Danielle fit the bill perfectly. The only part of her that was not perfect? She was Tommy's girl.

In a sense, part of me hoped that one day she would realize that my demeanor was slightly off or that I needed a hand on my shoulder, yet would she dare reach out to me?

Would she see me for me and only me?

Something inside of her sees Tommy for someone other than a brutish fiend, and I was not fully able to comprehend what it was that she saw in him.

Alec did cool down once Wendy and Stacey talked him out of trying to punch Tommy. Although deep down inside Alec knew that Tommy was not really trying to hurt him, but Alec's sense of pride was slightly bruised. One of his best friends, arguably the strongest one, just knocked him off of his feet. For a teenage boy, having your pride ripped out from under you is a rather slippery slope.

Fortunately, Alec was surrounded by two women who were strong enough to convince him that violence is not the answer. It truly was an accident and at that moment, Alec needed someone to remind him of that: luckily he was willing to accept two voices of reason that night.

Danielle and Tommy were standing close to her cherry red Toyota Celica and started to bicker about something. Tommy stormed off into the shrubs looking visibly angry, as always.

"I gotta take a piss," he shouted, waving his hand behind him.

"Fine by me," Danielle shouted after him somewhat sarcastically.

I had a bit of alcohol in me and too much confidence stirring in my core, so I did what I thought would be best in that moment: I sauntered up to Danielle with the swagger only a drunk teenage boy would have when trying to woo a woman.

She was rummaging through her car. Her left hand was pressed firmly on the passenger seat as she snagged some old papers and litter with her right hand.

I cleared my throat, and to my surprise she did not turn and meet my gaze. I tried it again and was met with just an anxious feeling stirring in my stomach. I tried for a third time and without turning around, she sternly said, "I am not ready to hear your apology just yet."

She thought I was Tommy.

'Danielle, no,' I started. 'It's me.'

"Scott?" She flipped her hair over her shoulder as she stood. Her black pants hugged every curve of hers as she rose.

'Hey.'

"Hey."

I thrust my hands in my pants pockets and waited for her to say something. She stood there curiously looking at me, wondering just why I walked over to her.

"So…" Danielle smiled and shut the door. "What's going on, Scott?"

A thousand words flooded my mind. I had no clue just what to say to her in the moment. Should I ask her how she is doing? Should I tell her that I have a crush on her? Should I see what she was cleaning out of her car?

'What the fuck? Like,' I paused to take a breath. 'Why are you with that guy?'

Yes, that was the perfect thing to say: tell a woman who just had a small argument with her boyfriend *why are you with him...* What could go wrong?

"Excuse me," she placed her hand on her chest, almost in a state of shock.

I just betrayed a guy who defended me and continuously took me under his wing. Why? All for a girl... well, a woman. Danielle. What is wrong with me? I don't know what prompted me to say that.

In all seriousness, who the hell was I? What would possess me to walk up to such a beautiful girl and say that? How could I speak in such a way?

Danielle's eyebrows shriveled and her eyes narrowed.

"What is wrong with you?" She grew incredibly defensive.

'I-' Before I could even explain, she cut me off and began to monologue.

"You *don't* know the real Tommy!" She snapped at me. "You just see one side to him, and it is not the side that shows the world who he truly is. You know, you just don't realize this, but he is the most amazing guy in the world."

We leaned against her car for a second and as she gleaned into my glazed eyes, I heard the words that would shake my soul. At the time, I just didn't fully appreciate each word that sprung from her lips as I do now.

"There is a side to him no one gets to see. You don't know how much he struggles all of the time. You have no clue what his family is like."

She got incredibly serious and grabbed my shoulder with her right hand.

Softly, she spoke: "There is always a story behind the story."

Something happened that night. Something, in that very moment, made me feel real. It made me feel that all of the misjudging I bestowed upon other people was actually a reflection of my own misunderstanding. I didn't realize the true gravity of the situation. I didn't take in every fiber of her existence as what it was worth. All I was doing in that moment was being selfish, and for what? Why was I so driven to be so judgmental, especially when I was always so misunderstood?

There is a story behind the story.

There always is.

Even if we don't see it. Even if we do not feel it or sense it.

There is always something on the inside that we do not comprehend.

Something is going on...

Something is being told in what is untold...

It is a story.

∞ ∞ ∞ ∞ ∞ ∞ ∞ ∞

The rest of the summer flew by mercilessly. I was homeless for my birthday, once again, which honestly didn't surprise me. I grew to truly despise my birthday because of how my mother treated me when I turned sixteen, and I honestly gave up on trying to change what my birthday meant to me.

Yeah, it was another year that marked my existence, but so what. I wasn't that special. I didn't truly matter.

Back at school I was up to my usual pursuit of chaos during the day. The guidance counselor found out I was on the streets and surfing from couch to couch to get some semblance of a good night's sleep.

The counselor called me into his office and pulled a chair up next to him. The chair's red padding looks like it had seen better days, but really who was I to judge?

"Scott," the counselor's tone had a special severity to it. "I am worried about you."

I was a senior and I had made it that far, so clearly he was not worried about my academics, or I would have been sitting in summer school the past few months.

"It's come to my attention that you aren't at home anymore."

A strong silence hung in the air.

Someone obviously opened their big mouth, but did it really matter? What was this guidance counselor going to do for me? What was anyone really going to do about my dear mother's habits? That's right…

Nothing.

No one was coming to save me.

I had to save myself and I was totally fine with that.

"Son, what are you doing with your life?"

How cute, I thought at the time, he's taking the fatherly approach with me. As if that would win him some authority over me. I crossed my arms and shrugged. A half-inebriated sigh fluttered from my lips.

"You can continue to sit here and act like a rebellious teenager, or you can let me help you."

He had a point. He did seem like he was trying to help, at the time he just didn't realize that I was drowning in so much turmoil that I needed more than a life preserver. I needed a whole boat to rescue me.

We sat and talked about my life up until this point, but of course I withheld the part about my mother abusing me constantly. No one needed to know about the ghosts of shattered glass that clung to my skin each day.

We came to a series of agreements over the course of the next hour. By the time I walked out of his office, I had a false sense of hope that someday things would get better. At the time, I did not know what my life would become. Then again, if you asked anyone whom I knew at the time, they would not have even guessed what my life would become today.

Anyway, as I walked out the heavy doors of Jamaica High School that day, I felt an overwhelming sense of relief. I had no reason to, honestly. It was just a conversation. Sometimes I guess you just have to put some of the fallen pieces back together, even though you are still picking up more pieces along the way. Life has a funny way of happening to you, even when you least expect it.

∞ ∞ ∞ ∞ ∞ ∞ ∞ ∞

Wendy or Stacey would come visit me at the grocery store. Oftentimes they would sit on the benches there and watch me ring up customers. Neither would stare or interrupt me, but I felt that they were watching over me. In a way, they were like my angels… although at the time I was such a devout Atheist because I had renounced Judaism for it was so closely related to my family. In hindsight, I would not have used the term angels then. Rather, I told people at the time that they were just my friends making sure I was doing okay. Some nights, Wendy would pick me up and drive me back to her apartment in Flushing. I would stay on her couch and her mom would fix me a hot meal, no questions asked.

At that point, Wendy and her mom knew my situation well and would not dare pry.

It was nice to be able to have some safety and security despite my parents' dismissal of their one and only son.

During one dismal Friday morning, Rebecca dashed up to me at school clutching her backpack.

"Scott, Scott, Scott," she seemed out of breath.

'What's up, Rebecca?'

"It's mom," she huffed. "And dad. They are going away for the weekend. You can come home and get your things."

I smiled, for at least someone in my family was looking out for me.
'When are they leaving?'

"This morning," she tugged on her backpack strap. "They dropped me and Sarah off at school and drove out to the Poconos."

I desperately wanted to go back to the house to pick up what was mine: my bed, my clothes, a few old records and trivial things. Rebecca even told me that since I left, nothing of mine was touched.

It was almost as if my presence was frozen in time within my parents' house.

Maybe my parents hoped that I would return someday, but I knew that my mother would never willingly welcome me back in that house ever again.

I gathered a bunch of my friends and marched up to the house with a glimmer of hope in my eye.

Part of me felt optimistic that getting my stuff back would redeem my sense of self.

As I was gathering up my clothes with Wendy, a few friends of ours invited other friends to join in taking my stuff away from the house. Before I knew it, people were bringing their friends over and everyone had a bottle of alcohol in their hands. People were filtering in and out of the tiny house without remorse.

Rebecca even joined in on the fun and could be seen weaving in and out of the crowd that formed.

"Uh oh," Wendy looked over at me with a box of clothes in her hand.

We looked around as loud music was playing from somewhere in the room.

Teenagers I did not even recognize were throwing up in the streets; chunks of bad decisions laced with bile floated towards the gutters.

In the morning when most of the partygoers were gone, I woke up to Rebecca, still wearing her t-shirt of the rock band KISS, throwing up violently in the bathroom.

A resounding knock at the door, followed by the voice of an angry middle-aged man, echoed throughout the trashed house. One of my parents' friends arrived at the house with court papers. He explained that I was getting charged with attempted murder along with endangering the welfare of my mother, her other children, and the pets in the house.

"What the hell," Wendy shouted as she pushed trash from her path. "Endangering the welfare of your mother, her children, and pets."

'Yeah,' I rubbed the back of my neck.

"You are her kid too, yet she threw you out with no problem whatsoever. Oh, and I am sure her goldfish here are in such danger," the tinge of sarcasm in her voice was apparent.

When Wendy and I brought my things back to her house, her mother said the charges were utterly repulsive.

On Monday morning I ran right into my guidance counselor's office and told him what happened. He managed to excuse Rebecca from her classes for the day so she could come to court with me.

Wendy's mother took off from work and sat in Family Court with us. The room looked nothing like it did on those fancy court television shows; the judge was not even on a podium and sat at eye-level with my parents as we all spoke.

"Well," the judge smoothed his moustache as he spoke. "Is all of this true?"

I shifted my eyes to the court appointed attorney I was given.

"Your honor," he straightened his tie as he glanced at me. "My client says he is not guilty."

By some twist of fate, this Family Court in Jamaica was a block away from the alley I slept in when I was living on the streets. I wonder if my mother would have shown some compassion, had she realized where we were.

"Sir," my mother screeched. "That boy is a menace."

As she began to point her finger in my direction and spew profanities in the courtroom, the judge smacked the gavel down.

"Ma'am," the judge started. "This sounds utterly preposterous."

The judge shifted his shoulders towards me and gazed directly in my eyes.

"Young man, do you plan on going back to the house?"

'No,' I peeped.

"You have been out of the house for a year, is this correct?"

'Yes, your honor.' I glanced over at my mother who stuck her nose in the air.

"Do you have a place to live and a job?"

Wendy's mother perked up and clutched her purse as she stood, "He is in my care, sir."

The judge looked over at Wendy's mother and smiled at her wholeheartedly.

"He is not coming back," the judge shifted his eyes to my mother. "So I will be giving you an order of protection for one year. Is that okay with you, son?"

When he looked back towards me, I nodded my head sternly.

As the conversation continued the stark reality hit me: my mother officially severed my umbilical cord.

I was no longer her child.

Wendy's mother ended up writing a formal letter to the court, stating that she would be taking care of me financially in addition to the job I had at the supermarket.

As the winter came roaring past us, the guidance counselor kept his promise and miraculously got me to graduate a few months early. I was gravely stunned that it actually happened.

When I looked out into the crowd of families that were seated in the library, I did not expect to see my parents. For clarification, no, they were not there. Also, this crowd consisted of every super senior's parents and siblings, which had to be less than fifteen people. I was practically alone in that library though a small sea, more like a puddle, of mortar boards and tassels stood before me. Loneliness in a populated room was rather becoming at this point. I did not expect anything from the world, and in turn nothing was given to me.

The typical graduation hymnal played over the speakers and the small stage was set. Walking across the room to receive my diploma, the name *Scott Zachariah Matheson* echoed between the walls as I made my way up to the podium to take my rolled-up piece of paper. I turned to face the people in the room and was met with one set of friendly eyes: Wendy's.

Wendy walked in while my eyes were downcast towards my shoes, and sat patiently while waiting for me to notice her grinning from ear to ear. Her presence was a welcomed surprise on this gloomy, frigid day.

"Sorry" she mouthed from feet away. "My mom-"

I couldn't make out the rest of the words, but I assumed that her mother was going to be there as well; she just could not get off of work.

The fact that she would even consider me on this supposedly monumental day was rather heartwarming.

See at this point, I hadn't seen Wendy for a few days, for I just flew back from Florida. After the miniscule ceremony, Wendy and I stood on the steps of Jamaica High School in the midst of a light snowfall that cascaded down the ornate architecture.

"How is Alisha doing?" Wendy asked with her hands in her pockets.

Although it may seem shocking to remain friends with an ex-girlfriend or ex-boyfriend, when two people just are not right for each other, it is better to communicate than to live in a perpetual state of anger. Sometimes relationships do not work out, but even though people may grow apart, at the end of the day friendship is more important.

That's what ran through my mind as Wendy and I recounted my visit with Alisha.

'Good, she's good, thanks.' The condensation hung in the air after I spoke.

"What did you guys do during your visit?"

The two of us began walking the long path to the steps of the school. The stone wall moved closer to us as I moved further away from the school I really never wanted to see again. I was content with graduating early, for I think I really needed to get out of the experience that was high school. I did not want to get rid of my friends; rather I think I just had to graduate early in order to feel like I was no longer a kid.

'We went to a Def Leppard concert. I have to say that even though Rick Allen only has one arm now, he is still a phenomenal drummer. It was incredible to see him in person.'

Wendy knocked into me slightly as we walked down the steps.

"Really?"

'Yeah.' I stopped and turned slowly as we moved to the edge of the steps. Jamaica High School was fading into the horizon and the frigid snow that was falling. It was almost as if a picturesque postcard could be based on this moment. I would have called this scene "The Liberation," for I felt so free leaving these four walls, knowing full and well that I would not have the crutch of high school to hide my youth anymore.

What life would hold for me, I was holistically unsure. Still, I had time to figure out what my life would become.

Danielle's words rang through my mind as Wendy and I walked out of the gates of the school and strolled through the neighborhood. Wendy's words seeped into my head, but the phrase "There is a story behind the story" kept pulling me along.

"You okay?" Wendy grabbed my elbow and the tracks that we left were fading due to the impending blizzard.

I would have been lying if in those moments I said I was okay, just worried, so I did what any emotionally scarred boy would do.

'I'm fine.' Those words seemed to calm Wendy's concern, though I knew that she was too perceptive to just accept that as an answer. She stopped prying and we walked to the car in silence.

∞ ∞ ∞ ∞ ∞ ∞ ∞ ∞

In the days that passed, I found myself scrounging for some semblance of normalcy. I was an adult now. I had to fully accept responsibility for everything that I would do in life. Sure, I was seventeen and was homeless before, but now I was seventeen, out of high school, homeless, and in need of something bigger than just a job at a grocery store.

I found myself a room for rent in Queens and a job at Aetna Life and Casualty in Lake Success, New York. It was just a short drive between my room and job, but I felt like I was living the real adult life.

I felt comfortable enough to reach out to my grandparents on my father's side and tell them about my "new" life. I called them up one day and Wendy drove me to the Bronx to see them.

As I knocked on the door, I could hear the pitter-patter of slippers move across the floor. The creaky floorboards of the apartment gave away my grandmother's presence as she scampered to the door.

"Ginger, who is it?" Hearing my grandfather's voice in person was soothing.

"Julian," she spoke, "It is our grandson!"

She opened the door and swung her frail arms around me. Her pink, slightly pilling housecoat rubbed against me as she hugged me.

"It is good to see you sweetie." Her genuine mannerisms made me feel welcomed.

My grandfather stood in the hallway arch on the far side of the apartment and boomed, "Well, Virginia, are you letting the boy in?"

We spoke for a bit and I told them about my experiences over the past few years and months. My grandfather remained stern while my grandmother's concern grew obvious in her furrowed brow.

The two of them held hands and listened, with plenty of interruptions, throughout the three hours that followed.

Eventually when Wendy came to pick me up, I told her that my grandparents agreed to let me borrow their car to take back and forth to work each day. The Oldsmobile Cutlass Supreme would be at my disposal, for my grandparents' concern for my well-being also came with wanting to make sure I could at least go back and forth to my new livelihood each day.

Wendy and I spoke about the conversation I had with my grandparents, and she seemed genuinely concerned when I told her about my sister.

Though my running away from home marked my inconvenient freedom, Rebecca was taking the brunt of my former abuse at home. Since my mother could not destroy my self-worth, she still had to take out her rage on someone. Rebecca was the unfortunate victim.

I felt bad for Rebecca, and as her older brother, I knew I needed to intervene soon or she might face the same fate I endured for years. Homelessness would not help Rebecca grow; rather it could stifle her completely. I did not want that for my family.

∞ ∞ ∞ ∞ ∞ ∞ ∞ ∞

As I delivered mail to the Aetna employees on Monday morning, I came across a woman whose entire cubicle was decorated in New York Mets flags, memorabilia, and merchandise. Being the witty punk I was, I just needed to make a comment.

'So you like the Yankees, huh?' I plopped her mail on her desk.

The woman swiveled in her chair, revealing her cherry red kitten heels and thin fishnet stockings. Her nail file rested in between the fingers on her right hand.

"Clearly," she muttered sarcastically.

'You know,' I began confidently, 'I was at the '86 World Series games. Uh. Games six and seven."

She smiled and revealed her pearly white teeth. The woman was mature but discernibly attractive. The Mets memorabilia was a great conversation piece, but she was clearly more fascinating than her cubicle.

"I'm Olga," she dropped the nail file in her lap and extended her hand. 'I'm Scott.'

"You sound fun, Scott."

I made my first friend in the office. I was the cute little boy and she was a mature, older woman who I most definitely thought was smoking hot. I had a huge crush on her, but like Danielle, she was way out of my league.

I was making $75 a week, my room cost $70 a week, and I had $5 left over for food. Olga seemed like the kind of mature woman who would be worth more than a $5 date on a Friday night.

I went home that day from work with a renewed sense of happiness. I may not have had much, but the solitary Schlitz beer my hall neighbor would leave for me seemed like the world.

Stacey came to visit and started to ask me every question in the book: "What the hell are you doing with your life? How are you doing? How are you surviving?"

I did not really think about any of the responses. Everything was crazy at the time and I just existed for survival purposes at this point.

My diet consisted of those cheap potato chip bags and beer for breakfast, lunch, and dinner. I truly could not afford anything else. I stopped at the corner store each day to buy my chips and scurry off to work.

Each day I would saunter by Olga's cubicle and flirt with her. She told me that she had a boyfriend, Dougie, who she lived with, but that never seemed to stop her from grabbing my thigh and squeezing it tightly as I sat on the edge of her desk.

This charade of innocent flirting continued for weeks. I kept to myself, and my pornographic magazines at home, and responsibility appeared to be rather fitting for me. I loved my crazy, messed up adult life that left me a few dollars shy from being homeless each week.

I would brag to Olga, the 34 year-old woman who took a liking to me, that I had my *own* room in Queens. I did not know if that impressed her, but she seemed genuinely intrigued by my youthful looks. I was a boy, nearly a man, who doted on her all day at work. I personally thought she was drawn in by the attention I gave her.

With my suave and debonair demeanor, I handed her my address on a wrinkled napkin. I winked as I told her, 'If you *ever* need to *come* by, here is my address.'

She seemed genuinely turned on by my gesture, and I was eager to see if she would take me up on the offer. The only female visitors I had in my room were Wendy and Stacey, and neither of them were even close to being my potential love interests.

∞ ∞ ∞ ∞ ∞ ∞ ∞ ∞

To my surprise, one brisk March night just weeks later, I woke up at 2:00AM to the sound of knocking at my door. I wearily peeled myself from the bed and teetered to the door in my underwear. The light from the hallway illuminated her silky blonde hair and tight midnight blue dress.

"Can I come in?" Olga's fingers wrapped around the door, she was eager to enter my quaint room. "Dougie and I had a fight. I can't go home."

Of course, I let her in without disdain.

We spent the night together wrapped in the cotton sheets. My skin pressed against the sweat dripping off of her in the heat of passion. We may not have seemed like a couple that would actually get together, but in those moments when we were intertwined in the sheets, everything just made sense for a change.

Danielle said there was a story behind every story, and that is the truth. Olga had a reason for coming to my room that night to be with me. Whether it was out of curiosity or because she was actually kicked out of her house at the time has always remained a mystery to me, yet she still ended up in my room and wrapped in my bed.

In the days that followed, she stayed with me and we continued our nightly fun rendezvous. I was engulfed in her intense sensual energy and her passion, and thought that I was the luckiest 17-year-old in the world. I was with a sexy woman, I had my own room and a car to drive, and I was free.

Though as with all experiences in life, freedom is not always free.

Remember, there is always a story behind every story... and this one was just beginning.

CHAPTER 8

November Rain

~

"Everything you say to me takes me one step closer to the edge...

and I'm about to break."

- Linkin Park, American Rock Band, Agoura Hills, California

Once I dove headfirst into Olga's world, there was no escaping. She was a sensual dynamo who refused to let me rest even one night. When she wanted sex, she got it, despite my willingness or not. She would tell me, "Oh you are seventeen; you can handle me."

Stacey and Wendy had an issue with her.

"How could you let a mature woman take advantage of you like that?" Stacey would constantly ask. With the chord to my phone wrapped between my fingers, I would rest at the edge of my bed and convince her that I was okay.

"Sure," she would retort. "Do whatever you think is best."

Her distinct sarcasm hung in the air. I was naive and young; I didn't listen to my friends' advice.

I met The International Beer Club in front of Jamaica High School one night after work. I had been drifting away from them ever so slightly, because my schedule and girlfriend were more conducive to my new lifestyle.

Olga gave me a bag of pills and told me to take them before she came home that night. I had them in my pocket when I went back to the high school, so naturally I took them while I was there.

While Danielle, Tommy, Alec, Stacey, and Wendy were drinking, my vision began evolving into a massive blur. Everything was getting dark, and not just because the sun was setting. I was being transformed into an entirely different state of mind.

What the fuck kind of pills did she give me?

"You okay, man?" Tommy moved towards me and rested a hand on my shoulder.

'Yeeeeeeee-' I began screeching and jolting back and forth erratically.

The group watched me trip over my own two feet and start screaming randomly. Wendy tried running after me and I threw myself onto the grass.

'ELVIS' I began shouting.

The group circled around me and began to chuckle nervously.

"What about him?" Danielle bent down as if she were talking to a small child.

'He-' I started to sob hysterically. 'He died, didn't he?'

No one knew what to say. I was too far gone to comprehend what I was doing.

Stacey decided to break the bad news to me, since everyone else was too terrified to do it: "Yeah man, Elvis is dead."

This sent me into a dramatic tailspin of tears and hysteria. To this day, I am unsure why I was triggered by Elvis.

I began having delusions of voices shouting at me and giving me advice. At the time it seemed like incredibly random voices and people, such as Abraham Lincoln, but I was particularly drawn to every word that came from his mouth. His messages seemed diluted and complex, but the voice that echoed in my mind sounded real. Wendy and Stacey's voices faded in and out, until I just up and left.

I ran to the car and gripped the steering wheel intensely. No one ran after me, but then again, I did not even know who anyone was at those moments.

I felt lost and found all at once. I was holistically broken and beaten into silence. Yet in the silence, I found clarity and a sense of cohesiveness. What was in those pills Olga gave me?

∞ ∞ ∞ ∞ ∞ ∞ ∞ ∞

Olga arguably thrust me into a world of chaos and confusion, which would spark my drug-fueled rage and explicit violence. I never physically injured anyone, but I would constantly crave alcohol and whatever drug Olga could get her hands on. I was hooked and she knew she could do anything to me.

I returned back to my room, our room actually, where she kissed me with such passionate indifference. I was hers. I was her property and she owned every drop of blood coursing through my veins. The only identity I had was one of complex delusions that she developed for me.

I was never truly sure what drew me to Olga until I grew older. Through therapy and a series of soul-searching discussions, I realized that Olga filled a void in my life. Olga was the one, mature woman who loved me and seemed to care for me. My mother did not care for me. I didn't really have any other older female role models in my life, so in hindsight I was drawn to what I could not experience.

Olga bestowed upon me a sense of fun and excitement that I never knew came with adulthood. I was so busy spinning my wheels in the mud, that I did not get a chance to drive: after years of being homeless and down on my luck, Olga was my feisty four-leaf clover. Though at the time I probably would have used different language to describe her, I saw Olga as a blessing.

Blessings are supposed to come with some sort of epiphany or miracle attached to them, but while dating Olga I was immersed in a state of ecstasy… this was primarily fueled by the drugs and cocaine she would expose me to regularly.

Night after night, I catered to her whim because I genuinely loved her and wanted to make her happy. Despite my blurred state of mind, she still convinced me that I was able to stand. With the last of the cocaine running out, she pushed me to see that getting more cocaine would send her into a jovial state of mind. She helped me get credit cards so that we could get more cocaine whenever we wanted to.

The two of us would do crazy things like go into Macy's Department Store, dash up the stairs to reach the cookie store on the third floor, and buy a $100 gift certificate with my credit card. I thought it was a brilliant way to get money for cocaine, because we would spend the $100 gift card on a $1 cookie, get $99 change, for you could not put money back on a gift card back then, and use the $99 cash to go buy drugs.

It was a perfect system, though I had no clue that I would be destroying my credit score for years to come.

Still, I would do anything for love, and I did everything she asked of me.

∞ ∞ ∞ ∞ ∞ ∞ ∞ ∞

After scoring cocaine that would tide us over for some time, Olga was too pleased with herself to just go home for the night. She needed some fun and she needed it now.

With her nose speckled with bits of white dust, she gazed at me and swatted my shoulder playfully.

"Scott-" her words dragged on and fluttered through the air, "we gotta break into Dougie's house and steal my shit back."

Now normally I would not condone illegal behavior, well, unless it had to do with drugs or alcohol or anything she wanted, but my mind was laced with cocaine. I was beyond the point of comprehending the balance of right or wrong.

We drove all the way to her old place that she had with her boyfriend and stood inches from the apartment door. The metallic letters gleamed in the hall light that swayed in the gentle breeze that flew in as the door slammed behind us. There we were, about to break into the apartment, without a lucid thought or concern for what was legal passing through our minds.

Olga pounded on the wooden door, hoping that by some miracle he would answer.

"That fuck isn't even home, damn asshole." Her voice faded in and out.

I turned and began looking around the hall. The lights flew diagonally in my line of sight. I was inhabited by the ghosts of pain and pleasure mixing with the cocaine and chemicals in my head.

My eyes fixated on the metal hilt of something hiding behind a glass case: it was an axe.

Perfect.

Just what the doctor ordered.

Olga pushed me aside with utter indifference. She ripped it from the case with extreme force and began breaking her way through the door. I stood there in absolute disbelief, but I knew that the sensations creeping up and down her spine were forcing her into this manic state of mind.

Olga leapt through the gaping hole in the door, which caused her to laugh even more maniacally than moments before.

Her chaos-fueled sickness was cured with the repetitive slamming of the axe against the solid wood. Something told me that Dougie was not going to be happy when he got home and saw this scene before him.

"Come on already," her voice droned on in the hallway as people poked their heads out of their own front doors. Upon seeing the terrifying masterpiece Olga created, they retreated inside and slammed their doors. No one batted an eye and not a single soul seemed to care.

They were all just inhabitants of the building; no one was truly living in it.

As I stepped inside, Olga began throwing black trash bags in my direction. Her placid demeanor was such a juxtaposition: she was fueled by equal parts rage and cocaine.

To this day, her wide-eyed glances and violently passionate actions still haunt me. My body is still adorned in the scars she gave to me during our heated arguments.

Gathering her belongings came and went without further incident, but deep down inside I felt somewhat guilty for breaking down Dougie's door. There had to be a story behind his story, just as there was a story behind Olga's story. She was not just doing this out of blind rage, but something else was brewing.

The two of us dragged everything she owned down the narrow, dreary staircases. We left through the same hole in the door we came through: almost as if leaving through his apartment door would symbolize, once and for all, her leaving her home.

As we trampled down the stairs, giggling and planning the rest of our night, she showed no remorse. She seemed happy, or at least what she would consider happy, for a change. It dawned on me that we probably left the axe cutting through the planks in his floor... as if a smashed front door was not enough of a sight, the axe sticking out of the floor would definitely make things worse.

∞ ∞ ∞ ∞ ∞ ∞ ∞ ∞

"He hit me a lot, you know," were the first words Olga said to me as we drove down the Grand Central Parkway. She was gripping the passenger seat almost as if it were a life preserver.

Another still silence hung in the air.

"Thanks for coming, I guess," she said as she gazed out the window. With each pothole we hit, her gentle sobs escaped her lips.

Our sole bedroom in Jamaica was her salvation. Though her and Dougie were trying to build a life together, a series of four walls and a leaky apartment ceiling were not her home. She was merely existing with him, not living with him. That is the difference, in some way, that no matter how much we try to make four walls and a roof our home it just doesn't fit... unless you have someone with you who is your home.

As we pulled up to where *our* home was, she wiped the tears from her eyes and smiled at me. We moved in silence as the two of us dragged her things into the house. The hallway was damp and dark, but I could always count on my one can of Schlitz beer sitting beside my door. The old man next to me never forgot me and always looked out for me however he could. That one can of beer had more love in it than anything my parents seemed to bestow upon me up until that point.

The two of us dropped the bags on the floor and crawled under the covers. I watched the blades of the ceiling fan circulate above us as she cuddled into my chest. I could tell the drugs were wearing off as she nestled closer to me.

Olga rested her tender lips on my shoulder and whispered, "Never let go of me."

Her eyes flickered in the dim light from the lamp on the nightstand.

'Never,' I muttered as both of our eyelids shut in unison and the calming murmur from the fan lulled us to sleep.

∞ ∞ ∞ ∞ ∞ ∞ ∞ ∞

Olga's white Buick Regal was a thing of classic beauty, just like her. Except no one could own her.

Well, unless you counted the cocaine.

The two of us were jamming to some amazing music in her car. The lyrics seeped into my mind, for I was turned on by the music she showed me. Her experience opened me to rock music I had never heard before, and it was an exhilarating feeling to watch the melody move through her.

The two of us were on our way to a Bon Jovi concert just living in the sounds that sprung forth from the radio. That night was the bittersweet symphony I needed to hear and enjoy, and Olga was the one person I wanted to feel every moment with.

We got to the concert and parked in the far corner of the lot. First thing was always first with Olga, so she naturally took out the cocaine and we took care of business. The lyrics to her favorite song, "Roundabout" from Yes, boomed over the speakers:

"Along the drifting cloud
The eagle searching down on the land
Catching the swirling wind
The sailor sees the rim of the land

The eagle's dancing wings
Create as weather spins out of hand
In and around the lake
Mountains come out of the sky and they stand there
One mile over we'll be there and we'll see you"

Hours later, we were barely hanging by a thread at the Bon Jovi concert. She was so high that the sweat beading off of her forehead mixed effortlessly with her hair as she shimmied.

If I hadn't grabbed her from falling over the ledge at the concert, this chapter would have had a very different ending. Age clearly did not matter in this relationship, although I was 17-years-old and she was 34-years-old, for our time was built on moments upon moments of the classic adage, "sex, drugs, and rock and roll."

∞ ∞ ∞ ∞ ∞ ∞ ∞ ∞

The two of us never blurred the lines of professional versus relationship at work, though we did flirt and play Uno in the break room constantly. Not a single person knew about our life together beyond the walls of work, and it was better we kept it that way.

Outside of work my friends were fleeting memories. The International Beer Club became a thing of the distant past. Wendy and Stacey would call me and ask to hang out, but I would always blow them off. Nights filled with Olga and cocaine were more appealing than just hanging around the park and drinking second rate alcohol.

Olga and I were living. She took me under her wing and would bring me to see local bands in these archaic dive bars. We were reckless adults, but we were fully grown up. The two of us were spending hours each weekend following the local band On-Line, snorting drugs, and drinking past any comprehension of who we were and what we were doing. I remember spiritually being in those moments thinking life was bigger than what I was doing. It was bigger than the drugs. It was bigger than people dying or living. It was... it was... I didn't know what it was.

There was something.

I just knew there was something I wanted to sink my teeth into.

I wanted to be someone.

I just didn't know how to get that.

Upon being immersed in the cocaine-infused lifestyle, I earned myself a front row seat to putrid actions and repulsive moments that I would rather forget. There are some things in life you cannot erase from your memory, no matter how hard you try.

Olga yearned for any ounce of cocaine she could get her hands on.

There were many dealers we went to and people we trusted.

Oftentimes, she would dispatch me on a mission to score anything I could find. While going out to get my hands on our fix, I never thought twice about my safety. I wanted to please her more than anything.

On one particular night after work, she told me to go to this new address in the midst of Brooklyn. She said that there was a new dealer who promised a lucid high.

As I drove all the way to East New York, Brooklyn, Billy Squier's lyrics to "The Stroke" blasted over the speakers.

"Now everybody, have you heard, if you're in the game
Then the stroke's the word
Don't take no rhythm,
Don't take no style
Gotta thirst for killin',
Grab your vial"

I let the beat flow through me as I got closer and closer to where Olga sent me. With my hand firmly gripped around the steering wheel, I found myself cutting down a side street.

My car bumper was eerily close to a jet-black Lincoln Continental; its windows were tinted and seemed to be opaque. To my left, there were a row of dilapidated apartments and three garages with their gates shut tight. Leaning against one of the garages was a young boy who was about seven or eight years old.

The Lincoln Continental made an abrupt stop and the front passenger side window rolled down.

Instinctively, I stopped about four or five car lengths away. Something told me that there was about to be trouble, although I was most likely just paranoid because I also needed a fix.

My gut told me to pretend I was just parking my car and not paying attention, but my curiosity got the best of me.

The kid walked up to the Lincoln and passed a wad of cash through the window. A hand appeared and dropped the gun in the kid's outstretched palms. It stunned me that a child was able to buy a gun off of the streets of Brooklyn. I shed a silent tear in honor of the death of that boy's innocence.

I realize I was being hypocritical, for I was on my way to break the law as well. I did not consider where I was or what the potential consequences could be.

Although I continued on my way to get cocaine, that moment haunted me for years to come. Something deep within me prayed that our world would not be filled with violence. However, at that moment something deep within me craved cocaine.

I shut my car door and scurried into one of the apartment buildings. The daylight was sealed behind me, as was my dignity.

As I climbed the steps all I could think of was the potential of cocaine coursing through my veins.

My legs brought me to the third floor and a wooden door at the far end of the hallway.

As my knuckles met the door, I heard footsteps approaching rapidly.

A small woman opened the door with her young daughter standing nearby. Though men were dominating the drug scene at the time, there were few women who were trying to make it as dealers.

This woman was one of those outcasts in society.

She was not your typical stay-at-home mom who remained docile. Her stature and the way she walked commanded respect. I was impressed that she seemed to be running the drug ring in this area of the city.

The woman was leading what appeared to be a lucrative business, for there were countless men who reported to her and moved her product. Small bags and pure bricks lined her dining room table.

She was the embodiment of female empowerment.

The woman's daughter walked with a limp as she moved about the room. The young girl was grinning from ear to ear and blinked at me sweetly.

"Come in, come in," the girl said as I walked into their apartment.

Something in my mind whispered that this was all wrong.

How could we live in a world where dealing drugs was a normal daily occurrence?

In hindsight, I realize that I was being judgmental and I had no right to be. After all, I was picking up drugs from this woman.

The woman could be running a legitimate and legal empire; however, she was using her acumen to line her apartment with cash from desperate addicts' pockets. Other men were standing around, but it was clear that they worked for her. No one seemed to cross her and I wondered why.

I wondered how her life's journey came to this point. Despite her situation, she seemed incredibly powerful.

I purchased the drugs and high-fived the little girl on my way out. She giggled as I walked through the front door.

With the drugs safely tucked into my pocket, I receded down the steps and back into my car.

Years later, I picked up a newspaper and saw a picture of the woman and her daughter on the front cover. They were shot and murdered in a drug raid that went horribly wrong.

I was heartbroken, but not because she became my regular dealer prior to her death: the respect I developed for the woman was unmatched. Her life might have been drastically different had she chose a different path; she had so much potential.

My hope for a better tomorrow was slipping from my heart's grasp.

These days blurred into one another and eventually left me with the stinging sensation that I was missing out on my family's memories: the good, the bad, and the tragic.

One day after work, I came home to a crumpled note resting against my door. Stacey was only pissed at me two times in her entire life: this was the first time. Her anger seeped through every word she penned on that faded scrap of paper. Although I had not been returning her calls, and I was running around with Olga more times than I could count or fathom, Stacey remained vigilant.

The note felt familiar between my fingertips, although it was doused in emotions I still never quite understood. I know my parents were incredibly harsh when it came to me and my well-being, but I never thought they would let another one of their children succumb to the same fate.

There, in black and white, my worst nightmares were actualized:

Rebecca overdosed on pills. She's at Schneider's Children's Hospital. Where are you?

Though I was definitely on something at the time, I remained true to my family values. I rushed to Rebecca's side, where I saw my enraged parents moping around the hospital.

"What the fuck is he doing here?" My mother bellowed and that same sense of trepidation from when I was sixteen snuck back into my bones.

'They are abusing her, keep them away from my sister!' I was shouting at the doctors and Sarah held her ears in the corner of the hallway. The colorful giraffe painting and array of balloons were a stark contrast of what was going on before our very eyes.

I called Child Protective Services on my parents, but obviously they didn't do anything. My parents still continued their years of mistreatment and abuse, unaware of what it was doing to our seemingly picture-perfect family...

But isn't that always the case? Sometimes people may not fit in your picture, but they always end up being the ones who get framed.

Life has a crazy way of playing out that way sometimes: you try to be one person, but the world paints you as a totally different one.

My mother made it seem like I was utter trash, though I was the one who constantly tried to save our family. No matter what I did, my mother never saw me as her own child. Call it what you wish, but I never felt like I belonged in her life.

Though biologically she was my mother, maybe I was never destined to be her child.

Walking towards my car, I felt a pounding in my chest. My breath became labored and rather hurried. The streetlight was dimming rather slowly and I felt a rush of nausea pushing into my gut. It took everything I had to block me from hurling directly onto my car.

Something was burning inside of me. Something was pulling me in two separate directions...

That something was the bond I had with Olga falling to pieces, and the sense that I needed a shot of bourbon to remedy the pain I felt within.

Something had to change, yeah…

Something.

∞ ∞ ∞ ∞ ∞ ∞ ∞ ∞

At this point, Olga and I were dating for over a year and a half. She moved into her own apartment, which was close to her family in Valley Stream, so naturally I followed her out there.

I got my own little place that was much nicer than the one-room place I had in Jamaica. I was so proud of myself when I brought Olga home with me to the apartment in Valley Stream, but she was not as pleased. She punched me in the face and smacked me across my arm: the bruises were "Proof of love," as she would say.

Despite the cocaine coursing through my system, I still had one last ounce of chivalry left; I never laid my hands on her.

There is a stereotype that runs rampant through our society: men won't come out and talk about non-masculine and seemingly shameful things like getting abused by a woman. Although I am not coming to the conclusion that what she did was abuse me, we did have a turbulent relationship at times. The cocaine fueled her rage.

Olga would often punch me in the face because she wanted that last line of cocaine. We would have crazy sexual experiences as a result of her debauchery, but at what cost?

Between her intoxicating love and my willingness to please her, I realize in hindsight that I was losing myself. I spent so much time trying to bend to her every whim, not noticing just how close I was to breaking.

When you are on cocaine or any sort of drug, it replaces every logical thought you assumed you could create. Assumption is overridden by the consumption of ecstasy that filters into your system.

Olga would threaten me with a knife, saying that if I ever dared to take the last drop of cocaine or fantasized about another woman, she would kill me.

With each passing day, I felt her presence creeping over my shoulder as the ghost of her spirit hung somewhere in the air. It was bitterly cold with and without her, and all I had around me was a very thin coat: no one else loved me the way she did.

She was within, and she was without. Still, the scratches that remained on my arm were the only physical entity marking she was there beside me without me believing she was a cocaine-fueled vision.

I abandoned The International Beer Club for Olga. My friends would stop calling to see where I was and if I was even functional. Stacey and Wendy would try reaching out constantly, but I would turn them away without a second of remorse. I could not fathom why they would want to associate with me: I was a grown-up. I was out in the world and had my own place.

I had a girlfriend who was my best friend and I loved dearly.

Almost nightly, Stacey would call and plead for me to spend time with the group.

With indifference in my tone I would reply that I was busy, for Olga's endearingly horrifying glances would remind me that I had everything I needed right there: Olga and cocaine were all I needed.

∞ ∞ ∞ ∞ ∞ ∞ ∞ ∞

Despite loving all things New York Yankees, I ended up selling valuable 8x10 autographed photos of members from the 1977-1978 team. Thurman Munson, Billy Martin, Lou Pinella, Bucky Dent, and a few other greats were dropped off at a pawn shop during one of my cocaine-induced rages.

It is not one of my prouder moments, but drugs make people do terrible and nonsensical things.

I did not need friends or possessions. I just needed Olga.

I figured she was all I ever needed.

∞ ∞ ∞ ∞ ∞ ∞ ∞ ∞

One night after work, I intended to go over to Olga's basement apartment. As I have said, during the day, she did not want to associate with me at work. She spent the whole day powdering her face and avoiding me. It was not like I could just go up to her at work, so I just waited in my grandfather's car a block away. She had strict rules that I could never deviate from: do not tell anyone at work about our relationship, do not come over if her aunt and uncle were home, do not take the last line of cocaine.

The list went on and on.

Nine times out of ten, she would sneak me into her basement apartment and let me stay the night. No matter what happened at work, I would come home to her or she would call me at some point. She was my life; so I knew we would keep in touch.

Today seemed different though. I must have been waiting in the car almost an hour at this point, and decided that I would just surprise her. I hadn't seen her car pass me, but she had to be home at this point.

When I pulled up to her aunt and uncle's house, her car was already seated comfortably in the driveway for the night. It was odd. She did not tell me her plans for the day, but if she were going to come straight home after work, why would she keep me out of the loop? Why wouldn't she tell her boyfriend what she was up to?

I scurried down the steps and knocked on her screen door. The light was on and I felt slightly anxious. I straightened my tie and took a deep breath: my shoulders slightly wrinkled my dress shirt, but I knew Olga would not care.

When her eyes met mine upon opening the door, she pulled her door close behind her.

"You are not welcome here," she boomed.

I pushed the door slightly and saw another man's shoes resting next to the couch. My eyes widened and she knew something about me was way off.

"Get away," she began backing up into her apartment and I pushed the door open all the way. "Stay away from me!"

I nervously combed my hair with my fingers and moved towards her, 'Babe, are you okay?'

She ran at me with a knife.

She tried to stab me.

Olga, of all people, tried to stab me.

I figured this all had to be a misunderstanding, or the drugs, yeah. Yeah, it was the drugs.

I looked down at my tie and saw the shredded fabric flapping around. She really did want to stab me. No. No. No. It was a mistake. It had to be.

"Man, I think you have to go." The man on the couch stood up and moved towards me. I froze, unsure of how to respond.

I did not ask any questions, for I trusted Olga dearly. I loved her beyond what it means to love someone, and I know she loved me too. I caught her eyes welling up as I turned and slammed the door behind me.

I did not know what else to do or where else to go, so I just drove home and sat in my apartment. I allowed the darkness to pull me into whatever alcohol-induced sensations awaited for me.

∞ ∞ ∞ ∞ ∞ ∞ ∞ ∞

"Hey honey, you okay?" Olga peered around the corner and approached me gingerly. I stood there with an abhorrent look on my face, unsure of what to say to her. She just called me "honey" at work.

'Hi.' I kept shuffling the mail in front of me.

"Hi. Hi? Honey, it is me." She rested her hand on my shoulder and grinned.

I smiled back instinctively and waited for her to respond.

"How about the two of us have dinner tonight at your apartment? Just us two." Olga slid her hand down my back, tracing my spine slightly on her way down. "We could find something to do together."

I could feel myself getting hotter and pulled slightly at my tie before clearing my throat. She loves me. Last night was nothing. Just nothing.

Olga disappeared back towards her cubicle, and I could tell that night was going to be a good night for us. I spent the rest of the day at work daydreaming about Olga and figuring out ways to make her happy.

∞ ∞ ∞ ∞ ∞ ∞ ∞ ∞

I puttered around the kitchen eagerly awaiting Olga's arrival. She was due to come at any minute, and everything just needed to be perfect for her. It had to be perfect. Just perfect for my Olga.

She crept into my apartment with a sultry "Hi Baby" and threw her bag and coat on the couch. Olga seemed to be in such a pleasant mood and even brought cocaine with her. It was going to be a great night. I knew it. I felt it.

Olga moved her way across the room and wrapped her hand around the back of my neck. I nestled into her neck and began to kiss her slowly. Olga's body loosened as she pressed against me and let out a gentle laugh.

She planted a sweet kiss on my lips as she fluttered her eyelids. Olga turned and receded towards her purse for a moment, allowing my mind to wander towards the ringing phone.

'Hello?'

"Scott, hey, glad you're home," Stacey sounded incredibly happy to hear my voice.

'Stacey, hey, how are you?'

"Well I will tell you how I am doing, later tonight that is!"

'What?'

"Scott," her tone grew happier, "A bunch of us are hanging out tonight. I am not asking you to come out, I am telling you that you have to!"

It was pleasant to hear her so joyful on the phone.

Olga cocked her eyebrow and hurried across the room.

"Who is that on the phone?" Olga looked very displeased.

I covered the receiver and whispered, 'Just Stacey, don't worry.'

Olga's demeanor grew impatient and serious: "Hang up," she boomed.

'Hold on, I-'

"No," Olga yelped. "Hang up now. This second."

"Scott, are you there?" Stacey's voice grew slightly concerned.

'Yeah,' I kissed Olga's forehead, 'Yeah I am here, Stacey.'

Olga grew outraged.

"Are you coming tonight? You're coming out tonight, yes you are!" Stacey was eagerly waiting for a reply from me.

Olga began pouting and stomping around like an insubordinate child. She did seem like she was looking forward to tonight, and no doubt she had some crazy cocaine-fueled party planned for the two of us, so I naturally had to comply with her wishes.

'Stacey, I-'

"No, you are coming out!" Stacey grew impatient.

'Stacey, Olga needs me. You can't just call me and expect me to come out and see you. You need to respect mine and Olga's relationship.'

"Respect you? Respect you!" I could hear Stacey's voice straining. "You spend every moment with Olga and I just want to see you. You have to come out and see us."

'No. Stacey,' I got incredibly upset: how could she just say she wants to see *me* like that? Couldn't she understand how important Olga was in my life?

"Yes, Scott." She retorted. She grew indifferent to my stern protest.

'No, Stacey, I am not coming out. Olga needs me. *Olga* wants me.'

A still silence hung between us.

"I cannot believe you! I ask you, I *tell* you that you have to come out, after everything, and all you want to do is turn your back on me and The International Beer Club."

'No, that is not-' she cut me off and grew angrier.

"No, that is what you are doing. You are disowning us, and for what? For Olga."

Olga heard that and instantly began crying.

'You know what Stacey; you are so far out of line. You *know* how much Olga means to me. If you can't accept that, then that is your problem.'

Stacey grunted and sighed, "Fine."

'Fine?'

"Fine, goodbye Scott, don't you worry about us. Don't you worry about me."

'Fine.' I said coldly. 'Bye Stacey.'

"Goodbye Scott."

As the receiver slammed down, and I slammed my phone down in return, little did I know I was sealing my best friend's fate... my real best friend's fate.

Olga kissed me and leapt on top of me.

"Who needs her anyway, honey? You have me." Olga wrapped her legs around me and began running her fingers through my long blonde hair.

The two of us kissed and began making our way to the couch, which became our spot for the next few hours.

Who needed to go out and be with a bunch of teenagers anyway? Olga was my everything, and I could not leave her, and I knew she would never, ever leave me.

∞ ∞ ∞ ∞ ∞ ∞ ∞ ∞

The next morning at work was rather quiet. Olga's aroma danced through my body and I could still feel every single one of her touches from the night before. She was inches from me, but I could not walk over there and touch her. Rules are rules.

"Scott," one of the secretaries called for me, "Someone is on the phone for you."

'Tell them I'll call back later.' My mind was elsewhere, and no one would call me at work anyway.

"Scott, it is your sister Rebecca. She sounds upset."

'Okay, I will be right there.' I dropped the mail and began my slow walk past Olga's cubicle, hoping her eyes would lock with mine even if just for a second.

The moment I picked up the phone, Rebecca's cries flooded my ears. I could only imagine what my parents were up to now.

'Hey Rebecca, calm down, what did they do now?' I rested my back against the wall.

"No, hi, um, hey Scott. Are you sitting down?"

'Are you in the hospital again?'

"Um," Rebecca sounded anxious, "Well, no, but, um."

'What's wrong?'

"It's Stacey."

'Oh, Stacey,' Rebecca must have heard the disdain in my voice, 'What did she tell you, Rebecca?'

"Uh, um." She cleared her throat as I eagerly waited to hear whatever excuse Stacey gave her for calling. "Scott…"

Rebecca's tone grew solemn and serious for a change. Something was up.

"Scott, there was an accident last night."

As Rebecca began explaining what happened, my mind started racing. All I could clearly make out in those moments were that The International Beer Club was hanging out by some train tracks last night. Stacey saw a drunken man get his shoe stuck on the tracks, so naturally she went to help. The man was belligerent and Stacey was trying to get him away from the path of the oncoming train. She was not drunk and she was just trying to help, but she didn't realize that her shoelace got caught in the tracks.

Then the train came.

The people who saw it said she was a hero. She died a hero.

She still died.

If I were there, she would be alive. I would have never let her get on those tracks. It would have been me. It would have been me.

It would have…

Tears filled my eyes and I could not breathe.

I left work without talking to Olga or anyone. I just ran. I ran far and screamed until my lungs gave out and I crashed to the floor.

In the days that followed, every media outlet printed that a bunch of kids were messing around on the tracks and got killed. It was not true. The media printed what they wanted the narrative to say, but everyone there that night said Stacey was not drinking.

She died trying to help. Everything was twisted.

I spent the days after Stacey's death with The International Beer Club. Olga was furious, but I refused to give into her; Stacey was dead.

And I was the reason she died that night. It was my fault.

If I was there, we would have never met at the train tracks to drink. Maybe we would have, I don't know. I just don't know, but she would still be alive today.

I blame myself, well, I did… in some ways. We all make decisions and that night she decided she needed to be on those tracks.

Our song, "Sweet Child of Mine" from Guns n' Roses, played over the radio as it began to rain. You can't describe those inconsolable feelings that purge from your system when losing your best friend, especially when you feel like you are the one who killed her.

∞ ∞ ∞ ∞ ∞ ∞ ∞ ∞

My body shook violently as it began coping with her loss. I was completely without a succinct plan. I was utterly heartbroken and battered beyond repair.

I stood at the edge of the tracks where she took her last breaths. I could feel her presence in the air: she died trying to save another human being.

How could someone be so selfless? How could someone just give their life for a total stranger? How could she leave?

The dirt beneath my feet dragged me deeper into this intense sadness within me. Stacey was one of the only people on this planet who could make me feel like much more than I was.

She made me realize that I could be a better person. *Could be.*

Her existence and her legacy could not go unnoticed. They could not be swept aside like the dust in the wind that materialized upon her departure from this world.

She wouldn't risk her life for two people, two souls, to be lost.

No. There was more. There had to be.

I had to be more.

∞ ∞ ∞ ∞ ∞ ∞ ∞ ∞

Olga stood mercilessly at the foot of my bed, smashing her crimson patent leather heels against my bed frame.

"Come on, Scott, wake up, get up," she was growing more impatient. Olga was not accustomed to waiting for me to peel myself off of the bed and jump into action. If she wanted something, she wanted it *now*. She wanted it right then and there, no excuses and no exceptions.

I groaned in an attempt to acknowledge her presence, but rolled over and succumbed to the comfort of my jet-black cotton sheets. My pillow was the only thing I could fathom to hold in the moment.

"Scott," she whined, "It's been days, don't you want to just get up and get out or something?"

'No,' I muttered through tears, 'Just leave me alone.'

"Scott," she boomed while ripping the pillow from off of my head, "This is not good for you. Come on, let's go out, get up."

'I am not going out until the funeral tomorrow, Olga, so just let me be.'

"Nuh uh, nope, no," she protested with utter disgust, "You are going to her funeral? Why?"

'She is… was my friend, my very good friend… and I should have been there for her that night. Instead, I am alive and she is dead.' Tears rolled down the edges of my eyes and cascaded onto the bed. 'Is it supposed to be like a sign or something? Why am I still here?'

"What are you talking about," she snapped, "Come on." Olga dug her ruby red nails into my leg and tried tugging me out of bed. Her strength was no match for my devout sadness.

"Fine," she screeched, "Stay there then. I'll call you tomorrow."

She left my room with a resounding thud. I shut my eyes and let the darkness fulfill my heart.

When my alarm went off in the morning, my dried tears clung to my eyelashes with such a reverberating reminder of the days that had passed.

I had to be there for Stacey today. I had to.

As I slid my freshly pressed suit on and tied my classiest tie, the man before me was not my reflection.

I had to be a new man. I just had to.

For myself and for Stacey.

∞ ∞ ∞ ∞ ∞ ∞ ∞ ∞

The rain rolled down my spine with such a purposeful chill. I stood watching everyone's sullen eyes dart between the Rabbi and Stacey's pine coffin, almost as if they were trying to make sense of what was happening and why it had to happen to such a beautiful soul. The truth is that there was no answer as to why this happened. Would there ever be any answers?

Thoughts whisked around in my head over what had happened days prior. I could not help but blame myself for Stacey's death.

Why did Olga have to demand that I stay home with her?

Why did I have to listen?

It wasn't anyone's fault, yet we try to make sense of the nonsensical by assigning blame to whoemver is within reach… and whomever seems like the easierst target.

It was unfair of me to pin the blame on Olga, yet it was just natural for me to be enraged by the very sight of her… even if she was not at the funeral with me.

The rain reminded me to clear my mind of everything but Stacey's funeral. I was here to pay tribute to her, after all.

I could feel Stacey's fingers interconnected with mine, though I knew full and well that it was just her spirit that now had to live within her friends and family. People can leave us unexpectedly. People can die all the time. People live on through the hearts and minds of others.

Memories never die.

The murmurings of her family's tearful tributes were interrupting all of the memories of Stacey that flashed behind my glassy eyes. There were so many beautiful thoughts that flooded my head. Looking down at my hands made me realize that it was like I could feel Stacey injecting herself into my body and watching over her own funeral.

I was within my body and without my body.

It became an indescribable feeling that I would never be able to duplicate again.

The Rabbi picked up the shovel from a mound of dirt and handed it off to a man I did not recognize. Stacey's body slowly began to descend into its final resting place, six feet below those who cherished her, and would always cherish her, so nearly and dearly.

As with Jewish tradition, the man tottered over to Stacey's grave, stood firmly in the damp ground, and twisted the shovel so he could hesitantly drop dirt onto her coffin. The family and friends of the deceased bury the physical embodiment of their loved one, so there is love in every iota of dirt that falls back into the ground.

When the man passed the shovel to me, I felt a wave of eyes glare in my direction. As I stepped towards the hole to bury Stacey, my tears mixed with the rain that was now falling at a steady pace. Her presence was growing stronger within me, almost as if to say, "Scott, it's okay, it's not your fault."

With a twist of the shovel, I spread my love and years of memories into the ground. The dirt became infused with tears, joy, laughter, sorrow, and the disheartening feeling that I may never feel the strong platonic love I had for her within another soul.

There was no replacing Stacey; not in this lifetime, or the next, or all those that followed.

An eternity of shattered hearts poured onto her coffin with a reverberating thud.

Upon looking into the ground, I could see the dirt embracing her gently, almost as if it was saying that it was okay for her to fall further into this great Earth.

The burden anchoring my soul suddenly floated to the surface as I felt a release of emotion. Tears exasperated themselves from my eyes as I drove the shovel into the dirt and began pushing it towards the hole. Everyone watched in amazement as years of true love and divine friendship amassed on the surface of her coffin, until she disappeared.

The center of the universe revolved around us in this very moment. We became the focal point of all of the spiritual energy in the world, yet I did not realize it yet.

Upon tilting my head towards the sky, the rain caressed my face as if it were captivating me, thrilling me, chilling me, both figuratively and literally, as if it were dragging me up above the clouds and beckoning me closer.

A rush of joy circulated through my veins.

Stacey, are you there?

Do you hear me?

Do you miss me?

I miss you too.

Do you hear my voice?

Can you give me a sign to show me that you are still with me?

Chills forced themselves up my spine, almost to replace the rain that tried to make a permanent home between the cotton particles clinging to my back.

Stacey rushed into my soul and compelled me to dig her deeper and deeper into her physical resting place, for she knew her soul would spend forever between the fibers of my every being.

The wet thuds that once echoed from the top of her coffin stopped. She was fully buried. I gazed up at the crowd with a blank expression as silent weeping filled the air.

There is no good in goodbye, and there is no "us" in trusting that she will always be with me.

What's left is faith… and that is all I could ever hope for.

∞ ∞ ∞ ∞ ∞ ∞ ∞ ∞

When I retreated back to my car, "Patience" blared on the radio as a reminder of my solitude.

"Shed a tear 'cause I'm missin' you
I'm still alright to smile
Girl, I think about you every day now
Was a time when I wasn't sure
But you set my mind at ease
There is no doubt you're in my heart now…
You and I've got what it takes to make it
We won't fake it, I'll never break it
'Cause I can't take it"

At that point, I really could not take it. I took a swig of alcohol from the metallic flask I had in my glove compartment, and began driving home.

The rest of the day was an absolute blur due in part to the tears that crowded my line of vision and the lines of cocaine that just seemed to keep seeping into each crevice of my body.

∞ ∞ ∞ ∞ ∞ ∞ ∞ ∞

As the alarm clock blared, I felt the pangs of loneliness etch further into my soul. Her loss was debilitating and painstakingly clouding my vision.

Tears became a veil of reassurance over my eyelids. Everything and everyone we could have become shattered between passing seconds.

I ask myself what you would have been doing now. I ask myself if you would still see the amazing friend you once said I was.

Shadows danced along the walls in an echoic performance of our final moments together on this earth.

I hope you would be proud of the man I have become. I hope you would cherish our moments as much as I had cherished you. Our tears are forever intertwined and plastered in the grand masterpiece that is our time spent together. A resolute statue stands frozen in time: praying that my life is your legacy. Praying that you always remember me, as I will always remember you.

And when I pray to God, I pray he watches over you as you look upon the memories you shed here on this Earth.

I will forever be a thread in the fabric of your memories, and you will forever be a beautiful soul in the historical epic that is my life's journey.

Stacey, I hope you can fathom how much you are missed.

...And I hope you realize that all that I am and can be has been built upon through the bricks you placed over the shattered foundation.

∞ ∞ ∞ ∞ ∞ ∞ ∞ ∞

My relationship with Olga was desolated at its core the night Stacey died. I just did not accept it or see it, for I was covered in a solid veil of misery and pain. I was drenched in far too many years of tears and chaos to accept my winding path of self-destruction. The selfish nature of my actions was a crass juxtaposition to all that I could be and influence in the world.

Sadly, it took Stacey's death to signify that there was a problem manifesting within my soul.

To make matters worse, I was not cognizant of the turmoil I was a part of...

And the papier-mâché chain of poor decisions continued to surmount any semblance of sense I could talk myself into.

Stacey's presence still lingers with me in each passing moment, and I only hope that she is proud of the man I became...

I can only have a little bit of patience that we will meet again and I could apologize in person...

"Nothin' lasts forever
And we both know hearts can change
And it's hard to hold a candle
In the cold November rain..."

Rest in Peace Stacey Durschlag
Precious Daughter,
Beloved Granddaughter,
Niece and Friend
February 9, 1973 - March 29, 1989

May every memory of you be a reminder that our lives are valuable for being a part of your existence.

CHAPTER 9

On the Borrowed Sands of Time

~

"Cars are crashin' every night. I drink n' drive… everything's in sight. I make the fire but I miss the firefight. I hit the bull's eye every night."

- Guns n' Roses, American Rock Band, Los Angeles, California

A faint noise in the distance disturbed my sleep. I popped up from underneath the blankets, moving heavily towards whatever was rustling in the other room. I was met with her rummaging through a basket full of toiletries in the bathroom. A sole prescription bottle with its crumbling label rested in her shivering hands. A look of disdain spread across my face. I motioned towards her and she whipped her head around to greet my gaze.

'Is that your medication,' I inquired groggily.

She stood glaring at me with a blank stare.

"It ain't yours, obviously," she ripped the cap off and slammed three pills down her throat. The hard gulp shattered the silence in the room. As I turned to leave, she reached for my shoulder: "There are 90," she shouted in whisper form, "Nobody's looking for them."

I broke from her grasp and sauntered back into the bedroom. I heard her footsteps receding towards the corner of the room. I plopped onto the bed gazing at the off-white wall that was teeming with chipped paint.

Olga was getting more arrogant and violent, but I was still drawn to everything that was her eccentric and lustful existence.

"Scott," she sniffled heavily, "Let's go out, just us."

I perked up and met her gaze. 'Where do you want to go?'

She sneered and tossed me a bottle of liquor from atop the dresser.

"We're going out, drink up and get ready for a night you *won't* forget."

Her love was an intoxicating drug, one that I was hooked on and refused to detach from.

I pounded down the bottle as she began lining up our latest intoxicating elixir.

Being sober was an afterthought. I felt numb, but I felt alive with cocaine coursing through my veins. Besides alcohol, cocaine became the answer to any question, it was everything I ever wanted and adored in life. It became my world, but I was the one spinning on an axis, and I would revolve around it until I passed out. I was sure it would kill me, and I was sure I would not even notice I died.

∞ ∞ ∞ ∞ ∞ ∞ ∞ ∞

My head was spinning. My heart was throbbing from the pit of my chest.

Once the bottom of a bottle is your only salvation, you know you fell off the path. Because the devil at the bottom of the bottle of whiskey knows there is no turning back.

I felt as if I just ran a marathon while lying down.

I had the innate urge to tear the first thing I saw in half.

I was restless in my pursuit of getting high, but at the same time everything inside of me screamed that it was so wrong.

Still, it felt oh so right.

Just so right.

I was yearning to catch another taste of the flavor that was so alluring to my senses.

At this point I was trashed beyond all belief, though I wanted more. I needed more. I had to have more. More and more and more and more of what Olga could conjure up.

She threw me a clean shirt and dragged her sharp nails along my chest. Almost in a cat-like stance and with a sultry drawl hanging from her lips, she muttered, "Let's go Scott. Life is waiting."

∞ ∞ ∞ ∞ ∞ ∞ ∞ ∞

I don't remember driving to Old Country Road, yet the next thing I knew we were surrounded by flashing lights and loud noises. My grandfather's car came to a screeching halt at the corner of some rickety bar: it was yet another place the two of us would go to score some good cocaine.

As always, we just needed to have more.

It was not uncommon that we would fight over that last speck of cocaine just to get ourselves through life. Still, though she seemed to thoroughly enjoy sucker punching me clear across the face to snort the last drop, she took on the demeanor of a kid in a candy store when she would get a fresh batch from the somewhat local and sketchy bar.

As she dipped back into the car and rocked against the velvet cloth, I could see her eyes rolling into the back of her head.

She was in a state of absolute ecstasy.

She was aching to let go.

My brain pounded against my skull in an effort to revitalize what energy I had left within me.

The bright lights from the bar read 2:30 A.M., which when combined with my diluted state, forced me to feel as if I were drifting in a sea of endlessness.

Death was but a construct, and I was not built to die.

I was born to live. I was born to run. I was born to breathe in air and blow hard.

Olga's words began slurring, but what I could make out before she knocked my shoulder was, "Drive already."

I spun around in a flurry of lights and the scent of distressed rubber filled the air.

Nothing made coherent sense.

Everything was happening around me, but I would not dare tempt fate and react to the facets of life.

Olga's voice grew more distant and before I knew it, we were entangled in a war between words. I can't remember what our fight was about, but I could recall her cursing me out and seeing her covered in powder.

Upon making the quick U-turn, I guess she dropped some of the cocaine into her lap. Her screaming became more wilder and more rampant.

The red and green beams from the traffic light were moving so slowly as they cascaded across my line of sight. A thudding from the passenger door marked Olga's exit from the car as my blood filled with utter rage.

I could not remember what she screamed before I heard her leave the car. As a matter of fact, I could not even feel my fingers gripping the steering wheel.

Everything was nothing, and everything was getting progressively darker despite the bright lights beaming into the car.

Immense anger flourished in every corner of my core. I had to leave.

I saw her carrying our cocaine away and knew she was not coming back. She did not need to. She had everything she wanted in her grasp and disappeared into the depths of the night.

Good. I didn't need the drugs. I didn't need her. I was on a natural high from earlier. The alcohol was permeating my veins and I was carefree.

I was untouchable.

∞ ∞ ∞ ∞ ∞ ∞ ∞ ∞

The radio blared a melody that excited the alcohol that was slurring around in my brain. The noises were appealing to all of my senses as the words ransacked every fiber of my being. I could not even begin to comprehend what was playing over the speakers.

The moment a flash of green light flickered across my eyes, I stepped on the gas and felt the curb kiss the tires. I cut the wheel and hit the gas as soon as I met the end of the entrance ramp on the Meadowbrook Parkway. I heard the engine of my grandfather's Oldsmobile Cutlass Supreme roar over my sweet sounds of intoxication.

In hindsight, I should have never gone out that night, but it taught me the value and the true fragility of a human's existence.

Out of the corner of my eye, another car was speeding towards the right side of my car.

I panicked.

I did the only thing my inebriated mind could comprehend at the moment: I swerved to the left.

My eyelids slammed shut and I heard a cacophony of metal crushing against a cement wall.

∞ ∞ ∞ ∞ ∞ ∞ ∞ ∞

The darkness on the side of the highway forced me to use my feet to feel for the closest sidewalk. I felt leaves crunching at my feet as I hastily stumbled through shrubs and past a series of chain link fences.

I was in the process of blacking out but moving forward.

I did not know where I was; yet I did not feel fear.

I did not feel.

∞ ∞ ∞ ∞ ∞ ∞ ∞ ∞

My fists pounded against a blue wooden door: its hinges aching to burst upon my vagrant thudding.

'Hello,' I shouted in a state of despair. 'Is anyone home?'

Absolute silence.

It was in the middle of the night; of course someone was home.

I slammed my palm against the door again, hoping something, someone would appear. It was a case of immense desperation.

A solitary light appeared against the white, flowing curtains. A small hand appeared against the glass windowpane.

'Hello! Please let me in, please!' I begged. I began crying. I pleaded. 'I need help! Help me, please!'

The person on the other side of the door sighed and responded to my desperate calls.

"Who," the voice spoke groggily, almost as if it were in a trance, "Who are you?"

The door was muffling the voice, but I could tell it was a female.

I paused for a moment. I didn't really know how to respond. All I knew was that my grandfather's car was somewhere behind me in the distance, and I was no longer with it.

We both paused, seemingly to catch our breath in unison.

'I was… I was in an accident. Please open the door.'

The woman creaked the door open gently and I burst into her dimly lit living room. I stumbled forward onto her sofa and let my body succumb to its comfort.

She seemed somewhat shaken, but not surprised.

Her presence was clear, though she was waiting.

Waiting.

Waiting.

Waiting for me to make a sound.

I turned, clearly panicked, and met the eyes of the woman before me. The quaint little house seemed to turn inward to her frame, and she appeared almost angel-like in nature.

"Who are you, young man?" She stood pensively glaring into my core. In hushed tones, she continued, "Do you know it is 2:30 in the morning?"

'Ma'am,' I was scared. 'I was in an accident.'

She said her name, but I could not remember it for the life of me.

'I'm Scott,' I responded.

My head began drifting slightly as I sunk to her living room floor. She grasped my face tenderly and spoke softly.

"Scott, Scott, are you still with me," she shouted in my face. In hindsight, I do not think she was really screaming, rather she seemed like she just woke up startled by my rapid pounding on her front door.

I had never seen eyes so emerald and pure before, but then again, I had never seen these eyes before.

"Scott," she boomed once again. I tried with all my might to open my mouth, but something was stopping me.

I focused for what seemed like hours on prying my lips apart, but all I could feel was… actually, I couldn't feel. Why couldn't I feel anything? Why are my fingers numb? Why are my eyes so heavy?

I bit my tongue accidentally while trying to find the words to say to her. After all, I was sitting in this strange woman's living room, but she did not feel like a stranger.

She felt like a familiar face from somewhere in my distant past.

We heard sirens ringing from outside.

"The highway," she said. She stood and walked to the window, pushing the curtains back to see the commotion happening outside.

Blue and red flashes of light flickered in the corner of my eyes.

She walked into the kitchen for a moment and I heard her bare toes touch the linoleum tiles.

What was she doing?

Where was she going?

Why was she content with a strange, clearly inebriated man sitting alone in her house far from the brink of dawn?

She hastened back into the room and audibly sniffed at my blatant alcoholism.

The taste of metal lingered on my tongue as the woman with the emerald eyes hovered over me as I sat on the taupe sofa. Finally, I concentrated all of my energy on splitting my lips apart. A breathy yet exhausted, "Where" escaped my slightly bloodstained mouth.

"Scott," the woman whispered. She placed a steaming cup of coffee in my hand; the porcelain clung to my fingertips tenderly.

With spots dancing across my line of sight, I realized where I was: the faint lights flashing in the windows, a silhouetted figure perched next to me, the defined lines from a gentle face contrasted with the dimly lit room. Sirens wailed as I felt my body jerk and spasm.

What did I do?

What did I do?

'Oh, yeah,' I realized, attempting to chuckle silently to myself… not like the woman sitting next to me could hear my internal monologue.

The beeping, the sirens, the panic grew louder. They echoed in my head as if they were trying to rearrange a melody. It was a delectable sound I had never heard before, but this would be the last time I would have the pleasure of conjuring sweet music ever again.

I felt my chest rising and slamming with every crisp word that formed from within me.

For a moment I clung to the chirping of the sirens, but the woman's voice cut through the noise. Muffled noises circulated within the room. Her compassion burst through the chaos as the sounds grew into a roar.

Then a yell.

Then silence.

'I was in an accident.'

We sat in silence as I let my words shift through my skull.

"Do you need to call someone, Scott?" Her voice ushered my fears away. Her calm demeanor and compassion were overflowing from within.

She led me into her kitchen: a picturesque breakfast nook lined by red checkerboard curtains, a white metallic stove with a pleasant tea kettle atop, wooden cabinets with small crimson knobs… I had trouble taking in the whole scene in my frenzied state.

A rotary phone rested on the wall parallel to the red checkerboard curtains.

"Call who you need to." Her voice grew more distant as I heard her moving back into the living room. She fluffed the pillows we were just sitting on, picked up a book, and read while I fished through my mind and tried to figure out whom to call this late at night. Back then, you remembered the phone numbers of people you knew and loved.

I called my grandmother. She picked up and had a difficult time understanding what I was saying.

I called my parents. At this point I had moved out, but I was hoping they would show me some mercy.

They slammed the phone down the moment I said, 'Dad, I know it's late, I was in an accident.'

An accident.

How bad was it?

I don't remember getting out of the car, and I do not remember having a seatbelt on.

I got out of the car somehow.

I just couldn't remember.

The alcohol and drugs were beginning to wear off.

I called all of my friends.

I called Olga.

I called anyone whose number I could remember.

It was a great night for everyone to play tough love.

Crunching metal echoed in my head as the woman before me pressed against my flesh with her hand.

"It will all be okay, Scott," sang from her soul.

I rushed out of the kitchen and out the front door.

As I walked back to the car, all of the laughter, the joy, the tears, and the memories slowly danced into the darkness.

Everything I knew was over, and everything that would have been escaped with the rise and fall of my bloodied tongue against the top of my mouth. A life was over and a new life had begun.

I should have died that day.

Should have.

The darkness swallowed me wholeheartedly and wrapped its arms around me, softly rocking me to a deafening lullaby reserved only for those on the cusp of death.

I approached the direction I came from, and saw the scene: my grandfather's car was smashed into the wall so hard that it appeared to be swallowed by the cement. An ambulance's lights were flashing. A tow truck's yellow lights were swirling and shrouded in mist.

I ran.

I flew back to the woman's house in sheer panic.

She was standing at the door upon my return, and ushered me back into the house.

We sat in her kitchen and she poured me another hot cup of coffee.

We had a heart to heart talk at 2:30 A.M.

We were strangers in the night that formed a common bond by simply showing some compassion.

Her words echoed slightly through my head. It was a sign that things had to turn around and that I needed to make some decisions in order to grow.

I left the kitchen and scurried out the door to face my demons. The woman with the emerald eyes stood at the door and waved goodbye to me. She wished me luck and said, "Until we meet again under better circumstances, Scott."

I smiled, waved and gently whispered into the night, 'Until we meet again.'

∞ ∞ ∞ ∞ ∞ ∞ ∞ ∞

As I planted my feet into the soil with each resounding step, I felt a deep burst of energy. It was almost as if I suddenly snapped out of my alcoholic and cocaine-fueled trance. All of the pieces of my life seemed to fit together nicely: and I realized that something was bound to happen... rather, something was happening.

When I reached the scene of the accident, my grandfather's car was gone. The police sirens had faded into the night and the ambulance had disappeared.

A solitary tow truck driver was parked close to the scene, his lights still flashing rhythmically in the night.

I approached him with great trepidation and prayed that he would not question how I found myself walking along the highway close to 3:00 A.M.

Radio static ushered me closer and closer to the driver's side window.

'Excuse me.' I peered into the front and saw the faint embers from a cigarette burning in the truck driver's hand. He shifted his head and took a drag from his cigarette.

The smoke blew past me and drifted in the wind.

A raspy voice emerged from beneath his massive hat, "What's up kid?"

He did not realize I was the one whose car was here probably just moments ago.

'Where'd it go?'

"Oh," he smashed the cigarette down onto the dashboard, extinguishing the flame, "The car?"

'Yeah, the car.'

"Bud, another truck just towed it away. You shoulda seen that thing."

I grew slightly uncomfortable: 'Why?'

"There was no driver, but whoever it was is lying dead in a ditch somewhere." He let out an exasperated whoosh and reached down into the car. His face disappeared from my line of sight.

'I was,' I spoke unsteadily. 'I was in that car.'

"Well," he rose again, letting out a few heavy coughs, "I guess you were in the backseat because nothing, and I mean, noth-*ing* survived in the front seat. Cops are scouring the neighborhood looking for a 70-something year old man."

'Oh, wait-- my grandfather, it's-- it's my grandfather's car, but I was driving.'

With a nod of disbelief, he pulled a card from his pocket.

"Alrighty kid, whatever you say," he presented the card to me through his open window, "This is the detective's card. Call him in the morning... they'll uh... they'll want to talk to ya."

I took it gingerly from him, worried that he was skeptical that I had, indeed, driven the car into the wall.

I was sure it happened though. I mean, how else would I end up at a stranger's house in the middle of the night? What if it was just a dream? No, it couldn't be.

How would I have ended up here?

I guess the driver saw confusion or some sort of fear register on my face, for he softened his demeanor.

"Hey," he said, lighting up another cigarette, "I have a phone, do you need to call someone to pick you up?"

I thought of the only person who might answer in the middle of the night: Wendy.

In a frenzy, I dialed her number and was somewhat surprised to hear her comforting and groggy voice over the phone.

"Hello?" What a wonderful thing to hear in the middle of the night: a familiar hello.

I explained to her where I was and what happened, and within minutes she jolted awake and exclaimed that she was on her way. The tow truck driver stayed with me and appeared to grow more compassionate by the minute.

The intoxication rushing through my veins subsided and I felt truly awake again.

∞ ∞ ∞ ∞ ∞ ∞ ∞ ∞

Wendy's Plymouth Scamp pulled up next to me and I jumped right in. At this point, it was close to 4:00 A.M. and the night was slowly morphing into a brisk, hazy sunrise. We talked for a while about what had happened, and part of her seemed skeptical. Still, she knew I had to be telling the truth: she heard the fear seeping through my voice.

We laughed a little bit and smiled all the way back to my small apartment in Valley Stream. I was incredibly thankful for Wendy, especially in those moments. She was the only person I knew before the accident that made me realize that I was important. She made me feel that I was still here for a reason... well, her and the woman with the emerald green eyes at least.

However, the moment we pulled up to the house, Olga stepped out of the front door and burst into a fit of rage.

"It is 4:00 A.M. Scott, where were you?" Her high heels tapped against the concrete. I suddenly hated the sound of concrete.

Wendy grew visibly upset and argued with Olga, "He was in a car accident, and where were you, missy?"

The two of them began bickering in the dusk, as Wendy's sensible words sank into Olga's cocaine-tainted mind. The morning dew started forming on the blades before us, as the scene unfolded between the two women. Wendy's eyes narrowed, as Olga's fury grew more powerful.

The exchange of words bounced back and forth between the two women until Wendy shifted her body towards mine.

"Scott," she yelled, "That's it, I'm done. She is no good for you."

"Me," Olga shouted, "Me?! What about you!?"

Wendy grasped my shoulders and through manifesting tears she muttered, "Good luck, Scott. Good luck."

As she walked away, I felt the world shifting on its axis for the second time in one night. Wendy's receding footsteps cut through my thoughts: she rescued me tonight, yet somehow, I was still drawn to Olga's diabolical intrigue.

I was convinced that Olga would be the death of me, and tonight, that almost was the case.

∞ ∞ ∞ ∞ ∞ ∞ ∞ ∞

They always talk about an afterlife, but do they ever talk about an after near-life ending experience? I guess that's what this state of mind is: a blissful feeling that tomorrow isn't guaranteed, so we have to make today count.

The kindness from this absolute stranger was the embodiment of a juxtaposition: as life itself seemed to come to a screeching halt, I was warming up to the idea that second chances and new beginnings are at the edge of every single circumstance.

As I woke up to the sound of birds chirping outside my bedroom window, I felt alive again.

'Everything is going to be okay,' I told myself knowing just how much I cried the night before. All of the pieces will fall, and I will pick them up and rearrange them nicely. They may be tattered and torn, bruised and broken, but they will fit together... maybe not in the physical sense, but they will be there.

I rolled over and pushed Olga's half-naked body off of my arm. She looked so peaceful when she wasn't filling her body with cocaine.

I pulled my jeans from the floor and ripped the detective's business card out of my pocket. I snatched the phone and moved towards the corner of the room, praying I would not wake Olga from her deep slumber.

"Hello Detective Robins," a strong voice boomed from the phone.

'Hi, hi sir. I'm Scott. I think you found my car last night,' I grew more and more nervous and it was clear.

"Boy, how old are you?"

'Seventeen, sir.'

A deep sigh came from somewhere within his chest, "Were you drinking last night? Is that how the car got that banged up?"

'No sir,' I chuckled, 'I don't drink. I am just seventeen.'

"Okay," he said skeptically, "but have you seen that car?"

'Detective, sir, a car snuck up on my passenger side and I swerved to avoid him. The next thing I knew I was frenzied and running for help. By the time I got back from calling for help, the car was gone.'

He believed me, and he told me where I could find the car. Detective Robbins explained that he had already called my grandfather and that I should connect with him and go to the junkyard.

The junkyard. Was the car that bad?

I frantically hung up the phone after thanking him profusely, then called my grandfather.

My grandfather was clearly panicked. We spoke for a few moments and he told me just where to meet him to go see the car. Olga's eyes cracked open and she was cognizant enough where she could drive me to meet him and see the car.

∞ ∞ ∞ ∞ ∞ ∞ ∞ ∞

As we pulled up to the junkyard, I could tell something was happening. It was a feeling that just burned somewhere deep within me. I heard whispers and voices creep from the recesses of my mind.

My grandfather's face was pale and ghostly: almost as if he saw a dead man wandering around in my body.

I finally understood the root of his distress when I saw the car: it was almost as if the car was a massive accordion. The engine was sitting in the backseat of the car. It was totaled, and there was no way that anyone could have got out of that car alive.

Then it hit me again: I somehow got out alive…

Except I did not know how.

Looking into the eyes of my grandfather, I realized that I was truly blessed.

It dawned on me that I was a walking miracle: the car was dead and destroyed, but I still walked this earth.

From gazing into the reflection of the remaining untouched portion of the body of the car, I realized that cocaine had owned me and I truly didn't own anything else.

My life was a gift from the heavens, or somewhere, or something.

I was walking around in the borrowed sands of an hourglass.

Every moment forward would need to matter, because there is a reason why I did not die on that day… in that car… alone and on the Meadowbrook Parkway.

My life had a purpose... or should I say, has.

Our experiences are a manifestation of who we are and what we will become... from being a stranger in the night opening her door to a confused young man, or to being on the receiving end of a compassionate opportunity to live again.

An important concept is so crucial to grasp:

Death is certain; life is not.

CHAPTER 10

Midnight Confessions

~

"We are young, wandering the face of the Earth, wondering what our dreams might be worth... Learning that we're only immortal for a limited time."

- Rush, Canadian Rock Band, Toronto, Ontario

In the days that followed the accident, I could not feel. A mixture of cocaine and alcohol ran rampant through my veins for far too long. Without it, I was devoid of emotion. I was trapped in my own body, sweating profusely to the nauseating sound of my heartbeat unable to determine which way to beat.

Cocaine was an illness that was coursing through my body, yet as it was leaving my system, I felt the pangs of sickness strike me down. I spent hours upon hours curled up in a ball on my floor, swimming in my own filth and despair. Every light was too bright. Every sound was amplified by the raging migraine that just would not let up.

The deafening silence pierced through my skull as a reminder that Olga, my true love, was adamant about not coming to see me.

If there were any signs that marked the impending doom that coexisted between our love and her forthcoming actions, this was it.

Retching, twisting, turning, and spasms were irreconcilable differences permeating my soul, yet in those moments I felt that my fateful moments that could have resulted in my death was a warning sign. I had to stop my frivolous lifestyle and begin edging closer and closer towards patience and peacefulness... yet peacefulness could only be attempted once I delved into fits of pain and suffering. At the end, I chose cocaine and opted for drugs to be my guiding light; if only I knew before I was tempted that I would be dealing with this sort of treacherous condition, if only...

In those moments between pangs of nausea and my stomach's insubordinate rebellion, I am sure I relished in the fact that I was there because of my choices and because of my insolence... yet in hindsight, I think I was just happy that the porcelain toilet was kind enough to cool my body upon melting to the floor each time I hurled.

The noises from those days still haunt me sometimes.

And sometimes when I look back on those moments, I realize that I really deserve to hear the echoic bouts of drug abuse ring through my head: it is a reminder to never tempt fate again... never again.

Like I said, Olga was not there even in the slightest. In the days that followed the accident, she did not call, she did not stop by, and she did not make an effort to show me an iota of compassion. Instead, she was set on getting her hands on more cocaine and alcohol... and she was more content finding out what was at the bottom of a bottle than holding me tight as I fought thoughts of relapsing into my old behaviors.

The first day of healing is arguably the hardest during any process whatsoever. To stand up knowing what had been coursing through your veins, and finally feel a tinge of hope is a drop of faith in an ocean of immense pain.

Yes, recovery is a steep road that some have to travel. Despite the innate feelings of loneliness that may traverse their soul, a person is never truly alone... for their soul fills any void of devout solitude that could permeate their existence.

Withdrawal has to be one of the most difficult experiences someone will ever have to face. When you have vibrancy coursing through your veins for so long, then just have to cut that sensation off forever... The loss is a nightmare in itself. Pools of yellow muck sat at the edge of all reason, as I thought to myself...

'This must be what it feels like to be unloved?'

∞ ∞ ∞ ∞ ∞ ∞ ∞ ∞

The phone rang and woke me from whatever deep state I was in. Olga's voice on the other side of the line was rather shocking, but then again who else would be calling me?

'Hello?'

"Hey baby," Olga's sultry voice echoed in my ear.

'Oh hey.'

My nonchalance must have come as a surprise to her.

"Honey, you need to come out. On-Line is playing a house party and we can't miss them. You know how much I love them." Her voice was droning on and on.

Despite her absence, I did not give her a second thought.

'Sure,' I murmured, trying to grasp at the clock on my nightstand. 'When-' I yawned, 'When do you want to go.'

"Meet me here at nine. Wear something nice. Do *not* disappoint me!"

She slammed the phone down and must have frolicked throughout her apartment while getting ready.

Okay, so she did still love me. She still remembered me.

I mean, she had to... right?

She called. She did call... and now we were on our way to another wild night of Olga's festivities... did I just call it wild?

'Hmm.' I stood in a deep state of thought for a moment or two. 'Odd.'

∞ ∞ ∞ ∞ ∞ ∞ ∞ ∞

Hours later the two of us were dressed to kill and crammed in between common strangers. The house the band rented was packed with people, and we were just two souls floating in the abyssal depths of crashing drums and the bass thumping over the speakers.

Olga was visibly excited while I stood close to her, unsure of how to respond to a room full of cocaine-fueled and alcohol-driven people. I thought detoxing was rough, but being in the epicenter of drugs and alcohol made my relapse look...

No. I swore off drugs and alcohol.

That accident was a sign from the universe, and I was not about to give up on myself. I was ready... for what, I don't know, but I knew that I could not take a sip of alcohol or do anything remotely close to cocaine.

I looked to my left and caught Olga wrapped up in a conversation with some people who were clearly blitzed out of their minds. She summoned me over with a single curl of her finger, so naturally I approached her with a sheepish grin.

Olga wrapped her arms around my body and started to laugh maniacally.

"Scott, baby," she began whining, "You don't look like you are here to have a good time."

'No,' I perked up for her sake. 'I am here to have a good time, really.'

If I said I was not there to have a good time, she probably would have begun screaming at me. I loved her; I didn't want her to get upset, especially at an On-Line show.

The music seeped throughout the split-level house. Many people were filtering in and out of the basement, where most of the action was taking place.

Olga began talking nonsense and leaning into me a little too aggressively. She released me and sprung towards the man who offered her a line of coke. I shrunk into the corner and tried to make my presence a little less known.

Sitting in the crowded, smoke-filled room my mind began wandering. There were about ten different conversations going on at once. I could not keep up and my head began to throb. I fell into a state of loneliness while watching Olga snort her prized white dust.

I felt all alone.

I was alone in the sense that though physically I was surrounded, the millions of thoughts running through my mind were violently colliding with my current, physical locale. Questions were filtering through me: Why am I here? What have I done? Why am I feeling the way I do?

I am young. Very young.

For my age, I have been through more situations and witnessed enough of this world's problems to just sit back and ask "Why?"

I am not sure what I am trying to say because I am a very confused person. Well, at least in this current situation I was. And in my life thus far, with the pain and problems I have seen and shared so far, I had to ask myself one question: "Why am I the one to feel and see so much, especially at such a young age?"

I am not sure of an answer. If I were sure of an answer then existing at that point in time would have been acceptable. I was in search of something, anything. Any reason. Any reason as to why I didn't die in that accident.

'Oh universe, send me a sign.' My whispering caught Olga's attention and she darted right over to me.

"What-" she stumbled and slurred her words. "What's with the face?"

'I'm sorry. I am just a bit distracted and-' She grasped my face and ripped me towards her line of sight.

"Pay attention to me," her pupils dilated wider and wider. I grew more aware of her looming fit of rage and for the first time, backed away from her.

'Okay,' I replied sternly.

"Loosen up already," she shrieked.

I gulped and began twiddling my thumbs nervously. I was highly uncomfortable. It was the first time I was discernibly uncomfortable with her.

I didn't know how to handle it.

"Get yourself a beer," she shooed me away with her hand and returned to her newfound cocaine buddies.

Unsure of what to say, I obliged and meandered into the kitchen.

A blonde woman was leaning with her back against the fridge: her leather jacket was perfectly placed atop her shoulders as she smoothly chatted with a group of rather eager men.

'Excuse me,' I said, motioning to the fridge.

Though slightly disgusted by my polite request, she uncrossed her arms and moved away.

I pulled the door open as the suction around the fridge became unglued from its disposition. The fridge was packed with alcohol and other unidentifiable goodies, but a solitary can of Budweiser teetered between the shelf and some rancid-looking food.

As I went to grab it, a tender hand slid underneath mine and snatched the beer nearly out of my hand. I turned to glance at who would grab a beer from someone and sure enough...

The blonde girl with the leather jacket had cracked it open and began chugging it down. Droplets of the beer spilled from her lips, and she made steady eye contact with me as she wiped her face.

'Hey,' I said, unsure of what to do.

"Finders keepers, *asshole*." She smirked and wandered off, beer in hand.

I shrunk into the basement and followed the sound of the drumbeat slowly trailing off.

What kind of trouble could I get into while watching the band?

∞ ∞ ∞ ∞ ∞ ∞ ∞ ∞

I slithered down the steps and into the depths of the crowd. The drum beat was rhythmically calling me closer and closer to the band. It was almost as if there were an invisible fishing rod reeling me into the vibrations of music emanating from the center of the room.

As my eyes fixated on the chrome elements of the drums, the music came to a screeching halt. I stopped in my tracks and glared at the band members.

"We are On-Line, and we'll be right back," the lead singer gripped the microphone and shut his eyes, almost as if he were feeling every quiver from the speakers move straight through his veins. The musicians began talking with people in the crowd and stepping away from their instruments, including the drummer.

Upon seeing me admire his set, he looked me in the eye and smiled, "You like 'em?" He was friendlier than I had expected, but then again, I am not sure what I was expecting.

'Yeah man.' I was in awe. 'I play a bit here and there, but I'm still trying to find a band, you know.'

"Here" the man handed me his drumsticks and moved from behind the set. "Why don't you try playing a bit? I'm exhausted anyway."

I looked at him with slight discomfort in my eyes: 'You want me to play?'

"Yeah man." He perked up and took a swig from a can of beer sitting atop a speaker. "Let's see what you've got."

He summoned the band and told them they had to get back on their instruments.

∞ ∞ ∞ ∞ ∞ ∞ ∞ ∞

"Alrighty boys and girls, we have a guest drummer here rockin' out with us." The lead singer shouted into the microphone. He turned towards me as I situated myself on the stool. "Dude, what's your name?"

'Scott,' I said humbly, unsure of what to do or say… well, I knew I was going to drum.

"Give an On-Line welcome and round of applause to our man, Scott." The lead singer raised his hand and counted me in.

I began playing an array of rock music that I knew the crowd would enjoy. I shut my eyes and just felt the vibrations course through me. It was a feeling unlike any other. It was a sensation that shook every fiber of my core.

It was magical.

It was breathtaking.

It was everything.

It was better than any drug that ever flowed through my system.

We fooled around for a few songs until the drummer re-appeared at the bottom of the steps. The blonde woman from the kitchen was hanging on him, almost as if she had an intense secret to tell him. She transfixed her eyes on my body, dragging her pupils up and down my jet-black leather jacket and torn blue jeans.

I was unsure what to make of the situation, but her disgusted demeanor made me feel like she intended to make me feel uncomfortable. It was working.

When the music stopped, I stood and thanked the guys for allowing me to play with them before I scampered back upstairs to find Olga. She was standing around a group of men who were inching closer to her with every laugh she tossed from her lips.

'Olga, hey, did you hear me play?' I approached her and grabbed her arm.

She pulled away from me and continued to laugh with the guys.

"Yeah, okay Scott," she said nonchalantly.

'What?'

"What, *what* Scott?"

'That was really me playing the drums.'

"Yeah, and I'm the Queen of England."

The other guys laughed at her sarcasm while she dug her verbal daggers further into my core.

"Why don't you go make yourself useful and find me a drink, can't you see we are talking?"

She was absolutely indifferent to my presence, and could not care more about my exciting experience. I honestly think she didn't even believe me.

It figures.

But I still loved her.

I moved my way back through the crowd of people and walked into the kitchen. After grabbing her a drink, I made my presence known to her again, only to find that she had a cold drink in her hand. One of her new friends must have got it for her.

It figures.

But I still loved her.

I made my way back down to where the band was playing and allowed the music to carry me through the rest of the night. I knew she would find me when she was done with her little escapades, and I wasn't worried about her having fun: she was clearly having a great time.

That's all that mattered to me.

∞ ∞ ∞ ∞ ∞ ∞ ∞ ∞

Days later, Olga was up to her usual antics again. She returned to being her sensual, caring self and stayed the night. Olga pressed her tender lips against mine with such meticulous force: "You know I care about you, baby."

We fell asleep and let the breeze from the window brush against our skin.

Finally, I felt a sense of peace within me for the first time since I gave up alcohol and cocaine. My life was turning around and I was not about to give up on love or myself anymore: I was a renewed man.

When we woke in the morning, I rolled out of bed and into the bathroom. My sister had contacted me days earlier and told me to come to her Bat Mitzvah, which was happening later today. I had my suit and everything ready, but something felt different: I was going to see my parents for the first time in a while, and I did not know just what was going to transpire between all of us.

For my sister's sake, I just hope that nothing overtly tragic was bound to happen this afternoon.

Olga was actually the one who encouraged me to go to the party. Though I had plenty of fear surrounding seeing my parents again, Olga held my hand and promised me that no matter what, she was going to be there for me. I trusted her at her word, which gave me the confidence to go through with seeing my sisters and family again.

∞ ∞ ∞ ∞ ∞ ∞ ∞ ∞

The party was filled with familiar faces of people who didn't even remember my name. Though my hair was much longer, my body much leaner, and my face progressively slimmer, the second I stepped into the room, my parents locked eyes with me. Regardless of how much time had passed, they knew their son.

And neither of them wanted me there.

A sickening feeling crept into my stomach.

"Hey Scott, you made it!" Sarah, my younger sister, darted up to me and wrapped her arms around me.

My parents kept their distance at first while my other sister, Rebecca, zoomed over to me with purpose in her eyes. The three of us chatted just like old times. I could feel their love and affection towards me seeping out through their smiles and excited bantering. Various people glared at me from across the room, for I am sure that my parents shared their perspectives on their "runaway, degenerate son." I could only imagine what they told the family about me. I hated that. The family only knew one side of the story, and they didn't know what my parents put me through.

I doubt that my parents would have admitted beating and screaming at me. They had to upkeep their picturesque image of community and family.

At the end of the day, I just didn't fit in their frame.

"Be an absolute gentleman, Scott," Olga nudged me towards a table and motioned for me to sit down.

The two of us kept to ourselves in the corner while everyone danced and enjoyed each other's company. We were perfect strangers to everyone but my sisters, and in a sense, I was okay with it: Olga and I were there for her, not my parents. The wandering eyes at the party would need to look away eventually.

That's when I would be able to breathe a bit easier.

My father sat across the room from me, surrounded by his band of firefighter buddies and snickering friends. The true treasure to the Matheson last name and legacy was arm and arm with a woman twice his age, and I was sure they were trying to figure out if I was sober or not.

Odds are, they just figured I was drunk.

Or deep down inside, they probably didn't care either way.

∞ ∞ ∞ ∞ ∞ ∞ ∞ ∞

Olga and I got up and danced for a while. We did have fun there; I am not going to lie. However, my father's displeased glances grew heavy on my soul, forcing me to respond in a way I am, to this day, not proud of. My mother made a comment to my father, which was loud enough for me to hear. Sarcastically, my mother screamed, "Ask my son: the doctor, the lawyer, the dropout."

I spun around violently and began to charge at both of them.

Olga tried grabbing my arm, but I slid from her grasp.

As I rushed closer and closer towards them a woman with gentle eyes stepped in front of my mother and father.

"Wait," she shouted.

I stopped short and froze. I did not know just what to do, but it was exactly what I needed to snap me back into reality.

We all stood glaring at each other, unsure of what to say next.

"Scott, please just wait a moment, before you do anything hasty. Just wait a moment," her voice was soothing and unlike any voice I had heard before.

She must not have been a family member of mine, because she was way too kind and sincere to me. Still, she knew my name.

"Step outside with me right now, just say goodbye to your sisters, and come outside with me," she held my hand tightly, almost how a parent would hold their scared child's hand.

Something within me told me to comply with her request. I kissed Sarah and Rebecca good-bye on their respective foreheads and told them how much I loved them. I saw Olga standing in the far corner talking with my parents; she was visibly flirting with my father a bit, but I could not stop to say anything at that moment. The mysterious, kind woman told me to go outside, and something drew me towards her energy.

I stepped out into the daylight, squinting at the sight of cars reflecting in the sunlight as they sped by. The woman was standing in the light, allowing every inch of her presence to be cloaked in the rays of sunshine that were an apt juxtaposition to what I experienced inside.

"Scott," she took on a somewhat solemn tone, "Over here."

I moved closer to her and she stopped me from speaking immediately.

"Let me introduce myself," she spoke sweetly.

"My name is Barbara Harmon..." a nervous tinge hung in her voice.

"And I'm your mom's sister. Scott, I am your aunt."

My mother never spoke about her family before, yet I felt a certain kinship with her. And so, the words, "Scott, I am your aunt" billowed through my mind as we sat on a nearby bench, talking briefly about who I was, who she was, and how I had a family I never really knew existed.

'We have a lot to catch up on, I guess.' I smiled and felt happy for a change. "That we do, my son," she patted my shoulder, "That we do."

∞ ∞ ∞ ∞ ∞ ∞ ∞ ∞

I left the party shortly after, with Barbara promising to call me in the coming days so we could go out to lunch together. It was nice to have a sliver of hope for a change. Something told me that Barbara was not lying. Something told me that I had a reason to be happy again. Something... something...

Then something else happened: The International Beer Club and I were not close anymore, but something told one of the guys to call me right away when they heard the news.

I would not have believed it, but it made the local news so it was obviously true.

While she was driving on the Long Island Expressway for one reason or another, probably rocking out to whatever was on the radio, a cement truck pulled up next to Danielle, and for one reason or another, fell over and crushed her car instantly. She did not feel any pain. It was sudden. It was quick. It was a catastrophe.

It was the toughest funeral I ever attended. It was the exact opposite of Stacey's, for while Stacey's was a Jewish funeral, Danielle's funeral was a huge Catholic display of respect and chastity. When the prom queen dies, everyone attends the funeral. Though I do not mean that in a derogatory or sarcastic way. Danielle was a truly angelic presence, and my last conversation with her was: "There's a story behind the story." Her wisdom is what I teach and preach to this day.

No one should ever judge a book by its cover.

Something changed inside of me when I watched all of her friends speak in church. Despite the crowds and lines of people miles beyond miles outside of the church doors, Tommy was nowhere to be found.

I found out that it turns out he was right: he never did end up graduating from Jamaica High School. To my knowledge, he ended up going to prison for a long, long time.

I wish he were wrong about himself, though deep within he seemed to know his fate long before we all glanced up at the ornate architecture of Jamaica High School.

And no, Olga was not with me when I went to the funeral.

I guess that is a bit of foreshadowing.

∞ ∞ ∞ ∞ ∞ ∞ ∞ ∞

The next day at work, I passed by Olga's cubicle only to find it desolate and empty. Her baseball memorabilia disappeared, her chair was lonely, and she was, for all intents and purposes, gone.

I frantically ran into our boss' office, only to find the secretary tapping away at her keyboard.

'Where is Olga?' I demanded.

"Why" the keys kept clicking as the secretary spoke, "Why do you care?"

I was flustered. Why did I care? Oh, yeah, I loved her and she disappeared.

"She transferred to Florida, Scott, she gave in her two weeks' notice well... two weeks ago, I guess," another voice boomed from the hallway.

I scampered out of the door and down to my car. I rushed to her apartment to find her moving boxes with the man I had seen in her apartment before.

'Olga, hey, Olga!' She did not look happy to see me, rather she looked like she was about to break down and cry.

"Hey, Scott, I was going to call, um-" Olga stopped short and began to tear up a bit. She seemed like she was trying to hold back her emotions, but then again this seemed like it was the first time I saw her sober in forever.

She told me she was moving to Florida and as soon as she could, she would send for me. Olga told me that she wanted to ensure that she had enough money in Florida before she moved both of us down there.

As if you did not guess by now, she never sent for me...

And this would be the last time we spoke.

∞ ∞ ∞ ∞ ∞ ∞ ∞ ∞

A week had gone by. Olga didn't call or attempt to contact me at all. She seemed like she was gone, and I guess I was okay with it.

Did I really have any other option?

I could feel pins and needles creeping up my spine. I could tell that day was going to be a difficult day. It felt as if someone wrapped their hands around my spine and just kept squeezing tighter and tighter. It was an uncomfortable feeling that left me numb and aching. I knew I couldn't do anything about it, so I just kept moving.

That day would have been our anniversary. Well, at least I thought. I don't really remember because it had been so many months since Olga and I had been together. Even when we were together, I don't think I would have been able to remember our anniversary considering I was higher than a kite each time we were together. Looking out the window at all of the people passing by, I wondered if I would ever see her face again. No, not in a dream, but in reality. Did she think of me?

Did she even shed a solitary tear when she left? I could go on forever waiting for the real answer as to why she left. I just couldn't live in limbo anymore.

I was unbalanced. I was stuck between two versions of myself: the drug induced one longing to see her again, and the one who was slightly sober and uninhibited by the puppet strings she placed on my back.

Again, a pain in my spine radiates towards my shoulders. If life has taught me anything so far, it is that if it is meant to be, she will come back. Until then, I will continue living. That is, if you define living as wondering what could have been and what may still be.

Lonely and without a single thing to occupy my time, I chose to drive over to some crummy little bar in Westbury. Its stench could be detected just from standing in the parking lot and was infested with cocaine worshippers like myself and Olga, so it was clear that the bar was the prime place to forget what's her name…Olga. My darling, dear, passionate… no, I couldn't do this.

I couldn't think of her.

I couldn't get caught up in yearning for her, especially since she just up and ditched me like that.

There is that saying, "The grass is greener on the other side," but I always seem to be that other side. I am always the one that ends up being the *other* person, for everyone wants to see what the other side is like…

But no one stays.

∞ ∞ ∞ ∞ ∞ ∞ ∞ ∞

I glanced into my side view mirror the second I got out of my car, smoothed my eyebrows out, and promised myself that I would not touch alcohol or absolutely anything else during the night.

Being around people would be good for me. Being surrounded by music lovers who just appreciated being in the presence of some good music would remedy my loneliness for a Thursday night.

When I stepped through the glass doors of the bar, I was met with an utterly depressing sight: other than the band members and the bartender, there was just one woman standing around.

Great. The blonde in the leather jacket from the party that stole my beer.

When I looked at her from across the room, I could feel her hatred seeping through her pores. She was disgusted to be in my sheer presence, yet the two of us were the only ones standing in the rickety bar on a Thursday evening. I had quit drinking and cocaine at this point, for my head was weighing too heavy on my heart, but I was looking forward to seeing On-Line perform. She gazed at me with a blank stare, almost to ease the awkwardness and show some sort of sign of hope that I would saunter up to her so she didn't have to spend the night standing alone in the corner.

Against my better judgment, I approached her. Her blonde hair whisked over her shoulder as she turned away, for she didn't seem to want to admit she was glaring at the one and only person in the bar.

With her head turned towards the neon signs above the bar still, she muttered, "You're Scott, right? We really don't need to go over cheap introductions. I'm Gemma."

I stood there silently for a moment, trying to figure out the next words that would spring from my mouth.

'Ok then,' I grumbled. She whipped her head back around, almost in confusion, because she couldn't understand why I actually agreed to something she said for once.

"Fine," she quipped, folding her arms and rolling her eyes almost simultaneously. We stood there watching the band set up in silence. I turned to the bar to get a drink to get me through what seems like it would be one of the most awkward nights ever. She contorted her body so she could watch my every move, almost as if she didn't trust me leaving her line of sight.

"Scott," she peeped, "Buy me a beer." I looked over at her in astonishment. She spoke, finally. I got myself a 7-Up, and her some no-name beer that looked mildly appeasing. She snatched it from my hand and proceeded to pound it back in true Gemma fashion. The glass made a reverberating thud when it hit the bar.

I will never know what prompted me to say this, but I met her gaze and said, 'Don't worry, we don't have to be friends, I just don't want to stand here in silence all damn night. Tell me you hate me or something.'

A breathy chuckle burst from her lips. Yet something in her eyes said we would be more than friends. Later that night, between the thick fog and soft leather that lined my back seat, her passionate lips confirmed my suspicions: she didn't hate me, she was just afraid to feel my body pressed against hers. Though that night, as our lips touched for the first time and I could finally see past those cold, dark eyes for what they were, I felt pure lust between her locks of hair that brushed against my tender touch.

In the back seat of an old car, in the parking lot of a rotting bar, I found peace between her gentle thighs. I had a feeling that from then on, we would be bound to one another forever.

The two of us sat engulfed in one another for a few moments. She caught my urge to contain the grin that was growing across my face.

"What is it?" She looked up at me with a blissful demeanor.

'Nothing, it's just…' I paused, trying to collect my words for a second, 'You look beautiful.'

She smiled and gave me a gentle peck on the lips.

Something felt right about Gemma being in my arms. Olga may have been physically gone for about a week, but spiritually speaking, she was gone far before I ever even realized it.

Still, Olga was a cherished memory that remains in a special place in my heart… where all of my past loves remain.

∞ ∞ ∞ ∞ ∞ ∞ ∞ ∞

Barbara ended up calling me less than two weeks from the first moment we sat on the bench and chatted for a bit. I told her that Olga left me and she said the love that I lost wasn't worth the cost.

Towards the end of our phone conversation, I distinctly remember her voice as she uttered the following words, "Scott, you can call me Aunt Barbara, I mean, if it is okay with you."

I agreed to meet her later that day, because it was not like I had anything else to do. Aunt Barbara and I walked through the streets of Manhattan and across the Brooklyn Bridge. It seemed almost as if we were reminiscing about our lives in the sense that we knew each other longer than what was actually just a few months.

Words melted into one another as I admired the friendship and bond that were forming between our lives. I was present to every syllable that hung from her lips and every story that she told through smile after smile.

As we approached the entryway to Brooklyn Bridge Park, she began to reminisce about her experiences as a child. Some stories about my mother were sprinkled here and there, but she was keen enough to focus her energy into what I needed to know and not what would sting or burn with relation to how my mother and I had been "getting along" as she so appropriately put it.

"Scott, this is Brooklyn Bridge Park, have you been?" Her eyes lit up the moment she saw the water before her.

'Yeah,' I chirped, 'I've been here a lot over the years. This is one of my favorite spots.'

"Spots," she jeered, "I have those too. Come," she motioned to the bench, "Sit."

We sat peacefully gazing out at the city and its bustling nature.

Boats scurried about in the water and you could hear cars honking from Manhattan.

It was a pretty comedic sight: Manhattan's juxtaposed energy from day to night as I had seen many times before in this very spot.

"My husband and I actually had our first date here in this very spot," Aunt Barbara was so happy to share that part of her life with me.

I was just as exuberant as her: my understanding of our family heritage was growing as we spoke into the sunset before us.

As we recounted moments of bliss and laughter, and moments of heartache and tears, I felt an inner sense of peace.

Where had she been all my life?

Why would my mother hide her from me?

How did my aunt know to find me exactly when I needed her?

It was beautiful and it was a true gift from the universe.

Aunt Barbara was finally showing me what it was like to feel just at home, and her hugs were a great start to finally feeling like I was no longer standing in the shadow of an abusive past.

I was finally home.

As the two of us spoke briefly about Olga, various thoughts drifted in and out of my mind: Do you see me? Can you even feel my presence anymore?

Or am I just an apparent apparition, forced to haunt your every thought because you knew, deep in your heart, I never truly existed?

But no, I existed in your soul.

And I always will.

∞ ∞ ∞ ∞ ∞ ∞ ∞ ∞

That afternoon was the first of many afternoons where my aunt and I would talk about life, my experiences, her beliefs, and most importantly, *our* family.

I guess this is a good place to talk about my mother's real story, for Aunt Barbara was the one who helped me put the pieces together. As Aunt Barbara and I sat in a dimly lit Brooklyn diner, she painted the picture of who my mother was long before I was brought into existence.

"She's not who you think she is," Aunt Barbara whispered in the shadows of the overhead lights.

There is a story behind her story. There is a story behind how she treated me as a child. My mother was raised in an Orthodox Jewish home and was plagued by her own abusive situation. Bruises adorned her torso and thighs while her face was always perfectly pristine: no one in the community could know about what happened behind the closed doors of a "perfect" family.

I was following in my mother's footsteps without even realizing it, for she was also kicked out on her sixteenth birthday.

"You see, Scott, your mom fell in love with a boy who was half-Christian and half-Jewish, but he was raised Christian... and your grandparents despised that," Aunt Barbara whispered.

'So, what happened to her? What happened to the boy?' I was at the edge of my seat finally learning about my family history.

"Your mother married him."

I swallowed hard. My father was the reason why my grandparents disconnected from my mother.

"Your grandparents could not handle a Christian boy dating your mom. They told her to leave him... and well, when she did not comply..."

I cut her off, 'They kicked her out.'

"Yes," she said solemnly.

Aunt Barbara grabbed my hand and looked me in the eyes: "Just know your parents loved each other deeply once."

'Once?'

My mother moved in with my father's parents and stayed there even after he was drafted into the Vietnam War. They even got married. Though my father's mother was compassionate and sensitive to the situation, she always said that my mother was just not right.

And so, the cycle of abuse continued... with me.

I never got to meet my mother's parents, for she never returned home after she left. That's the one difference I guess: I didn't stay away from my mother and father for long, and well, I guess that part of the story comes later.

"When your mom left, I was just thirteen. I did not know what was happening."

I gulped. My sisters probably did not understand what was happening, just as Aunt Barbara did not comprehend why my mother was gone.

"When I found out about you and your sisters, I tried Scott," her eyes began to water and she wiped away crisp tears. "I brought gifts, I waited on your block for hours, and your mother would shoo me away each time."

My perspective of my mother changed drastically. She succumbed to pain at such a young age and did not know how to handle her life... I guess we are one in the same.

Through tears, Aunt Barbara embraced me and apologized for what my life became. Yet in those moments I spent with her, I was happy she found me when she did and how she did.

It was almost like she was my guardian angel.

∞ ∞ ∞ ∞ ∞ ∞ ∞ ∞

Days after learning about my mother's story behind the story, I sat glaring out the bedroom window of my apartment. There were so many unanswered questions and so much I did not know about.

Who was I? Really... who was I behind the history my family hid from me? Who would I become in the future? What would I become in the future? What else did I need to know about my family?

What was I missing?

My mind drifted the moment my head hit the pillow.

A mind full of questions often succumbs to the melodic lull of stars bursting throughout the sky. There are so many wishes that are made on stars... I wonder just how many come true.

∞ ∞ ∞ ∞ ∞ ∞ ∞ ∞

I woke up at midnight to the sound of repetitive knocking. A female voice was calling out my name from behind the door. Olga had moved to Florida and left me, so I knew it was not her. Gemma had been ignoring me since our sensual encounter, which meant unless another woman was coming to find me; this unusual visit was going to remain a mystery. I chose to give into my innate curiosities.

I answered the door.

"I broke up with him." Gemma rushed into the apartment and flopped onto the couch.

'What?' I rubbed my eyes and slammed the door behind me.

"I had a boyfriend the night we, you know, were together," Gemma started, "But I got to thinking and realized that you are the one I want."

'Okay.'

"Okay?"

'Okay.'

"You don't want to know, what... like... anything? You don't have any questions?"

Gemma sat up and gazed at me with tears in her eyes.

'No. You want me and that is that.' I smiled. She seemed genuine. After dealing with everything Olga put me through and finding out about my mother's story, I knew that Gemma's appearance was a sign from the universe or something.

She seemed like she needed a bit of understanding, too.

"You need to know a few things about me though before we go any further," her heart rate must have increased exponentially at that moment. She began speaking rapidly and not making any sense.

I sat next to her and kissed her slowly, caressing her hair and face in the process. When she opened her eyes and softly exhaled, I could tell some compassion was just what she needed.

"I'm bisexual," her eyes teared up.

'I don't care what you are, just as long as you are you.'

"Really?"

'Really.'

We kissed again.

'Any other midnight confessions?'

"No."

'Okay.'

A long pause hung in the air. I opened my arms and embraced her, for I could tell that something within her needed that. I wanted to make her happy for some reason, and that hug appeared to be what she needed.

We sat locked in that tender embrace until she fell asleep on my chest. I naturally followed soon after, with her heartbeat keeping time with mine.

When she woke in the morning, she told me all about how she was in love with her female best friend and wanted an open relationship if we were to be together.

'Cool,' was my only response.

And the saga that is Gemma began...

∞ ∞ ∞ ∞ ∞ ∞ ∞ ∞

I didn't have the heart to live in the same place where Olga and I had slept together and partied night after night, so I quit my job and chose to move. I worked at an auto leasing company that had a place to live.

The dealership offered me a dingy room on the lot in exchange for washing the cars. At night, I would act as the security guard to ensure the vehicles would not be damaged.

In the morning, I would drive to their main office twenty minutes away to shave and shower. Before the workers would get there, I would lean over the sink and let the water drip over my head.

It made me feel alive despite everything that made me feel I was dying inside.

To a young man, it was a thrill to be surrounded by brand new cars. The leather seats felt miraculous against my skin as I moved them back and forth from the satellite lot to the dealership.

The metal cars provided a sleek background to my new lifestyle without Olga. I had a bunch of crazy parties there with Gemma, for we could let people into the lot after hours and we would spend hours dancing around in the apartment I had there.

Gemma would bring various women and men to the lot who she claimed she also had an open relationship with, and being a naive boy looking for love, I was fine with it. She snuck away hand in hand with a woman in red, so my eyes began to wander.

'Open relationship,' I muttered. 'Open…'

My eyes fixated on a woman wearing an aqua blue bra and distressed denim jeans. She's one of those girls you genuinely do not notice unless you are looking for her.

She stands in the corner like a wallflower in its appropriate place. Her decorum is cloaked in the insecurities she decoupages upon her face: the lipstick gluing together the broken pieces of her cracked face. It is a sullen reminder of where she once hung a bright smile.

Unfortunately for her, she became ensnared in a trap: a cage lined with phrases like, "But baby, I love you," and "I promise you" followed up by papier-mâché retorts from a seemingly happier time.

The archangel of death embraced her, but his grasp was too loose and she slid through his clutches just seconds away from an absolute disaster.

So she hangs there, like a dirty old coat stained by equal parts time and crushed food remnants: yearning for a seat at the table, yet hungry for nothing other than to be herself again.

I approached her apprehensively, unsure how to begin the conversation in a way that would settle the tension in both of our souls.

I lurked towards her, moving cautiously because I was so unaware of how she would react to my presence. I wanted her story. I needed to know her experience. I had to understand just why she was breathtakingly beautiful, yet consumed by silence.

'Hi,' I spoke timidly, trying to provoke a reaction.

She glared into my eyes and picked her hands up from her sides. She waved without making a noise, but it was clear she felt some sort of reconciliation for my attempt at being friendly.

Then it hit me. She opened her mouth and jumbled words fluttered out: Hi, I am Robin, and I am deaf.

We tried to communicate for quite some time and I tried explaining to her that I was in a band. She asked me what music I know and I told her I knew how to play the drums. Robin grasped my hand and dragged me to her car.

"Teach me music," she said in a broken tone.

'Teach me sign language then.'

She smiled and thanked me.

'How am I going to teach you music if you can't hear?'

"I can feel." She grabbed my hand and held it against her radio.

We turned on the radio and a Bon Jovi song just so happened to play. She turned the volume all the way up and said, "Tell me the lyrics."

She read my lips the whole time and I sang to her.

"You have a great singing voice," she chuckled.

'Well, I guess you have a great singing voice when you are singing to a deaf person.'

The two of us laughed and figured out the importance of vibrations: you don't need to hear something, for you can just feel it. Robin taught me that.

We connected on a whole different level that night, and I was happy about that. We ended up speaking every once in a while, but we drifted apart. I was thankful for meeting her and for learning from her.

Vibrations still play an important part in my life, though they certainly take on different contexts now.

∞ ∞ ∞ ∞ ∞ ∞ ∞ ∞

Gemma and I were having fun. It was a different kind of fun from what Olga and I had, but it was fun. The two of us spent plenty of nights getting into shenanigans at the car lot, but most importantly the two of us found a stronger bond than I had ever expected.

See, I was an atheist at this point, because I was so conflicted about Judaism.

"I'm a Lutheran," she explained. Gemma was also kind enough to tell me about her story behind the story: her life being raised Lutheran and how she was very committed to her family. Gemma would spend night after night eating dinner with her family before sneaking out to see me.

She was also the reason I ended up getting baptized in her family's Lutheran church. I did end up teaching Sunday school and about Jesus' powerful story.

Gemma helped to shape my spirituality and understanding of religion in the context of the world.

I distinctly remember sitting down with one of the pastors at her church and talking to him about the Lutheran religion. He said, "You could be gay, Jewish, uh, Muslim... You, you're welcome."

That's what I wanted to have.

"You're welcome. Everyone is welcome," echoed through my mind.

My aunt even gave me her blessing and condoned my religious exploration.

I had just experienced the accident a few months earlier and I was still reeling from what happened. I felt something was talking to me and that the universe wanted me to find out the truth.

Why did I survive?

Why did Gemma come into my life?

Why was I still here?

Being in church with Gemma and her family was a spiritual cleansing of sorts. The Rabbi at my family's temple told me to stop asking questions, but the Pastor at the Lutheran church wanted me to question things.

The pieces of my life were beginning to fit together for a change.

Pastor Frank told me that it was okay that I felt lost, for it meant that I could find myself again and again. Everyone can find themselves again and again; it just depends on where you choose to look. He was the one who agreed to baptize me with Gemma taking on the role of my godmother.

And Aunt Barbara was the one who told me to write a letter to my father when I wanted to change my name.

I was unsure exactly what to write, but I wanted to, in a sense, apologize for the pain I am sure I put my parents through. I let him know two things in the letter I wrote to him: I wanted him to know that I was becoming a different man (I mean, after all, I was getting baptized) and that I wanted to change my last name.

What do you say to the man who contributed to the life you are living? How do you even write the words that fail to build upon your very lips?

How do you define yourself when the world already defined you?

My father responded promptly through his own letter of sorts: he wished me luck and respected the fact that I was doing something with my life. Then he begged me not to change my last name. I had so much anger towards my parents. Their actions seared into my very memory. Though I sensed the desperation seeping through my father's very words.

You are my only son. You are my legacy.

I had never even heard my father speak those words.

*Even if we don't talk, I want to know that I
leave something in this universe that carries on.*

Suddenly, I had a new respect for my father. He knew that there was a legacy attached to the last name, the Matheson name, and out of respect to him and to all of those who wore the Matheson name before us, I kept the name. Even though I was angry with my family, there was a certain honor and respect that lived through my last name. There is a certain something that lives in every last name: a legacy. From that moment on, I knew I had to create and carry on a legacy... I was just unsure about what that legacy meant or what it would look like. I promised myself that I would never change my last name.

And as the water cascaded over my head and down my spine, I gazed up at the sky and thanked God and everything that brought me to this very moment. Gemma stood nearby and grinned as tears streamed down my cheeks.

People glance up because there's this idea heaven up, but the truth is you can glance anywhere because angels and spirits are all around you. It doesn't have to be up. We just think angels are up, because we know space is up. It's really intertwined into the energy of this planet and the universe.

Day after day I feel Danielle's energy and presence.

I sense that she is out there in the universe feeling genuinely happy. Her wisdom and story are being painted in the pages of this book, letter by letter and moment by moment. Her physical life was short, but still mattered exponentially.

As with everyone who has passed, their legacy lives on in the hearts, souls, and minds of the lives they touched.

The beauty they bestowed upon us and the lessons they taught us thrive in our veins, which leads me to ask... who are your angels? Have you thanked them for your experiences so far?

Would they be happy with whom you have become?

In retrospect, I know my angels are looking down at the journey I have travelled, and are probably shaking their heads, but filled with glee at the same time.

This soul is still developing and growing, and I have come so far... and we have so far to go.

CHAPTER 11

Born to Be My Baby

*"Before you cross the street, take my hand.
Life is what happens to you, while you're busy
making other plans."*

**- John Lennon, British Singer and Songwriter,
Liverpool, England**

Each time I opened my eyes, I saw a brand-new world. My own blood ran through my veins, though crimson rivers flooded with my past crept through every fiber of my being. I was the same old Scott Zachariah Matheson, but I was essentially an entirely new man.

Whether it was Gemma's version of love or my discovery of religion that helped me see the light is up to interpretation, but when you put this entire world into perspective every moment is part of a domino effect. When we choose to change something about ourselves, be it our name or our religion, how truly different are we? Do we walk amongst different streets entirely, or do we genuinely shift our mind so that it does not matter where we walk? Then do our respective lives become a multi-colored quilt made of dense fabric and sheer illusion?

Where do boundaries exist between the person we inherently are and the individual we are becoming?

Where do we cross those blurred white lines?

I knew where my boundary was drawn the moment Gemma spoke just a few words to me... but more on that later.

For now, I was swimming in the sea of opportunities my renewed faith filled my very core with, and I had no foreseeable reason to stray from the new beam of light I had found.

In an effort to become more stable, again, the key word there is effort, I chose to move out to a ranch-style house in Farmingdale. Its white shutters and sky-blue siding were akin to starting over. That's just what I needed. I needed a fresh start. I needed some semblance of home, even if it was not defined by four walls and a roof. To prevent my sister Rebecca from getting involved in any more chaos inflicted by my parents, I invited her to come stay with me and she happily obliged.

I had Gemma, I had Rebecca, and I had my Aunt Barbara back in my life. Everything appeared to be falling into place for a change, and I was not sure how to handle it.

Then Gemma and I hosted these parties called the Trash and Crash Bash.

Our version of normalcy was defined by loading countless drunks and party-goers in our living room and causing a raucous. You could almost sync your heartbeat to Metallica's early songs, which consistently boomed over the speakers.

When Metallica was not playing, my friends and I were rocking out to whatever crazy music we could conjure up. A few of us started a band called the Suicide Kings and would perform everywhere from dive bars to mine and Rebecca's living room. Gemma and I continued our wild adventures and had no worries whatsoever.

Since the accident, I had banished drinking any sort of alcohol though temptations were present. However, the parties were blind to my reservations. The insane celebrations continued despite my distaste for drinking.

Though I had no money, no direction, and no true path in life, my life was going great.

∞ ∞ ∞ ∞ ∞ ∞ ∞ ∞

On a brisk spring evening, Aunt Barbara came to visit suddenly. She knocked on the door so gently, but the crazy dog Rebecca and I adopted, Lassie, scampered off of the couch and straight to the door. Her caramel and white fur floated through the air as she leapt around.

It was a blessing to have Lassie with us, though I was clearly indulging in my pop culture fantasies. I wanted a picturesque life more than anything, and maybe subconsciously I was hoping that by naming my pet after an iconic dog, I could live a perfect life.

"Sweetheart, it's your aunt. Open the door please," Aunt Barbara's light brown hair bobbed up and down in the reflection of the small window centered in the door.

When I opened the door, she was holding a pan filled with chicken and rice in her hand. She seemed genuinely happy to see us and sauntered directly into our kitchen. She often came over just at the right moment: whenever I was feeling defeated or exhausted, she materialized almost out of thin air. Aunt Barbara was a genuine angel who never showed an ounce of selfishness, even when it seemed like she was on the verge of passing out from sheer exhaustion.

Rebecca, Aunt Barbara, and I sat around our dinky kitchen table and talked about all different kinds of things: how our respective lives were going, the future, and how to keep ourselves sane. She would always putter around our house, cleaning up just about anything that seemed awry or out of place.

After Rebecca would shuffle off to bed for the night, Aunt Barbara and I would sit on the couch and talk about Gemma, our family history, and just about anything that came to mind. Nothing was off limits. In hindsight, it is clear that she was a crucial voice that spoke to my soul, and still is in many ways. Her wisdom touched me in a way that no other person in this universe has been able to impact me. Her love still resonates with me in ways this world could never describe.

She is always with me. Always.

"Scott," she said one night, "How are you becoming the man you can be proud of?" She sat pensively awaiting a reply, while nestling against an old, tattered pillow.

We would sit on the sofa and talk about our dreams.

"It's always good to have a dream, my son, but it is also important to think about how you are constantly growing and learning."

Her words echo throughout my mind even now.

At the end of the night, she would slip a $20 bill in my pocket and give me a gentle kiss on the cheek. Each time, she would tell me how proud she was of me and how impressed she was with how I was evolving.

Moments with her fill some of my fondest memories.

∞ ∞ ∞ ∞ ∞ ∞ ∞ ∞

Gemma and I would meet up after I got out of work and just before dinner. She always had to be home for dinner, so that her and her religious family could say grace together. It was a beautiful tradition, but somehow it did not suit me. Her father was a stern and well-respected man in the community, and he never cracked a smile, nor did he show his emotions. His facial features could be used as a model for one of those handsome, ornate statues in the New York City public parks, and everyone would naturally respect him as a heroic icon.

Each night, Gemma would sneak back out of her house and come see me. We would rarely spend the night together, but if we did, she was always out the door and home by early morning.

Her turbulent methods of partying led us to some interesting moments, but we would always end up together by the end of the night. No matter what, she showed she loved me in her own way, and I would do just about anything to please her.

One night while the two of us were starting to get hot and heavy, the two of us stopped in the sheer heat of passion. The tail end of the summer was upon us, and she got up from the mattress to switch the ceiling fan on before we fooled around. As she stood on the bed, I admired her figure: she was petite, but something seemed off about her utterly perfect curves.

'Hey, Gem, can I ask you something?'

She dropped back down to the mattress and climbed on top of me, wrapping her fingers through my long, unkempt blonde strands of hair in the process.

"What baby," her lips ran up and down the crevices of my neck.

'Are you pregnant?'

She stopped moving, "What did you say?"

'Are you pregnant?'

She sat up abruptly while straddling my body. Her entire demeanor shifted.

"What? Are you calling me fat?"

'No.'

"Well, that's what it seems like you are doing." She moved off of me and plopped with her back facing me. She was rushing to pull her bra straps back over her shoulders.

'No, no, no.' I got very nervous. I did not mean to call her fat. I was just asking a question because I was curious.

"I-" her voice broke, "I am not fat."

I loved her for who she was and I was not trying to insult her. I truly did love her.

After that moment, I never questioned her again. Though she was getting a tad rounder, I knew that she may have just been stressing out or dealing with some family stuff she did not want to talk about.

That was cool, sometimes people do not want to talk, so we continued our nightly adventures between cuddling in the sheets and other activities.

∞ ∞ ∞ ∞ ∞ ∞ ∞ ∞

My days consisted of the same mundane activities: working my medical billings and collections job at some small company, then coming home to wait for Gemma to stop in.

Towards the end of November, she came barreling in one night in a state of hysteria. I could not understand what she was trying to mutter under her breath, but I made out a few words here and there. Nothing was making sense.

"I have some news," she finally said clearly.

'What's up?' I sat on the couch and patted a spot next to me in hopes she would sit next to me.

"Well, it's good news and it is also a bit of bad news, but I think-"

I cut her off and put my hand on her leg carefully. 'What's the news, Gem?'

She grew even more nervous, so I offered to take her out to eat.

We rode in silence all the way to the pizza place, but she fidgeted with her fingers the whole way. The two of us got out of the car and she froze.

"Scott, listen to me."

'What?'

"I'm pregnant, and I am due in two weeks."

The car keys crashed to the floor as a resounding silence broke throughout the room. I could not speak. I could not move. Everything moved in slow motion around both of us.

'Two weeks?'

"Two weeks, well about two weeks."

I was going to be a father. I was barely a man myself, and I was bringing a legacy into the world. I was beyond scared shitless and speechless. In school back then, there was no conversation about safe sex or condoms. We were all just having fun and living life. We did not think about the consequences or what ifs. We just lived paycheck to paycheck. We devoured any semblance of normalcy and life, for we were young kids walking in the shadows of grown adults.

We were not the ones who knew all of the answers, but we knew enough to get by… and for some, that was all that mattered.

Though much more mattered the second she muttered those words: I'm pregnant. I had to step up. I had to breathe. I had to come up with a plan for myself… and my… and for my child.

Questions fluttered throughout my head like butterflies escaping from a netted cage: I knew what existed beyond the borders, I just never thought I would cross them this fast and in this manner.

"Well, what are we going to do, Scott?"

'I don't know Gemma.'

I leaned against the car and watched the stars dancing above us. I shut my eyes slowly and let the noise from my rapid heartbeat fill my mind.

'I don't know.'

Some men have nine months to prepare to be a father. I had two weeks. How do you learn a lifetime of wisdom and insight in less than two weeks? How do you bring a boy or girl into the world and raise them to be a man or woman?

"People put their kids up for adoption to give them a better life" Gemma said, nervously playing with her hair. "No, that's stupid. It's our child."

I opened my mouth, but nothing came out.

"Scott," she said frantically, "I don't know what else we can do. My father would kill me if he knew about the baby."

I gasped. No one knew about the baby. Who could she tell? Who would she tell? She could not even tell me.

'Okay.'

"Okay," she screamed, "Nothing is okay Scott!"

Gemma leaned into my chest and began crying. I shut my eyes and just started praying. Every fiber of my being felt as if it were on fire, but all I could think about was the fact that I had two weeks to get my act together.

How do you pull yourself together in two weeks when all of the pieces of your life just shattered simultaneously?

Questions floated throughout my head with no remorse. I had to find answers, and find them rather quickly. I had a child, my child, who was counting on me... and I did not know who he or she was or who he or she would become. I just knew about his or her existence and just had to be the best person I could in those moments. I remained strong and considerate in Gemma's presence, for I did not know just how to respond.

We ate dinner, I asked her thousands upon thousands of questions, and the two of us ended up passing out on the quaint mattress we had on the floor of my small house in Farmingdale.

The walls felt like they were closing in on me. My mind was rushing to different places and the concerns building inside of me were mounting quite a war on my mind.

I stood up and started to shake. Gemma was still sound asleep and nestled up against the pillow and trying to let her unconscious mind wander. Her facial expressions were a mixture of blatant uncertainty and fear. She was showing on her face what my mind could not organize in those very moments.

I dashed into the bathroom and hugged the toilet. The porcelain felt rather comfortable against my sweltering face. As I wretched and heaved, I came to the realization that my child would be doing the same very soon. He or she would have nights where he or she would be sick and need me to rub his or her back. He or she would cry and not know what to do, and as a father I would need to do my best to… to… What was I doing?

What was I saying? What was I thinking?

Gemma mentioned putting our child up for adoption. How could we? How could we? I mean, neither of us could probably handle a child, but still.

My brain was torn. Every thought was built on the premise of what ifs and insecurities. Questions continued racing through my mind as the two of us snuggled on the mattress once again.

Everything was about to change, and I had mere moments to prepare for whatever came next… I guess you could say I was really living on a prayer at this point.

In the midst of the chaos I was immersed in, Gemma and I ended up getting free tickets to a RUSH concert. Our good friend Jackie got us front row tickets to see the Toronto, Canada-based band perform at the biggest concert hall in New York: Madison Square Garden.

Gemma and I were ecstatic to be in the presence of musical greats, and I wonder if Geddy Lee realized he was rocking out merely inches away from a woman in her ninth month of pregnancy.

Neil Peart's drumming was an utter thrill.

I wondered if everyone else in the crowd realized that we were about to be parents. I wondered if the world would become drastically different the moment that our child entered the world with a gentle wail.

The melody and beat of "Subdivisions" made me feel whole despite the looming presence of my child within the next few days.

Music had been my everything for years, and this moment would become a quintessential story in my life for decades.

Regardless of what Gemma and I would do, who else could say they were celebrating life at a RUSH concert on the eve of their life changing forever?

∞ ∞ ∞ ∞ ∞ ∞ ∞ ∞

One night when I just lulled myself off into a deep sleep, I heard rustling from outside of my window. When I heard an alarm going off, I jumped up. I looked outside and in my dreary, exhausted state; I didn't notice what was going on before my eyes. When I woke up in the morning and rushed out the door to go to work, I finally saw it: last night, someone had broken into my Toyota Supra.

The shattered window lay scattered in pieces on my front seat. The brisk winter wind whipped through my car and touched every bit of the fabric seats. The thief or thieves didn't get much, other than my dignity and a few loose coins in the car, but I felt like it was symbolic of everything crashing down around me.

How could I raise a child if I could not realize my car was being broken into?

With no money and barely enough sensibility in terms of what to do, I brushed the glass onto the floor and drove to work.

Each day that followed, I was counting my blessings and praying that when the moment came, I would know just what to do.

On December 10th, as I was just drifting off to sleep, I got the call. At exactly two thirty in the dead of the night, my phone rang and the noise shot straight through to my heart.

"Hey Scott, my water broke. I am driving to the hospital in East Meadow, Nassau something or another," her voice was cracking through whatever phone she called me on.

Half nauseated and half exhausted, I told her that I loved her and that I would see her soon. I hopped in the driver's seat of my Toyota Supra and did not bother to stop and think. The cold winter wind beat through the car as I raced down the block. The broken window, despite appearing a week earlier, still remained, as did my trepidation of becoming a dad. Everything I had and everything I was up until this point was going to make me the father I was about to become.

The cars surrounding me on the Southern State Parkway were just blurs.

My heartbeat was pushing past my chest and drawing me closer and closer to Gemma. Nothing was more important at this moment than her. Nothing in this world mattered but our child.

This moment, my child's birth, was everything and anything I needed.

∞ ∞ ∞ ∞ ∞ ∞ ∞ ∞

I don't remember parking my car. I don't remember asking anyone in the hospital where Gemma was. I just found her. My mind registered her heartbeat and her voice once I walked into the hospital.

'Hi,' a smile crept through my worried demeanor.

"Hi," Gemma looked relieved to see me.

As she was wheeled into a different part of the hospital, we held hands the entire time. The world was moving in slow motion.

"It's time." The nurse stood before both of us, probably thinking about how we were just two kids getting mixed up into something larger than both of our lives. Regardless, our child would be born just moments later.

At 5:38 A.M., we heard the doctor pronounce, "It's a boy!"

A boy. My son. Our son.

I stood there, watching red and pink blotches of fluid drip from his skin. The doctor and nurses scurried towards Gemma again.

'Oh God,' I muttered a bit too loud, 'Are we having twins?'

I saw something emerging from Gemma once again.

"Honey, that's the after birth. Didn't they teach you anything in school?" The nurses and doctor glanced over at me.

Seeing my son come into this world was a beautiful experience beyond any sensation that words could define. I saw life emerge for the first time before my very eyes. I was okay up until that point. However, the after birth made me reconsider fooling around during Science class in high school.

After birth is one of the most nauseating visuals after seeing a beautiful life enter this world.

"Let's splash some water on that face of yours," the nurse said as she led me out of the room. Gemma was laying on the bed looking up at the fluorescent lighting. I could only imagine just what was going through her head at the time.

I watched the nurse clean off my son and wrap his small, tender body in a blanket.

"What is his name, dad?" One of the nurses locked eyes with me. *Me.* I'm dad. I'm a father.

Days ago, Gemma and I were in a state of panic. Our fear was pushing us to consider adoption, though our options were based on uncertainty. Now, we were parents, and now he was a few inches before me. I fell in love with him instantly.

We had to figure everything out for our family.

'I don't know just yet.' I spoke stoically and was in a clear state of shock.

What would we name him? Did Gemma want to keep him?

I thought for a few moments: Should I go to work? Should I not go to work?

Gemma and I sat with our fingers linked: my right hand was brushing the pellets of sweat that were wrapped between her hair.

'I don't know." I whispered to Gemma.

"You don't know what?"

'I don't know if we can be parents.'

She smiled and rested her head against mine. In those moments, I could tell she felt the same way without even saying a word. She would just need to explain him to her family, which would be no easy feat.

I ended up calling out from work, coughing and choking while on the phone, of course, to deter them from thinking that I was lying about being sick. I was sick, but I was sick to my stomach. I was a father now and I was nervous beyond belief.

As the hours ticked by in the hospital, Gemma would take the baby in her arms and cradle him gently. The way she looked at him was how I felt about him: she loved him and we both knew it.

"He needs a name, Scott. What are we calling him?" She gazed up at me as I paced about the room.

'Bryan?'

"Why Bryan?"

'I really like the name Bryan.'

Bryan was the name of our favorite hockey player: Bryan Trottier, from the New York Islanders, had strong values composed of following his heart, tenacity, and teamwork that were truly admirable. I wanted my son to have those good qualities, for I did not believe I had the skills to be a role model back then.

In the years that followed, I ended up getting a job near the skating academy in Port Washington where Bryan Trottier practiced. Call it fate or destiny, but I would end up standing by the food truck outside the building with Bryan Trottier. The two of us spoke in such a nonchalant manner and it was a blessing to be in his presence.

It was moments like those that made me realize Bryan was meant to be a part of my life.

She smirked. "Well, Bryan it is then."

'Okay.'

"Okay."

As the late afternoon crept upon our little scene, she began to rock back and forth in the bed.

'What's wrong?' I looked up from a parenting book that the nurse gave us to pass the time.

"It is getting late. I need to go home for dinner." Gemma tried standing.

'What? Why?' She was confused as to why I was shocked.

"I told my family I had to go into work early. I can't *not* go home. They would worry."

'But you can't-' The nurse rushed in when she saw Gemma stand up.

"What are you doing? You need to stay in bed," the nurse boomed.

"No, no, no, you don't understand. I need to get home to my family." Gemma began pulling tubes and wires from her hands and arms.

"Your family is here." The nurse motioned to me and to the door, signifying Bryan who was now resting in the nursery for the night.

"I can't" Gemma began to cry. "I can't stay."

Gemma got dressed, despite my cries and the doctor's pleading, and drove herself home for family dinner. I stayed in the hospital and hoped she would come back the next day.

∞ ∞ ∞ ∞ ∞ ∞ ∞ ∞

Hours later, I was still sitting in the room where Gemma was once resting. I did not know what else to do. I had nowhere else to go. My son was in this hospital somewhere and his mother was eating pasta and meatballs with her family, probably panicking about giving birth just hours ago.

The hum from the fluorescent lighting grew dull, and I decided I could not sit still any longer. I removed myself from the wooden chair and let the pitter-patter of my feet carry me out into the hallway.

I saw a group of doctors and nurses nearby, so I began to walk towards them.

'Nurse,' I approached her cautiously and tapped her on the shoulder.

"What can I do for you, hun?" She was busy shuffling papers and putting away files.

'I'd like to see my son.'

She smiled and pointed towards a hallway: "He's in the Elyza Wing. Fourth door on the left."

'Thanks.'

"Sure." She went back to shuffling the papers around.

I walked down the hallway, which was deserted and dim since most people were already sound asleep for the night.

Bryan was sound asleep and bundled up just under the large glass window. He seemed angelic in nature, almost like a pleasant contrast to my childhood and life so far. I personally could not see him disappearing from my life.

In the morning, when Gemma reappeared at the hospital to visit him, I told her what I was feeling. She kissed me on the forehead and cuddled him into her arms.

"I know," She spoke softly. "He's ours."

We didn't have anything. We didn't have money. We didn't know what we were doing as parents. Still, we were going to do everything in our power to provide for and care for our child.

Our son.

We decided that Bryan would stay with me and my sister, for Gemma could not just walk into her house and announce she had *her* child with her. In the days that followed, Bryan slept on my mattress on the floor. He cried and whined at first, but by the second night he slept next to me, utter peace flowed through him.

While watching him sleep for those first few nights, I came to the stark realization that Bryan saved me.

When I first held him I was scared shitless, but I was responsible for his life. The first time you hold your child, your baby, you are just overwhelmed with love. I made him, well, I helped make him.

Despite everything I did in my past: drank, did God knows what kind of drug, and did other incredibly dangerous things, he was okay.

Bryan was healthy.

I was not supposed to be alive. I was supposed to die in that car crash, with my head melting into the solid concrete on the Meadowbrook Parkway.

Yet I was there, and there was a reason: Bryan was my reason.

I knew from that moment on that I needed to make something of myself. I did not want him growing up to see a man who was nothing; he had to see me succeed. He just had to. I just had to make him proud. I wanted him to see a father who would actually do something amazing on this planet.

When you have a child, you begin to look at life differently. You begin to see the world in terms of wisdom you could impart upon your child and the strength you can help your child build. You do everything and anything to see your child happy and successful.

The days of being a washed up nobody faded into the setting sun hours ago. Bryan needed a role model. Bryan needed me. Bryan needed-

My thoughts paused as he began cooing and rolling into the warmth of my body. I held him closer and smiled as I brushed my finger against his wispy hairs.

He is precious. Life is so precious.

I could not be another statistic in the grand landscape of this universe, so I figured that I would talk to my son about what I knew about life and what I hoped to learn.

'My sweet boy,' I whispered. His mouth opened slightly and a bit of saliva pooled at his tender lips.

'I want you to know something.' I looked at him in the darkness and began to tear up at how pristine he was both inside and out. 'I want you to know what to do in this world and I want you to grow up very different from my upbringing.'

I began to speak to him in hushed tones and with purpose.

As I started drifting off and slurring my words, my first bit of advice sputtered from my lips: 'Bryan, refuse to sink. Never actually give up. Be who you are. Love the way you want to. Love. Just love fearlessly and love like this. Do not *ever* give up. Do not let life ever be over...'

My words faded as my eyelids shut. The last thing I remember telling him were the three words that would cling to my soul for years and years to come:

'Refuse... to... sink...'

Part II:

The Reckoning

CHAPTER 12

What a Wonderful World

~

"I see skies of blue and clouds of white. The bright blessed day, the dark sacred night... I hear babies crying, I watch them grow. They'll learn much more than I'll never know, and I think to myself what a wonderful world"

- Louis Armstrong, American trumpeter, composer, and vocalist, New Orleans, Louisiana

"How is my darling baby boy doing today?" Gemma rushed into the room and scooped Bryan up in her arms. Bryan cheered and cooed at the sight of his mother, who promptly kissed me on the cheek and moved towards the couch.

Rebecca wandered out from the kitchen with some mashed peas in a paper bowl.

"You made it just in time for dinner," Rebecca's voice had an urgent raspiness to it.

As Gemma drew Bryan closer to her chest, she watched Rebecca itch her arm and glare at the clock.

"Do you have somewhere to be, Beck?" Gemma locked eyes with me and smiled coyly.

"Yeah, a few friends and I are going out for the night. Do you two need anything?" Rebecca began putting her purse over her shoulder.

'Nah, we are okay, thanks.' I smiled back at Gemma as she rocked Bryan gently from side to side.

Rebecca's eyes moved towards both of us as she clutched the knob to the front door.

"Have fun tonight you three," she shouted to us as she exited the house for the night.

For the first time in about 10 months, the three of us had the house all to ourselves. We spent the summer playing with Bryan at the beach and taking him to the park, but what the three of us desperately needed was a quiet night together. Our small, close-knit family needed quality time together, so we dusted off the stereo and turned on some music. The radio stations were not playing such exciting music at eight at night, but we made it work. Gemma found a Michael Jackson song playing on one of the stations, so we chose to dance around to the latest song he came out with. Bryan seemed to enjoy the lyrics as we moved him around the room:

"Now I believe in miracles
And a miracle has happened tonight
But, if you're thinkin' about my baby
It don't matter if you're black or white."

The music entertained Bryan, for his jovial demeanor was contagious to both myself and Gemma. We were not perfect parents by any means, but we were thrilled to have him in our lives. The two of us were arguably living better lives because of Bryan. Though the past 10 months were by no means a vacation, we still had each other and that was everything.

Gemma and Bryan moved towards the bedroom and kept swaying from side to side.

I heard Gemma gasp lightly and could feel a smile spreading across her face. I appeared in the doorway to see her and Bryan fidgeting with a new toy of some sort. The local church was paramount in helping our small family raise Bryan right. On top of Aunt Barbara's generosity and Rebecca's thoughtful babysitting, various members of the church brought over food, baby supplies, and plenty of toys for Bryan. We were able to survive because of the kindness and compassion of, well, strangers primarily.

I had no money to my name. I was practically living on welfare and on the verge of starving, but Bryan never knew that. Bryan had everything he could have ever needed, and he never knew about the sacrifices that Gemma and I made to keep him healthy and comfortable.

The church did so much for us in the eyes of God and in order to make a difference in the lives of their fellow human beings. They helped us get up on our feet when it seemed as if we had no solid ground to stand on.

I wished that somehow, in some way, and one day I could give that much hope to someone struggling. I prayed I could thank each and every one of those kind people individually, for the immeasurable faith the church members bestowed upon us was beyond what Gemma and I could seriously comprehend.

At the end of the day, faith and hope are what brought Gemma, Bryan, and I the energy to move forward each and every second. Without the sheer goodwill from the community, we would not have been able to survive for very long. Saying that we have immense gratitude towards them and the other kind souls who helped us does not truly suffice in the grand scheme of life.

Therefore, I try to remember the wisdom and generosity people have shown me, and put that positive energy forth into this world.

∞ ∞ ∞ ∞ ∞ ∞ ∞ ∞

With each night that passed, Gemma would come and visit before returning to her family. All this time, they had no idea that their grandson existed on this Earth. Her family knew about me and the relationship I had with Gemma, but they were inherently clueless to the fact that their daughter was dealing with two separate lives.

At home, Gemma was the perfect daughter who obeyed her family's wishes. When she was with me, she was a mother, my love, and a bit of a wild child. Gemma continued to upkeep our open relationship while taking care of our son.

We would still get into our fair share of interesting situations, but we were rather calm as opposed to our serious partying days.

Our family life and social lives did mix occasionally, for when our friends wanted to have a jam session as a band, we were always quick to host a more moderate version of our Trash and Crash Bashes.

One night the band wanted to rehearse some new songs in the living room, so I naturally told them that they could come over. We set up our instruments while Bryan was sound asleep in his crib and began to let the rhythm flow through us.

As I felt the vibrations seeping through me, I could not help but close my eyes and feel the power of the drums echo through my core. At the time, I was not using language that fully encompassed the spiritual nature I experience now, but the feelings were always there. Music moves you in a way that could only be felt through vibrations and often times lyrics: if there was anything that Robin had taught me all those months ago in the car lot, that was it.

I try taking some wisdom, lessons, and insight from everyone I encounter and apply them to my life in some way. In a sense, I have taught all of those lessons to my son in hopes that he carries the torch wherever he may go in life.

Some of the lessons I taught him I am unsure of how they impacted him, but occasionally I get to see my wisdom and interests reflected in how he views the world. Arguably, his love of music stems from being a part of countless jam sessions over the years.

As the Suicide Kings played in the living room (we did end up changing the band name eventually, but we did think the name was awesome), Bryan managed to make his presence known in the house. We stopped playing momentarily so that I could scoop him up from his crib, change his diaper, then bring him into the living room with some toys to play with as we serenaded him with sweet, classic rock music.

As the group played, Bryan found solace in the bass drum I was playing. Despite it being the loudest and noisiest part of my drum, he found it to be the most soothing. Clearly, he was a kid made in the exact image of his father. Bryan cuddled against the old t-shirts I had balled up in there to muffle the sound, placed his thumb in his mouth, and fell sound asleep. Unsure of what to do and unaware of whom to consult for a baby crawling into a bass drum, I did what any logical musician and parent would do: I kept playing.

Over the years, as long as Bryan fit into the bass drum, he would sit inside of it while I played. I am still stunned he never developed a hearing issue because of his love of finding himself in the loudest places possible.

Nevertheless, my adoration for the drums and music in general continued to thrive, and Bryan developed a very early appreciation for music.

∞ ∞ ∞ ∞ ∞ ∞ ∞ ∞

Aunt Barbara would call weekly and check on her nephew and his little angel, as she called him. She was so proud of me for being a responsible parent, and her approval and admiration were what helped me guide Bryan throughout his childhood.

She would continue to stop by and slide a $20 bill in my pocket when I was dealing with the most stressful moments. She would also bring over dinner and play with Bryan when I needed a second to breathe. Although Bryan was a blessing and a true miracle, every now and then I needed a moment to collect myself and reflect on where my life was going.

At almost a year old now, Bryan was up and running around the house without shame. As he waddled about his diaper would sway back and forth and his childlike wonder and innocence would get him into all sorts of trouble. I continued to remain fearful as to whether or not I was doing enough to keep my son happy and healthy, but I also wanted to ensure that Gemma was receiving enough love and affection.

Above all I wanted to make everyone happy and satisfied, and would do just about anything to make sure I was being the best person, man, and father I could be.

Gemma and I were just itching to get out of the house one night as a family, so we went where any family with a young child would go: a hockey game. Bryan seemed to enjoy watching hockey with me on television. More specifically, he loved watching the New York Islanders play. I think the cheering, different colors, and the noises excited him the most when it came to the game.

On that fateful Saturday evening, the three of us bought tickets to go see the game in action. Little did we know, the three of us would be biting off a lot more than we realized by going to a publicly televised hockey game.

Gemma and I were not the only people who attended the game with a child, for the Islanders were running a special promotion for families that night. We were able to sit back and enjoy the game on the rusted metal chairs as we took turns bouncing our beautiful baby boy on our laps.

The large screens overhead played videos of the usual occurrences at the hockey games: we saw the referees rushing about on the ice, we watched the players score their goals, and there were fun games that audience members were able to participate in on the big screens.

"Let's hear it for the parents who brought their youngsters with them tonight," the announcer boomed in a grand, comedic way.

Parents were holding up their babies while everyone ooh-ed and aah-ed at the screen.

"Look!" Gemma shouted over the crowd as she pointed to the screen.

Bryan, Gemma, and I were on camera and on the big screen. Bryan waved to himself as the people around us cheered.

Our little family made it. We were together, we were happy, and we were having quite a night to remember.

Yeah, it was quite a night to remember.

∞ ∞ ∞ ∞ ∞ ∞ ∞ ∞

I drove Gemma home and walked her to the door for the night. It was late, Bryan was sound asleep in his car seat, and our whole night was utterly perfect.

By the time she got home Gemma's parents were also out for the night, but it was eerily quiet in the house.

I retreated back to my car and waited a moment before I pulled away from the curb. Bryan's incoherent babbling filled the silence in the car as he snored and fidgeted in his tiny winter jacket.

Life, as I knew it, was absolutely perfect.

The stars up above were reminiscent of those that shined just about a year earlier when Gemma told me we had two weeks until we were going to be parents. A lot had changed so drastically since then, but above all I was so complacent and happy with how things turned out.

Years ago from that sudden moment, if you had told me that I would be a responsible and stable father, I would have thought you were lying. Yet as I inhaled the thin, cool air that night while taking Bryan out of the car, life and all of its perfections were in full bloom.

∞ ∞ ∞ ∞ ∞ ∞ ∞ ∞

The next morning, I stood in the kitchen sipping coffee while looking around. Bryan was sound asleep, the whistling from the radiator was ever so slight, and I was happy. I was genuinely happy.

The Sunday morning melodies of small children and families gathering together to go shopping or go to church filled the streets. We were just days away from Christmas and Bryan's birthday had just passed.

Bryan was a year old and he seemed like he was adjusting to life in his father's care incredibly well.

I waited for a call from Gemma to talk about what exciting plans our family would have for the day, but again it was eerily quiet. Rebecca was passed out in her quaint room and I had just checked on Bryan moments before. The phone lay dormant on the wall with the twisted phone cord just yearning to be stretched.

'Hmm...' I thought. 'Gemma usually calls by now.'

Assuming she must have been tired from last night, I retreated into the bedroom and flopped onto the mattress. She would be calling any moment. I knew that.

As I watched the ceiling fan spin around and around, the phone finally rang. I popped up and dashed back into the kitchen to hear Gemma's sullen voice on the other end of the phone.

'What's wrong?' I was worried about her and I knew it was too quiet. Something had happened and my mind instantly shot to the worst-case scenario.

"It's Bryan." Gemma's voice dropped as she likely swallowed rather hard.

Confused and consumed with worry, I pulled the phone cord far enough to check and see if he was still in his crib.

'Bryan is safe. He is here with me.'

"No," she sighed. "I don't think you understand."

'Then tell me what is going on.'

"Bryan-" she was trying to collect her thoughts. "We-"

'Gem? What is it?'

"We were at the game last night." She finally murmured.

'Yeah, I know,' I said matter-of-factly. 'I was with you.'

"We were on television at the game last night."

'Yeah, I know. It was a publicly televised game.'

"My father-" she started to cry. "My father was watching the game."

My heart sunk. My face flooded with equal parts fear and despair. Her parents did not know about Bryan, and they must have seen us.

The next few moments were a blur.

"I will mourn you for one day," Gemma said, partially imitating the stern voice of her disappointed father. *"Just one day, Gemma. Then I want to meet my grandson."*

I did not know what to say.

Life did not prepare me to get kicked out of my house at sixteen, nor deal with the abuse from my mother.

Life did not prepare me to crash my car into a concrete wall.

Life did not prepare me to live or to die by the hands of any misfortune I had encountered in the past.

Life certainly did not prepare me to become a father at such a young and inexperienced age.

Yet somehow, I managed to learn what I needed to do in order to survive... at least up until this moment.

At this moment, I was about to find out what it meant for a father to be enraged by another father. I was unsure what life had in store for me now.

Gemma and I spoke for a little while longer and she said that her father refused to speak to her. I would spend the rest of the day pacing and praying for whatever was coming next.

I hugged and played with my son in hopes that his happiness and laughter could deter me from the anxiety I was feeling deep down in my bones.

Still, nothing could take away from what I could only imagine her father was going to do to me next.

All I could do… was wait for the inevitable hammer to fall.

If only I knew what the hammer was…

∞ ∞ ∞ ∞ ∞ ∞ ∞ ∞

The next morning, that Monday, I called out from work in fear of what was to come. Rebecca woke up early and helped me change Bryan's diaper while wishing me good luck.

When we heard the phone rang, both of us jumped and scurried into the kitchen.

With Bryan resting against my shoulder, I picked up the phone and took a deep breath. Before I could even say hello or conjure up any words to say, Gemma's father greeted me with a stern "Hello."

'Hello, sir,' I said, unsure of what to do or say next.

"I-" his voice softened and sounded more understanding than usual. "I would like to know if I could see my grandson today."

I smiled and Bryan cooed.

"Is that my boy?" Her father did not seem disappointed or upset. Her father seemed really intrigued by who Bryan was and what he looked like, so I promised to bring him over after Bryan ate some breakfast.

"See you soon," her father spoke sternly, yet quietly before he hung up. Gemma did not get on the phone at all, but I could assume she was upset.

I packed up a bag for Bryan and the two of us shuffled to Gemma's family home. I hoped that her parents were not truly upset by the news.

∞ ∞ ∞ ∞ ∞ ∞ ∞ ∞

As we sauntered up the steps, Bryan resting patiently in his car seat, the cherry-red front door swung open.

"Where is he?" Gemma's mother squealed, practically ripping the car seat from my arms.

"My boy," Gemma's father stood close behind her. "Let me see my grandson."

The two of us walked into the house and were greeted with a few presents: toys, clothes, and books for Bryan.

Gemma's parents took turns playing with Bryan and laughing with him throughout the day, while Gemma and I nervously waited for her father's stern conversation about the importance of being responsible.

Eventually after hours and hours of avoiding us and playing with Bryan, her father sat beside me and put his hand on my shoulder.

"I could sit here and tell you all about what it means to be a father, Scott." His grip tightened around my shoulder. "But it looks like you have been doing a superb job of raising him for a year now."

I gulped and let out a short breath, 'Thank you.'

"No," he started, "Thank you."

We took a walk outside for a while and discussed Bryan's life so far. The entire time, Gemma's father smiled and kept his hands tucked in his pockets. I told him the truth about the day Bryan was born and how we were worried about what he and Gemma's family would say.

The wisdom he imparted upon me was something I eventually passed down to my son, and I hope that he carries it with him throughout his life: "A gentleman is always honest. No matter how difficult something is, no matter how strange a situation it may seem, and no matter what is going on, a true man must speak the truth."

We smiled at one another and retreated back to the house for a pleasant family dinner. I finally felt that we were all a family.

As we held hands around the table and said a prayer for the family, I felt connected to Gemma and each and every person at the table.

I guess all we needed was a bit of faith to carry us through...

We had each other and we had a strong connection now, and nothing else in this world seemed to bother us, for we were genuinely together at last.

∞ ∞ ∞ ∞ ∞ ∞ ∞ ∞

As the New Year fell upon us, Gemma and I realized that our salaries were not helping our situation.

Neither of us had enough money to sustain the family.

We were beginning to get hit with a plethora of questions: How will you survive? What are you doing to take care of your family?

The queries went on and on, and I felt that we had an opportunity we needed to take: the two of us needed to do something in order to get our lives together. I was working the collections job and barely surviving day by day. I was not happy. I was not truly happy. I was happy with Gemma and our beautiful son, but I was not happy outside of the four walls we sealed ourselves behind.

The mounting pressures were pushing at our walls and the three of us had to leave.

"We could get two jobs each," Gemma said one night over dinner.

'Two jobs? How could we afford to work two jobs and take care of our child?'

She knew I was right, but I didn't know just how I was right. I felt that we could not work two jobs each and take good care of Bryan. Rebecca and Aunt Barbara were kind enough to babysit when they could, as were Gemma's parents and family, but we could not keep living the way we were.

"My uncle said that he could get us a job down in Texas."

'Texas?' I sputtered from my lips.

"The cost of living is way cheaper down there, and we could afford to stay home with Bryan more often." Gemma began playing with her fingers and twisting her lucious, flowing hair. I could feel her nervous energy from across the room as I looked down at Bryan playing with a toy on the floor.

We had to do just about anything we could to keep our family alive and well. We had to survive. We had to keep going.

We had to do something.

We had no choice but to move to Texas and simply pray for a window of opportunity there.

Our luck just had to change somehow, so maybe it would change when we moved to Texas. Staying in New York seemed less promising day by day. Though Aunt Barbara and Rebecca would be closer to us in New York, the money we could make in Texas *could* save our family.

We were stuck permanently between a rock and a hard place in New York, and we were running out of options.

Our only option became Texas.

And with our only option came a slew of obstacles and chaotic moments, but hey, in the words of Bon Jovi and his latest album at the time:

> *"And it's hard to hold on*
> *When there's no one to lean on*
> *Faith: you know you're gonna live thru the rain*
> *Lord, you got to keep the faith*
> *Faith: don't let your love turn to hate*
> *Right now we got to*
> *Keep the faith*
> *Keep the faith*
> *Keep the faith."*

And so... we kept the faith.

With what little belongings we had to our name, we picked up and moved our family to the Lone Star state...

If only I knew just how lonely of a state it was, I wondered if we would have made the same steps as a family.

Still, time and time again, Bon Jovi's words echoed through my ears: *"Keep the faith."*

CHAPTER 13

Southern Hospitality

"Sometimes I thank God for unanswered prayers. Remember when you're talkin' to the man upstairs. That just because he doesn't answer doesn't mean he don't care. Some of God's greatest gifts are unanswered prayers."

- Garth Brooks, American Country Music Singer, Tulsa, Oklahoma

Texas was our chance to start over. No one knew us really, so we could rewrite the stories we were telling everyone back at home.

Gemma's uncle promised us that the job I would get when we moved here would be helpful for both of us and Bryan, and we had no reason to doubt him, but as with everything in life there is a story behind the story.

We did not belong in Texas, or rather, the locals made us feel as if we did not belong in Texas.

No matter where we went in that small town we were treated like outsiders. I guess it was rather uncommon for new people to move to such an obscure place in Texas, but we were there and we were going to make the most of it.

The most important thing was for my family to be happy. As long as Gemma and Bryan were happy, then I was content. I was thrilled. I was excited.

Actually, I was lying to myself.

Standing on the streets of Cuero, Texas, I felt something was missing: a fundamental piece of my existence, a sentimental element of my soul.

Gazing into the graffiti eyes of an artist's exasperated and hopeful image for tomorrow, I confirmed what I knew in the depths of my soul: a part of me was in New York.

Another part of me was in Texas: my physical body. My skin, my hair, my hands... but my soul was split in half.

Something just seemed so out of place here.

I guess that something or someone is me.

Although bridges were always my way of symbolically identifying the transformations I was dealing with in my life, the old cobblestone bridge on one side of town did not have any inherent qualities that satisfied my soul. On top of that, the bridges that stood over and near the highways were just empty reminders that I was either far below the expectations of everyone in Cuero, or I appeared to be high above everyone because I was, as they deemed me, a "Dirty yankee."

Some bridges have to collapse before they are truly completed, I guess.

Though as Bruce Springsteen always said, *"It ain't no sin to be glad you are alive,"* and I was glad to be alive. I was happy that my family was finally together and under one roof, even if that roof is a rental home that Gemma's uncle and aunt give you with the option to buy the quaint home.

What was I saying… oh, well, still, it was home.
Our home.

∞ ∞ ∞ ∞ ∞ ∞ ∞ ∞

There are some stories from my Texas days that should not be told, nor should they even be remembered. In many ways, this brief reflection is not instrumental to the stories I tell, for I still talk about them anyway. Is it not true that all of our experiences leave an everlasting impression upon us, and amount to whom we grow into as human beings?

Perhaps I chose to talk about these stories and even live my life like this at the time in order to build up to something greater. They are not my proudest moments by any means necessary, and I wonder if any of these people are still alive today. I wonder what happened to these people. I wonder if they grew from their experiences. I wonder if they ever had the chance to change their lives and took their own leap of faith.

I wonder what happens to all of the people who play an important role in our lives, then fade into the shadows of whatever path they choose to embark upon.

Part of me thinks that I chose to move to Texas with Gemma and Bryan because I wanted to run away from the ghosts of my childhood. The memories of my abuse still haunted me each time I glared down at my right hand and saw remnants of where my knuckles were graced with glass.

Still, no matter how far you try to run from your demons, they will always catch up to you.

Always.

The sheer truth is that the demons we call memories often live in our minds and in our souls. They will follow you everywhere you go.

It is up to you to put your memories and demons to rest, so that you may be truly happy wherever you may roam: be it a different state or a different state of mind, you choose the path you must take in order to live freely. Never tether yourself to a treacherous memory, for it will be difficult to live devoid of tranquility without releasing negativity from your mind, body, heart, and spirit. Well, at least that is what I have learned.

The house Gemma, our son, and I rented was about the same size as the house I rented in Farmingdale, though the land we lived on was much larger. The house was white with a shabby, terra cotta-colored roof, but we were holistically on our own.

As we were unloading all of our belongings from the moving truck, two police officers pulled up behind it.

The two of them, wearing crisp brown uniforms and reflective aviator sunglasses, strolled up to us in unison.

"Are you stealing, boy?" One of them said to me. He slowly removed his glasses and placed them atop his head.

"You know, we are a small town and don't like *strangers*," the other officer started to circle me. Gemma retreated with Bryan in her arms. The two of them dashed into the house, seeming somewhat fearful of the strong presence of local law enforcement.

'Sir,' I spoke humbly while brushing my hair behind my ear. 'We have just moved here from the north.'

"We get that boy," the first officer said. He looked me up and down and tilted his head in disappointment. "We still don't like *your* kind here."

"Yankees and northerners are not *our* kind of folk," the other sneered.

'I am not stealing anything. I am here with my family for a better life,' I shrunk towards the moving truck.

"Heh-" the second officer chuckled. The two of them began retreating towards their vehicle.

"That's what they all say, boy." The first officer placed his sunglasses back on his face and looked back at me with a stern distaste in his mouth. "That's what they all say."

Gemma wanted to move down here so badly and I could not disagree with the argument of starting fresh, but the drama from our lives in New York followed me in Texas. I was an immature kid who could not handle the responsibility of living with his family in a house far from home.

This eventually led to the destruction of everything I stood for and the demolition of my relationship with Aunt Barbara, the only family I truly ever had. I hurt Gemma's family deeply and damaged my fair share of memories with my growing family.

Samuel, Gemma's brother, was a tall, lanky man who always tried to make everyone laugh. He was a dreamer and an X-Ray technician by day, but at night he was a multi-level marketing salesman who was trying to create his pyramid-esque climb to the top of the world. He ended up living close to us in Texas and encouraging us to participate in this enticing, "create your piece of the pie" concept.

This almost caused us to lose everything we had and added onto the mounting familial problems seeping throughout our household.

Samuel's wife Patricia was just as personable and friendly as her husband. She welcomed us to Texas with so much love and patience in her heart. Patricia consistently invited us to church, because, as she said, "That is just what you do in Texas: you go to church."

Gemma revealed as we settled into Cuero that Patricia was the one who would get me a job with a collections agency nearby.

Though I was promised the world and promised a job, it turns out that some words and promises are just as fragile as glass when spoken… for the promises made to us with regard to Texas were broken swiftly.

When I arrived at Victoria Hospital, which was the next town over, the "folks," as they said, took one fatal look at the New Yorker with long blonde hair and a child-like grin and refused to hire me. I should have really thought through moving to Texas, but in reality, I was a victim of my own poor choices. Upon leaving the interview, I spent the twenty-five minute drive home watching the dirt from the single-lane highway disappear in my rear-view mirror. I could not help but think about the homelessness problem that we face in New York.

There are people sprinkled throughout the five boroughs, living in squalor and garbage, yet this road seemed like it had plenty of space.

The open road showed no mercy, but apparently neither did the streets of New York.

∞ ∞ ∞ ∞ ∞ ∞ ∞ ∞

The first fourteen months in Texas proved difficult. I was miserable and tried just about everything, or at least I thought, to get my act together and, as the Texans said, "Man up."

Cuero was split in half by a set of train tracks that ran directly into the desert. Their straight lines were akin to the division that split my heart directly down the middle: I wanted to make Gemma and Bryan happy, but I was also rotting away inside.

Bebe, a tan gentleman who was heavily into the music scene in Texas, was my hope at a fulfilling experience in the Deep South. He lived on the other side of the tracks, and I would frequently walk across them to have a jam session in his makeshift music studio.

The two of us would talk for hours and hours about the rock and roll music scene, melodies, harmonies, and the impact lyrics had on our lives.

He was a Bon Jovi fan as well, and I felt that we had a sort of connection that could not be severed by anything.

In the days that followed from my first meeting and music session with Bebe, my entrance at church was a rather unappealing one. Samuel and Patricia, along with their church-going friends, scolded me for going to the other side of the tracks.

"Do you know what kind of people live there?" Patricia snarled.

"Those people are not like *us*." Another woman screeched.

They continued to bombard me with comments about how the "poor" people and the people on our side of the tracks are vastly different, and that no matter what, I should not cross the tracks to see him ever again.

Though we were under the eyes of Jesus hanging on a cross, his sacrifices and hardships seemed to be lost in the muddled words of hate and ignorance.

I continued to visit the other side of the tracks almost weekly to play music with Bebe despite the discerning glances from Cuero's folks.

To make matters much worse, I made an attempt to start my own medical collection agency. It failed miserably. Gemma and I fell short of paying the rent each month, so Aunt Barbara would send us some money just so we had a chance at survival.

Aunt Barbara was always looking out for my family and I, but when she secretly called Samuel one day to talk about my experience in Texas, I flipped out. I was beyond furious and felt my world shattering once again. In my eyes, she was being intrusive and waiting for all of the pieces to fall, just so she can pick them up and tell me what to do.

I was so fearful of that.

I was petrified that the ghosts from my past would continue to catch up with me: my mother's actions, my father's words, and Olga's disregard for my well being.

I was caught up in a net of my own immaturity and pain. I didn't know wrong from right and even if I did, I wonder if I would have had the guts to stand up for myself and declare that I needed more help than expected.

I was pushing everyone and everything far from my arm's reach, to the point where even Gemma was slipping through my fingertips.

Eventually, Aunt Barbara started to call less and less. Each time she spoke to me, all I did was argue with her.

Then the phone stopped ringing and I was left alone with Gemma's disapproving glances and my own deteriorating self-worth.

We did have Bryan, and at the end of the day he was all that mattered during our time in Texas.

∞ ∞ ∞ ∞ ∞ ∞ ∞ ∞

Going door to door to collect money from people who could not pay their medical bills was the absolute antithesis of what I stood for, but I was desperate for money. The medical bill collections agency was not panning out to be profitable, and I knew deep down that everything about it felt wrong, but I was in survival mode.

We moved to Texas as a family to begin anew, and here I was chasing scraps and demolishing any semblance of who I was as a man.

I had started going to church regularly and I was newly baptized, so I did what I thought was right. I began to speak to God regularly and ask him for guidance.

I begged God for help starting my own business in order to support my family.

In hindsight it was my first wish that the universe heard and internalized, though at the time I did not think I was speaking to the universe. I didn't even know if anyone out there was listening.

Within weeks, I was back on the streets looking for a job again… that's when I found Reliable Finance, which was yet another collections-type company. I was falling into the role of taking from people without considering what was being taken from me in the process.

Reliable Finance appeared to be a rather reliable job and one that welcomed me with open arms. My long blonde hair remained steadfast on my head, and I had no intention of changing any of my physical features to please the kind folks of Texas.

Mary, from Yoakum, TX, was a mature woman with flowing gray hair and the supervisor at good ol' Reliable Finance. The personal loan company was nothing like the medical collections agency, for I was not going to collect money from those who were sick and at the verge of dying, but the business of taking was shaping up to be something stable.

"You're a cutie," Mary said while pinching my cheeks. "You'll be great for door-to-door collections, they'll all *love* you." She winked and walked away.

Her compliments and overwhelming kindness graced my presence each morning at work.

I never had an interest in Mary, though I thought that it was cool that a mature woman was interested in me. As a crazy kid, I was drawn into the affection she would give me considering the fact that Gemma was inching further and further away from me at home. Physically and emotionally, I felt I was losing Gemma day by day.

It is weird, but it seems like when we are younger it seems awesome that an experienced, older woman is into you. Yet as we grow and mature, you think you're cool if a younger woman is into you.

We put too much effort on age, when it really is not about age. It is really about a bond or connection you make with another human being. Though Mary and I had somewhat of a cool connection, it paled in comparison to any sort of *real love* relationship I developed in years to come.

I despised and truly hated my job. Working there became a burden on my shoulders. Mary was the only solace I had at Reliable. She took care of me and supported me. She listened to who I was and what I was about or could be about.

I was too young and naive to appreciate her at the time, but I carried her sense of compassion with me throughout my entire life.

"Appreciate what you have and keep fighting for what you don't have." Her words of wisdom echoed throughout every door I knocked on in search of loan payments.

I quit that job the day some guy pointed a rifle in my face and told me to get off his property. My life was worth more than what measly loan payments I could collect from people.

I don't think Mary ever truly understood why I just left her high and dry, nor did I ever see Mary after that day, but I still think of her wisdom from time to time.

I scurried back home after I quit and told Gemma that we had to do anything we could to get back to New York. As Bryan cried in an effort to diffuse our insolent bickering, Gemma held him close to her chest with a dull smile on her face.

"I know. I know," Gemma whispered in an effort to calm Bryan. She glared up at me, our son in her now-heaving chest, and reached out for my face. Her fingertips were cold and clammy.

"I know."

∞ ∞ ∞ ∞ ∞ ∞ ∞ ∞

In the midst of everything, Gemma, Bryan, and I needed to return to New York temporarily. My grandfather passed away suddenly and we boarded a plane to attend the funeral. Bryan was complacent and quiet the whole time we were flying up, almost as if he knew we were going back there to mourn the loss of his endearing relative.

Although I was a rude and disrespectful kid most of the time, and I was ignoring my dear Aunt Barbara, I still loved my grandfather and the family that made me feel as if I belonged.

Rebecca came to pick us up at the airport and something within me knew she was dabbling in drugs. To make matters worse, I later found out she was using heroin. I had already stopped my cocaine use at this point, but I knew this was a terrible situation for my sister to be in.

As a parent, there are very few moments where you can truly tell if your child is listening. There are instances where you see your child reflecting or processing the knowledge you bestow upon him or her, but to see it in action is an entirely different experience. While everyone was standing around after I delivered my grandfather's eulogy, Bryan broke free from Gemma's grasp and walked up to the casket.

Everyone froze in fear, unsure of what to do or say.

Did Bryan understand what was going on? Could Bryan fathom loss at such a young age?

Bryan looked down at his great-grandfather, gave a small wave, and said good-bye. Gemma locked eyes with me and began to sob openly. I stood there, tears streaming down my face, looking at my boy. Bryan waddled back over to me and grasped my fingers. While his heartfelt gesture caused a wave of tears among the friends and family who gathered around, a voice within me that sounded just like my grandfather murmured, "I am so proud of you."

As the rain fell outside, I realized the curse of a torrential downpour on depressing days of my life was alive and well.

∞ ∞ ∞ ∞ ∞ ∞ ∞ ∞

My Aunt Barbara saw me in passing while I was in New York, but she did not say more than a few words to me:

"I still love you, my boy," she muttered to me as I stood in the doorway to my grandfather's funeral.

I walked past her and lived in a state of utter melancholy for the days that followed. I blamed myself for Rebecca using drugs, for I felt that I abandoned her just like my mother did to me.

As Gemma and Bryan slept against my shoulder on the plane ride back to Texas, I had to find something, anything, to bring me home.

When we returned to Texas the two of us made an effort to rekindle the romance in our relationship and ignite a fire within our bodies through any means necessary. While still in my inexperienced, child-like state of mind, I thought finding another job and earning what I could, might help us shift onto the right path together.

I had to fix all of the pain I was causing myself, and those who I loved. Aunt Barbara did not deserve how I treated her. Rebecca deserved a positive role model in her life. Bryan needed a father.

I worked at a fast food joint for a brief period of time. When that did not serve me, or my family, I took a job in a factory working shifts of 12 hours on and 12 hours off.

The grueling work was tedious and painful at times, but I kept thinking about my family. It was a plastics factory in Victoria, and I took root each day in front of a conveyor belt line. The pink goggles and latex gloves I wore made me feel as if I was suffocating.

I would pick up the garbage bags that cascaded down the line and place them in the boxes next to me. This routine would drone on and on all throughout the day or night. It was the most miserable, boring, mindless job you could ask for. It was a factory cloaked in darkness regardless of how the sun attempted to shine.

I would get a fifteen-minute break every four to five hours, with the clock looming over me and my nauseated expression consistently.

Life was composed of unchained melodies in which I would wake up to the sound of an alarm clock, listen to the radio on my way into work, listen for the bell when I would get a break, and then wait for the bell that signified I could clock out for the day.

At the end of my shift, I would saunter down to the convenience store in the area and pick up a measly hot dog to satisfy my hunger; that was dinner at 6:00 A.M.

It was not normal. It was not living at all. It did not make sense.

∞ ∞ ∞ ∞ ∞ ∞ ∞ ∞

One morning while in such a rush to just start my day, a herd of cows planted themselves in the middle of the road. I honked my horn. I pleaded with them. I begged God to let me just get past them.

Nothing worked. No one heard me.

After arriving an hour late to work, I told the foreman that I had to wait for all of the cows to get off of the road. He laughed, along with the other workers nearby, and said, "That's just the southern hospitality our little ol' state has to offer."

Of course, it's hospitality when you are late due to cows.

Of course, it's also hospitality when you are belittled and looked down upon by townspeople.

Of course, it's common courtesy when you are treated like just another cog in a machine.

Later in the evening, weeks after I spent all of my energy slaving away in the factory, I stepped out into the midnight sky. It was about 3:00 in the morning and the small patch of grass that existed in the distance barely felt the cool, crisp sensation of dew.

My grandfather had recently passed away and that was still on my mind. I admired him and missed him, and wished that I could have spent more time appreciating him. That's the thing about loved ones who pass away: you do not often realize or acknowledge the memories you are creating while those cherished individuals walk the planet, but the moment their existence is a mere memory, life changes. The sensations we feel, their voices that comforted us, the look in their eyes when the person's pupils drifted over you in endearment, they are replaced by acknowledging a life that was hopefully well lived. We must individually carry on the legacies of our loved ones when they are gone, and cherish every fleeting second as it ticks on by.

I watched the carefully illuminated American flag waving in the wind. It flew high above on a pole and represented so much more than just a symbol of nationalism in our country.

I thought about my grandfather who fought in World War II. His bravery and courage carried him through even the darkest of nights. They helped him stand tall on nights just as the ones I spent at the factory: though sadness and longing were coursing through my veins, he carried on.

The red stripes on the flag were reminiscent of the blood that still persevered through my body. The white stripes signified the purity that embodied what all of us once felt and could feel again.

All fifty of the stars contrasted against the blue square in the corner represented individual declarations of independence: each star depicted a state that had its own story...

Everyone and everything carries a story behind the story.

I closed my eyes, took a deep breath, and darted towards the payphone.

"Hello," Gemma's groggy voice materialized in my ear.

'I quit. Come pick me up.'

She packed Bryan in the car and was sitting before me in the reflection of the moonlit night.

We drove down this deserted highway in the middle of nowhere. The farmland surrounded us on either side. I turned to her in the eerie silence and let my eyes drag along her defined silhouette.

I had a future. I had a life to live. I was worth more than the penniless jobs I was accustomed to.

I spoke the first words that materialized on my mind, body, and spirit: 'I am going to make something out of myself. Not this, but something.'

She didn't reply.

I vowed I was going to make my grandfather proud. I was going to make them all proud of me. I was going to show my son that we were not born to follow.

∞ ∞ ∞ ∞ ∞ ∞ ∞ ∞

To diffuse the tension brewing within me, Gemma, Samuel, Patricia, Bryan, and I went to the local county fair. There were various activities, small toys, the aroma of apple pies cooling in the wind, and children laughing along with the rustic banjos being played by amateur musicians on stage.

Bryan, Gemma, and I approached the carnival games, with my hopes of winning Gemma and Bryan a stuffed animal brewing within my budding confidence. When I finally tossed the small rubber ball into a stationary cup atop some old wooden box, I was thrilled to finally win at something.

I felt alive, and then I felt like an idiot. While northerners are accustomed to winning stuffed animals at a fair, I was now the proud owner of a live baby chicken.

Patricia convinced us that we just had to buy more chickens so that our new, precious chick was not alone.

Gemma seemed happy, Bryan was chanting, "Dada" over and over again with excitement brewing in his voice, and I had to take this opportunity to keep them happy.

The next day when I was walking through the local farm supply shop attempting to find something for all of my future pets to feed upon, I saw an advertisement for a Disc Jockey, or DJ, position at a local club.

I pulled the phone number from a small piece of paper hanging on the advertisement and considered that my luck was about to change. I knew music rather well, I was sure that local clubs and bars in the area were looking for someone with an ear for excitement, and I knew I only had one question lingering in my mind: What was the worst that could happen?

CHAPTER 14

Bottom's Up

~

"You were always so lost in the dark. Remembering you... how you used to be. Slow drowned. You were angels... So much more than everything."

- The Cure, British Alternative Pop/Rock Band, Crawley, West Sussex, United Kingdom

Bryan waddled up to me with an inquisitive look in his eye. I was wearing a midnight blue tie Gemma had picked out for me and I hoped that everything was about to go according to my master plan: I would get this job, I would make money, and we could move back to New York.

"Dada," Bryan squeaked. "Where are you going?"

'I have to go to work,' I kissed him on the forehead. 'I'll be home soon.'

He smiled and tottered back into the other room.

Gemma kissed me on the cheek and wished me luck, and I was out the door in seconds.

I nervously smoothed my tie as I drove up to a club called "Velvet Ropes." It sounded incredibly classy, considering the area was quite different from Cuero. Victoria was as close to an urban town as you could get without travelling for hours to get to major cities like Austin or Houston.

The club was a small white building with a fairly decent size parking lot. The thought of working as a DJ was exciting to me as it brought me back to my younger years of mixing songs with my friends in the International Beer Club.

The moment I walked into the club my life had changed. I was oblivious to the topless girl dancing around the pole on stage, because if I saw her when I immediately walked in, I am sure I would have turned around and ran right out. Fear and intimidation would have caught the best of me.

I was definitely far from my sexual prime and understanding the true concepts of making love. Anything sexual was frightening and uncontrollable, despite the fact that I had encounters with women before Gemma.

I asked a waitress at the bar for the owner and was introduced to Gina. Gina was a southern lady with a thick accent, young, and somewhat on the curvier side. She was very sweet and asked me about my experience with music. Gina explained to me that the club actually belonged to her father, but he owned several in Houston and was not around here much. She basically ran the day-to-day operations.

Gina showed me around the club and introduced me to the DJ booth. When I say this was not like the deejaying of old, I mean it really wasn't. The place was crawling with some CDs and a jukebox, and a "no brainer" to operate. There was a small mixing board in the center of the booth and the system was easy to understand in about two minutes flat.

She asked me about my taste in music and she seemed to appreciate my eclectic taste. She told me if I was hired, I would need to bring my own CDs and use them whenever possible. Gina said that I would have to work with the girls on the music for their routines and announce things like drink specials and silly catchphrases like "You don't have to go home but you can't stay here" when it was time to close.

I left the club excited because the job seemed exciting and promising. Still, there was a sense of trepidation burning in my core. The parking lot was empty when I walked out, but I still felt that I had a chance to finally earn some money to bring my family back to New York.

Then, in flashing neon letters, it hit me. I gazed up at the Velvet Ropes sign in the far corner of the lot and saw the phrase underneath, which slammed me right in the face: "Gentlemen's Club."

The routines Gina spoke about would be dancing routines, as in music the girls would strip to.

As I drove home, I was trying to figure out ways to break the news to Gemma. She would never agree to me getting a job at this club. There would be a million naked girls walking around and ogling at me day in and day out.

To my utter disbelief and shock, she was supportive.

We had a plan and that was to get back home. Gemma agreed that no matter what, we had to do whatever we could to support Bryan and bring us back to where we inherently belonged.

Desperation swallowed us whole. Neither of us had time to digest what was going on; we just both wanted a way out.

We wanted a window of opportunity and just about anything that looked feasible was plausible for us.

∞ ∞ ∞ ∞ ∞ ∞ ∞ ∞

On the eve of our fourth anniversary together, the phone rang rather abruptly. I had assumed that I did not get the job when I did not hear from Gina right away, for I figured that my long hair and New York drawl scared them away. However, Gina called and told me that Velvet Ropes could not wait to have me as a DJ.

My life each and every night until the day I drove back to New York would be an amalgamation of glitter, music, raunchy women, mistakes, and poor decisions.

I was living a shallow existence built upon drama and chaos, and this situation was not making my life any easier.

I dashed out the door around 5:00 in the evening and kissed Gemma on the forehead before I left.

"Go do this for our family," she shouted after me. I could feel it in her voice that she was upset we could not spend the night together, but I knew, deep down, she wanted to go to New York more than anything in this world...

Or so I thought.

∞ ∞ ∞ ∞ ∞ ∞ ∞ ∞

When I arrived with a handful of CDs in a plastic bag, Gina had the girls line up and introduce themselves to me.

"Everyone, I want you to meet our new DJ," Gina shouted.

The girls gathered around, doused in glitter and too much make-up for their own well being, and smiled.

'Hi,' I remarked coyly. I was unsure what to say or do.

One of the girls lifted her shirt up and revealed her breasts.

"Hey big boy," she remarked in a raspy voice. "I am Chastity."

I gulped.

Two of the girls, Starr and Christian, waved politely.

A blonde moved inches from my face and began to warn me about harassment:

"The name is Summer. So you know, harassment is a major concern in the line of work we do." She thrusted her hips into mine and started running her fingers down my back.

'Excuse me-' I began panicking.

"Shh." She placed her finger over my lips. "We are allowed to pinch your ass. It's okay."

It really was far from okay.

'For my family,' I whispered under my breath. 'For my family.'

∞ ∞ ∞ ∞ ∞ ∞ ∞ ∞

Standing alone in the corner, I became a purveyor of the cultural habitat I became immersed in. There were so many bodies scantily clad in whatever they were suddenly accustomed to wearing. It became a rather overwhelming sensation I just could not seem to shake.

My life was about to change.

The woman on stage was dangerously sexy. Her luxurious legs rocked backwards onto the stage with the rest of her tender frame. Men were launching money in her direction, at this unknown beauty masked in far too much makeup for her dainty age, yet there was something... something erotic protruding from her overall presence.

It was sensational and it was sickening all on one fatal swoop. I could not pull my eyes away from her devilish grin, yet something within me was burning. It was not a sensual burn, but rather a warning sign... a red light... a bad omen of sorts. It was only fitting that her name was-

My mind went blank mid-thought.

She approached me and my thoughts grew more perplexing and discombobulated. Her fingernails, crimson and glittered with what resembled diamonds, gripped the corner of the DJ booth.

"Hun-" her voice was stern, dark, and just as mysterious as her...

"Play my song on cue this time, 'kay sugar? The last guy always fucked that shit up," her eyes pierced right through my guts.

She would be trouble. I knew it. I felt it throughout my body.

"Chastity," another female's voice cut through the crowd.

It belonged to one of the most stunning faces I had ever laid eyes upon. Beautiful. Sexy. Classy. Jet-black hair. Perfectly proportioned. All of her walking towards me. Her smile glowed with the fervor of the sun. She was just naturally glowing, a stark contrast to the haughty image of the strip club. Her sultry voice rested in my ear as she wrinkled her perfect little nose for a split second:

"Hey," she grinned and extended her alabaster hand, "I'm Starr. What's your name?"

'Scott,' I spoke nervously, 'The name is Scott.' The second our hands touched I felt a rush of adrenaline push itself throughout my body. I was moments away from losing the ability to speak from just being in her sheer presence.

If Gemma could see me then, she would have surely knocked me right in the jaw. Who knows what my son would have said if he could even mutter more than four words. For love and for money… for our return to New York… I'm here for love and for money…

For Gemma… for Bryan… for my family…

"Your mind looks like it is fluttering elsewhere," Starr was still standing there, twisting her head in sheer curiosity.

'It's-' I began nervously.

"Is it your first time working in a club like this," she plopped her body joyfully on the stool near me. She leaned into every word I said. Starr was one of the most genuine individuals I had met since the moment I came to Texas.

There is no shortage of words when describing the beauty that was Starr: alluring, classy, perfectly proportioned from her long flowing hair atop her head to her delicate little toes. Her jet-black hair always swayed in tune with her hips that rock like an infinity symbol. If you watched her, her physical and spiritual beauty infinitely struck you. With a flick of her hips, she made you believe in heaven on earth.

Chastity was the exact opposite of the name she wore. Rather than be chaste and pure, she would take explicit joy in being the furthest thing from the embodiment of justice and all things right in the world. Her fire engine red hair appropriately warned you how she could burn you in an instant, and how dangerous she was, but if you were too ignorant to pay attention, you, too, would feel the wrath of her sirens.

I played the music that the girls asked for. I put on some different songs throughout the night that seemed to liven up the crowd. The men in the audience were throwing money around at the girls and shouting raunchy obscenities.

I felt miserable, but not because I was genuinely feeling that way. I felt miserable because the women were ordinary people who were not the personas they put forth on a stage for all to see.

We all wear masks and fall victim to false judgments; however, it is a stark reality we live in: we can choose to continue to identify as the victim, or we can stand.

While cleaning up for the night, Chastity snuck into the DJ booth. "Rough first day?" She whispered in a sultry voice.

I tried not to look up at her. I did not want her to lift her shirt again or do something off-color. She noticed how uncomfortable I was and began to speak to me in a rather normal tone.

We began talking about Gemma and Bryan along with our aspirations for New York. Chastity spoke about her family problems and gave me a bit of advice before leaving me to tidy up for the night: "Loosen up, Scott. Everything will be okay."

I left the booth soon after and drove home. Gemma and Bryan were sound asleep by the time I got in at 3:00 in the morning, but it did not seem to matter.

I made it through the first night.

∞ ∞ ∞ ∞ ∞ ∞ ∞ ∞

Every weekend there was a feature dancer that was on tour. That first weekend, Raquella Stroke was the first woman I worked with. She said that I had quite a collection of music and even gave me a $7 tip at the end of the night.

It was exciting. I was getting tips from the dancers and I thought I was rich!

Christian, one of the girls from the first night I started, dashed up to the DJ booth as I was cleaning up from my second day at work and began flirting with me. I was hoping that she would not begin acting just like Summer, and I quickly grew uneasy.

There was just something about her. Christian's short blonde hair and friendly demeanor did not seem to fit the stereotype of a dancer that floated around in my head.

As a matter of fact, the first thing I learned that weekend is that most of the girls were not just dancers: they were people. I began speaking to them one by one and learned a lot about their stories. One of the girls, Kyla Rae, had a loyal following of customers that her boyfriend Alexander did not like.

She also said that Alexander did not appreciate me speaking to her frequently throughout the night and after work. The two of us locked eyes from across the room; his brown eyes narrowed when he saw my long hair.

"Yankee," I saw him mouth from clear across the club.

"He has a gun, you know. We all have guns down here," Kyla Rae whispered.

I almost bolted from this job, too, but I was beyond exhausted. I had this voice inside of me that said to just move forward, get the money I needed, and get out of the south.

"Hey Scott," Starr's distinct voice broke from the far corner of the room. "A bunch of us are going to The Kettle to get pancakes. Do you want to come with us?"

Starving and ready to collapse, I did what any exhausted young man would do: 'Sure, let me just shut the lights.'

I was at the top of the world. A beautiful woman wanted to have pancakes with me at 2:00 in the morning, I was working in a strip club, and I was able to play music all night. What more could a guy ask for?

There were turbulent moments and enticing moments, but regardless my emotions were all over the place. The skeletons in my closet danced before me every single night, and I was never sure of anything that would happen at work other than the paycheck that was waiting for me at the end of the week.

Well, I was always certain I would see someone every night: Louie. He was a regular customer who always bought booze, but never sat up front launching money at the girls. We quickly became friends once he came over to chat for a bit.

Louie revealed that he hung out there every night because he had such a nasty case of insomnia.

"Life changes once you've seen the things I've seen," Louie said while tilting his drink into his mouth.

'I hear you, man.'

"No," he gulped. "You don't really. I was in Desert Storm. I watched bloodshed happen before me during an experience I wish I could forget."

The sound of Golden Earring's "Radar Love" blared in the background, but we stood in silence. His tone hinted that there were things that the government hides when it comes to war, which made me realize that the internal pain he was dealing with was running rampant through the minds of other soldiers.

He saw an actual war. I was just battling a war within myself. There is a story behind every person's story.

We spoke about his experiences as the girls shed their clothes. Men were throwing dollar bills at them like savage animals. Hooting and hollering filled the air and almost drowned out mine, and Louie's conversation.

Louie and I would continue our nightly conversations for months to come, but we knew our place in the grand scheme of what was happening in the club.

When Kyla Rae and Starr kissed on stage, I realized that nothing could truly faze me at this point. Still, I was intrigued by the glance that Starr gave me when she broke away from Kyla Rae. Starr's seductive wink in my direction did not make me feel uneasy, and this was the first time I felt a sort of weird sensation at Velvet Ropes.

Christian stayed after that night and began to open up to me about how she was stripping to pay for her chemotherapy treatments. She lifted her short blonde wig from her head and told me about her pancreatic cancer.

This shattered my heart beyond comprehension: she was human.

"I only have a few months left to live," she said. "I might as well make them fun."

I remember thinking that she was going to die and no one would hear her story. On her days off, she would travel by herself to Houston to get her treatment, then return by nightfall so she could dance and make money.

"We all fight battles within that no one knows about," she would remark nightly, almost as if it were her motto or saving grace.

The days that followed were just as eventful as the last, with my paycheck firmly clasped in my hand I returned home to see Bryan's gentle smile.

How hard could this routine be, especially when there was nothing routine about it?

∞ ∞ ∞ ∞ ∞ ∞ ∞ ∞

Louie called me up one night during my second week of work and asked if he could join Gemma, Bryan, and I for dinner.

Happily, we set the table for four and welcomed him into our humble house with open arms.

"So how do you two know each other?" Gemma asked while feeding Bryan.

"We met at work; I frequent there every night-" Louie replied.

"Oh." Gemma sounded somewhat intrigued.

"It's not what you think, ma'am," Louie began to backpedal his tone. 'Strip clubs are not what you think, Gem.'

Bryan grabbed a glob of mashed potatoes and shuffled it into his mouth.

"I know." Gemma shot me a glance. "I *know*."

We left the conversation at that and had a pleasant evening with Louie, though Gemma said that she wanted to come visit me at work within the next few days.

I saw no problem with it, for I knew Gemma was okay with the situations, however I was blindly unaware as to what fantasies were brewing in her mind.

∞ ∞ ∞ ∞ ∞ ∞ ∞ ∞

Sunrises and sunsets became mere indicators that a new day was starting and old news was fading away. Something felt awry, but I could not place my finger on just what was going on.

Life was happening at 800 miles per hour, and I was sitting in the fast lane just waiting to get bombarded by what came next.

Then Gemma walked into Velvet Ropes.

"Hi Scott," she approached me rapidly and gave me a kiss on the cheek. 'Hi honey.' I did not know what else to say.

We spoke briefly for a bit until Chastity made her way over to us.

"You must be Gemma, Scott raves about you!" Chastity interjected.

"How thoughtful of him," Gemma said in a hushed tone.

The moment their eyes met, I saw excitement flood through Gemma's expression. Recently, I had not seen Gemma look so happy, until she looked right at Chastity.

'Gem, this is Chastity.' My words faded. The girls were getting along quite well.

Starr sauntered over and began chatting with me. She had hinted at wanting to take me out on a date one night, but I always turned her down. She was gorgeous and all-around stunning, and the two of us seemed to have a connection, but I was too focused on getting Gemma, Bryan, and I back to New York.

Gemma's priorities seemed to change however, once she locked eyes with Chastity.

"Why don't you guys come out to The Kettle with us after work?" Chastity did not break eye contact with Gemma.

'We have to get home to Bryan.' I declared.

"Bryan is with Patricia and Samuel, he is fine for the night," Gemma seemed eager to spend more time with Chastity.

To make her happy, I complied with Chastity's invitation.

When we went out later that night, Chastity, her friends, and a few of the girls from the club started passing a joint around. I refused because I was clean at this point, but I felt that we were getting ensnared in a net that we just might not get out of.

Gemma caught that I was getting uncomfortable, and nudged me to relax.

Where were we all going? What were we doing?

When the sun rose through the window, we realized that we had been at The Kettle for hours and hours just talking.

The coming days would be filled with uncertainty, with Gemma joining the crew at Velvet Ropes almost nightly.

On the way home one night, Gemma and I began talking about how our lives were taking quite a peculiar turn.

Gemma glanced over at me and cautiously opened her mouth; "Did you ever think you would end up working in a club like this in Texas?"

'Not really,' I replied. 'But life is unpredictable.'

"Tell me about it," she smirked at me. "I mean, we're parents."

We smiled as she wrapped her arm around my arm.

Gemma leaned her head on my shoulder as we continued walking.

The stars glistening in the sky were vastly different from what we were accustomed to seeing in New York, yet I inherently knew we were looking at the same space.

It was all a matter of perspective and sometimes beautiful things can only be seen when you are looking up.

"Hey," the two of us stopped for a moment and Gemma began twiddling her thumbs.

'What's wrong?'

"I-" her voice was a bit shaky.

'Gemma, you can tell me anything.'

"I know," she sighed. "Do you think I should get a job?"

'What?'

"Do you think I should get a job at the club to help us earn more money?"

'I mean,' I smiled at her. 'What sort of job would you do there? Bartend?'

"Dance."

'Dance?'

"Yeah," her eyes began to search along my face.

We both paused for a moment.

'Is that something you would be interested in?'

"Um," she swallowed. "Yes. Yes, I think so."

'If that is what you think is best-'

Gemma was uncertain again, "I mean, you work there. You come home with a pretty good paycheck every week."

'Yeah, and it really isn't a bad job. Everyone there is nice.'

"I really like the girls and their stories. This feels right to me for some reason. I hope you don't mind," Gemma remarked.

'Mind?' I shifted my body towards her and tilted my head.

"If we work together, we can get a lot of money. We can get out of here faster."

A resolute silence stood between us.

'I agree,' I rubbed the back of my neck with my right hand. 'I totally agree.'

I was numb to what was happening nightly at the club, but she was right.

"We get to see each other and we can work together to help our family."

Gemma was dedicated to our family and creating a better life for us. She would have done just about anything for Bryan, and for us.

Later that morning, my worlds collided: Gemma applied for a job at the club. She would become Velvet Ropes' next infamous dancer.

Things were spiraling out of control and spinning rapidly.

Starr approached me three weeks into my job at the club and struck up a conversation. Out of the corner of my eye, I saw Chastity and Gemma flirting. I knew that Gemma was bisexual, but I did not know how passionately she felt about Chastity. Starr touched my face and tapped my nose with her pointer finger.

I later discovered that Chastity and Starr had some sort of silent yet obvious competition between them. It was respectful, though their allure commanded an audience nightly.

We continued our nightly tradition of going to The Kettle, eating pancakes, then going home to sleep for a few hours. Gemma's tips were growing day by day, and it was apparent that she knew what she was doing.

Our path to New York was getting closer and closer.

Though it is always darkest before dawn.

∞ ∞ ∞ ∞ ∞ ∞ ∞ ∞

One Saturday evening as all of the days were beginning to blur together, Starr approached me and said that Summer, a friend of theirs named Alonzo, Gemma, her and I would be going to a hotel nearby. When I asked why, she said that a handful of us were going to have a little fun.

The hint of excitement in her voice worried me. This probably led to the worst moment of my life.

Starr was seeing Alonzo socially, though he was married and clearly had feelings for Kyla Rae and Summer. Starr brought myself, Gemma, Alonzo, and Summer to one of the shabby rooms at this run-down motel.

My hands began to shake and the sweat pouring down my sideburns gave way to how I felt in those moments.

"Lighten up, it's an adventure," Gemma stroked my arm and smiled at me.

I still didn't feel any less anxious.

I was struggling to procure true happiness, so anything and everything secretly scared me. Even if I didn't make it fully known, I was still questioning everything.

Once the door shut behind the five of us, Summer began taking off her pants and leather jacket. She was standing before the four of us with her lace magenta thong peeking out from her tattered t-shirt.

I grabbed a beer from the counter and popped it open. I desperately wanted to drink it, but upon shifting my eyes to what was going on in the room, I placed the bottle down.

I was not going to sleep with anyone. My fear and Gemma's presence got the best of me. Though the moment Alonzo grabbed Gemma and began passionately kissing her neck and undressing her, I looked to Starr who was already in her matching red and black studded lingerie.

I liked Starr, I really did, but my heart was just not in it.

She pulled me close and started to kiss me, but I could not take my eyes off of Gemma and Alonzo.

Even after Starr and I had finished up, I could not pull my glance from Gemma and Alonzo, who were still going at it. Summer walked over and began to engage with the duo. Starr and I just sat and watched. Gemma appeared to be incredibly satisfied while I just looked down at my lap.

Something deep within me broke. I did not feel like I was enough, and I felt incredibly vulnerable in that room.

After that moment, I became eternally self-conscious about being with someone physically. I was a mess.

As if it could not get worse, Starr ended up telling everyone about it the next day at work. I walked in on everyone laughing about it, and began to get slapped on the ass and called, "Champ" by everyone there. Even Gemma.

She may have been joking, but my heart cracked into a few more pieces that day.

I always listened to everyone's drama and problems, yet when it came to an insecurity I was dealing with, no one bothered to consider my emotions.

Even at home, I could not face Gemma without feeling immense pain. She morphed into one of the dancers practically overnight, and though we slept in the same bed, we were thousands of miles apart.

∞ ∞ ∞ ∞ ∞ ∞ ∞ ∞

The following days were filled with snickers and sneers, and Gemma barely even spoke to me. We were inching further and further apart from one another, and our surroundings were not helping us.

The hardest part of coping with depression is standing in a room filled with people, but feeling as if you are all alone… and in all honesty, I was very lonely. Something unidentifiable at the time continued to be broken deep within me. There I stood watching everyone smiling, dancing, and laughing, and I must admit that I did all of that too, but behind my smile was deep-rooted pain. When I gazed over at Alonzo and saw him talking to Gemma, and touching her playfully, I grabbed a drink and pounded it down my throat.

I fell off the wagon after so much restraint, and I had never felt so ashamed.

The rest of the night was almost a total blur. I could barely focus on what was in front of me, because a haze of alcohol clouded my vision. How many drinks I had became the million-dollar question: 6? 8? 12? I think the only ones who could tell me were even more intoxicated than I was. It was really no surprise.

When I finally plopped down into a chair, I gazed around the room and was thrust into a whirlwind of chaos. Nothing made sense and no one even acknowledged my presence. I became an afterthought, a warm body in a crowded room… I just blended into the scene that was being painted in the room. I was just another flower perched in a fragrant meadow.

"Scott, you in there," I heard beaming through the air, "Scott?"

Chastity was standing right in front of me, but she seemed miles away.

"Hun," I saw her place her hands on my shoulders, but I felt nothing, "you good?"

Words were melting through my teeth, but I could not hear what I was saying.

"It's Christian… She's hyperventilating… Do something!" Her words were echoing around my head, but they barely registered on my face. My demeanor was caught between a flush of Captain Morgan and Ginger Ale and the pangs of righteousness that were trying to wrap around my twisted brain.

As the phrase "Do something" slowly crept through my head, I rose from the chair as if I were flying. I was being drawn to Christian's soul, which was crackling and dropping to the floor teardrop by teardrop.

Dazed and confused, I managed to find her against the wall shaking violently. The world came back into focus as I looked at her shattered eyes.

'Christian, can you hear me,' I shouted into her face.

She kept shaking violently and melting further into the floor. I grabbed her shoulders and snapped back into reality. The haze of alcohol that captivated me faded through her tears.

"S-S-Scott," she questioned shakily.

Her gaze readjusted to meet mine.

"I-I-I am s-s-s-so co-ld-d-d," she managed to murmur.

Her eyes were engorged in yellow and red pools of capillaries.

I whisked her into my arms and dragged her into the bathroom. Instantaneously, she wretched, right into the toilet. Her necklace clanged against the porcelain with such force as she continued to lurch forward. I held her as gently as I could despite how ill she was getting.

How much did she drink?

Would I vomit like that in a few minutes?

Was it just alcohol that plagued her body… or did she take something?

I steadied her body so she could readjust her feet. She fell back into me as I did the only thing I could think of at that moment: I held her. I cradled her head and shoulders as if she were a child. The tears that ran from her face and the breaths between her persistent heaving stopped me from worrying about where Gemma was at that moment. For now, I had a purpose: to save Christian from the depths of her loneliness.

"I can't," she shouted, crying as each letter fell from her lips, "I can't keep going on this way."

Her cries became more desperate with each passing moment.

'It is going to all be okay,' I whispered into the side of her head, 'I promise.'

My promises were no match for the violent vomit that spawned from her body and into the toilet bowl.

When she finally rocked back into my arms, I repositioned her so she could see my face.

'Sit up straight and give me your hands,' I extended my arms, palms facing up, so she could find shelter in resting her hands in mine.

She placed her hands on mine rather weakly, almost as if she was handing me her soul so I could repair it.

'Close your eyes, inhale through your nose and exhale through your mouth,' as the words eased out of my mouth, I felt the world shift on its axis. The universe was cuddling us at that very moment, almost to say, "Hold on, your life has a purpose, and you are about to discover it."

Christian sat there inhaling a new perspective and exhaling the pain. Eternity could have passed us by at that moment, and we would have never noticed. I felt sincere peace in watching her transform into something revolutionary. She was finding her center, her balance, before my very eyes.

She finally opened her eyes and wore a new disposition on her face. Her entire aura became lighter, and her soul was visibly different.

"Thank you," were the only words that came out of her mouth periodically for the next few minutes.

When we finally stood up and exited the rusty bathroom stall, she gave me a genuine hug and said, "You are a healer. You have more heart in your body than you realize… don't waste it."

Moments later she exited the bathroom and faded into the crowd again. There I stood, looking out among all the faces in the room and discovered that it is possible to be alone in a packed room, but it is also possible to find purpose in the slightest of moments and the smallest of actions.

I ran into the Men's Room for a moment to collect myself. Sitting on the sink, mocking me, glaring up at me, was about a gram of cocaine in a small baggie.

This was my chance. I was in utter and complete pain.

I gave up drugs already. I tried giving up alcohol, but the devil that lives at the bottom of a bottle of rum is so enticing. I heard the battle roaring within me.

Could I do this? Could I turn away? Should I even bother turning away?

I continued filling my mind with questions and slid the bag in my pocket. I figured that I would think about it and let the future version of myself decide my fate.

The door swung open and I raced out of the room. Velvet Ropes was in need of its DJ, and I had to work.

By the end of the night, Gina and I were the only two left in the place. Louie had left to try getting some sleep, Gemma was who knows where, and all of the girls retreated to wherever they called home.

I rushed back into the bathroom and dumped the cocaine down the toilet. Who was I kidding? I was clean.

And I always would be.

I was not going back to the man I was.

Being on cocaine is quite a high, but beating cocaine and recently overcoming alcohol create an even better high.

When I walked back into the main stage area of the club, I saw Gina sitting with a bottle of vodka to her lips.

'Gina, are you okay?' I approached her slowly and watched the tears stream down her face.

"That's a good idea," she mumbled. "Ask a crying drunk if they are ok."

Her tinge of sarcasm was humorous and unsettling at the same time.

The song "Just Like Heaven" from The Cure could be faintly heard in the background:

"You, soft and only, you lost and lonely
You, strange as angels
Dancing in the deepest oceans
Twisting in the water
You're just like a dream
You're just like a dream."

"My friend was murdered here at Velvet Ropes not too long ago." Gina began heaving and took another swig from the bottle.

We went through every grueling detail and talked through the night. It was a pretty powerful moment for both of us. I remember I wanted to help people. I was seeing a real side to humans in an environment that wasn't very healthy.

Gina pulled me in close and embraced me. It was about 5:00 in the morning and she sighed in relief.

"Thank you," she sobbed openly.

'Why are you thanking me?'

She pulled away from me and explained that I was the first person she could ever open up to and she did not understand why.

It was the first time I felt special, maybe ever. Despite the insanity and the turmoil, I felt at peace. That night led me to seeing a perspective that delved further into the "story behind the story" ideology.

We would continue to spend nights having conversations about her emotions, and I realized that I was in Texas for a reason.

I learned that even when people lose their best friends in a shooting, they are still able to keep moving forward due to the power of that person's legacy and energy in this world. It was one of the first times somebody told me: "I don't know how you, or why you came into my life, but thank you." The night before that court case, the clubs closed at two o'clock because that's the law and I stayed there for hours and hours, talking to Gina about how she could not believe the case was going to trial.

I always considered myself to be a caring and giving person, but that was a string of real powerful moments. Texas had a purpose. It was not just about sex, drugs, and mayhem. It was an introspective process through experience. My inquisitive mind ran rampant. It was about discovering questions like how do we fix the drug problem in our country? How do we fix the healthcare system in our country? What does the American flag that flies up above genuinely represent?

The moments matter. The stories matter. The stories of different individuals and the roles they play matter. The memories of what matters live on. The heartbeats and souls of those who walk and roam this planet matter. I am going to make sure they all matter with regards to whatever I choose to do in life.

∞ ∞ ∞ ∞ ∞ ∞ ∞ ∞

Gemma came rushing up to me at work one night. She was frantically calling my name, to the point where I thought something was on fire. She rarely spoke to me at work.

"Scott, Christian never came into work. Something is wrong," she shouted.

'Hold on, hold on, what?' I took the headphones off of my ears.

"She is not picking up at home either. Something happened."

I knew about Christian's situation and what was happening at home, so I naturally told Gina I had an emergency and ran over to her house.

As I stepped out of the club I was met with violent winds and bright lightning. I feared the worst: each time someone I knew passed away, the skies opened up and the rain was unforgiving.

I prayed that Christian would not be another person I would need to mourn.

Her car was parked right out front, but none of the lights were on in her house.

Something was wrong.

I tried the front door, and fortunately, because people in Texas apparently do not lock their doors, I was able to get in.

Christian was sobbing on her bed and throwing up in a bucket near her. I sat next to her, propping her up against my body, and just asked her to speak to me.

She did.

She asked me to hold her close.

I did.

Through her tears and the words that were spilling out of her mouth, she cried about using drugs, her chemotherapy treatments, and feeling lost in general. Christian fell sound asleep in my arms and I didn't go anywhere.

I slept next to her the whole night.

Come morning, she did not wake up. Christian rolled over and fell out of my arms. She did not budge, but she was still breathing. She was almost angelic, with her eyelids flickering like the fragile wings of a cherub. I got up and left quietly and never ended up seeing her again.

I found out months later, once I returned to New York, that she ended up quitting her job at Velvet Ropes and lived out the rest of her days in a hospital bed somewhere. She did end up passing away, but I found comfort in knowing that when it happened, she was happy.

Or at least her version of being happy.

∞ ∞ ∞ ∞ ∞ ∞ ∞ ∞

As I closed in on three months of being with Velvet Ropes, Chastity thought it would be a good idea to convince me to go to a tattoo parlor with Starr after work. The three of us were hanging out in the parking lot of the club. I was in the midst of filling the cracks of loneliness that persistently cut through my core, and I was blind to Chastity's actions. I later learned that she slipped something in my soda, for she thought I needed to loosen up. She later argued that it would be a good idea to have a bit of harmless fun.When we arrived at the tattoo parlor, I was incoherent and babbling. Starr and Chastity were not as wasted as I was, but they were both mildly intoxicated. I did not know where I was or what I was doing, but I knew that I wanted to get a tattoo on my shoulder.

One of the tattoos posted on the wall, a stone cross with the words "Rock of Ages" plastered on a banner that balanced in the middle of the image, spoke to me. I did not know just why, though I was recently baptized and drawn to crosses.

I don't remember getting it, or anything about that night for that matter, but I do remember waking up with a tender arm the next morning.

"It's cute, I like it," Gemma said as a grin climbed across her face.

It seemed as if I ended up with it for a reason, but it was a symbol that extended far beyond the cross: it was symbolic of the faith I had in the music I played and heard for years and years to come.

Everything happens for a reason.

∞ ∞ ∞ ∞ ∞ ∞ ∞ ∞

On my last night at Velvet Ropes, I wish I had the chance to take a picture of the scene. Louie was leaning against the wall telling me about his experiences in the war, the girls were making a killing in tips, and Gemma was resting at home with Bryan.

Life was not perfect, but it was exciting.

Gina's father walked in and looked incredibly irate. He was in town visiting the clubs and checking in with family, only to watch a massive scene unfurl in Velvet Ropes.

Two men got into a massive argument over Kyla Rae. When they began to throw chairs and tables at each other, I saw Gina gasp and reach for the phone. I felt it was my duty to protect the girls, who were practically standing in the middle of everything.

I jumped into action and began pulling the men apart, but by that time the police arrived to break up the fight.

The police threw me against a wall and frisked me for weapons. Gina ran over to protect me, but the officers claimed that I was the one who started the fight.

'Sir,' I yelled. 'I am covered in blood. I was trying to break it up. How could I have hit anyone?'

Gina's father's voice boomed over the scene, "He did it. The Yankee started it. I saw it with my own two eyes."

"What," Gina whipped her head towards her father in utter disbelief.

The two of them began to argue about my role in the fight, but her father refused to budge. He claimed that a "Yankee" could not be an innocent bystander.

He ended up firing me despite Gina's cries and pleas.

Even though the Civil War between the northerners and southerners ended over a century ago, the deep-rooted bias still permeated in the minds of some individuals.

I wondered why we all couldn't get along.

The police officers escorted me out and Gina's father banned me from the club for life.

To this day I have not stepped back in Velvet Ropes.

I ended up becoming a patient at the same hospital I was supposed to get a job at many months ago. People crave an exciting bar fight story to talk about their badge of honor, but all I ended up with was a broken toe.

This was not me. This was not making myself a better man. This was a nightmare, and I was praying I would wake up soon.

How do I rebuild from here? Where do I go from here?

I ended up having to stay at home and rest my foot, while Gemma became the primary breadwinner for our family.

She made the ultimate sacrifice for Bryan and me, and to this day I could never repay her. Gemma became rather proficient at dancing and was very popular. She left Velvet Ropes and began touring the different clubs around Texas. She would often drive two or three hours away to cities like Houston and San Antonio. I hated that she had to travel that far, but she vowed to do whatever it took to make enough to go back to New York.

"I will dance as long as I need to, just for us to get out of Texas, and we will put this chapter behind us," she said as she walked out the door during the first weekend she went on tour. She ended up pursuing a relationship with Chastity that existed both between the sheets and out in the clubs of Texas, but she was fighting incredibly hard for our family.

Each night, she would come home with at least $400, and that was just in tips.

She was not working to have fun or to party anymore like when we were at Velvet Ropes. Gemma was on a mission.

She was working to save money for our family. It was crazy, but her supreme sacrifice showed just how much she loved her son.

We were never really aligned, nor were we in tune too often, but she was the one who went out there and saved every penny for us.

Gemma would always call to check on Bryan when she was working incredibly long shifts.

Desperation hung on her lips as the shrill of giving up permeated her veins. Though that was it, she was giving up a part of herself.

Though miles apart, I could feel her heart shattering as if she were next to me.

No matter how close or how far, a confirmation of loneliness can be felt by anyone in the same predicament.

No matter how near or far. Sometimes distance makes it even more horrific, because you can hear "I'm fine" through the phone, but feel the pangs of unrighteous solitude between every passing breath.

It is sickening.

∞ ∞ ∞ ∞ ∞ ∞ ∞ ∞

After six months of her dedication and hard work, Gemma had enough money to get us home to New York. She dropped it on the table and let out a shrill.

"When we get to New York, we have to go our separate ways."

'We need a fresh start,' I glanced over at her and smiled slightly.

Neither of us argued, as it was a clear mutual understanding. The two of us needed to change for the better. This chapter of our lives was insane and beyond our wildest imaginations.

We needed a new beginning.

Gemma kissed Bryan on the forehead and walked into the bedroom.

I got up from the table with tears in my eyes. I dashed out the front door with no sense of direction.

I started walking aggressively down the street, rather devastated by how our conversation went. I could not understand how the words flew out of my mouth so poignantly. It was almost as if that conversation was long-overdue decades before it ever materialized on my lips.

Gemma's discomfort stung hard. Deep. Painstakingly. My heart was twisting in ways I never knew existed. She could never fathom the inordinate pain I was dealing with.

As my breath became exasperated, I sensed something… a rumbling in the distance.

I began racing the thunder from the merciless sky. I was huffing and puffing to keep myself from becoming drenched in the sudden storm. 'Why am I doing this? Why?' I said to myself as I heard my sopping wet feet hit the pavement.

Why am I doing this? For her? For me? For my body, mind, and spirit. I couldn't let my body succumb to these parties anymore. This drinking, these drugs, this lifestyle. I can't do it. I can't. I-

That last lightning strike did it. The sky opened up and water was dumped everywhere. It eradicated every thought manifesting in my head. I was drenched. The Texas rain wholly engulfed me. At least my tears were masked by the torrential downpour.

As my thoughts flooded my mind again while dragging my sopping wet frame through the rain, I realized that I have learned how crucial family is. Bryan. My son. My everything, always. I will try to be a loving father, though sometimes I wondered where my thoughts trickled off to. I'll spend a lifetime dedicated to his well being.

The love of a family is a bond that could never be severed. It can never be tainted or diseased. It is something I vow to uphold, despite the devout unrest lingering in my body. When push comes to shove that family bond, whether it be biological or through marriage, love is undying. Love is unchanging. Love fades slightly, but it never dissipates fully. It cannot disappear.

It will not.

It won't. It won't.

Love for family is the fabric that holds us together wholeheartedly. Love is what will be there when all seems lost.

Bryan, I love you. I will do anything for you.

As I stopped dead in my tracks in that traumatic rain, I gazed up to the sky. 'God,' I screamed into the rain, 'I hear you. I feel you. I get you.' In those moments, I felt my faith coursing through my blood. I knew, standing there in the rain that day, exactly what I had to do and what my purpose was.

My son, Bryan. I had to do right by him.

We had to get back to New York.

Within the week Gemma and Bryan were on a plane back to New York while I drove all of our belongings back in a massive moving truck. The metallic sign that said "Leaving Texas now" signified the first time I could breathe in what felt like years.

It was the summer of 1994.

As I exhaled and watched Texas fade in my side-view mirror, I was hopeful that life was about to get better.

Again, what was the worst that could happen?

CHAPTER 15

99 in the Shade

~

"Send up a signal. Throw me a line. Somebody explain 'this funny Valentine.' It might not be legal, but it sure ain't a crime. I'm one step from crazy and two steps behind."

- Bon Jovi, American Rock Band, Sayreville, New Jersey

Breathing in the New York air had a certain familiarity to it. The aromas of stale air, pollution, and garbage were pungent and a stark contrast to Texas, but they signified a return to some semblance of normalcy.

After experiencing Texas, I felt the need to call Wendy.

While I was down south, I discovered how awful I was towards her. Wendy did so much for me and was a phenomenal friend.

I lost her because I was fearful of Olga and losing what I thought was a healthy relationship.

Upon calling Wendy and hearing her friendly "Hello" on the other side of the phone, I felt that everything was suddenly okay again. The two of us talked for a while and I sincerely apologized to her.

She was thrilled to hear that I had a son, and I was happy to learn she met someone who truly loved her.

Wendy and I seemed to continue our friendship right where we left off, which made the concrete jungle seem less of a burden on my shoulders.

Although Gemma and I agreed to part ways the moment we got to New York, and I promised to take care of Bryan, the three of us ended up renting an apartment together.

She looked right through me. To her, I was a faint memory of what her life could have been if she chose to set aside her jealousy and give in to hope. If she could have only seen herself in the light that encompasses her soul, she would have understood.

Instead she sat in darkness, lurking in the shadows of remarks like, "you don't understand."

She was wholly unbalanced in every sense, for her compass pointed due south. The further she headed down that path, the harder her life would become. If you stand in someone else's shadow, while making excuses as to why you cannot emulate your own light, then every part of what makes you glow will fade.

The two of us were young and naive then; we needed to grow.

Savor your light, keep your light... just do not cast your eyes downward at another who is trying to create a better life for his family. Our family.

Our son.

We ended up finding separate jobs with different companies. Both of us were doing what we could to make ends meet, though we were in separate worlds with separate goals.

I began chatting with an endearing young woman at the insurance firm I worked for, Brittany, who seemed to be the exact opposite of Gemma.

Though Brittany was visually stunning like Gemma, she had a way about her that embodied the care and affection I had not been getting from Gemma. Although Gemma and I were still under the same roof, I really did not have such strong feelings for her anymore.

Bryan, Gemma, and I would eat dinner together as a family, but that is just about where our life as a cohesive family ended. Both of us cared deeply about our son, and tried our hardest to provide for him.

We hoped that he did not see our struggles and hardships. We hoped that he was still innocent enough to understand that mommy and daddy were just dealing with some tough stuff.

We wanted a better life for our son.

And we still wanted to have fun.

∞ ∞ ∞ ∞ ∞ ∞ ∞ ∞

Gemma and I got into a conversation about Brittany, which prompted a convoluted series of discussions. By the end of our two hour-long talk, we managed to come to the conclusion that we needed to change our lives up a bit.

Our conclusion?

We thought we should have a threesome.

In retrospect, I am not sure what either of us was thinking.

'Are you sure about this?' I began to fiddle with my fingers.

"Yeah," Gemma said confidently.

'I mean after-' she rolled her eyes. I could tell our minds reverted back to our days in Texas.

"Get over it, Scott. Just see if she is interested at least."

I called Brittany to see what she would say. Somehow, she agreed, and actually seemed eager to have this experience happen sooner rather than later.

We all chose to meet at a motel in a run-down Suffolk County town, and I felt the world shifting on its axis again.

There was so much anticipation seeping through the air as Gemma laid her eyes on Brittany. I stood there in the center of the room silently begging for either one of them to make the first move. Prior to this moment, the relationship between Gemma and I hung by a thread, waiting for that last push to combust and fizzle us out.

Though in this moment, I felt more alive than ever. Was it the blood rushing to my head at the possibility of keeping Gemma happy? What would I think next morning if this actually happened? How could I go back to work and see Brittany in the halls again? Some guys fantasize their entire lives about having a threesome with two women, and I was possibly going to live that stereotypical male dream within moments. I was petrified that we would be immersed in another Alonzo moment like in Texas.

I was suspended in a state of will they, won't they?

Then Gemma thrust her tongue into Brittany's mouth.

The verdict was will they: the two of them hit it off right away.

Gemma and Brittany's bodies began interlocking in ways that I could not have even imagined. They began their tumultuous twists and turns in the direction of the wall near the rickety bed, and my eyes began to fill with excitement. I think I did this. I think I made this happen.

At this moment, I was living the dream... but was I?

With her body forcefully pushed against the wall and Gemma's violent kisses embracing her body, Brittany motioned for me to come closer. I cautiously approached the women as not to disturb their sweet passionate release. Brittany grabbed my crotch with her tender fingers and drew me closer to her lips.

Skin was clinging to skin as sweat poured over our bodies.

With Gemma's touch cascading along Brittany's curves, eroticism controlled my every motion. I pulled Brittany's head closer to my face and embraced her lips once again. Somewhere in our maze of skin and lust, Gemma had already ripped off all of her clothes and my blue jeans. Was this really happening?

Moments later the three of us were blending into the strewn sheets and blankets that once rested peacefully on the bed. My fingers traced every inch of their bodies, almost as to preserve the moment forever and ever. Brittany's gaze was etched in my memory, and for once I paused in a true state of disbelief: I had made this dream come true. I snapped back into reality within seconds, for Gemma had already wrapped her hands around my thighs.

Heavy breathing and cries of exuberant passion filled the air for hours. It was another Alonzo situation, but I did not feel jealous. It was a perfect case of a double standard; however my anxiety was lulled into a sense of safety.

At times, I sat and watched both women crash into one another over and over and over again. If there was any doubt in my mind over what the term "hot and heavy" meant, I think our first night as a trio solved that problem.

Our lust was infinite, real, and wholeheartedly overwhelming. Three souls were intertwined in fits of violent passion and anxiety of whether we were truly pleasing one another... or at least that is how I saw this moment. A mixture of hot sighs and insistent groans echoed in my ears.

As our night dove into morning I would continue interlocking my fingers with each of theirs, leaving raunchy remnants of our night together along their thighs, torsos, breasts, and necks. Each of them made a silent agreement to cherish our time together as satisfaction filled the stale motel room, but this could have been a hopeful wish fusing into the depths of my erotic fantasy.

As natural beams of light reached through the mesh red curtains, the two women collapsed into my arms. Laying there, planting gentle kisses on both of their foreheads, gazing out into the dawn ahead of us, I became drenched in sweat and utter peace: this would happen again, and again... and again.

Passionate nights became our habit. Brittany and I would glance at each other at work, our blank gazes telling a secret story to one another about what debauchery we would participate in later.

Frozen soda bottles, neon vibrators, and pink-feather handcuffs would become our new friends. We were eager to get through the workday so the three of us could ram each other into the wall or launch one another into the sea of blankets and satin sheets.

We would have a year of continuous, fervent nights that morphed into exciting days that would consume every fiber of our being. Pounding hearts would be the melody of our sensual meetings, which were mixed with the soothing grunts and sighs of our powerful threesomes.

The breathy sighs and trembling thighs only ceased when jealousy cut between Gemma and I like a sharp knife.

The bitter cold and snow covered my shoulders when I had returned home from work one night. Earlier in the day, Brittany and I had agreed to go to a rock concert in New Jersey, only to get trapped in a maze of public transportation and terrible weather. Upon turning the frosted doorknob and entering our little apartment, Gemma's shrills jolted me further into the depths of the once still winter air.

"Where were you," she demanded an answer. Her foot was rapping against the hardwood floors now soaked in the remnants of an adventure-filled night.

'Like I said,' I began pulling my crimson scarf from my neck, 'Brittany and I were trying to go to that rock concert in Jersey, got lost, and wasted hours on trains and in bus stations.'

A still pause was shattered by her shrieking: "What about me?"

I stood in disbelief for a moment, expecting her to answer her own question.

At this point, I saw a small shadow creeping down the hallway.

'Gemma, it is late, keep it down,' I whispered to her in hopes of ending this argument she self-perpetuated.

She became more enraged, knocking down a lamp in the process of her launching her arms into the air.

"Scott," she shouted, "It's us. It has always been us and you should have remembered that."

'Gem, honey, I don't understand,' I stood frozen and puzzled inches from her warm body.

She picked up a plate and launched it at my head, which fortunately ducked just as the plate crashed behind me.

For a lack of better terms, she was utterly enraged. She had violent intentions despite being silently guilty of having sex and experiences with Brittany in my absence. In the past, we knew that at the end of the day the three of us would be entangled in stained sheets together, and that was all that mattered.

Then her words stung like daggers in my chest: "I'm leaving you."

Little time passed between those sharp three words and a gentle cry emulating from the corner: "Daddy? Mommy?"

Bryan had crawled out of bed, rubbed his precious eyes with his innocent little hands, and brushed against the walls of the hallway on his journey to find his life being decided for him.

A sting of guilt crashed over my body before I could even hoist him into my arms. Gemma's heartless demeanor stood in the far corner of the living room as Bryan rushed towards my legs in tears.

"Daddy, Mommy, don't go," he was still suspended in a gentle dream-like state, confused by whatever adult conversation had just tore through his little soul.

With him wrapped in my arms and listening to the throbbing heartbeats that were about to burst through my chest, I brushed my cold hands against his flowing blonde hair.

A beam of mercy shined through Gemma's hardened demeanor as a gentle phrase fell from her mouth: "Stay here until we can get our situation figured out."

One of our old pillows soaked in the memories from one of our threesome-filled nights was dropped onto the couch as Gemma retreated to what was our bedroom.

"Don't think about coming in here," were the last words that lulled me to sleep as she slammed the door and shut out any hope of us being a trio again. Bryan cooed and cried for a while in my arms while my tender grasp reassured him that I would always be there for him, no matter what. He was and always will be my little boy, and no one would stand in the way of my undying love for my dear son, not even myself.

From the moment I laid eyes on him, I knew I would risk everything and anything to keep him safe and assure him that he would always be loved, and nothing could break apart our bond: not a threesome and not this universe.

There had to be a way to make this family work. There was no more love in terms of Gemma and I wanting to be together forever, but there was a distinct love within our hearts. No matter what was happening between us, we loved our son.

We were young.

We needed to grow.

We had to figure out how to split up amicably without giving up our son.

In the stark moonlight that brushed over us on that beige couch, I reaffirmed to him that our family would always be a family. His little tears dripped down his cheeks as I serenaded him to sleep with soft and mindless melodies.

My son superseded any responsibilities I had towards other people, and this moment was my unspoken promise to him: I will love you forever and ever, my little boy you always shall be, and no other person will come between us, for it will always be you and me.

Bryan and I shut our eyes and let the night whisk us away into our fantasies for a moment, even if mine had just come crashing down moments earlier.

There was so much life left to live, and Bryan and I would always live it together.

My son deserves a better life than I have, and I will continue to uphold the promise of the two of us against the world: I will love you forever and ever, my little boy you always shall be, and no other person will come between us, for it will always be you and me.

∞ ∞ ∞ ∞ ∞ ∞ ∞ ∞

Gemma came to pick up her things the next day. When she was struggling to pick up some of the things she packed in slightly damaged cardboard boxes, I bent down and held her for a moment. She reciprocated my touch and we looked in each other's eyes for the first time in what felt like years.

'I'm sorry.'

"I'm sorry, too," she whispered into my chest.

As she stood to walk away, I caught a glimpse of her stomach looking a bit larger than usual.

'Are you pregnant, Gemma?' I should have learned my lesson from the last time I asked her, but last time I was not wrong.

"What did you just say to me?" She pivoted and her eyes widened.

'Is it mine?'

Gemma became enraged. It started a massive fight that just did not need to happen. She rushed into the bathroom and grabbed a pregnancy test from the cabinet.

"You want me to prove it? I'll prove it."

She took the test right in front of me.

As the word "Negative" appeared in bold pink font, I felt that she deserved so much better.

I didn't like the man I was.

I felt even worse than I thought I ever could feel.

"We're officially done," she tilted her head downwards and dragged a bag of her clothes out of the apartment.

As usual, questions filled my head:

Did I do this? Was I the reason our family fell apart?

The answer seemed to be yes, but it was a more painful sensation than just one syllable passing through my lips.

My tumultuous journey through relationships would continue.

Bryan was sleeping at the time, but I was thankful he did not see what I did to his mother. I felt terrible.

Sometimes when I think of those final moments of living with Gemma, I feel the urge to call her on the phone and apologize, but she has moved on and moved forward.

A year after she moved out of our New York apartment, she married her now-husband Ethan. The two of them have a beautiful family together and she turned her life around completely.

Gemma went back to college and got her degree in finance from a local community college in Arizona. She had opened her own bakery close to the Grand Canyon for a short time, which did incredibly well. After travelling around the country for some time, she ended up returning to New York to settle down.

I always hoped that my presence in her life did not hurt her or cause her pain, though I do know that everyone's experiences are composed of their own actions. She made her choices, as did I, and I pray she has nothing but positive energy in her life.

Gemma made so many sacrifices for Bryan, and myself, and I hoped one day she would be able to be repaid for all of her courage, determination, and tenacity.

As for Bryan, he saw his mother from time to time and spent many holidays with her. She never forgot about him though our relationship fizzled out.

That's the beauty of it all: relationships can collapse, but respect can still remain.

The lessons that Gemma taught me, even in hindsight, helped me become a better person.

All of the people who I encountered in Texas and up until this point taught me a lesson, and there are many lessons I am still learning.

After a few months I got settled in New York, and I called up Aunt Barbara. I had a lot of apologizing to do.

When I called Aunt Barbara, I was nervous. I did not know what to do or to say, but all I knew is that I truly missed her. I genuinely missed my aunt. I was sincerely sorry and I hoped that she knew I screwed up.

The phone rang three times and when she picked up, my heart sank.

"Hello," she sounded happy, and I prayed she would stay that way.

'Aunt Barbara, it's me,' I paused out of fear. 'It's me, your nephew, Scott.'

She chuckled a little bit and I could feel her smile seep through the phone.

"What took you so long, my boy?"

I began to tear up.

She sounded thrilled, "I missed you, too."

CHAPTER 16

Until Her Veins Run Dry

~

"I've begun evaporating right before your eyes. I just keep regurgitating my own demise."

- Sixx A.M., - American Rock Band, Los Angeles, California

The moment Aunt Barbara pulled up to Alley Pond Park, I flew from the bench and landed right in her arms.

"Look at you," she cupped my face. "You look so grown."

We embraced again.

'I am so sorry for everything I-' tears began streaming down my face.

"Do not say you are apologizing to me, show me your apology." Aunt Barbara motioned for us to sit at the picnic benches.

I happily scooted to the opposite side of the picnic table and grinned.

"Tell me everything I have missed. How is little Bryan doing?" She was overjoyed and could not stop smiling.

We chatted for a while about all of the wonderful things we have both been a part of. She sat there without any sense of judgment or malice. Aunt Barbara was just genuinely happy that I was back in her life.

"A strip club?" She remarked. I was waiting for her to say something else.

"Oh boy, that sounds like quite an adventure!"

She was indifferent to my livelihood, but she was considerate about it. Aunt Barbara was not trying to guide me one way or another, nor was she taking situations from my past and throwing them in my face. She was honestly being such a kind soul who just heard and listened to everything I said.

∞ ∞ ∞ ∞ ∞ ∞ ∞ ∞

After the two of us sat and talked for a while, she stood and grabbed my shoulder.

"Come, come," she said, pulling me with her as she kept walking. "We are going on a lovely walk through nature."

'Okay,' I was following her every whim, following in her footsteps until I could completely catch up with her.

"You're a youngster," she shouted jokingly. "Hurry it up, kiddo!"

We passed lush greenery and flowers that were eagerly welcoming the spring air. There were downed trees scattered about and some that were sturdy and tall. The trail we were walking was poignantly pleasant and I was eager to see just where we were going.

The two of us complimented nature in its holistic beauty. Every single tree, flower, bush, and element was gorgeous in its own respectful ways.

Chestnut-colored squirrels and picturesque chipmunks were frolicking over the stumps where rotted trees once stood.

"Everything has its own beauty about it," Aunt Barbara grabbed my arm. "Even the elements that have long passed away are beautiful in their own right."

I felt tranquil.

The two of us came to a mossy lake with rocks placed around it.

'Thank you.' I turned to her and rested my forehead on her shoulder.

"Heavens, what for?" She ran her fingers through my hair.

'For being you.'

She smirked and let out a breathy chuckle. Those words did not hold too much merit by themselves, but in the context we were in and having been through all that we experienced, it all made sense, or so I hoped.

We began speaking about life and nature. We talked about her job in the city and how she gets a chance to gaze out at the Brooklyn Bridge, the Twin Towers, various passerby's in lower Manhattan, and other things she found particularly quintessential to embracing the beauty of New York.

"Doesn't it feel good to be home?" She rubbed my back.

She knew the answer to that already; I think she just wanted to express how happy she was to see her nephew beside her again.

In the years that followed, I wished that I could experience those moments with her over and over again. Though we had plenty of walks through nature and long talks, only two of them distinctly stand out as a string of moments where I remember practically everything that happened.

This was the first experience.

The second would come years and years later.

∞ ∞ ∞ ∞ ∞ ∞ ∞ ∞

Being back in New York came with its fair share of adventures and excitement, but nothing compared to life back in Texas. In many ways, I was grateful for it.

Bryan was adjusting incredibly well to life in the north again, which was a massive relief.

Though Gemma and I were separated and living different lives, she still kept in touch with us and ensured that her son was being taken care of.

Still, the pangs of loneliness struck at my soul nightly: everyone was leaving and everything was changing before my very eyes. After hearing about the fall out between myself and Gemma, Brittany stopped calling all together. She did not want to deal with the drama surrounding both of us, nor did she want to be ripped into a situation where life became tense. When the three of us were entangled in the sheets or just having a conversation, things were working out well. However, the second that jealousy, rage, and anger were introduced into our relationship, our sacred bond was severed.

As I have seen time and time again, bridges can collapse.

And once they do, there is a sort of painstaking loneliness that occurs: how do you fathom the gravity of having an extremely chaotic life that crumbles at its core?

I figured that once I returned to New York, I would begin to amend the relationships I had with people who I dismissed or disregarded while in Texas.

I had been living with my sister Rebecca for a while before making the decision to leave for Texas, and I do not think I ever truly considered her well being when we were making the drastic move as a family.

Since I returned to New York, it seemed as if Rebecca was making a sincere effort to stay far away from me. I assumed it was because it seemed like I was just ditching her. We had such a strong relationship before I moved down to Texas, and I was going to try to do whatever I could to remedy the bond we had before my life took quite a crazy turn.

In an effort to extend an olive branch to Rebecca, I did what I thought was best: on a peaceful Saturday morning, I scooped Bryan up and decided we were going to make a surprise visit to Aunt Rebecca. After all, I figured, you couldn't really turn away your nephew, could you?

∞ ∞ ∞ ∞ ∞ ∞ ∞ ∞

On the car ride over to see Rebecca, Bryan was cheering and clapping along to the music we were listening to in the car. I can't distinctly remember what we were listening to, but I know it had to be a rock song. Bryan adored Bon Jovi, Poison, Mötley Crüe, Van Halen, and all of the classics that I enjoyed. Even beyond that, Bryan was accustomed to music that some hardcore rock fans may not have even heard of: Cinderella, Gorky Park, the list goes on and on.

I guess, in a sense, I exposed him to all of that music hoping it would impact him in the way it helped me.

Although I knew, for a fact, that Bryan would never have to face homelessness or half of the chaotic situations I went through.

No matter what, history was not going to repeat itself ever again.

As we pulled up to her house, everything seemed rather normal. The terra cotta potted plants were resting on the cobblestone steps, the front door had lush green vines surrounding it, and it appeared that everything was orderly and organized. It was somewhat of a pleasant surprise, considering when we lived together our house was not the neatest of places.

As Bryan and I approached the front door, I could tell he was excited to see his aunt. His little legs approached each step with the fury of a young man on a mission.

When he reached up to ring the bell, he stepped back and placed his tiny hand in mine. He was mumbling things to himself; almost as if he were rehearsing a speech he was about to make to his aunt.

When the door opened, the two of us were met with the glance of a man just about my age. His face was sunken in, his eyes were shallow, but you could tell he had such a kind heart.

"You must be Scott, Rebecca's brother, the family resemblance is uncanny," he said.

Bryan grinned from ear to ear and pulled at the door handle.

"And this must be your darling son, Bryan," the man opened the door and shook his little hand. "It is good to meet you both, come in." He pushed the door open so the two of us could walk in.

I shook his hand, which was colder than I had expected, and escorted us into the kitchen.

"I'm Rebecca's boyfriend Chris. We live here together, I'm not sure if she mentioned it," he had an anxious raspiness to his voice.

'No, she didn't, but it's good to meet you, man.' I pat him on the back as a means of showing my appreciation towards him.

We walked into the kitchen, which was also incredibly neat compared to what Rebecca and I had years ago. It seemed like she was doing incredibly well for herself, and I felt less worried about her at this point.

"Beck, come down here, you have a surprise guest," Chris shouted up the stairs that connected to a small hallway off of the kitchen.

"Okay, one sec," Rebecca sounded distant, and although she was upstairs, I felt something was slightly off. Just call it a brother's intuition, I guess.

The three of us sat in the kitchen for a little while, simply talking about things like my son's life so far and how Chris met Rebecca. The story itself seemed a bit odd, but I did meet Gemma in a bar with just the two of us listening to On-Line. Stranger things have happened, and my life embodied that phrase wholeheartedly.

Rebecca eventually came frolicking down the steps, already realizing that her brother and nephew were sitting in her kitchen.

"Well, well, well, aren't you a sight for sore eyes," she shouted, staring at both Bryan and I with her pupils extremely dilated.

"Aunt Rebecca!" Bryan jumped out of his chair and dashed towards her.

"Hello little guy," she hugged him and smiled. She was wearing a long-sleeve sweater and began itching her arms. This was red flag number two.

The first red flag should have been when I got to her house and noticed how neat everything was. She was never that tidy, and although Chris could have been the one who cleaned up, I never really saw Rebecca as being such an organized person. Maybe she had changed her ways since we last lived together just a few years ago, but I doubted it.

Something bigger was happening, and I just had to figure it out.

Rebecca's shallow eyes, her blatant fragility, and her constant itching were subtle signs that she was dealing with something. Her clean, well-kept house was a facade for what was genuinely going on behind the scenes.

We spoke for a few moments, but I got the sense that she was holding me at an arm's length.

"You should get going, Bryan looks tired," she said while rubbing her head against her shoulder. Rebecca was starting to speak rapidly and appeared to lose her balance a bit.

'We just got here, it's okay.'

"No, no, you should leave. You should go." Rebecca locked eyes with Chris, who promptly melted away into another room of the house.

Rebecca was physically pushing us out of the house and seemingly without remorse. It had been quite some time since we had really seen each other, but she could not be more resistant to our presence.

"You need to go now," Rebecca walked us to the door and opened it. "I am so glad you stopped by. I'll see you soon!"

The door slammed shut behind us and I heard her footsteps recede into the house. A strange car was parked across the street, with its driver just idling there. He was watching me walk to the car with Bryan following closely behind.

"Daddy, Aunt Rebecca missed us!" Bryan exclaimed with his innocent grin plastered across his face.

'Yeah,' I broke eye contact with the man in the car. 'Yes, of course.'

I felt bad. I had seen this scenario before. The guy in the car was a drug dealer and Rebecca needed a fix. I was sure of it. Both Chris and Rebecca had to be using. What sort of drug they were using, I was not too sure at that moment, but it had to be heroin or cocaine: the itching, the dilated eyes, her demeanor... All of the signs were there.

She's lost. She's in pain. She's pushing me away.

And I didn't know how to help her then.

I didn't know what to do.

My head was throbbing and I needed to collect my thoughts, but I had to stay strong. Bryan gazed up at me once we got into the car, and the first thing he said was:

"Daddy, are you okay?"

I wasn't, but how do you tell your five-year-old son that your life is falling apart and you don't know just how to pick up the pieces? How do you help others when you can't even help yourself? Why does life hurt so much? Why does everything seem to be spinning out of control, even when you think there is no set reason why the world is spinning?

Does it ever stop? Will it ever stop?

Looking in the rear-view mirror, I obscured all of my existential questions behind one that I knew Bryan would respond favorably to:

'Who wants ice cream?'

"Me," Bryan shouted. His worries were non-existent. He didn't need to panic. He didn't need to suffer. He was still pure and unfettered by adult responsibilities.

∞ ∞ ∞ ∞ ∞ ∞ ∞ ∞

Bryan sat on the curb with me as his chocolate ice cream cone melted down his petite fingers. He slurped every ounce of that ice cream up as I glared out into the parking lot with a glum look on my face.

All of these years, I thought I had it tough. Yet when I left my parents' house, dabbled in drugs and alcohol, and continued to fight the demons in my head, I still had Bryan. I had the light of my life sitting before me, but what did Rebecca have? What love was extended to Rebecca while I was busy shattering my heart?

I was not there for her and though I was lost beyond belief, she was standing in the darkness all alone. As her big brother, I could have been there for her. I knew better, and I could have prevented this path she was tumbling down.

I should have known the moment she was admitted into the hospital years ago that her path was going to lead her here.

But I was selfish.

But I was ignorant.

But I didn't consider the consequences of my actions and how it could hurt her so badly.

I felt sick to my stomach.

"Daddy, do you want some?" Bryan raised his cone towards my face.

'No thank you, sweetheart,' I grinned at him and patted his head lightly. His wispy blonde hairs were slightly caught in my own fingertips.

Our family could have supported her. Our family could have helped her, though in actuality, they did not help me even in the slightest. They could have made amends for years of their ignorance by extending her a helping hand, but their grasp clearly fell short.

She was coping with a much more difficult battle and one that would probably run her directly into the ground if no one stepped in. Despite my one-time bout with alcohol during my Texas days, I was clean. I am clean now. I battle every single day to stay balanced and stray away from past crutches that held me up briefly and dragged me down.

The deep-rooted depression growing within me was hard to manage, but this internal fight would not be executed in vain. One day I would get better. One day I would be better. There would come a morning when I didn't feel like I was on the verge of breaking down with every passing second.

It takes a lot of strength, and I really did have a good life when I look at what I was dealing with and going through.

I was lost, and I was looking for someone else to find me.

After all, that's what I thought love was: someone just finding the real you once and for all.

My sister's road was rough, and though my road was tough, I was still walking. I just hoped that there was something I could do to help her, but in those moments when she pushed me away, I was unsure just what to do. I asked this time and time again, but how do you help yourself from drowning when you don't know how to swim? And then how do you help someone else from drowning when you are sinking seemingly further and faster than they are?

We're all lost in our own way, just waiting to be found, but at the time I thought people had to just find each other… not considering the fact that people could discover ways to help themselves. It may take time, diligence, and a lot of different efforts, but you can save yourself.

I did not know that just yet, and clearly neither did she.

∞ ∞ ∞ ∞ ∞ ∞ ∞ ∞

I was weaving a pattern of finding people that did not align to who I was or who I wanted to be. I was a lost soul, although I didn't comprehend the language of the soul at this point in time. I was still learning and growing, and I was in desperate need of a guiding light.

I had Aunt Barbara, who I was thankful for, but I needed someone else.

I needed something else.

I needed a clear purpose and to ignite the ambitious nature I knew I had growing deep within me, yet I still had to find my own way.

Although Bryan and I were doing quite well for ourselves, I was still crying every night. I never let him see how destroyed I was by losing relationship after relationship, and he seemed to be happy.

That's all that really mattered. His happiness was paramount to everything I was dealing with, and I knew that as long as he was living a good life, then in reality, so was I.

While closing in on over half of a decade of a relationship, I did truly miss Gemma. She was caring and sweet at her very core, but she just didn't love me like I loved her. Well, in actuality, I was still searching for what love was.

My mind was littered with questions: Why is it that loving someone means you must let them go? Why is it in order to grow and become healthy, you must crash and fall apart? Can a tragedy bring about wonders you never fathomed?

It's ironic that God is there even when you don't ask for God... in actuality, that is a true blessing.

Irony, or something like it, exists when prayers are answered in the words of a song, the feeling of air brushing against your face, or in the message of a stranger just passing by.

Why is it when you try to express love to someone, it could destroy the relationship between two people forever?

How can someone think they have come so far in life, only to learn they are still trudging through the challenges they may not even know they are facing yet?

Life is so short, but there is so much to learn... and in moments that seem perilous or tragic, we are more eager to learn than ever before... or are we frozen solid?

Do we stand still and just wait for life to crash into us like waves from an ocean of memories, or do we move with the ebb and flow of the tide?

I loved Gemma, I really did, but we both loved in different languages and were unwilling to learn just how to translate everything that was going on.

We did not listen, we did not talk, we just were.

During one of our final conversations as a couple, she expressed that once I grow and become a healthier person, I will not want her. Maybe she is right... I guess she was right.

I had to grow up.

Will I ever know of a true relationship, a trusting relationship, a true love? Does anyone truly hold the key to my heart and my spirit?

This pain has to stop eventually. I am pushing my feelings far away when I should be addressing them. In order for me to be a better person in the future, I must stop the craziness inside of me. I am a lost soul that is weak. My head is a monster that must be tamed.

Is there any hope for me? I guess time will tell. When a person is so stuck, so lost, and so scared, they should not be getting into another long-term relationship. Unfortunately, in those moments of pure weakness, I was blind to that.

I did not see anything beyond the pain I was in.

Then, as the phone rang one night in February of 1997, I thought that I just had to take a leap of faith.

So, I jumped... and little did I know I would land in a situation that would open my eyes just a little wider. It's funny how the world works: just when you think you are sinking, a life raft appears.

And with that... I floated just a little bit longer.

CHAPTER 17

I Finally Found Someone

~

"We started over coffee, we started out as friends. It's funny how from simple things, the best things begin."

- Barbara Streisand, American singer, actress, and songwriter, New York City, New York

As I said, the phone rang on a bitterly cold night. On the other end of the phone was my friend Natalie.

"Hey, you can't say no, we are going out to a party," her tone was rather confident.

'No, but thanks though,' I went to hang up the phone, but her voice drew me back into the conversation.

"This is not up for debate," she remained persistent.

I had known Natalie for years, through the music scene and from random gatherings, but this was the first time she called me and practically demanded that we go to a party.

'I don't have money.'

"I will take care of it, don't worry."

'But someone needs to watch Bryan, and-' she promptly cut me off.

"I am sending my sister over to watch him for the night. You have no excuses. She's coming over in 30 minutes, just get ready."

I had no clue what else to do except to abide by her wishes.

Within a half hour her sister was there to watch Bryan, and Natalie and I were out the door and on our way to the party.

∞ ∞ ∞ ∞ ∞ ∞ ∞ ∞

The two of us arrived almost simultaneously at this local bar. Natalie told me that we were there to see a Rush cover band perform. The actual band was from Toronto, but this band had members from all over Long Island. They had a rather large following, and I was particularly drawn to their music.

They were a pretty decent cover band, but I desperately wanted to play on stage with them. It had been years since I got a chance to play drums on a stage like that, and I missed being able to make sweet, sweet music.

The band played for a while, then opted to take a bit of a break. Playing for long periods of time on a stage can be incredibly grueling, especially when you're really into the music.

When the band members stepped off of the stage, Natalie turned to me and said that she was going to grab me a soda. I leaned my back against the peeling red walls and sighed. It had been the first time I was really out since Gemma left and probably even before that.

Michael Jackson's "Thriller" began playing over the speakers above us, so I naturally had to sing along:

"No one's gonna save you from the beast about to strike."

I was tapping along to the beat and waiting for Natalie to reappear, when a clearly inebriated woman with short, raven-black curly hair stumbled on top of me.

She practically jumped right into my arms.

"I am so sorry," the woman said, slightly slurring her words as she pushed off of my abdomen.

'What the fuck,' I blurted out, not knowing what else to say.

"Oops," she let out a cute little belch, which showed how far gone she seemingly was.

'Who the fuck are *you?*'

Natalie rushed back over and placed the drinks on the table near me.

"I'm Elyza," the woman playfully ran her fingers along my leather jacket.

Stunned and slightly intrigued, I chuckled and replied, 'I'm Scott.'

I was unsure of what to do, but Natalie was grinning from ear to ear while sipping her drink. I began talking with Elyza for a while, for something about her seemed incredibly different from the women I had encountered in bars in the past.

As we were talking, my younger sister Sarah walked in and threw her arms right around Elyza.

"Elyza! How are you?" Sarah's warmth radiated throughout Elyza's body as the two embraced.

Sarah acknowledged my presence, but she looked much happier to see Elyza than she was to see me.

The three of us talked for a while as Natalie faded into the crowd at the bar. Somehow Sarah and Elyza knew each other from work, and I felt that the world put us together for some incredibly strange reason.

Hours went by as I watched Elyza pound down shot after shot of alcohol. Though she was trashed, she still had a certain ebb and flow to her. Her movements and dancing were more fluid than the water shifting around in my glass.

Elyza grabbed my hand and pulled me in to dance, to which I happily complied.

As we moved around and around, her hips gyrating directly into mine, I felt free for a change. I had loosened up and felt every rhythmic beat from the drums and every strum from the guitar.

We both moved as if we were the only two in the room, and I felt that in those moments, we were connected in a way that could never be translated into words.

"Do you want to get out of here?" Elyza looked at me with bedroom eyes and ran her fingers up the back of my neck.

'Sure,' I gulped. 'I mean if that is what you want to do.'

"I want to." She drew me in closer. "I *want* to."

I was so incredibly nervous due to my track record of past relationships, but I gave my regards to Sarah and Natalie before I dashed out the door with Elyza.

The two of us ended up heading back to my place, where Natalie's sister and Bryan were passed out cold on the couch. We snuck right past them quietly and started fooling around in the bedroom.

As she ran her hand down my leg, I stopped her and looked her right in the eyes.

'Are you okay? Do you want this?'

She looked back at me and grabbed my face. "Yes, I do." Elyza kissed me on the lips and pushed me back towards the bed.

'Okay.' I stopped her again. 'We are not having sex unless I get a condom.'

"Wow," she moved back slightly. "That is incredibly responsible. Okay."

I ran to the local 24-hour pharmacy and bought a box of condoms, then darted back into the house and into the bedroom.

After Bryan, I always used a condom and always had the willpower to stop what I was doing. I would never not use a condom unless I was sure of two things: I was definitely, truly, and deeply in love AND I wanted to be a parent with that person. I knew that they would be both incredibly rare to find and if I was ever in that scenario, I knew it would have to be the ultimate, truthful love. I knew I would just feel it.

The first person I was with since Gemma, even though I was in a very unhealthy state of mind, was Elyza. While the two of us were getting ensnared in the sheets, I told myself that I was going to be a good man.

Love, sex, and physical actions had to be approached with a lot of caution. I had a lot of anxiety building around those three concepts. As a result, moments when I am getting physical with someone became very special to me.

In the passing seconds when Elyza and I were first intimate, that's what was going through my head: Am I being a good man?

I just had to be. I needed to be.

∞ ∞ ∞ ∞ ∞ ∞ ∞ ∞

The next morning, I woke up to Elyza resting in my arms. The two of us were still covered in sweat with our skin touching one another's. I moved her quietly, pulled my pants on, and went to check on Bryan and Natalie's sister.

The two of them were still sound asleep on the couch. I was grateful for that.

I grabbed two bottles of water from the kitchen and retreated back into my bedroom.

Elyza was sitting up with the blanket wrapped around her chest.

"Hey," she smiled at me.

'Hey,' I offered her the bottle of water.

"Thanks."

We sat there for a few moments and I offered to drive her back home.

On the way the two of us talked about nonchalant topics like the weather and the band from last night, until we reached her place.

"So..." she stalled in the car for a moment.

'So.' I rubbed the back of my neck, where just hours ago her fingertips rested.

"I don't know what to say really."

We both started to giggle like little children, until I shifted my body to look directly at her.

'Do you want to hang out again?'

"Yes," she leaned over and kissed me on the cheek. "Yes, I would, thanks Scott."

She jumped out of the car and darted right into her house.

I rested my head on the steering wheel for a moment, trying to collect my thoughts.

'Wow.'

I did not know what to make of the last 12 hours. I went from being incredibly upset over Gemma, to being at a party, to bumping into Elyza and getting intimate with her, to driving her home and asking her to hang out.

My rollercoaster of a life seemed to be climbing to a high point: the one night stand I had ended up lasting for... quite some time.

∞ ∞ ∞ ∞ ∞ ∞ ∞ ∞

I returned home and in the days that passed, I told Elyza about my life before I met her. She was very accepting of my past and even encouraged me to write a letter to Gemma. I was trying to fill the void of emptiness that pressed against my core, and Elyza somehow knew that. So, this is what I wrote:

"Dearest Gemma:

I have been trying with much difficulty to write the perfect letter to you. My whole life has been so painful that every time something bad happened in our relationship I would try to control it. I was so scared of losing you that I used every method, no matter how unhealthy, to keep you in my life. I was willing to ignore the situations we were in, despite the fact that deep down I knew you were not in love with me. The way I have been acting was unhealthy. I have had no respect for myself and I did not love me. I have been a lost soul who did not know what life was about. I now realize that you must choose to do what you have been trying to tell me for quite some time now. I will miss our long conversations and the time we have spent raising Bryan. He is honestly the best thing that has happened to me. I know I have dreams to fulfill but I do not know what they are. I want you to know that I am trying to learn what it means to respect and communicate in a relationship. Maybe one day we will be friends and have better communication. Send my love to everyone.

Love Always,
Scott"

I needed to be saved, and Elyza was there to save me. I was just blind to the bigger price I would have to pay. If there was anything I learned in life, it was that you need to heal yourself before you do anything else, though I was not able to see that at the time.

Still, Elyza and I blossomed together, and I am thankful every single day for everything she taught me. Our life together was developing into something truly beautiful.

Elyza convinced me that Gemma and I were never meant to be. She felt I needed to accept this fact, and though I expressed it to Gemma in a letter, I had to move on.

I never sent the letter to Gemma. I just tucked it away in a drawer somewhere and ended up unearthing it when I moved somewhere along the line.

Elyza said I needed to be a strong person and that it was okay for Gemma to move forward. I had to see things differently.

I needed to be a whole person before I gave myself to someone. I had officially decided that I did not want to be with Gemma ever again. I knew it had been over for a while now, but once I committed to it in writing, I felt relief.

I needed to be strong and find a dream to pursue. At the time I thought maybe it's my passion for drumming. I really had not focused on that as much as I would like. I just knew I did not have the skills. I needed to practice.

I could not compromise myself or anyone else to follow my dreams.

I kicked drugs and I was strong then. I can be strong.

No matter what, I had to pursue a dream for myself, and just refuse to give up.

I had to refuse to sink once and for all.

∞ ∞ ∞ ∞ ∞ ∞ ∞ ∞

Elyza was exactly what I wasn't and was just what I needed.

Shortly after we started seeing each other, and I mean within about a week and a half of our first encounter, her father passed away.

When I found out her father passed away, I wanted to be supportive. Elyza seemed to have a lot of friends, so I decided to show my support by attending her father's wake. I thought I could just slip into the crowd and not really be noticed. She had no idea I was coming. I thought it would be sweet and supportive to surprise her.

No one knew me there, which was fine, especially her boyfriend, or should I say "supposed" ex-boyfriend. When I walked into the funeral parlor, she flashed me a look of surprise. Not the surprise of happiness by my show of support, it was more like the surprise of "What do I do now?"

All her friends noticed me right away and all of a sudden, I felt like I was in an unneeded spotlight. Elyza ran up to me and begged for me to lay low. She asked me to respect her wishes, which I obliged.

A few moments later, Elyza shuffled me out to the parking lot and told me she was so happy to see me. Elyza genuinely said that she appreciated me coming.

I later found out in a phone conversation with Elyza that her boyfriend proposed to her that same night. She said she didn't mean to shuffle me away, but her "ex" was there and she didn't expect him to come.

In addition, since no one knew about her and I, she was uncomfortable and didn't know how to handle the situation. I told Elyza not to stress it and I understood. I only wanted to support her and assured her I was there if she needed anything.

The part that did sound odd to me was that her ex-boyfriend apparently proposed out of guilt because he had promised Elyza's dad that he would propose to her before he passed away.

Apparently in a rage, Elyza broke up with him when this did not happen.

In hindsight, I wondered, 'Did he know something I didn't?' Did she have unresolved feelings?

I wish I had been more insightful at the time, but for the first time in my life, I was the "other guy." I wasn't the man that Gemma wanted, or Mr. Cool that stole Audrey upon my return from camp, or even my friend from my second-grade nightmare.

That was good enough to sell me on wanting to be with Elyza and to turn a blind eye to what should have been obvious.

Little did I know, this was a pattern that Elyza would follow in the coming years of our relationship.

∞ ∞ ∞ ∞ ∞ ∞ ∞ ∞

After Elyza's father passed away, she took a leave of absence from her job. She worked at a community-based social service type of agency as a Social Worker.

Her leave of absence was so she could fly down to Boca Raton, Florida and spend some time with her mom, as she was mourning the loss of her husband. Their family was small, yet very close-knit. Her brother lived in California and her mother lived in Florida; they were all she had in her immediate family.

The next three months were a whirlwind full of ornate pleasures and intense memories. I flew to Florida to visit Elyza three times.

I remember one night when I was on the phone with her, struggling with emotions about Gemma, Elyza let out a somewhat maniacal laugh and the next minute there were plane tickets waiting at the airport for me.

I was in the midst of a major emotional breakdown, and Elyza nurtured me and took care of me. She was being sweet and loving, which is what I needed, and within three weeks of our first encounter her letters to me were about her declaring her love for me.

She said I was "the one," but we would "take it slow," since I was basically "damaged goods."

Those were her words.

We never did take it slow, and made our relationship pretty official from that point on.

In hindsight, I never stopped to mourn the end of my relationship with Gemma, or to come up for air.

I was too scared to be alone and Elyza was a viable option. She was fun and crazy. It seemed harmless.

To this day I do not like being alone, however I have learned the quality of being alone and taking the time to find myself. I have learned about not rushing into relationships, allowing them to breathe and grow... something that if I had done then, may have saved me from tons of grief.

It is so important to take the time to learn yourself and the person you intend on spending your life with. Without taking it slow, you leave room for major pitfalls. Then again, perhaps I would not be where I am today if it were not for those lessons and the immense hurdles I have not spoken about yet.

Would I change what I went through if it meant not being where I am today? How ironic, but I do not think so.

I got slightly sidetracked there for a moment, but the bottom-line is this: I loved going to Florida to see Elyza.

Each time I would visit her, we would go on "healing walks," where we would talk about life, problems, and struggles I was having. It reminded me of my days with Taryn and Lana. Ironically, I had lost touch with Taryn many years prior to this, but was told she was living in Boca Raton. Elyza helped me try to find her during my visit, but we were unsuccessful.

We talked about Taryn on our walks. We talked so much about me. We never spoke about Elyza. Now I realize she was counseling me, but was not in tune to that then.

On one of these walks, and during my second trip to Florida, Elyza announced that her and her mom decided to spend a week in Cancun. We decided that when she came back, she would meet me in Orlando for a pre-arranged trip I had planned with my grandmother, uncle, Bryan, and Aunt Barbara. I didn't think anything of their little trip, but figured they needed it to help with the bereavement process.

When she was in Cancun, we spoke once on the phone, surmounting a $450 phone bill for what was possibly a half-hour talk the most. We were crazy, but we were in love.

When Elyza met my family in Orlando, they all fell in love with her. She immediately became a Social Worker to the entire family, which my family definitely needed.

Elyza attracted dysfunction because she embodied elements of it, though everyone saw her as fun and energetic. In a sense, aren't we all dysfunctional in our own way?

During her last week in Florida, I got into a fight with my new landlords in New York who were very noisy. The place where Bryan and I were living started disintegrating before our eyes. The roof began to leak, the bathroom was falling apart, and the landlords were indifferent to everything. It was a horrible living arrangement in a not so great neighborhood, so Elyza came to the rescue and contacted her landlord for me.

I had a key waiting to her apartment and moved in before she even got home from Florida. That was probably the biggest mistake

I ever made but I was miserable where I was and with whom I was as a person.

When Elyza told me where her apartment was, I saw it as a sign. It was in Le Harve, which is right between the Whitestone and the Throgs Neck Bridge. Being between the bridges seemed so symbolic; I wondered, 'Was I back home at last?'

Maybe it was a good, safe, and familiar place for me to start reconnecting with who I was or wanted to be. The bridges were my home, but Elyza and I were living together before we even got to know each other. We were living together before I even knew who I was.

When she returned from Florida, things seemed great. We went for a drive out on Long Island and then I was blindsided with the news. I have replayed those few moments over a million times in my mind.

As we were driving around and taking in the beautiful summer sun, Elyza said she had something to confess to me. She admitted that while in Cancun she found someone.

She pursued his affections for a week.

I was crushed and had flashes of Gemma all over again, but as I calmly pressed for details, and as Elyza openly and vividly described the sexual escapades she had with her Cancun lover, I decided I could not face this pain again.

My mind, body, and every facet of logic twisting through my brain shut down. I was on Route 110 in Farmingdale driving eastbound in the middle lane and I felt my head was on the verge of imploding.

In an effort to push the pain away, I forgave her on the spot as she swore it was over. She said she wanted to be honest with me and start our relationship off the right way.

How funny does that sound?

She thought I was amazing for forgiving her, telling me it was eating her up inside and she was so distraught that she may have hurt me.

Elyza vowed it was her last hurrah before settling down with me because I was "the one." I accepted that as a justifiable statement, as I wanted someone to want me and I could not bear the pain of Elyza hurting me.

I couldn't bear the pain of going through another heartbreak.

Her Cancun lover called once and she told him it was over, and I took that as a good sign. I remember the night of that phone call.

Elyza raved on about how amazing a girlfriend she was for telling him it was over and all I could think was "Why did you even pursue someone else?"

Then I quickly pushed it away in an effort not to deal with the ulcer my life was causing me. What I really was doing was protecting my broken heart from being permanently damaged.

I should have run for the hills.

The moment Elyza told me about her Cancun lover our relationship ended; it just took me years of hiding, pushing my emotions away, and figuring my pain out to admit it. It took me years to reopen the wound and face it head on.

Our love was a love that did not fit whatever standard definition this world calls upon, but then again neither of us could truly define ourselves anyway.

All I knew was that Elyza was right: I had to find a dream, I had to find a passion, and my current job was not helping me fuel my ambitions even in the slightest.

∞ ∞ ∞ ∞ ∞ ∞ ∞ ∞

Even though I should have learned my lesson when it came to insurance companies and medical billing jobs, I found myself back in the same situation when it came to my professionalism. I was working at the corporate office of a home health care company that seemed like the largest health organization in the nation.

I despised this job as well as many that came before this one, but I was good at it. My job was to find and speak to insurance companies, and then get them to pay for services we rendered to patients in their home. Day in and day out, I was responsible for millions of dollars in claims and services.

Something about the whole situation seemed wrong. I saw payoffs and illegal activities happening behind the scenes. I saw backstabbing and how the industry cared more about money than people. It was sickening, literally.

The medical field professionals were great at making money for themselves and hoarding all of it. No one who called to collect the money ever saw any of it. We were running around and digging up dirt, yet we were the ones who were continuously getting buried.

The stress of working up to sixteen-hour days at the company was weighing heavily on my body. Though many aspects of my life seemed like a metaphorical ulcer, I developed an actual ulcer and was still dealing with negative emotions from Gemma.

Though I was only in my mid-twenties, my stomach was bleeding profusely. I needed to be saved from the monotony and desolation I was slowly succumbing to.

Once the company asked me to collect from incredibly sick and poverty-stricken senior citizens, everything spun out of control.

I got in trouble countless times for being compassionate with senior citizens. I would spend hours on the phone talking about their lives and situations.

In a sense, I became a counselor for them. I listened to their problems and concerns. My boss became furious when he found out these seniors were calling me, their bill collector, to talk about their day.

Morally speaking, how do you take money from elderly and sick people who do not have anything?

I felt the urge to help them instead. Something deep within me said that I was in the wrong business. At the time, everyone was in the business of understanding you took a job to have a job. If you were not happy, then it was your problem.

I was quickly learning that this was not the case at all.

There had to be more to life.

∞ ∞ ∞ ∞ ∞ ∞ ∞ ∞

The misery was piling on and I felt that I was on a locomotive that was about to jump the tracks. Between Gemma, trying to learn how to be a good man, and everything else that was building up at the base of my skull, I knew I had to find a way out. Elyza saw that and began pleading with me.

I was a mess. Again. Though Elyza was there to pick up the pieces.

"The social service agency I work with is having a community service event soon. I want you to help with it," Elyza rolled over in bed one morning and started to rattle off everything I had to do.

I was exhausted and confused, but I listened.

She was working with hundreds of youth who would be setting up a Memorial Day parade throughout some communities in Queens.

At first, I was apprehensive. I could not imagine being there at all, let alone helping out.

Begrudgingly, I decided to go along.

How weird is it that sometimes you make small decisions in your life, and these end up being the fabric of the quintessential moments in your life?

I was not supposed to be in the bar with Elyza that night we met, but there I was. I was not supposed to work in a gentlemen's club, but that helped to catapult us back to New York.

What is the worst that could happen at a charity event?

∞ ∞ ∞ ∞ ∞ ∞ ∞ ∞

On that fateful Memorial Day, we started incredibly early in the morning. Elyza brought me around and introduced me to so many people. My head was spinning and it wasn't even 7:00 in the morning just yet.

While helping to set up, I met countless teenagers who were quite interested in talking with me. They were so open, honest, and considerate. They reminded me so much of my own troubled past. I spent the day with them setting up chairs and tables, playing on the basketball courts, and handing out flyers.

Throughout the day we shared stories, bonded, and for the first time ever I felt… different. People were looking up to me.

Maybe they saw something in me that I did not comprehend just yet.

The local councilman saw me working with the teens and approached me.

"Young man," he said, wandering up to me.

'Hello sir, how can I help you?' I smoothed my hair and smiled. I did not know what else to do.

"I am so impressed with how you work with those kids, are you a social worker?"

'No sir,' I laughed. 'I am just here to help out.'

"What a pity." He shook his head.

'No, not at all, I work in home health care collections.'

He laughed, "You should be working with kids, not pushing papers."

The man walked away and Elyza ran right up to me.

"Do you know who that was?" She looked as if she were in awe of me.

'Not really, he is a politician, right?'

"He's the councilman who funded this whole event." Elyza dragged me to the side of the basketball courts. "You're phenomenal at this."

'This what?' I turned back to the kids who were calling my name.

"*This*, working with the kids!"

'Okay,' I said nonchalantly.

"We will talk about this later." She raced off to the next task she needed to handle, but did not forget our conversation.

Later that night, she said I was a natural and that I needed to become a social worker. She said I would have to go back to school, and I promptly stood up and walked away from the table.

'You are *not* getting me to go back to school,' I stormed towards the bedroom.

She stood in front of the door and narrowed her eyes. "I want you to look into it."

'I haven't been in school in about ten years, how can I go back?'

"You can," she put her hands on my shoulders. "And you *will*."

It took Elyza about six months, but when she came home with the college application in her hand, I knew that she would have her way no matter what.

How weird is it that sometimes you make small decisions in your life, and these end up being the fabric of the quintessential moments in your life?

CHAPTER 18

Are You a Tree?

~

"Lift your head up high and scream out to the world, I know I am someone and let the truth unfurl. No one can hurt you now because you know what's true. Yes, I believe in me. So you believe in you."

- Michael Jackson, King of Pop, American singer, songwriter, dancer, Gary, Indiana

Some days the mounting pressure felt unsurpassable. It was a sinking feeling, only to be cured by Bryan's airy giggles and innocent smiles. He was the breath of fresh air I consistently needed in order to feel my countless efforts and late nights were well worth it.

Sitting at the table, writing what could well be my thousandth paper, my eyes hesitated to stay open. A full day at work and school proved to be quite the challenge... but there was Bryan.

His little vroom vroom noises filled the air with joy and laughter. The small toy car he was pushing along the table made divets in the wood. A once mighty tree marked by an indulgent little car enthusiast.

"Dad," he yelped. The small red car flew across the table and over my papers.

"Daddy, a car!" He was excited it flew into my path. A teensy smile crept across his face. Small giggles escaped his body.

I grinned back at him and slid the toy across the table. Somehow, in someway, his unfiltered bliss made me feel that this was possible.

This journey would be for him, for us... a reminder that no matter how old you are, you deserve to pursue your education... to pursue your dreams... to shine a light for others.

Elyza was relentless in her efforts to get me back to school.

Before I enrolled, I was reamed out by my bosses for helping the elderly again. My ulcer was getting worse. Tears were streaming down my face uncontrollably, and when she begged me to try one class, I knew I had to take her up on at least trying school.

She convinced me that I could change and that I needed to go after what I wanted. The problem was I just didn't know what I really wanted.

School scared me. College scared me.

Yet the moment I entered my first English class at college, my fears melted away. I loved it and became engrossed in getting an education and taking as many classes as possible. Exploring different elements of knowledge made me feel as if there was something burning deep within me. I naturally asked a lot of questions, and I finally had an environment where questions were welcomed. In theory, I thought that the more classes I took, the sooner I could help people to make up for lost time.

I took a job working for Elyza, who was promoted soon after to director of another program at the social service organization. I slid right into the position of being her very visible and well-respected Director of Community Service. Suddenly, I was running a program for 300 kids.

I felt way in over my head, but once the head of the company put his arm around me and said he saw something in me, I had an overwhelming sense that I was in the right place.

"I have an eye for this," the owner said. "You may not be able to see this yet, but you are going to do great things in this world. You're going to do it your own way. I am not sure what it looks like, but you'll get there."

My life was actually changing.

In a few short months, I became president of the Social Work Council at Adelphi University. I ran events on campus and was involved in just about every and anything that crossed my path.

Bryan, who was more aware of my life and passion for schooling, also took note of my change in behavior and different outlook on life.

I had big dreams and an even bigger vision.

I was working seventeen hours a day on top of going to school.

It was Elyza who brought me into this new realm of possibilities, and so I did what I knew was best for Bryan and for Elyza…

∞ ∞ ∞ ∞ ∞ ∞ ∞ ∞

My hair was whipping in the wind, wrapping tenderly around Elyza's head as she rested against my chest. The Manhattan skyline looked absolutely stunning, especially with her nestled against me.

"Scott," she whispered, "Scott, what are you thinking?"

A smile crept across my face, 'You're beautiful, Elyza.'

I felt her whole body relax into mine.

Brooklyn Bridge Park had been so monumental to my life so far, and it was about to become another quintessential part of my story. Elyza was about to make Brooklyn Bridge Park part of my undying love story. Would she say yes? Would this make her feel sincerely loved? Would this take us to the next level and beyond?

Only time would tell…

And it was time…

'Elyza,' I started, taking her hand and leading her to the center of the stone path.

Our bodies were the epicenter of Brooklyn Bridge Park and our hearts were in line with my aunt's building. I could feel her presence wrapping around me, encouraging me to take this next step.

'Elyza,' her eyes gleamed in the exquisite sunset.

"Yes, Scott?" Her hands began to heat up as I drew her closer to me.

'I love you.'

"I love you, too," she whispered in such a sultry way that made it seem like it was just the two of us in that park. Our park. My spot.

I pressed my lips against hers and bent down on one knee. The world stopped for a moment as I reached into my pocket and pulled out the ring box.

I looked down at the black velvet box as her hand tensed in mine.

Her eyes filled with tears and she was whispering yes before the words could even spill from my mouth.

This was the beginning of a beautiful new chapter in our collective lives.

My words fluttered around my head and her joy became audibly louder in my mind.

"Yes, yes, yes, Scott, yes," she was glowing.

As we embraced and kissed in the watchful eyes of Manhattan's skyline and the Brooklyn Bridge, it was clear our lives were about to blossom into an amazing journey.

Our original one-night stand was just one night after another of love overflowing into the next day, and this just solidified that.

∞ ∞ ∞ ∞ ∞ ∞ ∞ ∞

"Are you sure you are okay with the two of us just being alone?" Elyza's voice grew more anxious by the minute.

'Bryan was going to be alone with you eventually,' I twisted the phone cord around in my fingers. 'I can't make it home from school in time. Please pick him up.'

"Well, what do I do?"

'You have worked with kids before, just talk to him.' I began signing papers as people put them in front of me. 'Elyza, you can do this.'

"He's your son though and-"

I cut her off, 'He is *our* son. You are *my* fiancée.'

I could hear her smiling through the phone.

"Okay, okay. I'll make him some of those dinosaur chicken nuggets for dinner."

'Do what you do best, my love, I'll talk to you later.'

"Okay," she sounded exhausted, but less apprehensive. "I love you."

'Love you lots, I'll see you when I get home.'

The event I ran went off without a hitch, however when Elyza was driving Bryan home, he ended up getting sick all over her car. When I came home later that night, I scrubbed her car until the stench was out.

"I am so sorry, Scott," she began tearing up a bit.

'I am sorry you had to smell hideous, regurgitated school cafeteria food in your car.'

We laughed it off, but we both knew that this was the moment that marked Elyza's official introduction into our small family since the two of them made a memory that would surely last a lifetime. I loved Elyza, and I know Bryan really did, too. Elyza was paramount in raising Bryan to become the man he is today, and I hoped they both knew how much I loved them so.

∞ ∞ ∞ ∞ ∞ ∞ ∞ ∞

There were days when being a father, a student, having a full-time job, along with balancing a relationship and trying to have a somewhat normal life were difficult. At the end of every day, I would look forward to coming home and seeing my best friend's smiling face. No matter how tough each day was, seeing Bryan made everything better.

Once when I came home rather late, Elyza said that Bryan refused to come eat dinner and refused to leave his room. He said he only wanted to talk to me and me alone.

At first, Elyza thought that it was something she did, but I assured her it had to be bigger than what meets the eye.

I approached his door cautiously and knocked carefully.

'Bryan,' I heard rustling from behind the door. 'It's me, dad, can I come in?'

"Yeah," I heard Bryan say through tears.

I came into the room and saw him lying on the bed under a bundle of blankets.

'What's wrong, buddy?'

"They said things," he sniffled, "About me in school."

'What kind of things?'

He started sobbing again. As a father, I was devastated. You never want to see your child cry, let alone anyone else say anything about your son.

"They were saying my last name is Moth-" he sniffled again and let out a yelp, "Mothman!"

'Oh Bryan,' I pulled him closer to me. He was crying uncontrollably now, and to this day I cannot forget this conversation:

'Bryan,' I rubbed his back in an effort to soothe him.

"What daddy?"

'Are you a tree?'

"What," he looked up at me, his pristine tears rolling down his cheeks. "Huh?"

'Are you a tree?'

He was confused. I paused and spoke again.

'Are you a tree?'

"What?"

'I said, are you a tree?'

He chuckled a bit, "No?"

'If I called you a tree Bryan, what would you say?'

"I would think you were crazy."

'Why?'

"Dad," he laughed again, "I am not a tree."

"Yeah," I said proudly. "And you are not any other word that anyone else will ever call you."

He hugged me and stopped crying.

'If anyone ever calls you names, just think of that word, 'tree,' and realize something.'

"What's that dad?"

'Stay grounded in who you are, and the world will respect who you are. It may take time, but stay strong, kid.'

Elyza appeared in the doorway with tears welling in her eyes. Bryan jumped off of the bed and ran directly towards her. He embraced her and she knelt down to pick him up. As she scooped him up in her arms, he nestled his head into her shoulder and said the words that made her realize just how much she meant to him: "I love you."

She gazed at me and started crying.

Sometimes, we realize who matters to us just by seeing the compassion they bestow upon us. Whether we see it outright or not, sometimes the most loving and endearing moments our loved ones give to us are hidden in the words they say or actions they do. Regardless, love comes in many shapes and sizes, as does the word family, and we knew that our little family was special. Bryan had two sets of parents that loved him dearly, and no matter what, Gemma, her husband, Elyza, and I had to join together to show Bryan exactly what it meant to be a family.

Miles away or inches apart, families are families because of the size of their hearts. At the end of the day it is not about money or what expensive things we can give to our children, it is about the love that we show them, the care we give them, and the moments that we share with them.

∞ ∞ ∞ ∞ ∞ ∞ ∞ ∞

The day Bryan was baptized, all four of his parents were there: Elyza, Gemma, Ethan, and me. The four of us re-defined family, for Elyza was officially Bryan's godmother and Ethan was officially Bryan's godfather.

As the four of us stood up there with Bryan, we smiled at one another.

Elyza leaned over to Ethan and whispered, "It takes a village to raise a child."

She was not wrong.

As Gemma placed her head on my shoulder and rubbed my back, she held Ethan's hand and said, "That's our boy."

Then Gemma grabbed Elyza's hand and looked her right in the eye. She stood there and rubbed her hand for a moment, and then Gemma softly said, "Thank you."

All four of us smiled and embraced, for we knew we were raising quite a special young man.

Our young man.

It was fitting: Gemma was my godmother when I was baptized, and now we were all standing there when Bryan was baptized. In a sense, our lives were coming full circle, and we were experiencing life in a whole new light.

In a sense, you could say that my life was shaping up to resemble an infinity sign: no matter how far I travelled, I would always be brought back to people, moments, and places to show just how far I had come...

And just how far I had to go.

That's the beauty of life: sometimes things come full circle, and we do not realize it until we can fully see what our life is becoming.

If relationships break up, there does not need to be a sort of stereotypical, "I hate you, you hate me" situation. Just because society dictates one thing, it does not mean that thing is what you must create.

Relationships can come from a place of higher consciousness if you allow them to do so. We don't have to mold ourselves into a box. We can live outside the confines of a box. We can be whatever we choose to be. We can love one another and accept one another and we can all make a difference.

∞ ∞ ∞ ∞ ∞ ∞ ∞ ∞

In the months leading up to our wedding, I sensed that something suspicious was going on with Elyza. I could never place my finger on it, but we would get into these fights where she would lock herself in our bedroom and we would talk it out, but there was an aspect of our relationship that happened behind closed doors that was unhealthy.

Still, after going through my relationship with Gemma, I wanted security and stability. Elyza provided all of that.

I wanted somebody to be on the right track with.

I wanted a teammate and a true love.

I think the saying "love is blind" blends in well with this story, but the truth is that this love was not the "love" I truly wanted. I was still searching for love and in the process, I found Elyza. However, I was still healing and developing.

With a dysfunctional state of mind, I set forth on a journey of growth, in which my relationship with Elyza assisted me in finding myself. She knew it all along too, which is why I think she pursued other people from the get go.

She liked me, maybe even was attracted to me, but she knew me well enough to know I was growing leaps and bounds. Elyza knew when I found myself; I may discover a whole other world. She knew it might be a world that did not include her. I think at one point she decided to help me unconditionally with this idea in mind, but as the years unfurled and I became more engrossed with rebuilding me, she began to stray.

I think her straying was a way to protect her emotional vulnerability. I think at the very least on a subconscious level since she felt I was going to leave her, she may as well as have someone on the side waiting for her. I always knew there were other men and always questioned her, but she would deny it.

In one instance, she was in our bedroom and she said that she met this guy and there was something about him that bothered her. She said she felt as a social worker she had to help him. However, when she said it I got this weird feeling in the pit of my stomach. Perhaps it was the way she said it. Perhaps, it was how I knew about what happened in Cancun. Perhaps it was because I knew deep down that she was not happy.

My insecurities became overwhelming. I was wholeheartedly uncomfortable with my body, and I sensed that she picked up that my confidence was diminished. My mind always drifted back to my experiences in Texas, and I thought I would never be able to get over that situation.

Then there was an instance when she found out I was still friends with Chastity. At first, she was okay with Chastity being in my life, but the second she found out that she was a dancer from a Gentleman's Club, Elyza warned her to never call again.

And we never ever spoke again.

Elyza was jealous, but then again so was I.

It was an unhealthy time for both of us.

I would sit in bed and cry myself to sleep, but she said she still loved me.

Our love was just a different kind of love.

∞ ∞ ∞ ∞ ∞ ∞ ∞ ∞

On the eve of our wedding, Elyza showed how much she loved me through giving me a gift that lasted well over two decades after that point. Earlier in our relationship, the two of us went out to a karaoke bar.

At first, I had said, and pardon my language, 'Fuck that, I am not into karaoke.' Yet the moment she got up on stage, I realized how phenomenal of a singer she was. I sat there all night, making fun of the way she controlled the stage, for I told her the truth: 'You need to be the lead singer in a band.'

She took that statement literally.

She took out an advertisement in the local paper, and before I knew it, a guitarist was playing "Hit Me with your Best Shot" by Pat Benetar in our basement.

We got married in August, soon after we had a band together, and we played our first show a few months later.

We went from playing for senior citizen homes, to volunteer organizations, to bars, and we gained a following. Our band, Outlet, ended up playing charity functions and helped raise hundreds of thousands of dollars for various organizations.

Over time, Gemma ended up moving around the country and found herself back in New York. Gemma's husband Ethan was our bass player for quite some time, while Elyza was our lead singer, and I was drumming. Our conversations were not about my past with Gemma, but rather we were all friends. We were all there for Bryan and we were a family.

When Gemma and I were together, we were not in a healthy situation, but we still learned to respect each other and became friends. At the beginning, communication was difficult, but over time Gemma and I joined together in harmony.

We harmonized together in life and in the band, and life was quite a sweet melody…

For the time being, at least…

CHAPTER 19

A Thin Line

~

"I need to know that things are gonna look up 'cause I feel us drowning in a sea spilled from a cup... I want a reason for the way things have to be. I need a hand to help build up some kind of hope inside of me."

- Train, American Rock Band, San Francisco, California

The conversations that lingered between Elyza and I grew even more distant with each passing day. I knew, deep in the crevices of my brain, that I thought of Elyza as my savior and guiding light, but then there was what happened when that light dulled with each harsh word that flew forth from her beautiful lips.

It was agonizing. I was in utter pain.

It seemed that nothing I did pleased Elyza even in the slightest.

When the phone rang, I felt a deafening chill run up my spine: it was either my sister calling to tell me something about Bryan or Elyza clamoring to get my attention. It was Elyza.

Somehow her car was towed from the area of Scarlet Middle School and she needed me to pick her up right away. As the Director of Community Service at The YM & YWHA, I was constantly out and about, but being able to help Elyza reminded me of the true love we had for one another.

I snatched the umbrella from next to my desk, hopped in the car, and drove in the drizzled rain to where she said she would be waiting.

The radio was inundated with traffic reports and illiterate static, yet I found something soothing in what resonated between the jumbled songs that played. It set a nice, reassuring tone that no matter how distracting or unclear something is, beauty still exists deep within: it is just a matter of moving or adjusting the frequency.

∞ ∞ ∞ ∞ ∞ ∞ ∞ ∞

When I finally reached Elyza, she seemed incredibly upset. An incredibly passionate and rather discombobulated argument sprung up between the two of us, and it dawned on me why she was in such an obscure area at the tail end of the afternoon:

'Wait a second, were you with Frank?' I grew rather volatile but tried to keep a calm demeanor.

Elyza was flustered instantly, "What? Why? Scott!"

'You were... you were in the school together?'

"Scott, this is ridiculous. My car broke down!"

'Well, where is it,' I questioned her. The thunder rumbled louder above our heads.

"Where is what?"

'Where is your car?'

"Okay so it got towed. Scott, I do not need to explain this to you. I do not need to explain anything to you!"

I was lost in thought and caught between the raindrops as they smashed down between us.

"Just give me your keys," she yelped, holding out her hands, "I am going home."

I passed her the car keys and she drove off, flustered and without me. Great.

I guess I would have to find her car somehow in this rainstorm. Fortunately, I had her spare car keys in the event she ever needed them. Still, how would I find the car in the middle of Queens.

As the rain came pouring out of the sky, I found salvation in a small coffee shop blocks away from the school. The poorly lit sign barely illuminated the name of the place, and I had hoped that whatever I was getting myself into was going to be welcoming enough to keep me hidden and sane for a few hours.

A small bell rang as the door slammed behind me; my soggy shoes were leaving a wet path across the linoleum tiles that lined the floor. What a way to make an entrance. A small woman adorned a frown across her face as I approached her cautiously.

A raspy, fractured voice emerged from the woman with such force: "Ya gonna mop that up, hun?" I could feel my body folding into itself rapidly.

"Hun, don't worry," she motioned her hand towards the raggedy mop in the corner, "I had nothing else to do in this ol' shop." She began walking towards the mop, leaving me cold and alone at the counter.

A dark figure rose out of the corner of my eye and approached my dripping frame. I was petrified that whatever it was would dig me further into the depressed state I was in.

The figure rested its arms on the counter and muttered, "Elaine, before you get your panties in a wad, get this poor guy something to drink."

When I whipped my head to the left, all I could see were flaming red lips and the outline of some sort of nose under a raven-black hood. She plopped onto the stool two seats away from me, and continued nursing a steaming cup in her hand.

Elaine, the repulsed woman, dropped the mop with conviction and shot me a dirty look. With a sigh, she uttered, "What'll ya have, hun?"

'A medium-sized coffee, black,' I humbly murmured, 'Please.'

She rolled her eyes into the back of her head and turned towards the half-empty ceramic coffee pot. Thunder and lightning were arguing just outside the window.

The shadow to my left was tracing an invisible infinity sign on the counter, almost as if she was forcing her negative energy into making it a perfect figure eight. I inched closer to her, ready to ask why she was sitting alone in some run-down coffee shop on a Friday night. The yellow wallpaper in the corners were peeling and seemed to creep towards Elaine's frustrated demeanor.

The shadow's eyes drilled daggers into my soul when she looked up. Though I could barely make out the color of her eyes or other features, the deep red bruises on her face were clear as day. The heavy rain complimented this woman incredibly well, and it was an unfortunate reality.

'What, what happened to you ma'am,' I spoke in a hushed tone so I didn't alarm Elaine during her grouchy coffee-pouring process. My tears were starting to fade upon realizing that this woman needed more help than I did at that moment. My hero complex rushed to the surface, but nothing else came out of my mouth.

"I don't need you to try to fix me, bud," she quipped almost instantly. Elaine turned around and started to charge at me full-speed. With fear creeping up my spine, the shadow lunged and defensively extended her arm across my chest.

"Lainie, leave the guy alone. I'm sure he isn't having a good day either," her eyes dragged along my silhouette with sheer pity. Elaine dropped the coffee cup in front of me and squinted a bit.

"Leave my girlie alone, you hear, hun," she said with such conviction. Elaine turned away and scooped the mop up.

I turned back to the shadow woman who re-positioned herself on the stool. She seemed more at ease now. As her head drifted up to meet my sunken eyes, she opened her mouth slightly. A breathy sigh came out.

'I know how you feel-' as I started speaking she cut me off with her sharp tongue.

306

"No, no you do not," she retorted through tears. Her hood dropped from her head as the bruises became more visible. They were enormous and decorated her entire face.

'Scars make you beautiful,' I whipped back.

"Well, then I am the prettiest person in the whole fucking universe," she shouted at me sarcastically.

There was a momentary pause as tears started to stream down her face. I had never seen eyes so emerald and pure before, but then again, I may have, but I could not recall from where.

Softly, I moved closer to her and whispered, 'It's your soul that makes you beautiful. Now, you may be shattered, but he didn't break you.'

Her expression softened slightly, as she whispered, "Well, Gandhi, thank you for your wisdom."

'You're very welcome, miss…' I paused for a moment to see if she would respond.

"Morena," she said, extending her hand, "The name is Morena."

I extended my hand in solidarity. 'Scott's my name,' I became half-confident that I could help her through whatever was going on. My concerns about Elyza's wrath melted away as I suddenly had a purpose: I had to help this young lady out. We moved over to a table with the exterior awning's abrupt waterfall as a backdrop.

'So, you seem like a damsel in distress,' I said, stirring my coffee so a faint clinking noise could be heard to break our silence.

"I am not a damsel in distress," she quipped mockingly, "I am a warrior princess whose crown fell off temporarily." A small smile cracked through her hardened exterior. "You aren't here to inflate your ego by playing hero."

I chuckled slightly. 'I am not trying to play hero-'

"Yeah, you are," she shot back instantaneously.

'No.'

"Yeah, kiddo, you are."

I was taken aback by her attitude. 'Did you just call me kiddo?'

She murmured a quick, "Mhm" as she sipped her drink.

'I am trying to help you, because it looks like those hurt,' I yelped.

"They are battle scars, and they may fade, but they don't heal." She was a tough little cookie with emerald green eyes that were the perfect juxtaposition to her crimson-coated face.

A pensive look came over my face as I caught myself staring into her soul. I could not help but feel torn about her situation; though bruised and badly beaten, she appeared to be solid as a mountain: no one could move her. I felt some sort of weird connection to her as she continued glaring at me with determination.

"So, what's your story," she uttered through a smirk, "No one comes into Casey's unless they have to."

'Casey's,' I questioned.

She shifted her weight and tucked her left leg beneath her. "Casey's," she motioned around the room, "This excuse of a coffee shop."

'Oh,' I said embarrassingly, 'This place is something else.'

Elaine perked up from behind the counter for a moment as Morena glanced in her direction.

"Casey's was Elaine's husband's lifelong dream. When he passed away, she did everything she could to keep it up and running. 30 years later, she is still here," Morena began swishing what was left of her drink around the interior of the cup.

I sat in awe for a moment at this woman's demeanor. Despite the bruises across her face, she didn't seem to care about herself. She was fixated on everything around her: the raindrops racing down the window, the door creaking slightly, Elaine's whereabouts... Morena was focused on everything and nothing at once.

I watched her eyes dart around the room until I expressed concern for her, 'What do you fear, Morena?'

She sat in silence for a moment with a blank look on her face. "Nothing," she started, "I fear nothing." It sounded like she told that lie a thousand times. Somehow, I think she was beginning to believe it for a change.

'You must fear something,' I tilted my head towards her, trying to pry an answer from her lips.

She grinned slightly and asked, "What do you fear, Scott?"

It took me a moment to conjure up a response. What did I fear? What did I know? Could I come up with an answer that would appease this woman?

'Loneliness,' was the first thing that flew from my mouth.

She placed her hand over mine and curled her fingers underneath my grasp. "Well, Scott," she softened her tone, "You have a friend at Casey's."

We sat and continued talking after that moment. Morena seemed like such a mysterious figure; within an hour of knowing her she knew a lot about me, but she was a mysterious and seemingly selfless shadow in a coffee shop. I did not know what to make of her.

I felt I could be open to this stranger about my fight with Elyza, for Morena did not seem like a threatening creature. As I began explaining my relationship with Elyza to her, Morena propped her elbow on the table and rested her chin in her hand. She seemed intrigued by me.

It was quite odd.

A long dramatic pause cut between us as I released the words, 'I feel so worthless and alone' into the air. I think this was the first time I admitted how I felt about our relationship, I mean, after all, she was cheating on me and I could not do a single thing about it.

Morena whisked her hand in my direction and grasped my forearm. "Come with me, now," she announced. Her small body pulled me across Casey's and into the Men's Bathroom, which was equally as run-down.

I had no choice but to follow this woman on her sudden journey. Morena stopped me in front of the crusted-over mirror and pointed at it, "What do you see?"

I stood for a moment and came up with the first thing I did see: 'You, me, and a whole lot of grime.'

Her eyes narrowed as they rolled backwards.

"Scott," she said through an angry laugh, "What do you see?" She pointed back at the mirror.

I gazed at my reflection for a moment and came up with the next thing I could think of: 'Myself. Wet, exhausted, and grumpy.'

We turned and looked at each other as she placed her hand on my left shoulder. She spoke again, only with more pause and purpose this time, "What do you see?"

I responded with, 'Myself. Wet, exhausted, grumpy, and standing in a dirty Men's bathroom."

"What do you see?" She spoke again.

'Myself. Wet, exhausted, grumpy, in a dirty Men's room with you telling me to look at my reflection. Morena, I don't understand.'

"Look again," She remarked with a softer tone.

I glared at myself and noticed my blonde hair obscuring part of my face. I brushed my hair behind my ear and sighed.

'I see myself, wet, grumpy, tired-' she cut me off as I was about to trail into the Men's bathroom part of my speech again.

She pushed me closer to the mirror so I could get a better look at myself.

"Look past what you see as obvious," she whispered, "Now, what do you see?"

I gazed into the mirror and caught the reflection of flickering fluorescent lights this time. More of my surroundings came into focus as I captured this moment in my memory. Here I was in a bathroom with a strange person in a crummy coffee shop, and I couldn't help but ask myself how I got here.

Oh right, Elyza's latest tantrum.

'I see a man trying to become a better dad and a better husband,' I started, 'I see a man who needs help, I see a man who throws his heart and soul into everything, I see a man who wants to begin again, and I also see a man who does not know how to.'

Morena stood in silence for a moment while she collected her thoughts.

"Ok," she said matter-of-factly.

'Ok?'

"Yeah, okay, that's it," she backed away from me and leaned against the cracked lime green tiles.

I stood and glared at her with a confused look across my face. Why did she do that? Why did she pull me in here? What did she expect me to say?

"I can see you're trying to justify why I did that," she shrugged her shoulders, "I'll tell you when you're older."

'Why me,' I asked her.

"Why not you," she responded with sincerity.

The two of us exited the bathroom as I still wore the perplexed look on my face. What was her purpose? Why did we meet? Why did I feel connected to her suddenly?

Elaine was wiping down the counter with a red-checkered rag. The rain was slowing down and our drinks were losing their steam. I looked at the sunset that was peering between the clouds. How long was I here for? Would Elyza notice I was even gone?

Morena and I returned to our seats by the window and sat in silence. Who is she? What was she? Why did she care? Did she care? So many questions whizzed through my head. My heart could not take any more turmoil.

I stood up abruptly and explained to Morena I had to leave.

"See you soon," she said, almost as if she knew I would be back.

'Take care of those bruises,' I responded. She cringed at the mention of her face. It was like for a few hours she forgot about whatever havoc was brewing in her mind and her life.

"Take care, Scott," she said amicably.

The tiny bell chimed behind me as I rushed out of the short oasis I created for myself. I knew someday I would be back here, I just didn't know how soon…

Or if I, indeed, was ever going to be in the presence of that peculiar woman again.

Upon exiting the coffee shop, I peered down the block and saw a blue Honda at the edge of the street. On a hunch, I clicked Elyza's car key remote and the car's lights flickered. She was on the wrong block, her car did not get towed, it was there before me.

I guess it was just my luck.

I hopped in the car and drearily drove home, only to find Elyza reached our answering machine a few hours before I did and received the news first.

∞ ∞ ∞ ∞ ∞ ∞ ∞ ∞

When I walked in the door, Elyza wrapped her arms around me with tears welling in her eyes.

"Thank God you are home," she muddled through tears. I wiped the tears from her eyes and implored her to tell me what happened and why she seemed so devastated and elated all at once.

Our dear friend, Adam, committed suicide.

He was the first police officer of the millenium to pass away.

And somehow this story unfolded just hours after what happened between Elyza and myself.

∞ ∞ ∞ ∞ ∞ ∞ ∞ ∞

A solitary light shone through the crack in the door.

All I could see was her silhouette drifting between the windows. She paced fervently, the wooden floorboards echoing her concerns as she did her dance through the night.

I glared up at the ceiling, its settling cracks tracing the cracks in my heart. She was fading. She was drifting away.

'Are you coming to bed?' I waited anxiously for a response. She was silent.

A pitter pat pitter pat noise was all that resonated throughout the house. A faint echo that acted as a reminder that Adam left too soon before his time.

We spend years traversing bridges in their own right and their own respect: a link between souls and their humanistic frame.

But when one leaps from a bridge, all words seem to be severed at the core of their morphological echoes.

We search for lifetimes for an answer, knowing that we have the ability to chase passions and dreams as long as we remember we are born to run. Still, some people do not realize the gaping hole they leave if they take their path and try to erase it before their story is told.

No matter what question is asked in terms of a person's lifetime, suicide is never the answer. I knew that Elyza knew that. We just hoped that Adam would have remembered that as well. For he left the world with a reminder that help is within arm's reach, even if that reach extends across a thin blue line.

His passing became a beacon: one of solidarity and one of hopefulness. His life and legacy did not fade and his memory is constantly floating in the hearts and minds of those who knew him and were touched by his presence.

Weeks upon months, Elyza and I would spend time helping his wife Penny with various things around the house and beyond. We would pick her three sons up from school along with Bryan, and keep them at the house until Penny arrived home from work. Things between Elyza and I seemed to grow stronger, and it appeared that we were closer than ever before.

One night while I was watching the four boys play in the living room, Penny came to pick the kids up early and brought in a small box with a bow placed neatly on top.

"Mama Mama Mama," the little ones chanted: they were nine, ten, and twelve years old, which was rather close to Bryan's age, but they still longed for their mother to come pick them up so they could all get dinner together.

"Let mama talk with Uncle Scott for a second and we will get going, okay kiddos?" Penny kissed each of them on the forehead and they trotted back into the living room as the two of us walked silently into the kitchen.

'Hey, I don't know how they got so wired,' I said wistfully, 'It isn't like I fed them ice cream after school or-'

Penny cut my words short with her laughter and said it was no bother, she loved to see them smiling and laughing again. It was late June 2001 at this point and we were just winding down for the upcoming summer.

"Hey, Scott, this is for you," Penny gently handed me the box and waited patiently for me to open it. "I know it must be crazy to handle the four boys day in and day out."

'Penny, don't worry about it,' I responded while untying the box. The bow was a gorgeous blue and gold masterpiece. 'You didn't have to get anything for me for caring for those little angels.'

"That's the thing," she said, "they are little angels, yes, but you are an angel."

I lifted the lid of the box to find a pristine porcelain statue that sang from somewhere deep in my soul. Five little figurines were holding hands, their angelic wings barely touching and their little halos placed perfectly on their heads.

'Penny, what is this?' I was in awe.

"This, Scott, this is the circle of angels. You have been a part of my circle of angels since Adam's passing, now I want to ensure you are protected as well. Thank you."

Penny and I embraced in the kitchen, and I am sure she could feel the tears streaming down my face.

The circle of angels, I loved the name. It touched me deeply.

I had a circle of angels.

CHAPTER 20

The Lights Went Out On Broadway

~

"It's different than it was before. Now we need it even more. Fire's falling from the sky. Innocence just said goodbye. It may never be the same. Maybe it was time to change. A time to grieve. A time to cry. A time to live. A time to fly… Another reason to believe"

- Bon Jovi, American Rock Band, Sayreville, New Jersey

When I got home, Elyza was nowhere to be found. If her stuff weren't strewn around the house, I would have convinced myself that she left me for good. That didn't seem like the case… well, for now at least.

I have been pouring my soul into being a light for everyone else, but who will light my way? I certainly don't think it is Elyza, for she seems just like all of the others: another case of love me then leave me.

I caught my face in the mirror as I walked down the hallway. My blonde hairs were frolicking about on my head. School was weighing heavy on my mind, Elyza's latest and greatest actions were messing with my head, but all I could think about was the mysterious Morena. Why? It was the early 2000s, and the world could have ended with Y2K's supposed doom, but here I was, not living the life I had hoped for. I was counting down to the days when I would find true love; only I didn't know when that countdown would stop.

I had to push all of this energy and passion I had into something positive. I can't just waste away while trying to find the next love of my life, if she was truly out there. Is she out there?

The slam of the front door dragged me back to reality for a moment: Elyza was finally home. The melodic plop of her bag and sigh from a long day's work reminded me that she really had a rough life, and I was definitely making it more difficult for her. Did I ever truly have her heart?

"Hey," she was surprised by my presence, almost as if she forgot I existed until that moment.

'Hi,' I said.

The two of us glared at each other and she rushed to embrace me.

"You are the one still, Scott." She was whispering into my chest.

'I know, I know.'

We stood there in the center of the room with life revolving around us slowly.

"I love-" I pressed my finger to her lips gently.

'You don't have to say it.'

"No, because I feel it." Elyza smiled, stood on her toes, and kissed me on the cheek.

The rest of the night was a bit of a blur and as the summer followed, I felt pieces of myself fading behind Elyza's persistent absences during obscure hours of the night. Regardless, she still assured she loved me and we continued our relationship.

∞ ∞ ∞ ∞ ∞ ∞ ∞ ∞

As September rolled around, it seemed as if everything was shaping up nicely. Elyza seemed to be perkier than usual and our relationship appeared to be blossoming into something truly transcendental.

I had hope again. I had faith. I had a small family that was close-knit, and we were together. Aunt Barbara and I had been going on long walks to talk about existential questions. We were bonding and I finally felt that I was living a life I was supposed to be experiencing years and years ago.

Positive thoughts and the conversations I had with my Aunt Barbara helped propel me towards finally having a career opportunity where I felt that I could actually help countless teenagers.

The principal of a city high school hired me to be their school's Social Worker, and I could not have been happier.

On my first day of work, September 11, 2001, I had just dropped Bryan off to school and drove home to get ready for my first day. I was rehearsing everything I would say to the students and my future fellow co-workers. I was thinking about how I would set up my office and what I would do to encourage students to seek out my advice.

I had four years of experience working with youth and I was still considering starting my own business.

As I finished preparing my lunch and started walking out of the door at 8:40 in the morning, my cell phone rang.

'Hello?'

"Hello my boy, are you ready for your big day?" Aunt Barbara's warm voice was such a comfort.

'Hey, I guess so. It's been a long time since I felt that I could make something of myself, so yeah, I think I am ready.'

"I am so proud of you." Aunt Barbara's infectious smile could be felt through the phone. I got into my car, shut the door, and plopped my lunch bag on the passenger seat.

I did not have my Social Work degree yet, but I was well on my way. Today would be the first day in my life that I would genuinely make a difference.

Aunt Barbara reassured me that today was going to go incredibly well.

"I have faith in you," her tone was gentle, like the symphony from a baby bird, and suddenly I felt an intense sense of calm. I was about to thank her for her wisdom and for everything she had done for me up until this point. I was grateful for the positivity she brought to my life regularly.

Then, at 8:45 in the morning, I heard a loud crash over the phone.

Then there was complete silence.

'Aunt Barbara, you there?' She worked in lower Manhattan, so odds are a car had backfired or something was going on floors below her window.

"Scott," her tone transformed into a more somber sensation. "Something is going on, I'll call right back."

She hung up the phone and I was left in a state of confusion. Something was wrong. Something was awry.

I turned on the radio as I did every single morning and was met with the answer to the lingering questions spinning through my head:

Approximately a few minutes ago, a plane hit the North Tower of the World Trade Center in lower Manhattan. We will have more on this developing story shortly.

Images of a small plane struggling filtered through my head. I thought about all of the people in the building who must have seen the plane coming and started running. I thought about the passengers on the plane. I thought about the scene unfolding and how tragic of an accident scene it must be.

I called my Aunt Barbara instinctively.

"Hello," she picked up instantaneously.

'Hey, is everything okay?'

"Yeah," she seemed somewhat nonchalant. "I think it was a small plane that crashed into one of the Twin Towers. It's odd though."

'What?' I was stopped at a red light and began tapping on my steering wheel.

"My building shook."

'Your building?' The light turned green, but I didn't move. She was less than a mile from the Twin Towers, but you could see them from her office window.

I started driving a bit further down the road when the second plane hit. This was no accident.

I do not think that even the most eloquent language in this universe could fully fathom or capture what that second plane sounded like over the phone.

The air was filled with fear and destruction. Time stood still and the sheer panic on my face melted into my lap.

The world changed at that moment for everyone and everything. Listening to an explosion through the phone was deafening. My spirit shattered in tandem with the crackling windows that radiated down the south tower.

"I have to go. I love you." Aunt Barbara hung up the phone and my heart stopped beating for a moment.

I turned the news back on, as did probably everyone on the planet. My phone rang again and I was praying it was Aunt Barbara. It was my new job.

They said not to come in.

'You hired me to be a Social Worker, what do you mean don't come in?'

"Don't come in," the woman said. "We're under attack. We don't know what's going on. We're assessing the situation."

Then there was a solid click. She hung up.

∞ ∞ ∞ ∞ ∞ ∞ ∞ ∞

I hung on every single word of the monotone voice now blasting over the radio. I began driving towards Manhattan, unsure of what my end goal was. I needed to help however I could. I needed to be there for people. I had the inherent urge to ditch my car somewhere in Queens and run into Manhattan.

Bryan's echoic voice penetrated my mind. I could hear him crying for his father somewhere in the distant future. I could sense his fear from miles away.

The city was being locked down.

People were being evacuated out of Manhattan in droves.

I called whoever I could think of, including my friend who lived out in Massapequa near me. He was an officer with the New York Police Department. He went in right away.

I responded to the urge growing in my soul and started driving to the Queensboro Bridge. I figured that would be the quickest way to get into Manhattan, but as I drove closer and closer, a man in half of a uniform was standing in the middle of the road blocks before the bridge. He looked like a police officer, but he was wearing jeans and a fluorescent NYPD jacket.

He told me to turn around and go to a safe place.

Life as I knew it shifted in a matter of moments.

I put my car in reverse and watched the solemn faces of people covered in dirt and debris walk past me. Public transportation must have been shut down and there must have been mass hysteria flowing through the city.

As I watched, the hollowed eyes of New Yorkers scanned crowds of people as they wandered the streets of Queens.

I took a deep breath and pulled over somewhere. Elyza called and we started to come up with a plan.

"I think we should pick up Bryan and drive to Canada." I heard the trepidation in her voice.

Thick clouds of black smoke were blowing east through the borough of Queens. It had to have been coming from the Twin Towers.

The radio blared over Elyza's cries:

The World Trade Center's Twin Towers have collapsed. Debris and smoke are blanketing the city. Ladies and gentlemen, we are under attack.

Elyza's voice faded back in: "Toronto is a big city. We can hide there. I heard fifty planes were taken over by terrorists."

This was no time to freeze and wait for life to happen.

This was not the moment in time where I would just throw my hands up and panic.

I pulled the visor down in my car and took a good, hard look at myself in the mirror.

'We stay,' I told Elyza. 'We stay and we live as New Yorkers, and as United States citizens.'

I can't remember what Elyza said in response to my assertion. She was equally as worried as I was, but as with every individual, we manifest emotions differently.

We could have been on the verge of World War III. We could have been immersed in an attack on the White House. We could have been dealing with any number of tragedies that could have been erupting all over our country.

In those moments, I believed time would tell what would come of our nation. I took solace in remembering that we were, indeed, the land of the free and the home of the brave.

There were a multitude of patriotic sentiments manifesting throughout my conscious mind. I drove, in somewhat of a daze, back to Massapequa and back to the quaint house with red shingles that Elyza and I had recently moved into.

As I passed towns, cars, people, and trees, the same environment I had seen many times before, I felt different. A strong sensation was burning in my veins, and it was nothing like I had ever felt before.

Courage was coursing through my veins. Faith in my country's leaders, and in the individuals who lived and breathed the same air I did, was running rampant through my soul. My heart was pounding from my chest, but it was pounding to the beat of heroes who would be marching into the city to protect and care for those who were injured in the attack that happened today.

Souls would be relying on each other to stay strong. We, as a country, would need to remain steadfast. No matter what was happening, we had to redefine the words unity and community in our country.

We would all have to step up.

We would all have to face the world with our hands resting on our hearts and the melody of the National Anthem serenading every last drop of the fervor we had within us.

As I got out of the car and walked up the steps to my house, I looked at the large white symbol, 11A, which juxtaposed the ruby red shingles of the house. I paused and turned to the American flag that was waving in the wind in the distance, its vibrant colors were clear as day despite the halo of gray that shrouded every solemn fiber of the world we now had to become accustomed to.

I closed my eyes and let the words of the National Anthem flow through me:

"Oh, say, can you see, by the dawn's early light,
What so proudly we hailed at the twilight's last gleaming?
Whose broad stripes and bright stars, thro' the perilous fight'
O'er the ramparts we watched, were so gallantly streaming.
And the rockets red glare, the bombs bursting in air,
Gave proof through the night that our flag was still there.
Oh, say, does that Star-Spangled Banner yet wave
O'er the land of the free and the home of the brave?"

We are the free. We are the brave.

These colors of patriotism and valiancy will not run.

We are Americans. We are all Americans. We are New Yorkers. We are the future and we are going to uphold the strength of the American people no matter what happens in this country.

I opened my eyes and saw the effervescent flag briskly whipping through the air. We are proud. We will stand tall. We will not succumb to tragedy.

We are individuals, and united we stand in the face of adversity.

Our world would not bend or bow to terrorism, not then, not now, not ever. We do not negotiate, we communicate, and we show who we are in our acts of valor.

We are the legacy of all of those who perished before us, and the individuals whose souls left this planet before their time and at the hands of others.

We are the living, we will continue to live, and we will continue to stand, united.

I retreated into the house and put my palms on the wooden dining room table. I glared at my reflection in the mirror and shed a tear for those whose physical journey ended today, although their spiritual journey and legacy would live on.

This was the dawn of a brand-new era, and we the people of the United States would continuously build on tranquility, justice, and liberty in this country.

∞ ∞ ∞ ∞ ∞ ∞ ∞ ∞

In the months that passed, I collected the memories of 9/11 and the stories of those who represented our country that day in the crevices of my heart.

We did not hear from Aunt Barbara for about 48 hours after the attack. She was a first responder, and a former registered nurse, who bravely rushed to the scene as it was unfolding. She spent every single day of her life for the next six months pulling bodies out of the rubble.

She embraced heroism and her role in this universe as a savior. For those six months, she was breathing in the aftermath of screaming people, desolation, tragedy, and chemicals. Unfortunately, Aunt Barbara got sick as a result of her efforts, but she did not make her illness too well known.

Three months after 9/11 happened, I made my way into lower Manhattan to see the damage with my own eyes.

The news was reporting images of tattered flags flying above Ground Zero. There were visuals of people covered in dust traveling through the streets. People had to walk across bridges to get out of Manhattan because trains and tunnels shut down. The transportation tunnels that once ran below the towers were crushed when the towers fell.

Bryan was silent about 9/11 for months. As a child, how do you fully comprehend what is going on in the world, especially when the news is plastering images of blood, destruction, and gore across every screen and newspaper imaginable?

Why would anyone do something so devastating to so many people?

The world fell to its knees, and we had to pick each other and ourselves back up.

While I walked through the streets of lower Manhattan three months after the tragedy, I was devastated.

The smell of flesh hung just below my nose. Tears shattered onto the floor with a resounding thud. The new chapter was beginning, and the old one just went up into vibrant flames.

I felt my core crumble at the sight of debris and loose paper from months prior float through the air.

I could not fathom how anyone would wage such a war on others and on themselves. To plan and create an attack of this caliber was a massive act of incongruence upon the inherent strength we all carry within us. This was an act of violence. This was an act of anger.

This was an internal war that was projected onto the souls of those who represented the citizens of this fine country.

The energy and lives of those who were impacted by the destruction of the Twin Towers in New York, the attack on the Pentagon, and the demolition of Flight 93 on the same day, would not fade to gray. Hope remains. Faith remains. Strength remains.

We are free.

We are innately free individuals.

We are humans, regardless of borders or the land we come from, and we all must work together to uphold holistic human values and do so on a daily basis.

And if anyone or anything tries to challenge the facets of human decency, there is much to be developed and created in this world...

There is always a story behind the story.

There is always a bridge to be constructed, created, or strengthened between souls, communities, and societies.

Above all, we must come together.

No matter what, there is a will and there is a way.

And when a door closes... one must open a window of opportunity.

CHAPTER 21

Building Bridges

"You can't start a fire. Sittin' 'round cryin' over a broken heart. This gun's for hire even if we're just dancin' in the dark. You can't start a fire without a spark."

- Bruce Springsteen, American Singer-Songwriter, Long Branch, New Jersey

Every single morning after 9/11, I waited to hear my phone ring with good news. I was praying, sometimes overtly and often internally, for the high school to call and tell me they were ready for me. I was fully prepared to jump in and do what I could to support the children of New York City, especially on the day the sky filled with ash and remnants of fleeting hope, yet I was told to wait.

I was done with waiting.

I wanted to do what always burned deep within my core, yet I was told to wait: don't come in to work, wait. This does not work right now, wait.

How much waiting could I commit to?

How much patience could I uphold before I broke down?

The waiting game was not something I could play anymore. Once I realized that my willingness to help others and my innate, considerate nature had to be brought out into the open, I chose not to be a pawn entrenched in societal notions.

Life was taking me down a road I had not traveled before. In the wake of a tragedy that was wrought with anxiety, fear, and much trepidation, there were countless questions and few answers. As our country was ensnared in adversity, I hoped to provide some semblance of clarity; our youth and our country deserved it.

Then, about a month and a half into "waiting patiently," the phone finally rang.

A woman's stern voice beckoned to me: "You can come into work today."

I threw the outfit that I wore for my original first day back on and dashed out the front door.

Life began again on October 30, 2001.

∞ ∞ ∞ ∞ ∞ ∞ ∞ ∞

As I walked through the thick, abysmal doors, no one greeted me. I carried boxes of books and folders in, only to be met with a flurry of high school students rushing to and from classrooms and hallways.

No one cared.

No one acknowledged my presence.

If I were a fly on that wall in that very moment, which I might as well have been, I would have embraced each passing second slightly more than I did. There would have been a certain essence of tranquility in enveloping myself in my new environment. I would have been able to dive further into elements of my new surroundings had I appreciated the silent freedom I was granted in merely walking in the building alone.

Yet, in those moments, I felt that this was the beginning of some sort of bureaucratic whirlwind. Who does not welcome a new employee at the door in the morning? Who opts to hide away in an office or classroom, merely carrying on with their day as a means of fulfilling a job, not a life's true calling?

Regardless, I chose to walk into the main office and search for a place to drop my boxes.

With a thud, I made the first of many echoes throughout the halls of that building.

"You Matheson?" A petite woman with miniscule glasses glared up at me.

'Yeah.' I matched her nonchalance with a bland expression.

"Room 339 is yours. You can head on up. Make sure you move your timecard when you come in and out of the building, and we *won't* have any problems." She retreated into another area of the office.

The bustling and movement in the hallway died down, so I instinctively made my way to the third floor.

My eyes dragged along the numbers on the wall. The classrooms looked drab and bleak.

It seemed that if the rooms were this dull, the students would be bursting out of them by any means necessary in search of help for their various issues and concerns.

The jet-black numbers contrasted with the wooden door that stood before me: 339. Three-hundred and thirty-nine. I had hoped it was the first sign of many that would grace my presence as a Social Worker.

I dropped the boxes before me and grabbed the doorknob. A chill flooded down my spine as I took a deep breath.

My entire frame heaved as a sigh escaped from my mouth.

'Here we go,' I whispered.

The door somehow opened on its own.

A teenage girl with long chestnut hair stood before me with her hands on her hips. She had sincere eyes and a fire-engine red t-shirt on.

"Well, it's about time," she all but demanded.

'What?' I pushed my boxes into the room with my foot. Dust from the floor fluttered into the air.

"Do you realize that I have been cutting class for the last month while trying to wait for you?" She threw open the top box and started to rummage through it.

'Who-' I circled her and let my eyes wander through my new office. 'Who are you?'

"Oh," she picked up a coffee mug and placed it on the table behind her, "I'm Mandy. The social worker who used to work here told me to teach you the ropes."

'Oh.' She shook my hand.

"You're Scott Matheson, it's good to meet you." She had a refreshing tinge of spontaneity in her. I could feel her positive energy radiating from her core.

We began talking while we unpacked the items from my boxes. She placed the books on the shelves on the far wall, but Mandy did not toss them haphazardly. With each item she removed and brought into the office, she glanced around before she put it in its seemingly rightful place.

She shared stories about her mother and father's struggles. We spoke in detail about her younger siblings who she tended to regularly.

Mandy's maturity became more apparent with each word she spoke: she was a graceful human being sheltered in a fractured cocoon of a teenager's body.

"Come on," she placed the last book on the shelf. "Let me show you around the school.

Mandy took me on a tour throughout the building, which included a comprehensive list of where I could find troubled students in the neighborhood. She also explained to me the teachers she thought were understanding and made an effort to tell me which of the teachers she felt were far from caring.

It was a true treat: I got a glimpse of the school I would be working in from a student herself. I was inspired by watching a student show me around the school, for it confirmed what I knew for so long: even students can be leaders when given the chance.

The two of us spent days exploring parts of the school and finding students who needed counseling. By the end of the first week, my office was jam-packed with stories of students who had self-esteem issues, eating disorders, family troubles, and so much more.

By day, I was in the midst of a carousel: I watched the children enter my office sometimes feeling lower than low, but by the time they left, I could see their demeanors and emotions being elevated before my very eyes.

It was happening.

I was a Social Worker.

I was making a difference.

∞ ∞ ∞ ∞ ∞ ∞ ∞ ∞

When I arrived home, sometimes far beyond the moments where the horizon faded to darkness, I was equipped with countless stories about my day, my students, and whom I was helping.

Bryan always scampered up to me and plopped next to me.

"How was your day, daddy?" His cheerful smile made any chaotic day better.

'It was good. How about you, bud?'

He proceeded to tell me all about his friends, his experiences, and how great of a day he had.

It was refreshing to see how much he was growing before my very eyes, and every chance I got; I would pause and just admire my son. His life came to be because of decisions I made years prior, and I could only hope that my decisions since his birth have reflected the better man I was trying to become.

I only pray that he sees his father as a role model and someone to look up to.

Elyza burst through the bedroom door and shrunk down into a chair opposite Bryan and I. She had a magazine in hand and was peering over it to see what we were talking about.

After half an hour of sharing stories about life and school, Bryan ran to the bathroom to get ready for bed. Elyza and I sat awkwardly avoiding each other, but for no apparent reason.

'How was your day?' I un-crossed my legs and rested my right arm on the sofa.

She sat in silence for a while until the magazine dropped from her hand.

"It was okay, I guess." Elyza appeared as if she was trying to be interested in me, and my day, but something was clearly on her mind.

'Do you-' I started to speak, but the phone rang. She zoomed from the couch into the kitchen to pick up her cellphone. I could hear murmurs of what she was saying, but it was difficult to make out the conversation.

I got up and began puttering around the house. I felt as if she did not want me to know about what was going on, so I went about my business.

After hearing Bryan shuffle off to bed and shut his door, I made my way out onto the steps. The brisk night air ran through each strand of my hair, whisking its allure through the pensive thoughts that filled my mind.

I was inundated with questions as usual, but I was entranced by the beauty of the night sky. Just a little over a month ago, I was standing on these very steps gazing up into a different sky. I would spend hours and hours standing on these steps watching the world float by. Thoughts of where my relationship with Elyza was going filtered through my mind. Sitting on the steps would provide me with an entirely different outlook of the world, but I was always perched upon one of the same steps.

The evening brought a new voice to Massapequa at night, for the suburban neighborhood's noises would simmer throughout the course of the night. By day, the laughter and jubilance of children would flood the street in the early morning and at three in the afternoon, but I was not able to hear those sounds anymore. I was at work by the time the kids would begin their daily routines. As a matter of fact, by the time the children retreated into their respective houses, I was still at work.

I was privileged to hear the chirps of crickets or cicadas, or whatever wildlife existed after the moon cast its shadow upon the water tower nearby.

The American flag slept in the distance, while I watched the headlights of cars flash by as they cascaded down our block.

I closed my eyes and inhaled the night air. I exhaled the darkness within me, and the trepidation fluttering in my core.

∞ ∞ ∞ ∞ ∞ ∞ ∞ ∞

Upon returning back inside, Elyza was nowhere to be found. I had not heard her leave the house, nor did I see her leave in her car, so I assumed she had to be somewhere.

I tiptoed into Bryan's room carefully and kissed him goodnight. His rosy cheeks were barely noticeable in the shadows, but as his father I knew him well enough to know just where he would position himself in bed.

He adjusted himself slightly and smiled, making me feel as if my gentle sign of affection would usher him into a peaceful night of sweet dreams.

Elyza was still somewhere in the house, though I could not discern where. Therefore, I listened to my exhausted body and strolled into the bedroom. It must have been about twenty minutes or so until Elyza flew into the room crying hysterically. In retrospect, I heard the fight. I heard the breakup happening between her and another man over the phone.

In those moments, I did not think to say, "Oh no, my wife is steeping out on me."

She was my wife, so I did what any loving husband should or would do: I embraced her and whispered in her ear.

As she heaved and sobbed openly, all I could muster up was, 'Everything will be okay.'

Fortunately, everything was.

∞ ∞ ∞ ∞ ∞ ∞ ∞ ∞

At work, it was a normal day in a fast paced, emotionally intensified atmosphere. The setting was a small office on the third floor of a school building.

As a social worker who was coordinating a leadership and counseling program, my door seemed revolving in nature... There were tons of adolescents, tons of emotions, tons of issues, and best of all an abundance of inspiration.

There was something incredibly special about youth who were given an opportunity to voice their opinions in a constructive and an innovative environment.

During these early years as a new social worker, I was looking to make a huge difference in this world. I wanted to give youth an ear, as well as empower them to believe in their dreams.

I had no idea that on one particular day a young student would suggest an idea that would ultimately be the catalyst to years of HIV Awareness work, additional leadership trainings, teen-led conferences, and the creation of a manual to implement in schools across the country.

The student approached me and said she was a "peer leader" and she was trained by an organization in the city to teach other peers about HIV awareness. She said that she thought it was an issue that there was no education plan in her school.

She was upset that many of her friends were not making healthy decisions.

She asked me if she could do one training for the students in my program. I have to admit that the idea struck a personal chord in my heart. I had recently lost a friend to HIV and another youth leader I was working with had lost her mom to HIV as well.

It was an issue dear to my heart and that I wanted to take on. I thought to myself, if we could only educate our youth in an innovative manner, maybe they will listen and we can stop this virus. Perhaps that innovative manner was to be taught by youth their own age.

Thus, an entirely new era of youth leadership and empowerment was born and continued to blossom for years and years to come.

Day in and day out, I was thinking about ways to integrate youth leadership programs into schools across New York City. I was building school curriculums, inspiring teenagers to create and implement different lessons, and staying incredibly late at night to make sure the kids had a safe place to stay after their classes ended.

We created our own community.

We created our own family.

We shaped our lives in molding one another's thoughts.

In giving students a voice, I was able to create my own voice. This led me to walk down a winding path of question after question, but through it all the pain and agony I felt was dissipating: in helping the kids find their way, I was able to find my own way.

Though I had quite a long way to go…

∞ ∞ ∞ ∞ ∞ ∞ ∞ ∞

Towards the final days of the 2001 - 2002 school year, Bryan would come to the office and hang out with the kids. He would hide on the couch under their jackets and bags and they would love spending time with him.

It was inspiring to all of us.

Bryan got a chance to see his father in action for a change, and he seemed to love it.

The office had a glass partition with a hole in it, which was created by a former student from years ago, who punched the glass. Its fractures and radiating cracks were a constant reminder that lives were lived long before I came into this office, and now it was my turn to help students realize their full potential was within reach.

I would hold sessions in the smaller part of the office, while the groups would take place in the larger section of the office.

Between Bryan's presence and the uplifting work being created in the office, I felt my passion was finally flowing freely.

With the end of the school year, my first official school year as a social worker, I had a lot of hope. Elyza was happy that I was back around again and we started going to concerts together.

The two of us got tickets to see Aerosmith, which was one of our favorite bands to listen to together for their music livened up my spirit unlike any other band. Bon Jovi was and has always been my favorite band, though there is something special about an Aerosmith song.

We were able to get backstage passes to the show because the piano tuner for Aerosmith, Uncle Ernie, worked with myself and Elyza at a number of local agencies in New York. The two of us would sit for hours upon hours and listen to him tell us how proud he was of his nephew, the one and only Steven Tyler, the front man of Aerosmith, who took his love for music and brought it to stages across the world.

Uncle Ernie would gleam with pride as he told us fascinating stories about Steven Tyler, and the two of us would thoroughly enjoy seeing the pure happiness that spread across his face each time he would talk about his nephew. We heard about amazing adventures and ideas Steven Tyler would be a part of while growing up, knowing that all of these stories led up to the fascinating concerts and performances he would amaze audiences with.

All of the people who knew Ernie naturally called him Uncle Ernie.

He was in his eighties, yet he never ceased to recall days of when he was in an orchestra as a kid and was involved in the music scene. He was so well respected that after countless Aerosmith shows, Elyza and I would show up, call backstage, and tell people that we knew Uncle Ernie. Each time, he would happily invite us backstage to see what was going on and meet the band.

Uncle Ernie supported the local community churches, which later became home to a music program that I would run in the future called Rock Ur Heart Out. It was a somber, quiet loss to the music community when he passed away at 94. I consider it one of my biggest blessings and honors to have known him and be in his presence. Supportive family members like Uncle Ernie are paramount in any aspect of life, including the music business. Each and every one of the members of Aerosmith are so down to earth, and it is probably because of the support they received from their family members like Uncle Ernie.

Elyza and I were able to meet the band on multiple occasions, which was one of the highlights for each of our musical passions.

Steven Tyler is as funny in person as he is when he expresses himself on stage and on television. His mannerisms and actions in front of fans, his friends, and family were beyond amazing, and I was fortunate to see his persona in action and become a part of an experience that could last a lifetime.

There was a man hanging out backstage with us after one of the concerts who was chatting with Steven Tyler. Elyza stood in awe of Tyler, with her push-up bra and lace-lined tank top nearly pushing her breasts in everyone's face.

I watched Steven Tyler talk to this man who he knew by name, which was rather admirable. He is famous and making time for his fans, friends, and family. Mid-sentence, Steven Tyler stopped and turned towards Elyza for, let's face it, she was hard to miss.

"Everybody stop… stop… everyone," Steven Tyler yelled.

We all looked at each other and asked why.

"Jimmy, do you want to know how great it is to be a rock star?" Steven Tyler grinned from ear to ear. His smile was contagious to the other people standing around.

Steven Tyler turned to Elyza and outright says, "Would you mind if I autograph your breasts?"

Elyza, without fail, responded, "I don't mind at all."

He then took a permanent marker from someone's hand and signed her breasts. I don't think she took a shower for an entire week after the situation occurred.

Seeing that young guy's face light up when Steven Tyler signed Elyza's chest appeared to light up his whole life. People have the ability to make or break someone's day, and the power of music can genuinely inspire some pretty amazing moments.

Finding your passion in this world could mean all the difference. For me it was living my life through drumbeats and helping kids, but I soon found out my passions did not cease there.

I wanted more from life, and well, I had quite a lot of living to do.

∞ ∞ ∞ ∞ ∞ ∞ ∞ ∞

Towards the end of the summer, I was excited to finally get back behind a drum set and perform for a crowd. It felt like it had been too long since I had been able to express myself musically, and I was thrilled that Alley Pond Park could be the quintessential backdrop for my latest music adventure.

Naturally, while the band was setting up, Aunt Barbara came to see what we were up to and remained at the park throughout our entire concert. We had a nice turn out, but by the end of the show, there were very few people left to hang out with us.

Aunt Barbara remained.

She looked paler than usual, but she was clearly overjoyed to see me, as she often referred to me as her "favorite nephew" in the flesh. Aunt Barbara and I had continued our almost daily phone calls to each other to talk about life and our experiences, but the school year provided us with less and less time to connect during the week.

It's not that we were growing apart; it was that we were both dealing with some major situations in our respective lives. I had just finished my first school year as a social worker and I was preparing to graduate with my Master's Degree in Social Work. Aunt Barbara was working diligently at what became known as Ground Zero: the site where the Twin Towers once stood.

Both of us were steadfast in our efforts to help people how we could. We were each working long days and often spent hours talking on the weekends about what we were finding out about ourselves.

Aunt Barbara never got mad at me for not calling her during the week, for we each knew the responsibilities we had towards those who needed us most.

She liked hearing stories about my students. She enjoyed hearing all of the pain in my soul leaving my body. Most of all, she really liked hearing from me.

As the two of us sat in Alley Pond Park, I was scraping the brick red paint that was already chipping off the picnic table. In a sense, I think that was my way of channeling nervous energy into something.

"Do you know how proud I am of you, my boy?" She spoke softly.

'I sense it, Aunt Barbara, I really do.' I looked up at her and stopped chipping away at the paint.

We spoke about Bryan and Elyza; she talked briefly about her husband who I very rarely saw. More often than not, he was not around when I spoke to Aunt Barbara on the phone.

The two of us pondered various existential questions throughout the next few hours we spent together. We waltz back and forth between the tables and wooden fence that rested precariously by the parking lot.

As the sun was setting on our conversation and the warm summer night was upon us, I looked over at my aunt for a moment. She was not well, but she did not want to make it known. There was something about her energy or her aura that was off slightly.

'I have to get this giant garbage can into my car, could you help?' I picked up the plastic can and tried waving it around for a moment.

Aunt Barbara smiled naturally and moved towards me. The two of us gripped the can and tried to ram it into my car. We turned it every which way, but the can refused to maneuver into the car.

An onlooker may have glared at us from afar and watched this scene unfold before us. They would have seen two fools trying to smash a large plastic garbage can in a car, but much more was happening. The two of us were creating bittersweet memories that I would reminisce about for years and years to come.

After about fifteen minutes of trying to slam the trunk on the can, the two of us leaned against the car and laughed. Aunt Barbara wrapped her arms around my left arm and began tracing my Rock of Ages tattoo with her pointer finger.

"Always keep the faith, Scott, not just in others, but yourself." Her voice sounded more somber than usual. It was like she knew what was coming.

'You know I always do, Aunt Barbara.' I looked down at her and smiled.

She glanced up at me and grinned.

"My boy." She kissed my arm gently.

'My *aunt*.' I leaned my head against hers.

"Never give up," she rubbed against me slightly. "Never give in."

'I know,' I said. 'I know.'

"I love you."

'I love you, too.'

We grinned and watched the golden summer sun disappear behind the lush trees.

September was just around the corner, and I could feel we were both ready to get back into our routines of helping people and doing just about anything we could to honor the memories and legacies of those who perished on 9/11.

Hope was on the horizon, and we did not need a sunrise or sunset to truly dictate that.

CHAPTER 22

Bridge Over Troubled Water

~

"I'll take your part when darkness comes and pain is all around."

- Simon and Garfunkel, American Folk-Rock Duo, Forest Hills, New York

September brought about a new era of faith and hope. The kids were lined up at my door on the first day of school, almost as if they were waiting all summer to tell me about their progress or situations.

I was excited to get back to work, for I felt that the conversations I had with the kids were building up to something bigger. Something was happening within all of us as we spoke about life from an outside the box perspective.

Two students in particular, Jake and Lita, were the epitome of an 80's couple. Jake was one of the first students I ever worked with when he was in elementary school. When I was still working with the social services agency and Elyza, I was called to connect with a student who had very severe ADHD. I was told that I would be a good role model for him and could support him.

We connected and had a wonderful time together.

By chance, he ended up in another program I was a part of when he was in middle school. The social service agency had a community service leadership program that worked with the kids once a week. Jake was one of the kids who were in my class.

Fast forward to my first job as a high school Social Worker, and there he was again. During my first week of school during my first year at the high school, he came to my office and thanked me for everything I taught him.

Jake, Lita, and Mandy were the ones who helped fill my office each and every day, and they were the ones who helped me assist hundreds of kids.

Jake and Lita met in high school and were definitely born in the wrong era.

Each morning they would come into school and blast 80's music over my speakers. They were head over heels in love with one another, and I jokingly teased them for seeming like characters in a classic 80's movie.

The two of them frequented my office and spoke about their relationship and communication issues. Each of them struggled with familial situations and challenges, but they both knew exactly who to come to if anything was going on.

There were countless cases of students who were unique in their own way. There were stories of students who were bright, insightful, and mature, just like Mandy, and were clearly leaders in their own right. The kids needed a platform. They needed guidance. They needed someone to help them see their inner selves and what they were capable of doing.

While I was talking to Elyza about all of this over dinner one night, she smiled and continued stirring her pasta with her fork.

Bryan chimed in with a full mouth, "Dad, that sounds great!"

Elyza looked over at him, "What sounds great Bryan?"

"Dad is going to help them find their voices," Bryan perked up.

'I just don't want to start another business or something and have it fail, especially with the kids involved,' I grinned at Bryan and Elyza.

"It won't fail this time," Elyza began, "You're ready."

The three of us continued to speak about what it would look like if I started an organization to help kids. Elyza was incredibly supportive and kept throwing different ideas at me.

I pulled out a pad of paper and a pen and began jotting down whatever I could.

'This could be a reality,' I was getting lost in the words on the page.

"This will be a reality." Elyza grabbed my hand and looked over at Bryan, "The kids need something to believe in."

After Bryan went to sleep, Elyza continued to talk about ways to structure various programs and ideas. The two of us were curled up on opposite sides of the couch just letting our thoughts flow.

I paused for a moment and looked up at her, she had picked up her own pad and pen and started to write things down.

'Thanks, Elyza.' I watched her eyes rise to meet my gaze.

"Of course." She grinned slightly and returned to what she was writing.

In a matter of months, I would be starting some sort of non-profit agency.

I would finally get a chance to do even more good things for this world. It was just a matter of time.

∞ ∞ ∞ ∞ ∞ ∞ ∞ ∞

October flew right by as I took case after case and helped students find their way. It turned out that a lot of students ended up counseling each other while I was working one-on-one with some individuals. The office was overflowing with leaders and creative thinkers.

It was such a beautiful sight to see.

At the beginning of November, I was sitting in the office talking to a bunch of the kids about my dreams of starting a non-profit agency. They were so excited about it and they began telling me what programs and ideas I should take into account while I got the agency up and running.

We all went back and forth about stories and names for various curriculums and programs.

The kids were taking an active role in shaping my dreams.

The youth before me were helping to pioneer what I hoped would be global ambitions and a reality that would shift the world of education.

As we all bounced ideas off of each other and spoke about how to create an organization that could reach millions, there was one thing missing: a name.

There was an organization that I dreamt I could become, which was already helping youth with various services. The Door was based out of Manhattan and was consistently evolving and assisting kids that were sitting before me in my office.

"The *Door*?" One of the kids said. "What kind of name is the door?"

We all chuckled at the way in which she spoke about the organization's name.

'I get it,' I started. 'What about the door? You walk through the door and then what? What if the door is locked?'

"Ooh," one of the guys yelled, "Let's name your non-profit *The House* or *The Lamp*."

"*The floor!*" Jake chimed in.

"*The ceiling!*" Lita yelled.

"Yeah," Mandy said, "or *The Window*... like *The Window of Opportunity*."

We all froze. As we exchanged glances, we started smiling at one another.

Windows of Opportunity. That was it.

'Mandy, you did it!' I jumped up and hugged her. We had a name for our program.

"In Spanish, it would be *Las Ventanas de Opportunidades*." The kids started to laugh at one another.

We were already thinking globally.

I started to develop my purpose and took it to the next level. I was on the verge of something big. While at the high school, I was meeting amazing professionals. I got to speak to amazing families. I learned so much about what being a social worker really meant.

I honed my counseling skills. I was crafting my leadership skills.

I was building programs, I was writing curriculums, and the voice I was bestowing upon youth was also strengthening my own voice.

We were creating magic on a daily basis, and it was escalating on so many levels.

When I finally spoke with Aunt Barbara over the phone and two weeks into November, we both had exciting news to share. Her unstoppable nature was paramount in pushing me forward with my non-profit agency idea.

Through coughs and with a strained voice, she mustered up the courage to say, "I am so proud of you, my boy."

Her affection radiated through the phone.

'Thank you, Aunt Barbara.'

"You should do this. You should start your company."

'Nobody's going to listen to me though.' I shrugged slightly.

"Why is that?" She said with an inquisitive inflection in her voice.

'No one will listen to a long-haired punk kid.'

"Scott, you are way more than that," she began. "You are a treasure and a sincere soul who is just embarking on his journey into the world. Keep the faith and stay strong."

'You're right.'

"I know." We laughed and she began to cough.

'Are you okay?' She picked up the concern in my voice.

"I am just a little sick. Don't worry about me."

She brushed off her persistent coughing with some excellent news:

"You will never guess who I met with a few days ago." I could tell that she was having a hard time containing her excitement.

'Who?'

"I met with your mother."

'What?!' I had just recently seen her when I went to check in with my sister Sarah, but she barely spoke with me.

"You heard me right. We had lunch for the first time in 30 years and it is truly amazing how the universe works. We cleared the air and we're going to have a positive relationship now."

'Wow,' I was stunned and thrilled at the same time. 'I am truly happy for you.'

"She is a genuinely good person, Scott, always know that."

'I know,' I started to tear up a bit. 'I hear you.'

"I am up in Rhode Island now, we are going to be here for a few weeks just relaxing." She was referring to the house her and her husband had in a small town on the water in Rhode Island. The water gave her some peace, and I could tell she needed to rest.

'That's good,' I said. 'I'd love to visit sometime.'

"You will," she remarked. "One day."

I yawned and rested my head against my left hand.

"I love you, Scott. I really love you." A subtle pause rested between us.

'I love you, too. We'll talk soon.'

"Of course we will. Goodnight Scott."

'Goodnight.'

I hung up the phone and felt so happy for her. She was rekindling a relationship with her sister, which meant that my relationship with my parents had some semblance of hope lingering on the horizon.

Then a few days later, on November 18, 2002, her husband called me to inform me about what had happened: Aunt Barbara slipped into a coma because of her illness. She was ill and she did not want anyone really knowing, but because of everything she breathed in during her rescue efforts on September 11, 2001, she developed a very nasty sickness.

I fell to my knees and screamed.

She was brain-dead.

I drove up to Rhode Island that Monday night just to see her.

Aunt Barbara was resting peacefully in bed with a respirator hooked up to her face. She could not breathe on her own, but the steady chirping from the heart monitor meant that her heart rate was holding steady.

In my eyes, she was stuck between the balance of life and death. I held her hand and felt her slight warmth radiating through my body.

Without a clue what to do, for let's face it, I always asked my aunt about what next steps I would take, I did what I thought was best. I drove

344

back down to Queens to help the kids I was working with. I planned on driving back up to Rhode Island over the weekend to sit with her, and the students who I worked with were incredibly supportive of my emotions and what I was going through.

I had to be there for the kids, as she would be if she were in the same situation.

∞ ∞ ∞ ∞ ∞ ∞ ∞ ∞

On November 24, 2002, my aunt, Barbara Harmon, passed away. She was taken off of life support and her physical journey on this planet ended.

Her legacy, however, lives on.

Elyza, Bryan, and I drove up to Rhode Island for the funeral, which was heart wrenching and devastating. Aunt Barbara was my family. She was the one who helped me see my purpose and life, and she was gone.

I was at an utter loss for words.

The funeral was beautiful in its own respect, but I had a difficult time comprehending my emotions in the days that seeped by.

Rhode Island's seashore was a perfect backdrop for honoring the memory of someone so special to me. Her house was ornate and like something out of a mythical fairytale: it was quaint enough to reflect her lifestyle, but majestic enough to conjure up the genuine, enchanting nature of Rhode Island.

While everyone was sharing beautiful memories about her in her own living room, I excused myself quietly from the house. I walked down to the rocks to watch the waves crashing slowly against the barriers situated at the end of the street to prevent the Atlantic Ocean from ravaging the small town.

As tears rolled down my cheeks, Elyza materialized next to me.

For a few moments, neither of us spoke a word. She could sense my innate pain rippling through my core.

"You know, you need to do something in her memory." Elyza grasped my hand and laced her fingers between mine.

'She always,' I cleared my throat. 'She always believed in me wanting to create the company I always dreamed of.'

"So do it," Elyza began. "And do it in her name."

'Windows of Opportunity...' I swallowed again. 'The Barbara Harmon Institute.'

She was never able to see what I created, but her confidence in me brought Windows from just a dream to a stable reality.

Nothing can replace or bring back the thousands of lives that were lost as a result of 9/11, but I knew I would do everything in my power to honor the legacy she created. I would do everything I could to respectfully cherish the memory of all of the souls who lost their lives as a result of 9/11 and its aftermath.

First impressions can be so powerful and leave an imprint on you that can last a lifetime. Not only did my Aunt Barbara encompass bravery, guts, and class, she was and is the light who shined so I could see the path my life would take. Bravery, guts, and class are adjectives that do not do justice in describing the incredible woman I felt blessed to call my aunt.

Words cannot describe, nor explain the type of person my aunt was and what she has meant to our family and me. No matter what was going on in my life – good, bad... or insane, I knew I could always count on her. Even if it was a quick call on our cell phones, she always made me smile.

In a generation where the term "family" can be difficult to define, Aunt Barbara taught me the meaning of it, the importance of fighting for it, and the beauty of appreciating it.

I often turn to music and songs for inspiration. There's a line in a Celine Dion song that states: "*With a little faith, love can move mountains.*" That line and song truly capture my aunt's spirit. She never gave up, always stayed strong, and put 100% of her heart into everything.

I always thought my life was crazy and hectic, but after one conversation with Aunt Barbara I felt better, because there was someone out there who was doing more than me. I don't think she ever stopped. Truth be told, I look up to my aunt with the highest respect and try to model myself after her.

I have so many memories of my aunt, and will continue to cherish them forever and ever because of what she means to me.

On September 11, 2001, I was on the phone with my aunt when the second plane flew into the World Trade Center. I knew she was scared, but I was amazed at how her poise and character stood tall during and throughout this tragedy. I remember all of the fear of that day, including the thought of losing my aunt prematurely. It was a thought that was scary and came along with feelings I did not want to deal with. It renewed and strengthened our relationship and I was thrilled and thankful that I did not lose her. I never knew I would have to face the fear of losing my aunt again, and this time for real, only 14 months later.

I will cherish every moment we shared together, though there were too few of them and how I wish I could have so many more.

I will miss you Aunt Barbara and I thank you for teaching me that I can make a difference, for empowering me to follow this dream of creating Windows of Opportunity, and for giving me so much more than you will ever know.

∞ ∞ ∞ ∞ ∞ ∞ ∞ ∞

When I returned to New York, I visited Brooklyn Bridge Park to reminisce about one of our first memories together.

There is something about the walk alongside a bridge that can answer the questions of a lost soul.

There are so many moments and memories on that promenade. I remember my aunt, who was more of a mom to me than my own mother, telling me about her first date with the love of her life as we walked across the Brooklyn Bridge. The way she told the story with reflection and passion was so romantic. I remember thinking to myself I could never walk that bridge again until it is with the right person.

In the days that followed her transition from life through death, I also walked our paths at Alley Pond Park for hours. I would waltz into one of the many diners we used to meet in and allow my eyes to search the faces of patrons there. Still, she was physically gone from this world. Still, I was faced with the abhorrence of a life cut short just as it seemed like the sun was rising.

And in the shadow of her passing, all I could do was bring my pensive mind to graze upon wonderings that I conjured to ease my pain. What now? Where do I go from here? How do I manage to fill a gaping hole in my core that was once diluted by her infinitesimal wisdom?

The air surrounding me was thicker without her life to breathe faith into my consciousness. Her words were the crisp, dewy raindrops that bead upon blades of grass: mornings exist without her, but now they carry a sense of austere loneliness.

A sense of purpose was burning and building within me.

That's the amazing thing about God and the universe: life manifests itself in many ways. From a spiritual perspective, I truly believe God does not control the bad things that happen on this planet. We have freewill, we have energy that transmits between souls, but I do think God, the universe, source, whatever you choose to call it and whatever you choose to believe in such as faith, shows you that when you listen to your soul, you can make beautiful things happen out of bad situations. Windows of Opportunity is just that.

Windows of Opportunity, or WOO, is an outpouring of positivity and love from years of experiences and lives being lived.

And it always will be, for it honors the life and legacy of Aunt Barbara.

∞ ∞ ∞ ∞ ∞ ∞ ∞ ∞

In early December 2002, on the eve of miraculous miracles to come, I had a dream that I was on top of one of the Twin Towers. It was inundated with illustrious lilacs, which were a vibrant purple shade, and was truly beautiful. Aunt Barbara walked among them with me. She held my face and told me that I had big things to do.

Before I woke up, she whispered to me that I had to keep moving forward.

"I am always with you," were the last words I remembered her saying before I woke up. My purpose was cemented in my brain: Windows was going to happen for her and for the kids.

The next day at work, a tragedy struck our school: a student of ours, George, was in an unfortunate accident at the Bayside Marina in Queens. Somehow, he was crushed between a few of the boats there. The news reported that he and a bunch of the kids were drinking and doing drugs, but of course the media got it all wrong. Other people, adults actually, were drinking and getting involved in illegal activities near the kids.

His friends were devastated.

Since they were all musicians, I asked them if we could all honor his memory by holding a benefit concert in his memory. We would call it Musicapalooza and have all of our student musicians and artists perform.

His friends happily agreed and took leadership roles to construct the event. In a matter of weeks, we were able to proudly honor his memory. The entire situation reminded me of what happened to Stacey, and I knew that I had the power to turn a terrible tragedy into a positive situation.

When Stacey passed away, I returned to Jamaica High School and asked the principal if we could hold a memorial to honor her memory. Although we made an excellent case, he said that the memorial would promote alcoholism and reckless behavior. Stacey was not drinking that night and she was acting heroically, but misjudgment was prevalent.

I argued with the principal, yet he refused to budge.

The media had it all wrong. The principal had it all wrong.

There were two systems failing miserably at pursuing the truth.

A bunch of students from Jamaica High School ended up leaving a graffiti memorial in her memory on a brick wall by the field where we used to hang out, but the school quickly painted over it.

History was repeating itself, although now I had a chance to grab the pen and rewrite the story. My presence had the power to shift the systems that failed so many years ago. I was a tadpole swimming in a sea of dysfunctional bureaucracy, though I had the innate feeling my influence was growing by the second.

The Musicapalooza festival ended up taking place annually to honor George's memory and raise money for the school and various charities along the way.

It was just a small act that radiated through a mourning community.

It was something positive and empowering that the kids could use to express themselves and cherish their friend's memory in the process.

∞ ∞ ∞ ∞ ∞ ∞ ∞ ∞

As 2002 was coming to a close, Elyza started to drift away from me again. I was finishing up school and was about to host a plethora of charity events with my college, Adelphi University.

As Bryan and I were packing up to go see the charity football game at Adelphi University, Elyza decided she just did not want to join us.

Whether it was because she was going out with one of her supposed "friends," or she was just tired, at this point I did not care. All I knew was that I had a vision now. I had a dream brewing inside of me that could not be silenced even in the slightest.

Nothing was going to stop me from pursuing this dream.

No one was going to stand in my way.

The world was about to see the drive, stamina, and hope I had brewing within me.

It was time I woke up.

While sitting in the stadium with Bryan, I stopped for a moment and looked around at the faces of the fans. They were excited and cheering because they truly believed in the 11 men running around on the field. They truly believed in their team. Those 11 men may be strangers to them, but they give the fans something to believe in. We do that. Everyday. By standing in a classroom and posting online, we ignite a fire that burns for miles and miles. We stand up with silent cheers echoing through our kids' hearts and minds.

Their passion and glow are why we do what we do.

We get them when they are young, able to be transformed. We see them at their best, their worst, and we help mold them. The country is our student population. The world is our classroom. We are educators of the universe. Let the bell ring loud, far, and wide, for class is now in session. Systematic change will happen now and for years to come. Our politicians, as our teachers, have a duty to encourage us and show us the way. The time to start this ripple of knowledge is now.

Why wait?

Our students, our country, need us more than ever. It starts here, it starts with you, it starts with me, it starts with WOO. Windows of Opportunity.

Class is now in session.

Part III:

The Rebirth

CHAPTER 23

Too Late For Love

~

"Standing by the trapdoor aware of me and you. The actor and the clown – they're waiting for their cue. And there's a lady over there. She's acting pretty cool. But when it comes to playing life, she always plays the fool."

- Def Leppard, British Rock Band, Sheffield, United Kingdom

Elyza's love is like water: slipping through my fingers leaving me temporarily cleaning up the mess of her aftermath. She douses everyone in the exuberance that is her personality, but failed to recognize that her love, or lack thereof, caused a tsunami of despair and destruction in the path that followed her.

Aunt Barbara's favorite Simon and Garfunkel song diluted the immense pain I was feeling over Elyza:

> *"When you're down and out*
> *When you're on the street*
> *When evening falls so hard*
> *I will comfort you*
> *I'll take your part,*
> *oh, when darkness comes*
> *And pain is all around*
> *Like a bridge over troubled water*
> *I will lay me down*
> *Like a bridge over troubled water*
> *I will lay me down."*

Bryan was young, but he understood the pain I was going through. I am sure he sensed that I was hurt by some sort of emotional strife, but I doubt he was able to tell that I was depressed over Elyza.

I made a serious effort to keep a smile on my face, but with every passing moment, I felt myself slipping into a deep depression.

Elyza chose to participate in a transformational leadership conference in Manhattan, and I was happy for her. The two of us were still living together, but it felt that our marriage was crumbling at its foundation.

At the end of her first day of the conference, she asked me to meet her in the city for dinner. I was hopeful, but I was unsure what the night would entail, so I complied and began praying for the best.

My prayers seemed to be answered to some extent.

While the two of us sat down for dinner, she asked that we have an open conversation about our relationship. I was slightly confused about what that meant, so I asked her to clarify just what she wanted to talk about.

"I'm not going to judge you, and you can say anything you would like," she sat with her hands folded on her lap.

'Okay,' I said wearily, yet optimistically.

"I need you to be honest and I want you to know," she swallowed hard. "I have been unfaithful, but we have worked through all of our problems so far."

I ran my pointer finger up and down the edge of my glass of water, unsure of what to say next.

"If our relationship is going to get to the next level," she grasped my hand, "We really need to work on this."

The two of us locked eyes and it seemed like everyone else in the restaurant faded away.

'If you want me to be honest,' I adjusted my legs and leaned closer to her. 'I think I may have a crush on a lady at work. I'm confused. I don't... I don't really know.'

It is a really strange thing to admit, since you're not supposed to be attracted to anyone else when you are married.

Without missing a beat, she replied, "Awesome. Doesn't this feel good? We can work through that. We can talk through that."

Our dinner arrived and the two of us started to eat. It was amazing. I was on a high. I was honest and there wasn't a fight.

Everything felt great until day three came.

At the end of her third day at the conference, I picked her up and she was silent. During the car ride through Manhattan, I looked over at her and waited for her to say something. About twenty minutes passed and she finally spoke as we were crossing the 59th Street Bridge into Queens.

"What do you mean you like a lady at work?" She snapped.

We had a gigantic fight that lasted three hours, and I was left wondering just what her transformational leadership conference consisted of.

I had to swallow my dignity and hope that Elyza's sudden outburst of anger would dissipate as the night went on.

Our relationship was falling apart and I felt that I was losing control again. I did not know just how to make Elyza happy, and all I kept focusing on were Bryan and my new job as a social worker.

The only other thing that seemed important was growing Windows of Opportunity's programs and curriculums. In order to hide my emotions from Elyza and Bryan, and in my attempt to mourn Aunt Barbara's passing, I gave all of my energy to Windows of Opportunity... and I felt I was truly starting to make a difference in the world.

Some may say professionally I was at my strongest, but personally and emotionally I was about to give up on life. I was a walking oxymoron. I was either going to stay with Elyza and be miserable, or leave her and be miserable. Either way, I still did not have what I was looking for.

Calendar pages were flipping before my very eyes and I felt that time was speeding faster and faster as I arrived at work each and every day. The students I was working with came to me about ideas for a conference, so naturally I listened to them and helped them plan it.

Before I knew it, they were creating workshops about eating disorders, HIV awareness, self-esteem issues, and just about anything they could conjure up. We solidified a date for this conference and got permission from the high school to host it during a school day. This transformed before our very eyes as we started inviting other high schools in the area to our building.

We ended up having over three hundred students come to our school for a fully student-run conference on a Friday afternoon in the dead of winter.

It was exhilarating; it was passion and love in action.

∞ ∞ ∞ ∞ ∞ ∞ ∞ ∞

In addition to working with the kids at the high school, I was about to graduate from Adelphi University with my license in social work. I was the president of the community service and outreach program on campus, and I was working in tandem with the fraternities and sororities on campus to produce large-scale events and charity benefits.

One of the young women from the Sigma Delta Tau sorority, Crystal, was rather outspoken when it came to putting together events. I was in awe of her persistence and passion, and spent plenty of time with her and her sorority sisters to develop programs and events on campus. Lara, one of her friends, worked with the two of us often to establish a voice for charity organizations at Adelphi University.

Crystal, Lara, and I were working diligently to organize a 9/11 memorial for all of the lives that were lost less than two years prior in the senseless tragedy in Manhattan. Our school was just miles away from Manhattan, and we knew that so many people who lived and worked there still needed support and guidance from the events that unfolded not too long ago.

While we were working together to coordinate different events, Crystal and I started to get very close. She was thankful for my friendship and opened up to me about her experiences growing up.

"I had cancer as a child, and I went through remission, but my life was never really easy," she was forward with what she went through.

She reminded me of my friend from middle and high school, Lana, and I saw first hand what she had to deal with. I could only imagine what Crystal went through.

After hours upon hours of conversations over coffee and tea, Crystal admitted that talking about it was therapeutic.

I was thankful that she confided in me, so she did not have to carry the burden of her emotions around any longer.

I hoped that one day I could find someone who would listen to me. I hoped that I could find someone who was non-judgmental and was willing to just listen. It was difficult to find someone who understood how to speak to the voices within my soul.

Then she reappeared again: the woman from Casey's with the kind eyes that seemed to see something deep within me.

As I was walking into a small coffee shop near Adelphi University, a familiar voice rose up above the small crowd of college students.

"Hey sunshine." She just stood there with her head tilted, waiting for a response.

'Morena.' I froze for a minute and smiled instinctively.

"Where have you been, Scott?" She held out a cup with green tea and motioned for me to take it.

Wearily and skeptically, I took it from her hand.

'How did you know I would be here or want this green tea?' I sipped it.

"I don't know," Morena looked out the window at the passing train. "Just a hunch, I guess."

I hid my grin behind the cup. I don't know what it was about her, but something in her eyes and how she carried herself made me feel that I was safe... even though she was practically a stranger.

'Um…' I looked at her wistfully, 'Do you have just a few moments to-'

"Listen?" She smiled at me. "Yeah, I can listen."

We walked out of the coffee shop and leaned against the small ticket booth attached to the train station.

'It's my wife, Elyza,' I began. 'We are having some issues and I don't really know what to say to her.'

"Why not?" Morena put her hands in her coat pocket.

I told Morena all about what had been happening between Elyza and I, and throughout the whole hour, Morena just sat and pensively pondered everything I was saying.

'I love Elyza,' I remarked. 'But I don't know if it is true love.'

"True love is when you can't imagine your life without a person."

I looked at Morena who was leaning against the wall now.

She spoke softly: "It is when you look at someone and see a side the world does not have the privilege of seeing. It is doing something nonsensical because you can and because you want to. It is the smell of a new book. It is a cherished memory, it is a place, and it is someone who is home."

We stood in silence for a few moments.

Morena finally opened her mouth, "Is she home?"

'I don't know.' I guess in a way I was always searching for "home." At that point, I didn't know what a "true" home looked like or what it even consisted of.

Sometimes Aunt Barbara seemed like home, but I didn't think of her in terms of the typical "home."

The truth is, deep down inside, I was consistently looking for love. The idea of being in love as a "power couple" was always enticing to me. I yearned to be in a relationship with someone who not only made a house a home, but someone who treasured and valued me for who I was and what the two of us could become together.

I admired political couples like former President John F. Kennedy and his wife, Jackie. The two of them were taking the world by storm. Each of them was an icon in his and her own respect, but they were setting new standards. I wanted that. I craved it.

I needed it.

Yet, I felt that although Elyza complimented my professional growth and leadership, I sensed I was starting to surpass her in different ways.

I also sensed that she was cognizant of it and fearful of what would happen.

She was also interested in and pursuing other men.

I had to keep searching. I had to keep trying.

I had to find the essential "one" who everyone always spoke about. People throw the term "he is the one" or "she is the one" around, but do they ever truly know?

How do you know when you find the one? What does the one look and feel like? If you are with someone and they do not seem like the one, then do you leave?

What if you lost your chance with your "one" person?

Morena watched as questions filled my head, but they all sputtered and melted away before they could grace my lips.

It was a painstaking reality: would I always be in search of home? Would I always be yearning to find the other half of my power couple?

"Hey," Morena's voice permeated my line of questioning. "You look like you are getting stuck in your head."

She was not wrong.

'I am just thinking, that's all.'

"Thinking about what?"

'My life. My choices.' I looked at Adelphi University, which was partially obscured by lush greenery.

Morena placed a hand on my shoulder.

"Give it time, Scott. The path will get clearer. On a clear day, you can see forever."

Suddenly, the train station was bustling with college students and commuters. I moved to the side slightly so people could get to their cars or move past. When I turned to ask Morena something, she mysteriously disappeared.

It figures.

Another woman who vanished and who remained quite a cognitive conundrum disappeared.

This was becoming the story of my life, but I was looking forward to reading it.

For in reality, I felt myself growing from deep within my core, I just did not realize it in those pivotal moments.

∞ ∞ ∞ ∞ ∞ ∞ ∞ ∞

I was fearful of the next chapter.

Trepidation was consuming every ounce of hope that was brewing within me. What would my life look like in the years to come? What would result from mine and Elyza's persistent bickering?

How was I becoming the man I wanted to be?

Who was I trying to be and why?

I began pondering just what my purpose in life was, and if there even was a purpose.

When I shut my eyes and tried to reminisce about good moments from the past, I constantly went to a scene that my Aunt Barbara shared with me years prior. The two of us ventured into Manhattan's Central Park to see a musical artist, Paul Simon, while he was on his tour. We had just met and were trying to bond over what we both loved: music.

Aunt Barbara was trying her best to peer over the heads of people watching him perform, but since she was so short, she just kept dancing around on the tips of her toes.

I offered her to perch upon my shoulders so she could see, and with one hopeful hoist into the sky, she was able to see the concert much better. The two of us were able to experience Paul Simon perform "You Can Call Me Al," one of her favorite songs, in person. We laughed, we danced, we sang, and every passing moment became etched in the epitome of "the good ol' days." I just wished I were able to fully cherish that moment. I wish I took more pictures of her smile.

I wish we had more time together.

The somber reaction to her memory drifted from my mind as the clock in my office clicked with each passing second.

Crystal and Lara were undoubtedly waiting for me to show up at Adelphi University so that we could put some last-minute touches on the 9/11 memorial event. Day by day, I was seeing the wonderful side of humanity: we were all coming together to honor and cherish the memory of those who passed.

A sense of patriotism flourished within me: I was a part of an event that was showing respect to those who were no longer walking this planet, and those who sacrificed so much to save lives the day of 9/11.

The sacrifices continue and the legacies live on.

Later that week, the 9/11 event was a somber, yet hopeful transcendence of what it meant to be a survivor. We all had so much to be grateful for as New Yorkers and the pathfinders of a better tomorrow.

The band Elyza had created with me, Outlet, was able to perform at the event. Five hundred people sat before us, clutching white candles that were burning to commemorate those who could not physically be there.

We chose to open with "It's My Life" from Bon Jovi. The lyrics were a poignant reminder that we were all living. We were all moving forward. We were all united, despite the tragedy that loomed over our heads and weighed on our hearts each and every day.

> *"It's my life*
> *And it's now or never*
> *I ain't gonna live forever*
> *I just want to live while I'm alive*
> *(It's my life)*
> *My heart is like an open highway*
> *Like Frankie said*
> *I did it my way*
> *I just want to live while I'm alive*
> *It's my life*
> *You better stand tall when they're calling you out*
> *Don't bend, don't break, baby, don't back down."*

I just wish that Crystal had been able to continue to carve her path as a survivor and creator of life.

Her cancer returned with a vengeance, and she passed away a month after.

Crystal was one week shy of preparing for a charity event for an organization she supported dearly: Friends of Karen. The organization is dedicated to helping children who have cancer, and were there for Crystal and her family when she was dealing with her battle.

She always said she wanted to do something to show her appreciation. This event was what she hoped would help her show some of her gratitude and adoration. With her passing, Lara, Sigma Delta Tau, and I ensured that Crystal's legacy would live on.

I went on to run the NY Fundraising Chapter for the Friends of Karen organization and in Crystal's name. A future New York Senator worked with us and, at the time, he was just finding his own way in the world. All of us were featured in an article in the paper, and a plaque dedicated to Crystal still exists on Adelphi University's campus at this very moment. I even had the prestigious honor of authoring the words adorned on the plaque.

I guess that was my first attempt at literally etching my thoughts in something that could never be destroyed or erased.

Over the years, the future politician became better known, and I faded into one of the millions of faces he must see each and every day.

I promised myself that if I ever went into politics, I would do my best to remember everyone who helped me here along the way. After all, I had come so far thanks to so many beautiful people, and I knew that I really had a long way to go.

My winding path was just taking a turn for a new adventure, only I did not know it yet.

∞ ∞ ∞ ∞ ∞ ∞ ∞ ∞

The weeks were flying by before my very eyes, and I had no way to slow down the pace in which my life was progressing.

I was coming to a number of realizations and revelations. I would say life was spiraling out of control, yet I knew that I was making strides in building Windows of Opportunity and a better world for Bryan and the many others who would grace my life.

After 9/11 and losing my aunt, I think I threw all of myself into Windows of Opportunity. I launched myself headfirst into this company that I felt was a necessity in this world. It was in memory of my aunt and I had to honor her memory.

Still, I always struggled with balancing relationships and work. One of Elyza's number one complaints in our relationship at the time was that I was gone for hours during the day.

One of our major fights happened because I was not there for her. I spent 18 hours a day building and creating the organization for the kids.

I was pouring my heart into the programs and curriculums. Elyza was there when the idea of Windows of Opportunity was born, but while it was blossoming into something huge, she was growing into an entirely different person. I got into this type of work because of her.

She inspired me.

She opened the door to my interest in going back to college and I took off.

When I finally realized the path that I wanted to be on, there was no stopping me.

We were not, by any means, perfect. Elyza entered my life when I needed her the most, but both of us were growing like branches off of the same tree: our paths were laced with similarities, but stricken with differences.

Love, in the context we each needed it to be in, did not exist between us. I searched for love for many years. I was on the verge of entering a brand-new stage in my life. I was done.

The search was over.

There would be no more searching for love.

I decided I would just dedicate my life to the thousands upon thousands of kids who needed my help.

It may sound odd, but I actually thought I could be a male version of Mother Theresa, or even the next Gandhi.

During one of our last major fights, close to the eve of a Musicapalooza event up at the high school, Elyza stormed off. To my surprise, she sent me an e-mail that night. I was stunned she actually wanted to correspond with me, and then it hit me.

It hit me hard.

It slammed every crevice of my core: the e-mail was not meant for me.

By accident, she sent me the words that were meant for another man.

"I'm lying to my husband" were the words it began with.

She ended up revealing that her weekend business trips were actually clever disguises to meet up with a man whom she was seeing.

At that point, I knew in my heart that our marriage was nearing its end. This was the final nail in our coffin.

I was not mad.

I called her.

We spoke for a bit and I felt the pangs of loneliness shock my core.

When I tried to sleep, I began having violent dreams. With each passing moment, they were vivid depictions of a life that was not fully actualized.

Each time I woke up in the middle of the night, I was fearful of what would occur next.

I would shut my eyes and pray that nothing would jolt me awake suddenly. Yet with each flicker of my eyelids, another horrid vision clouded my mind.

∞ ∞ ∞ ∞ ∞ ∞ ∞ ∞

I had a dream I was floating on a small raft in the middle of a body of water. Gazing around, all I could see was the skyline of Manhattan and remnants of the New York nightlife.

Someone, a man I did not know who was dressed in business attire, snatched at the edge of the raft. He was clawing at the edge of the rubber raft with his fingernails; each scratch dove straight towards my core.

"You were destined to be here," hung on his lips as the fishhook ripped him further into the water. As I sat on the life raft, trying to grasp at his hand, all I could see was him dropping further into the ocean with pride in his eyes. The last words I would ever hear him say were: "it was meant to be this way."

As the raft drifted on, I could see the air bubbles getting smaller and smaller. Looking northeast, I glanced at the sunrise easing over the horizon: a solitary sign that a new day would bring minimal peace to the seemingly metaphorical shipwreck left behind.

Though the colors painted across the sky were a symbol that I could bring new light, if only I could get over the guilt of seeing him drown and feeling guilty that I couldn't save him. He could have been me. He could have been anyone I know or was trying to help.

In being your own hero, sometimes you are blind to the fact that someone else's villains are roaring close behind.

Maybe my troubles and insecurities were beginning to dissipate, but others were struggling far more than I could imagine.

Maybe, just maybe, my dreams were a manifestation of pain and anxiety that were running rampant in my mind.

Maybe those visions would fade once I came to terms with what I had to do in order to make myself happy.

∞ ∞ ∞ ∞ ∞ ∞ ∞ ∞

How come when I am faced with adversity or have questions and doubts that fill my mind, I end up here?

The bridge was only half visible some mornings: that day was one of them. The fog mercilessly swept across the top of the Throgs Neck Bridge. As I strolled down the path at the nearby park, I couldn't help but reflect on my past with Elyza.

I guess that may be because I was about to face another major change in my life.

I was constantly choosing work and volunteer opportunities over my own marriage. Elyza hated that job most of the time.

She respected who I was and was becoming but hated that she was married to it and to her all at once. She couldn't fully support me, which I can sort of accept and understand, then again, I was unsure if that is what drove her into another person's arms. From the very beginning, she told me that I should find a dream and chase it… didn't she? Didn't she tell me to be all I can?

Was there a fine line to her support like a contract that read "Just don't become better than me? Just don't piss me off? Just make sure I get what I want first and then you can be what you want?"

Regardless, Elyza's lies were weighing heavy on my shoulders.

The cool mist flew off of the water as the waves hit the rocks on this early April morning.

Despite Elyza's viewpoints on me and despite the fact that both fog and divorce were on the horizon, I knew the answers were within me.

I have come far and accomplished a lot, with many thoughts and stories unfolding along these shores. I am going to continue to move forward, with my new life, my new relationships, and my renewed faith.

Even on the days when I was unsure of my life and purpose, I was still able to find peace in the picturesque image of the bridge and the sloshing water that nestled against the shore.

I rushed back to my car and decided to drive around for a while. The answers to everything I was looking for grew within me, and I knew that within a few hours I could feel like an entirely different man.

∞ ∞ ∞ ∞ ∞ ∞ ∞ ∞

Dropping the bag onto the floor, I felt the weight of the world shift. Alone again, naturally, but as it was told to me on the phone that night: I exude independence. "It's lonely at the top," rang from within my soul, almost as if those words were pulling me closer to the floor.

The lyrics to Bon Jovi's "Lonely at the Top" echoed through my soul:

"I just couldn't live with what was left for me
And I couldn't run far enough from the truth, what's the use
Yeah, it's lonely at the top
Happy's one thing it's not
Before you know you find yourself alone and looking down
No one there can help you stop before you hit the ground
It's lonely at the top."

I sat in the middle of the kitchen for a bit and looked down at my rough and calloused hands.

'Greater good,' I muttered into my heaving chest.

I gazed up into the rickety light fixture dancing above my head.

'All for you, and you don't even realize it,' escaped my mouth almost as easy as inhaling and exhaling the air I breathe each moment.

The shadows from the fan brushed the walls as I dropped completely onto the kitchen floor, glaring at my surroundings.

'Soon,' I whispered, 'very soon.'

The sound of letting go is absolutely deafening. Though it can often be filled with utterly bitter screaming or blank silence, it could be heard throughout a person's entire body.

Although she was miles away in another person's arms at the time, I would like to think my signature on the dotted line jolted her up for even a moment, just so she could feel a little bit of pain from the years of part-time love she gave to me.

It truly surprised me when I signed the divorce papers, merely because this was the first time I could breathe freely. I felt about 120 lbs. of weight being lifted off my back knowing that she no longer owned me anymore.

And love would never own me again.

∞ ∞ ∞ ∞ ∞ ∞ ∞ ∞

It was supposed to be perfect. What seemed like a million lifetimes from my search for answers as an adolescent came down to a single teardrop that rolled off my cheek.

I didn't expect to cry.

I had thought about that moment many times in the past three or so years.

I thought about it even more during the past twelve months: our divorce.

What would it be like? How would I feel? Would a raging fight ensue?

I tried to fathom what the experience would be like, but I never imagined that the moment would come before a major event for my students.

I rushed to Musicapalooza to help the kids set up for the night. The bands were pouring in and bringing what seemed like droves of equipment with them.

As I made my way backstage to see how everything was progressing, I heard a massive argument ensuing outside of an emergency exit. I rushed out to see what commotion was happening and saw a handful of teenagers arguing about music.

Words were jumbled. Voices were strained.

A young woman, who was clearly related to one of the teens who were arguing, tried standing in between the arguments that were getting more heated.

When one man swung at the drummer, I stepped in and grabbed his fist.

'Boys, are we okay here?' They all looked at me, and my long blonde hair.

Not a soul spoke in those moments, and I tried to stay as calm as possible. As we spoke, our conversation became peaceful in nature. The band chose not to perform that night, but at least none of the kids were severely injured.

"I appreciate your help," the woman put her hand on my shoulder.

'It is not a problem.' I smiled at her.

"Seriously, thank you." She grinned back at me.

'I'm Scott,' I extended my hand towards her. 'I am the school's Social Worker.'

"I'm Shirley," she shook my hand. "I work for the school system as well."

We chatted briefly and I disappeared into the ambiance of the Musicapalooza festival. Her words of appreciation seeped through my body.

The voices in my head were growing louder, and as the bands played, I thought about all of the lives I was saving and just who was saving me.

It was the circle of angels, a group of guardians who were looking out for me from the heavens, hoping that I was living the life I needed to lead.

Regardless of where my personal life was going, I had to think about Windows of Opportunity and the work I would do for thousands of kids that I would meet.

The rock music fluttered through my ears as I watched all of our students move and twist to the melodies rapidly moving through them.

I was there for the kids, and that was all that mattered...

With a rather nostalgic and pained sense building within me, I let out a sigh.

Yeah, that was all that mattered.

CHAPTER 24

Every Child Deserves a Window of Opportunity

*"How many times can a man turn his head
and pretend that he just doesn't see?"*

**- Bob Dylan, American Singer and Songwriter,
Duluth, Minnesota**

Young people of today have the skills and the smarts to handle the world they inherit. But they don't have the essential confidence in their vision and potential. Without empowerment, they cannot do their best work. This means it's time to change our schools, change our communities and change our minds. Youth are the leaders of today and tomorrow.

"If we fix the school system, we can fix the world" became a mantra of mine. I lived the saying, I breathed the saying, and I was committed to throwing every ounce of hope and energy I had into creating and developing Windows of Opportunity - The Barbara Harmon Institute.

Youth can make a difference, and I was watching them do so before my very eyes. If they wanted to put together a conference, they made it happen.

The kids just needed a spark to help ignite the flame within them, and I was happy to help them see everything they were capable of along with so much more.

2005 was the year of Windows of Opportunity, and I was hopeful that Aunt Barbara was looking down at me, along with the Circle of Angels, and proud of the man I was becoming.

I was so far from perfect, but I was the perfect person to bring students a platform to stand upon.

While working in the school system, even for this short time period, I realized that our youth were being disempowered. Good intentions from youth were being squashed by educators and were being told that their problems were "too big to handle."

I was shocked.

I was appalled.

I was concerned.

Though most importantly, I was ready.

I was ready to take on whatever was coming next. I was ready to inspire youth to lead, to grow, and to develop.

With a mindset that is based on the premise of "nothing can get solved," then how would anything get resolved?

With this mindset what is the collateral effect on their families, our communities, nation and ultimately the world? Are our local and world leaders even contemplating this?

I watched daily as the focus of education weighed heavily on passing standardized tests, forced memorization, and a regurgitation of textbook facts. Youth seemed to become versed on how they may work their way through the system and get out of school as soon as possible.

Does this genuinely create the intellectual leaders we need to achieve the goals of our world? Sadly, I found that youth just wanted to run home and escape this monotony by getting lost in a video game, or surfing the web aimlessly.

When do the real thinking and problem-solving strategies begin?

Should the goal of schools be to make sure everyone could get a 100 on a test? Should schools be focused on the monetary gains for high grades, or should they be focused on empowering youth to be world thinkers, personal achievers, and grounded in creating a road map to personal goals?

How did we get to the point we are at now?

And how were we getting out of what we were forcing our youth into?

There needs to be a shift in what is possible for youth in the areas of leadership, empowerment, self-esteem, school performance and career planning; a shift from disempowerment, differences and indecision to possibility, tolerance and opportunity.

This became the mission statement of the non-profit agency that I founded, Windows of Opportunity. This agency was teeming with purpose and a history of designing and delivering successful, innovative empowerment programs and workshops for youth that were developing their leadership skills from various platforms.

The need for a global conversation was growing.

The world was about to hear about programs from Windows of Opportunity, and I was hoping that the world was ready to listen.

If youth are to be the leaders of today and have the capacity for deep analytical thought and problem solving, our education system must become grounded as an empowerment-based system.

The sole intent needed to become to have youth learn the answers to the following three philosophical questions:

Who are you?

What do you stand for?

How will you transform that into society?

I shared these ideas with Morena, who just seemed to keep bumping into me in coffee shops, parks, and the most random of places. Just as I was always about to decompress, find some inner peace, and disappear into solitude, she was there.

Morena was becoming a realistic apparition who seemingly materialized out of nowhere. She would seep into the background of society once we spoke, and I figured that a woman like her was too mysterious to figure out.

"I'm just a placeholder," Morena would say as she flickered her emerald-green eyes.

'I don't get it, for what?'

"Something," she would look into the depths of my eyes and whisper the same words each time I asked her the same question about who she was in my life: "I am the placeholder for something bigger in your life."

I preferred for her to just be straightforward, but it seemed that all she was accustomed to was speaking in puzzles.

Nothing was ever clear-cut with Morena, and I sensed that it was part of her mysterious allure. No one was ever with her, I very rarely saw anyone interact with her, and anytime I would try to bring up the bruises that were adorned on her body the day we first met, she would change the topic.

I could never tell just what she was hiding, and I think she preferred to keep it that way.

During one of our conversations that started at Alley Pond Park and ended in a small coffee shop nearby, she looked me in the eyes and said, "Isn't it about time you forgive yourself for your past?"

Then she left.

In a sense, she was right. Nightly, after I put Bryan to sleep, I was busy beating myself up over nonsense. I was caught in a cyclical trap of feeling sorry for myself, feeling lonely, and praying that I could do the right thing.

Occasionally, I would glance out at the stars of the new small apartment that Bryan and I had moved to in Hicksville. The two of us were living on our own and trying desperately to keep moving forward.

Well, at least I was.

Bryan was doing incredibly well in school and life: I was trying just about everything in my power to be a good man and role model for him.

I just hoped that he knew that, could see some of the lessons I was trying to teach him, and was able to internalize the good, mindful core values I attempted to impart upon him.

At this point, Bryan was a teenager. He was close to the same age as the students I was working with at the high school.

Bryan would spend countless hours helping me create programs and volunteer with the high school I worked at, when he was not playing football at his own school, of course. I always made it a point to go to every single one of his games, for I knew that my family was who I always wanted to see sitting in the crowds of my high school handball and lacrosse games.

I wanted Bryan to have what I never experienced, and overall, I hoped he would have a much better life than I would.

His teen years were progressing nicely, or so I hoped, and I was thankful that he did not seem to notice my personal struggles and suffering.

Like I mentioned earlier, I was lonely. I had Bryan, so I was never truly alone, but I wanted the other half of that power couple I always yearned for to just appear. I was tired of waiting. I was exhausted from nights of tossing and turning, just wondering when she would appear.

Yet in the dim hours of the morning when I looked out at the shadows cascading around my bedroom, all I could see was my reflection in the mirror.

The solitude on my face was very becoming.

I always had the feeling I had to sacrifice love for the bigger picture. I wanted love and I wanted growth, but I could never truly find an equal balance between the two.

I always lost.

I would stare at the Spiderman 2 poster I had hanging in my office at work. One of the kids once remarked that it seemed to capture my soul perfectly: the word "Sacrifice" was draped across the bottom of the image of Spiderman and Mary Jane swinging through the city.

The lyrics to Train's song, "Ordinary," would usher my mind into a brief, trance-like lullaby to quell my loneliness:

"And when the world is on its knees
With me, its fine

And when I come to the rescue,
I get nothing but left behind
Everybody seems to be getting what they need
Where's mine?
'Cause you're what I need
So very but I'm anything but ordinary"

The question was, who was she? Who would be the one who would rescue me? Was I destined to be alone forever?

In pursuing my dream of creating a better future for countless youth, would I truly have to give up finding my quintessential "one" true love?

These questions and more plagued me day by day.

And they never seemed to want to dissipate.

After all, as Spiderman said, "With great power comes great responsibility."

∞ ∞ ∞ ∞ ∞ ∞ ∞ ∞

"What does your soul say, Scott?" Morena leaned into her hot chocolate, which was piping hot.

The falling leaves from October 2005's damp weather paralleled how I felt on the inside: the tears I cried always touched a part of my core. I was acquiescing into a state of mental disparity, though I tried my best not to show it on the outside.

'What do you mean, my soul?' I clutched the paper cup and leaned back in the chair. I had been bumping into Morena so often and in such random places, that we chose to meet at least once a week at a quaint bakery in Queens.

At those very tables, we would have countless conversations about strengthening my voice that always seemed to speak from within.

I do not know what it was about Morena, but she was a prevalent pain in the ass that seemed to know just how to speak to me. She spoke my language, even though I was not very fluent in hers. We both spoke English, this is true, but the two of us were speaking in a manner that lit a spark from deep within me.

"Your soul is who you are," she began. "It is a quintessential part of why you do what you do, whom you choose to be, and what you aim to create in this world."

'Quintessential?' I looked up from my cup.

She smirked, "You use the word all of the time. I figured I would try it on for size."

'And how does it feel?'

"As if I am stealing your words."

'Well,' I leaned in. 'Sometimes you do truly take the words out of my mouth.'

She wrinkled her nose, smirked, and narrowed her eyes. "Can we focus on your soul here?"

'Soul, yes, soul.'

"It is all about soul."

'Thank you, Billy Joel.'

"You're very welcome, *anyway*, it is all about what you feel on the inside. It is about what your inner voice says to you and what you choose to listen to. If you do not listen, then you will not know what you want."

'Well,' I sipped some coffee. 'What if I do not know what I want?'

"Then listen closely. Listen harder. Listen with intent and proceed."

'That makes no sense.' The cup echoed a bit as it plopped to the table.

"Then you have to listen with more intent."

Morena looked out the window at the cars passing by.

'Why don't we ever really talk about you, Morena?' She was still staring out into the world.

"Maybe," she glanced over at me. "Maybe, just maybe, no one focuses on you. Maybe, *just maybe*, it is time all eyes were on you."

'Oh.' I was not sure how to respond to that.

"Sometimes, it is all about sacrifice."

She put her fingertips on the window, but she did not leave any smudge marks on the glass as she ran her right hand down towards the floor.

Sacrifice. I knew that word all too well.

The two of us spoke a while longer and she made her mystical exit into the bustling Queens streets.

'Soul?' I let my breath linger on each letter that stemmed from my mouth. 'Soul.'

∞ ∞ ∞ ∞ ∞ ∞ ∞ ∞

Back at school, we were creating conferences and curriculums that embodied youth empowerment and leadership.

Our programs did not discriminate against any sort of social constructs built within the school. We had students who were seen as popular running our programs. We had kids from broken homes, shelters, youth who were exploring their sexual identity, you name it.

My soul felt as if all of these programs were leading to something bigger than all of us. Yeah, that's right, I started truly listening to my inner voices and doing what I thought would be best for myself, and the youth I worked with at the same time.

Balancing my life was not easy, but it was worth it.

Windows of Opportunity was developing HIV prevention workshops, lessons, and curriculums.

We were on one of the most popular youth television networks in the United States, MTV, and we were promoting our training programs and safe sexual practices. The kids were taking the torch and running full speed ahead.

There were not many safe sex and HIV prevention workshops, so we looked like the pioneers and advocates for a well-informed world. It became our guiding light: we were speaking about problems that plagued teens and tried our best to educate them on protection.

The kids were creating program after program under the umbrella of Windows of Opportunity, and educational experiences were growing moment by moment. It was an exhilarating feeling to watch leadership spring forth and become a major part of our youth's lives.

They were empowered.

They were excited.

They were breaking out of stereotypes and doing what they thought was best.

Countless youth were stepping up and designing programs freely and without much trepidation. In the battleground that consisted of their lives, these kids were stepping up out of the trenches and facing the world headfirst.

They were not going to war with the stereotypes that people were putting forth, rather these kids were waging a war against whatever limitations or boundaries they thought they had.

They were setting new standards.

They were breaking through the boxes they were once placed in.

Their families were getting involved and their communities were gathering around them. As the months progressed before us, the Dream Out Loud Conference was soaring to new heights. Parents, families, and volunteers came out in droves to show their support.

There are countless stories of families who have impacted my life over the years, though their stories are not mine to tell. They could never be told eloquently within the confines of this chapter, but to say I am grateful for all of them is an absolute understatement.

Windows of Opportunity was created by youth, for youth. It was an organization for the people and by the people.

It was something that we could have never imagined, yet created based on the premises of strength, poise, growth, dignity, and constantly yearning to be more, see more, and do more.

The non-profit agency became my voice in the world, which was holistically represented by the courage of our youth to have their voices heard.

It was beautiful to watch programs and curriculums blossom from the depths of everyone's souls.

It was utter perfection with regard to how willing the kids were to step out of the shadows and into the bright lights of our community at large.

It was, and is, a sense of unity that emerged from a window of opportunity.

...And it always will be what it is: a series of windows of opportunities.

∞ ∞ ∞ ∞ ∞ ∞ ∞ ∞

Though Windows of Opportunity was taking off in some very major ways, I still took time to address what is one of the cornerstones of my very existence: music. I was still attending countless Bon Jovi concerts and various rock shows here and there.

Despite mine and Elyza's divorce, we were still performing together at Outlet shows and keeping the melody alive.

Elyza and I were good friends with a past, and I never considered her to be my ex-wife. We were musicians and we were social workers, but most importantly, we were friends and that was a crucial aspect of what made Outlet's music sound so invigorating.

Elyza and I were given a chance to star as actors in a music video for Queen Rose. I helped write the script for the video and spent a lot of time helping to prepare for the shoot, which would take place in Central Park.

On the coldest day of the year, I was dressed in about three to four layers of clothes, shivering at just about every chance I got, all to have a part in making history.

The video was supposed to be about racism and building a bridge to peace, and it was truly a transcendental, musical moment that I could not forget. I was grateful Elyza and I were able to be a part of it, and I was also thankful that Queen Rose allowed my students to join in the production as well.

My yearning for music did not end there.

In an effort to travel and see what existed beyond the borders of New York City, I flew down to Florida to meet up with an old friend from college and see Melissa Etheridge live in concert. She wrote a lot of songs that spoke to the voices in my soul, and I treasured how amazing of a singer and songwriter she was.

Naturally, I pulled my friend, Camilla, backstage with me in an effort to try to meet the great Melissa Etheridge. She was standing on top of a bar, with glasses of alcohol shifting and sloshing around. People were screaming her name and I just wished that I could get her attention. It was then that I met Trace.

After the crowds began to thin out, we waited for quite some time before a guitar tech emerged from backstage. He was looking around and caught our eyes.

"Hey, you guys from around here?" He called out to us.

'Not really.' I shouted back.

Camilla perked up and moved towards him, "I am."

The guy smiled and extended his hand.

"Hey, I'm Trace," Camilla and I gave him a warm handshake. "I know this is going to sound really crazy, but we have a bunch of like, fan stuff, and we would be happy to give it to you if you could give us a ride back to the hotel."

We went out to a bunch of bars.

We ended up back at Melissa Etheridge's hotel and were hanging out in the room next door to her.

We went on her tour bus and were able to see the essential rock and roll fantasy exist before our very eyes. There was a box of cold, leftover Domino's pizza sitting in a box near her bed, which I snatched before I plopped down on a chair.

I finished the pizza and shifted my legs. My eyes were wandering around the bus in a star struck manner, I was intrigued by all of the stories she lived through within these walls.

As any fan or child-at-heart would do, I took a running leap onto her bed and glared up at the ceiling. It was covered in mirrors, which only gave me an idea of some of the fantasies that happen on that tour bus.

Life was happening before my very eyes, and I let the lyrics to Melissa Etheridge's song, "Giant," sing to my soul:

> *"I am a giant*
> *And you will not make me fall*
> *And you will not make me crawl*
> *I am a giant*
> *And I'm not alone*
> *Winds of change have blown*
> *And the walls come tumbling down*
> *And I've learned from my mistakes*
> *Picked myself up off the floor*
> *I have learned just what it takes*
> *Now I am stronger than before*
> *And we are standing side by side*
> *We are determined now to win*
> *We have come too far*
> *And we've got the scars*
> *And we are never going back into the shadows again."*

Never. Again.

It's officially time to embrace who I am, and truly refuse to sink.

CHAPTER 25

Breaking the Habit

"I can't let this life pass me by. In a blink of an eye it ends. I can't let my tomorrows decide what I am in this life. It's like committing slow suicide."

- Scott Stapp, American Singer-Songwriter, Orlando, Florida

My professional life was soaring further than I could have ever imagined. I was creating the man I never thought I could be. I was growing into this amplified image of myself. It was difficult to fully fathom the differences I was making in the lives of youth at the moment, for even though I could put on a brave face in front of the world, I was struggling.

The ghosts of my past still haunted me. They were shaking every ounce of my core internally, and my guilt wrought through every crevice of who I once was.

Even though I was trying my best to move forward, I was still haunted by what my family was experiencing behind closed doors.

Four walls and a roof could only conceal so much pain and pressure before everything came crashing down.

I was fighting and clawing my way to get out of the oppressive and repressive state I was once in. However, while I was rising from the dirt below me, my sister was still begging to emerge from the depths of the hole we were once both in.

I could not leave her.

I had to go back for her.

I had to save her.

Cocaine and depression lined my pit of despair, while she was drowning under the weight of who knows what. Heroin seemed to be her flavor of the "weak", but then again, she was not weak. She was strong. She knew, deep down in her heart, that she had to rise above.

∞ ∞ ∞ ∞ ∞ ∞ ∞ ∞

Bryan, Elyza, and I decided that we were going to go out one night for dinner. Elyza remained in my life despite our divorce, and over time the two of us became more proficient with regard to communicating. After all, it seemed that what was lacking in our relationship, above everything else, was the ability to talk to one another.

So many people say that communication is the key to everything, and we internalize that idea in many different ways, but there is a massive difference between someone's intentions and someone's actions.

Elyza attended a number of transformational leadership workshops, which helped her open up and verbalize the thoughts brewing in her head.

She approached me and we started having honest conversations about our lives, our relationship, and everything that did or did not happen between the two of us.

As the three of us, Elyza, Bryan, and I, sat at a glossy wooden table housed in the corner of a diner, I felt peace. It was a strange feeling: I was spending so much time building Windows of Opportunity, which did seem to parallel my own personal growth at the time, I was blind to the intrapersonal relationship that I had to build between myself and my soul.

Bryan's sky-blue eyes were glowing with excitement as he told Elyza all about how he was doing at school. He was proud of himself. He was developing and growing before my very eyes.

He was, and always has been, my everything.

Bryan saved me when I thought I was about to teeter over the edge, and I was trying to do everything in my power to make him a good man. I was trying to make myself a good man for him. I was trying my hardest to become someone he was genuinely proud of.

Each time he said "dad" in a sentence, I could not help but stop and smile at him. He was the epitome of life and love, and I prayed that Bryan would continue in his pursuit of growth. I was hopeful that he would never see the strife and struggle I was still dealing with, and I was grateful that he did not have to lead the life I grew accustomed to as a child.

As I saw the world evolving through glances at my son's eyes, my phone rang.

It was my younger sister, Sarah.

Panic and fear inundated her tone, and I was unsure of how my life was filled with such stark contrasts: one moment I was in awe of my son, the next I was hearing devastating news from my sister.

"Scott, Scott," she was panting. "You have to help."

My mind went blank.

"It's Rebecca."

My heart sank.

"She is in jail."

A flurry of questions shifted into my mind. I watched Bryan and Elyza smiling at one another, trying my best to hide the sheer trepidation that stirred within my mind.

Why was she in jail? What happened? Where were my parents? What was going on? How did this happen?

How could I let this happen?

'Where is she?' The solemn tone cut through Elyza and Bryan's conversation.

Within an instant, the three of us were in the car and off to a police precinct in Queens. Sarah said she would meet us there, but I was nervous.

What would I do?

My son was confused. How would I explain this to him? What do you say to a child as his innocence is slowly draining from his very precious eyes?

I figured honesty would be the best thing I could use to speak to my teenage son.

Elyza sat with her elbow resting against the passenger side window and balanced her fingers in her mouth. Her other hand was firmly gripped around my right hand.

Bryan saw the scene unfolding before him, and I am sure a plethora of questions filled his head.

In what felt like forever in a second, we reached the precinct.

∞ ∞ ∞ ∞ ∞ ∞ ∞ ∞

We flew into the precinct, begging for someone to point us towards where Rebecca was being held.

One of the men in uniform pointed towards a desk, where another officer was standing and reading through some paperwork. I politely excused myself and introduced myself to the officer as Rebecca's brother.

"She's higher than a kite, man," the officer bluntly said to me.

I was devastated.

She got caught.

It seemed like we were at the point of no return.

Elyza pulled me to the side and told Bryan to sit in a plastic chair by the corner. She became incredibly protective and wanted nothing but an explanation in that moment. Elyza did not blame me or make it seem like I was the one who forced Rebecca into this downward spiral.

"What do you want to do?" Elyza gripped my arm in an endearing way.

'I'm going to talk to the officers, stay here with Bryan.'

I pulled away from her and she released my arm almost instinctively.

Sarah burst through the precinct doors and hugged me tight. She was clearly panicked and distraught by what was going on.

She hid behind me as I spoke with the officers, which truly made me feel like an older brother. I was protecting my sisters as best as I could, and my parents were, not to my surprise of course, nowhere to be found.

We stood there for a while and spoke with the officers. All of them seemed to feel sorry for Rebecca, who was shouting and rambling on from within the holding cell.

She was screaming mine and Sarah's names and reaching through the bars. An officer told her to get back, and I could see the desperation in her eyes. She was sick.

Rebecca was beyond ill, yet medicine could not remedy her current situation.

"What do you want to do?" One of the officers asked.

'Pardon me?' I was confused.

"What do you want to do? You know you can bail her out if you really want."

I turned back to see Elyza consoling Bryan. He was not crying, but the two of them were having what looked like a long talk about what was happening. I was thankful Elyza was there with us.

I thought about my past. I thought about the years and years of abuse I endured, which was probably similar to what Rebecca was dealing with…

Only I made it out.

After a long, dramatic pause, I looked over at Sarah. She was tearing up and was having a difficult time comprehending every action occurring before her very eyes.

'Keep her overnight.'

"You will do no such thing!" A voice boomed from behind me.

It was my father.

"She's my daughter, and you will not make decisions for *our* family." He was red in the face and rather stern.

'She is my sister. This is *our* family.' Elyza stood up and rushed behind me. She clutched Sarah's hand in hers.

"*You* are no longer part of *this* family. You don't belong here." My father's fit of rage echoed throughout the precinct. It seemed as if everything had stopped and everyone was looking down upon our scene.

'She needs to detox in prison. This is for her own good.'

My father's face became flushed with fury.

My mother materialized behind him, slithering around his frame in a way that rivaled a snake's slick motions.

"You don't know what is *right* for *our* daughter," she hissed.

"You think you are some *hot shit* social worker?" My father turned his head.

I was coming from a place of love, yet my father and mother could not fathom it. They were blinded by what they did to me. They were obscured by the rage burning within them.

Yet despite all of this, they also chose not to bail her out.

The next day, I heard from the officers that she spent the night vomiting and crying in the prison cell. No one attended to her pleas and whimpering. All she had was a bucket and her solitude.

It was lonely at the top, sure, but it was even worse at rock bottom.

Yet in the desolate hours that built upon one another, she was healing. The process through healing is not always sunshine and positivity: it is often wrought with agony and laced with epiphanies about facing our own insecurities.

Through the night, Rebecca was entertaining her own metamorphosis: she transcended addiction and pain through a mixture of resolute silence and coming to terms with her actions.

When she was finally released from prison, my family and I put her in the best rehab program in New York.

She looked as if someone had thrown her into a literal pit of despair and dirt, yet she clawed her way out.

For the next thirty days, she spent day after day coming to terms with her demons. Each and every day, Bryan wanted to visit her at the rehab center. Rebecca and Bryan were always so close; for I am sure that he remembered everything she did for him as a child.

Children tend to know who genuinely cares for them and their well being.

Rebecca always loved Bryan and Bryan always loved his aunt.

He never judged her and gave her nothing but unconditional love. With his fingers interlocked between hers, he made all of her difficult moments fade away.

The special bond between the two of them reminds me somewhat of my Aunt Barbara and I. Though Aunt Barbara and I never truly addressed it, it was almost like we had a language of our own. We understood one another and truly cared, although sometimes I felt like a thorn in her side.

She still loved me.

And Bryan truly loved his Aunt Rebecca.

Watching their conversations and interactions, no matter how near or far I was to them, made me smile from the depths of my soul.

∞ ∞ ∞ ∞ ∞ ∞ ∞ ∞

Thirty days later, Rebecca officially vowed never to touch drugs again. At this point, she has been sober for decades and her veins are free from drugs.

She is free.

Her liberation had to be surmounted by a series of unfortunate events, yet she is still alive and thriving.

In the years that passed, Rebecca spent day after day using her survival as a means to rebuild her life brick by solid brick. She was moving forward with her life and became heavily involved in physical fitness. Rebecca promised herself that she would never go back down the dark path she was once accustomed to.

While I was still at the high school in Queens, she came to my office to offer her story to my students. After school hours, she was sitting and talking with many of the youth volunteers who dedicated a part of their lives to leadership, empowerment, and building Windows of Opportunity.

Rebecca began her conversation with a deep sigh and the words that I never thought I would hear: "I sat in my feces and urine for two days straight. I was covered in vomit and guilt for longer than I think I could remember."

I felt tears start to stream down my face.

"And I know I will never turn to drugs again..." She paused for quite some time. Rebecca shut her eyes and was holding back tears.

"And I have my brother to thank." She pointed at me and smiled, which made me feel as if I was truly part of the family again.

She went on to talk about the most disgusting and disturbing moments of her life, and through it all she was brave.

She was poised and smiling, knowing that through sharing her story she was freeing herself from pain in the process.

Almost an hour later, when Rebecca was done telling her story, there was not a dry eye in the house. She tilted her head downward and smiled, while the kids sat silently. We were unsure of what to say or do until she looked back up at me.

The kids began to clap and she glanced over at me.

She mouthed the words "Thank you."

I rushed up to her, embraced her, and whispered, 'I love you,' in her ear.

She never told the story again. That was the day she buried her story into the same hole she emerged from. She couldn't tell her story over and over again, and I do not blame her.

Rebecca moved on.

She grew and transcended the pain she once swam in, and she did not drown.

It must have been a silently exhilarating feeling for her: she was able to rise when she fell, and she continued to rise throughout life.

∞ ∞ ∞ ∞ ∞ ∞ ∞ ∞

Her boyfriend, Chris, who was with her the night she was arrested, did not travel the same path as her.

I only wish he had the strength to rise as well, but sometimes we are weighed down too heavy by our own demons.

Chris and Rebecca moved upstate after she got clean, but he continued to struggle through everything that plagued his soul. Their respective lifestyles no longer served them.

He got involved in something that no one in the family ever quite understood, which sent him away for a few years. When he ended up coming out of prison after half a decade of living in both a mental and physical jail cell, he was never the same.

Sacrifices are made regularly.

We even sacrifice our well being and the ability to stay strong because of the magnets that guide our internal compass. Chris did not get a chance to live much longer after getting released, for his soul was dragged through such a deep and desolate series of moments in his lifetime.

It was a sad day when we found out that Rebecca and Chris had officially parted on their own respective paths.

It was an even sadder day when we found out that Chris could not chase the monkey on his back, and he passed on from this life to the next.

He was never able to find the peace and innate happiness that existed deep within him. Everyone has different demons to grapple with in their lives and within their souls, and it is not always easy to translate your energy into a language that even you can understand.

When you are unable to connect to what soothes your soul, what you are about, and who you are in the context of this universe, it is tough to find the faith brewing within yourself.

It is quite a challenge to find who you are sometimes. It is demanding to call upon whatever burns within you while trying not to extinguish the flame.

I should be dead. There are many people who could have died as a consequence of their actions.

Yet they are still here, so many are still here…

I am still here.

We still walk this Earth because the sand in our respective hourglasses are still brimming with life. Time has not run out for us. It is a gift and a treasure to remain in such a conscious state in this atmosphere.

The stories of our survival will be written in the stars. However, they are not just stories of surviving addiction. They are not stories of surviving illnesses or challenges beyond our wildest dreams.

Our lives are stories of faith. We exist beyond the scope of the metaphysical, for we are the embodiment of hope, strength, courage, expanding our souls, lessons, existential learning experiences, and much more.

Our stories are proof that we have the capability of becoming a better planet.

It is time we awaken and choose to reveal the inherent gifts we have within us.

It may take quite some time to unwrap and pull back the countless layers of who we are, yet we are in there… somewhere, just waiting for our inner voice to tell us that we are more than what meets the eye.

We are more than life itself.

As Bon Jovi said, many years after these moments took place, in his song "We Weren't Born to Follow:"

> *"We weren't born to follow*
> *Come on and get up off your knees*
> *When life is a bitter pill to swallow*
> *You gotta hold on to what you believe*
> *Believe that the sun will shine tomorrow*
> *And that your saints and sinners bleed*
> *We weren't born to follow*
> *You gotta stand up for what you believe."*

It's time to take a stand.

CHAPTER 26

Shine

"Give me a word, give me a sign. Show me where to look, tell me what will I find? Heaven let your light shine down."

- Collective Soul, American Rock Band, Stockbridge, Georgia

"How is your sister doing?" Morena's hair wrapped around her face in the brisk wind. Alley Pond Park's trails were oddly empty for a beautiful, yet windy spring day. Another school year was coming to a close, and I still felt empowered by the magic and mystery of the insightful conversations I continued to have with students.

'She's doing well. She came to my school a few days ago and actually shared her story with my students.' We continued walking down the path.

"That's rather courageous."

'Rebecca has been through hell and back, and she was using her challenges to inspire the kids.' I grinned.

"Huh," Morena turned to me. "I guess it runs in the family."

She picked up the pace and began walking towards a small body of water in the middle of the park. Morena glared out at the water, took a deep breath, and smiled as she exhaled.

'What's on your mind?' I waltzed next to her.

"Nothing." She sounded resolute. "Nothing for a change."

'That sounds hard to believe.' I looked out at the water, attempting to see what her eyes were fixated on.

"It does not hurt to clear your mind every once and awhile."

'No, it does not.'

We stood in silence for a moment, until she turned towards me.

"Where does your soul go?" An angelic-like glow materialized around her body. The way the sun hit her shadow made her appear to be something she was certainly not.

'What do you mean where?' I looked at her irises, which were submerged in an opaque pool of white.

"Where does your soul go when you want to feel happy?"

'I don't know. I guess it comes here.' I gazed around at the blossoming trees.

"Well, then, when do you feel you are happy?"

I paused for a moment. Just when I think I know all of the answers, Morena asks me something stoic and spiritual like this.

'When I am with Bryan.' Naturally, I loved spending time with my son.

"Think of when you are independent of other people. I know you love Bryan dearly, but when are you happy and alone with your thoughts." Morena moved forward towards the water.

'Oh.' I paused again. 'Well, when I play music.'

"Just play music?" Morena looked back at me.

'Well, more specifically, when I play the drums.' This was a constant definite in my life.

Music.

When I was in a state of despair, I turned to the words of Bon Jovi and countless others to usher me into a more positive mindset. I have always had a strong connection with music, playing the drums, and just listening to the lyrics of songs.

Morena led me over to a short stone wall near the water. She sat and motioned for me to join her.

"Close your eyes," she murmured. "Inhale the fresh air, exhale and listen to the universe."

I shut my eyes and listened to the sounds around me: a chirping bird, the rustling of the branches, and Morena's breathing, which was slowing.

It was a calming moment for me, especially after a series of challenging situations, both professionally and personally, consumed my life recently.

"Tell me," I could feel her moving closer to me. "Tell me all about when you first felt music coursing through your veins."

I exhaled.

I inhaled.

I exhaled again.

"It was my uncle who pushed me to feel the vibrations of music move through me." Although Robin had introduced me to vibrations in her own way years ago, my uncle's love for music helped establish the foundation for my ever-evolving experiences.

I reminisced about my uncle's role in my life. He performed in a band called Rhapsody that I always looked up to as a child. I wanted to be them. I wanted to be like him. They always played in famous bars in Manhattan like Rosie O'Grady's.

My uncle actually bought me my first music album, Stevie Wonder's *Hotter Than July*. I listened to his song, "Happy Birthday," constantly. I fondly remember when my uncle took me to an Elvis impersonator show. I loved Elvis. I loved listening to Jay Black and the Americans' "This Magic Moment." My uncle's band did an excellent rendition of the song.

Everything about music made me happy. No matter what I was dealing with, music was my salvation. It just always has been.

I was overjoyed when my uncle decided to join the band that Elyza had created as a wedding gift: Outlet. I was in awe of him. He played an electronic piano, which was always set up close to my drum set, and it was such an honor and a total thrill to see him perform with us.

My uncle nurtured my innate love for music. He took care of me and everyone around him. His pure soul radiated through both his love for music and his adoration for sharing his gift with other people. Music was in his blood. Music was his life force.

Him and my father established my genuine respect for melodies, lyrics, and all of the attributes that come with music.

The famous voices of deejays like Cousin Brucie, Jack Spector, and Don K. Reed enticed my spirit. Norm N. Nite and Bob Shannon also helped me develop my love for rock n' roll, and other aspects of music that inspired me to play the drums.

To this very day, I thank my uncle and father for instilling the gift of music within me.

I let the stories of the past fill my heart and soul. My mind felt at ease for a change. Music gave me the avenue to keep progressing forward, even in moments when I thought my life was about to take a turn for the worse. There were quintessential moments when I could distinctly recall my appreciation for music as a pervasive presence in my life.

Although I was an utter outcast in temple, for I just had to ask questions all the time, of course, I did get a chance to play the snare drum during services. My uncle was actually the one who bought me my first drum set.

In middle school, I wanted to play the saxophone badly. A song with a saxophone solo in it always radiates down my spine. When it was my turn to try playing the saxophone, my band teacher said that someone else was going to be playing it. Once, I drove my band teacher crazy because the other drummer in the class and I took it upon ourselves to have a drum solo at the end of a song. Though he threw a chair in sheer frustration, I was unafraid. The education system should not be composed of individuals who are so quick to bring negativity to the youth they are meant to educate.

We need to raise the standard of education, and this moment made it clear that something had to be done.

As for those moments, however, I just let the music flow through me. Morena's voice became more soothing as I spoke, "Tell me more."

I continued to share about the local bands I encountered.

Throughout every stage in my life, I was involved in some sort of musical endeavor: between bands with my friends such as Dutch Kills, Good Intentions, Suicide Kings, Central Time Zone, Wayne Foundation, and Tequila Mockingbird.

The manager from Dutch Kills took me under his wing. They were excellent and almost became famous, but Soundgarden ended up getting signed to a label in their place after a grueling contest and a series of live shows sponsored by the label. Dutch Kills was offered a deal, but they refused: the label wanted them to change band members though they remained loyal to one another.

That's the beautiful thing about true musicians: they stick together.

The lead singer of the band spoke softly, but his voice was powerful and commanded the room. Each note he sang was an absolute juxtaposition to his usual speaking voice, which was a poignant reminder that we all have a strong voice deep within us. Sometimes, it just takes the right time or place to bring out that voice.

The music industry needed Dutch Kills to become a part of its illustrious cultural impact. Each melody the band created had the potential to move mountains, but I guess their fame was not written in the stars.

It appeared that every aspect of systems in our society needed an absolute overhaul of their core values, but as with some situations, everything just needs to align.

Thinking of the band allowed me to reminisce about the stunning girl in high heels and leather mini-skirts, who would religiously shimmy up on stage and introduce the band; now Gemma's movements were just ingrained in my memory.

Central Time Zone consisted of some of my best male friends with a thrilling alternative rock tone. I could go on and on about how wonderful they all are.

One of my favorite memories was when Outlet, Central Time Zone, and a new band I was working with called TCBT joined together to perform for a charity benefit.

I was given the chance to play drums all night and with all three bands. My arms were incredibly sore that night, but my heart was in a state of utter euphoria.

Wayne Foundation was a blues-rock band that pushed my skills to the limit. One night I had the flu and felt like throwing up, but I remained on the drums and clung to my sticks until the end. Dedication ran through my veins.

We had the opportunity to play a show in Hampton Bays out on Long Island, where I was introduced to the guitarist's good friend. He innocently asked if I was the new drummer because he knew the band wanted to get rid of the old guy.

I was the old guy.

That was when I found out I was being fired.

I was devastated and did not see it coming, but I was appreciative of the experiences I had with them.

Tequila Mockingbird was based on Harper Lee's infamous book *To Kill a Mockingbird*, which also resonated with my soul. As Harper Lee said, *"People generally see what they look for, and hear what they listen for."*

Music did that for me.

Music was my true religion.

I worshipped devoutly upon picking up a set of drumsticks.

I opened my eyes for a moment to see what Morena was doing, as her presence seemed very distant to me.

She was standing at the edge of the hiking trail, looking out into the distance.

'Morena,' I called after her. I rose and rushed to her.

"What do you think?"

'About what?'

"Finding your true happy place."

'Music is not a place though.' We were standing perpendicular to one another.

She placed her hand on my chest and closed her eyes when she connected to my heartbeat.

"Do you feel this?" A still silence permeated the air between us.

'Your hand, yes.'

"No, I mean your heartbeat."

396

'Oh,' I felt bad for a moment. I should have realized what she meant. 'Yeah.'

"This is your metronome. As long as your heart beats, you, too, beat on to your own rhythm."

She was right.

Music did flow within me and music was the connecting thread that remained between my soul and other souls.

The revelation was reminiscent of what I remember from one of my favorite movies I used to watch with Wendy growing up: *Eddie and the Cruisers*. I was always drawn to the characters Eddie and Wordman's relationship: Eddie provided the music and Wordman provided the lyrics.

I inherently knew that I was a holistic representation of music; I just had to find someone in this universe who could embody the spirit of the lyrics that contributed to the growth of my soul.

She was out there.

Somewhere.

Maybe she was just beyond the purview of my very eyes.

∞ ∞ ∞ ∞ ∞ ∞ ∞ ∞

When I was younger, most of my fondest memories were laced with facets of music. I once found myself wandering through a record store and came across a horrifying face: it was dark, scary, and beyond my curious imagination.

I bought it, took it home, and listened to the music.

The name on the album was Billy Joel, and he was singing about a "Piano Man."

I was sold. I was blown away. The lyrics and melody were transformative.

His words touched a part of me that other music could not reach. Though Frankie Valli was one of my favorite artists, for my father adored his music as well, I was enamoured by the rock n' roll genre and the sensations that shivered up my spine when I listened to the various melodies.

Rock n' roll spoke to my soul in a way that always drew me to a place that felt similar to home.

Morena and I continued to move through the woods. We would stop and admire nature in its most natural forms.

Alley Pond Park was no stranger to beauty. The conversations Morena and I had only augmented the enchanting atmosphere around us.

"When have you felt the most pain when it came to music?" Morena was digging deeper. She wanted me to explore myself, and my soul, yet it was difficult to read her intentions. Why was she always asking so many questions? Why would she be so keen on having me express myself and peel back the layers of who I was?

Just what did she see in me in those moments?

'Why do you want to know?' I was intrigued by her.

"I don't need to hear it," she began. "I need you to hear it. I need you to listen to yourself and your soul."

'Well,' I gazed at her. 'I will tell you.'

She grinned coyly.

Music brought me confidence, it brought me hope, it brought me comfort, and it brought me strength.

Even during times when I was not feeling my best, music connected me to the voice deep within my core.

Outlet used to practice in a dingy rehearsal space we called the dungeon. It was a room at the end of this long, dark corridor in the basement of a real estate office. Though it appeared to be a terrifying place, I managed to make it even more abhorrent one night.

The bassist we hired, who ended up dating a woman I set him up with, turned out to be an abusive imbecile.

After finding out what he did to her, I practically attacked him. Again, it was not one of my finer moments related to music, but it was a defining moment.

Regardless of how I was feeling, I would always advocate for other people.

Elyza followed me out and told me to relax as I chased the guy down the basement corridor and out into the street.

I went berzerk, lost my mind, and screamed, 'This is my fucking band!'

To this day, I have never seen someone run away from me so fast.

To this day, the band lovingly teases me about my not so reserved moment.

Back in my youth, around the same time I discovered Bon Jovi and Van Halen, Mötley Crüe arrived on the scene.

To us kids, all we knew was that parents and adults enforced that we were not allowed to listen to the "Crüe." Once people saw the pentagram on their posters and albums, they assumed the band was full of devil worshippers.

When I was playing handball one afternoon with a friend in College Point, we ended up walking back to his house and hanging around his room for a while. Upon walking into his room, I saw it hanging there on the wall: a Mötley Crüe poster with a pentagram beaming down towards me.

The words plastered across the poster read, "Shout at the Devil."

I glanced over at my friend and asked what the band was truly all about. We listened to Mötley Crüe's second vinyl album, and from the moment I heard the lyrics, I was hooked.

The opening dialogue at the beginning of the album was the same as the start of the book of Genesis in the bible.

Each word resonated with the idea that good overpowers evil in the world. Mötley Crüe expressed that although the world has become evil, countries were weak, cities were morphing into slums, and wickedness was rampant, there is hope.

Mötley Crüe's lyrics inspired a spark within me. It was as if the words in each of their songs were waiting on a revolution:

The opening dialogue even preached:

"Those who have the youth
Have the future"
So come now children of the beast
Be strong
And shout at the devil"

Religion and faith were laced between their songs about debauchery and chaos, and despite the abuse at home and fear inside; there was a message from a higher power.

It meant that there was something, a power deep within all of us that can combat the evil in this world.

There was a story behind the story in each of their songs.

Several albums later, as the lyrics continued to resonate with me, the original recording of their album Saints of Los Angeles began with whisperings of the Lord's Prayer.

The band was so misunderstood.

Many judged them for their appearances and not for what they sang about. There was a solid message in their songs, but countless people were blinded by the darkness they seemed to emulate.

So much was hidden behind the words they spoke.

So much quivered deep within me.

We continued to walk the trail again and discuss when my great-grandmother passed away. I was twelve years old and my mother refused to let me go to the funeral. I can still smell my great-grandmother's cooking and feel the crushed leaves beneath my feet. I would go to her house and leap off of the roof and into the piles of leaves that neighborhood children would help her rake onto her lawn.

Those days were gone now.

I had remained in the house with my younger sisters while the funeral took place. It just so happened that throughout the weekend Michael Jackson released his music video for "Thriller" on MTV. Zombies and guts were plastered across the screen for me to watch. It was a lengthy display of blood and gore, which contrasted what my mother wanted me to see.

Michael Jackson's music resonated with me throughout my life. The melodies of Madonna, Hall and Oates, and Mötley Crüe had their respective roles in my journey as well.

"Hey Jude" from the Beatles and "Stairway to Heaven" from Led Zeppelin also held important roles in my life. They were the strings that were woven together to establish the fabric of my very faith. There are plenty of songs that helped me establish who I am, and they quickly became the soundtrack to my life.

We reached the end of the trail again and started to move towards the edge of the park.

Still, our conversation seemed like it was just beginning.

"Hey," Morena put her hands in her pockets and looked up at me. "How about we walk around a bit more?"

'Morena,' I stopped for a moment and put my hand on her shoulder. 'Why do you do what you do?'

"I don't know." She winked.

It was like she knew her purpose or path already, but she did not want to reveal too much… or anything at all.

We stood there smiling at each other for a bit, until Morena asked me to sing the first thing that came to me.

'You want me to sing?'

"Allow the voice from your soul to say something."

The first thing that came to mind were the lyrics to "Shine" from Collective Soul. It was my favorite song to perform on the drums. While playing the song, the band always elevates to a centralized vibration: we all rise together during the song. I extended my hand to Morena and she placed her hand in mine. We moved closer to one another and began to dance.

'Give me a word
Give me a sign
Show me where to look
Tell me what will I find
Lay me on the ground
Fly me in the sky
Show me where to look
Tell me what will I find.'

Morena responded with a line before I could even muster up the courage to sing the last few words,

"Oh, heaven let your light shine down."

'You know the song, too?'

"Who doesn't?" She laughed.

'I am clearly not too great of a singer.'

"You don't have to be to translate the words in your soul."

I removed my hand from hers and stepped back to take a look at her.

'You're not real, are you?' I tilted my head.

"I am as real as you want me to be." Morena shrugged.

'Why did we talk all about this stuff?'

"Music?" Morena asked.

'Yeah.' I stood there, waiting for her to answer me.

"Sometimes what you are searching for is not exactly what you are looking for." She looked past me, almost as if she was talking to someone else. When I turned to see who was there, she disappeared.

I stood in Alley Pond Park alone with my thoughts.

I think the point of this whole experience was reflection: music plays a really large role in my life. Music saved my life. Bon Jovi saved my life.

His music kept me going and gave me hope. There is not a day that goes by that I am not attached to music in some form or way.

Music, in all its shapes and sizes, eloquently depicts the language of my soul. It pervades societal customs and norms.

It also permeates how friendships and relationships are established, strengthened, grow, and proceed forward; especially when those relationships are augmented by communicating openly.

∞ ∞ ∞ ∞ ∞ ∞ ∞ ∞

Elyza and I were slowly becoming very good friends. Despite our past relationship challenges, our love of music and performing redefined who we were. We kept moving forward as a band and as a cohesive whole.

For some time, Bryan's stepfather was our bass player, which meant that Gemma regularly attended shows. Our respective pasts were diminished by our love of music and our individually renewed sense of who we each were.

Music had the power to bring us all together.

Music also brought Bryan to new heights and new places. I got the chance to see him perform in Manhattan at the famous Carnegie Hall and twice at Lincoln Center. His love of bass, and music in general, helped him grow and expand his soul as well.

Deep down inside, I know that Bryan's front row seat in his mother's womb at the RUSH concert played a role in his love for music, too. The day before he was born, he had a chance to hear one of the greatest rock n' roll bass players of all time, Geddy Lee. From that point on, it seemed like Bryan's adoration for music would transpire into something magical.

At countless concerts our band, Outlet, put on over the years, Bryan and his friends performed on stage with us.

Our band members came from all walks of life and different experiences: our love of music connected us all in the most unlikely of places.

Outlet's guitarist was in a Christian rock band and was always drawn to 80's music. We met at basketball games and baseball games where our children mutually played together. The blues rock guitarist and the bass player in our band did not have an ego, and proved themselves to be two of the most peaceful men in the world.

In what felt like seconds flat, we were booked every single weekend. We played bars, clubs, parties, charity events, you name it.

We did charity shows for multiple biker groups and performed at all of their clubhouse shows. Their loyalty to our music was truly unmatched, as so many members of the group would travel across New York to see us play.

∞ ∞ ∞ ∞ ∞ ∞ ∞ ∞

On the night of one of our largest events, a $100,000-raising charity event, Outlet was getting ready to take the stage with our group of spiritual musicians. I had always felt excited about performing as a band, but this situation seemed intense. I was on the cusp of getting over my sister's struggles, I had been grappling with how to balance relationships in my life, and I was intrigued by Morena's persistent disappearances and appearances.

My mind was racing, though my heart was healing.

The music within me was fluttering forth and my voice was getting stronger.

Elyza rested her head on my shoulder moments before we were about to go on stage.

I sighed and thought about how far music had brought me over the past few decades. Music was my catharsis and I could not be more grateful for music.

Windows of Opportunity was on the verge of something major, and I had the renewed faith and confidence to bring it to the next level.

I stepped onto the corner of the makeshift stage at what would be one of our largest concerts ever.

The screeching rails beneath me were echoic of the past few months. The noise was beneath me, but when it grows louder and louder, some may succumb to it.

It almost happened. I almost gave in. Yet something inherently grew within me and told me I was not allowed to give up. A rush of love fell over my body. I felt the universe holding me and telling me that everything I experienced brought me to this level of compassion, human ability, and growth.

Despite all of the negativity that had been overwhelming and consuming at key times, these key times existed as a means to unlock the next passage, the next part of my human soul… the emergence of more.

Music had always resonated with me and clung to the broken bits of my soul. Music had been a guiding light when words failed to materialize.

Upon stepping on stage, moments before the music would need to flow from me, I was shaking. I felt faint and the light around me was encompassing my peripheral vision. I would have probably panicked if I had the time, but no… I would not. I could not.

This was meant to be. This was kismet.

This was the final release of all of the negative energy that had been burning to a crisp. Those flames would be extinguished. They just had to be.

As the voices of the crowd crept closer to the moment, the denouement of a series of soul-developing moments, I took a breath and stepped into the line of sight.

I felt an abundance of anticipation and resolution, but it was not coming from me. The energy in the room shifted.

Once the first beat sprang from my drumsticks, screams erupted in the room. I remained steadfast, as I knew this would be it. This was the moment. This was me.

I was shedding my final layer and stepping into the sunlight.

The rest of the song flowed from within with the ferocity of a coursing river.

My pulse heightened and I was, in those moments, ready. Ready to take on whatever may come. Ready to accomplish each step to move closer to universal illumination. A collaboration of souls beckoned and brought together that very moment.

A majestic collection of noise burst from the crowd. I held back the sheer joy and tears.

I was home in my own skin.

What resonated the most was the message I received within my soul, which summed up what happened in humanistic terms:

"You walked out today fearless in the face of what the whole world judged you for years, and you stood and performed and the universe channeled its cheer for you through the souls of that audience."

Souls were just electrified by a few moments of my music propelling forward... imagine when I really speak.

Empowerment for humanity rests in our hands; it's time to lead with my best foot forward.

CHAPTER 27

Red Tape and Sacrifice

~

"After all you put me through, you think I'd despise you, but in the end I wanna thank you, 'cause you've made me that much stronger."

- Christina Aguilera, American singer, songwriter, Staten Island, New York

Professionally speaking, I was about to reach the peak of who I could be in the context of our community at large. I came to terms with my past, I was looking forward to the future of the non-profit agency, and I felt that my life was about to elevate to an entirely different realm of possibilities.

Though life has a funny way of working out.

Just when you think you are at the top, sometimes you realize the sincere fragility that rests just below your feet.

I guess the pervasive theme here is that you just have to keep rising from the ashes, like a phoenix, until you can genuinely fly high.

My life was, and continued to be, one massive question mark after another.

Many new ones appeared over the course of time, but my inquisitive nature is alive and well. Life has an incredible way of creating questions and answers that linger on the tips of our tongues, yet words are often the last line of defense when actions are prevalent.

Answers often appear throughout the ripples of time and space, and tend to lead to soul-enriching revelations. With each ripple of time that passes, a new journey arrives. Tenacity, choices, consequences, lessons, and blessings are sure soon to follow.

The stickiness that my body was patiently trying to endure gave way to the evidence that it was another hot summer day in late August. The one window of my bedroom is propped open with an empty water bottle in a desperate attempt to allow some air in. The room is your typical off-white bedroom, though I often look at these four walls as a colorful solitude from my past life. The red curtains add brightness to the room and are slightly parted in order for me to see what type of day it is when I awake each morning.

What I normally see is the side of the house next to me. The houses around this part of the world are on top of one another, but at least I can tell if I need to grab the umbrella on my way out or not. Since living here, I never take my surroundings for granted. I appreciate all aspects around me. I particularly love the far-right wall that is merely a piece of sheet rock screwed into the frame. It blocks off what I respectfully describe as one of the many catacombs of this home.

To the left of this sheetrock are my three empty dressers, which consist of white formica and are up on rocks to avoid further water damage from the many floods that happen here in Bayside, New York, a town blessed with a balance of scenic streets, within a hustle and bustle environment.

I am not sure why I actually keep the dressers as I have all my clothes in large plastic containers along the right wall when you enter the bedroom. It is a system that works well for me and the dressers just take up space, not that I really need the space. The tops of the dressers do act as a display of artwork or a container for personal items: whether it is loose change, or one of my prized possessions, an empty shoebox, they made me feel as if I had a permanent home.

The bed is a full-size bed that takes up much of the room, but is centered nicely. A large television that is turned on its side acts as a nightstand on the left-hand side of the bed. Revealing portions of the depths of my personality are placed on this fallacy of a table in the readings of *The Secret* by Rhonda Byrne, *The Unauthorized Biography of Rene Angelil – The Making of Celine Dion* by Jean Beaunoyer, my own personal attempt at a poetry book that has a quote on the front that states *"One instant is eternity; eternity is the now"* by Wu-Men, and a tour guide book of Ireland, a bleak reminder that I wanted to travel the world one day and make a real difference inspiring the masses.

I also had a box here that is 5 3/8 inches wide by 8 3/8 inches tall in which the contents are symbolic of the culmination and purpose for my existence. The sum total of these objects captures almost every depth of who I am.

All that is missing is a Bon Jovi catalog of songs and it would paint the whole picture.

The year is 2007 and my morning started the same as it has many times in recent months. Rolling off my sheets, and as my feet hit the ground; I thanked the universe for all of my blessings. I wondered what this day would bring as each day of my life is full of wonderful and incredible experiences. Even if nothing is planned, something magical happens.

Even at certain points of my life when people would look at me and assume that I had a good life, it can't compare to present day. I never thought life would come to this. Not while I was going through what I have gone through. The light at the end of the tunnel is awe inspiring, especially when one thinks they are lost in that tunnel forever. I guess this is the story of my time in the tunnel.

Later on in the day, I got into my black 1999 Chevy Monte Carlo. The scratches and dents ever so slightly added character to the car. I am relieved cars can't talk. The memories and stories of what has occurred with this car could probably be a television series in itself. The car is the one possession I own that is my pride and joy. It has its dents and scratches, created by some of those untold stories, but to me that car is a piece of art. It doesn't always start because the self-starter shuts down the car sometimes, only to restart three minutes later.

Of course, it always happens when I am in a rush and it is truly a pain in the ass.

There is no smoking allowed in my car, but it has a few cigarette burns in the seats. The seats are a dark grey, almost black. The windows are a dark tint, almost illegal. She has been good to me and at 135,000 miles she is still going strong. The only thing I don't like about the car is the console. It is broken and always driving me nuts.

Other than that, the car is almost everything to me.

I practically live in it.

Many people who know me say I am very sensitive and more like a female than a male, but if there is one male macho stereotype about me, it is my Monte. I love that car.

I began my drive to Hicksville to pick up my son Bryan from high school football practice. He had been through the ringer with me, and had adjusted quite well to life. He is easy going, but focused and determined.

I think I am a good father, but I won't be able to fully measure that until he is older.

We have a communicative relationship and can talk about anything. We respect one another and I love that about us.

Hicksville is about twenty minutes east of Bayside and is considered to be the suburbs. It is a nice town but has been getting overcrowded over the past ten years. There is an influx of an Indian culture that has been settling in Hicksville for the past ten years and I often wonder how a culture picks an area to migrate to here in America.

Hicksville is large, with a major mall directly in the middle of it, several restaurants, and huge business. Throughout Hicksville are winding streets that create an image of a gentle and friendly community of homes, however, most neighbors don't know each other and you are lucky to get a wave or a hello if you see a familiar face during the course of your day. It is actually the same way in Bayside. It is kind of sad to me that society is heading in that direction… unfriendly, unknowing, and not caring.

To some it may seem like your ordinary, monotonous day, but for me, I realized it was anything but boring or routine. In fact, it was special and I realized in those first moments of this drive what the magical component of the day was to be.

With the windows down, I had Bon Jovi's new album, *Lost Highway*, blaring at decibels as if I wanted all of Bayside to be impacted by this band as I have been through the years. In a strange contrast though, I had lyrics from Melissa Etheridge's song, "Similar Features," pounding through my mind.

I know, not even following the same rhythm as Lost Highway, but that is how my mind works sometimes – just a bunch of mumbled songs and a beat that never stops.

"Now the paint is still wet in your do it by number dream."

That Melissa Etheridge lyric perfectly captures how surreal the realization of what my life has finally become. With Melissa in my head and the Monte blaring with the up-tempo guitar riff on Lost Highway, I stared out my rearview mirror only to see the reflection of my past behind me. For unbeknownst reasons, I knew the time had finally come.

The enchantment behind today was that this day would mark the beginning of telling the untold story. It would be the day we would begin the new journey; the day the ups and downs, the ins and outs, the dreams and nightmares are finally told.

The real story of my life can and should be told.

∞ ∞ ∞ ∞ ∞ ∞ ∞ ∞

I still considered myself to be in my youthful prime, as I believed with all my spirit and being, that age is just a state of mind. The mind is a lot stronger than most of us realize and you can be young and mature or mature and young… if that makes sense.

However, as I glared through that rearview mirror and into the past, my memory brought me back to a time that I still cannot fathom how I allowed it to affect me the way it does.

Dates and years are vague to me, but certain things you cannot forget: the swing of a bat, the sound it makes when it connects with your body, the ragged edge of glass cutting you in rage, the sound of a body being dragged down the stairs by a fist full of hair, the screams in the night, shadows of parents arguing over financial matters as I lie awake in bed listening to the teardrops roll off my face.

Confused and lost were my dearest friends growing up and they have kept close to me like my own shadow through most of my life.

Everything seemed to finally be going well… what could possibly go wrong?

∞ ∞ ∞ ∞ ∞ ∞ ∞ ∞

The program I was running up at the high school was utterly magical. I was doing a tremendous amount of work inside the school and helping the community simultaneously. I was working with a lot of families, with after school programs, and Windows of Opportunity was thriving as a part-time program that took place at night.

Nothing I did after three in the afternoon ever interfered with what took place during school hours.

They all loved me at the high school and were consistently praising my work… that is, until there was trouble and questions materialized.

Then they turned their backs on me.

I began working at the high school with some pretty amazing administrators. From 2001 to 2006, I had a phenomenal supervisor who supported all of my endeavors with the students. I was the golden child. I was seen as magical. I was on the front page of local papers and bringing the school to new heights.

I was held on a pedestal with my mindset flushed with positivity.

Then funding got cut.

Then different district level administrators came to the school.

That's when the fire started.

We had a set calendar of events, which consisted of workshops, conferences, trainings, and events that eclipsed any negativity students were experiencing.

However, my new administrator seemed to have other priorities.

We met during one of her first days at the school and I explained all of the amazing things our youth were doing.

"Keep doing what you are doing," she assured me.

She told me she worked at the middle school level and that there would be some transitional things to consider throughout the year, but that nothing would get in the way of our work.

Months later, I would be caught in the biggest professional challenge of my career.

We began planning the annual Dream Out Loud Conference and began to send out invitations, as we did every single year. Suddenly, the new administrator did not approve of what was happening.

She claimed we were running the conference without her permission and became infuriated.

'You told me to keep moving forward,' I was respectful when I spoke with her, but she seemed incredibly distraught.

After a long pause, she demanded I send an apology letter to all of the schools we invited and to rescind the invitation.

The kids were working really hard, yet she was indifferent. I called all of my contacts and told them what was happening. I sent the letter and planned on running the conference behind her back.

The kids were all depending on me.

My principal and one of the assistant principals in my building told me to go ahead with the conference. They supported me despite what the new district level administrator and supervisor told me to do.

Once she caught wind of the conference, she showed up and saw three hundred kids running and participating in workshops, trainings, and different ceremonies.

Though she was appalled, I figured she had no real power over me, or the kids. Yet she never revealed that her position within the city's district education offices was a rather lofty one.

She did not like me.

She did not like how I defied her.

She became the epitome of a system structured to limit the voice of students.

To her, the system was a set of rules scripted in black and white.

To her, we were breaking every single rule in the book she so sternly abided by.

This golden child and man on a pedestal became public enemy number one seemingly overnight.

I honestly did not see the impending war or that I fed into what would occur, I just hoped that my intentions to help youth would overpower any misunderstanding or malice that would befall the conference.

To this day, I wonder if I would be where I am now if these events did not happen as they did. Were these moments blessings in disguise? Were these moments meant to be?

I never really knew.

∞ ∞ ∞ ∞ ∞ ∞ ∞ ∞

When she interacted with kids at the conference, she appeared to be blown away. She began calling her friends, who were administrators, and told them to come to the conference. She led them around after speaking with the kids and took full responsibility for the day's events.

When she and the administrators left, she turned to me and grabbed my arm. With a smile spread wide across her face, she looked me in the eye and said, "Never disobey me again, or you will regret it."

A chill ran down my spine.

Something was just not right.

Days later, I would find out just how she treats people who disobey her. When I walked into work, I was promptly summoned into the office by my principal, assistant principal, and a handful of detectives. My supervisor, the woman who told me not to disobey her, was standing front and center.

"You're in big trouble, Mr. Matheson," her eyes were filled with spite.

I could feel the hatred seeping from her skin.

"You are stealing from the school system." The words hung on her lips like icicles hanging from a roof.

There was a website I designed that was promoting programs from Windows of Opportunity. She found it and said that if I did not take it down within 24 hours, I would lose my job.

Windows of Opportunity was drastically separated from the high school, yet she saw the non-profit agency as a means to dig a metaphorical knife in my chest. She continued to scream at me in front of a man who would always defend me, and my position in the school. He stood there in silence.

They all did.

Even though I complied and pulled down the website, I felt my stomach churning in ways that seemed unimaginable.

I walked up to my office with a blank stare on my face.

I was about to be ensnared in a vicious cycle of bureaucracy: the system was broken and so much had to change. Everything had to change. It just had to.

Though I was distraught and in a silent state of panic, I was struggling to wear a mask that obscured my true emotions. I spent the day going through the motions of what I had to do: I was petrified by the misnomers and threats the woman bestowed upon me, but I did not know what else to do.

The kids were asking what was wrong, but I could not even speak.

How do you say that you feel like your entire life shattered and collapsed before your very eyes?

I went directly home after school and threw myself into the sheets. The sun set while I was busy letting tears stream down both sides of my eyes. The last thing I remember was shutting my eyes and praying to just wake up. Was this all a nightmare? Was this karma for my past? How could this happen?

Why me?

Why?

∞ ∞ ∞ ∞ ∞ ∞ ∞ ∞

I woke up at some point around one in the morning. It was not even a full day since my world came crashing down, and yet all of my work seemed to have faded away.

Standing around a group of teenagers yesterday, I found peace with the fact that I will forever be alone… and that is okay. To hear, "I am so proud of you, you are such an inspiration" from a kid going through massive issues, it was electrifying. To know your stress and struggles project as strength and salvation: how do you even comprehend that?

Could you ever?

415

It wasn't until I got in the car after being ignored by various adults I work with that I realized…

In becoming my own hero, I had to be forced into a state of independence.

So much for family and support, right?

Everyone will hope for the best for you, until you start to do better than them. It is heartbreaking. Yet at the same time, it is refreshing to see that I am clearly making somewhat of a difference.

Even if that difference means owning the strong tendencies that are so becoming of me. To be perceived as headstrong or annoying is an absolute honor, for I know that my efforts are creating a shift in the fibers that weave together the foundation of everything I am working towards.

And if in the end I am the only one standing my ground because all have either misjudged me, abandoned me, cast me aside too soon, or misconstrued my intentions… then I will need to accept who I have become. If it is meant to be, it will be… but no one said it has to be a fairytale ending.

After all, fairytales are just tails: the end of innocence and reality as we know it.

Carry on; carry on as if nothing really matters.

∞ ∞ ∞ ∞ ∞ ∞ ∞ ∞

The days that followed were agonizing. The months that followed were painstaking. I had to hide how I was hanging by a thread. Bryan saw me crumbling, but he could not figure out just what was wrong.

I was wandering through Alley Pond Park hour after hour.

I held a series of internal dialogues with myself and my soul: Wear a mask so they can't see your pain and agony. Hide in the shadows so you don't have to face the true reality of everything. It will take a while, but when the water rushes through, the levees break.

And as your eyes flood with sadness, don't let them see you cry. Don't let them see you crumble under the oppression of everything you have gone through. Don't let their words seep into your mind and crush you.

Don't let this pain destroy you forever.

Don't let the sun go down because of your heavy heart.

You will rise again.
You will bounce back again.
You always do.
You just have to.
You can survive; you have survived.
It isn't a bad life; it is a bad day.
Sharp words will drive daggers into you.
Heal.
Release the anger from your wounds.
Survive.

    Survive.

        Survive.

The lawsuit against me, and Windows of Opportunity, carried into 2008.

Solitude in Alley Pond Park was my salvation: it was there where I could be with my thoughts and pray for my Circle of Angels to help protect me.

Morena would appear now and then, but it seemed like she sensed the devout sadness stirring in my soul.

On one chilly day in February, with my breath materializing before me, I found myself somewhat lost in the park. The trails blended together and I could not figure out where I was. Spinning around, my eyes dragging along every tree and broken branch, I dropped to my knees.

I cried.

Hard.

What would possess someone to attack an individual who was actually helping children? I was not doing anything illegal. I was giving students a voice.

And still, that was not good enough.

Was I ever good enough?

Did anyone truly see me for who I was?

"Hey" a voice sprung from up in the trees.

I looked up and saw Morena perched on some rather low-hanging branches. She had the same, pristine smile that she usually did, but something seemed different. Her demeanor and expression reminded me of the days when Stacey and I would chat in *our* tree.

It was her energy. It was like her presence was calling upon me to rise.

"You okay, kiddo?" She let one of her legs hang from the branch. Her back was resting against the actual tree.

'Yeah.' I wiped tears from my face. 'Yeah.' I stood up so she didn't worry.

She sniffled for a few moments: "Do you smell that? It smells like crap."

We both laughed and I could not remember the last time I felt even a little bit of happiness.

'Why are you up in the tree?' I tried deflecting my sadness.

"I don't know," she said. "I just really like being up here."

'Stacey used to do that, you know.' I put my hands in my pockets and leaned against the tree she positioned herself on. 'We would sit in the first few branches for hours and talk about music. Now that tree has grown so high that even if I tried, I could not get into Stacey's tree.'

Morena looked down at me as my blonde hairs were seeping into the bark of the tree.

'I really miss Stacey.' The tears began streaming again.

Morena climbed down the tree and stood before me, almost in one poised motion. It seemed like she floated down to stand beside me.

"She is always with you." Her tone was soft. "Always."

'I know.' I sunk down into the mud beneath the tree. The ground was nearly frozen solid.

"What happened, Scott?" She sat down in front of me.

I proceeded to pour my heart out. She was willing to listen and I was willing to release everything bursting from within my head.

Through tears and with a heavy heart, I spent the next hour or so weeping about what this woman was doing to me.

She was destroying my career. She didn't care.

She was not thinking about the kids, she was carving my heart into shreds because she was caught up in an archaic rulebook.

Was there even a physical rulebook?

Throughout my gut-wrenching, soul-shattering catharsis, Morena just sat there. She listened. She was indifferent to the weather and was formulating a response.

After I finished speaking and was left dry-heaving in the slush and freezing weather, she tilted her head and spoke just a few words: "What does your soul tell you to do?"

I burst into tears again.

'My soul,' I had a hard time catching my breath in the frigid temperature. 'My soul is desolate. It is empty. It is silent.'

"Then listen more intently."

'I...' I began gasping for air. 'I can't hear. I can't breathe.'

"Come," Morena stood and grabbed my hand. "Let's get you a nice, hot coffee."

∞ ∞ ∞ ∞ ∞ ∞ ∞ ∞

We sat in a coffee shop near Alley Pond Park. I was shivering and could barely wrap my fingers around the cup.

Morena sat there, her legs tucked under her, looking out the window.

All day I had been ruminating about the phrase "It is lonely at the top."

It really, truly is at times.

I thought back to years ago when I worked with other individuals. They would nitpick and call me names, pinch me, and treat me like the scum of the Earth.

That has always been how my life unravels.

However, despite the cloud of sadness raining over my head, I find solace in the work I do. I am there for the kids. I am there for the mission. I am a mere pawn in the game, but pawns can rise.

All of this will be insignificant next year.

All of this will be insignificant two weeks from now, or so I hoped.

Their hatred and jealousy will grow, but I guarantee that a light is shining. It shines somewhere and in some form.

The kids see the goodness in me, and shouldn't that be all that matters?

It does suck to be hated though.

How do you go from working with someone on a professional level, to treating them like utter crap? That is really mature. But I knew all of this. I saw it and felt it.

Come Monday, I knew I would walk in with my chin up and with a black cloud hanging over me.

I will have to obey her, my supervisor.

For after all is said and done, they look at me with green streaks in their souls, but when called to rise they shackle themselves to false pretenses and shallow promises.

This too shall pass.

It has to.

∞ ∞ ∞ ∞ ∞ ∞ ∞ ∞

I came back to work day after day wearing a false smile across my face.

I watched the clock. I watched the door. I was watching my back, since no one else was.

I was living in a perpetual state of, "When will they get me?"

February passed.

March passed.

April passed.

May passed.

June arrived, and I was still under investigation.

It ate at me regularly and I was disturbed by the mind games the woman was playing.

"Don't disobey me" haunted my nightmares. Her voice echoed through my soul and I was suffocating.

I was freaking out and I was getting sicker by the day. The stress from all of this took me down hard and fast. Everything I taught the kids did not permeate my mind. I could not apply it to myself, for the daunting nightmares were extremely loud and incredibly close to my heartstrings.

I figured I was going to die from humiliation.

Did this make me a fraud?

I was helping thousands of kids, but this seemed to be how my life and my career were about to end.

What next?

What now?

My life was in utter dismay, and I thought it was all about to end when I was called into my principal's office.

Him and a handful of executives smiled, straightened out their suits... and explained I was going to be charged with another offense: inappropriate conduct and behavior with students.

After months of pain they were not just coming after me, but the children and families I worked with as well.

This was it.

My pedestal was in shambles.

∞ ∞ ∞ ∞ ∞ ∞ ∞ ∞

Kids and families were brought into the principal's office to be interviewed. Families were visited at home.

The investigators and my supervisor were going for my jugular. They wanted me to bleed out and drown in my own sacrifices.

They were asking families if I was inappropriate with their children. The kids were getting scared and were crying openly. Every single one of them said the exact same thing: "Mr. Matheson did not do anything."

I received a letter in the mail stating that Windows of Opportunity was being sued for $4 million.

I placed the letter down on the counter, ran into the bathroom, and vomited.

All of the lives I changed were about to be submerged in turmoil, and I could not help them.

Within thirty days of the second investigation, I was standing at a gas station looking out at the other cars before me. What were the stories behind the people standing here?

Who else was struggling with something dark and horrifying?

My cell phone rang and my heart dropped… what's next?

A kind voice from an investigator seeped through the phone. He told me that he did not understand why these investigations were taking place, told me to stay strong, and graced me with some news.

"You're obviously doing something right," he said. "I just wanted to call you personally and let you know that the inappropriate conduct charge is being dropped."

Days later I felt like I could breathe again when another investigator told me the first set of charges were dropped and that they realized I was truly innocent.

'Okay,' I figured, 'Now can I live again?'

Once again, I found out that taking a breath meant just gasping for air.

Though months had passed since the start of my first investigation, and just a few mere days past since the second set of charges were dropped, I got yet another phone call.

I may have been innocent from the start, but that meant nothing in the eyes of a new set of investigators. Apparently, my case file ended up on someone else's desk, and he chose to re-open the case.

They still wanted the $4 million. They still wanted to bury me.

They wanted to take Windows of Opportunity down.

My immune system was shot. I could not breathe. I was minutes away from ending up in the back of an ambulance and I was unbalanced.

My supervisor's vendetta was so relentless.

Her mind was a gun just waiting to take its shot: she was locked and loaded.

The summer was filled with desperation and looking for a way I could heal.

∞ ∞ ∞ ∞ ∞ ∞ ∞ ∞

By the fall of 2008, crunching leaves cackled beneath my feet. Trying to run would help me to no avail, and I knew my opinions were holistically limited in every aspect. Voices flooded my head: some familiar, some idealistically innocent in their intent. Still, I knew the choices I made had to be my own.

Who was I becoming?

Could I always live in a state of perpetual fear like this?

What sort of energy was I committing to myself and my future?

More importantly, I wondered if I even had a future.

Back in my office at the high school, I was numb.

Sitting, legs intertwined and tucked under my body, I was slowly discovering the overwhelming fear that radiated throughout my system. The other faces of kids in the office looked quizzically upon my anxious demeanor and watched me tremble with exquisite horror of the reality we were facing.

I sat tapping the armrest to my right, eyes searching the room for some sign of joy. All I could see were shallow recollections of what could have been, and the stark reality of what was.

I helped the kids I could, but I felt my days were numbered.

After school, I sat by myself looking at the word, "Sacrifice" plastered across the bottom of the Spiderman poster.

Sitting alone in an enclosed space, I started feeling the existential dread seep into each crevice of my brain. Not a single soul could fathom all I had been through and all I had seen. I once heard someone say, "Wear a smile and not a single person will sense something is wrong."

Oh, if I only knew then what I know now.

To walk through a hallway and be treated as a disease, to have honest conversations with a person and have them all but spit in your face, to be in a room with people who look right through you as if you are a massive jerk or piece of crap. To be holding on by a mere millimeter of a slender piece of thread: dangling… just waiting for a hand or a glimmer of hope to keep you alive and awake.

But it does get harder with each passing moment. At times, it seemed as if there is no end to the agony. It seemed as if more weight was being progressively added stack-by-stack, slander by slanderous word.

When does it become too heavy to bear?

When does it become so ingrained and painful, that something has to happen?

Where is the light within? Where is the voice within that says, "You'll be okay, just hold on…?"

No. There is just utter silence.

There is just pain. A deep-rooted pain knowing that you harness so much potential, yet are contrasted by the devout burning sensation enveloping your soul.

Hurt shivers down my arms and picks up the tiny hairs along the way.

"I hurt myself to see if I still feel," echoed through the small room. Johnny Cash's pain is almost as drastic as what rattles in my mind right now.

What have I become?

Everyone I know does seem to go away in the end.

The smile I wear rests in my palm, drenched in blood and deep-rooted in the missing pieces of everything and everyone I once had and held dear.

I wanted a new beginning.

I called up a few friends and connections. I had plenty of people who wanted to work with me in different after school programs and such over the years.

"Be strong" is the best and worst advice anyone could give. Strength implies having the capacity to lift the weight or burden being placed before you. Still, we must uphold a certain sense of decorum that shouts to the world, "Hey, look at me, I am fine!" Meanwhile everything inside of you wants to just shrivel up and scream.

I knew it wouldn't always be this way.

The pain dissipates and the sun will rise majestically into your soul. Your heart will fill with the tenacity embraced by a better, brighter day. There is solace knowing that this moment is not finite. This moment is not the be all and end all, nor is it remarkably close to the denouement of any of the dramatic plays that rip the mask off to reveal the penultimate scene.

We were not born this way. We were not born filled with hate and discontent for one another. This was taught. This was learned. This was the indirect impact of a scowl that lasted too long. This was the direct result of telling someone, "No, you are just not good enough." This was the unraveling of the ribbon of society as it was clasped from the fingertips of a mistaken villain.

Yet in consequence, the mistaken villain manifests a new identity filled with misjudgment and hostility.

The rising conflict did not need to exist this way. No. The hands of time may not be able to reverse and submerge us into a realm of a past that can be reversed. No. Though we have the exquisite reality that higher consciousness hangs in the teetering balance of who we could become or aspire to be, and who dares step into a transformative state.

We must not be disillusioned by the horrors spewing from the mouths of those with a low vibration. We owe it to ourselves and the world to live in a state of extraordinary: to be authentically ourselves and represent the voices of the people like us who are still clawing their way out of banality.

It is time to rise above. It is time to reset the boundaries slammed before us. It is time to bring the world to a level of higher consciousness that seemed unfathomable.

Seemed, but isn't.

Seemed, but sewn together through the fabric of life betwixt with time.
Seemed... but still standing.

So be strong... because the best and worst experiences of our physical lifetime exist because we experience them.

I believed in my vision.

I believed in my sacrifices.

∞ ∞ ∞ ∞ ∞ ∞ ∞ ∞

Phone calls have changed my life time and time again. I chose to resign from the high school I was working in because the negative energy was seriously destroying my soul.

My friend called me within twenty minutes of leaving a message for her. She offered me a job as an after-school director of one of her programs, with a staff of fifty-five people to supervise and six hundred students to enlighten.

I would also receive twice as much of a salary than what I was making at the high school.

Naturally, I accepted the job. I had to run away and this was my way out.

I drafted my letter of resignation, which was given to students during my last official day at the school.

This chapter in my life was about to take a serious pause. It was for the best that I left. I had to regain some semblance of my mental health and sanity.

The weight of this burden and walking through the doors of the high school each day was simply horrifying to me.

When I left the building for the last time, I was free from the agony, but not from the guilty image I seemed to conjure up.

The anxieties from the charges were put on hold, yet my pain was far from being over.

I put the fractured pieces of the mask together and kept forging forward... I had to... I just didn't have a choice.

Once again, I was making yet another sacrifice.

CHAPTER 28

God Bless This Mess

~

"Hey God, there's nights you know I want to scream. These days you're even hard to believe. I know how busy you must be, but Hey God... Do you ever think about me?"

- Bon Jovi, American Rock Band, Sayreville, New Jersey

A crinkled copy of my resignation letter was stained with my tears. It was lying in my hands, looking back at me with such great disdain:

"Lift your head up high and scream out to the world, I know I am someone and let the truth unfurl. No one can hurt you now because you know what's true. Yes, I believe in me. So you believe in you." - Michael Jackson, "Wanna Be Startin' Something"

I will not bog you down with quotes like I usually do in my blogs and writings. Sometimes less is more, if you know what I mean.

I guess this is intended to be the last letter I ever write as an employee of this education system. Yes, for those of you who do not know, and I apologize that you are finding out this way, I have been afforded an amazing opportunity that comes at the most perfect timing in my career. I have accepted a new position at a wonderful agency that will allow me to continue building Windows of Opportunity, Inc. as well as being given the chance to train youth in the five boroughs of NYC. I will be helping 8 times the amount of youth I was able to help at the high school. Please note that this has not been an easy decision for me by any stretch of the means. Those of you close to me know that I have been working six nights per week on top of what I do for the high school, so I can continue having the finances to build Windows and be in a position to obtain this new full-time job.

I have agonized over this change in my life for some time now. The joke around the office has always been "Scott says he is leaving again, and he is still here. He is never leaving!"

I think I have always known that even though this has been the best job I have ever had, that my world was not going to end in room 339, and in my own way, I have been preparing you for my announcement that started on Friday.

I learned so much from all of you... about me, the world, and how to be a better human being. I learned there are a lot of ignorance, hatred, and ills in this world that needs to be changed. I realized I am only one person and even though you have all been so supportive, I sometimes feel like an army of one... and it has been a long and tough battle.

No, I am not giving up and never will. I will always Keep the Faith. This decision has come at a time that I feel is necessary to reposition myself to accomplish what I set off to do in the beginning: Change this world for the better. As I said on Friday and will continue to say in my final days of working at this high school, this is not goodbye, as I will be expanding Windows of Opportunity to five nights per week and will finally have the freedom to create positive change my way: head on and on a large scale.

So, I leave you with this parting gift – my thoughts in a final letter... a way to tell you what I am feeling, what I want you to think about, and a way to set the record straight once and for all.

I am digging down deep for this one.

My words are carefully chosen and my mind and heart is an open book. I am giving you the best, and perhaps the worst, of me.

There are so many thoughts that have run through my head over the past few months. I have done a lot of reflection, shed some tears (because of those I will miss seeing on a daily basis), and did a lot of soul searching. Life is like the wet paint on a do it by number puzzle: just an unfinished mixture of beginnings and endings that run together... that when completed, if ever completed, is supposed to tell a story.

Ahh... so, what am I getting at?

We are still painting our story, and my departure is just another piece of the puzzle. Allow this to be the closure we need individually so that we may all move on to new beginnings. By talking about the work students have done, honoring it, and seeing its significance, it will free us up to open the windows to new opportunities... and new beginnings. Closure serves to tie up or sever loose ends, quiets the mind even when questions have been left unanswered, signifies the end of an experience, and acknowledges that a change has taken place.

I could go into a whole soliloquy about the past seven or so years, going on eight, but I am hoping you will all do that in your responses. I have set many goals for the high school, myself, and for Windows of Opportunity.

We have achieved most of them, fell short on a few (but learned tremendously from those shortcomings), and changed some ideas along the way. Setting goals for ourselves, if we think about it, is our mind's way of admitting we need change, and then sets us off in the direction towards that change. We have set goals for ourselves and this program that is extremely idealistic, and when dealing with such strong ideals, you will get supporters and naysayers on your journey.

Also, when trying to obtain such high ideals as we have attempted in this high school over the years, we have found that some things don't work and some things don't make us feel the way we had hoped to.

Our goals have been fierce and strong, and some, such as the creation of Windows of Opportunity have been slow and careful. By embarking on the path of Windows of Opportunity slowly, I have had the chance to look around and consider other options as we all grew and learned together. I have had time to examine the underlying values (you all know how big I am on teaching values) of what Windows of Opportunity was about and found ways to manifest those feelings, whether it looks exactly like our initial goal or not.

We have created many programs that I feel, actually, that I know, are going to impact the world in a major way. I feel confident in the path we have taken, the slowness in building the agency, and in the foundation we have created. Just like a great band, we tackle one audience at a time; building an army of supporters who know the difference we bring to their lives. All the bands that do this are the bands that have longevity. They are the bands that have jealous haters as well, but over all have many that love, adore, and respect them.

That's what counts in life.

Life doesn't always give us the opportunity to anticipate or prepare for a big change, and we may find ourselves overwhelmed by what is in front of us. But let's choose to look at what we have accomplished one thing at a time. Maybe it was a session, or a class, or an event. Maybe you took something from the program and it helped you three months later when you found yourself in a weird predicament. Take a second to look at these things.

Look inside you and you will realize that you have accomplished quite a bit.

You will also see that you have changed for the better and that you had all you needed inside of you this whole time.

As our time and unprecedented accomplishments at the high school come to an end, I pray you have the tools necessary to give back to those around you and your community. You all know I am big on community service and I will set up a community service program at Windows of Opportunity, but always remember to give back because of the success you have achieved. If you are a peer leader, you are always a leader. Enjoy who you are and use those skills in all of your walks of life. I hope that my words and your experience with me, and the community, have left you inspired, energetic, equipped, and empowered for a life that you dream about.

You must remain vigilant in moving forward, ignoring those that don't believe in you, and forgiving yourself for past mistakes. Learn from your mistakes. Stay true to yourself and your hearts' dreams. Don't settle for less than your full potential. Look beyond your current definition of success. Make sure you remember to have a balance in life, especially when it comes to your career, love, and money. There is much more to life than career and finances, though this is important. You must, and I stress MUST have inner happiness – no matter how long it takes, it is something you should never give up on trying to obtain. This is something that my experiences at the high school have taught me along the way.

Always strive for what it is you want. Life is too short. We see it all the time. We teach it in our trainings. People are dying daily from HIV, cancer, accidents, and so on.

We have lost too many people along the way.

Keep that in mind as you complain about how much high school is left or that Mom and Dad are in a bad mood after work...

We learn everyday. Be open to learning. Some of life's best lessons will not happen in the classroom (though you should all go to class!). The school of life continues way past the walls of high school.

Life doesn't begin or end there, as is the same in your homes.

No matter where you are in life it is never too late to start new: to refocus, to take another path. It is never too late to learn and grow and even take your successes (such as I am doing) and build on them.

Grow to a higher level – you have all you need – THROW AWAY the LIMITATIONS OF OTHERS!

Ignore their negative opinions, and their ignorant viewpoints.

Those who judge you, especially when you know in your soul you are right, aren't worth your time or energy. They will try to hold you back or take you down.

Why? Who knows? Maybe it is jealousy?

They are like the bullies in the playground or even worse – they are like cyber bullies – who hide behind their anonymity. If you know in your soul you are on the right path, don't let the naysayers take away your dreams. You have all the tools you need to flourish – to grow and to reach heights without limits.

Life is a war out there.

You may lose a battle or be a victim of what seems like a hidden attack with a hidden agenda, but don't let these setbacks defeat you. It is just a momentary battle. Go out and win your war!

It is what I live my life as and it's what my life stands for.

That has never wavered.

It is what Windows is all about.

Anyone else who says otherwise about our successes and how we accomplish them or says anything about the dreams you or I fight for, just does not get it!

Forget them.

They will never win, even if they think they are victorious.

In this world we live in, there is a good versus evil concept. This is the war on life I was writing about a moment ago. It is okay to look at the world this way.

Let us face the facts here. Some people are angry and hate certain things in this world. It is that inner anger and rage, whether it is at themselves or the world around them, that makes people jump to conclusions and fight back. It is okay to be angry and express your emotions of injustice, as long as you aren't looking through a narrow looking glass and you have ALL your facts.

If you don't, hold your judgment.

Ask questions. Go to the source. If you think your family hates you, sit down and talk to them. If you think your boyfriend will cheat on you, tell him how you feel insecure. If you think people are crushing your dreams or don't believe in you, ask them why?

Maybe you will get some insight about yourself, but remember just the same, you don't have to accept their viewpoints. Always follow your heart, your soul, and your passion. This is what life is about. Do the good you dream of doing.

BE THE CHANGE YOU WANT TO SEE IN THE WORLD!

And don't waver when people judge you or try to take you down for being that change. People should be ashamed of themselves for trying to put you down or take you out for the good that you are and that you do.

Your life should have no limits.

You have all put your hearts not only into our projects and my dreams, but into the lives you wish to have. Every session, every group, every moment in the high school and outside of the building was about creating the life and world you wanted. If you hated (and believe it or not, we have plenty of haters — kids and adults alike — who just don't get what we get) what we did that's okay too, because you are only going after the life you wish to create for you and your world.

As long as you didn't hurt people along the way you should never be ashamed or feel bad about creating and chasing your dreams. If you did, however, try to hurt people or judge them in a negative light, then I challenge you to take some time and reanalyze your actions.

Perhaps it is too late because what is done is done, but you can always change who you are and grow from the mistakes that you made. The truth is that we are all learning, and it is very difficult to tell, when looking only at the exterior of a person, what's going on inside. Often we look at a situation, as I have taught in class many times, and jump to conclusions.

If two men in bandanas speed up to a convenient store and jump out to run in… it does not mean they are robbing the place. Perhaps one was injured and needed to get a Band-Aid. You just never know and if you passed judgment and don't have the facts (and saying "I know! I just know! I can tell!" is NOT HAVING THE FACTS!), then you have more than likely handled the situation unjustly and unfairly.

You may have even caused unnecessary pain to others. If you understand this concept it is never too late to apologize to the ones you hurt, or if you have too much pride, learn from the situation.

Maybe if you speak to them or those you judged you would actually learn another perspective that you hadn't seen. It may even change your previous thinking radically.

Whoa, I didn't mean to get on a soapbox there. Don't get me wrong here at all. I am not mad at those who hate me, and what I did for the school. I know what you are all saying... but I mean it. Like I said, I did a lot of soul searching this weekend.

We all know people who fail us, try to take us down, and keep doing so. Forgiving them doesn't mean you're supposed to deny the facts, pretending they didn't happen or don't matter.

Forgiveness sees the failure for what it is but refuses to hold people emotionally hostage until they've paid for it.

I forgive these people.

I must forgive them for real change in this world to take place. For Windows of Opportunity to do what it has started to do. I must practice what I preach and stand for good values. Real forgiveness occurs when you have chosen to forgive, versus having a positive feeling towards forgiving that person.

Feeling forgiveness is usually slower than choosing to forgive. Don't rush the feelings. Let your will to forgive lead your actions. Your feelings may have to catch up later. I am still hurt by what some people have done to the programs I ran with students in the school, and what they have said about me, and my students through the years, but I forgive them all, as I know the truth.

What I think of me, the programs I ran at the high school, and Windows of Opportunity, is far more important than what naysayers have to say or think.

I choose to live up to certain standards and ethics. I do my best all the time. I live by my own significant set of values.

When you live by your values, what others do has little effect on your emotions and choices. Though competition can seem like the road to fulfillment, proving yourself to others is not nearly as satisfying as setting and accomplishing your goals. There will always be those who have achieved more than you and those that have achieved less.

You measure yourself fairly. You reevaluate your goals and successes. You know who matters in your life and whose opinion counts.

The ones who truly love you are whom you should be listening to… as well as yourself.

Well, I have been writing this nightmare of a letter for hours now, so if you are still with me I commend you and I leave you with some final thoughts to ponder: You have all come to me for guidance and help in basically, to give it an umbrella term, in becoming better people. Becoming a better person in your own eyes is a whole-life project; it is a journey to become optimal, and thus you should focus your step-by-step efforts on multiple areas of your life.

Since you likely know which qualities you consider good, growing as an individual is simply a matter of making an effort to do good whenever possible. Respect should be a key element of your efforts. When you acknowledge that all people are deserving of compassion, consideration, and dignity, you are naturally more able to treat them the way you yourself wish to be treated.

I want you naysayers out there to focus on that sentence.

Let me repeat that… I want you naysayers out there to focus on that sentence.

You will become a more active listener, more helpful, and truthful. Going the extra mile in all you do can also facilitate progress in your life. Approaching your everyday life and responsibilities with an upbeat attitude and positive expectations can help you make the world a brighter, more cheerful place. Finally, coming to terms with your values (there is my favorite concept again) and then living by them will enable you to introduce a new level of integrity and dignity into your life.

As you continue to grow, take pride in your success, in memories that were made as a result of our programs, in the experiences you may have had with Windows, and in your own life. Be proud of learning who you are and re-learning about who you are as a person. While you may never feel you have reached the pinnacles of awareness you hope to achieve, you can make the most of this creative process of transformation. Becoming a better person is your choice and is a natural progression in your journey of self-awareness.

I will miss you all and will not say goodbye, as I am not leaving this world for years to come. I am here in the community. Windows of Opportunity is flourishing and is in eight school districts. I am amazed at the growth and I know the agency will continue to flourish.

And I hope you will all continue to share in my dream with it.

With the utmost respect,

Scott Matheson

It was devastating to me that this was the legacy I would leave behind for my students. My principal and assistant principal must have looked at this letter and tossed it aside, especially after seeing how long it was.

However, something told me that my students and the families I worked with read the entire thing.

I was hoping that somehow, somewhere, someone was going to be impacted by my words. I may not ever be able to experience the aftermath of the amalgamation of letters that plastered the page, but knowing that someone might pick up the letter and read what I wrote meant the world to me.

I just hope that the readers of the letter would never suffer as much as I had at that point.

∞ ∞ ∞ ∞ ∞ ∞ ∞ ∞

I spent most of my days looking over my shoulder. I was hopeful that the lawsuit from the city would not impact all of the potential good I would be creating in this world.

It was agonizing and ate at my core.

How long could I allow my mind to wander to such a dark place?

On top of all of this, I felt that Windows of Opportunity desperately needed a home. We needed an office and we needed a building to work out of.

While I was at an Outlet rehearsal with Elyza, she assured me that miracles happen.

Bryan was incredibly supportive of my dreams as well; he told me that when the time was right, Windows would find an official home.

During one of our walks, Morena assured me that the universe works in mysterious ways.

"You never know," She remarked while leaving me at the coffee shop one day. "The universe is kind to those who live relentlessly in pursuit of liberty."

'Liberty?' I called after her, but she was already out of earshot.

Had I known what I know now, I would have understood her comment at that moment. I was so absorbed in hiding from the lawsuit to internalize any of her apparently paradoxical wisdom.

As I placed the paper coffee cup in the trash and began my trek out into the street, a familiar voice rang from down the street.

I squinted to see who was calling my name, but the faces on the street were unknown.

Then a former graduate of the high school, and a former peer leader from the Dream Out Loud Conference, appeared before me.

"Mr. Scott! How are you?" He embraced me.

'Randy,' I smiled. 'It's good to see you man.'

We began catching up and leaned against his car, which was a really old, beat up, and horrible looking station wagon.

'Dude, this car is-' He cut me off.

"A piece of shit? Yeah…" he hit the roof of the car with his palm. "I know."

I proceeded to tell him about what I was up to: working with the after school program, handling the lawsuit still, and about how Bryan was doing well on his high school's football team.

"If you know anyone who needs someone for theatre work or music shows, could you tell them about me?" He said.

Something inside of me told me to talk about finding a home for Windows of Opportunity.

'Definitely man, and if you know anyone who has an office space for Windows, let me know.'

Randy grabbed my shoulder and began laughing, "Man, it is a good thing we bumped into each other."

I shrugged, 'Why?'

"You should check out my mom's church!" He got very excited.

'Your mom's church,' I laughed. 'You mean the church your mom goes to?'

"No, no, no," he shook his head. "My mother is a Reverend at a church!"

I tried obscuring my laughter. I looked at his black t-shirt with a pentagram on it, the black nail polish on his fingertips, and his hair that was equally as long as mine.

'Randy, you take rebellion to a whole new level.'

"Yeah," he shrugged and put his hands in his pockets. "My mother tells me that all the time."

We finished off our conversation a few minutes later and he handed me her phone number.

After a short phone conversation with her, and with a promise to give her $100 a month towards the church's expenses, Windows of Opportunity was able to call Queens Community Church its home.

Randy's mother invited me to attend a Sunday service to see what the church did for the community. I happily accepted the invitation and told her I would see her that weekend.

∞ ∞ ∞ ∞ ∞ ∞ ∞ ∞

Come Sunday morning, I found myself lying face up in bed. I was contemplating all of the universe's seemingly connective actions:

The after-school program I was working with was run by a Jewish religion-based organization.

Queens Community Church was inviting Windows of Opportunity into its house of worship, and I was not keen on having Windows be affiliated with a religious organization.

Let's face it: the last time I was in church had to be when I was with Gemma. I was not going to church regularly and I was questioning everything. I was delving deep into some complex spirituality-based level of thought. I was exploring different ways of looking at life, especially since the lawsuit was weighing so heavily on my mind, heart, and soul.

I was very in tune with having Windows of Opportunity promote unity, but at what cost?

Did I really want to call a church Windows of Opportunity's home?

Could I continue to establish a voice in the community through a church?

Is this going to be the beginning of a new chapter for Windows, or will it be the final chapter?

My mind raced with notions of community members of different faiths rejecting the youth programs because they were associated with one specific house of worship. I felt my body shaking and my fingers started to tingle: everything I wanted for Windows was either within reach or sliding away from me.

It was horrifying.

My over-analytical mind thrust my heart rate into a new realm, and I was barely able to keep up with what this meant for the futures of countless youth.

Before I could catch up with my over-active mind, I looked over at the clock and realized I was already thirty minutes late to the Sunday service at Queens Community Church. I leapt from the bed in a panic and bolted towards the shower: if I was going to be fashionably late, I might as well appear fashionable.

I darted out the door and found my mind continuing to race as I drove down the streets of Queens.

Despite the lawsuit, despite my past, and despite my mixed emotions, I was about to potentially grow Windows of Opportunity on a much larger scale. I dreamt of Windows of Opportunity almost nightly.

I would let my mind wander down streets and avenues of New York City. I could almost feel the winds of change gracing each pore on my face. Yet was this a pipe dream or a constant reality?

Was this about to be the moment where I could look back, from decades into the future, and say that this was the next big step?

Would this become Windows of Opportunity's story behind the story?

I parked my car in front of the church. Its exterior was covered in warm red bricks and some slightly fractured white shingles on the side. The roof looked like it needed some work; but overall, it looked like a rather sturdy building. It seemed as if it were grounded in both faith and futility: though I was going to have to make my way into the building in order to see what the future had in store for me.

The asphalt was sturdy, yet it was doused in divets and bumps.

Clearly, the building had been standing for quite some time, but this could mean that it was a beacon calling community members directly to it.

I approached the front doors cautiously, took a deep breath, and tugged at the door handle.

Once inside, I felt the energy from the universe shift. It was almost as if I walked into a new realm.

The front hall reeked of mildew, but promise. I was unsure of what to do or say in those moments.

Services had long since started, so I made my way through the double-paned glass doors and into the sanctuary.

All eyes were focused on the minister, Randy's mother, who was in the middle of preaching the word of God. No one turned to look at me or acknowledge my presence. I felt holistically invisible in those moments, so I chose to sit in the last pew.

My eyes were drawn to the sunlight melting through the ornate stained-glass windows. They were marvelous, for lack of more elaborate terms. I could go on and on forever discussing the illustrious details of each and every single window, but the one that caught my eye the most was the dove surrounded by light situated at the center of the pulpit.

The dove's wings spread clear across the circular window. Its purity was breathtaking and exquisite. I was drawn into the story of how that dove came to be. While the sermon was being read, I was locked directly into the amber eyes of the bird.

Everything within me echoed the sentiment that the bird's journey was parallel mine. It kept beckoning me, as if its innate messages were indicative of a metamorphosis that remained within my soul and its own.

The crystal blue and lavender pieces, in conjunction with the sepia and ruby pieces sprinkled behind it, were such a calming sight to see.

Clasped in its beak was a single branch, maybe an olive branch or a twig, which could be indicative of the bird's willingness to build a new nest for itself.

I wanted to build myself a nest.

Queens Community Church could be my very own nest.

It could be Windows of Opportunity's nest.

Was this it?

As I sat admiring the stained glass, I heard some familiar words being read to the crowd. It just so happened that the moment I walked in and sat down, Randy's mother was reading the description of Windows of Opportunity from my website.

It sounded amazing.

As each word left her lips, I found myself gaining more confidence.

She said that Windows of Opportunity would be occupying space within the church as she smiled at me.

No one seemed to protest or have any issues with Windows' mission and vision, which made me quite happy.

It seemed as if Windows would be welcome here after all.

∞ ∞ ∞ ∞ ∞ ∞ ∞ ∞

Once the sermon ended, I found myself wandering around the sanctuary. I traced the outline of each stained-glass window with my intrigued eyes. I was not sure just what I was getting myself into, but this place seemed lovely.

Randy's mother walked up to me and shook my hand.

With a soft voice, she spoke: "It's wonderful to meet you in this church, Scott."

'Thank you.' I shook her hand.

As we engaged in idle chitchat, two people approached us with purpose.

"I want you to meet Paul and his wife Eve," the two of them, an elderly couple who appeared to be somewhat friendly and warm, sidled up to me.

They each shook my hand and greeted me with a sweet, "Hello," although something seemed very off with the interaction.

After a few moments they walked away and Randy's mother pulled me aside.

"Paul is a member of the church's board and Eve is his wife." She was whispering as to not raise suspicion.

'Okay.' I did not really know what else to say.

"I told them you would be renting space here in our basement, but I want you to come to me with any problems or concerns."

'Okay.'

"They are not the nicest people. I don't want you having *any* trouble, do you hear me?"

I nodded in agreement, for I was unsure of what else to say.

I caught myself latching onto every word that came from the minister's mouth. She began showing me around the building as the members sauntered from the sanctuary.

As we entered the basement and I rested my eyes on the stage, I could see a large music program performing on that very platform. I could see a sound booth being built to house new music equipment. I could see events happening within the building.

When we went into the office, I could see a wooden desk being filled with curriculum plans and students' work. I imagined binders being displayed across the wall.

It was magical. It was all ours.

It was officially a brand-new start.

It was, in every essence, a window of opportunity.

∞ ∞ ∞ ∞ ∞ ∞ ∞ ∞

Everyone left the building and I found myself wandering the church's halls. Over the course of the next decade, I would be moving through the halls in search of myself and my soul. We were home.

We were caught between the confines of four walls and a roof, but the possibilities were endless.

This would be my spiritual hideaway.

This would be where I found myself and found a place for my students as well.

This was where I would share countless memories, programs, and exquisite visions.

All for $100 a month and an exciting dream to share with the world.

While walking alone through the building, I found myself meandering back upstairs to see the sanctuary. It was doused in elements of natural sunlight and hope.

This could be something; this could truly be something.

I re-entered the sanctuary, but this time I was completely alone.

As I walked up the aisle and to the altar, the feelings that flooded my soul were reminiscent of a bright future. I felt that I had been there before. I had walked this path before. I was accustomed to struggle and strife for so long, yet in the moments that preceded my walk up the aisle, I was free.

I was free.

I was liberated beyond the lawsuit and the relationship issues that plagued my soul.

It was almost as if I was completely starting anew.

The bird in the center of the stained-glass window was looking down upon me, almost as if it were God himself shedding his light upon my soul.

I would be reborn in this church. I would be caught between a conflict of what is truly spiritual and what is genuinely religious, but all I knew was that everything would soon make sense.

It just had to.

∞ ∞ ∞ ∞ ∞ ∞ ∞ ∞

As I was leaving the church and locking up the building, Bryan called me on the phone.

"Hey dad," he sounded elated.

'Hey buddy.'

"What's going on?"

'Well, I think I found a home for Windows of Opportunity.'

"Finally," he sounded relieved. "I knew you could do it dad!"

We talked for a little while longer about the church and what he was up to, but I could tell he was ready to rush out the door on some sort of adventure.

"Dad, is it okay that I go out to lunch with this girl from school?" He sounded excited.

'Sure, go ahead.' I smiled. He was carving a path of his own and becoming a joyful young gentleman.

"Thanks, I love you, dad."

I paused and turned back towards the church.

'I love you too son.'

The sun was eclipsed by the steeple on the roof. A massive white cross contrasted the light shining down.

"Hey, stranger." A familiar voice rang out: Morena.

'Hey, how'd you find me here?' I was genuinely confused.

"I guess it is just a gift." She looked like she had been walking around for a while.

I learned not to question her habits or actions by now.

'Do you want to see where Windows of Opportunity will be calling home from now on?' I motioned towards the church.

"Sure," she grinned. "I would love to."

We went back towards the church and unlocked the door. I felt the same energy shift as I did when I first walked in, and I was sure she sensed it as well.

The two of us walked into the sanctuary and her eyes instantly fixated on the dove. I began to explain to her my dreams for the church: countless music shows, youth programs, and support groups.

All throughout my honest depiction of my vision, Morena seemed to embrace the presence of something in the room.

'Morena,' her back was facing me. 'Are you listening to me?'

She paused for a moment and turned to meet my gaze. Her eyes were almost like an iridescent white.

"It is beautiful." She seemed at peace. All of the philosophical thoughts that floated through her head came to a rest at the adjoining of her eyelids. Morena sighed deeply and looked back at me.

'It is home.'

"Is it though?" Her nostrils flared up.

'I don't know...' Suddenly I was unsure of what to think. 'I mean, I think so?'

"Give it time." She brushed her fingertips along the pews as she made her way back up the aisle. "Time."

∞ ∞ ∞ ∞ ∞ ∞ ∞ ∞

What I did not realize is there was a lot of drama and plenty of low-vibrational negative energy clouding the true energy of the church. After a year of lonely nights in the sanctuary, countless soul-wrenching conversations between me and Morena, and succumbing to the abandoned church's energy that was only used by members on Sundays for a few hours, I began to realize what was happening.

Randy's mother chose to leave the church and encouraged me to talk to Paul if I wanted to remain there.

I panicked. All I knew about Paul and his wife, Eve, were that they were not nice people. That was the first thing that Randy's mother said to me on the first day I came to the church.

When I was wrapping up with one of my programs for the night, Paul called saying that he was going to visit me at the church. I felt the pit of my stomach drop further and further into the abyss.

Paul, the man who I was told was "not nice," was coming to speak to me. What did this mean? Would Windows of Opportunity be pulled from the church?

He arrived and sat down with the few kids who were still in the building. They were talking to him and he appeared to be rather sweet and insightful.

After all, even if he was not nice, he appeared to be a man of God. He had to be rooted in some sort of cultural and spiritual values.

"These programs are quite lovely, Scott," He put a reassuring hand on my shoulder and patted my back.

'Oh, thank you, I appreciate it.' This would be the first time we spoke practically ever.

"Of course! I love seeing people fill the halls of this church, especially children."

I became bashful suddenly. I did not know what to say to him or how to approach the conversation of keeping Windows of Opportunity in the building.

"Listen," he paused for a moment. "Don't let me keep you, I just wanted to say that you can stay at the building and keep the community coming into Queens Community Church."

446

'Thank you,' I was happy. 'And don't worry. I will make sure that I pay you next week.'

Paul stopped in his tracks. "Pay me, why? What are you talking about?"

I was confused. 'The $100. I paid the Reverend every single month.'

He looked at me with some disdain in his eyes. "What?"

'I will have the cash next week. Please don't worry.'

"Worry?" He wrapped his arm around me. "Son, we were not charging your organization to work with us."

I froze. Where did the money go? What was the Reverend doing behind my back?

Paul and I sat in the chairs outside the sanctuary and just started talking.

We discovered that there was a story behind the story after all: Paul and Eve were good people. Paul was a delight to speak to and he admitted that his wife was a little bit wacky, but extremely caring.

The Reverend was pocketing the money I gave her each month. She wanted to establish a certain level of fear between me, Paul, and Eve, so that I would not ask questions. I guess the Reverend figured that it would never come to this.

There is a story behind her story, but it made me wonder about the last year.

Still, Paul and Eve accepted me with open arms and became big sponsors of Windows of Opportunity. They became my friends and family, and always accepted me as their own.

There is still hope.

There is still faith.

Though this world may be filled with some people who are solely interested in bettering themselves, there are individuals who look to do the universe's work.

I intended to share my light and life with the Queens Community Church and with the world.

Before I knew it, I became a member of the church's Board of Directors. Windows of Opportunity and the Queens Community Church entered an enlightening and mutually beneficial partnership.

Paul talked me into becoming a Chaplain at the church and I found myself in classes. I became an ordained minister through the Universal

Life Church and started realizing just how soulfully enriching life at the church could be.

Windows of Opportunity became grounded in the essential elements of the church and everyone knew my name.

Outlet came in to perform shows, kids were leading music programs, and everything seemed, well, perfect.

And for once, perfect sounded absolutely perfect to me.

CHAPTER 29

Alegria Espiritual

"When I fall in love I take my time. There's no need to hurry when I'm making up my mind. You can turn off the sun but I'm still gonna shine and I'll tell you why."

- Jason Mraz, American Singer-Songwriter, Mechanicsville, Virginia

The lawsuit's ugly intentions were still looming over my head. As months progressed, I would sit awake at night with Bryan watching nearby.

"Dad, do you need anything," he would watch me in the dim beams of moonlight that emulated some sort of holy presence.

'No thanks, Bryan, I'm okay.' I rested my hand on his shoulder.

He would turn away slightly, hoping to catch a grin materializing on my face.

"Okay," Bryan retreated towards the door. "If you need anything dad... *anything*, you would tell me... right?"

'Yes,' I flashed a smile in his direction. 'Of course.'

He walked out of the room and into the kitchen.

Although the pressure from the lawsuit was bearing down on me, it seemed like something else was bothering me. Something else was weighing on my soul; I just could not fathom what it was.

I was a few weeks away from finding out the truth about Paul, Eve, and the Queens Community Church, but that was just not it. I spent the night pacing the floor and anxiously trying to see what my soul and brain were processing.

Then, the next morning, I found out Olga passed away.

I didn't even know what made me think of her, but before I knew it my Circle of Angels were expanding.

I got some sort of impression from deep within the universe and wanted to look her up. I was across the street from the building where we used to work together at the time, and I sensed that something was off.

I just didn't know that it was her.

I found out that she passed away at the age of 49: it was the same age my Aunt Barbara was, except Olga had colon cancer.

She succumbed to her illness rather quickly and did not suffer much, which I was happy about. I had called the phone number I had of hers, which belonged to her house in Florida, and spoke with her boyfriend-turned-husband.

He was saddened by what happened, but he did not really remember me too well.

Olga ended up getting clean. They had two puppies together, but never had any children. Her obituary echoed the life of a woman who turned things around, yet her story was tragically cut short.

That's what worried me: what would my life be like at 49?

Would I fade into the sunset alone, or would I be surrounded by Bryan, and a darling wife of mine?

Would I ever find anyone?

All I knew was this one, coherent truth: Death is certain, life is not. At least that is what the accident told me. This is what was imparted upon me the night that I stumbled into that stranger's home.

I wondered where she was now, but part of me thinks that her grace and kindness still walk with me. Her emerald-green eyes seemed to be ingrained in my core, and part of me thought that the woman was somehow still watching over me.

Nevertheless, I was truly sad when Olga died, for I never got closure. I was always under the impression that we would meet again. I hoped that we would bump into each other nonchalantly and talk about how much we had grown since our relationship.

The days of clubs and drugs had long passed at that point, and it would have been wonderful to sit with her someday and just talk.

However, someday never comes.

Nevertheless, I was truly sad when Olga died, for I never got closure. Long ago, I was under the impression that we would always be together.

Morena and I spoke about this notion. I told her how upset I was due to Olga's passing. I created this story in my head that because she loved me, she knew that without the world of cocaine and without her, the older woman, being in my life, I would become something in the future.

Maybe she was wrong, but maybe she was right.

Maybe I was just making everything up in my head.

Maybe she was implying that by leaving me alone in New York, I would stand a fighting chance.

This was a gift, in a sense, from the universe.

In all honesty, I was grateful that Olga left me. I was blessed for she did love me, or at least I interpreted her actions in that way, but my soul was better because of the experience that was her.

"So," Morena said, leaning against the fence at Alley Pond Park, "How do you feel about all of this?"

'She's with me.' I looked up at the fading fall sun. 'She is always with me.'

"The Circle of Angels," Morena said it so confidently, and I believed her.

'Yeah.' We were both looking up at the sky now.

"Yeah."

I just hope that Olga is in a good place now, one free of fear and the things that tethered her soul to cocaine.

In a religious sense, I hoped God was looking out for her. I hoped that God forgave her for everything she did down here on Earth.

Olga does genuinely have a good soul.

I always hoped to visit her grave in Florida, but I never got the chance. I guess if it is meant to be, it will be.

Her body rests in Tampa, Florida. Someday, I'll find her again and thank her for everything she did for me. I would thank her for indirectly, or maybe even directly, setting me on this path.

If Olga were in the car with me the night of the accident, I am certain she would have died. She did not deserve that fate, and clearly, nor did I.

I sensed that the drugs ended up catching up with her body and spirit, which is why she died so young. She had a good life, or so I would like to think, up until her death, but I sense she is okay.

Now, in death, she can live.

I had grown so much since my days with Olga. I am not the same person I was that night when I crashed. I do not do drugs, I don't drink. I became a stronger soul.

I thank God for that accident. I thank God and the universe for everything that has been bestowed upon me. I was spared to tell my story and spread awareness, and, well, I guess I was spared for much greater things in life, but I will get to that story eventually.

I had a fresh start.

I had a long way to go.

I have a true purpose.

∞ ∞ ∞ ∞ ∞ ∞ ∞ ∞

I still longed for the other half of my power couple fantasy. It had to be a reality and it needed to happen soon, and this is what I told myself in order to bring Windows of Opportunity to the next level.

Yet, little did I know, the possible other half of my power couple was on the verge of appearing before my eyes.

Elyza called me one night, begging for me to meet with a young woman who was interested in offering companies marketing services. The woman was about to graduate with her degree in marketing and was desperately trying to find someone, anyone, who would be interested in having her display a company of some sort on quite a major scale.

That's where Windows of Opportunity came into the picture.

The woman was working with a man who was very interested in her and knew Elyza well. He was trying so hard to impress her and find her some clients to market, which sent him to Elyza. She reassured him that Windows of Opportunity would accept the marketing services, and so he set up a meeting.

I sat eagerly awaiting the young woman's presence at a coffee shop in Woodhaven. It was located in a high-class shopping mall where people would travel to in order to gather up the finest clothes and accessories.

I had faith that this interaction would be good for Windows. After all, we were creating conferences, curriculums, programs, and trainings; it was about time that they were marketed properly and with intent. Youth around the world needed to experience the wonder that is Windows of Opportunity, and maybe this woman could help us go to that next level.

I could only hope.

She flew into the coffee shop with folders in her hand: she seemed flustered, but was breathtakingly gorgeous. Though you could see the anxious look in her eyes, it was clear that she was there with a purpose.

This woman was there to make a difference.

We locked eyes and I felt my heart melting. I thought that I finally found someone who could just walk into a room and captivate everyone in her path.

Her gaze was mesmerizing. It was almost as if I could get lost in her majestic, exotic beauty. She was elegant and individual in her own way.

Her presence in the room was exquisite in only a way she knew how to maneuver.

She made her way over to me, realizing that the longhaired blonde man must be me. I stood and did not realize that I was practically towering over her petite body.

'Hey,' I mustered up confidently. 'I'm Scott.'

"Nice to meet you," she spoke with a thick accent. "I am Faith."

Faith. I always stood by the words "keep the faith" and there she was. It was meant to be. She was meant to literally walk into my life.

We spent the next three hours talking about Windows of Opportunity's programs and history. I found myself telling her all about who I was and how I hoped to keep expanding Windows' influence on education.

Faith sat there, her head resting in her hand, intently listening to each word I said.

"You are a very smart man, Scott Matheson." I loved how her accent put an extra exotic flair on everything she said. Faith spoke in detail about what she thought about me, and my programs so far, and would occasionally flutter her eyelids while looking at me.

I had been alone at this point for a while. Elyza was the last person who I married, let alone dated, and I was unsure of what I should do. After all, Faith and I just met, but I could tell there was some sort of strong display of raw, positive energy between us.

I just wondered if she felt the same way.

'So, tell me,' I leaned in closer to Faith from across the table. 'What's the story behind your story?'

She giggled nervously, unsure of how to answer the question.

"Do you mean you want to know about me?" Faith coyly shifted her body in the chair.

'Yes,' I spoke confidently. 'I want to know who *Faith* is.'

She laughed again and regained a sense of decorum. Faith's eyes dragged along my body, and I could tell she was trying desperately to figure me out.

"Well," she leaned her body across the table and reached out towards me. "I want to know more about the story behind Scott."

Our fingers were touching, but it felt more like an innocent grasp than anything.

Still, this was the first time a woman touched me since Elyza. I felt my body tense up instantly.

'You'll just have to get to know me, then.' I could not believe I just said that. Where was this suave version of Scott coming from? What was I doing?

Did I know what I was doing?

Did she feel the same energy as I did?

"I want to know the spiritual side of Scott Matheson." Faith fluttered her eyelids again. Was she picking up something between us?

This was the first time I actually felt something, anything, since the lawsuit reared its ugly head.

Truthfully, I was nervous. Questions flurried through my mind as if it were snowing flakes of fear intertwined with intrigue in my mind.

What was happening?

'Spiritual?' I tilted my head. 'What do you mean by spiritual, like, religious?'

"No," she laughed, but not in a condescending way. "Like, your soul. What happens in your soul?"

My soul. She wanted to know about my soul.

Who was this woman?

She was gorgeous, she was intriguing, she was brilliant and knew a lot about marketing... and she was sitting before me.

Why did I still feel slightly uneasy about her presence?

What was I doing?

She continued to speak to me about the marketing material she wanted to create to bring Windows to the next level, and that's when it hit me: I needed the other half of my "power couple" to want to marry Windows as well. I needed someone who would throw herself into every project and program of mine with purpose, with passion, and without trepidation.

I needed someone who would be my professional equal, as well as someone who would also love me unconditionally.

Though in reality, did I really know the meaning of unconditionally loving someone at the time?

Faith seemed to fit exactly what I wanted in a partner, and that physical energy seemed to be so strong between us. Then she hit me with the words that stung my soul: "I should tell you, I am married with two kids."

My heart sank.

"Though I should tell you-" her eyes wandered off as she tried collecting her thoughts. "My husband has a girlfriend who he has lived with for years. I married him so he could get citizenship here."

What?

What?

Wait…

What?

I did not know how to respond to her, so I just sat up and let out an, 'Oh, okay.'

How suave and debonair. *Okay.* Come on Scott, you are better than that.

"I just figured I would tell you." She seemed upset suddenly.

'Thank you,' I told her. 'For telling me your story.'

Shit.

Shit.

Shit.

Now what?

We spoke for a little while longer about Windows of Opportunity, and then I leapt into my Monte Carlo and drove off. My head was spinning. How could I find someone so intriguing to me, yet she seemed so far out of reach?

Now what?

My mind raced as I drove down the Cross Island Parkway to get home.

'What is wrong with me?' I shouted. I slammed my palm against the steering wheel as my head flooded with thoughts of failed relationships and the overwhelming presence of the lawsuit.

Then I crashed my car head-on.

∞ ∞ ∞ ∞ ∞ ∞ ∞ ∞

This would be the second accident caused by a girl.

Although I hit a cement wall, yet again, I was okay. The car was… in one piece… but my ego was bruised.

I know I am serious and letting my heart open up when I let judgment cloud my thoughts. Still, even as I sit here now and write specifically about a person, all of those feelings from our first meeting together flush through my soul.

It is no secret that I've spent years looking for love, getting into bad relationships, making mistakes, growing and learning from relationships, and trying to find the right person.

The cops came and took an accident report, but I knew that I was truly the one at fault. No one else got hurt, and I was thankful for that.

I never want someone to suffer as a result of my mistakes or missteps.

I called Bryan and I told him I was going to be late.

I was thinking of whom else I should call to tell I was okay, but no one else came to mind.

Except Morena.

I looked through my phone to see if I actually had her number, but I didn't. It was weird. It was strange.

I had known Morena for quite some time, and yet I did not have a way of contacting her. She always found me.

She seemed as if she couldn't be real.

We had our weekly coffee meetings scheduled, but something inside me said that I had to speak to her right away. Morena was the only person I could trust with talking about my soul and my inner thoughts at the moment.

What was I doing?

∞ ∞ ∞ ∞ ∞ ∞ ∞ ∞

Later that night, Bryan embraced me as I walked through the door.

"Dad," he was clearly concerned. "Are you okay?"

'Yes, of course I am.' I hugged him. He was getting a lot taller and I could not see him as the little boy I used to carry around in my arms anymore.

"I got worried." He looked outside and saw the car banged up a bit. The hood of the Monte Carlo was missing some paint and other attributes.

We sat and talked for a while, but I was still preoccupied by Faith's presence. I needed answers. I had to find out what was happening.

What was my inner voice trying to say?

Days later, Morena and I met up at the coffee shop near Alley Pond Park.

'Her family totally would not accept me.' I started. 'She is 25. She is 13 years younger than me. I am not from her culture. Her family is important to her and-'

Morena cut me off: "Stop making excuses."

'Making excuses? Making excuses!' I was flustered.

"*Yeah,*" she quipped sarcastically at me.

'Okay.' I took a deep breath. 'Maybe I am making excuses, but-'

"*But... but....* But nothing." She seemed disgruntled.

'What's wrong?'

"Nothing. Just nothing."

'Morena... what-'

"Why are you doing this to yourself?" She crossed her arms.

'Doing... what?'

"You are sabotaging yourself. You know you are interested in her, so just go for it. What is the worst that could happen?"

'I don't know... she does not want me?'

"How will you know unless you take a chance?"

She was right. Morena was pushing me to decide, to just make a move, to do something.

'You're right.' I sat back and looked out at the leaves cascading down the window.

"No, I'm Morena." She smiled sarcastically. Morena constantly used humor to hide her emotions, though I could still see right through her. She was transparent, almost like a ghost.

Maybe she was not real.

'Hey,' I thought about wanting to call her. 'I never realized this, but I don't have your cell phone number. I wanted to call you the other day and-'

"You wanted to call me, why?" She adjusted herself in the chair.

'I wanted to... talk?'

"Oh." She seemed surprised. "I'll give it to you."

Looking down at her number in my phone, I considered the fact that she must be real. She has a phone number. We are in a public place and she is drinking hot chocolate, as always.

People can see us, right?

She is here interacting with me and had to interact with someone to get our usual drinks.

'Maybe I *am* losing it,' was a thought that crossed my mind.

Morena and I finished our conversation and I went off to run a youth program in Brooklyn Bridge Park.

I was always running around doing something.

For one of the curriculums, the kids in the youth program wanted to do a photo shoot for a marketing promo that Faith was going to put together. As we stood in the park, posing and taking various pictures, we were all laughing and talking about how we were going to get *very famous*.

A guy approached me, in an attempt to be tough in front of his wife and child, and asked me to leave. He seemed to insinuate that this wholesome and fun photo shoot was offending his family.

"You don't belong here," he boomed. The kids looked at me with fear in their eyes. They seemed partially upset that someone would dare interrupt our program.

"It's a private park," he pointed to the sign that said: "RESIDENTS ONLY."

As to not cause a scene, I packed my equipment and left. I was offended and hurt, but I did not want any trouble. The lawsuit was still pending, and this was the LAST thing I needed: someone potentially getting violent with me in front of the kids.

It just amazes me how a person's perception can truly be off the mark.

It is an observation of humanity in general mixed with my personal experiences, and it does really eat at my soul.

The guy saw me as a threat, and yet, I continuously try to be the nicest and most giving guy possible. There is something about society that saddens me at times.

Every time I think I have all of the answers, something happens.

I guess that is life…

But it does not have to be this way.

Things change.

They always do.

∞ ∞ ∞ ∞ ∞ ∞ ∞ ∞

Faith and I spoke on the phone quite often. We were planning plenty of marketing material around the curriculums and programs that Windows of Opportunity was offering.

Faith was also very keen on sharing her insight into what she deemed as, "Developing my spiritual side."

459

She is the reason I became so open to developing my sense of spirituality, which, in turn, led me to become the man I am today.

For her, I am eternally grateful.

As I said, we would talk on the phone for a while expressing our thoughts on the world and life in general. The two of us began to delve into a realm I was unsure of and unaware of. Faith was reciting quotes from a book called *Joy* by Osho. His words brought me to realize there was an entirely different school of philosophical thought when it came to the soul.

The first quote she read to me, with each letter floating from her tongue in only a way her exotic accent could deliver them, was this:

"Happiness has nothing to do with success. Happiness has nothing to do with ambition; happiness has nothing to do with money, power, prestige. It is a totally different dimension. Happiness has something to do with your consciousness, not with your character."

'That is beautiful,' I paused and let the subtle static from our phones hum between us. 'Did you write that yourself?'

She reminded me that it was a quote from Osho.

Faith and I would continue digging into Osho's words and insight. She was the exact opposite of what I was in terms of spirituality in those moments: I was still finding out about who I was, while she seemed to be very comfortable in her own skin already.

Her energy was just mesmerizing.

There were multiple occasions where I just wanted to give in to what Morena told me to do. I had to stop making excuses. I had to bring myself to find the courage to just go for it. I had to just say something to Faith, yet my history between Starr and the other girls from my Texas days filled every crevice of my brain with nervous energy.

I still had repressed feelings from that night.

I never got a chance to get past worrying about my romantic and erotic energy, if I had any, really, became the larger question at hand.

Regardless, I wanted to love Faith and show my affection for her in a way that transcended sexual energy. I wanted to spend every moment showing her that she was whom I wanted to spend my time with.

It's crazy, I know, that in just a few conversations I thought I knew what I wanted in life, but love is love. Passionate love could occur between two people, but I didn't just want that. I wanted love in all of its forms. I wanted to feel her reaching into my soul and caressing each tender idea that fluttered into my head.

I wanted her.

I wanted all of her.

Or did I just want to be loved?

In reality, I could not say any of this to her at the time.

In my eyes, she was both within and beyond reach: no matter what I did or tried, I did not think I could please her emotionally, physically, sexually, spiritually... though I did not realize I just had to evolve a bit more in order to love both her and myself fairly.

As our phone conversations grew more in-depth about spirituality and about marketing strategies for Windows of Opportunity, I found myself getting ensnared in what seemed like a perpetual trap: I wanted her, but I was afraid to do anything about it. I sensed that she realized this as well, yet she did not want to come to terms with what either of our emotions meant.

Then one night, during one of our long conversations, I went for it.

I always fantasized about having the "power couple" relationship materialize before my very eyes. This could have been the moment. This could have been my one shot.

However, as I walked around the sanctuary aimlessly brushing against the pews while engaged in our phone conversation, I was blind to the different layers that come with finding that true love.

With the idea of wanting to make the universe a better place, I was not acknowledging the power that existed between us. When two people acknowledge, accept, and channel their inner power into a bigger vision, that is when souls truly expand, inspire, and empower.

In those early moments in mine and Faith's relationship, or lack thereof at this point, I was still solely focused on my ego.

As I said, I still went for it.

'Faith,' I took a bit too long of a pause in our conversation. 'What do you think of a guy like me?'

She laughed for a moment, which caused me to panic. Why was she laughing? What was she thinking? How did she interpret what I just said?

'I just want to make you happy,' I gave her a little something else to work with while she crafted a response for our conversation.

"Scott," she began, "There is a huge difference between happiness and joy."

What was she saying? I was asking her about us in terms of a relationship, and something deep within her prompted this sort of conversation.

"Joy is a place you can stand in," she continued. "Joy is an emission of energy toward others. You can bring joy to people, you can't always bring happiness to others, so you have to make yourself happy."

This was not the answer I was looking for, yet it was the one she bestowed upon me. It was earth shattering in so many ways.

'Okay,' I was unsure what else to say. 'Then what is love?'

She took a deep breath and let her thoughts roll from her lips and through the phone: "Well, I can tell you what love is not. It is not something you can physically hold and touch. It is energy. Love is universal. Love makes the world go 'round."

I nodded intently and sat down in one of the pews. I looked at one of the prestigious stained-glass windows, but since it was dark all I saw were the glass pieces being transformed in the shadows of pure darkness.

"Love is something that happens between couples because you feel like you are flying. You feel like you are on cloud nine. These love ideas and comparisons we make as humans are not understood in plain English."

She tried searching for the words in those moments. Her native language was Spanish and since she was born and raised in Ecuador, and then taught herself English at sixteen-years-old, the language barrier seemed to hold her back from fully expressing herself in those moments.

"Love is the fuel of souls expanding. That is why we are on this planet. We came to truly learn what love is and we learn about it through lessons. The energy expands in one person so that other people can feel this energy."

In an effort to try showing her that I understand what she meant, I tried adding onto her thoughts: 'Love breathes life into us.'

"Yes," she shouted. "Then, in turn, we breathe life into love."

'Love is God,' I looked at the cross before me. 'Or whatever your concept of God is.'

The two of us sat in silence over the phone. I did not expect the answers she gave to me, nor did I realize we were going to talk about all of this.

Nevertheless, I felt that the conversation was warranted. My soul was expanding through everything she said to me, and I had a feeling this was going somewhere.

I felt compelled to tell Morena all about this the second I hung up with Faith.

Faith and I agreed that we would speak more about this in person tomorrow when we met to discuss marketing strategies face to face, and I was thrilled.

I dialed the number that Morena gave me in the coffee shop and was met with a depressing tone on the other end. A lull sprang through the phone and I sat there, confused as to what was happening and why this would happen.

In a monotone voice I heard: *"We're sorry. You have reached a number that has been disconnected or is no longer in service. If you feel you have reached this recording in error, please check the number and try your call again."*

Maybe she was not real after all…

∞ ∞ ∞ ∞ ∞ ∞ ∞ ∞

As Christmas approached, I was becoming more aware of the potential that Queens Community Church afforded me with. Paul and Eve turned out to be much nicer than expected, which in the long-run told me that I always need to trust my gut and find out the truth before making judgments.

There is a story behind the story, and the one that Randy's mother tried to tell me about Paul and Eve was not true to who they were.

Regardless, I began building a relationship with both of them and enjoyed their company immensely.

For the holidays, Paul and Eve were incredibly keen on having Outlet perform a Christmas-themed show at the church.

Elyza and the band were thrilled that we would be able to perform for the community and the members of the church. I will always remember that night as one of our most memorable Outlet concerts, although it could be argued that every single Outlet concert is unique in its own special way.

Though I finally found out the truth about Eve, I quickly realized how angry and abrupt she would become. As the band performed that night, she tore us apart screaming that we were devil worshippers and defacing the church's altar with foul music.

Wendy's husband even came on stage dressed as Santa Claus, and I was thankful that she was still a part of my life all these years later. Her family was my family, and I am eternally grateful for her.

Despite the frivolity and laughter he brought to the children, it was not good enough for Eve. As the kids danced around and celebrated the joy of Christmas, she remarked that Santa was Satan, but spelt with different letters.

I took a deep breath and reminded myself that everyone sees things from different perspectives.

Though I saw Outlet's performance as something that sparked joy and innate happiness, Eve saw the whole situation from a different lens.

Who was I to judge? After all, I lived my life being inundated with misnomers and misjudgments. I could not consciously criticize someone for having a perspective different than mine.

Still, something just did not seem right. At the time, I could not put my finger on it. Maybe my mind was clouded by the lawsuit hanging over my head.

Maybe I was scared.

In hindsight, I just knew I wanted to make the church my home.

The building itself carried plenty of history within its walls: the stained glass windows were donated from Germany, and before that the building was rumored to be pivotal in the World War II era.

In contrast to my views of the church, many of its members were leaving in droves.

Paul admitted to me that night that the church had to be revitalized.

Someone had to breathe life into the church. Someone needed to save it.

Between the youth programs bringing kids in and out of there, and the concerts that were held occasionally, I truly felt I could be the one.

I could save the building.

It still had a heartbeat, for I was the one bringing blood and oxygen to the heart of its operations.

Paul and Eve made me feel as if I could go the distance.

As long as I was willing to walk the line, I figured the church would not plummet into a ring of fire.

How many people get their own church?

How many people get to become a part of building something awe-inspiring?

In the months that followed, I would sit in the sanctuary and embrace the energy it emitted. It was a refreshing feeling: I was constantly blessed by the magical positivity that would embrace me as I thought about my life within the walls of the church.

The sanctuary became a part of my consummate whole: my soul was growing at a rate that did not exist before and my understanding of spirituality was changing rapidly.

I would pace between the pews of the sanctuary and consistently ask questions out loud. I hoped that God could hear me. Honestly, I hoped that someone would hear me.

I spent so much time trying to reject the experiences that were a part of my childhood, my religious upbringing included, yet while meandering through the pews I could not help but reflect upon my life. I did not want to be associated with the concept of religion, but I could not help but think about the possibility that God brought me to the church.

The dust glimmering through the stained-glass depiction of a saint echoed the solitude I was currently feeling. I allowed myself to introspectively reach within my soul. When I closed my eyes, I drifted to a place where Faith's hand was intertwined in mine. She kept whispering sweet phrases in my ear, which became clearer and more soul enriching with each passing moment.

Faith is spiritual and her thoughts were outside the box. She was still in the initial stages of exploring who she was and her purpose in the world, but I could tell that she was genuinely someone special.

We were finding comfort in exploring our own souls together.

We were diving into a realm that just scratched the surface of who we could become.

She had her own business, which meant she was a rather busy and leadership-conscious woman. Faith was exploring who she was and she was highly educated. At this point, Faith had only been in the country for about eight years, and she taught herself English while clinging to her Ecuadorian culture. She was a self-made woman who was strong in every aspect of the term.

Faith owned any room she walked into with such poise and grace.

She seemed like the perfect match for me.

As I prayed and spoke to whomever would listen out in the world, I realized a difficult epiphany: I thought I was truly falling in love with Faith. Each phone conversation, each meeting over coffee, each glance we shared… it was drawing me closer to her.

Yet regardless, I sensed that the passionate tension that lingered between us was going to remain in the balance of who we were and how we would interact.

∞ ∞ ∞ ∞ ∞ ∞ ∞ ∞

Days before a major event Windows was running, I was on the phone with Faith when I received an e-mail that one of our sponsors could not make the donation that he intended.

I was mortified.

I did not want to disappoint the youth who worked so hard to put everything together, yet I was at a loss.

Faith assured me that she knew how to get donations for us, and promised she would get everything together within a day.

She did not fail.

The night before the event, two of her million-dollar business clients gave her a stack of cash. She was overjoyed when she called me and asked to meet in a coffee shop parking lot to give me the envelope of cash.

The sexual tension was building in the back of my head, but I was so exhausted from staying up all night for the past few days that I barely picked up on the signs she was dropping before me.

We sat facing one another in her truck: she was sitting in the driver's seat, running her right hand up and down her thigh and occasionally brushing up against her frilled skirt.

We began engaging in idle chitchat about each of our respective days. It was almost as if she was drawing me in with her eyes, screaming at me to take that first step towards what might be.

466

Faith's voice took on a more effervescent tone each time I tried to get out of the car. The moment she would see my hand drift towards the passenger door handle, she would blurt out something to attract my attention.

Even in my exhausted state, I could sense that there were some heavy flirtatious feelings building between us. I became immersed in her energy as she gazed longingly into my eyes. Her eyelashes were fluttering before me in a way that I sensed was trying to communicate that my departure from the car would signify that I didn't want her.

I wanted her so badly though. I wanted to know more about her soul, her energy, her light, everything. I hung on every single word that came from her mouth in an effort to look for a sign.

I was unsure if she wanted me physically. Faith enjoyed our conversations, but memories of my sexual encounter with Starr clouded my judgment. I could not handle the laughter and the commentary again.

My anxiety shot through the roof of the car, yet the raw, physical tension between Faith and myself mounted.

Feelings of anger juxtaposed with happiness, the sensations of blood flowing through my body, panic, intrigue… they all floated through me with the urgency of what was about to happen.

Though in my mind, I was building up the courage to get out of the car and leap into my Monte Carlo.

"Are you okay?" I was sure she noticed the sweat building atop my eyebrows.

'Yeah,' I muttered nervously. The loud gulp I took after I spoke must have tipped her off.

We sat in resolute silence for a moment until she reached for the dial to turn on the radio.

The slow, ethereal lyrics to Dashboard Confessional's song, "Vindicated," ushered in a vote of confidence in my soul.

"Hope dangles on a string
Like slow-spinning redemption
Winding in and winding out
The shine of it has caught my eye
And roped me in

467

So mesmerizing so hypnotizing
I am captivated
I am..."

Our eyes became entangled as the heat seeped into every crevice of our respective souls.

We tried to keep our conversation going, but when I reached the middle of a remark about the past few months, Faith's eyes captured mine.

Another thick silence stood between us.

"I don't want you to get out of the car," her voice was alluring and sensual.

Her accent drove me wild.

'I don't want to get out of the car,' I inhaled deeply, then exhaled with the next word clinging to my moistening lips... 'Either.'

She smiled as her cheeks filled with varying shades of pink. Faith seemed as if her temperature was rising with the elevated energy in the car.

Her aura was intoxicating and I sensed the innate longing dripping from her mouth.

We drew each other in closer and closer, until I could see every pristine pore that rested upon her face.

Our breathing was syncopated and growing more in tune with one another. She forced her fingers through my hair and tilted her head, so that her lips were directly in front of mine as she spoke: "I want you."

The windows began to fog and I could hear my heartbeat bursting through the sensual silence that still managed to pulsate between us.

I whispered slowly, as to savor this moment: 'Then come and get me.'

Our lips crashed upon one another and I could feel soft moans emerge through her mouth. Our bodies started to intertwine as the music on the radio faded into the distance: our heartbeats were the only thing we could mutually hear as she climbed on top of my lap.

Faith was in command.

Her movements became more forceful, alluring...

I wished that in those initial moments, I could have slowed down a lot more. I would have wanted to taste each flavor of her: her skin, her tongue, her sexual prowess.

Our clothes came off and notions of Starr and Gemma flooded my head. Faith could see that I was getting flustered, but she pulled me in closer anyway.

Her movements were intimidating, yet deeply erotic. Faith was unwavering in her commitments to pleasure and passion. She was the utter essence of sexy. The sultry look she kept giving me was emotionally stimulating.

Faith's shouting was growing louder and louder as my hands travelled up and down her thighs. It felt as if we were both transcended into another world.

I did not feel the threat of the lawsuit shooting daggers into my back anymore. All I could feel were her nails passionately digging into my skin.

Our moments were entrenched in the rhythm of our mutual affection. I am often at a loss for words when I think of this moment, for our climactic moment of will-they or won't-they resulted in a dance that was echoic of a passionate, spiritually enlightening encounter.

There was absolutely something there between us that night. Even though the event was the next day, I went home and I was restless.

I could not sleep, for when I closed my eyes all I saw was Faith. All I heard were her pleasurable moans drawing me deeper into her soul.

I couldn't wait for her to get to the event that next day, for I was rehearsing my first line to her in the mirror all morning and afternoon.

Doubt flooded my mind.

My palms started to sweat.

When she walked into the room, my heart sank. All of the conversations and emotions from the past few months clouded my judgment. How did we get here? Where do we go from here?

What was I doing?

She looked stunning in a long, flowing white dress that hugged the curves of her body perfectly. Her hair bounced as if there were a fan directly pointed at her.

Everyone looked at her as she made her way towards me. She had an overwhelming sense of confidence, which made me look at myself and realize that I was not worthy of her.

My heart was pounding faster.

Faith looked at me jokingly and told me to behave. To me, it seemed like a code for "You can take this dress off later."

I desperately wanted to impress her. I yearned to be her everything, because in my eyes, she seemed like she was deserving of any and all love I could give her.

Still, I was incredibly torn.

In the presence of her energy, being exhausted seemed to slip from my mind. I was on the verge of falling asleep with every passing second, but I knew that I had to pull through at this event... for myself, and hopefully so she would see how dedicated I was.

I drove her home and we sat in silence for most of the ride. I could feel the tension building between both of us, but nothing happened.

She smiled, and I sensed that there was some sort of insecurity hidden within the darkest depth of her eyes.

Before she got out of the car, she grabbed my hand and glared into my eyes. As her mouth opened, I was petrified. What could she possibly say? What was she mustering up the courage to say?

"Your name is Scott," her voice had a tinge of melancholy in it. "But if I could go back in time, I'd convince your mom to name you Adonis. It's badass and it means extremely handsome man."

I looked at her with a blank stare.

"You're at a crossroad in life where you gotta say fuck it... and from now on you come first. The people you put first in WOO will never give back what you do for them, because no one can give you back a more prominent form of caring."

She sensed the overwhelming sadness enveloping my shoulders.

We sat in silence for a moment as she pulled her hand away from mine.

"This is going to be a good year for *Adonis*. Stop living in a fog. You do your job well, but you must worry about today's issues today and tomorrow's issues tomorrow. We have already lived life and died many centuries ago, we've been through heaven and experienced it, and through some magic we are living our second life right now. Now is the time to 'redo' life."

Faith got out of the car and I could see one of her parents standing in the doorway of their dimly lit apartment.

Still, she shouted back to me: "Do what makes you happy. Not anyone but you. New beginnings. And I promise I will try and do the same with you and for you."

The car door slammed shut and I felt my hopeful demeanor exit the car alongside her.

∞ ∞ ∞ ∞ ∞ ∞ ∞ ∞

I texted her the next afternoon when I woke up.

As the day dragged on, the agonizing reality set in: she really did not want me. The summer flickered by like the tapering recession of a candle's flame.

I got the message.

I don't know exactly what had happened between us during that first physical encounter, but I did not imagine that night in her truck.

I thought the chemistry and energy were strong.

I found myself wandering Alley Pond Park again, in hopes that I could find an answer.

All I found was Morena.

Confusion and a devout sadness flooded my soul.

My shattered and tattered heart had been through so much, and giving up was starting to sound like a feasible option. The battle scars I wore from past loves, or at least what I thought was love, started to mount at the boundary of my eyelids.

As the tears strolled down my face relentlessly, Morena watched me unfold before her very eyes.

"There, there," she patted me on the back. "You can't fake chemistry."

CHAPTER 30

Espera Un Poco

"The day reminds me of you. The night hides your truth. The earth is a voice speaking to you: Take all this pride and leave it behind 'cause one day it ends. One day we die. Believe what you will. That is your right, but I choose to win. I choose to fight"

- Creed, American Rock Band, Tallahassee, Florida

As the new decade arrived without remorse, I felt the clutches of another decade of soul-searching rear its ugly head.

Do I truly think this decade was ugly? Absolutely not.

However, I ushered in the decade with a sinking sensation that the "Power Couple" partner I was looking for was not going to materialize before me.

I might have said, 'It is what it is,' with every painstaking moment that passed, but I would have been lying to myself.

Things were not what they appeared to be.

Faith had disappeared for about seven months at this point, though the lawsuit continued to persist. Three years of tremendous anxiety stood behind the phrase, "It is what it is," and no one could tell me otherwise.

The nights when I could muster the courage to crawl between the blankets, like a boomerang I would shoot back up out of fear and anxiety.

One night in particular, I woke in a panic and jolted from the bed. The words "Remember, stand your ground" clung in my memory like a crystallized harmony. The clock was blurry, so I felt I must have still been dreaming. A wave of nausea pooled in my core as I rushed to the bathroom.

Standing over the sink, I brushed crisp water upon my cheeks. The sensation brought my vision some clarity. Upon looking up, I was not alone in the bathroom. Almost 10 or 15 ghostly figures stood behind me, patiently watching me. Some faces were aged and sunken in. Others were fresh and nearly glowing. I recognized most of them.

"Scott," the leader spoke, "please protect yourself from your emotions." I stood in awe of the faces before me. They came.

'Tell me what to do,' I asked politely.

They swayed momentarily and Aunt Barbara stepped forward. "Dear, you know how. Thank you for hearing us last night. Keep walking Alley Pond for clarity."

'Why?'

"You are a mere vessel for our intentions. You will wake up. You will foster hope and courage and devout faith. We are more than a circle. We are a community.

Another voice shot forth: "You are not crazy. You see. You see all of us." Danielle was standing before me.

Stacey's voice echoed through the room: "You feel our heartbeats mingling with your own. Be patient, for in education there is veritas. Truth. Be the solace. Be the light. Reign over your emotions without stepping into the blinding light. They hold no physical or emotional merit over you."

The room was illuminated in blue cosmic shadows floating in a circular motion. Everything was before me. Everything.

"Promise you will stay strong." Aunt Barbara's voice was vividly moving around in my mind.

'How?'

"Promise."

A sympathetic echo of melodic no, no, no, no, nos filled the air. The angels smiled.

'What do I do? Say? What-,'

They faded before an answer could spring forth. I thought I was hallucinating.

However, the sensation I felt in my soul was real. Their light is real. My devout beliefs in them carry their legacies onward.

My light is within me. It always has been, despite the fire that burns around me a fire still burns within.

'Why me?' I muttered to my tear-filled eyes in the mirror, yet I was absolutely certain that no one was going to respond to my question.

I promised them I would stay strong. I promise that I'll attempt to maintain my strength. I am not going anywhere.

I can't.

I am standing my ground against darkness.

I had to refuse to fall down.

∞ ∞ ∞ ∞ ∞ ∞ ∞ ∞

"Dad?" Bryan's voice permeated my exhausted existence. It must have been an incredibly late football practice for him, for I did not expect to see him standing before me as the television hummed to the tune of static.

He plopped down next to me on the couch as I sat up. "Are you okay?"

'Yeah,' the remote and one of Windows' curriculum manuals fell from my lap.

"Are you sure?" He scooted closer to me.

'Yeah, yeah. I just fell asleep while waiting for you, bud.' That was the honest truth.

"Okay. When are you going to Toronto?" Bryan bent his right knee and began to knead at his right foot; he was always hard at work, just like his father, and I don't think he ever took the time to rest or relax. Then again, neither did I.

Like father, like son.

'Tomorrow night.'

"Who are the people you are working with again?"

'United Global Shift.' I reached for the remote and allowed the static to dissipate into the recesses of our tired minds.

"That sounds pretty cool."

'Yeah,' I put my arm around him. 'You going to be okay for a few days while I'm gone?'

"Of course, dad," Bryan was a great kid. I already knew the answer to that question, but I still had to ask.

∞ ∞ ∞ ∞ ∞ ∞ ∞ ∞

It's not everyday that you travel to Canada for a leadership conference and leave your teenage son at home.

I was excited that Windows of Opportunity would even be represented in a room filled with empowering speakers and dedicated individuals. From the moment I started Windows, I silently prayed for it to become a well-known entity in New York, and now the potential existed to officially have WOO create a global impact with revolutionary thinkers.

My mind wandered to such lofty and idealist places at times, I consistently wondered if my dreams would ever come true. Nevertheless, my thoughts kept expanding.

For my entire life, I was belittled for asking questions or being inquisitive in general. There was an inherent feeling that was burning inside of me, which told me that United Global Shift would not judge me for my curiosity. Rather, they would help me make the necessary shift that I so desperately needed in my life.

In the weeks prior, I was trying to get Windows on the map. Elyza was on a television show for her Social Work efforts, and a woman on YouTube was looking to interview me.

Much trepidation followed me, for the lawsuit did not seem to be letting up. Still, something told me to keep pushing forward.

It is funny how one decision that you make has the potential to change your entire life.

I wanted to be on the show.

I figured it would be a great marketing strategy and could define Windows in a professional sense.

As day broke over the horizon, I found myself sitting in Francis Lewis Park trying to clear my head.

The benches were solid and cold, though the water was calm. In a sense, the scene at the park was echoic of my life at the moment: everything around me seemed frigid, but I had to muster up the courage to stay calm no matter what. The weather, or external factors, could not and should not taint the passion burning within me.

I had to keep going, no matter how frozen I felt. Oftentimes, I seemed immobilized by the dismay surrounding my departure from the high school.

Still, despite my pain and agony surrounding my decision to leave the first job I truly loved, I knew that everything had to be happening for a reason.

Life had to keep being lived regardless of the dark clouds following me around.

That ideology reverberated through my core daily.

Just…

Keep…

Moving…

I left Francis Lewis Park and met the interviewer at a coffee shop in Long Island City. The two of us hit it off instantly and she asked that we film the interview at a place where I felt most comfortable.

Something told me that the Whitestone Bridge would be the perfect spot to talk about Windows of Opportunity. Francis Lewis Park was a gorgeous setting naturally; adding a discussion about WOO to the bridge's historical implications seemed incredibly appropriate.

The following week I would be recorded in an interview that would mark a professional turning point for me.

However, what stood before me would prove to be a monumental icon of both leadership and empowerment: United Global Shift.

∞ ∞ ∞ ∞ ∞ ∞ ∞ ∞

I boarded the plane to Toronto on an early Friday morning flight. Fortunately, the trip would only take me about an hour to complete, which gave me plenty of time to reflect introspectively on everything I had been going through.

The skies were painted with vivid reds, oranges, and yellows, as the midnight blue and indigo shades faded into the distance. The plane provided me with a window to as far as the horizon would reach, and I was grateful for every breath I took while admiring the sky.

Maybe Toronto would provide me with some clarity or peace I could not feel while on land.

The lyrics to Frankie Valli and the Four Seasons' "Walk like a Man" played through the earphones on my iPod:

"Walk like a man, talk like a man

Walk like a man my son
No woman's worth crawlin' on the earth
So walk like a man, my son."

Maybe the song was right: are one woman's vile and perturbed attacks on a youth program truly that destructive? Was she worth it?

My instant response to those questions would have been 'Yes,' however; I knew that although her actions and the lawsuit were destroying me, the voice within my soul said otherwise.

I had to listen.

I had to truly let myself be present for Windows of Opportunity, and not for the comments or actions that others would try to plague me with.

Deep down inside, I knew who I was.

Maybe I even knew who I would become back then, I just was not willing to admit it yet.

After letting my eyes rest for what felt like only a few minutes, I heard the overhead announcements declare that we were about to land at Toronto's International Airport.

The Canadian flag waved abruptly in the wind, almost to signify a pivotal turning point: the wind was moving the flag, but it still clung to the pole. The flag still remained grounded despite every outside force trying to rip it from its foundation.

That was it: I had to stay grounded. I had to remain steadfast and move towards promoting the values, vision, and mission of Windows of Opportunity.

It's all about shifting systems.

As I launched my backpack over my shoulder and shimmied out of the plane, I breathed in the fresh Canadian air.

It was a stark contrast to the smog that shifted through New York City, though I know each location had its wholesome effect on my existence.

Within an hour, I was surrounded by brilliant, amazing, and gifted lightworkers who had a rather spiritual side to them. I felt welcomed by their presence and what they seemed to want to offer to non-profit agencies like myself.

Everyone in the room was surrounding a woman with pristine skin and a seemingly open heart: Grace. She had silky blonde hair that extended past her hips and was speaking about "Shifting the system" and "Changing the system."

That's what drew me in: the energy in the room.

Grace and I locked eyes for a moment, and I got lost in the essence that was her chocolate brown eyes making contact with mine.

I was caught in the ebb and flow of the rhythm in the room. Everyone seemed to be on the same frequency, as if their hearts were all beating in a syncopated fashion while I was trying to learn about who I would become and what I would help Windows of Opportunity become.

Being surrounded by people who are like-minded and eager to make a difference in the world does something to you and your soul.

In a sense, it expands a part of who you are.

The process of educating your mind with enlightenment fills a hole within you that you didn't even know existed, and it does not slam you in the face abruptly.

It is an awakening of parts of you that lay dormant within who you once were, and introduces you to who you are.

By the time I ended up doing the interview the following week, my whole perspective on what I wanted to say about Windows of Opportunity changed. I was set on reshaping my language.

I was in the process of translating the ideas of who I was and what I was all about. Slowly but surely, I was grinding down all of the experiences I went through during all of these years. I was whittling down my negative experiences into the raw, unfettered existence that hid deep within.

There was a bigger vision regarding where I was going, I just did not realize I was lighting the path to get there the entire time.

It was all due to conversations I struck up with Grace while at United Global Shift. She was one of the individuals who helped me see what I could become.

We became casual friends; she was the smartest person I knew at the time and we would talk about such elevated thoughts. Those three days of speaking with her made my head spin, but Grace was, in essence, opening me up to another realm of energy and consciousness.

Grace was the one who introduced me to the term, "Lightworker," which made me believe that I, too, could become one of these energy shifters on the planet. She told me she lived in the middle of nowhere amid this place called Vancouver's Sunshine Coast.

Her life and intelligence were floating through my head as I spoke about Windows of Opportunity, and I think her vision, tenacity, and leadership were what brought me to speak as eloquently as I did that day during the interview.

At one point during the video interview, I turned towards the Whitestone Bridge and looked out at my future. Building bridges was something I always considered to be a quintessential part of my life, and maybe this was what the lawsuit was doing: it was possibly building a bridge between who I was and all I could become.

∞ ∞ ∞ ∞ ∞ ∞ ∞ ∞

I was persistent in trying to reach out to Faith for quite some time, though once I realized that I could write what would become one of

Windows of Opportunity's longest-running leadership curriculums, Project Evolve, I felt the confidence brewing within me.

All of my conversations with God and the world in the sanctuary were about one of three things: the lawsuit, the agency, and Faith.

Then one day, the two of us finally connected and went out to an Indian restaurant for lunch.

It was like some of my prayers and ambitions were finally being answered. Though I was excited and nervous, I mustered up the courage to talk to her about what had been happening between us over the past few months.

Faith flashed that coy, yet assuring smile at me.

'Why are you avoiding me?' I looked at her pulling on her sleeve and interlocking her fingers to obscure her slight apprehension.

She began to talk to me about various relationships she was in and all of the stuff happening between her and her family. Faith also made it clear that she only wanted to be friends.

"I don't trust the energy between us and I don't want to hurt you," she was gesturing at us furiously with her hands.

Inhaling deeply, I did what I thought was best at that moment: 'I get it.'

Though I was trying my best to hide it, I told her that everything was fine and of course we could be friends. She smiled and I played the situation off as if I did not care.

At that point, I figured there was no chance for me and her.

So many months had passed, so I did what I thought was what she wanted.

I gave up on thinking she would ever want to be anything more than pals.

'I do hope we could salvage our friendship,' I extended my hand and she cautiously shook it.

Faith seemed slightly disappointed, whether it was in herself or in me I could not tell, however I figured that this was how things would be from now on.

Then we left the restaurant.

∞ ∞ ∞ ∞ ∞ ∞ ∞ ∞

We talked about how she was confused about us. Faith was panicking, but tried not to show just how much fear was brewing on the surface.

Somewhere between her ranting's and ravings, I saw the vein in her forehead pulsate from its surface. Her exquisite smile became more cynical yet oddly demure. She was half repulsed by what came out of her mouth, though the other half yearned to tear from her body and form its own robust character.

Her motions and gyrations were confusing me rather quickly.

Faith's voice droned on and on. There was no end to her rambling once it started, but a sliver of hope flung itself into my path.

"If I wanted you, I could have you anytime I want," she peeped.

I stalled right there in the street, idling on the remnants that just sprung forth from her lips.

"I'm waiting,' I retorted. I could see her eyes morphing into slender daggers though her back was facing me.

"You're-" she paused to pick up the pieces of the conversation: "You're waiting... for what?" A tinge of curiosity clung to the still air between us.

I drew her in with every breath; 'You heard me.'

She stood firm and wrestled the words out, "Say it to my face."

I inched closer, unsure what this challenge would mean to her. The words escaped my mouth ever so slowly: 'I'

The distance between our bodies grew shorter. Her face became steadfast.

'Am,' crept from my lips.

The last word stood between the point of no return: 'Waiting.'

I was playing with fire, though the flame seemed to be so tempting to touch.

Her narrowed eyes looked incredibly desperate. She could not fathom what just happened. A challenge. A breaking point.

A breaking point snapped in the balance of will she merely bend?

Or would she fall and shatter to the ground?

A piercing echo flooded our minds. It was registering on her face.

Waiting...

Waiting...

Waiting...

Wai-

My thoughts were thrashed into the base of my skull with the tactful swoop of her wrist. Her hand rested while clutched around my neck, just tight enough to pull at my emotions.

She does not and will not back down.

"Decide," she quipped, swishing my body against the brick wall: "now."

Our eyes locked in dead silence. Violent whispers dripped from her lips, each moist letter drawing me into a lulled sense of fear with hints of excitement.

"Pick your poison, Scott," her voice had a sudden raspiness to it: "Dare to dance with the devil?" One of her eyebrows leapt up onto her forehead.

'Hun,' her hand dropped, as she knew this challenge was forcing her into a state of false security. 'You are an angel,' a small grin and sarcastic glance pooled on her face.

A pause separated us with a sense of eagerness: 'but I will knock that halo clear off your head in one thrust.'

She laughed nervously and tottered back before winding up and snatching my wrist towards the alleyway.

In one fatal blow she pressed her lips firmly against mine and tugged on the back of my hair. Seconds away from my face, she glared purposefully into my eyes: "Whose halo was thrusted off now?"

Her courage was far too fierce to handle with just one kiss.

So I took my chance and went for it.

We crashed upon each other and a light burst above our heads. A symphony beckoned. Wings fluttered around us in the form of birds ascending above the gray city.

Faith bolted down the block, my hand clutched in hers, as we dragged each other into the depths of a tumultuous night ahead. We rushed down city blocks and down backstreets. A steel door stood between us and our undivided selves.

A wholesomeness clung in the air as we ascended the stairs, unlocked the door, and burst into the living room of my apartment.

The last thing I remembered was Faith's name escaping my lips before the night descended upon our souls.

∞ ∞ ∞ ∞ ∞ ∞ ∞ ∞

The next morning, I awoke to her exhausted frame standing in the doorway, a cup of tea steaming on the nightstand, and the knowledge that we didn't sleep together... last night, that is.

"Did you miss me, lover boy?" Faith kindled the teacup in her hand, just waiting for my reply to burst forth.

I summoned her closer to me with just one curl of my finger. She glided closer and closer to me and placed the cup on the nightstand.

I sat up and inched near her ear, brushing back her chestnut hair in the process.

'Maybe it is you who missed me.' I could feel her body collapsing into mine. We rolled back onto the bed and she met my gaze with a longing stare.

"I missed your touch, my darling," a sultry tone emerged from her voice.

'Hun-' I said, sensuously pulling her hips closer to mine, 'I missed yours too.'

I sprung up and dove closer to her hips, facing her body directly in the process. As my hands eased up and down her body, I could feel her moans growing louder and louder. In the depths of my mind, I was fearful that I would not make her happy, yet she seemed to be living in the moment.

Fortunately, neither of us needed to be anywhere that day, and honestly, I do not think either of us cared, as the hours grew longer and more passionate.

I guess I was going to keep the faith after all.

We rolled around in the sheets and blankets for quite some time, allowing the day to usher us into whatever was about to happen next.

"Scott," she rolled towards my exhausted body and became entangled in the sheets.

'What?' I wrapped my arm around her and pulled her head closer. I kissed her on the forehead and cherished the memories we made together.

"There is a song called, 'La Nave del Olvido', but I like to call it 'Espera Un Poco' because it reminds me of you. It is by Jose Jose."

'Okay,' I drew her in closer. 'I don't know it. Why don't you sing it to me?'

I let my gentle kisses drift up and down her body as she whispered it to me in Spanish, but I translated the song days after, and found out what it meant:

"Wait,
The ship to oblivion hasn't sailed
let's not condemn what we have been through on the shipwreck
for our past
for our love, I beg you
Wait,
There are still springs within my hands
to pamper you/fill you with brand new caresses
that would die in my hands if you were to go away
Wait a little, a little more
to take away my happiness
wait a little, a little more
I would die if you go away
Wait
I still have joy to give you,
I have a thousand nights of love (that I would like) to give you,
I give you my life in exchange for staying
Wait,
I wouldn't understand my tomorrow if you go away
And I even accept your love if you were just pretending (to love me)
I would adore you even if you didn't love me."

We sat up, face to face in bed at this point as she let the last words leave her lips:

"*Wait for a little more…*"

Faith kissed me and I found myself crawling towards her until I was positioned right over her body. She laid under me with minuscule tears dripping from the edges of her eyes.

'It's beautiful,' I told her. 'Why that song?'

"I-" she hesitated slightly. "I felt so guilty, but I knew that something was between us."

We kissed softly for a moment until she placed her hands on my face.

'Faith,' I rolled next to her. 'I understand.'

"I think I love you, Scott."

'I think I love you too.'

We kissed more passionately and I could feel her smiling between our sweet release.

She was back.

∞ ∞ ∞ ∞ ∞ ∞ ∞ ∞

I continued my strolls with Morena in Alley Pond Park and often spent hours alone in the Queens Community Church sanctuary begging for answers.

Faith came back to me, so I figured that someone was out there listening to my prayers.

Still, I was scared shitless and found myself scribbling in one of my many journals to find clarity:

"Walk in Faith" - II Corinthians 5:7

Dear Father,

It has been a long time since I prayed to you in this manner, via pen to paper. So much time has passed since I wrote in this secret journal. This journal exists as a dormant and secret element of my soul only because I'm scared to express the spiritual insights I struggle with. After my last journal entry, this book got buried in boxes inside what we call the Minister's study, which is referred to respectfully as "the office", or "WOO headquarters."

More than a year has gone by and there are very few days, maybe I can count them on one hand that I have not sat in the sanctuary where I rest now writing to you. Jesus, my spiritual guides, Celestial Spirits, angels, and so forth, I pray you read the words I etch into this paper straight from my core. I pray to you daily for deeper answers, soul development, and a closer relationship with you. I appreciate all of the beauty you have bestowed upon my life, and I am grateful for the strength you continue to grant me.

I have been trying to grow spiritually to the point of wanting to recognize who I am. I continue to produce opportunities while embracing your name. I try to be a source of faith and inspiration for all around me. I balance my own development in your image, for I know your light shines upon me. The blessings you have given me, even the ones rooted in deep human pain, I am grateful for.

The lessons throughout my life have been blessings, though they often do not feel so. I had feelings for Faith, she left, but she returned. Our last ending was not pretty to my soul, and then she returned at the perfect time.

Did you send her back?

I sense her trepidation and something is off, despite her saying that she loves me. I am eternally grateful for the beauty of the lessons this relationship is teaching me. A light switch has turned on in my soul that is telling me what I deserve and who I truly am.

You have filled me with such a deep awareness and love, that it is difficult to relax at times and be in the moment. Faith is trying, and perhaps that should be good enough. During our relationship prior to and after her disappearance, I wrote 200-plus pages of exploration, pain, and sappiness that I suspect I'm going to erase as I move forward. I am so scared with all going on around me. I do not know what my future holds.

I am not ready to be this new person. Who is this new person, after all?

I am not ready to lose my career or my dreams.

I come to you at this moment father, as I am sure you are aware of, with a very heavy heart.

You have taught me so many lessons about love. Through this pain you are teaching me about love for humanity… love for another soul…

and love for myself, this is very clear, but it does not subside the pain.

I have grown to the point in which you know exactly what I want in a person. I am confused, but I am not confused. I have a very good thing going with Faith, and I do not want to mess things up.

She left. Hurt me. Came back. Requested a friendship. And now we are back. Should we have stayed friends? Should I disregard it as growing pains in a good relationship? Or is it fear of some sort… on both our parts? We really could never get our act together from day one.

I know I must trust in you, walk in faith, and let go. If this is truth, it will happen in due time, your time. You have sent to my life the most beautiful spirit to help me discover a better relationship with the universe than I could ever imagine.

Our souls connect and I am pretty sure she is aware of it, which is why I don't comprehend what is really going on between us.

Reality scares me.

The truth? Father, what is the truth?

I have so much love inside of me that I want to give it to someone and share it with someone, which has led me to the simple fact that I cannot stop thinking whether that perfect person exists…

I love Faith very much, but in the secrecy of these pages, I admit that fear still harnesses some of the energy in my soul.

Maybe I don't know better. Maybe I can't see your lesson or your message.

I don't always see the light, or know your way. I also believe things happen for a reason.

Faith is here, now, for whatever reason you see fit. I believe Faith loves me on some level though I sense an underlying deep sadness; an unexpected sadness towards my soul that comes from within her. I hope I am wrong.

Faith is definitely a spiritual soulmate to some degree, but my soul tells me there is more. Am I wrong Father? I dream still of the unknown while simultaneously fearing the loss of today. With all that said, I know I cannot control anything.

I know that if it is your will, it shall be done. I also know I cannot and should not show the intensity of my love anymore... it scares anyone I love away... something I pray for asking you to shield me from myself. With this knowledge, it is still difficult for me not to pray for human desires. Father, I really don't know what to do.

With anything. With love. With Faith. With this lawsuit.

Faith is smart, classy, and has you clearly in her being. She has these beautiful life saving dreams and incredible family values. Yet she does not think it can align to who I am, and my values.

She does not always show who she is but has opened up to me. There is endless good to her as there is with me.

We both agree the angels are speaking to us. Perhaps she needs time to pray and process and I should walk in faith, knowing if it is truly what is meant to be and in my soul, it will happen. Somehow, praying to you in this writing format makes me feel better and reminds me of my faith. I was scared to write about all my fears, because somehow that makes it real. What do I do if I lose my career? Faith will surely be gone then.

I'm an open book but maybe I should close myself off a bit? Do I say too much here? Write too much? Father, do you hear me?

I want to be true to who I am, even if I do not know what that fully means all the time.

As I close my eyes, it is as if the Holy Spirit just completely went through me. I hear, "Wait… she will come and you will know." Father, I pray that YOU are there for Faith and I, and you help to nurture our souls.

I pray that I keep focused and keep my feelings at bay so that I do not add more pain and struggle to Faith's precious heart and mind, until a time that you deem fit, that will benefit us both spiritually and divinely. I pray for strength and a positive outcome to this lawsuit. I pray that you help all the souls around me to continue to grow, individually and together. My soul is truly telling me many mixed messages, The love that is, and that I wish could be, are overwhelming my spirit. Thank you Father… No matter what the outcome.

Thank you for her being in my life.

I am so blessed.

∞ ∞ ∞ ∞ ∞ ∞ ∞ ∞

Though the lawsuit seemed relentless, I finally got called into the Conflict of Interest Board Court House. It was almost parallel to what you would see on one of those television court shows.

There were big block letters that hung in the hallway to signify that people were, indeed, there for the Conflict of Interest Board case you were dealing with.

It was almost comical.

At this point, it had been about three years since the case started and I was still sick to my stomach.

The court case was finally being heard, and I was out of the high school for about two years already, but I was still shaking down to my core.

I had so much going for me now: Faith was being incredibly supportive of me during the case's proceedings, I was in charge of two after-school programs, and $7,000 in court fees later, I was about to defend myself.

It was all because of the supervisor who I hoped and thought would want to help expand programs for the youth in Queens.

Instead, she was trying to bury me.

I figured I was never going to work in the school system again.

I was done.

It was a miserable experience that almost cost me my soul and my life.

The countless hours I spent praying and meditating, the days I spent wandering through the woods at Alley Pond Park ready to throw up, the bad dreams, the fear, the anxiety I had over potentially losing my license and my career...

Potentially not changing the world...

Every question, every pitfall, every painstaking moment... It led me there.

Who was I?

What was I about?

Days upon days of a deep-rooted depression, strife, and struggle were weighing heavy on my shoulders because I knew that my soul was good. I was a good guy who really wanted to do good stuff in this world.

Yet I was being sued for millions of dollars because one woman misunderstood me, and my intentions.

It didn't make sense to me.

Little did I know at the time, the universe was giving me the introduction to an immense lesson about my values and vision.

I was really going to take a stand against injustice and misunderstanding.

I just had to.

A long wooden table sat before me as I began to plead my case.

The lawyers from the school system pulled out pictures from my original website and smashed them down on the table.

I sat pondering whether this was real life or just fantasy.

"Mr. Matheson, we will continue pursuing this court case for years and years to come, unless you can tell us about these pictures," the lawyer pointed shamelessly at the images.

'What?' I sat up in the chair. 'These pictures of kids from the high school?'

"Yes," the man snapped. "They are on Windows of Opportunity's website *and that* is a *conflict of interest.*"

'Okay.' I was genuinely confused. 'I never saw a conflict of interest policy.'

The lawyers all looked at each other for a moment.

'I never signed a conflict of interest policy.'

One of the men in suits stood up, "Why are these pictures posted on your website, Mr. Matheson?"

I looked at my lawyer and stood up with my hands resting on the table. 'You want to know why they are posted there? They're actually posted there because I did not know how to design a website and put them there as placeholders until I knew what I was doing,' with exasperation overpowering my voice, I let out one last remark: 'Sir.'

The men looked at each other in disarray. They were flipping through files until another man perked up: "Do you have permission to have any of those pictures?"

'I had verbal permission from the kids and the parents.' They looked at me blankly.

'But you know this. The investigators asked if any of the parents were against having pictures posted. I told them as I will tell you now: obviously, they were not against anything I did.'

There were pictures of kids working with homeless families.

These were pictures of kids working, separating clothes from a clothing drive, and putting them in bags for people who needed them.

"Okay," one man said confidently. "You need to be fined for this."

'Okay,' I responded. 'What does that even mean?'

"This is a $1,500 fine because you do not have signed permission slips. Verbal permission and working with parents do not suffice."

We looked at each other for a moment.

This was the system.

What programs and schools actually get parents to come out?

So many people complain that parent engagement is one of the most difficult tasks in a school, but I was able to make it happen.

Just because I did not have signatures, they wanted my money.

I wanted to scream.

I wanted to leap across that long table and get right in their faces.

Instead, I just shut my mouth.

'Okay,' I spoke again. 'What are my options?'

"You have two," one guy said. "You can pay the $1,500 within 24 hours or we can take you to court and this will be more serious."

'If I pay the $1,500, am I blacklisted from the school system?'

The men looked at each other and laughed.

"Absolutely not," another man said. "We have a lot of people in your situation that go back to work the very next day."

My life was a miserable existence for three years just for this moment.

"You can still work with the school system too, you just need to get Windows of Opportunity a Vendor ID. Here is the phone number." He walked the piece of paper over to me.

That was it.

After digging into my bank account, it was all over.

I barely had money at the time, but the universe handed me this gift.

Within a day, the school system had their check and I had a contract with another high school.

I was left wondering why we can't shift the way we think.

Bad storms kept rolling in, where life makes you stop and look at everything, yet there is still the potential to rise.

Faith in ourselves will make us rise again.

The systems we are a part of do not make sense if we wish to truly have peace on our planet.

I want to change this world.

I want to rid it of confusion and disillusion.

∞ ∞ ∞ ∞ ∞ ∞ ∞ ∞

My soul was leaking stamina despite finally feeling liberated. Upon returning to the sanctuary, I wrote this letter:

"God's way of answering the Christian's prayer for more patience, experience, hope and love often is to put him into the furnace of affliction."
- Richard Cecil

Dear Father,

This gets so difficult at times.

I am struggling, which confuses me because I simultaneously feel stronger and closer to Spirit than ever before.

I have faith in what I do not see and desires of love from the depths of my soul. My confusion lies in whom I am supposed to be in certain situations, and I try to simply be a person with your inner light and spiritual love. As you see I sometimes fall short, and it happens more often than I choose to admit.

I take things personally and I soak them in and quite often wear a mask, even to myself, so nobody can hear me screaming inside. I love everyone and this world, and the things I see make me sad.

It hurts me deeply when I see a system add to someone else's pain and confusion. When someone's intentions are pure and loving, it is devastating for one to end up with less than what is deserved.

It shakes my foundation and my being, and halts my moving forward, though I do not know why.

I half suspect it's because love is the energy behind having faith and rising up, and when it feels absent, or needed, I tend to fold, yet fighting to be truly noticed. So many people think I have it together, and to some extent, especially since the growth of our closeness, I feel I do, and I am truly blessed, and I have no choice but to truly let it go and let God.

My heart and my feelings are true.
I do not want to inflict heartache on anyone's soul. I only want to be a very real source of empowerment and inspiration. I can only do that with you in my life.

What am I supposed to do? Not care that my friends are struggling?

Not care that I think I love this girl and still not be sure if she's the one?

Am I supposed to walk away and shut off my feelings and just be an instrument, a vessel of your work?

Am I getting it wrong?

Is there balance?

I know the purity of who I am.

Is it wrong to ask for a specific blessing? Is it wrong to feel true happiness around? Is it wrong to wonder if there is a higher love that can be an arm's length away and not just an attraction or any kind of natural love, but a deep, spiritual, fun, loving, life-altering, world-changing, passion?

I know thy will shall be done.

I accept that and I do praise you.

Thank you.

∞ ∞ ∞ ∞ ∞ ∞ ∞ ∞

An amalgamation of the crumbling pieces of my soul were falling back together again as I walked down the street.

My soul has been littered with the misnomers of those who chose to focus on the intentions of others as opposed to the respective lights that glow within them.

For months, I have endured hearing about how I am supposedly stealing from the school system, how I am not to be trusted because I am associating with certain people. I was too demanding, not in the right place, taking things too personally, doing "everything" wrong, doing "too much," then not doing enough, being scolded by sudden armchair experts on my life and experience, and I am sure if I listed everything, we would be here for quite some time.

Yet despite this manifestation of negativity, not a single person who has spread something defamatory of my character has come up to me and bothered to ask, without some sort of intention or end goal, "Are you okay?"

I have worn a mask seemingly made of steel to hide all of the emotions I have felt surrounding the sudden chaos and confusion I was thrust into. Each day I have had to process everything and progress without flinching, because if I did, I was "too emotional."

If I didn't react, I was cold-hearted. I have had to walk into rooms and meetings where I knew I was the most hated person in the room, sit down, and be professional despite the glances and whispers.

I have had to cheer on and encourage youth secretly, for if I did it publicly, then suddenly I would appear to have some hidden agenda. I have had to make myself devoid of all emotion because if I spoke honestly, I was too crass.

I have had to run up, down, and around so much, that I went months without eating anything between five o'clock in the morning and sometimes between seven or eight o'clock in the evening. I busted my rear end behind the scenes for days upon days, only to be shut down by sheer rudeness, disgust, and utter disregard.

When being called a supposed "know-it-all" who is too overbearing, I revealed pieces of myself to try to prove who I was... then I quickly learned that some believed I was just lying.

Well, after these few years, I must say thank you: I did not need this validation or reminder, I did not warrant this scarlet letter on my chest or these knives in my back. I did, however, do what everyone says you SHOULD do... "Be yourself," yet being yourself apparently isn't good enough for all.

Well, after all of this, I say thank you.

Thanks for the months of persistent hushed badgering, humiliation, and hatred. I'm trading in the mask for a pair of roots.

This tree of mine has been planted with the intentions of making a better future for our children and developing a more understanding world.

I'll branch out, away from all this negativity and hurt, stronger because I know what it feels like to be kicked down and slandered without regard for a person's willingness to genuinely help.

To genuinely be there.

To be a sincere and honest person.

If you are looking to continue spreading malice, then good luck dragging your own body out of the hole you're digging further and further into.

If you are looking for the truth, then look right here.

Stand before me and ask for what I have honestly been saying for these past few months. Look me in the eye and tell me how repulsive of a human being I am, talk to my face like how you talk behind my back, then try living with knowing you tried to tear down another human being.

Tried.

Think twice before you knock down another human being... for when you mess with one who has been further than the depths of hell... understand that his light is that much more resilient than you know.

This fire does not and will not burn out.

Passive aggressiveness, hostility, backstabbing, vanity, or pride will not extinguish this passion.

I was bent to the point where I broke... but by now, I have the distinguished honor of picking up pieces knowing who is truly there for me, caring, and supportive. I was told to quit, so I will... quit allowing the shallow words of others penetrate all I have worked for to honor our children. I was told to give up, so I will... give up the burdens that dragged me to my kitchen floor for the last of the countless times where I sit to contemplate my next tear-induced progression forward.

Just know these tears were not gifted to you as a reward for your jealousy.

No.

For your jealousy I say stand up and face your insecurities, not my abilities. Let the sharpest words try to cut me down. I'll stand, in my stubborn existence, bruised and bleeding... awaiting the day you will rise and fight to kindle the light within your own soul.

So bottom line, keep going and you'll get burned for trying to extinguish someone else's flame. If you're ready to make a better experience for yourself... then just wake up.

And to the past few years, I say:

'Amen.'

CHAPTER 31

Amen

~

"With an ironclad fist, I wake up and french kiss the morning... while some marching band keeps its own beat in my head while we're talking about all of the things that I long to believe. About love and the truth... and what you mean to me."

- Bon Jovi, American Rock Band, Sayreville, New Jersey

The relationship between Faith and I began to take flight. Within a matter of days, she decided that she was willing to make a commitment to me. Faith sealed her decision to stand by my side with a beautiful letter:

"Love's Commitment"

Spoken or unspoken, love is the greatest, most compelling of all human emotions.

To me, loving is a total commitment; a complete surrender of the heart, the mind and the soul. Loving is one's deep and intense concern for the life, well being, and security of another.

If, perhaps, you have some special needs, I will make every effort to achieve their fulfillment for you.

If, at times, you feel lonely, I will try to cheer you and dispel your loneliness.

If you ever need to share your innermost thoughts, you may pour your heart out, and I will listen.

If you ever need sympathy, I will try to comfort you with my words, my touch, and my presence.

If your needs are understandably intimate and human, I will share your sleep and be together with you in the intimacy of your dreams.

But only the commitment of my love will make this possible.

- Faith

In my love-conscious state of mind, I began realizing that Faith's presence was lifting my emotions up. At first, I thought that she would not keep coming back to me.

Though day after day, she would call me up and talk with me.

Once when she called, I was working at a school in Brooklyn not far from her house. Faith asked if I could meet her in the parking lot of a diner to just connect with her for a little while.

I enjoyed that.

When she wanted something, she was rather quick to ask me.

Faith consistently made an effort to talk spirituality with me, and dive into just about any topic of conversation she pleased. We had a deep spiritual and soulful connection, and I loved the philosophical conversations we had.

We talked about life, meditating, and thinking drastically different from so many people.

This was the main source of our attraction for countless years. Regardless of how hectic and chaotic my life was at the time, I was honored she would call me. From the sultry raspiness in her voice, I could tell she really needed me.

We would go to Little Ecuador in Queens and enjoy Ecuadorian cuisine. The two of us had deep conversations about traveling to Ecuador together one day, and each time we met up I could feel her energy consuming my soul.

I was enamored by her essence, drawn into her presence, and never wanted to leave her side.

∞ ∞ ∞ ∞ ∞ ∞ ∞ ∞

As my days grew longer and time with Faith consisted of passionate late night phone calls, I was excited by the visions I had for the future and the path I was embarking on.

Life was good.

I was my own version of happy, although I was consistently exhausted.

As I was working in my apartment one night, I enjoyed the silence that encompassed my soul. I was longing for Faith, but I knew that she was busy with her business somewhere in Queens.

Bryan was out with his friends and I had time to reflect on just how far I had come since the lawsuit. It was as if a burden was fully removed from my shoulders, but it still lingered in the shadows of whom I was growing into.

I heard a knock on my apartment door, which prompted my imagination to snap back to reality.

Faith stood in the doorway, her eyelids flickering at the sight of me, with a gentle sparkle in her eye.

'Hey,' a smile instinctively appeared across my face.

"Hey, can I come in?" She asked, though she was already through the doorway and into my apartment.

I shut the door and left my hand there for a moment when I turned around. Faith's eyes caught my trepidation, but I was silently excited to have her in my presence. I did not expect her to just appear at my apartment, but I was not going to question what she was doing in Bayside, Queens.

"It's just us now," she said as she glanced over her shoulder in my direction. I felt her body slowly rocking against mine though we were clear across the room.

"Now what," she questioned, finally turning her body so we were parallel to each other. I longed to grasp her flowing caramel hair hard enough to draw her closer, but passionately enough so that she would naturally drift into my embrace. I couldn't just say, 'I want you, I need you,' to her.

I mean, it's just too cliche. I had no idea what to do other than shift my gaze to the window.

The growing awkwardness was divided by some question she was asking, but I was too transfixed on whatever was outside to even care. No, that's a lie, I did care - I was just too nervous to make a peep. Reality slammed into my head hard once I caught her glance.

I recognized those eyes before, but in movies and in television shows, never directly in front of me: the flickering eyelids, her eyelashes kissing one another gently before popping open again. These were bedroom eyes. She wanted me so badly, but did she really?

I longed for her to melt upon touching my skin. I prayed she would collapse into my arms once we kissed. It had been so long since I had even been touched, let alone held, that I was hoping she would tell me what to do.

I hoped she would move me in a way only she could. I needed her to see how I just longed for her body to press against mine - even for a second, even for a moment.

502

"Scott," she quipped, "Maybe I should just get going?" There was a slight inflection in her voice, almost as if she were asking to stay or asking to leave. I couldn't make the same mistakes I have made in the past. Fuck, I couldn't go for it. I was too timid, too antsy, I was too… whatever, nervous or something.

She pushed her body away from the table she somehow ended up leaning on, and grasped her bag. It swooped over her shoulder and my chances were fleeting out the window. Fuck, fuck, fuck, do I make a move?

'No, don't do it,' I muttered.

Her face dropped. Fuck, I said it out loud. Well, there goes my final shot of the night.

She smirked slightly as her eyebrows raised. What was that? That look… it was something totally new.

Her legs moved to the rhythm of my heartbeat. Inching closer, and closer, I had to go for it… maybe.

"Well," she smiled innocently and extended her arms as if she was waiting for a hug. We embraced for a moment, for I released from her grasp out of fear. My hurried breathing gave it away. I was terribly nervous.

"You're nervous, aren't you?" she giggled a little bit and stepped back to see my face trying to relax. I couldn't lie, but I couldn't admit to anything.

'Nervous about what?' the chuckle gave it all away.

"I'm heading home now, I'll call you in the morning." She re-adjusted her bag and flashed me a sweet smile.

Her hand softly brushed past mine and I blurted the first thing that flew into my mind: 'You can't fake chemistry.'

The last word hung in my mouth, hoping she would gather a reply.

Her eyes flew to mine.

"What," she asked nervously. This is it; I have to do something.

I slowly let the words flow out onto my lips, with a pause leaping in between: 'You' 'can't' 'fake-'

Her entire body slammed into mine and our lips crashed upon each other's like waves against the shore. Our heartbeats synced to the ticking clock in the room I forgot existed; each second drew us closer and closer.

Her hands were inching slowly up and down my back, pulling me tighter into her small frame. With the meeting of our lips, a spark was lit.

It was a fire that could not and would not burn out.

She did it; she made the first move.

I knew she could feel the grin creeping across my face.

"Surprised," she whispered with the same grin spreading across her face.

A long pause hung in the air, for I felt her waiting on what words would come next.

'Relieved,' I whispered.

Briskly, she locked her fingers between mine and pulled me closer to the table. Though moving backwards and at the risk of ramming her body into the table, she did everything with grace and purpose. She wanted to drag me into her every will. Within moments, she collided with the table and jolted my body closer to hers. We kissed again, but with more vigor, more passion, and more stamina - telling me that I would not be spending the night alone on this hazy evening.

In a swift motion, she launched herself backwards onto the wooden table and called me closer and closer without a word. As my breaths started caressing her neck, I could feel her body quivering and dropping to the table.

I was climbing further and further onto the table and over her body, running my fingers through her golden hair, which was strewn across the table. Upon raising my head directly above hers, our glances locked in what was about to be one of the most genuine nights of our lives.

"Scott," she spoke softly, almost to preserve the moment forever.

I dragged my eyes along her tender body that was inches below mine.

'What,' I whispered, grinning from ear to ear.

"Your fingers are pulling out my hair," she struggled to say, almost as if she was trying to mask the pain of follicles of her precious hair being torn from her scalp.

I picked my hand up in a panic and repositioned it next to her shoulder.

The moment that happened, she shot her hand up to my cotton shirt. Her gentle hand showed immense passion as she wrapped her fingers around the black fibers and forced me closer to her face. Our lips met again, but this time it was much wilder than I could have ever imagined. With each twist and turn of our skin, I felt myself flying above the clouds. It was almost as if I was standing above it all, gazing down at our intimate meeting and cherishing the moment for what it was: beautiful.

∞ ∞ ∞ ∞ ∞ ∞ ∞ ∞

Amen

The next morning, I woke up alone. I could still feel every moment from last night on my body, and I longed to hold her once again.

As my foot dropped to the floor with a thud, I was hit with the reality that last night went a lot longer than I had realized. I dragged my body towards the kitchen and gazed at the full coffee pot steaming on the counter. Was she still here? It was a possibility.

I snatched a maroon mug from the cabinet overhead. The other porcelain mugs sang as I gingerly arranged them in case she wanted to grab one. I stand tall at 5'11" and I sometimes have to lurch onto my tiptoes to find what I need. At about 5'2" she will definitely need to leap onto the counter to even attempt to discover where the mugs are. What if she looked through my kitchen already? What if she looked through my apartment while I was sleeping?

I poured myself a cup of coffee and made my way around each of the rooms. The bathroom door was slightly ajar, and I tried my best not to disturb the floorboards in case she was in there. I doubt she would leave without waking me up. Though she is petite and gentle, she would have certainly made some sort of noise as she perused around.

The bathroom door creaked slightly under the pressure of my fingertips. It was empty. She was but a mere ghost in my apartment: an apparition of a passion-filled night in the midst of a life of spiritual solitude.

There was no note, there was no sign she had even graced my presence. For all I know, she could have been but a pleasant dream to juxtapose my loneliness.

'Oh wait,' I realized: the coffee pot. She was real; she was here.

Complacently, I sat upon the table in the kitchen. Our table; our spot. As I pensively sipped the coffee, I caught hues of pink, yellow, and orange creeping over the poignant trees. Last night, I peered out that window considering life's beautiful moments, and now I have another one to cherish.

I am in awe of the wonderful melodies that the music of life has to offer.

Running my fingers over each imprint in the wood, I understood just how breathtaking this table was. The oak I sat upon was once a tall tree filled with its own memories and heartaches. Sitting atop it, I see how much we are alike: we each have our purpose and re-purpose in life and we stand strong. In a sense, I feel some guilt that this once towering creature is sitting in my kitchen, hidden away from the beauty of whatever forest it originated from, but as in life, it has a new meaning: this is the place where two souls became intertwined. This place is special and this place is just as paramount as any lush forest or arboretum.

This is a place of growth.

I decided that I would take today to cherish all of the beautiful moments I could encounter. I leapt off the table and sauntered back into my bedroom. I had to go to my bridge.

While sitting at the bridge, I was contemplating the magical gifts that life has to offer. Each precious moment is a treasured experience, one that cannot be replaced or duplicated as it flutters by. We are all part of an elaborate scene that plays out over days or decades, and as each minute ticks closer and closer to the denouement, we uncover our true purpose and passion.

With every

passing

minute.

"Somebody had a fun night, huh," a voice crept from somewhere in the near distance.

Morena stood before me, wearing a light blue trench coat and holding two cups of steaming hot chocolate.

"I figured you already had your morning coffee, so I thought some chocolate would be suitable," she spoke matter of factly, almost as if she could see the passionate encounter I had with Faith merely hours ago.

As she handed me the cup and perched herself next to my exhausted frame, she rested her head on my shoulder for just a moment. Morena shrugged slightly and whipped her black scarf over her shoulder with her free hand.

"You know you get that look on your face," she said confidently, pressing her lips to the cup and slurping slightly.

'What look do I get on my face, miss know it all?'

"That look like you had a rather *passionate* night with the one and only... "

We paused and in unison sang the same word: Faith.

A gentle squeal came from the now joyous Morena. "Ooooooh, someone had a *good* night, *and morning I presume?*"

As I stood and walked away, Morena seemed to skip behind me with such a sing songy vibrancy that could typically be expressed by giddy children leaving school for the day.

'Mo, come on, we have a company to run,' I said, trying my best not to kiss and tell.

"Come on Scott, did all that pent-up energy just burst?" Her eyes widened.

I paused for a moment but could not contain myself, 'Yes.'

She shrieked with excitement as the two of us wandered out of Francis Lewis Park and into my car.

∞ ∞ ∞ ∞ ∞ ∞ ∞ ∞

Morena and I sat around the table in our quaint office at Queens Community Church.

The walls were covered in large pieces of paper. The words and drawings pointed to the dedication we spent years upon years on.

All of Windows' curriculums were planned. Our programs were outlined in scribbles and hieroglyphics that only we could understand, though we knew that in working tirelessly, we were building a future.

At the time, Morena and I just did not realize how big that future could be.

Surrounded by paper and inundated with sketches of logos for programs that were about to expand, I looked up from the scattered work before us to look at Morena. She was perched on the chair, one leg tucked under the other, eyeballing various documents while leaning her left arm against the table.

'Mo-' I placed what I was holding down on the table.

"Yeah," she did not even bother to look up.

'What do you see in this?' I gestured towards the mess before us. 'What do you see in me?'

She looked up from what she was reading and glared into my eyes.

"Why do you ask?"

'I don't know.' I really didn't know why I was asking at that moment, but I felt like I needed to say something.

"You are looking to me for validation." She placed the paper she was reading on the table.

'Well, I-'

She cut me off: "Stop doing that," she spoke sternly. "You know you are worth more than your self-doubt."

'I mean,' I rubbed the back of my neck. 'I know the lawsuit is over, but I still feel like I can't shake what happened.'

"Three years is a long time to deal with being judged."

'Yeah.'

"I hear you, Scott. I do."

'I know,' I got flabbergasted. 'Forget I said anything.'

"No." Morena got up from the chair and floated over to me. She placed her hand on my shoulder, and her warmth radiated through my body. It was an overwhelming feeling.

'Why not?' Miniscule tears dripped from my eyes.

"Because you should never compartmentalize what you think. Be yourself and express yourself."

'So then why don't you ever talk about what you are going through?'

She smirked, "Because there is a bigger picture at stake here."

Morena motioned to both of us with her pointer finger. I did not understand what she meant by that.

Part of me wanted to question Morena as the seconds cascaded by, but I didn't want to know what she meant. My head was filled with questions as it already were, I did not need to fill it with even more confusing thoughts.

"Be patient." She saw my mind starting to fill with thoughts, and though I would not stop thinking about her comment, Morena knew I would dive back into our work in the next few minutes.

Although our conversation ceased, her words still clung to the forefront of my mind.

What was the bigger picture? What did Morena know? What did Morena see?

What was I even thinking?

Before Morena departed, we cleared up the whole phone number debauchery. This time, she made sure she called me from her phone to prove that she was not giving me a faulty number again.

That woman used to confuse me to no end.

However, once I opened my mind and soul to understanding that the universe was placing situations in my path for one reason or another, I stopped letting Morena's mysterious actions clutter my mind.

It took years to get to that point, but more on that later.

Regardless, Faith was on my mind.

A lot.

Her figure would move ceaselessly through my mind no matter what I was doing.

Everything in my life was Faith: the scent of her in my sheets lingered for days, the conversations we would have on the phone would twist through my mind regularly, and I was finally admitting to myself that my future looked like it would be spent holding Faith in my very arms.

At last, my love had come along.

Then the phone rang and my heart sunk down to my core.

∞ ∞ ∞ ∞ ∞ ∞ ∞ ∞

Faith was panicking because she thought her son was being bullied in school. She pleaded with me to meet with him and talk about what was happening.

I sat there thinking how honorable it was that she chose to reach out to me when she was upset.

I was looking forward to fulfilling the image of "father figure" in the lives of her two sons.

Though I knew her situation, I never asked why her husband was not genuinely there for her or their two children. I figured that she would tell me in due time.

Faith's behavior became peculiar. She was telling me how she would meet up with me because her thoughts allowed her to believe I anticipated her presence in my life.

Suddenly, I felt like a charity case.

I was beginning to rot from the inside out: part of me always thought she was looking forward to the intense feelings that existed between us.

Though as perfectly and surely as the Earth revolves around the sun, she was pulling away from me as if our love was not a true gravitational force.

I began to pace the pews in the sanctuary, asking for assistance again.

I needed guidance and support from the Circle of Angels and all who would listen.

Oftentimes, when Morena was not organizing something in the office, she would saunter up the steps and catch me speaking to the angels.

"Be patient" would echo from Morena's lips to God's ears.

Though I sensed in some way that she was right, fear still permeated my soul.

I always wondered what would happen if Faith caught me pacing back and forth like this in the church.

In hindsight, I guess Morena was astute and in tune with the universe, for Faith ended up shifting her energy once again.

∞ ∞ ∞ ∞ ∞ ∞ ∞ ∞

I am not really certain how to explain what happened.

Faith and I met at the dog walk in Forest Park.

She wanted me to meet her there, hang out with her son, and go get some ice cream afterwards.

Faith was true to her word when she said she wanted me to meet up with her son. It honestly made me feel special in her life, and I liked that.

I wanted her to see me as a special person.

When I entered the park, she was behind a juniper chain link fence wearing a tan trench coat. Both of her sons were there playing fetch with their dog.

A deep breath separated me from what felt like a step into forever.

I approached her with a false sense of confidence adorned on my face, which morphed slowly as I began to speak with her son. He seemed to be drawn into my energy instantly.

Her eldest son and I chatted for a couple of hours with Faith nearby. Occasionally I caught her coy glances and felt the warmth of her smile.

The four of us, and their dog began a tender stroll through the park. It was fun, exciting, and enjoyable.

There were moments where I felt weird, but in an oddly pleasant way.

Then it hit me: it was Faith, her two kids, their puppy, and I. We were an instant family.

I have to admit it was scary.

We were all laughing and living in the moment that was that afternoon. Our group walked through Forest Hills, Queens, to an ice cream parlor with an outdoor seating area.

Faith, her sons, and I laughed, talked, and shared stories about our respective childhoods. Of course, I left out the dark parts of my past, but I was sure Faith could pick up on my energy shift as I reflected on my experiences with my parents and sisters.

As we climbed into her truck, remnants of the night Faith and I shared a romantic embrace flooded my mind.

'Did you guys have a good time?'

"Yeah," her youngest son perked up and grinned from ear to ear.

"Mom," her eldest son inched forward in his seat. "Can we all go bowling in two weeks?"

I glanced at Faith for approval and she responded, "Of course, baby."

The kids cheered.

Excitement and trepidation rushed through me once again.

All throughout the day, I was struck by how wonderful of a mother Faith was. She was genuinely beautiful inside and out, which led me to fall even harder for her.

This was really someone who would make a phenomenal life partner.

As we drove closer to the park to pick up my car, I turned to her as the kids were passed out in the backseat of the car.

'Did you have a good time?'

The red light from the traffic light beamed down upon her.

"Yes," she smiled and grasped my hand. "Yes, I did."

Faith and I had a silent, unwritten understanding: we were both running businesses and swamped when it came to our schedules. Maybe that was why whenever we were alone together, the compounding sexual tension from our respective lives flowed freely from us with no questions asked.

As I drove away in my car, I thought to myself that this was insane.

Though I did just have a wonderful afternoon with her family.

How could I not fall in love with her?

As the evening closed in upon my eyelids, I realized I could not stop thinking about her.

Three days later, I found myself staring at the unanswered texts I sent to her.

I was petrified to say these words out loud to Morena, but I knew that she was not going to judge me for my emotions.

'Hey Mo,' I muttered as the two of us sat at the table at the church.

"Yeah, what's up?" Morena glanced up.

'I feel like I have fallen in love with Faith.' A silence clung to my words. 'I think.'

"You think?"

'Yeah,' I sighed deeply. 'I don't know.'

∞ ∞ ∞ ∞ ∞ ∞ ∞ ∞

Something still rooted me firmly in feelings of trepidation.

As the spring was coming to a close, I found myself flopping on the couch late night after late night watching sappy movies.

Tears were streaming from my face without remorse as I shoveled popcorn into my mouth.

It had been a little while since I heard from Faith, but I knew that I truly cared for her. I prayed hard that I would see her during the weekend, though I was petrified that I was not going to see her.

The next morning, I woke up to a text from her.

Finally.

Thank you, God.

She wanted to meet me that night, so I sprung to my feet with sheer excitement brewing in my soul.

Though I was happy, I managed to rain on my own parade in moments. Tears started flowing again: What if she was going to meet me to say that she was scared and couldn't see me anymore?

The worst thoughts were seeping into my mind, but my day was still driven by the thrill that I would, indeed, see her that night.

As we sat down over dinner, she said she needed help writing a confidential, yet important letter.

I wanted her to fall for me. I wanted her to embrace me with the same love I felt for her.

I could only wish.

'I thought you didn't want to see me anymore. You haven't been responding to my texts.'

She laughed.

"Babe," she began. "My phone was damaged and I wasn't getting anything."

Faith flashed her new phone towards me.

I was driving myself insane for no reason.

Our conversation transformed into a discussion about her week. I just let her speak because the sound of her voice was soothing my soul.

Sadly, from the tone of her words, I realized that we were not on the same page. Although it seemed like we were reading from the same book, she was chapters away from our true love story being actualized.

We laughed with intent and enjoyed each other's company regardless.

As we hugged goodbye for the night, I was praying the universe would interfere as it did this morning, for I missed her.

I really, truly missed her soul next to mine.

Instinctively, I drafted a text message that I ended up sending her.

'Hey Faith. I was thinking about something you said tonight. I know you have to figure out things on your own, but I think we should talk more. Maybe the right relationship is a higher version of spirituality that exists in the right friendship. And if that is true, you will know the guy is thinking of you and loves you always, for it is built into the foundation of the friendship. I could be wrong, but the thought crossed my mind and I wanted to share it. I had a great time tonight, as always.'

She responded rather quickly, which caught me off guard.

"Always."

One word. That was all the text said: "Always."

She loved me. I was sure of it.

The energy was there.

∞ ∞ ∞ ∞ ∞ ∞ ∞ ∞

We spoke on the phone the next day and she still maintained the same energy as the night before.

'Hey.'

"Hey," I could feel her wide smile drifting through the phone.

'I think what you are doing for your husband is amazing. What you have endured and what you have done for the love of your kids is beautiful.'

"It is all part of the bigger picture," she said nonchalantly.

The bigger picture, just as Morena said. Whoa. She did see something. 'It's beautiful.'

"You're beautiful," she responded. A silence hung between us.

What came out of my mouth next shocked me for years to come:

'When push comes to shove, although he is driving you nuts, you are still doing what is right by your heart's standards.' I paused for a moment to let my words seep into her soul. 'That's one of the things I truly love about you.'

I could not hide my feelings.

Our early conversations about Osho, our respective inner lights, and our mutual philosophy of seeing the world through a different lens was what attracted me to her at the beginning.

My immaturity and fear held me back from actualizing my true feelings for her, and I originally pushed her away because I was closed off emotionally.

I was confused because she was so right for me, but I was living in the wrong mindset.

Now I see it clearly.

Now the fog has cleared.

Yet when will it stop raining?

When will the sun shine down upon us?

"Scott," her voice broke. "I don't know what to say."

'The way you run your business, how hard you work, and what you value is in complete alignment with me.'

"We do have the same work ethic and it is incredible," her voice shook.

'If I had to share about my past mistakes, I know you would understand.'

"The past does not matter."

'Faith,' I mustered up the courage to profess how much she meant to me. 'We feel right.'

Then I heard a click: she hung up.

I remember last summer was horrible without Faith.

I remember the night before the event and everything that unraveled after that.

I was so excited to explore the possibility of the two of us being a couple. The thought of "us" floated through my mind daily.

From the depths of my soul, I knew I wanted her by my side. It was something about her aura and energy that always pulled me in.

Yet once again, I felt the fear creeping over my shoulder.

My soul felt out of place.

She was so eager to write a letter defending her husband's citizenship within the country. Faith put aside the differences her and her husband had, so that her children could have a father figure in their life.

Though as the hands of time brushed past, I was the one who was playing a larger role in their life. Meanwhile, her husband ran off to be with someone else.

I thought I could be the one.

Why is it that I consistently go the extra mile for someone who would not move an inch to satisfy my soul?

Then again, what do I want?

Am I craving the skin of another to rest against mine, or am I truly listening to what my soul needs?

Why do all of these questions flash before my eyes?

Why?

Why?

Why?

There is this dark, dreary side of me that I genuinely hate. There are parts of me that I deem despicable, yet I hide my insecurities in the shattered crevices of my soul.

How can you have so much love in your heart and soul, yet hate parts of you?

In moments of desperation, with a flood of tears beckoning to rush forth, I called Morena. I did not know what else to do.

To my surprise, she picked up right away.

"Hello sunshine," she chirped.

'Hey,' I knew she could hear my sobbing, but part of me didn't care.

I could be myself with her and she did not judge.

"What's wrong?"

'Nothing, I'm just upset.'

"What happened? Let's flush this out."

Without hesitation, I told her all about what happened with Faith. I was spilling words from my soul that I didn't even know I felt at the time.

There was a certain cathartic wave that came from speaking to Morena.

Morena sat in silence as she listened to me talk for about twenty minutes straight.

'Well?' I shouted once I finished.

"Well what?"

A long pause hung between us, and I was worried she would hang up, too.

'What do you think?'

"Listen," she whispered softly. "Listen to your soul. What does it say?"

'It says,' I sniffled. 'It says to give up.'

"Never give up on someone who sets your soul on fire, you know that."

Fourteen words. That was all it took. Fourteen words.

And somehow, I felt better.

Faith did set my soul on fire, yet I was the one caught up in the flames.

"What did you do to make yourself happy today?"

I didn't know how to respond to her.

'What do you mean?'

"Happiness," she paused. "Do you genuinely know what happiness is?"

I was caught up in an unraveling series of sounds.

'No.'

"What are you worried about when it comes to Faith, Scott? Like, what are you really concerned about?"

I did not hesitate: 'I don't want her going back to her ex. I think I love her.'

"Okay," Morena said. "Love her and trust her enough to allow her to make her own decisions. She needs to learn."

I did not necessarily agree with that, but what was I supposed to say?

'I really do care about Faith.'

"Scott," she started. "At what cost? Isn't your soul worth more than what your mind says is happening?"

I did not understand the question at the time.

"Be patient," Morena said again.

I pulled the phone away from my ear, which abruptly started vibrating. It was Faith.

"Time will tell what she will do," Morena said. My mind was wandering as I fought between hanging up on Morena or rejecting Faith's call.

'Morena, I need to go.'

"See," she paused. "She called back."

How did Morena know? It was almost as if she was standing beside me, yet I felt she was miles away at the time.

I wiped the tears from my eyes and picked up the phone.

'Hello?'

"I'm sorry." Faith's voice shuddered, as if she were embarrassed.

'I am too, I guess.' I did not want to admit I was sorry for thinking she had disappeared again.

"I hung up because I didn't know what to do. I am confused. We are years apart and worlds apart. How do we manage that?"

'I don't know. We just do.'

I was praying she would stay with me. I was praying she would come over and leap into my arms.

"I do love you and I love me too. I love my family."

I didn't know what to say again.

'I know.'

Life constantly changes; everything changes.

How do we embrace change?

There were so many questions on the edge of my lips: Will you ever not be a part of my life? Could I ever love another person as deeply as you? What does my intuition truly say about you?

None of them manifested from my mind to her ears.

I know that I am destined for greatness. I sense it. It rattles around in my brain.

This moment, I thought to myself, will have to change. I know I am going to be in other countries and places. I know that I can walk through fire and clear a path for this universe.

Those were truths I held to be self-evident at the time, though my insecurities were loud.

I know in my heart and soul that I need someone by my side. She has to be passionate, she has to be strong, she has to be loving. She needs to have her own determination and strength. We need to be equals and we need to be balanced.

I want someone classy and beautiful both inside and out.

If she knew the tumultuous difficulties that wrapped around my soul in those moments, I was sure she would have hung up again.

"I love you. I do. I just don't know how to make it work."

'Let's make it work,' I took a deep breath to quell my anxiety. 'Together.'

"Things are better when we are together," Faith started to tear up on the phone, and I could tell that my soul knew her soul's pain in that moment.

Confusion and insecurities may be loud, but there is more to life than the troubles we think we must succumb to.

There is hope, and there is faith.

In those moments, I made a silent promise to her: I was going to love her every minute, every second, and every day of our lives. Angels were protecting us, for if they were not, why would she keep coming back just as we were on the brink of shattering our hourglass?

'Together,' I exhaled and took the leap of faith I knew I could always take. I found the one; she was the one.

"Together," she collected her thoughts and began to air her insecurities freely. Our conversation progressed deep into the night...

And so together became the mutual place where our souls would lie.

CHAPTER 32

For Youth By Youth

~

"Half my life is books, written pages. Live and learn from fools and from sages."

- Aerosmith, American Rock Band, Boston, Massachusetts

The following journal entries catalogue my adventures that took place during 2011. As Windows of Opportunity was growing on a global scale, I could feel my personal relationships evolving to new heights. On some level, I sensed that Faith was getting worried about me travelling across the globe, literally, and chasing my ambitions without remorse.

I missed her while I was away, but I figured that since we had been together for so long, the distance would only bring us closer together when we were in the same physical space.

Bryan was going off to college and for once I was going to be completely by myself in the apartment. Some nights after my work with one of the after-school programs, I would come home, heat up a frozen dinner, and catch up on whatever mindless television show was on.

Then Oprah Winfrey's program flashed before my eyes.

I made a promise to the universe once I saw that television special: she was starting a school in Africa, and I was going to do anything and everything in my power to bring one of the HIV programs from Windows of Opportunity all the way across the globe.

My words stretched all the way from deep within my soul to brand new heights.

I ended up winning a grant from a phenomenal company, which gave me a year's worth of professional marketing and consulting services.

This would be the first grant of many that Windows of Opportunity would receive, which made me truly feel that my Aunt Barbara and the Circle of Angels were overjoyed by my commitment to youth leadership.

The woman who was in charge of the company was inspired by what Windows of Opportunity was doing, and since she was working with the United Nations in Africa, she promised to take me to Nigeria with her for a week to present leadership programs to the youth there.

My dreams of taking Windows of Opportunity across the globe became a devout reality.

WOO became a worldwide endeavour.

∞ ∞ ∞ ∞ ∞ ∞ ∞ ∞

There was no doubt in my mind that I was an emotional wreck over this trip. I hadn't felt that way since I was eight years old and my parents dropped me off at sleep away camp for the first time ever.

I spent the first 48 hours of that camp experience crying.

All these years later, I felt the same apprehension and genuinely feared the unknown.

Will I come back? Will the plane crash? Will I be kidnapped?

These were the stereotypes that my friends and my colleagues innocently and jokingly planted in my mind. Still, they did not know the effect it was having upon my soul.

There was so much to do in New York and here in the United States, and so many people to work with.

Intention upon unattended intention filled my head.

Yet, my mind and my heart were telling me that I had to make the trip.

Something special was going to happen to me and to Windows of Opportunity halfway around the world… I just wasn't sure of what it was at those pivotal first moments of my journey.

Day 1

I am currently 41,000 feet up in the air. I woke up and the satellite map in front of me shows that our plane is over Africa.

I cannot believe I am doing this.

This past month has been rough on me emotionally, and I have been very in tune to the fact that I am stressed.

This month has been building up for many months, but I didn't know how much I was struggling until these past 48 hours. I didn't realize this trip was going to lead to an emotional breakdown, philosophically speaking that is.

Despite my fears of going on this trip, I dug deep down and listened to my faith and pushed through my fears.

I trust Beck and Half-Full, the company that gave us our first grant. The preliminary information she has shared with me about coordinating this leadership program sounds intriguing. Beck told me we are here to work with a company called Nagode and that their story is quite phenomenal, as they have an inspiring vision that is growing while they are trying to break the cultural divides of the country.

I always wanted to go to Africa and conduct leadership and empowerment work, and here is my dream coming true. Now that we are over Africa and I have been on this plane almost 11 hours, I feel a little bit better and less apprehensive.

I miss my friends and family and keep thinking about them non-stop. Maybe this experience will refocus me.

It is 3:41 in the afternoon here, 5 hours ahead of New York, and it is -75 degrees Fahrenheit outside the plane according to this map.

Can it really get that cold? I wonder why that is.

We are getting ready to land soon so I am going to go sit with my thoughts and prepare for this journey.

I hope you will join me.

Day 2

I decided not to tell anyone I am writing a journal on this trip because I wasn't sure if I was going to share my thoughts and opinions with everyone. I am currently sitting in my hotel room at The La Cour, a gated community with 24-hour security.

I feel very safe here but if it was not for Nagode, their obvious hospitality, and assistance already within this short time, I would have been a bit more fearful.

Touching down was an interesting experience and my eyes were already wide open.

Lush grass fields surrounded the runway and the view during my descent consisted of dirt roads intertwining what appeared to be a series of rundown shacks. There seemed to be one main concrete road in the center of everything, but there were mostly dirt roads.

I was taking photos left and right, as I was amazed at what I was seeing. I am in total tourist mode. I guess you can't take the photographer out of me.

A picture tells 1,000 words and it is a totally different world out there.

Out of the corner of my eye I saw a smile. I think Beck was amused at my photo taking, because she could see the impact Nigeria had on me starting to flourish. This is her fourth year coming here.

I wonder if she is used to this or if she has different perspectives from coming here consistently. I will have to process this with her.

Half-Full is so nice too as Beck said that we would have plenty of time to work on discussing Windows of Opportunity, and how we will overcome our challenges and grow as an agency.

That has me very excited.

Going through customs, there was a gentleman at the airport waiting for us that assisted on getting us through quicker. We were escorted through the airport, which I almost wasn't allowed out of because they didn't like the dates on my immunizations.

Our escort talked us through this small blockade and then Patrick, our driver, met us. Patrick is a huge, tall guy and was super nice. As a matter of fact, everyone I came across today has been extra nice.

Security guards at the airport carried very large rifles and there was a mildew smell in the air when I got off the plane. It reminded me of my old basement apartment after a flood. It's funny what smells we associate to other things in our lives.

Getting into Patrick's car was the beginning of the real adventure. Lagos (where we landed), the airport, and the streets were totally crowded and chaotic.

People outside the airport stood in a semicircle waiting for their visitors to come out the door. There seem to be a lack of rules on the road. People are speeding, buses that resemble vans have people hanging out of the windows, motorcycle taxis are zipping by, people are walking while balancing large items on their head, run down homes and stores that are far below poverty standards line the streets, houses on stilts sit in the water, and the culture of the community pervades the hustle and bustle of the people rushing to get from one place to another.

My senses and social work observation skills are on total overload. There are more people here than rush hour at Grand Central Station.

New York City on a busy day pales in comparison to the amount of people all over the streets. I could see why that article I read in Bloomberg News says that there is so much crime here, but with all the protection and special treatment we have I feel totally safe. It doesn't look like anything or anyone can get through Patrick, but I hope we don't have to put that theory to the test.

I am totally immersed in learning about this culture now that I am here. There seems to be a different use of the English language here and certain words stick out to me.

Instead of the phrase "my wife is pregnant," I heard "my wife has a baby in the womb." There are other examples but to me it seemed more civilized with no slang or cursing.

Well, at least I haven't heard any yet.

It is almost 8PM here. It is time for dinner and prepping leadership packets for tomorrow. I will process my emotions later tonight when I get back to my room.

This is a good opportunity for me to get grounded again. I know in my heart I am supposed to be here, but I do miss everyone back home.

∞ ∞ ∞ ∞ ∞ ∞ ∞ ∞

It is now 11PM here, 6PM New York time. We just finished preparing for tomorrow's leadership program but it seems fairly basic tomorrow. This is Beck's and Half-Full's client so I am following her lead as co-facilitator.

The real marathon of workshops and trainings will be Friday through Monday, which I think I will be thankful for.

They say when you are busy that time flies, but I am definitely feeling homesick and excited at the same time.

Is that even possible?

I want to check back in with everyone in New York and see how things are with Morena who is handling Windows of Opportunity in my absence, but my phone seems to be coming in and out of service.

I will wait until it charges.

Thank God Beck had an extra converter here, as the plugs here are different. The power here keeps going out as well. It goes out every so often for a few moments and then comes right back on. The first time it happened I was spooked but then I was told it was a regular thing.

It had something to do with the fact that the country doesn't have the same power output that we have in the United States. We are leaving here at 8AM tomorrow morning (3 AM New York time) so even though I slept on the plane, I think I need to try and sleep again.

The way this trip was planned was perfect because in my mind it feels like we lost a day traveling here and we will gain a day coming back. Either way, it is still a week, but thinking this way makes me feel a little less homesick.

∞ ∞ ∞ ∞ ∞ ∞ ∞ ∞

I cannot sleep. There is so much on my mind – it's processing time for me. Why was I so emotional before I left? I am sitting here in Africa!
It is so surreal. I cannot believe it.
There is pure insanity going on outside these guarded walls.
I feel like I am in a heavily guarded compound, though it is a really nice compound with very good food.
This trip was courtesy of Half-Full and Nagode. To me, that means someone sees Windows of Opportunity as an asset. Someone understands that we are building something that can impact so many around the world.
I know I am good at what I do, but back home things are super challenging in my life.
Maybe that is the point of me being here.
Learning about this culture and this world may put that world into perspective for me. I dreamed and envisioned I would be here in Africa one day and now I am. I am so thankful for that.
I truly believe this was in the cards for me and even though I had to struggle on my journey, the universe has allowed my dreams to come true. Seriously, there is $2.19 in my personal bank account and Windows of Opportunity's available budget is at an all time low.
What do I do?
I fly 7,000 miles away from home and my loved ones to do the work I believe in, to impact others, and to help them to dream. I may be down and out but I will never give up, nor should anyone else.
I am sitting here thinking about how thankful I am to all my friends and family who have been patient with me this past month. One of our clients did not pay us for our services and that put the agency in a real bind. Yet, everyone has been super supportive and patient.
I am a very lucky person and extremely grateful.

I have an amazing team at Windows of Opportunity and I want to be spiritually stronger for them and for myself. My faith this month is being tested and I will not waiver.

This is who I am.

The work that I am doing defines me.

I do not want to be a shadow of my potential; I want to surpass it.

I want to reach all my goals and beyond.

I want to help youth realize and reach their potential.

One day, I want to have a wife and family. I want to build an incredible life that my kids can be proud of and give them a world that is awesome to live in.

I am going to go call the United States now and check in on them, and then I am going to go read my notes again for tomorrow so I am fully prepared and focused.

Day 3

Wow. That is all I have to say.

Day Two has just come to an end. It is now 10:30 pm here (5:30 in New York).

I thought today was going to be an easy day, but it was jam packed and silently emotional. It started when I woke up at 7 am and by the time I got to Beck; it was 8:06 am. I was supposed to meet her at 8 am.

I hate being late, especially on the first day. I should not have stayed up writing last night, but it was so hard to sleep.

I felt really bad.

She didn't say anything but we skipped breakfast so we could make sure we could get to Nagode headquarters on time. We were scheduled to do an opening session with the group, and then meet with whom I think are the owners, Maneesh and Baldeep. (Later on that day I found out that Maneesh was the owner and Baldeep was the CEO).

On the way to the headquarters, we drove through the poorest part of Lagos, a town called Oshoti (pronounced Oh Shoot). Despite the horrible pun within the name of the town, it was a perfect reaction to what I saw.

It is so difficult to describe in words.

The streets were thin in width, with two imaginary lanes heading in opposite directions. The community is poverty-stricken and in complete chaos. People were selling things on the side of the road in what we would probably call a flea market. Cars and motorcycles were beeping at each other continuously as they would try to pass one another. Cars would cut one another off while trying to not hit the scattering pedestrians in the road.

The streets were lined with hut-like structures that had business signs on them like Toyota and Hyundai, but sold random used parts. There were countless motorcycle and car parts to be purchased, as there seemed to be a market for the many broken down vehicles on the side of the road.

The rugged dirt road leading up to Nagode was bumpy. It was just pure culture shock to me driving through these streets.

When we got to Nagode, the company was behind a large gate. It was not a fancy building at all, but I got the sense from the area that it was one of the biggest and nicest buildings to work in. It was completely opposite of some NYC office building built to thrill a person the moment you walk in.

From the second I stepped out of the car everyone was super nice and welcoming. The first question I was asked was how I slept last night. I thought that was nice and I wondered if that was the Nigerians' way of saying good morning.

Nath (short for Nathaniel) and Michael were the first people to greet us. They all seemed so excited to see Beck again. It was obvious that she did some great work with them in the past.

This got me excited to be a part of the leadership work we were about to embark on. We conducted an opening session and met many people from the management team. Afterwards, we met Baldeep and Maneesh in their office.

I was so impressed with them as human beings and I hope I get to know them better.

Their office was not fancy at all. As a matter of fact it reminded me much of the office and rooms we use at the Queens Community Church. I was thoroughly impressed with their set up. There was a sense in the air and in the conversation that as the main management team, they deeply care about developing their team as human beings and helping them move forward in their personal and professional lives.

There are no smoke and mirrors here. It is very authentic; it is all about the journey, the work, and the vision of this company.

Little did I know the real adventure was just about to begin…

∞ ∞ ∞ ∞ ∞ ∞ ∞ ∞

I think I experienced the scariest moment of my life.

We left for Ibadan right after our meeting with Maneesh and Baldeep.

Patrick was our driver again and Nath was in the front seat. They engaged us in wonderful conversations about culture and leadership. The car was flying at 90 mph while weaving in and out of traffic on bumpy roads. Poverty-stricken towns flickered by our eyelids.

Questions and emotions plagued my mind as we discussed why these towns are the way they are, the political climate in Nigeria, and thought-provoking questions such as "If you could have any 5 people at your dinner table, living or deceased, who would it be and why?"

Of course, my answer included my Aunt Barbara, as I wonder what she would think of me traveling in Africa right now. Then we came to a checkpoint and an officer with a rifle made us come to a stop. Most cars were just driving past us.

Patrick rolled down the window and I felt my heart palpitating.

Was this the moment my fears were going to come true?

The officer asked Patrick for ID.

Begrudgingly, Patrick dug through his pockets and ripped something from his wallet. He handed him a card and asked the officer what the problem was in a stern tone.

In my mind, I wondered if it was normal to speak to an officer that way. Still, my heart was slamming through my chest so rapidly, that I could barely process the question.

Then the officer turned his eyes towards me. He shifted his gun towards my face: the barrel was dark and elongated, but I felt that one solitary slip of the finger could have ended this story right then and there.

I would have been halfway around the world cloaked in my own blood.

My fingers were trembling and I almost jumped out of my skin when he spoke.

In a loud nasty tone, his words cut directly through the pain permeating the depths of my chest: "Who is he?" All I could think to myself was, "Why me? Why did he have to point at me?"

Suddenly, I was transported back to Texas.

The days of travelling door to door collecting money from those who were sick transcended to the forefront of my mind, and I figured that my life was about to come full circle. Only this time, the click from the trigger would be the last thing I would ever hear.

The tense feeling shook my core. I thought I was going to die, for my mind instantaneously shifted to the dramatic side of the situation. Patrick replied to the officer something that I couldn't understand (I think he was speaking Nigerian) and the officer said "I need you to pull over to the side of the road and speak to the officer over there."

I could tell Patrick was getting angry as he exclaimed "Why!?" The officer pointed to the other rifle-bearing officer and said, "Just do it!"

I didn't think my heart could beat any harder or faster until I saw what Patrick did next.

He responded to the officer by slamming on the gas pedal. Two officers with rifles tried to step in front of the car and Patrick just drove through them!

As the scent of rubber wrapped around my nostrils, all I could think was "Oh my God, Oh my God, Oh my God!" There were probably some other inappropriate phrases in my mind too, but all I could think was this was a scene out of an action movie.

Beck was nervous too, because she asked Patrick if we were going to get arrested and he said "For what? That was stupid. They aren't coming after us."

Nath kept looking out the back window and he appeared to be right.

They weren't coming after us.

My heart was pounding so hard for a few minutes after the entire scene unfolded, but I did all I could to keep a professional demeanor.

I was most definitely scared.

I learned later on that due to the extreme poverty in the region, people would often dress up as officers, or the officers themselves, would carjack or rob people for their money.

Patrick had the good sense to know this and was protecting us. Thank God.

When I learned that, I realized how lucky we were to have Patrick with us. I would trust my life in this man's hands any day of the week.

I do have to say I was impressed with how calm Patrick and Nath were. It made me think that they are immune to some of the shocking moments we have in the United States, for in their life these are just cultural norms.

I knew what I was experiencing and seeing was so powerful, and who knows if I will see this ever again.

529

I have this feeling I will and that there is a lot of work to be done, but at this moment I just want to observe and learn as much as I can.

I am a little less homesick now and a little more intrigued and eager to learn. When we got to the conference center where the bulk of our trainings would take place, the scenery changed. Once again, we were behind large compound fences with a massive security presence.

Once behind the fence, all I saw were juxtaposed conditions.

It was breathtakingly beautiful, a stark contrast to what was really right up the road.

Our room was also behind an additional locked door, which to my understanding is like having a VIP suite. I have to be honest: I don't think I ever felt this safe in New York. The treatment we are receiving is amazing and I am ever so grateful for it.

Outside this compound and in the villages, I think I would have a different feeling and experience. As a matter of fact, I cannot wait until Sunday because our security entourage is taking us to the marketplace. That should be a phenomenal experience.

Some notable sites today:

A gigantic billboard hanging outside the window had pictures of outhouses on it that said "SHIT IS SERIOUS BUSINESS."

I thought it was the funniest thing I would ever see, but then I realized it was so awesome because the billboard was tied into a recycling campaign that was introduced in Lagos. It is a pretty awesome initiative.

The scenery outside the walls of where we were working was strange to me, but it was a cultural custom in Nigeria. Kids walking barefoot through dirt and rubble, goats and rams walking in the middle of the street, garbage burning in the road, and hundreds of people, including kids, walking up to your car and trying to sell you things were normal.

I guess it is a lot like the people in New York City who walk up to your car and try to wash your window or sell you a water bottle. However, this seemed a lot more intense. I am not even exaggerating. Kids as young as seven and eight were walking the streets alone. I would love to get them in our Spread the Word Leadership program.

The rest of the day was spent preparing for the next 4 days of workshops. We are talking full days, probably 16-hour days by the time it is completed.

This is going to be an exhausting, but a powerful experience. I am looking forward to it. This is when I am at my best. It will be a shift for me not to be running the workshops, but I am looking forward to assisting in their facilitation alongside Beck and supporting the work that Half Full is doing.

I think time is going to fly by from this point on.

∞ ∞ ∞ ∞ ∞ ∞ ∞ ∞

I cannot believe I am actually here. This is Africa. I am 7000 miles away from home. Our life in the states is not bad at all.

I always have been a person of faith, but I now see more than ever that I am exponentially blessed.

The Nigerians are all awesome people, however, the poverty, overpopulation, and what comes along with that way of life is heart wrenching to me.

I don't know how much time I will have to write and reflect from this point on, but if I can I will.

Day 4

It is 7:22 AM and I won't be late today.

It is time to focus and be strong.

It is time that Africa learns about Windows of Opportunity and we start to build ways to inspire Africa. I feel like this is the beginning of something special for Windows.

I don't know exactly what yet, but I know it begins this morning. It is time to do the work we were created to do.

∞ ∞ ∞ ∞ ∞ ∞ ∞ ∞

It is 18 hours later.

I just walked into my room and I am so exhausted, but I want to get these emotions down on paper while they are fresh in my heart and soul.

Today was so powerful.

When we walked downstairs this morning (Beck has the room next door to me), our security, and entourage (I love saying that) were waiting for us.

The hardest part of today for me as a professional was that this is Beck's gig, and I did what I could to help her process activities with the trainees. It was so awesome to watch Half Full in action.

I learned so much from her presentation. We have very similar styles to presenting and we teach the same material, but it was inspirational to get another perspective.

As a side note, corporations should book Half Full to strategize and move their companies forward.

My eyes are closing so I am going to make this quick.

Highlights from today that stick out in my mind: Birds flying vertically straight up out of a tree and diving back into the tree (quite humorous and entertaining to watch), some bug attacking me, our Gecko friend that attended our leadership conference, I conducted an amazing counseling session "Scott Style" with one of the staff members that was pretty cool, two pieces of chicken and a protein bar was all I had time to eat, watching Nigerians and Indians dancing together which I think is a great message of what Nagode is trying to do (one of their goals is to bridge the racial tension between Nigerians and Indians while developing Nigerian leadership), everyone dancing with one another, a Michael Jackson song playing (and realizing it was so cool to see his impact around the world – everyone loved when Michael came on in between some of the other cultural songs), learning about the youth and crime issues plaguing Nigeria, the lack of help, guidance, empowerment and support for their youth, watching 127 hours, and the most major impact of the day has to be me really getting grounded again about who I am, what I stand for, and how I must put that in this world.

I am so grateful for so many of my little blessings.

Every single one of them.

There is a contrast here between church and youth issues: there is so much faith woven throughout this country but they are plagued with these issues.

Not one single issue in my life compares to this.

My emotional breakdown and challenges pale in comparison to this. I will never have a breakdown again. Nagode is inspiring me. The people of Nagode and the work they do is a catalyst to me looking at Windows of Opportunity and asking some questions that we need to answer.

What is the vision of Windows of Opportunity?

What is our mission statement?

Does everyone involved with Windows of Opportunity know our mission statement?

Can they recite it?

Can I recite it?

Do we eat, sleep and breathe our mission?

Do we buy into it or is it just an amalgamation of fancy words?

What are our agency values?

Integrity, Acceptance for all, and what else?

Our mission I know is to create a shift in the way we empower youth through innovative and impacting programs, but what else?

What is our vision? To inspire and empower youth on a local, national, and international level — to be the leaders of today. We are innovative, impacting, interactive, inspiring and inclusive... and now I want to add integrity to that.

We need to improve the culture within Windows of Opportunity and empower our leaders to create more leaders and improve upon who they are.

I realized today that even though I think Windows of Opportunity does great work and has great programs, I have lost focus and vision, and quite possibly for many years.

I have been reflecting all day on who I am and what my values are.

My life changed today and Windows of Opportunity is going to be what it was created to be.

I am coming home reborn and refocused.

There are still 3 more days to go and I am thrilled to be here and excited to get back on that plane to come home and reinforce Windows of Opportunity, while bringing my new perspective to everyone.

True authenticity will be in all we do, build, and impact.

I cannot wait.

Day 5

19 hours of work today, but I am totally energized.

This isn't work for me. This is passion.

I cannot explain the transformation that has taken place in me this week, especially today.

I feel completely opposite of what I have felt all month and what was building inside of me since probably last April.

The highlights for today are simple:

We discussed youth movements and Windows of Opportunity's future in Africa. This is not just a dream or a goal. This is reality.

The owner of Nagode and the CEO have a major vision and I know they want to make it happen. If any company in Africa can do it, I know it is them and I sense their true passion and authenticity in working with us.

They actually offered me a job, asked us to stay on an extra day, and even extended a thank you gift to me to see Tony Robbins, one of my inspirations (and a guest at my dinner table activity earlier in the week).

I had a few conversations with both Maneesh and Baldeep and they are truly inspirational and caring. I completely look up to them and I am so grateful for them taking the time to pass their wisdom to me and share their stories.

I had a prayer done for me and the work I do that was like no prayer I ever heard or felt before. During the prayer the youth I worked with was called my ministry; it was so passionate and so pure. I felt the energy go through me as we spoke.

How can a country be so poor but so purely happy? Everyone here is so grateful to be alive.

I came here for a reason.

I preach faith everywhere I go and those who know me see that. It's on my license plate to my car: KTF 88... Keep the Faith 88. It's in my daily discussion, but somewhere along the way I lost the true meaning of faith along my journey.

Today I found it again; I truly and deeply found it.

If I wasn't so eager to get back and work on our Windows of Opportunity initiatives, I would have stayed, but I am so grateful for everyone in my life back home that I want to see them and tell them personally.

Today's workshops and activities were so much fun. Beck navigated some challenging leadership and empowerment moments. I trust in this process and I am trying to take in the moments because I know some sort of story is being born here.

It is the people, not the poverty, that gets to my heart more and more. It is their authentic love for life. It is completely different from western culture.

I am so incredibly blessed to be here.

I need to get some sleep.

I will be back on a plane in just 46 hours, refreshed and ready for a new start!

Day 6

This will probably be my last opportunity I have to reflect on paper while in Africa.

I have been reflecting daily and constantly.

Today started with a text message from the states that woke me up: I was so thankful to get that text message because I slept past the alarm.

I must be physically and emotionally drained, though I hunger for more knowledge. I guess two 19-hour days of amazing workshops and assisting an amazing company help Nigeria move forward will exhaust you.

It is funny how I can sleep through an alarm, but instantly wake up when I hear my text message beep. It's funny how the mind works.

I had a dream about a church being built and Windows of Opportunity having an office there that had global programs.

It seemed so real.

This morning the workshops at the IITA conference center were amazing. I shared a student from my leadership program's story and how she is now running for Miss Teen New York and representing Nigeria with pride.

The student's journey and Windows of Opportunity got an ovation, and I had a sense of pride for all our youth and the work we do. I enjoyed sharing our stories and having them well received halfway around the world.

So many pictures were taken, contact information was exchanged, and I made so many new friends — all of whom are doing something special for their country.

Then our adventure back to Lagos began.

I have to admit I was nervous we would come across more potential carjackers, but that did not happen at all.

This time Patrick, (our bodyguard, driver, awesome bargaining business tycoon, and most importantly our friend) was escorted by Vivian, who was our 2nd bodyguard and local fashion guru.

Vivian has an amazing story as well, being that she is the only woman in an all male company; this was another gap Nagode has been trying to shift. Anyone could see why: she holds her own, is well spoken and intelligent, and is passionate about developing her leadership skills.

Patrick and Vivian were our tour guides through some of the poorest and poverty-stricken areas I have ever seen with my own two eyes. I questioned Vivian about how young the kids are who come up to the cars, and she explained that based on the poverty the families need them to start selling as early as the age of 7.

Sometimes they go to school and go straight to selling on the streets afterwards. Many families find stuff to sell in front of their homes, so the kids will get things from their parents and bring it straight to the main roads to get the potential customers from ongoing traffic.

Patrick bought bread from a young child who could not have been more than 9 and when the kid received the Nira (Nigerian money) his face lit up. Patrick said something to the kid in Nigerian that made him smile even more.

Seeing that smile had a profound impact on my soul.

I can't explain it totally, but I felt at that moment I would most definitely be back here to do some serious leadership work.

I was told later on that 50% of Nigerians are children with no formal education system. There are also poor teachers, no leadership skill building activities whatsoever, and nothing is being done about it at all. Our education system in America is bad in my opinion and is damaging to youth and their self esteem, but having no education system at all has to be even worse.

There were parts of our ride home that were stifled by traffic jams, but Patrick maneuvered through it in ways that you would never see in the United States.

I felt like I was on a ride in Disney World; it was totally fun when you stopped thinking about how many people were close to your car.

I think he took a different way back to Lagos because I didn't see any checkpoints on either side of the road. I wondered if it was because it was Sunday, which is a very big religious day in Nigeria where many go to church, or if it was because he was protecting us. I'd like to think it was both.

What I did see though were roosters, goats, rams, a man walking down the road completely nude, people urinating on the side of the road, stores made out of wood that looked like little shacks, and a lot of oil trucks.

Apparently there is no middle class in Nigeria, just very rich or very poor people, and most of the wealthy people get their money from the oil business.

It is so hard to take this all in and process it but I took so many pictures.

The drive was long so Beck and I had a lot of time to talk, reflect, and process. This led to a conversation about creating Windows of Opportunity's vision statement and working on our strategies, our action plan, long term and short-term goals, and the time frames needed for all of the above.

We talked about my personal transformation this week that I was not expecting to occur. We talked about how I was going to move forward personally as a leader and empower our staff at Windows of Opportunity.

I do not know the official wording for Windows of Opportunity's vision statement yet but it will look something like "To empower youth leadership on a global scale to impact global change." Of course global includes all of our efforts locally and nationally, which can be developed simultaneously with our overseas efforts.

Several of our programs have international potential for impact and in the world of technology bridging our leadership efforts will be extremely easier than we think. Nagode is already discussing having Windows of Opportunity in Nigeria and other places like Dubai. We already started our connections with the Embu Youth AIDS Advocates in Embu, Kenya, and I have a very clear vision on how to make this all happen. However, I need to have meetings with all my team members and process my thoughts with them.

Of course, I have strengths and weaknesses, as we all do as human beings, so I need to reflect on my weaknesses and fill those gaps.

I feel so confident and stronger than ever. I know this is a new dawn for Windows of Opportunity and I am so excited.

Our next stop was the marketplace. What an amazing, cultural experience.

The bumpiest and dirtiest dirt back roads were taken to this market. Sellers at the market would jump out in front of me "Mister, just come here and see with your eyes. I won't bother you for money, I just want you to see with your eyes."

Everyone in the market place was friendly, just overly anxious to get the sale. It reminded me of when I went to the marketplace in Cancun. It was the same there; just this was a lot poorer. The craftsmanship in some of these booths were phenomenal. The prices were so cheap too!

This is where Patrick became the business tycoon. He talked every single seller down in price. If Patrick didn't like the price (and he never did) he would make us walk away. A few moments later the seller would come running, agreeing to the price, saying "Take It!"

Every single time played out like that.

It was pretty cool to watch but I felt bad as well. I would not have minded paying the original price, as that was cheap as well. If the sellers got too pushy, Vivian handled them and settled them down. I couldn't get over how bumpy the back road to the marketplace was. There were a lot of holes and rocks, which forced Patrick to drive slowly.

Then we went back to our original hotel, La Cour. Now that I have been here a week, I see this as a luxury hotel.

I jumped into the shower immediately and then met Beck to do another video blog. We have been video blogging all week to capture some of the work we were doing. Then we were off to dinner with Baldeep and Maneesh.

We stopped at Maneesh's home for appetizers, and met his wife and kids. They were amazing. His kids, age 8 and 12 I think, are brilliant, friendly, and well spoken. I was so impressed. His son wants to help people for a living so perhaps we will train him at Windows of Opportunity to coordinate programs as he gets older. I could see that happening easily. We had an amazing conversation at dinner (a restaurant in the nice part of Lagos called Fusion) and I learned so much more about Nigeria. The crime is focused around the poverty and the need for money, but generally there is no murder. Cops will pull you over for money; Internet schemes (you know like the ones you get emails for I am lost and need money to get home) bring in $2 billion a year into Nigeria (I don't understand how gullible people are) and the carjackers will let you go as long as you give them money.

It is a turbulent society that needs a lot of services. The feeling at the table was that the answer lies within our youth and in mobilizing and empowering them. Maybe somewhere on those streets and dirt roads there is a 7-year-old kid running up to cars while questioning his destiny, knowing that this cannot be what his life is all about. Maybe he wants more. Maybe he is praying, dreaming of a better tomorrow. Maybe one day he will find Windows of Opportunity and together we will make that dream happen. Maybe one day when that boy finds Windows and joins our leadership training, I will *share with him this blog entry: my story on Windows of Opportunity's first trip to Africa.*

It has been a phenomenal week. I went from that emotional breakdown, to utter rejuvenation, to augmenting my role as a visionary in such a short period of time. I cannot wait to get on that plane tomorrow to my loved ones.

It is just another day now.

Day 7

We left the hotel at 7:30 am to go to Nagode's corporate office to run workshops all day for the staff that missed this weekend.

We have 8 hours to get 41 hours worth of training completed.

Patrick was there waiting as always, and I knew this was the start of a long 2 days.

While driving to the office, I absorbed all the sites I could, never wanting to forget the impact this trip has had on me. For some reason, I actually can see myself coming back here on a regular basis.

When we got to the office, we began to set up Beck's daunting task of cramming all this empowerment into a short period of time. This was not going to be easy at all.

It was here that my weariness began to set in.

We didn't eat much at all today, which is our usual mantra as we are fully engaged in getting our job done.

We said our goodbyes to all the staff and I realized I was going to miss them. Their courage, drive, and determination as human beings and individuals truly inspires me.

Patrick took part in today's trainings and I thought it was amazing to watch him blindfolded in our team building leadership relay race. I thought since he was so good at weaving in and out of traffic that he would find being blindfolded a severe handicap, but he embraced it and performed amazingly.

The team came into the room at the end of the day and gave us more gifts, which was unexpected. They gave us an African statue and pictures that are beautiful. I can't wait to put it up in my apartment to have that daily reminder of strength and courage, along with my entire experience here.

Empowerment, Embracing and Executing were the themes of this leadership weekend, and I experienced all 3 themes on a deep spiritual level.

Then Patrick whisked us away to the airport. We had a scare there as Beck lost her phone while our bags were being searched in customs, but she found it on the floor 15 minutes later. It had fallen and slipped under one of the search tables. We then had to go through three checkpoints before we could board the plane, but during this time I had the opportunity to reflect and discuss more of my leadership skills and vision with Beck.

She helped me flush out some great strategic possibilities for Windows of Opportunity and myself.

It was all very exciting and inspiring. I will always cherish this trip; I know it.

Day 8

The flight home was smooth. I watched Fast Five and then slept most of the way.

Four people got sick on the plane. One of them passed out in the aisle and grabbed onto Beck's arm on the way down and the other was a boy to my left throwing up in a bag.

This is something that I think would have bothered me a week ago, but now I just prayed for them to get better. I don't think anything can get to me anymore.

∞ ∞ ∞ ∞ ∞ ∞ ∞ ∞

Opening my eyes to realizing we were in the United States was such an amazing feeling, but I am apprehensive on how I tell this story so that people can realize and feel the profound impact this week has had on me.

I don't know if my words here, or the pictures on our social media pages, or the video blogs, will capture it.

After we went through two more checkpoints in Atlanta, Georgia and seeing that "Welcome to the United States of America" banner, I was excited to get home and continue restructuring Windows of Opportunity to do the work it is going to do.

∞ ∞ ∞ ∞ ∞ ∞ ∞ ∞

Beck's husband was so nice to drive me home. Seeing New York was a thrill, but also a little upsetting for me. We truly have so much abundance here and we take so much for granted.

There is so much over abundance here, but I guess as Maneesh shared with me, overabundance is okay, but it is what you do with that overabundance that truly matters.

Just like he is doing, he is inspiring a company to shift the perception of a country and inspire all of Africa. This is truly an amazing story. Inspiring Africa through global success is Nagode's vision and it is already coming true, as they have also inspired me to inspire those in the United States.

I called Faith the moment I landed, but she sent me straight to her voicemail.

It was odd: I figured that since I had been away for a week, she would be vying to speak to me.

I had hoped that she would meet me at the airport, but I knew that she was probably busy at work.

Though exhausted, I gave everyone hugs upon my arrival and began to share my experience. I can already tell that this impact on me is going to extend to Windows of Opportunity, my friends, and my family as I give them all of whom I am.

The globe is truly our workplace.

The Day After

I am sitting on a rock wall entrenched in the beautiful serene landscape in Alley Pond Park, Queens, New York.

I come here often for quick walks, to reflect, and to think through challenges in my life. This is something I plan on doing on an ongoing basis to keep my mind and body healthy and focused.

Beck from Half Full just texted me to check in on how my first night was back in New York, and to see how my reflection is going.

"The world seems so different now" is what I told her.

Queens is different.

This park is different.

Maybe it is just my outlook on life that is different.

541

I have a very clear vision for Windows of Opportunity now, more so than ever before. I have an incredible team that is going to expand and join me on this journey, as I will join them on theirs.

Our agency has a staff with incredible passion, with strong core values that include integrity, acceptance, respect, and the drive to make a difference. I want to empower youth on an international level to impact global change.

I have a very clear strategy on how to do this.

The culture, the language, and the philosophy of Windows of Opportunity is evolving and we are ready for the next steps. We have 9 years of incredible accomplishments and successes that I am so very proud of.

There is a lot to do here in New York, in the United States, and around the globe, which does seem small to me now.

I feel so overwhelmingly blessed that I have been given this opportunity to do the work that we do, to open up windows around the globe, to create opportunities for youth, and to shift our planet.

Windows of Opportunity is going to survive much longer than the days of our lives, and I am grateful to be at the helm in the beginning of its birth. It takes a village to raise a child, and with Windows of Opportunity being our child, I thank you all, here in New York and around the globe for being our village.

∞ ∞ ∞ ∞ ∞ ∞ ∞ ∞

I tried calling Faith again, but she did not pick up. She had to know I was home by now, but I sensed that there was a steady indifference in her willingness to see me.

As my mind wandered, Morena's voice jolted me, though it was in such a peaceful manner.

"Hey sunshine, how's it going?" Her smile lit up my soul.

'Morena!' I leapt from the rock wall and embraced her.

"I missed you, too," she embraced me in her arms. "We have work to do."

The two of us walked through the park, and she read my journal as we wandered around. I continued to call Faith and text her, though her responses seemed to be holistically non-existent.

Morena and I walked all the way to a coffee shop nearby and sat watching the news flicker on the screen.

One of the global news networks reported that the place where I was staying just days prior was bombed in a terrorist attack.

Several people lost their lives. Countless individuals were injured.

This had a profound impact on me, which fueled my passion even more.

The blessings surrounding me, and my vision, were clear.

I dropped the coffee cup in a trash can near by and extended my hand:

'Morena,' I spoke sternly. 'It's time to get to work.'

"Let's do this!" She reached for me and I pulled her up.

∞ ∞ ∞ ∞ ∞ ∞ ∞ ∞

I called Faith while Morena and I were shuffling through paperwork at the church, but upon finally speaking to her, she felt cold and distant. I was thousands of miles away from her in Nigeria, yet while my feet were firmly planted on United States' soil, the consummate distance between us was unbearable.

Was this my new stark reality?

Would I have to trade off having Faith for maintaining Windows?

I guess time would tell the rest of the story.

∞ ∞ ∞ ∞ ∞ ∞ ∞ ∞

I returned to work promptly and continued to run my leadership programs.

Last night I spent hours upon hours twisting and turning through the sheets… alone. Loneliness was becoming my partner. We would spend a lot of time together, getting to know each other intimately and without remorse. We were the power couple.

No, I could not do that. I could not forget the luxurious touch of Faith, no matter how much she hurt me and tore at my already tattered soul.

I think pursuing Faith's soul has me confused. Women confuse me on a deeper than ordinary level.

Even on this field trip with the St. John's students, I felt I couldn't focus. The counselor from St. John's is breathtakingly stunning: her long white skirt and precise denim jacket fondly remind me of my high school sweetheart. Both of them are striking in their own respect, both Guyanese, and both remind me of a strong sense of innocence. Still, though she is tempting my heart, I cannot help but revert back to pleasurable thoughts of Faith.

When Faith and I spoke on the phone last night, it sounded like she was in the arms of another man.

In these moments, I could guess where she was.

Maybe she was back with her ex.

Maybe Faith was spending time with her *other* man. Other. As if I was her one and only... no. I couldn't think like that. Faith would realize that she needs me. Faith would realize that she longs for me just as I do for her.

My love for her could have gone beyond the bounds of where she placed our love. Even now, I can distinctly feel her essence flowing through my soul.

She texted me. She asked me for help. Despite the fact that she was probably resting in the arms of another, I had to help. It was a sense of passion, duty, and a responsibility towards her. A sincere soul reaching out to a hopeful soul... a genuine case of wishful thinking... only she was the wish I longed to have come true.

Yet sitting in the abysmal darkness of the movie theatre, I could not help but avert my eyes to the gorgeous counselor once again. The slit in her skirt drew my attention to her figure: her soul was sweet as was her frame.

How could I like both of them at the same time? How could I miss and long for both of them in one fateful swoop?

Maybe I should dismiss the feelings I have for both of them. Maybe I should just give into the relationship I am building with loneliness.

Maybe, just maybe, I need help. Is it possible to like or adore two different people at once? Is it? Is it?

Hello, is anyone out there? Can anyone help me?

Again... no answer from the universe. Only long pauses and bleak silence. Maybe this is the answer.

Maybe in silence, there is a soul connection.

I needed to meditate on all of this again. I needed to allow myself the space to feel. Maybe I needed to feel myself, to feel every last crevice of what lingers in my soul...

But what if what lingers in my soul is just that… faith?

I hoped that if anyone is out there, I hoped that they would see my dilemma. 'Please answer my prayer,' drooped from my mind.

I begged, 'Please?'

Again, there was just silence.

∞ ∞ ∞ ∞ ∞ ∞ ∞ ∞

I turned back over in my bed sheets; the dawn crept over and through the window so effortlessly. In turning over however, I saw the apparition of love gently usher itself into my soul. Despite my spiritual pain and repression, the face staring back at me in the bed was just my own.

Please answer my prayers. Please help me.

Please.

∞ ∞ ∞ ∞ ∞ ∞ ∞ ∞

2012 arrived and began to dwindle just as swiftly as it fluttered into my life.

Faith was wavering.

We were together, and I sensed that there was another man, but it was never truly confirmed. I forged forward with my vision for WOO, while she continued to run her business.

Each time I would speak to her, she would make excuses for why we could not meet or she would merely evade my calls and texts.

Morena assured me that time would tell what would happen, and I chose to accept her words.

However, that did not mean that it hurt any less.

This emotional rollercoaster continued, until Hurricane Sandy reared its ugly head towards Long Island. People were losing everything: their faith, their homes, their hope, their jobs… and I knew Windows of Opportunity had to step in.

A lot of our volunteers traveled to places like Far Rockaway and southern parts of Nassau County to help clean and rebuild the beaches. We helped people believe again, and I felt that my life was starting to represent a beacon of hope.

It was a year filled with pain and many challenges, especially with myself... But when looking back on this year I learned so much about myself, love, dreams, vision, the world we live in, my friends, faith, and the incredible depths of the human spirit.

Within a year's time, it is amazing how much can open your eyes to an unimaginable transformation. There were moments I never dreamed I would have to face.

Out of these challenging moments came the realization of incredible blessings and treasures that have changed my life forever.

Some of the best memories and most teachable experiences of my life were created out of the darkest moments I faced this year. I was in a transition period between trying to love others and love myself equally. To be completely honest, at the time I was still working on how to understand how to love.

True friendship is rare and I am blessed for those who took the time to reach into my world and give me the mending gift of a beautiful connection.

Dreams can experience a wholesome rebirth. It's never too late to step into something or experience what the world has to offer.

I also became present to the fact that I am far from perfect and despite whom I show the world I am, and what I try to do for others, I still have some old demons lurking around. I need to continue working on my self-development, which I think will be a lifetime journey.

Hurricane Sandy, the Sandy Hook shooting and the death of my former student day's prior left a profound mark on my soul.

Our world has its challenges and we are only going to get through it as ONE, working together with our DIFFERENCES and our ANGER put to the side.

Seeing old students and new ones, staff members, and people from all walks of life work together for the benefit of mankind is an example of the blessed hope that we as a world can live in peace... But knowing in the same neighborhood where we were pouring our heart and soul into helping those who lost so much, that only a few blocks away I would have a former student shot and killed brutally, just reminds me that our work has only just begun.

2012 was a year of pain.

It was a year of hope.
It was a year of friendship.
It was a year of love.
We are now in the age of transformation individually and collectively.
We are all a community.
We are all a family.
We are all love.
We are one.

∞ ∞ ∞ ∞ ∞ ∞ ∞ ∞

As the dial tone rang throughout my eardrum, my heartbeat nearly created its own lullaby. Dropping to the floor, knees folded below me, hands resting on the floor, I exasperated some incoherent babble.

I called Faith to see how she was doing, and I accidentally interrupted a date she was on.

She was leaving me. She was cheating on me.

"It's over" were the last words that rang through my ears before she disconnected our call.

'How could she,' were the only audible sounds that could be discerned from my latest fall from grace. You wear a mask long enough, once you take it off; it is hard to gaze at the face of someone who vanished years and years ago. Tears streamed down my face with utter persistence, almost as if in this picturesque movie scene, I was the villain with the dirty little secret and the hero with the epiphany all in one.

Every hero has their tragic flaw, and every villain has their exquisite back-story. For me, I don't know which one this falls into just yet. I am still learning.

The lies she told me were mounting, and I felt trapped between doing what was right and going with the ebb and flow of the tragic reality before me.

Were these lies she told me, or realities that I just could not accept?

Regardless, I stretched my body across the floor and glared into the spinning fan blades overhead. With each rotation, my eyes widened. What if this was my life? Spinning and spinning in circles until the blades either flew off or the electricity was cut.

Either way, the devout horror was that I was stuck spinning and spinning in circles...

But the cage door was about to be thrust wide open.

'Be your own hero,' sashayed from my mouth and permeated the air with great confidence. My voice gained a solid ground, 'You'll always be alone, so just be your own hero.

As New Year's Eve rolled around, I sat in the sanctuary all by myself. No one else, not even Faith, was there.

She made an excuse that she had to take care of things without me.

The wooden pews were doused in the bright, yet somber lights of the sanctuary. Though my love seemed to encompass every decision I attempted to make, Faith still did not seem to want me.

In those painstaking moments as the clock ticked towards a new year, it seemed that no one wanted me.

∞ ∞ ∞ ∞ ∞ ∞ ∞ ∞

2013 was proving to be a challenging year so far.

I found myself wandering Alley Pond Park frozen and in a state of shock.

The park bench at the end of the trail became a subtle recipient of my solitude.

I sat there for some unspecified amount of time, allowing my breath to materialize in front of me as a reminder that if I am still breathing, I am alive.

Inhale beauty; exhale negativity.

Easier said than done. Somehow, "me, myself, and I" became my unsettling mantra. If holding out for a hero was what I had to do, then why do I have to claw and cling to hope?

But clinging has its limits.

Gripping the wooden planks of the park bench reminded me that pain is inevitable.

But suffering is optional.

Yet, if suffering is, indeed, optional, why did its power have a firm grasp around my soul?

Its clutches were intense and unnerving. Have I lost it all? Did I lose everything and was just too blind to notice?

The instance my warm tears surfaced, the cold brushed upon them and pushed them further down my cheeks.

A shiver flew up my spine, almost as a chilling reminder that my solitude did not mean I was completely alone.

No, I am not alone.

I never am.

Morena appeared beside me, almost instinctively. She didn't bother to ask what happened, she just sat beside me and put her hand on my shoulder.

'How could you be so speechless when there was so much left to say?' Were the only words that sprung from my soul as we sat on that bench. Images of Faith danced through my head.

There was no other way to muster up the courage to say that the ghost of Faith's heart follows me effortlessly, almost as a reminder of what could have been.

Questions drifted through my head, as if Faith was standing before me and I could speak freely:

How do you sleep?

When he presses up against you in the depths of a moonlit night, when he intertwines his fingers in yours, when he rests his head on you in the midst of a blinding rainstorm, I wonder if you remember how it felt to feel my essence against yours.

Do his lips taste the same as mine?

Do his hugs fulfill your soul as deeply as mine have?

Do you notice that my presence was a gift to creating your higher self, or are you just naturally accepting of feeling so low?

How do you sleep knowing you shattered my heart?

How do you sleep when you are lying to your soul?

How do you sleep when you realize you made your own bed and it is time to lie in it?

May you never feel the pain you put me through.

May your skin not shrivel when our eyes lock.

May your soul still find peace in pleasing his glass ambitions.

And now when you lay down to sleep, pray to the Lord your soul to keep. And if you rise before you wake, then pray there's no other heart you break.

∞ ∞ ∞ ∞ ∞ ∞ ∞ ∞

Nothing breaks like a heart. As I was laying face up glaring at the ceiling of the sanctuary, I couldn't help but let the pristine tears jet from the edges of my eyes.

How is it possible to feel so alone?

How is it possible to stand idly by and watch your world get ripped out from under you?

I would feel sick, but I don't know if I can feel anymore.

I say I can be my own hero, but what happens when the hero within me is distorted and beyond repair?

Will I make it?

Will I be okay?

Is it possible for me to survive this… or will this be the final blow to compliment the desolation of my existence?

If tears and whimpers are made in front of shallow existences, could they ever be validated? Then again, who needs validation from someone you used to know.

Let me pray, oh Lord, to your infinite divine light. For my faith is falling short and my mind is getting weak. These words I bear in my soul are a burden that I wish to speak.

Yet in this universe, the words seem to fall incredibly short…

I called upon whoever would listen in the sanctuary to usher me from the state of despair I was in:

'I am hoping this prayer gets to you, angels, as I don't know if you are hearing my silent ones. I know you see my tears flowing all morning. Today I am hurting. I am asking you for my one dream to come true. I want this hurt to disappear. It has taken me a long time to figure this out with all our back and forth, and it all made sense to me. She was perfect for me. We were good and it was flowing well. And I know I am perfect for her. Please help her remember that chemistry and energy between us. It still has to be there. It was not supposed to end. Not this way. I thought I had finally figured this out. Please please please hear my prayer and answer it in the affirmative.'

∞ ∞ ∞ ∞ ∞ ∞ ∞ ∞

Faith agreed to meet me for dinner, but all I found when I arrived at the restaurant was a letter from her.

She didn't stay long, as the host in the restaurant said, but Faith left a letter.

As I opened the letter, rose petals spilled from the pages, as if the pages released the truth of an old love story. As I picked them up they did not fall apart, but still feel new and silky, as if this true love has never really died:

Dear Scott,

I know this letter may be hard to understand and confusing at times. I, even at this very moment, am confused myself and don't know if I am doing the right thing, but I am going to try my best to explain my feelings. I hope, no, I know, that you will be able to understand and respect them.

You have asked me a couple of times whom I love more, you or the new guy I was seeing. I was silly to say I didn't know. Of course, I love you more, because I love you more than anything. This was never a choice between you or him for me. This is a choice for myself. Yes. I love him and may be willing to see where things go with him, but I know realistically that things may never go anywhere. Please do not, for one second, think that I am leaving you for him.

There is no easy way to say this, I need to let go of you and I need to take a leap of faith for myself and find out who I am on my own. I need to stop feeling guilty for my actions and start trusting myself. For all I know, I may be making the biggest mistake of my life. I may realize that 50 minutes, 50 days, or 50 years from now if it is true. But I know now that loving someone does not always mean you belong with them. And how will I ever know which path is right for me until I know which path is wrong? I need to take risks and chances and make my own mistakes. Please understand that you have done all of this. You have made your mistakes and have grown from them, and now I need to do the same. You have been in longer committed relationships than I have, and so it's easier for you to feel when something is right and not want to let go.

There are a few things I would like you to know. The main one being that I will always love you no matter what, even if we are never together again.

You were my first real true love. You taught me the true meaning of it, and I will never forget that. I will never forget anything we have been through together, nor do I regret any of it. I would not change anything from the past few years. Also, I would like to keep your ring if you do not mind. I may not always wear it or wear it on my ring finger at least, but I never want to let go of it and the memories that come with it.

The next thing I want you to know is that you have done nothing wrong. You have been the best boyfriend that anyone could ever hope for. Please do not ever think otherwise or let anyone else make you feel that way.

The last few years have been the best of my life. I am who I am today because of you and your love. No one has ever made me feel as beautiful, strong, important, respected and as loved as you have. For that I will never be able to thank you enough.

I am going to miss everything. Especially the little things. The way you grab my hand and kiss it in the car. My birthday cake under the bridge each year. Your massages. I know I may never find someone who loves me as much or as well as you do.

The last thing I need you to know is that you are a beautiful person. In every way. You are one of the rarest souls I have ever met and there will never be another you. Please do not ever give up on your dreams, and I will always support them too. Do not let this pull you back. You are a strong person. I want you to be happy, to have love. I know you say you will wait for me forever, but if someday you need to move on from me, though I am sure you think it is impossible now, please do so. And do so knowing that I will understand and wish you the best of everything this world has to offer. Do not regret anything. Live your life.

The hardest part in all of this is the pain and hurt I know this will cause you and has been causing you. I am so sorry. Please believe that is the last thing I ever wanted to do to you. But it will pass. "Do not cry because it's over, smile because it happened." As much as I am hurting right now, too, I will smile every single time I think of us and all we have been through.

I know that after hearing my feelings and knowing how much I love you, it must be difficult to understand then why I am doing this. I don't fully understand myself, but I know now that it is what I have to do, no matter how hard, whether it be for a little while, or forever. Nicholas Sparks is much more eloquent than I, so I will end this letter letting him explain it.

"You and I were different. We came from different worlds, and yet you were the one who taught me the value of love. You showed me what it was like to care for another, and I am a better person because of it. I don't want you to ever forget that… you are my best friend as well as my lover, and I do not know which side of you I enjoy the most. I treasure each side, just as I have treasured our life together… The reason it hurts so much to separate is because our souls are connected. Maybe they always have been and will be. Maybe we've lived a thousand lives before this one and in each of them we have found each other. And maybe each time, we have been forced apart for the same reasons. That means that this goodbye is both a goodbye for the past ten thousand years and a prelude to what will come… I'm not bitter anymore because I know that what we had was real. And if in some distant place in the future we see each other in our new lives, I'll smile at you with joy and remember how we spent the summer beneath the trees, learning from each other and growing in love. The best love is the kind that awakens the soul and makes us reach for more, that plants a fire in our hearts and brings peace to our minds, and that's what you've given me. I love you. I'll be seeing you."

Faith

∞ ∞ ∞ ∞ ∞ ∞ ∞ ∞

The paper crinkled in my hand to signify the fragility of the situation. My heart had only known pain for so long, and Faith seemed like the right soul for my soul. She seemed to complete me in ways that only we could understand, and I thought I was happy. I thought she was the one.

Little did I know that when I said goodbye before I left for Nigeria, she was gone… long gone.

Our love was breathtaking and soul shaking, yet even if I were to write out our story, where would I begin?

At the time, I did not consider myself to be a writer or an author, yet I wanted so eagerly and desperately to express who we were and what our future would become.

There is a sense of captivity competing with the freedom echoing throughout my soul. A captive secret that has somehow managed to survive the beatings and roadblocks on this open highway we identify as true love.

553

The passion and intensity that burns through my veins and is transforming the man I was growing into is credited to one Ecuadorian lady, who gave us a chance.

She saw something in me, and I hoped that we could have been the ultimate love story, but time needed to lace itself between our cohesive journey.

As I pondered what I thought was the quintessential love story, I found myself traveling through various natural landscapes.

I love going to Oyster Bay on the North Shore of Long Island. The houses are exquisite and it is a sense of country life tucked away in the pocket of the craziest place on Earth: New York.

There is one particular trail nestled in the woods that I love to get lost on. It is close to Mill Neck Manor, an old mansion that now stands as a School for the Deaf. It's been a home to many of my tears in the past, especially during moments when I couldn't get to my real thinking spot at the Brooklyn Promenade.

Whether I was crying on a rock while reading the 6th installment to *The Green Mile* by Stephen King, contemplating my emotional agonies, or watching Faith walk in heels through the brushes and wood bridges and rock paths with grace and ease, it's a place that holds many memories.

One particular memory is one I choose not to focus on often, as I can still smell the smoke that ensnared my clothing.

It is also the same memory that makes writing this book so much more difficult.

I could hear and feel every footstep through the path.

The last time I was there was when Faith and I were frolicking around the woods. I stopped at the love tree with all the initials of couples in the past carved into it. I wondered how many of those couples still existed.

I wondered if Faith and I were going to still exist after that day.

I knew we would in spirit, but I wondered about the reality of our situation.

I wondered if I was going to have my dreams destroyed.

I put the bucket down.

The matches, lighter fluid, and journals stood in the bucket like a potential crime scene was about to be created.

∞ ∞ ∞ ∞ ∞ ∞ ∞ ∞

It bothered me that I was on my hands and knees, in the dirt, wondering if our relationship was going to be forced to seek closure, and I couldn't find the initials we carved last time we were there.

My life was mayhem.

Was I about to burn the truest love story of all time?

After a few moments of wallowing in my pain I trudged on towards an open field where Faith and I said we wanted to make love one day. We fooled around at this open field the last time we were there, and it seemed the perfect spot as any to get rid of the journals.

I knew when Faith and I met, and as our story began to unfurl, I wanted to tell our story. I started a daily journal that told everything from spending quality time together, to whom in her family was questioning our different walks of life, and who was supporting us.

It told our daily activities and went into the details of how this incredible love was forming. It was some great writings and reflection to the pain, confusion, and joy I was feeling all at the same time, but now it was time to burn it.

As I watched my words shrivel up and smoke fill the sky, I swore I would never write again. Faith's words rang over and over in my head… "You can't burn memories that are in your heart and mind forever."

The matches teetered in my hand as the fire roared.

The bucket's reflective surface proved to be the perfect window into my own future: I wanted love, but I refused to let another woman into my life.

I could not live with the pain of another relationship.

No one else could ever have my heart again…

As I walked back to the car and let my head slam against the back of the seat, I turned on the radio and heard "Something to Believe in" by Poison:

"No regrets
In a time I don't remember
In a war he can't forget
He cried forgive me for

555

What I've done there
'Cause I never meant the things I did"
And give me something to believe in
If there's a Lord above
And give me something to believe in
Oh, Lord arise."

Maybe that was just it: I needed something to believe in.

If I were to ever let anyone else back in, they would have to care for and accept my soul…

Or I would quicker choose the crackling fire before me once again.

If only I looked into that fire and genuinely listened to my soul…

If only…

CHAPTER 33

Adiós y vaya con dios

~

"I'm done hatin' myself for feelin', I'm done cryin' myself awake, I've gotta leave and start the healin', But when you move like that, I just want to stay."

- Sam Smith, British singer, songwriter, London, United Kingdom

Shadows danced along the bedroom wall. My mind was far beyond the point of understanding the very essence of the pain Faith bestowed upon me. Being holistically shattered was becoming somewhat of a comforting melody looping over in my skull.

The moon cast its beauty onto the street below. The window gave me a front row seat to its striking habits: each night the moon would strike down upon the sidewalk. Without fail, it was always there. Sure, the clouds would sometimes mask its true intentions, but nothing would stop the moon from glowing.

Nothing.

Not the fact it is alone in the sky. Not the fact that it could only come out at certain times. Not the fact that it was only showing just one side of its adorous existence.

The moon was its own strength. Its own beauty, stamina, and balance of life.

Without darkness, we could not fully appreciate the light.

Or could we? Do we habitually lie to ourselves and argue that darkness is an appropriate balance or foil to the light? Do we trick ourselves into accepting the darkness too much?

Who are we fooling? Who are we trying to fool... ourselves? No, we shouldn't. We can't. We must overcome the negativity festering in our souls, and encourage ourselves to emulate the true light we *know* we possess. We must own our individuality, own our bravery, own the courage to stand and refuse to fall.

We hold innate magic in our souls. In the palm of our hands it sits, just waiting for the right moment where we can release it into the world for others to adhere to it and glow majestically as well.

Moonlight and sunlight have the same power, as do we: we are uniquely beautiful. All in all, we are the sky, the stars, and the ones who will stand.

We can't exist for the sole purpose of neglecting our soul's wishes.

Not Faith, not Gemma, not Olga, not a single being or love (or lack thereof) can mask or obscure what I know I can become.

I feel the fire building and burning within me. I can be more. I can be everything, everyone, and anything I imagine.

Tomorrow is a new day, and tonight is a faint memory with each passing second.

Reality drifting into a dream. Passion is permeating our souls and is manifesting into something more.

I am going to be okay. I am going to find divine love, but for my own soul and my own existence... for my own life's sake.

I am worth it.

I truly am.

∞ ∞ ∞ ∞ ∞ ∞ ∞ ∞

The next morning, I jumped in the car and began my journey to Stony Brook University. It had been so long since Bryan and I had one of our in-person, heart-to-heart, father-son conversations.

I knew I had to see my son.

Everything in my body pulled me towards his innocent presence. Bryan was the source of my pride and innate happiness, and I had to see him right away.

As I drove out towards the eastern part of Long Island, I was ensnared in a sight that dulled my excitement.

The condensation building on the window echoed the devastating scene on the right: tears welled in the eyes of the woman standing on the side of the road, a tan truck flipped on its roof, blood clearly raining from the windows.

Four cars stopped in the abysmal show mounting for a performance on the Cross Island Parkway. Sirens wailing in the far future: the carnage mounting through the onlookers passing their judgment.

The woman dropped to the floor as a group of men surrounded her. She saw the entire massacre unfold before her as she patiently drove to her forgotten destination.

Forever in her mind would be the crimson depiction of a skull slamming against a windshield and ejecting from the flipped vehicle.

All I could think of as I drove past, avoiding eye contact with the preliminary responders, was that hitting a concrete wall was my second chance... while the woman clutching the guard rail heartily gained a second chance at revival, yet could not see it at this very moment.

Clouds obscure our true potential, but when the rain clears and the sun rises once again, will you drown in the puddles or glide through the pain?

I hope you remember me. I hope you call out my name in the darkness one day, and I hope you realize how breathtakingly painful it is to release the dead petals of our roses from their glass case.

It was a tale older than time itself, but beauty fades…

As I continued on my journey out to Stony Brook, I let my mind wander far enough to where I still had control of where I was going, though I was ruminating on the true definition of love.

I loved Olga.

I loved Gemma.

I loved Elyza.

I love Faith.

I love Bryan…

There is an exquisite difference between all of these relationships: they have given me a new perspective. Each person taught or continues to teach me something about myself, and who I can become.

That growth and that extension of my soul are parts of me that are continuing to evolve.

Though some days I struggle to understand the lesson or meaning playing out before me, I am learning. I am still learning.

I am continuously evolving into a brand-new version of myself, and my story is far from over.

Our story was far from over.

∞ ∞ ∞ ∞ ∞ ∞ ∞ ∞

As I pulled up to the diner where Bryan and I were about to meet, I let my head rest on the steering wheel for a moment. My eyes felt heavy, though it was still incredibly early in the day.

There is a line in a famous Aerosmith song "Dream On" that reads *"Half my life is books written pages."*

What if the pages of the journals I kept became a book?

What if my story ever made it past the purview of Faith's mind?

What would it look like if my experiences were unfolded on blank pages for all to see?

Who would read my story?

Who-

My train of thought was interrupted by loud music that swooped into the parking lot. "Don't Go Away Mad (Just Go)" from Motley Crüe, blared through the approaching car's speakers:

"Seasons must change
Separate paths, separate ways
If we blame it on anything
Let's blame it on the rain
I knew it all along
I'd have to write this song
Too young to fall in love
Guess we knew it all along
That's alright, that's okay
We were walkin' through some youth
Smilin' through pain
That's alright, that's okay
Let's turn the page"

The music turned off and I locked eyes with the driver: Bryan. Let's be honest, who else would be blasting Motley Crüe in the middle of Stony Brook?

Here I was thinking that I was about to embark on the ultimate love story with Faith. I had no ideas that I would be starting a new journal or chapter in my life.

Perhaps this was a new journey of self-discovery.

I could not help but catch a peripheral glimpse of my past: the journals I kept from my days with Faith burning in a bucket surrounded by trees.

The last journal I have with any notion of our love in it remains tucked away in my nightstand, which has a final, blank page that sits at the back. I wanted to keep that page blank in the event Faith's heart had found its way back.

Most of our story lays drenched in the evaporating tears of my memory now, for the rest of our words doused in love and passion dwindled to an insurmountable heap of ash.

The wind blowing through the trees reminds me that life goes on and moves quickly by. I never thought that our love story would have a final chapter and in my heart it still doesn't. Even as she moved on, I thought we were embarking on the ultimate love story. We overcame almost every challenge we faced in the name of our love for one another. I guess I am moving forward though I truly believe that this love is so real and so strong, I haven't seen the last page yet. I don't know what tomorrow will bring or even today. I am questioning so much about truth and spirituality.

Yet through it all, as I question love and my soul's place in this world, I can't help but glare in awe at my son's growth and prosperity.

We embraced the moment we respectively exited our cars.

In my eyes, Bryan was the true definition of unconditional love and growth, and always would be.

The two of us made our way into the diner and he began to excitedly express everything he was going through.

Sitting across from me, I couldn't help but watch his eyes glow as he told me stories about how he was doing at Stony Brook University, his hopes, and his ambitions.

My mind still wandered over to Faith's merciless and sensual memory. We were exploring this realm of love and now I wonder if it was all a farce.

I now question if all I did for her, as "perfect" as a boyfriend that I tried to be, actually hurt her, not giving her an identity of her own, though I thought I did. I wasn't controlling. I was just trying to be loving, but I held on tight.

Now she has broken away.

I cannot say I blame her, but I hoped one day we could rebuild.

Do I need to loosen the grips of love?

Did I not celebrate her path?

The daily moments of love must have been suffocating to her. Had I known loving someone so deeply would have hurt them so much, I would have held back. It was not communicated to me, and I did not see what was going on. Though when faced with the beautiful soul of Faith as a potential life partner, I was overfilled with a feeling of gratitude and blessings.

She loved me like no other at the time, which honestly now makes me question if I understand love or what I deserve at all.

She says I taught her how to love, when in actuality it was she that taught me how to love.

Faith opened a world of spirituality to me. Was that fake?

I may have had my experiences, trials, and tribulations, which led me to Faith, but I never knew love until I learned it with her.

The last time I really thought love was "real" was Olga, though that was blinded with drugs and alcohol. Gemma and Elyza were what I needed at the time, but not laced with the feelings of "true" love, rather it was a matter of survival and fun.

A waitress walked over to our table and began to take our order. I almost found myself so deep in thought, that I nearly forgot I desperately wanted breakfast.

"Bryan," the waitress chirped, "you didn't tell me you had a brother!"

I grinned and watched Bryan's eyes roll into the recess of his mind.

'I'm his *younger* brother,' I responded. The waitress laughed and rested her hand against the table.

"What can I get you, hun?" She winked at me.

Bryan interjected, "I'll have scrambled eggs and a buttermilk waffle, please."

'Can I have two eggs over easy, with a touch of salt and pepper, a side of turkey bacon, and some lightly charred toast?'

The waitress winked at us and walked away.

Bryan rolled his eyes and laughed: "Seriously, dad?"

I grinned.

"I mean," he started. "You do look young, but–"

'Bryan,' I sipped my water. 'It's all about your mindset.'

"Uh-huh," Bryan laughed.

'As long as I think I am young, then I am young.'

The waitress came back and had a conversation with us. Bryan frequented that diner almost weekly and made plenty of friends there.

It was a heartwarming feeling: here he was, out in the world, connecting with people and finding his own way through life.

I was consistently proud of the man he was becoming.

As for me, I had become rather proficient at hiding my pain and just trying to move forward.

I was trying to build something, but without the right partner, I figured, why should I try to force anything?

I just pretended to be okay.

Maybe there is someone out there who matches my vision, or maybe not, but at the time my soul was so fragile that I was not certain who I was without Faith.

I was sure I had to move on and move forward, but Faith was the closest thing to true love that I had ever known.

It seemed that every relationship was teaching me something about my journey... I just wondered if I would ever reach a destination.

As Bryan and I continued catching up, we reminisced about childhood memories and spoke about how I would be going to Haiti with Windows of Opportunity next week. Fortunately, Bryan did not really remember our days in Texas, and I preferred to keep it that way.

Overhead, Billy Joel's song "Movin' Out" cut through our conversation:

> *"Anthony works in the grocery store*
> *Savin' his pennies for someday*
> *Mama Leone left a note on the door*
> *She said, Sonny, move out to the country*
> *Workin' too hard can give you*
> *A heart attack (ack-ack-ack)*
> *You oughta know by now (oughta know by now)*
> *Who needs a house out in Hackensack?*
> *Is that what you get with your money*
> *It seems such a waste of time*
> *If that's what it's all about*
> *Mama if that's movin' up*
> *Then I'm movin' out."*

It was wonderful to watch him transform into my little boy for a few moments. The music moved him in a way that I always hoped would impact him. He seemed to have the same appreciation for music as I consistently tried to instill in him.

If nothing else was clear in my life, at least it was somewhat obvious that my son turned out to be a phenomenal human being.

At the end of the day, isn't that all that matters?

As long as we raise our children to be global citizens who appreciate and are cognizant of the impact they have on this world, then is anything else really that much more important?

∞ ∞ ∞ ∞ ∞ ∞ ∞ ∞

The following week I was sitting at my kitchen table, watching about eight inches of snow drifting outside my window. Twenty-four hours from that point I would finally be landing in Haiti on behalf of Windows of Opportunity's Project Evolve adventure.

As the snow continued to fall, I felt Bryan's presence on the forefront of my mind. I was especially thankful for all of the times the two of us played in the snow or basked in Bryan's childlike innocence.

It is amazing to see how much changed over the years.

While sitting and admiring the condensation building on the window, I started the journals that would catalogue my trip to Haiti:

Day 1

The last 6 months have been surreal and I have learned so much about leadership. I have learned about the true character of other people, the love that people will bestow onto you if they truly believe in you, and the difficulty behind multitasking and balancing it all.

My heart had to learn about love the hard way, but if I had to go back in time and was given the chance to change anything about my journey, I know that I would not do anything differently.

Tears, laughter, fights, inspiration, long hours, running non-stop, ruffling feathers, losing contracts, intense emotions from the unexpected, adjusting schedules, disappointments, balancing programs, financial and fundraising struggles... the list goes on.

It was tough, and there were many days that I wondered to myself, is it all worth it?

The answer is in the details. When I see the first kid smile, when the final coat of paint rests on the door of a spiritual institution, when we shake hands with important dignitaries, when we take the success and empowerment we

have here at Windows of Opportunity in New York and spread its message...
the answer is a resounding yes!

I never know what these trips are going to bring and I cannot describe
how my soul works, but I never gave up on moving forward.

Something is pulling me forth.

Something within my soul is pulling me towards Haiti.

I don't know if it is going to be one kid, a single moment, a program, a
church, or something at a school, but I know my soul is saying you must go,
for my life is going to change.

It has to.

So much has happened in the past year, both personally and professionally,
and every moment, good and bad, has been a true blessing.

24 hours to go and my cell phone is blowing up with well wishes from
people and I thank each of you from the bottom of my heart.

Your support means more to me than you can imagine. At the moment
I am writing this I am speaking to Queen Rose, aka Roswitha, who I did a
music video with a few years back called "Building Bridges." The video was
about bridging the cultural gaps between races and cultures, and promoting
love and innate values.

We are all one, and it is something I believe in deeply. As for my direct
team that is physically joining me, nobody knows each of your individual
struggles and stories that were lived through in order to get here.

I thank you for overcoming, balancing, and joining me for this chapter
of my journey.

I feel blessed to be part of this chapter of your journey as well. For those
of you who could not make it and have my back, you are there with me in
spirit in every moment and every experience, which I will surely bring back
and share with you.

Now, I have to go play Tetris with my luggage and the gifts we are bringing
to the youth there, and then bundle up and go shovel this snow.

Day 2

Exhausted and sore, I cannot find the energy or words to write the myriad
of emotions I felt as we touched down in Haiti.

On only one-hour sleep, and after hours of shoveling what felt like a few feet of snow, I am in 90-degree weather, and it is hot and humid.

From watching our plane being delayed in New York due to the weather, to spending four hours on the plane writing and choreographing tonight's event, to tearing off the layers of clothes I had on in Haiti, all I could think of was throwing myself into staying in the moment, and catching what I can muster up in thoughts, so that I may share it with the world.

There is so much to write and say about Haiti already and the trip has hardly started. For starters, from just my perception I can already tell that there are so many untrue stereotypes.

I'm not sure where the fear of coming here stems from, as I have already met so many wonderful people with big hearts. It leaves me to ponder what is our perception of a developing country, of an area that had a traumatic situation, and what is society's definition of poverty.

It is surely a different way of life here.

People here seem to want to meet us, and welcome us as if we are all one big family. So many people on the plane were there to come and help in Haiti. It was a plane full of higher consciousness-driven and dedicated people.

The Haitian people seem so very grateful to receive us. Today was an intense and long day, though it was spiritually fulfilling. My exhaustion is making it hard to process and write, so I am sure my writing will get better as the week goes on, but let me see if I can get some thoughts out now as I force my eyes to stay open.

This morning did not begin well. We were running late as usual and on almost no sleep, I chose to park in long term parking at JFK Airport. If you have ever been there before, locating it can be difficult, and I found myself at a more expensive lot than I originally found online.

As my frustration grew, mostly from exhaustion, I decided to ask someone at the tollbooth for help, but as I stepped out of my car, I slipped on the ice, pulled my back, and I was in pain! I couldn't stop though, so I had to keep the pain inside and move forward. I thought to myself that I must try to stay positive, but to tell you the truth it was difficult at that moment. When we finally got to the check in and we were speaking to the agent, we heard Dafna, our film director, shouting across the airport "don't check in! don't check in yet!" I truly thought something was wrong, and it turned out she needed to check her shampoo and conditioner into our bags because she could not get them in through customs.

I laughed at this and couldn't help but tease her about where we were going and how she "needed her special shampoo." I am glad Dafna is a good sport and she joked with us all.

The morning only became more comical.

We boarded and found out the plane was slightly delayed. Since we were waiting there, other planes landed, leading people to board the plane who almost missed this flight. As more people boarded, the flight attendant announced, "Let's hope this is it." Maybe this is the wise ass in me, but I think that is one of the top ten things a flight attendant should NOT say overhead on a plane about to take off.

The flight was weird because everyone basically chose their own seats and were changing their seats up until the moment we took off. There were many college kids on board going to Haiti to do mission work, so it was almost like a laid-back free-for-all. I never witnessed a flight like that and it was kind of cool. All we were missing was a DJ and some alcohol, and I may have thought we were at a frat party. The truth is what I overheard from the conversations around me was passionate youth wanting to go make a difference. I felt as if I was in the right place and Windows of Opportunity is here for a reason.

Once we got to Port Au Prince, the capital of Haiti, and I heard the captain announce that it was 90 degrees, a sense of exhilaration washed over me. I think that was the first moment in the past 6 months that it hit me: I was in the Caribbean. We walked off the plane into immigration with a Creole band set up playing music to welcome us. That was strange because I felt for a moment we were walking into a vacation. I wanted to tip them but I realized I didn't get to an ATM back in the states because I was spending so much time shoveling and rushing around. Mistake number one: I came to a developing country without money on me. What was I thinking?

After we got through customs, my eyes were taking in all of the exquisite scenery. Dafna had already been schmoozing with people on the plane and we had the camera rolling and interviewing people in the airport for our documentary. We were interviewing a musical group from Connecticut that was made up of teenagers who visit orphanages in Haiti and play music for them. The one teen boy said it was his eighth trip to Haiti. He went on to explain about stereotypes and I knew we had the trailer already shot for our *movie and we weren't even out of the airport! What he said was powerful and I looked at these kids and thought to myself: "This is leadership. If they keep coming back, there must be a reason. What is everyone afraid of?"*

I was excited to see if I would get the answers to these questions.

A few moments later, Patricia Brintle, the Founder of From Here to Haiti, was in Digicel to pick up a local cell phone for her trip. As she was doing that Dafna, Kishner, and myself were standing in the taxi area. We found ourselves in a friendly conversation with a Haitian man who was trying to teach us French.

We were laughing, sharing, and trying to communicate, and I felt such a humble sense of him wanting to welcome us to his country.

I immediately laughed as I tried to envision someone in JFK International trying to teach someone English at the airport. Would that ever happen in a friendly manner? Never… and that is almost sad to me. Maybe we should all be this friendly and welcoming wherever we go.

The rest of the afternoon and evening were an utter whirlwind of challenges and emotions that almost left me feeling quite the opposite of excitement. I felt a roller coaster of emotions coming on, and on some level, I guess that is what it means to be in the moment. I wondered "what am I doing here," but in the same breath today has been a tremendous learning experience already. I am in for a lot this week, and I can already feel my life is going to be impacted deeply.

I don't know what is happening, but I feel something big is going to happen. When I went to Nigeria, I knew what my goal was for Windows of Opportunity. This is different though. This trip, when it comes to the direction and possibilities that Windows of Opportunity is heading in, almost doesn't fit into the puzzle neatly. Yet, I am here, so I know there is a reason.

I am just going to walk the path and see where it takes me.

We met up with Dr. Leveque, the VP of From Here to Haiti, and we all piled tightly into a car and sped around the streets of the capitol, visiting, and meeting people important to our trip.

Yes, we saw poverty and earthquake damage, but not how I envisioned what we were going to see. I cannot exactly explain it, but it was like the poverty and earthquake was a silent backdrop to a much bigger story here.

We went to a hardware store where we purchased supplies for the projects we fundraised for. It was cool to see first hand who was supported by our fundraising efforts.

We stopped at the church where we were supposed to do an event and then went back to the hotel and out for dinner. As dinner came, we were contacted that the show was going to start earlier than we expected and that we were going on first. This added some unforeseen stress to our evening, as we took our food to go (this was bad because I had not eaten all day already) and ran back to the hotel to get the clothes for the fashion show we were having, and then jumped into a cab… I am sure one day soon we will laugh at what happened next, but our cab driver got lost, and we ended up at the show… but two hours late.

There was so much confusion and traffic, and it surely impacted the flow of the show and the stress of the evening, but all in all, it was a tremendous learning experience. At the moment it was not fun, but I could tell by looking at the team, with each stressful moment that went by, we were professionals and were going to deal with whatever came our way. We got to see much of the congested city in our overcrowded lost cab; we witnessed the poverty and an influx of cultural differences.

It's hard to process it all in this exhausted mindset, but there was so much coming at me constantly. I am still processing what happened tonight but it was definitely a deep learning experience. I am proud of what my team attempted to do and how they met the unanticipated challenges along the way. My favorite part of the evening was surely after I got off stage and a 7 year old Haitian boy approached me and told me he thought I was great. I asked him if he wanted to be a model one day and he said that he did.

I told him not to give up on his dreams and we took a picture together. If you impact only one life it is enough, and I have a feeling we are going to impact many more. I have a great team here and we are going to have fun. The filming has begun already and everywhere we turn, I feel like we are on a film set. We went back to the inside of the church and interviewed the priest. That was quite an experience, and I realized this is going to be my first film with subtitles.

When we finally got back to the hotel very late tonight, we ate our cold food that we took to go hours beforehand, debriefed the evening, and spoke about what was to come next. We vented professionally and discussed the impact we were feeling already. It was a rocky start to this trip, but a good start.

I cannot keep my eyes open any longer. I am finally going to sleep. I will reflect more tomorrow.

Oh yeah, and Happy Valentine's Day… Good night.

Day 3

As I lay here at 8:26 pm it feels like 2 am, and quite honestly it is going to be difficult to find the words to describe today, as well as the personal and professional impact this trip to Haiti is having on my soul.

I think I'm having a much deeper reaction.

Not a negative or a positive one, but different from the normal. Maybe I should start with the last thought in mind, and work my way back to some of the beautiful blessings and stories of today.

It was a long travel day full of meeting and shaking hands and having conversations with very important people. After problems with our flight and almost not getting to Jeremie, and a coarse road trip through dirt roads that were extremely bumpy and rough, lined with homes that appeared to be huts at times, I saw not just "poverty" as we would envision it, but I saw a sense of culture and a way of life.

There was a man standing on the side of the road holding two dead chickens and trying to sell them.

The roads at times, especially in the towns that are a little larger, are lined with kids and adults trying to sell products to make a living. A real sense of entrepreneurship is engrained in a "I'm just trying to survive mentality."

We ended up in CarreFour Sanon at St. Francis Xavier Church. It is pretty much at the top of a mountain and if I could put it in terms of what we can relate to, the entire town is maybe a block long, with the center of the town being the church.

Surrounding the church in the nearby hills are many small hut-like houses and habitats where everyone lives.

As you pull into this "block" the first thing I saw, and added to my deep impact of today's emotions, was the roof half completed that we fundraised for. There were welcome signs to receive us posted all over the place. After meeting the Father and his staff from St. Francis, and a much-needed lunch, and then a much-needed brief nap, I walked over to the church we so feverishly fundraised for.

The roof was almost completed and that is one of the reasons I support From Here to Haiti so much, as they hire local workers to assist in the rebuilding projects, which in turn adds to their sense of the workers' empowerment and accomplishment, since they are a part of this town and this church.

As I walked around the church, and watched people work with pride and love, I felt a presence. It was a sense of "this is what it's all about." It was not euphoria, but finding the right word or phrase is difficult.

Maybe it was a sense of accomplishment.

I sat in the self-made, very uncomfortable, wood pews made of 2x4's without a back slant and I reflected in my mind, in a meditative way, every step of this journey to Haiti.

I thought about my first meeting with Patricia Brintle at Lollipops Diner in Whitestone, NY when she presented the idea. I thought about all the events, the meetings, the planning, the mistakes, the blessings of what this learning experience will do for Windows of Opportunity, who supported me, who didn't quite get what we were doing, the challenges, and how we forged ahead despite. The truth is, as a leader I do not mind being completely visible and willing to communicate openly about this.

I made several mistakes along this journey from the beginning, and I was not pleased with many of the challenges faced along the way. Sitting there, in this church, seeing all these moments as I stared at that roof, being physically there to see the culture of these wonderful people have a place to find hope, love, and family… to see the beauty of that moment, it was truly priceless.

To sense the lessons of the last two days, made all of this worth it.

I thought about the fashion show last night and my conversation with Kishner earlier today as we processed the event together. There were truly two blessings that came out of that show. We were frustrated in the moment with all that was going wrong and the challenges we faced in running a real show, but the first blessing included the fact that despite the challenge, our team came together to attempt something that was near impossible, but we didn't give up. We were going to do what we said we were going to do.

However, the second blessing is even more important. I realized subconsciously that I was stereotyping, thinking that since I was in a developing country that we can put on any show and it will be great.

How wrong could I be? Well, there is some sort of saying in Haiti, and I am sure I will not quote it correctly, but it basically says you cannot give a Haitian a plantain and tell him it's a banana.

What I learned last night is when Haitians put on a show, they put on a show! From building stages and lights and sound, along with 500 people, it was the real deal. As I stare at this roof, I can't help but reflect on how this trip is already having a valuable impact on who I am as a leader.

I made this trip about Windows of Opportunity's journey and the Project Evolve Program. As I sat in that church and processed who I am and my journey in love and faith, I wondered if this trip was the universe, spirits, or God's way to teach me a very deep lesson.

I know leadership development.

I know how to teach it, how to inspire, empower, and make a difference. I know how to create programs and curriculum. I know how to stay in the moment.

I think Haiti is supposed to teach me, inspire me, and bring me back to who I truly am. It is to serve as a reminder of the miracles around us everyday...

Speaking of miracles, I do have to share with everyone the other miracle from today. Just about an hour down the mountain was our first stop at Jeremie. Jeremie is a much bigger town that really simply has a Mardi Gras and Louisiana feel to it. This is always something that stands out to me, even when I was in Nigeria.

The way of life here is so different, and we see "poverty," but they are blasting music, dancing in the streets, living life, and seem to be somewhat happy. In Port Au Prince last night, it seemed like a block party every other street, with BBQs and all.

There was a positive vibe all around.

In Jeremie we had to make several stops for provisions and to meet people. At the first stop we had to stay in the car as Patricia and her husband Joe ran to get the items we needed. There were two kids that came to the windows begging. We had nothing to give as two of our suitcases didn't get on the little puddle jumper from Port Au Prince to Jeremie, due to the plane having too much weight on it.

We were told not to give in to the kids begging because if we did, everyone would rush the car. This one girl, no more than 10 years old, stayed with her hands glued to the windows just staring at us.

It broke my heart.

I was told by Kishner, (our amazing cinematographer, who is quite the visionary and a native of Haiti) that many of these kids, even if they have a home and a place to live, will come to beg because this is all that they know. Giving them something justifies or enables them not to do something perhaps more substantial.

573

It is the perfect example of how they (and all of us really if you think about it) have the power and drive to do something, but if not provided the "window of opportunity" (excuse the pun, I cannot help myself) we will stay stuck in the same feeling helpless routine.

They aren't trained or taught how to believe and dream.

This was another real powerful lesson for me. The girl did not leave the window until we drove away about ten minutes later. I just could not help but ponder what was in her mind, and wished that she could be in my leadership class.

We then met the Mayor of Jeremie, who was quite amazing, and agreed to come to CarreFour Sanon this week so we can interview him for our documentary film.

What mayor does that?

Keep in mind the population of Jeremie is 31,000 so it's a bit larger than some of the villages we are going to.

I couldn't get over that.

He is coming to us?

First off, we could not get to our mayor if we tried, never mind coming to us. He spoke to us about his shirt that he had on. It was Haitian fashion and with pride he stated that he had that shirt for 25 years. Such a different view than what comes in and out of fashion annually in the United States.

We met the mayor in a gated area, which seemed like some government building, and we had onlookers from the above building that gawked in awe. This only heightened my awareness to the importance of the moment we were in. It was the first time that Patricia from From Here to Haiti met him as well, and his time and gratitude was quite humbling.

I am looking forward to interviewing him this week.

Lights just went out. No generator or power. The place runs on some sort of inverter batteries at night. It's pretty dark. It is time to go to sleep.

Day 4

Today was another beautiful day of cultural blessings and filming.

I am currently beyond exhausted, even though we have stayed put in CarreFour Sanon.

I woke up and took a cold shower. As a matter of fact, it is my 2nd day of cold showers. Hot water is a luxury and water supply is limited. Due to the fact that many have to shower, you have to wet your body, shut the water, lather up, and then rinse. It has to be quick, which you actually do not mind because it is cold water and the weather is hot and humid as well.

It is Sunday morning and there was a big mass today where we were to be introduced to the community.

Overnight there was a much-needed rainstorm, which was apparently needed because there is a drought here. So, I ran to the church prior to the mass. My first thought was concern because the roof was not complete yet and how I saw the workers and cleaners yesterday preparing feverishly for this service.

I felt bad that they worked so hard to get the building ready, and the rain must be inside the building and ruining all their plans for the morning.

When I arrived at the church, I saw this older woman who apparently walked up the hill barefoot and her feet were all muddy. She washed her feet clean in a puddle just outside the rear entrance to the church. The surface below her feet was not concrete but more like hardened clay.

There was no frustration on her face. There were no signs of fatigue, but rather there was a joyous appearance that she had made it to church. I then realized that the workers came back in to prepare the building, there was a sense of resilience as there was no doubt that church was going to happen.

I felt as if rain, hurricanes, or earthquakes just didn't matter. Weather shakes you up a bit, but then you move forward.

I later discovered that many of the people at church, which was mostly populated by youth, come from far away. Some have to climb eight or nine hills.

They have three sets of clothes: church clothes, school clothes, and play clothes. The church and school clothes get hung up immediately when they get home. We spent the service filming and I was told that in our honor the youth choir was singing, which does not happen weekly. The name of their choir was "Echo of the Angels," which has a beautiful and spiritual ring to it.

They truly sounded like angels.

One of the youth members was the conductor and it was explained later on that with each service the choir members take turns in who the conductor is so they each get an opportunity to have the leadership empowerment experience.

How powerful is that? I think it is genius and not a bad idea to implement somewhere at Windows of Opportunity.

It goes along with the concept that we are all leaders.

As we were filming, I got a clip of this 2 or 3 year old dancing and once she realized the camera was on her; she froze in fear. It was so adorable. We decided that the message of our documentary film is breaking the stereotype of "poor Haiti" and finding examples of this is not a challenge at all, especially in the smile of a child, or the words of the Father, or the faces staring on in hope.

As a matter of fact if we had come down here with the intent to do a movie on "poor me I suffered from the earthquake" we would have a much more difficult time finding footage. The spirit here is ingrained in everyone I meet. Their gratitude for a t-shirt or a piece of candy is tremendous.

Kishner, who is from Haiti and then came to the US, looked as if he was being transformed back into his childhood as he became elated with hearing old songs and watching the youth perform.

After the service, Kishner and I hung around the church and did what we do best. We connected with the kids. Somehow, we turned our hang out session into a film workshop and we taught the kids how to pose and shoot.

The kids were thrilled to hold the camera. I did not speak their language of Creole but we somehow connected, with many of them holding my hands in a gesture of respect or perhaps admiration. Then came my sunglasses. This was so great.

Apparently, I learned that sunglasses here are considered a luxury item, and all the kids wanted to pose with my sunglasses.

Of course, I obliged and it was so great to see their excitement. I want to go and collect a bunch of sunglasses and send them here with their picture watermarked with the Windows of Opportunity and From Here to Haiti logo.

The ideas in my head for Project Evolve are so overwhelming and I know I have to put the brakes on and rebuild the infrastructure of Windows of Opportunity first and foremost. However, there are some very easy things we can do back home that would have a tremendous life changing experience for the youth here.

Hindsight is 20/20 and the truth is perhaps this should have been the plan from the beginning.

Perhaps the goal should have been for me to come to Haiti, scout the projects, meet people, troubleshoot, get ideas, and then bring it back to the team and the world.

I think that is going to be the Windows of Opportunity and Project Evolve model moving forward. I, and maybe a board member or Project Evolve Directors, will go scope out the area and project first, brainstorm what is needed and who the team should be, and then plan very carefully.

This trip has been amazing and it is only Day 3 and it is pretty much not what I expected.

I've learned so much today.

The youth here took a few minutes to warm up to our presence, but then they would not leave our side. I found here that the grades here are opposite than in the United States. Their grade 12 is our 1st grade and they count backwards. Once they reach the first grade, because their education is more intense, it is considered equivalent to an Associates Degree in the states.

Then they can come study in the United States and some do desire this.

There are colleges in Haiti, but there is an underlying question on the quality of the teachers and their training. The teachers in general are extremely underpaid, but I think there is still satisfaction that they have a job and purpose.

That's my opinion from just some observations, but I could be wrong about that. In the private schools, two of which we are visiting tomorrow, there is a rule to "pay what you can" weekly. The idea behind this is that as parents you have to pay something to send your child to school, but when your child graduates the parents in return have a sense of pride that they paid for, and were instrumental in, getting their child an education.

I love the fact that their tuition is not a set fee and it comes more from a place of love and empowerment.

Does this sound like a "poor" country to you?

It is almost as if we can learn some things about values, love, and our youth from Haiti. It is hard for me to stand here and think about their philosophy and not feel some shame about our education system in the United States.

Their philosophy drives these families, who live deep in the mountains, to work in order to gain pride and love. If you have $10, great. If you have $5, fine. Your kids get educated. There is a flip side to this of course. The love is real and the values are deeply positive and hopeful, but it is a "financially" poor country that is rich in spirit. Where we are now there are no doctors. If one of us was to get injured or sick it may take two hours to get a car up the bumpy roads to us and then down to Jeremie to a hospital that is not well equipped.

I guess that makes me somewhat nervous. Especially since I agreed to help the workers on the roof tomorrow.

I am excited about that. I want to speak to my former student, Dr. Danny Davids and his family for advice and suggestions, because I was told if we did a medical mission here that 500 people from all around would line up prior to sunrise in order to receive assistance. We could do it at the church and stay in the parish here.

Father Samedy, who we interviewed today as well, has been completely gracious and the hospitality is amazing. We are getting a wonderful varied experience in Haitian cuisine: plantains, snapper, sour sod, some awesome banana like drink, and so much more.

There are three sit-down meals a day with all of us and it feels like a sense of community and family when we eat. The truth is I do not have three meals a day back home, and definitely not sitting down for valued conversations, unless it is some kind of meeting or work and counseling related.

This was kind of nice, and reminded me of my early childhood, which is yet another deep feeling of how I take different aspects of my life for granted.

Breakfast and lunch here are very heavy. It is not a shock for pasta to be on the breakfast table. Dinner is very light, but to be honest by the time it comes to dinner I am still full from breakfast and lunch because there is so much food. I am enjoying trying their way of cooking.

We are being well taken care of at St. Francis of Xavier, and I wonder if I could even consider this "roughing it." There are not the amenities we have like hot water, water pressure, and electricity, but it's kind of nice. Patricia at From Here to Haiti said that we are lucky for this and that our next stop will have a much different cultural feel to it, and possibly closer to what we originally thought we would experience. She explained that you never really know what accommodations you are going to get on these trips, but the fact that there is always somebody there to help you out is nice. This is all okay though, as I am prepared for anything and it just doesn't matter.

I am here to learn and I am open for the full experience, no matter how rough it is. The impact so far is amazing to me so I am just trying to be present in the moment.

Tonight at dinner, Dafna did the grace prayer in Hebrew and we ended the meal with a prayer in Creole. I love the fact that we are in a Catholic building and they are respecting other cultures and opening arms to the other nationalities and religions we brought on our trip with us.

There is a beautiful ongoing lesson here in acceptance.

After dinner, out of nowhere, Canaval, a Haiti-wide celebration that I believe marks the beginning of the Lent season, is celebrated in many ways. A marching band came through this "one horse town" dancing and celebrating. I got out on the street and danced with them, which was obviously a very funny sight that is unfortunately on video.

It is one of the things I love about Haiti. It seems to me that people just break into song or dance on cue and out of the blue. You never know when some cultural outburst or celebration is going to happen.

My attempt to dance was an effort to join in this feeling of being free; it was a celebration of life no matter what obstacles lie in your path.

There is something truly beautiful about this piece of their culture. It happened at church after the service was over with the kids. It was in the airport, and now tonight. I cannot help but get this warm feeling inside when it happens.

As this night comes to a close, Kishner and I, who are staying in the "male" room of the rectory, are dumping footage onto the external hard drive we brought with us. We have over 300GB of footage already and it is only day 3. I am exhausted but totally engaged in this miraculous experience, but I would be lying if I did not admit that there is a piece of me that is yearning for a nice cup of tea. I am definitely detoxing the caffeine, as my headache is bad, but that is fine.

A good detox is needed in my system.

We live like kings though.

We should never complain again.

We do not know what we truly have… and I feel like people here do know what they have and more. When you have almost nothing, what is left but our spirits and our souls. Maybe that is where the problem lies. Maybe we just need our spirits and our souls and the "rat race" is not necessary. Maybe if we get back to basics, within ourselves, we will find the celebration that is life. So much less, can be so much more. Interesting thought to lay my head down to.

Good night.

Day 5

I am taking a break from a very extensive and exhausting day.

Finally, there is some tranquility to search my thoughts and process these moments as I am hiding out in the back of the rectory and sitting on these stone steps. Through the palm trees and looking far down the mountain side and out into the crystal blue Caribbean Sea, one may think for a moment that we were on vacation or at a resort, but if we rewind the day, you would surely see that this is far from a luxurious getaway.

Our day has been a fast-paced grueling adventure full of heart-felt moments that we came to Haiti in order to experience. I have not taken a shower yet as the day started full-force at sunrise.

The rooster crows and the town is up and moving. There was another bad storm last night and I am hearing chatter of roads possibly closing. On one hand the sounds of the storm on this mountain are so very peaceful, but it is debilitating to travel. The talk is that there is a chance this can compromise the flow of the trip and we may not get out of here or to our next destination.

It feels odd to me to not have that option and ability to leave when we want.

We awoke this morning to still not getting two of our bags from Tortug Air, which in my opinion is a horrible airline. One of the bags had all our gifts, donations, and t-shirts to give out, so that is a bit frustrating as well. The bags are being held hostage at the Jeremie Airport for luggage tags we do not have because Kishner's brother has them in Port Au Prince. He was going to bring the bags up when he flew over to meet us, however Tortug Air messed up his ticket as well.

Travel here is so difficult and it is truly hard to explain. I completely understand now experiencing it why Patricia was telling us to get our tickets from Tortug Air far in advance.

Once you live through this experience, you do finally get it.

If I ever come here again, I will travel and plan so differently.

You need to have a "go with the flow" type of personality, as well as be able to relinquish any control issues you may have, to absorb and appreciate the challenges here. You have a terrain here that is difficult to drive, and there is one flight per day from the capital to this region and back. The airline was in trouble once with the department of tourism and went almost bankrupt.

Couple all of this with the storm making the roads treacherous, and we have a possible issue on our hands.

Truth be told, the story goes on and on, and gets quite complicated, and honestly this could have all been considered negative energy and destroyed our trip. However, very quickly we are learning that there is a positive spiritual resolve throughout this entire team that overcame the challenges we faced at the beginning of this trip and turned every "negative" into a beautiful blessing and learning experience.

Today, as I self reflect, has had a tremendous influence on my own values, on who I am, as well as how I want to carry myself and Windows of Opportunity from here on out. I do not know how famous people who are in the spotlight do this all the time.

Today I feel like a rock star and Patricia stated for all intents and purposes we are. The day was an instant explosion of what felt like stardom as all the kids in the nearby hills and schools knew who we were.

It is Monday here, and all of a sudden, this quiet small village was swarming with kids. I could not believe how many children came to this small place. There are two schools nearby. One belongs to the Sisters, and one to the actual church. I awoke to so much happening all at once. We had to prep all the film stuff and meet up with the workers at the roof to help finish that project. We rushed over there to discover that this second storm caused so much water damage that the roofers were delaying their arrival until the sun was higher and things could dry up.

We met with the person in charge that I called the foreman. We discussed how we would help, what to do, and we made the brave decision to get up on the roof to assist in finishing it. Since there was a delay in this happening for a few hours, we decided to walk down the hill with our team and meet all the grades in the school.

At first, we stopped at their original school building that was destroyed by a hurricane. It was then that I realized that Haiti is not just about the earthquake that we automatically associate it with, but they are often ravaged with multiple storms. As I looked at the fallen cement and worn out beams, I daydreamed about rebuilding that school with real Internet access and then running our Project Evolve program through Skype.

It is a huge job though that would run us about $60G so I will not go there. It is not feasible, reasonable, and out of our range, but perhaps one day.

Seeing this structure in the ruins that remained left an aching in my heart and a wish to have more financial resources. A school here, a school in Kenya, our leaders in New York, developing leaders in Canada and the UK, which will lead to global conversations and solutions just seems so possible to me.

Anyhow, as I came back to reality, we got to their new improvised school and all the kids in every grade were so well behaved and so responsive to us. They stood when we walked in the classroom and all said hello in unison. It was so great to see "Windows of Opportunity" and the money we raised for the church written on their blackboard. Their classrooms were in these little wide-open huts; with makeshift desks and underneath their feet were nothing but the soil of the forest.

The students there seemed eager to learn and were excited to say in unison 'Windows of Opportunity" and "From Here to Haiti" as they were learning English. It was in this very instant I felt a tear well up in my eye because even though we did Nigeria, this was the moment of realization that I knew in my heart we were truly a global entity. Father Samedy later said to me in Creole "Wherever I go I will not forget Windows of Opportunity."

I felt his words in the depths of my soul.

I felt the harmony of the youth echoing "Windows of Opportunity" fill me up with joy. This is the right direction for our agency. I just know it, and yet I still think there may be some more magic to come. Haiti has been full of surprises.

What could top this?

The time we left the school coincided with recess for the youth. They followed us back up the hill to the rectory and we ended up teaching them how to play 2-hand touch football. The education was mutual as they taught us some Haitian playground games. There were moments I made sure I stopped and looked around, soaking it all in, especially the amazement I had with my team. Dafna was playing catch with the kids, as was I, Kishner was playing some game I think was called "We-Wa" that reminded me of duck duck goose. The kids would all hold onto us. One particular child was amazed by my tattoo, and others would grab our skin and stare at it, or pet it slowly as if they were in amazement with the different tone. None of us felt uncomfortable and none of us denied the youth their curiosity. We communicated not through language, but through the concept of fun and play, which I see now as a universal language across all cultures.

The youth eventually returned back to school from recess, and we headed directly to the church to finish this roof once and for all. The girls worked on churning cement and I climbed a ladder that was handmade from wood. I have to admit I was nervous starting with the climb, as the ladder was splitting and did not look very safe.

Getting up on that roof was very scary. I honestly do not know how I made it up there. Balancing myself was very difficult as you can only walk on the nails hammered into the beams. There is a video of this that I am sure is going to make it into the movie, or at least the bloopers, because it is very funny. This is not a work site that would pass OSHA regulations, but this was not about being official.

This was about hope and blessings. The workers were barefoot. They walked on the roof as if it was nothing, and worked with passion and pride. They wanted to finish today for the Bishop's visit tomorrow. Everyone pitched in and the job got done.

That would have been enough to call it a day, but we are not done yet. Our bags finally arrived from Jeremie airport and in the nick of time, because once the students were released from school they headed straight towards us, wanting to spend more time with us, and excited to extend that recess play.

They found us and even brought us a gift of fruit that had been picked from the trees. We returned the gesture with candy and they were extremely happy! We spent a long time with them and had long talks and we eventually had to disappear into the rectory and try to hide, or they would not leave.

We spoke to them at great lengths, and worked on their English, which they seem eager to participate in. It is nice to see youth enthusiastic about bettering themselves.

As we were forced to "retreat," I wondered if this was the rock star lifestyle… retreating into the safety of a gated community where the people eager for a few moments of your time cannot get in. The youth here were truly great and we spent as much time with them as possible. The rest of the day was consumed with taking pictures, filming, and great conversations.

Now it is time to meditate on Windows of Opportunity and my future.

Day 6

Last night after dinner, we had our usual "reflection" with Joe, Patricia, and the team. These are moments I am beginning to truly look forward to. This conversation in particular was a very detailed and informative discussion on the hierarchy of the Catholic Church, how it functions, as well as its own particular leadership challenges. It was explained quite graciously by Joe and in a way that helped me to truly comprehend the church.

This morning I was very grateful that Joe shared with us in such a way because it created the impact and importance of what was happening around me. Today the Bishop Emeritus visited us, which is a big deal because "technically" he is a step down from The Pope. Theoretically, especially since a recent Cardinal was appointed from Haiti, this man could be eligible to be the next Pope. I mean, it is much more complicated than that, but the point being is this was an extremely important figurehead that made the trip to meet us because of the work we were doing in Haiti. He made his way up the rough roads to bless the completed roof and hold a special mass in our honor. As he arrived, I could feel the excitement in the air shift, and the village became transformed with anticipation.

The church was packed for our celebration and with mostly kids from the local schools. There was singing and dancing at the service in honor of the Bishop and the new building, and the mass was interpreted into English for us. The Father stated that from this point on he was an official member of *Windows of Opportunity* and *From Here to Haiti*.

He praised our work, thanked us, and I will admit I had tears in my eyes.

I was completely overjoyed with the gratitude and could not help but feel the difference we all made deep in my soul. Following the mass, the Bishop granted us an interview and sat with us during lunch. We spoke of leadership and he shared with me some of his experiences, as well as exchanged ideas about programs for *Windows of Opportunity* to do in Haiti. I don't know if I would have fully felt the impact of this particular conversation or moment if it had not been for Joe last night. I speak to so many people about leadership and ideas often, but to be sitting here with this important religious figurehead, and be present to what was actually being said, was beyond sanctifying.

He has the power to make real change and shift systems, and was willing to not only have that conversation with me, but support Windows of Opportunity in moving forward with our vision in Haiti.

It doesn't matter who you are, or how important your position is, but when you get down to it, and people truly understand what Windows of Opportunity's mission is, they get what we are trying to accomplish. I think people realize in all walks of life with all religions, in all countries, with all ages, we need a sense of who we are, the ability to find that, grow from it, and be empowered to put that into our world.

Whether it is with our own personal life, our family, or community service locally and globally, we want our planet to be a better place to live. I think we are all under this misconception that life has to be a certain way because we cannot help it, and it frustrates me the messages we often get from society.

I think innately we know there is more. We need to start building the tools to search for that inner light, whether it is through our curriculums or programs. In speaking to the Bishop, I was taken in by how important and respected he was, but as we shared this conversation, I saw beyond that into his words and heart.

I saw just a man behind the prestigious position that simply wanted to make a difference and provide youth with faith to overcome whatever obstacles were in their way. It was common ground but we were from different walks of life.

Somehow this resonated with me deeply.

I am not Catholic but there is a mutual respect for cultures and spirituality this week. I respect whom I was speaking to and the conversation we were having. We were thinking outside the box, and that is what our world needs.

Our exchange empowered me to want to speak to more leaders around the globe, but one step at a time.

The rest of the day was an exhausting whirlwind of playing games with all the local kids and filming interviews for the documentary, but not without a dark cloud of another hurdle closing in. The remainder of the day was sidelined with some unfortunate and challenging travel news. The travel issues have been ongoing since before this trip even started, and continued when we arrived.

Certain decisions have to be carefully planned out back in the states when coming to Haiti, and even then, things may go wrong, as we found out today. We are basically stuck here for the time being. There is no car, and the flight on Saturday we had booked from Jeremie back to Port Au Prince, for some reason has us on standby.

We did not see that when the tickets were ordered, and part of the reason this happened is because we booked our flights late. With the country wide festival Canaval gearing up, and Tortug Air charging us double for tickets and messing up our flight information, it looks like there is no way we are going to get onto that flight. They are saying we may not get out until Monday, and this may not happen either. As we searched and discussed some possible solutions, there is an opportunity for us to leave Haiti tomorrow, but I am committed to finishing this trip, especially after all the fundraising we went through. Something tells me I must press on despite this stress, as you never know what is around the next bend.

Most of our team have commitments back in the states and cannot afford to risk being stuck here Saturday, so it looks like our staff will diminish the second half of this trip. It appears that it will be down to Patricia, Kishner and myself.

In my mind, I joke that I will feel like the 3rd wheel, as Patricia and Kishner are both from Haiti, but even with the internal joking, I believe this triggers the start of feeling somewhat homesick.

Of course, I must keep this to myself, as this is a professional venture and we have a mission.

In my heart this comes first and I must push my unexpected sadness aside. This trip has been challenging every step of the way, but this team has been phenomenal and is truly trying to go with the flow, despite the fact that they must feel exhausted from having all these obstacles thrown at them.

They are stepping up, absorbing all the beauty and blessings of these challenges. There is a positive resolve in all of us, but this particular challenge today was definitely a tough one not to focus on and let consume us a bit. We really needed a solution, and I felt a little beat up for the team as I could see clearly that Windows of Opportunity did not do the best planning to avoid this. I was sad that this realization was impacting the team. I keep saying this but I truly learned so much from the past six months and to take on global programs, you need a very meticulous, thorough approach.

We were driven and passionate with the best of intentions, but we left some holes in our approach. Thank God we have Patricia and her organization here, or we would be at a total loss.

There is a current battle in my mind as I am excited in wanting to do more in the coming week but as I lay here my focus seems to be pulled towards my negative thoughts.

I am feeling alone and the homesickness builds inside of me. I wonder what Faith is doing right now.

I am thinking about the kids today who only have one meal a day, but our hosts are making sure we have three. I am thinking about how at that one meal, the children only eat a little, and then they put the rest in a bag to take home to their families who have not eaten at all. I am thinking of this teen boy Edan, who does not have shoes, is approximately 14 years old, but shows up to be our assistant on all the film projects. He is so shy but just wants to help out, and feel a sense of belonging with our team. He didn't say this, but I can see it in his body language and efforts.

You do not need to speak the same language to feel somebody's passion and drive to want to make a difference. He has so much leadership potential and I know I will never forget him. I am sitting here thinking about how I can be a much better leader myself: how I get lost sometimes, what it takes to refocus, and what I need to do in order to ground me in my vision.

I am glad I am here in Haiti and I am thankful that the universe has provided me with this beautiful experience to make sure I learn a valuable lesson about personal and professional relationships, as well as some tough introspection about who I am. All these blessings I embrace but as my eyes grow heavy on this hilly mountaintop, I sense the distance between here and home, feel alone, homesick, and a bit somber.

Everyone has dealt with this stress and are in their own space trying to cope, so it is best to keep to myself for the time being. Tomorrow is a huge travel day and will change the emotions of this entire trip.

Let's see what gifts the universe has in store for us tomorrow.

Day 7

If a tree falls in the forest and nobody is around does it make a sound?

If the highest level of achievement in a remote village is becoming a teacher, does a child know how to develop other dreams and passion?

If you are staring out of a hole in a cement wall used as a window, staring into another run down structure that appears empty with some debris, and wondering about your friends and family back home, do they know and sense how home sick you are?

There was a deep sadness in my soul as I awoke this morning for my adventure to a new village and a new chapter was about to begin. I felt fear in my heart and a weeping inside of me, but I was not sure where it was coming from.

I had my suspicions, but the emotions were too consuming to find the right words. There is a sense of disorganization in Haiti when it comes to the roads and travel. There remains this overwhelming uncertainty about whether we are going to get out in time or not, as we originally planned, and I am feeling my control being taken away from me.

Sometimes I come across confident due to the way I plan and hold my vision in the work I do, but this morning it was hard to stand in that realization, and I am forced to trust the universe in what is to come. It is a scary place to be internally, but perhaps this is God's lesson for me today. Dafna left three days early due to commitments back home, and she could not afford to be stuck in Haiti.

I could have left today as well but I am committed to this journey and something deeper than the pain I am feeling now is telling me to stay. This internal conflict is messing with my balanced emotions, but I must give heed to it, and move forward.

Today was mostly a travel day, but it has been some adventure.

Where we are staying in Les Abricots is a stark contrast to the accommodations we had in CarreFour Sanon. I thought that was roughing it, but this is an entirely different level of "roughing it." It reminds me of my childhood days of Boy Scout camping and getting lost in the wilderness.

As we left CarreFour Sanon at 7:45 am this morning, Edan, the boy I wrote about in the last blog who has been helping us, woke up early and came to say goodbye to us, even though school did not start for a while. He was so shy and quiet, yet every time we seemed to need an extra pair of hands, he would pop up out of nowhere.

As we said our goodbyes, I truly felt bad for him. We were from separate languages and separate cultures, but there was a connection here, especially between him and our cinematographer Kishner. I think he looked up to

Kishner because Kishner was born and raised in Haiti, came to the United States, and has now returned to assist us on this film. I was wondering what he was thinking now.

What were his dreams? Did he have any? What did he feel about us leaving? I am definitely going to send him something. He needs a pair of sneakers to play in. I really cannot forget to do this and let New York City swallow me back up when I get home.

As we proceeded down the hill for one-hour to get back to Jeremie, we witnessed swarms of youth coming off the hills and walking what appeared to be miles. Education is a major core value to Haitians. It appears that everyday what we would see as obstacles is normal for these youth, so it is accepted and with no complaints. We have our youth that look for reasons to get out of school, and these youth are walking miles to learn, or will pick up rocks and sticks to assist in rebuilding their school that came down from a storm. It is quite refreshing and a different way of life.

Once we got to the airport, which is a dirt road and a very small two-room building, we dealt with the confusion of whether or not we could get Dafna on this puddle jumper back to the capital.

Remember the Mayor who was supposed to visit us in Carre Four Sanon? Well, he never made it up there, but he surprised us at the airport, which I have no idea how he knew we were going to be there, but we jumped on the opportunity to interview him on the spot. Out came the camera equipment, boom poles, and we jumped to action. The Mayor apologized for not coming up but he had recent back surgery and could not handle the roads. He wanted to honor his commitment and showed up at the airport to speak with us. Again, we know that would never happen in New York City.

I have to admit it was hard to stay in the moment, as being at the airport with the option to leave, but knowing I was staying, created a buildup of difficult emotions inside of me. Dafna has been a great addition to the team and I was sad to see them go. I do not think anybody could see me struggle as I forged ahead to try and stay focused on the work. Once the interview was done, it was time for Dafna to board the plane, along with Joe as well. I made sure my sunglasses were on as I felt my eyes well up in tears.

Half my team was gone and I was missing them.

I missed home.

I stood on the runway and I looked up at the pristine sky, trying to hold back my feelings that were quickly overwhelming me. I felt like that little boy in 2nd grade that freaked out and had a crying anxiety attack because my parents left me at sleep away camp.

As I stared into the sun and watched the puddle jumper disappear into the sky, I said, "Ok God. New chapter. Let's move forward making the best of this - being open to all the beautiful culture and experiences around me. You never know what the universe has in store for you, so let's go find it."

I did everything to hold this back from being obvious. I knew I had to clear my head because I was presenting workshops the next two days in Les Abricots and I will be in my zone, doing what I know I do best. It is great to be working on this film and building the roof, but educating and empowering youth is where my passion comes alive. I need to trust in that. I am concerned about presenting with a cultural and language barrier but that is beside the point. I really need a sharp mind so I can focus and run the best workshop I can.

At that moment, as our shrunken team climbed back in the truck, and as we headed back to Jeremie, I was feeling overcome with loneliness.

The trip just feels different.

It is almost like we had gone back to the states, and returned to Haiti for trip number 2.

My mind is so overwhelmed. Kishner and Patricia are so awesome and are great to travel with, but they have a common bond of being Haitians and knowing the language. That's okay though because they are my friends and I do enjoy the time I am spending with them. It is a new trip with new eyes that I must open up. It is a new journey. I am trying to be positive despite this odd hole in my soul that I feel deeply. Traveling through this dirt road, I stare out the window wondering what is next. It is very hot on this journey and I am very hungry.

The Mayor had invited us back to his home, which that sentence alone is such an amazing honor. Let me relish in that for a moment: "The mayor had invited us back to his home." The hospitality and respect here runs deep. We had to decline because of our schedule. We stopped at the Bishop's home in Jeremie before the very long trip to Les Abricots. There was an extremely large concrete structure that was about 10 stories high with no walls, and when we inquired about it, we learned that it was the foundation for a cathedral that was paused in its building efforts. There were no walls but there were stairs that went up to the bell tower. Of course, the roof of the church was not scary enough, so we decided to trek these flights and film the climb to the top. When we finally reached the top, the fear was so worth it because the view around us was breathtaking and spectacular.

It was called The Cathedral of the Miraculous Medal.

I have no idea what that even means but it sounds like a cool name. Then we got a tour of the local hospital where the Vice President of From Here to Haiti donated some hospital beds. At this point my caffeine withdrawal headache was building and I am pretty sure I was hallucinating about Starbucks. That sounds like such a "spoiled brat" statement. We are spoiled. I need to get back in shape, especially if I ever come back here. I feel you need some strength to handle all the walking and bumpy roads.

We began to head to Les Abricots, which was a rough two-hour drive. I remember saying when I was younger if you blindfold someone and drive into College Point they would know they were there because of all the potholes. Well, let me tell you something. College Point roads are very sophisticated compared to these!

These weren't even roads! They were rocks and bumps carved out through the ups and downs of cliffs and deep into the mountains. We kept stopping along the way to take pictures. Much later on I realized the Father of the next church we were staying at was the one who was our driver. He looked extremely young to be a Father and I am sure we will speak to him about that further. We stopped at a cliff to pay respects to another Father who lost his life falling off of it accidently. Then I learned that within this beautiful greenery there were many fires burning. Kishner was very passionate about taking pictures and videos of this because there are people burning a forest for coal so they can make money, with the cost being that there will be no forest in ten years if this continues. When you see the pictures, this will break your heart, as the scenery around us is extremely beautiful. What is beautiful about Haiti will no longer be beautiful. Finding and meeting Kishner was truly a blessing. We are quickly becoming friends and seeing Haiti through his eyes adds to the experience ten-fold.

At one point we jumped into the back of the pick up truck, through the extremely bumpy road, trying to balance holding on for dear life. We did this in order to get some better photography opportunities. My behind hurts but it was worth the moments we got on film. When we got to Les Abricots I realized their village was slightly bigger than Carre Four Sanon, and could almost be considered a small town. As we drove in I was not sure what to expect, so I continued to observe intently with an open mind. Things here seem more French in culture.

When we got out of the car, people we did not know who kissed us hello on each side of the cheek greeted us. I was taken back by this for a second but then realized it was customary and cultural. The accommodations had a completely opposite feel than Carre Four Sanon and if we thought we were roughing it then, surprise surprise. I feel now Carre Four Sanon was the lap of luxury. Here this home is cement blocks, no air, very hot, and feels like camping. The positive side is our hosts are amazing, and there is water pressure. The water is still cold, but I will take the pressure in this hot weather. Kishner originally told me there was hot water here, but I quickly found out this was not true.

He is totally hilarious.

The toilets here do not flush. You have to fill up a bucket of water and dump it in the toilet when you are finished. The Father had two dogs that I quickly became friendly with. We walked up a hill as soon as we settled in to see the site next to the church's school where we donated our fundraising money to for the completion of their "sanitary block," which is their word for bathroom. They were very behind on construction but that is okay because our team was cut in half. They still plan on finishing the project with the local church members and the workers they hired before we leave. I am sure we will help where we can.

However, as you will tell from the pictures and videos, I will be very impressed if that happens. One should never doubt the human spirit and there is definitely spirit here. What is impressive to me is how far our donations go and it is extremely clear that it is not just for supplies but for the spirit we infuse into the local workers who feel blessed to have this "window of opportunity" and be asked to be on a project that benefits their village. To me, their wages are so low, but to them, they were making a good day's pay and making a difference.

I am still feeling extremely sad and homesick but staring at this beautiful jet-black star filled night I am trying not to be homesick and be open to all possibilities. I had a great heart to heart conversation with Patricia tonight who is a wonderful woman and the Founder and Director of *From Here To Haiti*. She is a good person and has a good soul. Her words put me more at ease, and I am not even sure if she was aware of what I was feeling internally.

Tomorrow is a new day as I currently slide under the mosquito netting around my bed and try to fall asleep to the sound of the Caribbean Sea in the not too far distance.

Day 8

I awoke this morning with some apprehension and anxiety about today's events. I go to sleep tonight a changed man, astounded by what a difference one day can make in someone's life. Today is one of those quintessential days that you will sit back and reflect on, realizing you are not in control, but it all of a sudden makes sense.

It is in that thought and realization alone that fills my existence with validity, confirmation, and purpose.

I awoke to the sound of the sea and the village wide alarm clock, which is a 5 am ringing of "whom the bell tolls" across the town. They, too, believe in hitting the snooze button because about 20 minutes later the bell rings again, leaving me with the thought "What is going on? I didn't expect this!"

With no lights on and no sunrise yet, I began to hear the swarming of people outside getting ready for 6 am mass and the day that awaits them. I believe there is a mass every morning here.

Still feeling slightly homesick, I knew I had to clear my mind for the work ahead of me and for one of the main reasons I came to Haiti: to run our empowerment and leadership workshops. My goal, and the request from the school principal I spoke with yesterday, was to instill hope in youth who live in complete poverty.

She wants me to reach these young minds that have almost nothing, who are thankful if they receive one meal a day, and show them that they can have dreams too. It was up to me to inspire these youth. My job was to show them the world does not begin and end tucked away in this remote mountainside they call Les Abricots. That is a pretty tall order when my realization at the moment was how difficult it was to travel here with the horrible roads, as well as the comprehension and acceptance at this point that we do not even know if we can get out of here.

Of course, the principal was metaphorically speaking, but I couldn't help but think this was going to be a difficult message to express when I was feeling pretty stuck myself. I was scared and needed to clear my head. I was worried about the cultural barriers and I knew deep inside this was a big test for my global vision.

This was the moment I knew would make or break my true Project Evolve vision, and I was starting to feel the pressure build inside of me.

I spent the morning meditating and trying to put my head in the right place. I asked and prayed for light. I asked for a sign. I am so happy when my prayers are answered so strangely, yet in a way that is undeniable.

We had to eat breakfast quickly so we could go to the school Paradis Des Indianes in time. We were told that they had a magnificent ceremony outside the flagpole every morning and we did not want to miss it. We scoffed down breakfast and for a moment I wish I could stay at the table because I literally had the best eggs I ever had. So fresh and moist, I just wanted to eat more, but we did not have time. It was a long bumpy drive to the school that we had to go around the side of the mountain in order to get there, in which I would learn later, was just a short hike up a steep hill, which would have made more sense to take. When we finally arrived at the school, I was not sure where we were going. I kind of just followed Patricia and the Father, knowing they had obviously been here before.

The conversation I had in my head was a struggle about my feelings of being homesick, and who I was as a presenter in Haiti. I was praying for that inner light.

As we walked down the path and made a left-hand turn; I was not sure if we were walking into the school or not. I would soon realize that we were walking into the principal's home. That left-hand turn was the hand of the universe sending me the first of many messages and realizations today... It is a moment I will never forget for the rest of my life and I am not sure words can capture it all...

As I stepped into the house, and glanced across the room and took everything in, I literally laid eyes on paradise. The view that met my eyes was exquisite, unreal, and shook the ground I stood on. What I saw was pure beauty that filled my heart in a way that made all my doubts go away, placed a smile in my heart, and said to me "everything is going to be okay."

We literally walked into nirvana, a stark contrast to the world around us. Leave it to us New Yorkers to search a poverty-stricken country and find the nicest house with the most breathtaking views. We met the interns at the school who were quite gracious and welcoming. I found it interesting that this school was literally in the middle of nowhere, and had interns from other parts of the world who I would discover later keep coming back to this school to work. This tells me something already about the character and allure of where I am, and it leads to me having the feeling that I do not want to leave. From the middle of "nowhere," I felt like I was finally "now here."

Wasn't I homesick just 5 minutes ago? Well, it only gets better.

It was time to do the workshops. I presented to over 80 kids in a classroom that has never done group work. We presented for almost three hours, with Patricia interpreting and joining in on the presentation. It was apparent to me that Patricia was enjoying the workshop, as were the youth.

The interns and teachers were watching as well, and I could see them absorbing our message and challenge to open their souls. I was on point, and doing my thing. It was tough with the language barrier, and it interrupted my normal flow somewhat on how I process with groups, but it still worked. The Principal, Mica, stated that she was very impressed and she was taking notes herself. She said the kids here do not think for themselves and do not have hope. They are always told what to do and think. I thought to myself how this does not sound too far off from the youth in America, and wondered if silencing our youth's potential was a global pandemic. The youth had never seen or experienced anything like Windows of Opportunity, and the principal felt they needed more of this. We only scratched the surface of what we do, and we were immediately invited back.

She has 13 schools spread out across the mountain servicing 3,500 youth, and would like me to present at all the schools. I was asked to go to one school where there are 150 students who have no shoes at all.

I want to do this and go back on a fairly regular basis. Finally, I could feel the universe put this Haiti puzzle piece into perspective. It felt so good to present here and I was in complete alignment with the passion the staff has here. I cannot really put this feeling into words, but in the moment that you experience something, you do not need to speak the same language, you can just be in that moment and know the truth.

Truth transcends words. It can be felt. It is more than powerful.

You know it's a story, the universe's story, and you are one of the characters. You see it unfolding and you feel blessed that you are a part of this moment of your life. That is what I felt today. That is what I felt while presenting. This is what I felt sharing with Mica and her interns and her teachers. This is what I felt while filming. The universe gave me my sign loud and clear, telling me that I must come back here and set up Project Evolve formally, and that I must continue to go global. You never know what is around the next turn on this path we call life. I know my next step is to find business partners that want to sponsor this educational initiative. The only cost will be the travel, about $700 per trip to impact 3,500 youth.

No other expenses.

Who would not want to sponsor that?

Maybe I can create some sort of advertising and office plaque if I can find companies to send me here twice a year. I am just talking randomly here, but if you were in my shoes, and experienced what I did, this would all make sense to you.

The rest of the day we filmed in the hot sun, with the breathtaking scenery backdrop. I think Kishner and I were having the time of our lives shooting this scenery, knowing we were getting an incredible opportunity to be here. We interviewed an intern named Marie from Paris who was also a filmmaker. She has done some great work that she shared with Kishner and myself, and was there studying for her Doctorate in Anthropology. When we shared with her our story of how we may be stuck in Les Abricots, she mentioned two scientists who were studying there that were driving tomorrow halfway to the capital. She suggested we catch a ride with them, and we all of a sudden knew we were saved! Kishner called his brother who would come meet us at the halfway point and get us back to the capital.

We were going to by pass the issue of Jeremie, and go straight to our Delta flight. We had a plan to get home, and the day seemed to just keep filling up with miracles! The principal Mica shared her story on camera next. She was so awe-inspiring. She shared about how she started these schools in the mountain when she discovered these kids had no education at all. She is 77 years old and built 13 schools!

That is beyond phenomenal!

After meeting her there is not a single person at any age that can tell me that something is impossible. She was such a great storyteller that we ended up filming over an hour of her sharing so much! We can do a film on her alone!

It was so hot and humid, we were exhausted, and we were dripping sweat. The thought of New York snow was long forgotten. Despite the extreme weather here, my mood was at an all time high.

It is amazing to me how much 24 hours can make a difference in your life. I felt my passion ignited. There was no power all day, and my cell phone battery had died. At sunset, Kishner and I descended down the hill on foot, and I could not get the day off my mind. I kept running the events of the day over and over again. As we got to the bottom of the hill, the trail let us out on the beach of the Caribbean Sea. It was getting dark, but we knew what we had to do. We stopped and got Patricia, and walked back to the beach.

We knew we deserved 5 minutes of fun to wash down this sweat and we dove into the Caribbean Sea for a 5-minute night swim. It was exhilarating being in this beautiful ocean staring up at the starry sky.

Life all of a sudden seems to make sense. The possibilities and opportunities were endless. The last 6 months were worth today alone.

I feel completely blessed.

Haiti has this allure that is undeniable. The roads are rough and the people are poor but I beg to question, "what is poverty" if you have such a deep sense of inner happiness and will even walk two miles up hills and mountains to get to your school. I wondered which of these youths were walking back the two hours thinking to themself what kind of leaders they could be.

Were they for the first time ever thinking about their own dreams?

As I finally lay my head down from this long day, with the quiet sea echoing throughout my thoughts, I run through the miracles of today yet again. I stand in the power of these moments and realize my fear to be so sure and confident of something. If you asked me yesterday if I would come back to Haiti, I would have said yes, but with some apprehension and better planning.

Today, however, it is not only a resounding yes, but I would love to be back here for April, and to do staff development in October. I would love to help these youth become leaders the right way and empower their souls to bring Project Evolve solutions to their dear Haiti. It is as clear as day now, it is only the beginning for us.

Thank you, universe.

Day 9

I awoke prior to sunrise this morning with an excitement that was two fold. The town bell symbolized it was time to begin our long journey home, but my enthusiasm wanted me to run up the hill to the school that impacted my life so deeply just a day earlier. I wanted a taste of Paradis Des Indianes one more time, as I knew I would be back, but did not know how long it would take.

Talk about confusion.

Wednesday I wanted to be home so bad. Yesterday changed my life and today I have apprehension about leaving here. I feel like a transformation of my soul has taken place.

I knew I had to plunge forward, return to the states in order to do the work I do best, and build our global vision from that vantage point, but for some strange reason, I feel like I am leaving a piece of my altered heart behind.

Patricia at From Here to Haiti is such a dear soul. She stated that when her husband left on Wednesday, she felt her heart break, but now her heart was breaking even more because Kishner and I were leaving as well. Patricia stayed behind to finish business and was confident she would get on the plane in Jeremie. We would reconnect in the capital to take Delta back together. I felt a bit guilty leaving her in Les Abricots, but I knew she was in good hands and safe. She is tremendously admired wherever she goes in Haiti and seems to be in high demand. She is living her passion and doing incredible work. If Windows of Opportunity were not my passion, I would go work for her.

As we drove back to the school at approximately 7 am, I had a knot in my stomach with my conflicted feelings. I confuse myself sometimes with the way I overanalyze everything; some say it is my downfall as a Virgo. I think I am just caught up in the life changing moments the universe gifted me with yesterday.

Either that, or I am just insane.

The truth is when things seem right, I question if they are too good to be true. All the puzzle pieces are laid out in front of me and it is my job to figure out how to put them together. I know I am leaving here with so many answers in my heart but with a puzzle that still needs to be completed.

We spent the morning at Paradis. Kishner went to film the students, and I spent some time with the interns learning more about the multiple schools throughout the mountains. I worked with one class that was not scheduled and saw a moment of bullying as one kid was picking on another kid in line. Well, you know me! All I could see was a teachable empowering moment and how my sticks n' stones curriculum can be implemented here. I also learned they are in need of HIV education. One of the interns Marie was telling me that I must come to the school in the mountains that has 150 kids and how none of them even have shoes to wear. She feels they will really respond to my leadership approach. Another intern Nicholas was showing me how he uses donated computer parts to piece together a workable computer to teach the kids how to spell, speak Creole, and English. He showed me one computer that was pieces of a laptop wired to pieces of a monitor and console. He was quite resourceful and I was very impressed. He stated the Internet was horribly slow there. and difficult to get on. I wish I could bring them high-speed Internet so I could communicate more easily with the school and the students.

Part of me wondered if I would ever see them again, but part of me knows I obviously will. Things like this do not happen by accident and the impact we had must be followed up on. I could not help but think of some of the potential sponsors I reached out to who would not give us support or Haiti support based on their own stereotypes, and wondered if they would have a change of heart seeing what goes on here and the impact we have already had. I hate to sound like a broken record, but we are really onto something big here at Windows of Opportunity. Locally and globally, we are all one and connected.

I truly wish I had the support of some of those who turned their back on me and did not believe in me, and I hope to attract new sponsors and funders who support our vision and work...

"Stay in the moment, Scott," I said to myself and focused on soaking it all in. There was discussion of me returning in April and if funding allows it I will be there, but there is a part of me that knows the revamping of Windows of Opportunity is going to face severe challenges when I return. I am not sure how to fit Haiti into the bigger picture yet, but I know it fits somehow.

However, Windows of Opportunity needs my leadership at the helm and fully engaged, fully focused, and steering the ship with no distractions. If I choose this, there will be sacrifices and no time for much else, and I know this to be extremely true with all my heart. There is a twinge in my soul with that reality, but despite the changes I must accept, I would love to squeeze in a return venture here for a few days. I walked around the school grounds one last time, talked to more kids, and finished up my conversations with the staff. I promise to work on my French before I come back.

As we drove away, I instantly felt the same feeling I felt Wednesday. Homesick. However, this time I knew it was not for the United States.

I fell in love with Haiti.

The rest of the day is hard to explain and my conflicted thoughts consumed me and what I was able to truly take in. The journey back to the capital was treacherous and long. We piled back in a truck with the scientists that we met, and the driver was hallucinating that he was in the Indianapolis 500. Now that may sound great to someone who is in a rush to get out of a country but if you can picture this: the bumpy roads, the twists and turns through the mountains, no guard rails, long drops off the mountain side that look like something out of *The Fast and Furious* before the car explodes... well, then it becomes a bit less exciting. Not to mention, here I am an American who feels completely safe with Kishner, who is from Haiti and speaks the language, but when I look over at him and I hear him muttering under his breath in fear "Oh my God," then I knew I was in trouble.

Later on when we got to Cayes, the halfway point to the capital Port Au Prince, we joked about it. I think it was easier to joke then because we made it and we were alive. What we saw on this road was unreal. We saw bulls running toward the car; roads being blocked off for dynamite blasting, our hair and body full of dust, and tremendous amounts of poverty. We were filming away and taking pictures.

Once we got to Cayes three or four hours later, I wanted to take everyone out to lunch to thank them for their hospitality. I didn't have money on me so we walked into a bank and asked the rifle holding security guard if they had an ATM. He said yes, and pointed to a desk. What is normally a two-minute transaction in the states literally became a loan process. It took us about 30 minutes to withdraw $250 from my account. Paperwork, several signatures later, and standing on the teller line, we finally were given the money. It was something like $11,000 Gourdes, and I guess that was seen as "big money" as I heard someone at one of the establishments refer to a $50 bill. The thoughts on what I take for granted resonated with me on a high-vibrational level. This thought stayed with me on our walk back to the restaurant and throughout lunch. I felt it deeply and was present to the lessons happening within me. My eyes were open and I was soaking it all in.

We switched cars into Kishner's brother's truck and all I can say is thank god for his brother. Such a nice human being that drove the six or seven hours to meet us and take us back to the capital. He was going to get us out of Haiti before Canaval and the universe seems to continue working in our favor. We realized today was Kishner's birthday too, and I made sure we all wished him a happy birthday. I am sure it was not how he wanted to spend it, but then again, he loved the drive through all the towns and his country. I could tell he was reminiscing about his childhood and really loving the moment he was in.

Though this trip was treacherous and rough so far, I couldn't ask for a better opportunity to see most of Haiti that wasn't planned in our itinerary. The drive was about 10 hours in total from when we left Les Abricots, and for you locals it's the same as driving to Toronto from NYC.

We went through numerous towns, with tons of culture and sites and I learned about them all. I realized once again that Patricia, Kishner, and Manuel (Kishner's brother) were amazing tour guides and passionate about sharing with me.

There were a few things that stood out to me on this part of the road trip. First of all, the roads got smoother and I was so thankful for that. Bumpy in some parts, but I was relishing in the fact that I could finally get somewhat comfortable. Of course, you would think that would be the end of it and we would have a smooth ride...

Something had to go wrong to add to the travel adventures of the week. All of a sudden, we lost the muffler to Manuel's truck and his tire was almost flat. As he pulled to the side of the road and rolled down his window, he was asking the locals in Creole where the nearest auto shop was. He was told down the road so we drove a bit further, and we pulled up to a hut-like corner with no garage. Manuel explained about the muffler and the next thing I know the worker throws down a plastic mat, slides himself under the car with a small torch and some wire hangers, and welds the muffler together. Here I was thinking we were going to be stuck for hours and not make it to our plane, but the muffler was literally fixed in 15 minutes flat for a charge of $15.

Can you imagine?

That would have taken hours in New York and been a few hundred at least! While we were waiting the 15 minutes, I got to see the drums being set up nearby for a voodoo ceremony. There are so many stereotypes around voodoo in Haiti and from what I understand it is not what we think. I am looking forward to seeing Marie's film on this. She had to work hard to be trusted and brought into that community, so it will be interesting to see what truth is discovered. That is in alignment completely with the vision of our film as well, and I think the approach I am going to take with future film projects. I want to capture the true story behind what people see so that we can break the stereotypes on all levels of society. We stopped somewhere to get some kind of homemade fudge and I asked Kishner why some of the stores had such long names. He actually pointed out one particular store that had a long name and he said the name of the store was "Groceries."

I didn't get it at first and he explained that Haiti is such a spiritual country that they actually put a proverb or saying like "Praise the Lord" first in the store sign, followed by the name of the store. This is their idea of having God and faith in all their endeavors. There is spirituality and faith all around here. It's on the storefronts, walking the streets, in the ceremonies and celebrations, at the schools, and much more. It's a constant vibration of keeping the faith.

What's not to love about Haiti?

Several hours later, in much darkness, we finally pulled into the city-like vibe of Port Au Prince. I have to admit I was exhausted but elated to know we were a step closer to home. I got a thorough tour of the capital through the eyes of Kishner and his brother, which was a delight. I saw their version of Times Square, their soccer field, and much more.

We couldn't find a hotel at first, but finally did. The hotel had Wi-Fi and a comfortable bed, and I could not help but feel like God was giving me a gift for enduring this road trip. I got online and quickly saw I had a ridiculous amount of Facebook messages and emails. I decided to not get sucked back in right away to social media and just put up a status to let everyone know I loved them.

We went out to dinner for Kishner's birthday to a chicken place and we sat, talked, reminisced, joked, and had a great time. Now I lay here, downloading today's footage, ready to get the day started tomorrow, pick up Patricia at the airport, and finally head home. I am still missing Les Abricots, but I am anxious to get to New York and see everyone, as well as go full force with the future of Windows of Opportunity.

Hopefully this will be smooth, but I won't feel comfortable until I am on that plane!

Day 10

I worked very late last night transferring footage onto our external hard drive, so even though I am excited and a bit anxious to return home, I am very exhausted and feeling a bit disconnected from myself.

There are still things I will need to get off Kishner's camera when we get back to New York, but I have almost all our material. The footage we took is immense and I am excited to go through it. It is mind-boggling and I am going to need some tedious hours set aside to do this. I am beginning to think that this documentary is much larger than we anticipated, and we may need to come back to Haiti in order to film more.

So many people and professionals are interested in what we are trying to create. There are other points of views we did not get into this movie yet, that I feel we must get on camera in order to produce a well-rounded message. There are other ideas I have and I need some time to mull it over. It is insane how you have a vision, and as you are marching towards its completion, it takes on a whole new heartbeat.

Maybe by the WOO Film Awards in August we will get a trailer done, but definitely not the full length feature. Maybe we will, but we will see how it goes. We have not even created a title yet but we have definitely have toyed with some ideas. It has to be different, and something that draws the audience in to the message that challenges the stereotypes that most people have of Haiti.

I fully love the whole process of creating a story on film with a solid message and something with this intended impact should be done correctly. We are thinking about doing a version in English, French, and Creole, which are basically 3 films. I am getting a headache thinking of that undertaking.

As I awoke the sun peeked through the window, and my deep thoughts of the past 9 days led me to take a final thought provoking stroll up the stairs and to the rooftop of the hotel here in Port Au Prince. I feel blessed as I stand *out in the hot sun knowing that somehow we made it back to the capital. It is truly a miracle being here and knowing that we accomplished what we set out to do.*

I decided to take some silly videos of myself talking about all these feelings and thoughts I have.

Why not? I am all alone on this rooftop in the middle of another country.

I am sure this moment of childish quirkiness will not make the movie at all but I wanted to get some of my serious viewpoints down while they were fresh on my mind. From the rooftop you could see major cracks in the foundation of the building and later on we learned that this very building was going to be torn down and rebuilt due to the Earthquake damage.

I had not really thought about the earthquake much since I was here, because there is a much bigger story going on around me. I think the Earthquake just attracted light to this country. I can see that most visitors sense this and that realization keeps bringing them back to help and be immersed in the breathtaking culture of Haiti. I guess the help here never got to buildings like this one because they had to prioritize and deal initially with what did come down and the enormity of that cleanup.

The ones that were standing stayed operational until later notice. Four years have gone by and this hotel is still open for business despite the obvious impairment. That realization did not make me feel very safe. I am glad I did not see this structural damage before I went to sleep.

As I stood on that rooftop and looked out at the mountainside, it looked like the favelas of South America I saw in the movie Fast and the Furious. I don't know if that is what they call them here, but it looks exactly like that. They were very colorful and lit up the mountainside like one of Patricia Brintles' paintings from her charity art show she has every year. I thought to myself "I wish I had the Monte here," but then I really thought to myself "Haiti is so beautiful."

Yes, there is poverty, but all I keep seeing over and over again is a sense of pride. It appears to me that the people of Haiti see their inner beauty and do not use money as a factor that justifies their identity or develops their souls. They identify through education, health, hospitality, and spirituality. Their incredible spiritual beliefs stretch from Voodoo to Catholicism. They do have environmental issues and basic necessity issues, as well as a massive internal and external infrastructure that needs to be built. Despite this necessary reconstruction, it seems to me that Haitians are hard working people, even with the limited resources they have.

From an outside observation, it seems to me that the entire country is working together to forge forward and overcome their limitations to build a better tomorrow. I am not sure I have sensed or felt that anywhere else. I detected the emotional shift after Hurricane Sandy in New York and of course after 9/11, but it is different here. You see half built roads, dynamite explosions to make way for a new street, makeshift business that lines every block, and a hustle in the steps of many.

It seems chaotic at times and if you aren't looking for the "story behind the story" it may even seem out of control, but upon observation I sense the passion of these citizens. One of the interns from Paradis Des Indianes, Marie, whom we interviewed, actually said something that stuck with me. She said that Haiti has its problems, but she finds that it is a complete country. They have their good and their bad, but the good is just as apparent and present as the challenges.

This trip has really opened my eyes. Haitians are welcoming and grateful, and remind me that there is no reason to be anything less. We all have our demons and struggles, but to embrace the negative is so counterproductive. However, to stride towards the positive despite personal roadblocks, is the lesson I hope stays with me. You never know what is waiting for you around the corner. I was exhausted; emotionally overwhelmed, and facing challenges, but who knew I would turn the corner in the middle of a mountainside and find unexpected beauty.

Who knew I would find thirteen schools that want to work with Windows of Opportunity? Who knew that despite our long history of success this was actually becoming a new beginning that is truly groundbreaking?

I count my blessings this week and all of the blessings of who made this trip possible. I cannot wait to go back to the states holding these lessons deep in my soul and focusing on becoming a more improved leader. Many people do not get what I am about and misjudge me, and I am sure that will still happen, but it is okay.

We are all human beings and have our challenges. Time to get off this rooftop. I'll be back in a few...

∞ ∞ ∞ ∞ ∞ ∞ ∞ ∞

We just boarded Delta with 14 minutes to go before takeoff back to The United States of America… Prior to that, and from the moment I climbed down the rooftop, the morning led to an adventure. Of course, it was supposed to be simple, but why would just going to the airport, meeting Patricia, and getting on the plane for a nice ending happen smoothly?

We got a tour of the market place where I learned to haggle for some souvenirs. Once the vendors saw that we were going to spend money we were surrounded by sales people giving us their best pitch. There was incredible artwork that lined the street and I almost took a piece home, but I just could not narrow down which I wanted, nor did I want to bring that on the plane.

Then a 20-minute drive to the airport became an hour in traffic. Traffic and crossroads with no signals and mass mayhem. It was completely fun! I think that is when the stress began to build. We saw a lot sitting in traffic and I was taking it all in, wondering when I would be back. We went to a food market near the airport where Kishner thought I would be scared but it became a great experience as I watched how people begged us for money, and saw the vendors cooking in front of us.

Patricia's plane showed up an hour late in Jeremie because it picked up some famous star for the Canaval ceremony. It was totally insane and stressful, though part of me was laughing on the inside at the continued absurdity we were attracting in our travels. I knew we would be able to laugh about this for years to come. Patricia got in an hour later than she was supposed to and we thought we were not going to get on the Delta flight. With the time ticking, she finally made it off Tortug 'Air and we raced over to the main airport. After all we went through, the bulls, the dynamite, the 10-hour drive, constant dust blown in our hair, and so on, to get here, we almost didn't make it because "someone famous" was coming in.

I was seriously laughing to myself with that thought, and if I had to stay in Haiti to wait for Patricia, I would have had no problem with it, but as I got on this plane, I did feel a big sigh of relief and accomplishment!

I am going to try and rest for this flight home. I will do one more blog with my after thoughts, but here is my last contemplation before I close my eyes for an attempted nap; I truly cannot wait to come back to Haiti and I hope that my return will be in April. There is a lot to do in order to make that a reality, so I am going to need my rest before I put the pedal to the metal.

I have much to tackle upon my return and I am ready.

Day 11

*"Up the steps of the church, through the fields in the dirt, in the dark I
have seen, that the sun still shines for the one who believed."*
— Jon Bon Jovi

I have a few "thinking spots" in NYC that I like to visit in order to gather
my thoughts. Some of them are obvious and many people — especially the ones
close to me, know the places I escape to. The Brooklyn Bridge Promenade, the
second bench on the Brooklyn side of the Brooklyn Bridge Walkway, Central
Park, and The Whitestone Bridge are a few of those locations.

However, I have one, which nobody knows about, and that is where I sit
now gathering my afterthoughts.

The temperature is 54 degrees and dropping — a stark contrast to the 90 we
just came from. Flying into New York City has proven to be more difficult
than I imagined. As we came in over the Rockaways, you could see some of the
damage still inflicted from Hurricane Sandy and the aerial view thrusted me
back into last year when the heart and soul of Windows of Opportunity and
our newly formed Emergency Response Team rose to action. They got down
and dirty, put their gloves on, sweated in the nitty gritty of the wreckage,
ran their events, worked in shelters, and made a huge difference. I realized
how blessed I am to have so many good souls surrounding me. We are not
large enough to make a difference everywhere yet, but we are doing more
than can be expected. I am proud that we do it all with passion and vision,
and not with a huge budget. Whether it is local based tragedies or global
initiatives, we have a tremendous vision, which is happening and unfolding
before our eyes.

If you actually take a step back and look at the enormousness of what
we are accomplishing one program, one event, one trip, and one child at a
time, it is awe-inspiring.

The puzzle pieces are powerful. I just need to get in front of the right
investors and business partners because once you comprehend this mission
and see our vision, there is truly no reason not to invest.

As I touched down at JFK International Airport I had a sense of anxiety
I never felt before. For those next six hours back in New York City I faced
a series of emotions that I struggled with deeply. I drove by and visited the

usual sites. I drove to the church because there was a *Rock Your Heart Out* show happening, drove past a Starbucks, and eventually to my home. Though it all seemed familiar, it felt very different. It seemed to have all changed, or perhaps it was me who has changed.

Even being at the church and watching the bands do their thing, I knew it was their little magic moment in this spot of the world. Does it stop here or is this the start of a model for programs elsewhere?

The admission price to get into the show was more than one days pay for a Haitian. We have electricity to run this show. The power in Les Abricots is going out at this time. Why am I seeing these things? Why is this standing out? Why can I not stop thinking about this? More importantly, why am I "FEELING" this?

I am proud of all these initiatives: *Rock Your Heart Out, WOO Films, Project Evolve,* and the list goes on, but I am missing something. Something feels very different, or maybe needed.

I am not sure. The programs at *Windows of Opportunity* are all magical and about to come together in a way that I am not even sure I can fathom at the moment. I went on a mission to help the world and I think I found something much bigger.

Perhaps I found a new beginning.

It is bothering me today how much I own and have available at my fingertips, compared to the people in Haiti. In actuality, and I don't mind being completely visible again, but we spent a fortune on Haiti. I even had to take out a loan to cover some expenses, so it has left us in a financial bind that I foresee kicking our butts a little bit for at least a month to a month and a half, maybe even longer.

I know the resilience and support of my team will get us through the aftermath of my "risk taking for the sake of vision," but even with that, I cannot and should not complain.

I have a dresser and a closet full of clothes. They have three outfits in many homes. I remember moving into this new apartment with so much apprehension and not liking it at all, but now I see it differently.

I looked around when I got home, took a long hot shower, and counted all my blessings. I feel like I live in a mansion and unless I get married and have children, I do not need more than I have now. I honestly feel like I have too much. My car is "luxury" to me... and speaking of luxury, I turned on the radio to hear a commercial about a new car being the "ultimate luxury," how we "deserve" luxury, and we should buy into this idea of without luxury we "haven't made it."

I don't know why but the commercial is gnawing at my soul.

Why do we need more?

There are enough resources and food on this planet to take care of everyone, unless we all hoard it up for ourselves. Perhaps I am going to an extreme and I guess it is okay to want more out of life, but at this moment I am bothered by all these realizations.

Perhaps the struggle I feel is the overwhelming number of people I see who do not embrace their blessings and stay stuck within negative energy. Life is simply way too short and we are tremendously surrounded by and drowning in abundance.

Therefore, what is the reason for the deep misery lingering within me?

Ironically, the hypocritical side of me finally caved today and I walked into a Starbucks. I saw a long line and I stood there for a moment and stared at it. I asked myself why am I here, and thought about the kids I saw back in Haiti.

I turned around and walked right out of Starbucks.

I hope I do not go back.

Money seems different to me as well. Spending it has more meaning, and the thought of having it seems to be from a place of blessing. I cannot purchase one thing without this feeling of guilt and realizing how far this can go in Haiti. I do this for the most part anyways, but I wish I could only spend my money on our programs becoming more impacting and far reaching. I was trying to figure it out off the top of my head, but I have easily put in over $200,000 of my own money into Windows of Opportunity in the past 10 years. We have paid our dues for sure, and now it is time to step into the next level of our existence, locating long term sustainable funding sources.

I go back into the New York City schools tomorrow and I cannot wait to share with my new leadership class my experience in Haiti. Doing the workshops at Paradis Des Indianes was definitely the highlight of the trip, but working on the roof, meeting the gracious people in so many villages, and working with the students was so incredibly impacting for all that were involved.

I am so very very deeply grateful for my team who went with me. They endured a lot and stayed strong. They deserve all the recognition they can *get. My team back home is my heart, soul and backbone to every step I take towards fulfilling my vision. My aunt up above, who Windows of Opportunity is named after, The Barbara Harmon Institute, must have hand picked each of them for me because they are each a heavenly blessing. Last but not least, Patricia, Joe and the family from From Here to Haiti, they are doing God's work and they are angels on this earth. You have my undying support. I know this will be the first of many trips and adventures in Haiti.*

All I can say is God Bless and always, always, always Keep the Faith…

∞ ∞ ∞ ∞ ∞ ∞ ∞ ∞

A dark cloud seemed to follow in my shadow for the days that followed my return from Haiti. I was inundated by a wealth of overabundance, and my mind kept reverting to Faith's situation.

She had a new man in her life, but that did not make me want her or love her less.

The remnants of her love lay crystalized, frozen in time, awaiting the moment that she wakes up and recognizes what she has become. She lies in the dark depths of the recess that exists between them: the empty spaces where laughter and sunshine once beckoned them closer.

My mind began to think of what she was currently dealing with and how she would internalize the situation. In my mind, she stands in the shadows, longing for his touch and commiserating in the devout solitude that is their undying bond. She often misses his grasp just before the dawn, as they lay a few feet apart yet miles away with regard to their soul connection. Though inches from one another and greeting each day with their respective smiles, nothing can compare to the broken feeling he left her with when he looked her in the eye and said, "You don't see me like you used to."

I don't know. I may just be jealous that she did not want me then. Maybe our love was just an illusion. Maybe it was not a part of reality, but rather it was my mind's way of searching for and looking for love.

My heart felt as if it were a few beats short from everything I could accomplish. Despite being in Haiti and experiencing all of the spiritually enlightening moments there, I still felt that I needed the other half of my power couple persona near me.

If I were brutally honest, I would like to be a cross between Christian Grey from *Fifty Shades of Grey* and Dominic Toretto from the *Fast and the Furious* series. Each of the men are sexy, strong, powerful, and full of sturdy family values.

I came from a very harsh upbringing and until I met my Aunt Barbara for the first time at the age of 19, I had no idea what family meant.

Since then I struggled with its meaning and the search for it. Whenever I came close, I ended up getting hurt or allowing myself to get hurt for just the idea that I may have a family. I think I built Windows of Opportunity partially as a way to fill the void of not having a family.

Outside of Bryan, even the family I try to reconcile with is dysfunctional at best and I'm not as close as I would like to be. I partially became a social worker to figure that all out and make sense of my life and this world. I love them but we aren't close... And I miss my Aunt Barbara more than words can conjure up.

I truly wished for this idea of family.

Faith seemed like she could be my real family.

This feeling in my heart and in my soul was not just a profound love for Faith, but of her world. Faith's family, and her sons somehow crept into this dream that I wished for.

As the days progressed forward, I was scared of my feelings for Faith. I had actually never been that scared. I was scared because I did not want to lose her. I was scared because she was the closest thing to family that I had at the time. I was practically raising her boys. They came to me and not their dad. I was scared because I saw so much potential in our relationship and I wanted her to see the same.

I loved her family. I understand family was important to Faith and she never thought I fit in as an "American" or a "gringo" as she playfully used to call me... but I wondered if she would let it be my family as well?

With questions and hope flurrying throughout my mind, the storm that my thoughts brought upon me resulted in the manifestation of something I did not realize would happen right away.

I got a text from Faith.

∞ ∞ ∞ ∞ ∞ ∞ ∞ ∞

'I don't know what to do,' I paced back and forth glaring down at my phone.

Morena was laying down on one of the pews, gazing up at the stained-glass window on the side of the wall.

"Is channeling your nervous energy into pacing the floor going to give you an answer?" She raised her right arm up as she spoke with her hands. I found myself walking to the pew in front of hers and sat down.

'What does this all mean?' I was getting caught up in the logistical thought of her actually texting me.

"She texted you," Morena spoke softly. "Maybe you should just text back."

'Yeah,' I started. 'But what do I say?'

"Well, what did she say?"

I fiddled with the phone for a moment until her words illuminated my screen. 'It says… hey.'

Morena sat up abruptly. "Is that all it says?"

'No, there is more.'

Morena rested her head on the pew. She was glaring over my shoulder to try to catch a glimpse of what Faith wrote.

'She wants me to call her as soon as possible. What does this mean?'

Morena thought for a moment, then replied: "Let me see that."

I handed her the phone and saw her hit the "Dial" button on the screen. I was calling Faith.

Oh shit, what was I going to say?

Before I could think, Faith's voice permeated my head.

"Hey handsome, how are you?" Faith seemed happy to hear from me. What could that mean?

We spoke briefly, but she said that she wanted to meet me for dinner to talk.

My mind was clogged with questions. I could not even begin to think about what any of her words truly meant.

Before she hung up, she asked if I could do her a favor. With that tinge of sensuality in her voice, she asked if I could pick her son up from school.

∞ ∞ ∞ ∞ ∞ ∞ ∞ ∞

612

I promised, and the next day I cancelled all of my appointments because I needed to be around for him.

Morena shook her head in what I figured was disbelief when I did this, but she did not say a word. She was oddly quiet and let me do my thing, even though I could tell she wanted to say something.

Faith texted me to remind me to pick up her son, and followed up with a text saying that her father said he would be able to get him instead.

I ended up assuring her that I could handle it, so she told her father to just head back home.

I brought her youngest son home, and the two of us ended up doing homework and playing board games until her older son arrived. As I waited for her to come home, she called her older son and told him that the three of us should just eat and not wait for her.

I ordered some pizza for all of us and we sat on the couch for hours.

After a few hours, she returned home with her boyfriend in tow, which made me realize that she really did not want to see *me*.

Faith *needed* me, but not in the context I expected.

I left quickly and found myself racing the thunder outside her humble family home. I felt my footsteps slamming the pavement, one after the other, as I moved faster. My breathing was labored, but I wanted to beat the rain and get far away from her house. I forgot where exactly I parked my car in Ozone Park, but I knew I had to be close.

I kept running anyway.

I try so hard to be a loving, caring person, but I always end up being ensnared in some sort of challenge.

The rain came pouring down and I felt my body give way to the rushing waters.

Though drenched and upset, I knew that Faith put me back in her life for a reason. I had to prove myself. I had to show that I was going to be there for her and that I was reliable.

I had to be a better man.

∞ ∞ ∞ ∞ ∞ ∞ ∞ ∞

In the months that followed, Faith continued to call on me. Morena continued to run Windows of Opportunity with me, though she was a very silent partner in the day-to-day operations of the company.

Mother's Day was just a few days away, and I so desperately wanted to show Faith that I appreciated her efforts as both a successful businesswoman and mother.

Naturally, I felt the need to go above and beyond and bring her flowers. At this point, I had been caring for the boys and helping them with homework and such as often as possible when they came home from work. Her sons loved me and were used to having me around quite often.

I ensured that the flowers were "friendship flowers," but Faith did not want to hear it. The moment she saw them, she grew angry, launched them across the room, and forced me out of the house.

I was at a loss for words.

I had no idea how to apologize to her without making her feel upset.

Despite my feelings that I had put in a box for her, my "soul" intention was to make her feel supported and cared for. The flowers were an expression of our friendship, and were not an attempt to win her love or shower her with gifts.

I loved her in the romantic sense, but I knew that I could not show it, ever. Now, I was extremely sad and very confused by her reaction.

Faith stopped texting me, and calling upon me to help her.

Before this moment, she was okay with me bringing her favorite salad all the way to where she was working in Manhattan and she accepted my assistance as I picked up her sons and helped them with homework, but nothing was enough.

I was never enough in those moments.

I thought we had a chance at a higher consciousness friendship, but her anger pushed me so far from her purview, which made me feel holistically insignificant in her life.

There was a gaping hole in my heart and directly through my soul.

Morena tried to convince me that my actions were pure and that my intentions were good, and though I agreed with her, I grew angrier with each moment.

I became Faith's puppet. I was her support when she was lonely.

She did not want me.

She really didn't want me.

All hope and all faith were totally lost.

It took me a while, but I came to the realization that she was using me.

After all of this, it hit me: I am done with relationships. It would have to take someone unbelievably amazing, someone who could move heaven and Earth, to convince me otherwise. To be honest, I can't put myself in any sort of romantic space again because of this deep-rooted pain.

If anyone special truly existed, I feel like time would have to stop. There would be no way that anyone could top the love I had with Faith.

The tears flowed out of me.

I stopped hearing from Faith all together.

She was running away again and there was nothing I could do to convince her otherwise. So many youth were looking up to me for support and guidance, yet I was crumbling at the sheer thought of Faith's disposition towards me.

I am surrounded by all of this greatness in my life, but there is no one to share it with.

I felt so very empty inside.

Could you imagine what my life would be like if I truly had everything?

What would it look like if I had someone by my side?

I think I could change the entire world.

With the right partner and the right team, I could do absolutely anything I wanted to.

What's wrong with me?

Should I stay stuck in this mindset, or do I move forward?

Should I stay positive?

Should I be the man I know I am and leave this broken heart behind?

What if I just refused for my heart to be broken ever again?

The only thing I need to complete my life is love, yet Faith did not want me.

I fell apart in the sanctuary of the church day after day. In utter silence, my cries echoed through the church.

Despite my efforts, I was holistically alone.

Tears edged themselves out of the corners of my eyes and welled in the base of my neck. Faith knew how much she meant to me.

There was a haunting energy that remained in the room whenever our bodies were not touching.

The silent yearning we had for each other permeated the air.

The spiritual connection dangled precariously on the exterior of our souls.

I was imagining her wrapped in the arms of another man. Caught in the lie that was the raw passion between them. Tangled in the strings that barely held my heart together, which she ripped the day she walked out and forgot to say her final, heart-wrenching, soul-splitting goodbye.

I'd spare her the pain jetting through my body... "Adiós y vaya con dios" were the words that recalled years of memories shifting into the dimly lit room. Her ghost was still unravelling in the bed we called ours.

I was caught between the teetering balance of the pain that I was fearful I would succumb to and the urge to fight to stay alive. I was trapped in a cage where I could see freedom, but the padlock on the door reminded me that I was just a shitty existence, a step away from ending it all. I was snared in the raging waters that flooded my every second. I was a moment away from the edge of a knife: An inch from falling deeper into a hole I couldn't dig out of.

"If you have to contemplate it, then don't bother," hung in the air as tears welled in my eyes. A faint memory shattered to the floor as the glass ceiling rebuilt itself strategically to block me into a fervent tapestry of generations of oppression.

I couldn't exist. I couldn't be who I am.

The stinging loneliness of always being the second, third, or seventh choice.

The harsh reality that regardless of who I am deep down inside, I would never get to see what I deserve.

Or maybe this is what I deserved?

Or maybe this is what my purpose was supposed to be?

An example. A dreaded shadow fostering the soul of something bigger.

"Smile though your heart is aching... smile even though it's breaking..."

The weight of those masks burdened my shoulders. The cloak unraveling and melting away in my fingers.

Silencing my tears to hide the trace of sadness.

Pondering if I could adorn the mask for much longer without launching it clear across the room.

Being the bane of existence.

Closing my eyes and seeing the steps on the dark cover of my eyelids.

Praying for protection.

Hoping for a cure to a disease that is nonexistent.

There was no closure. There was no end in sight. There are days upon days feeding into weeks and months of miserable invisibility: the realization that I was nothing and no one wrapped into a disappearing shell. A passing moment reminded me that I am. An inch, a hair, a soul. A piece of a larger puzzle that does not exist in this realm.

A crackling tear streaming down my cheek reminded me that I was real. I was someone. I was not a thing.

A sniffle shattered the silence. Loneliness in a crowded room feels so wholeheartedly contrastive.

An escape hatch needed to appear. The next chapter needed to start. For this one smelt of dead roses that never existed and appeared as crumpled tissues dancing around a diploma that would never match its frame.

This dramatic scene needed no introduction. This parted sensation needed no further explanation.

Dare I choose the first door?

Dare I choose the second door?

What if all of those doors never matched everything I knew I could be or have? A solitary key to end all sorrow hung in the wind, though reaching it was so hard.

I was not as I seemed. I was larger. Stronger. Harder. Yet the weight bearing down upon me was too forceful in its entirety. The burden harkened a cry. I would follow it.

And I would become something I need not be: a shadow or a shell.

Darkness in the midnight hour succumbs to the tears within my soul.

An extinguished flame wrapped in the ashes of a dampened candle.

The wind still calls to rise... and so I try.

Yeah, I try. I have to.

One more light could not go out.

Part IV:
The Awakening

CHAPTER 34

The One that Got Away

~

"And these were our words. Our words were our songs. Our songs are our prayers. These prayers keep me strong, and I still believe."

- Bon Jovi, American Rock Band, Sayreville, New Jersey

Faith's absence left a gaping hole in what once was a broken, yet finally actualized, soul. I figured that maybe love was never going to find me. I assumed that maybe I was never meant to be in a relationship. Maybe, I surmised, I would always dance to the tune of being forever alone in my own skin.

Essentially, life was uncertain and I was on the verge of moving forward without a partner by my side.

For once in my life, that actually seemed okay.

A lot of people from Windows still didn't think I should give up so easily. Though they were not pushing me towards Faith, they were encouraging me to keep the faith. They told me that I should not give up and should keep looking.

Bryan would even chime in on what I should do.

"Dad," he would always begin with an endearing tone. "Why are you doing this to yourself?"

'What?' I would try playing stupid to deflect my emotions, but I could not shake the truth from my shoulders.

"Dad, you care about everyone else and you always look out for everyone," Bryan paused. "Who looks out for you?"

I didn't know the answer.

I mean, Morena had helped me through so much this far, but Morena was not close to the "power couple" image I had brewing in my head.

My soul was yearning for someone who could be my equal. I ached for someone who could complete me in every essence of the notion.

I found myself wandering the sanctuary day after day and night after night.

The stained-glass windows were drastically different at night, though the spiritual energy still lingered within the confines of the walls.

My prayers began to grace the walls of the church once again, as I searched my soul for what I should do.

I had been walking around with a heavy heart since losing Faith. It had been about six months of sorrow at this point, but with the New Year starting shortly, this sense of a "new beginning" did not fill my heart with hope.

I wondered: 'Will I ever have a good year? Will my life ever make sense?'

I sensed in my soul that I would not have been able to connect with God and develop my spirituality, if it were not for the love I felt with Faith.

Still, that notion needed to be swept to the side if I intended to find my purpose in life.

I needed hope. I needed strength. I needed answers. I needed-

At that moment a resounding thud from the far end of the room spooked me: someone was walking into the church.

Footsteps made their way up to the sanctuary as a voice crept around the corner.

It was Eve.

"What are you doing here so late?" She seemed stunned to see me there.

'Oh,' I dried my eyes. 'I was just, I was just praying.'

"Oh, okay." She looked at me blankly for a moment.

I sat in one of the pews and rested my chin on the one in front of me.

"Well, I will leave you to it." Eve retreated into the darkness as I heard her start rummaging through papers in the church's office.

The energy, the attraction, and the spiritual connection between Faith and I were so strong for so many years. I could sit and argue for hours that it was the ultimate love.

Why did things unfold the way they did?

What was I missing?

Was I ever really sure of anything?

I guess, in some way, it was supposed to happen that way.

There was something much bigger going on there and we were both being prepared for it.

She may not have been ready to face her demons, and I knew that I was also struggling, but it looked like there was no need for a partner in my life.

To trust someone again and bare my soul to the universe, well, that woman would have to be beyond special. There would have to be an overwhelming number of signs and unwavering strength from the universe in order to be with someone else.

I knew, somewhere deep inside, that Faith would return.

She always did before, but that time she was just taking longer than usual.

I had to pray. I had to process.

The door to the church slammed shut, and I could tell that once again I was alone with my thoughts. Eve left and it was just me, myself, the spirits, and the angels around me.

I felt the Circle of Angels there with me, although it appeared that I could not see their physical presence.

I felt blessed to have the sanctuary all to myself. The energy in the room spoke to my soul in ways that could never be articulated.

It was quite possible that Faith and I were really this incredible love story, and this was part of that love story.

Maybe whomever she chose to date would be a part of her development. Maybe what she went through as a child contributed to the woman she is today. Maybe seeing my life and experiencing it through her soul, and in return not being able to handle who we were, was part of our cohesive development.

Maybe, I figured, that is what relationships are all about: being a venue to learn about your own soul.

It sure did feel like a lesson was brewing in the strength of being alone. I did want to spend the rest of my life with her, but whatever will be will be.

If what we were going through then would help us maintain a solid foundation in the future, I figured, then we needed to be apart in order to grow. Our relationship would embody every essence of the word "faith."

There needed to be clarity. There needed to be a certain level of guidance.

As D.B. Harrop, a famous author, once said: "Have a big enough heart to love unconditionally, and a broad enough mind to embrace the differences that make each of us unique."

That being said, it is important to share your story and passions with the world. We are all on this road through life. We have all of these tremendous thoughts and feelings inside.

Why not get them out in the most beautiful and expressive ways possible?

Why not go for it? Well, whatever "it" is anyway.

∞ ∞ ∞ ∞ ∞ ∞ ∞ ∞

It had been quite a journey: a search for love, a discovery of faith, and a tale of finding yourself.

I have learned a lot of tough lessons, but I feel my soul has grown from it. Emotionally, I had been dragged through the mud and felt absolutely desolated at times, yet these experiences have molded me.

Every conversation matters. Every person I have encountered matters, and in hindsight, I realize I did not treat everyone in my life fairly, including myself.

I found myself pondering more questions while in my resolute and self-inflicted solitude: Where do our life stories come from? Who makes up your story?

Each person who has walked through my life contributed to my story, but can other people say the same?

I do not believe that the universe provides accidents. Relationships, whether good or bad, can waltz into our lives and create an avenue to learn something deeply about ourselves.

Moments, and people who grace each of our moments, all create a story of rare blessings. Sometimes we are able to see these blessings, while other times we shut these blessings out for we do not relish in all that they can become.

That is what happened between me and Alessandra.

∞ ∞ ∞ ∞ ∞ ∞ ∞ ∞

I believed life was all about love, and that love is an incredible energy. I think we attract people into our own lives when we emit similar energy, and like all things in life, energy changes from time to time. Sometimes you are in alignment with a person, and sometimes you just aren't.

I devoutly believe that is what happened between Alessandra and I.

When I was at an event that one of the after-school programs was running, a woman with flowing chestnut hair approached me. She was short in stature, but you could tell she had a big heart just from her approach.

"Hey, I was told to come to you, you're Scott, right?" The woman was perky and appeared to be excited.

'Yeah,' I kept fiddling with some paperwork. 'I'm Scott.'

"I'm Alessandra, I'm one of the volunteers here today."

'Okay, well, just sit tight and I'll let you know what we need.'

I did not mean to be curt. I did not intend upon Alessandra walking into my life, especially when and how she did.

Alessandra was watching me out of the corner of her eyes and twirling her hair around her finger. I was unsure of what to make of her, but I knew that she was watching me.

I looked up from the clipboard and asked if she was okay, but she just responded with a faint "Mm hmm" and continued watching me.

"Scott," one of the kids motioned for me to walk over to him. "That woman is totally flirting with you, do something, man."

I smiled and rubbed the back of my neck. 'No, she is not.'

"Yeah, man, she is. Go back there and ask her out."

'No,' I whispered and pulled him aside. 'I'm not dating anymore.'

"I know," the kid said. "So, ask her out."

I rolled my eyes and turned to head back over to the table, but she was directly behind me.

"Go on," she muttered. "Ask me out."

What was happening? Who was this woman?

Again, more questions flooded my head.

Alessandra sat and told me all about her passion for bands like Bon Jovi and Def Leppard, which was certainly up my alley, however I was filled with such trepidation about letting her in. She managed to slip her phone number into my pocket, and I sat in the sanctuary with the piece of paper in my hand, wondering if I should take a leap of faith.

I called Morena on my way to the church, and she somehow managed to make it there before I even left the event. When I arrived, Morena was patiently waiting on the steps outside of the church.

'I don't know what it is,' I looked over at Morena as I fiddled with the keys to the door. 'She seems like she is crazy about me.'

"Well, with all of your *endearing* qualities, it does not seem like a surprise." Morena tucked her hands in the back pockets of her jeans and followed me into the sanctuary.

I took my usual seat in the pews and began to pray.

'Can I emotionally handle this, Morena?'

Without skipping a beat, she moved closer to me: "Are you asking me, or are you asking your soul?"

Instantly, I grew defensive.

'I just asked you, Morena, did you not hear me?'

"Well," she did not return my unpleasant tone. "Ask yourself first. Then ask the world. Be comfortable in your own skin before you rush into getting hasty with someone else."

'I am not getting *hasty*,' I quipped at her.

She looked at me with her eyebrows raised.

"Okay," Morena plopped down a few pews away from me and began to run her fingers across the wood.

It was in those moments that I chose to take the leap of faith.

Within seconds, Alessandra's phone number was in my hands and I was calling her.

"Are you sure about that?" Morena chirped.

I paid no attention to her and continued to dial the number.

Alessandra seemed so happy to hear from me, and I was surprised that she seemed thrilled to actually hear from me.

We ended up scheduling a date together, for she had won Def Leppard tickets in some sort of MTV Unplugged contest.

In the days that followed, the two of us ended up on television since we were seated in the second row of the exclusive concert.

Occasionally during the concert, she would look over at me and smile. I thought it was creepy, but little did I know at the time, she was savoring our moments together.

At least I would like to think that was what she was doing.

Our mutual love for music led us to a Def Leppard concert at Coney Island in the baseball stadium there.

After the show, we had so much fun that neither of us wanted to go home. She was laughing and touching my arm repeatedly, which signified that she seemed quite interested in me.

Security guards kicked us off of the field after the end of the show, so we began to walk around the stadium until someone found us and told us to exit through a random door on the side. The two of us had no clue where we were, but the next thing we knew, we were staring down the members of Def Leppard.

The two of us met the entire band and started to talk to them as if they were not celebrities. Rick Allen, the drummer of Def Leppard, began to chat with me about how his wife was from Queens. Alessandra and I tried containing our excitement, but you could tell she was in awe of the entire band.

Rick Allen and I began to talk about his charity agency, and I told them about Windows of Opportunity's Rock Your Heart Out music empowerment program. We spoke about how I would love his company and Windows to work together, he told me who to contact at his company, and at the next concert in their tour, Alessandra and I were able to get backstage again to talk about all of this.

Alessandra and I stood in Rick Allen's dressing room as the three of us spoke about his accident. As a kid, I was reading about how Rick Allen lost his arm in the newspapers, however I was actually getting a chance to hear about the story from his own lips.

To say it was an exhilarating feeling to be in the presence of one of your drumming heroes is an absolute understatement.

Despite losing his arm, Rick Allen continued to drum. Though he spoke about the pain, the struggles he dealt with, and overcoming his adversity, one message stood out in my mind: it is literally possible to overcome anything.

The heart and human spirit can create absolutely anything.

∞ ∞ ∞ ∞ ∞ ∞ ∞ ∞

Alessandra's fun and free nature helped me see myself in a different light, though I was not cognizant of how I was actually treating her. The way she adored me could be seen for miles, though I was still reserved and struggling to live within the confines of each of our special moments.

When we went to see Bon Jovi in New York City, she almost got stuck in the subway car door. The two of us laughed for hours, and the moment reminded me of that last day I spent with my Aunt Barbara.

Once we got to the concert, something drew me to the giant American flag in front of us that stretched out across the first ten rows.

The first song Bon Jovi performed, "Undivided," somehow tugged on my heartstrings. I did not know what it meant at the time, but I felt fully present in that moment.

I knew I would never forget that moment or that day. It would live in my soul for all of eternity.

Though we had been dating for months, every time I looked over at Alessandra, I did not feel what I felt with Faith.

It seemed as if Alessandra's love and companionship was a cheap version of the soul-enriching love I had with Faith.

Maybe that was my problem: I was too busy comparing Alessandra to Faith, that I didn't cherish her for who she was.

Alessandra tried to love me, but I was so sealed off from who she was at the time. The two of us had a beautiful picnic in the park once, and Alessandra even tried to set up a few surprises for my birthday. Though she knew I hated the day and everything it meant to me, she still tried to make me happy with a cake and my favorite snacks.

She desperately tried to be whom I needed, and she was perfect in every essence of the word, but I was not ready.

I blew it.

∞ ∞ ∞ ∞ ∞ ∞ ∞ ∞

Alessandra showed up at my after-school jobs quite often and slowly grew to hate the work I did. She was very jealous that I spent so much time with the kids, while I left her to fend for herself regularly.

She would show up, her jeans wrapping around her curves ever so slight, tapping her long fingernails against the doors and windows where I was teaching, pleading to know when I would be leaving work.

It got to the point where I wouldn't pick up her calls anymore.

Then it got worse:

She began sleeping very late, she started to call at all hours of the night, and she would cry when I would not give her attention.

To this day, I panic when it comes to balancing everything in my life.

I want to give people all of my love and attention, but it is hard to do that and to maintain my health at the same time.

The mounting stress swallowed every inch of our relationship.

Then she gave me an ultimatum: "Scott, it's all or nothing."

Those words stung my mind and continued to crush my soul.

Did I love her? I think so.

Did I show her? No.

I chose "Nothing."

She cried and left gifts at my mother's house in College Point, though I continued to ignore her and disregard her emotions.

Then, one day months later when I started to feel really sick, I started having heart problems. I figured I could fill the void of my loneliness by calling her and asking to be friends with benefits, but she slammed the phone down in my ear.

Alessandra was an awesome and perfect woman, but I did not appreciate her for all of who she was.

In hindsight, she was probably the most fun and exhilarating person who I dated, and when I say dated, I mean that I never did seem to fall into an "I love you" stage with her.

I was too naive at the time and too close-minded to see what she meant to me.

I will always regret how I treated her, and I hope that she realizes how much of an impact she had on my soul.

In a different time and in a different place, I am sure we would have worked, but I was too stupid to realize that.

The two of us were made for each other, or at least I think that is what could have been if I actually gave her love a chance, but I know I screwed up our love.

We had this odd story that proves how alike we were, though I am unsure if we were ever truly in alignment: the two of us would name squirrels that climbed around outside of our windows. When we were kids, we found solace and peace in nature.

It is unfortunate that our compassion could not transcend into a healthy relationship.

As the lyrics to "Blaze of Glory" from Bon Jovi flowed through my ears, I could not help but think about the perpetual impact that I was leaving on Alessandra's heart:

> *"You ask about my conscience*
> *And I offer you my soul*
> *You ask if I'll grow to be a wise man*
> *Well I ask if I'll grow old*

You ask me if I've known love
And what it's like to sing songs in the rain
Well, I've seen love come
And I've seen it shot down
I've seen it die in vain
Shot down in a blaze of glory
Take me now but know the truth…"

I realized that I would always love Alessandra and that she would always hold a special place in my heart. She was the perfect girl, but the timing was definitely off. I do not know the damage I inflicted on Alessandra, but if she could see these words right now, I would apologize profusely.

I don't know what ever became of her story, though I am sure that she lived every moment of her life to the fullest, regardless of who was in her life.

In the sanctuary, I found myself praying and speaking to anyone who would listen again. Though I was very closed-off in the relationship I had with Alessandra, I still felt immense pain once I finally shut her out.

"Why don't you just speak to her one-on-one?" Morena stood at the edge of the pew, waiting for a response.

The words shot from my mouth like daggers ripping further into my soul.

'Why do you always have to start an argument, Morena?' spewed mercilessly from my lips, forcing the tears to the edges of my eyelids.

Morena sat in absolute silence. She pulled her sleeves down to hide the superficial scars that burned into her patiently distraught frame.

Everything she did was in slow motion: her eyelids turning downward before she cast her eyes towards the left, her pupils growing in size as she exhaled the pain, her slender sniffles hiding between the naturalistic breaths that expelled from her body. She was wholeheartedly broken to her core, yet she was resisting the urge to let the pieces go. She clung to them with such might, almost hoping that her existence would not be defined by another man's ignorance and misunderstanding.

Morena was brilliance and beauty wrapped into one, but the whole world casts a demeaning eye on a woman with passion and fervor coursing through her veins. Yet, something in her yelped.

It was a sign. It was a voice.

It was a resilient heart and a growing soul.

'Morena, what have you done to grow your soul today,' I quizzically awaited a response.

Clearing her throat almost instinctively, she glanced up and met my eyes: "What?"

'What have you done for yourself?'

"Scott, I..." she begged her soul to find the words she so truly needed to say, "I... I have never heard that question before. No one has ever asked, well, no... no one has ever asked me that."

A grin crept up, wrinkling her pristine cheek. Her tears melted away. Years of pain faded in between the breaths that escaped into the air.

Morena and I glared at each other for a moment. My hair fluttered in the wind as hers whipped around her line of sight. We kept walking through the trails of Alley Pond with purpose: growing our own souls through the small steps we would take. I told her she did not have to answer the question. I told her she could think about it. Still, an inquisitive side to her nature peeped between her drying eyes.

"Scott, let me ask you the same thing: what have you done to grow your own soul?" She wrapped her body around the billowing winds, catching a flighted sense to her aura in the process.

Her eyes glowed and her entire spirit took to the skies. At that moment, I had realized no one had asked me that, ever. Not a single person. Not a single lover from the past, spiritual or not. All it took to open my eyes was another broken, shattered soul... whose scars dove further than the depths of the ocean.

And there we stood, grinning like idiots in the woods, realizing that we both needed to wake up.

And dawn was on the horizon.

CHAPTER 35

Higher Consciousness

~

"Maybe there's a God above, but all I've ever learned from love was how to shoot somebody who outdrew ya. And it's not a cry that you hear at night, it's not somebody who's seen the light, It's a cold and it's a broken Hallelujah"

- Jeff Buckley, American singer, songwriter, guitarist, Anaheim, California

Life changes when you realize that you should truly appreciate everything you have. Absolutely everything can change in the blink of an eye: your relationships, your health, and your mental well being… the list goes on and on.

Why is it that we have to lose what we have in order to genuinely realize what could have been?

I am not just talking about Alessandra, Faith, Elyza, Gemma, or any of my relationships. There is a bigger picture manifesting here, and I was blind to everything as I was living my life.

I was clinging to hope as a sort of hope-a-holic. Is that even such a thing? If so, that sounds utterly pathetic. I do not want to fix the world. I want to expand it. I want people to find their light and what they are made of. We need to shift systems, not change them. Life has to be translated from a disempowering mindset to an empowering one. So many systems need revamping.

Education is key because it springboards society into so many other systems. We have to start there.

I was scared though. I wondered, 'How do I give up fear?'

I always wanted to please everyone and that stopped us from growing as a company. The world was demanding my kindness and my soul, but I created that space. It brought me to ask: How do I stop it? I didn't want to stop helping people.

How could I balance it?

I couldn't let anything stop me. I couldn't let people mess with me. I couldn't let my heart be messed with.

I was scared to be alone.

How could I be what the universe intended me to be while dealing with what I had to deal with in everyday life?

How do you emerge from being just a raindrop in the ocean to being an entire wave?

I had lived my life in the reflection of all that I knew I could be: Standing in the shadows of a towering deity that exists solely in the eyes of the fallen, and a shattered existence wallowing in the puddles of self-pity and faltering righteousness.

I stood before people not as I knew I could be, but as a faint portrait of a masterpiece: a faded canvas scrapped long before the artist could ever paint his imagination onto the hearts of many and souls of few.

Maybe this was my fate.

Maybe this was the existence that was predetermined for me.

Maybe this was how the light burns out.

∞ ∞ ∞ ∞ ∞ ∞ ∞ ∞

In the shadow of my overwhelming depression, not many people seemed to remember I even existed.

It was interesting, since I worry so much about the feelings of others; I figured that my phone would be ringing off of the hook.

Though it wasn't.

In the end though, I know I will always care about people even if they do not care for me.

At the time, I probably didn't even have spare time to let things like that bother me at all. Life is way too short and I am getting a taste of that fear as I grow older.

If I did not awaken my soul and appreciate the small blessings, such as the people who loved me and go above and beyond for me, then my entire story would have ceased long before it needed to. There were still people in my life who tried to help me dig out of the funk I was in.

Morena would call occasionally, but I kept sending her to voicemail. Part of me worried about disappointing her or not being able to express myself to her.

As pellets of rain dripped down my skin, it felt that my memories were springing forward with such a violent force. It was as if the angels were saying, "Do you see the lessons? Do you realize your full potential? Are you hearing our messages?"

Through strife and struggle, I was blind to the ambition and growth circling around me. I was succumbing to the loss I was naturally accustomed to.

I lost my apartment in Bayside when the landlord passed away. He was an elderly man who was kindly renting out a basement apartment to me. Though it was illegal, it was small and it was a place where I could rest my head at night.

With my finances spinning out of control, because every penny I made was being funneled directly into Windows of Opportunity and its programs, I was homeless again.

I moved my things into the attic of the Queens Community Church and slept in my Monte Carlo. Though the car was no place to call home, it was cozy and often warm.

It was supposed to be temporary, but I was not able to dig myself out of the financial turmoil I was already in. Money flowed right out of my pockets and into my programs' accounts. Students were succeeding while I was silently suffering, and I was okay with that.

My long nights of working in the church's office led me to pass out on the table, which eventually led to countless nights sleeping on the floor of Queens Community Church.

To try to maintain some semblance of hygiene, I kept a ratty old towel with me and washed up in the sink. I joined a local gym to shower each day, but I swallowed every ounce of pride I had left in order to keep moving forward.

I was surviving, not living, at this point.

I kept wondering: Did I forgive everything that happened with the lawsuit? Is that what was holding me back? I knew I had to forgive if I am to heal. My career was almost crushed, but things turned out okay, I made it through. However, I felt I lost my edge.

Life was different than it was before. I didn't feel good about it. I needed to commit to myself to feel better about everything, but I did not know how. I thought I was okay. Then all of that stuff happened with Faith. Then Alessandra.

I felt like people judged me silently.

How could I let go of this pain?

I was hurt and I was allowing that to be my primary focus. I was frustrated. I was too distraught. I needed to breathe.

It is okay to make mistakes. I know that now and I have made many. Vision without technique is blindness. I had to keep building on what I knew. I needed to follow my soul and the messages I was getting from the universe.

The world was occurring to me through the lens I had on, so I had to remember to change those lenses from time to time, or be open to the lens of other views, which led me to the fact that I needed to be open to changing my perspective.

That was the hardest part. I had to put myself in the places that gave me the most potential. I needed to work in a school or schools that allowed me to build and explore different concepts.

I needed patience, planning, and perseverance. I had to value the person I worked with, as much as the work I did within a system that had to be created to support both simultaneously.

I knew if I could figure out how to connect with my passion, it would bring me to a deeper place of empowerment. I had to learn to reframe every challenge and problem into an opportunity and a blessing.

I had to stop telling myself I was wrong for my thoughts and my feelings.

∞ ∞ ∞ ∞ ∞ ∞ ∞ ∞

For months, I caught myself dreading the fact that I had to leave work. I was preoccupied with work and inspiring youth during the day; however, I hid away in the catacombs and attic of a building I hoped could one day house countless youth programs.

One night in the midst of the summer, I was sweating profusely in the church attic. The air was oppressive and stale, and I could not tell if I was struggling to breathe due to the atmospheric pressure or the weight of my own choices.

Somehow, I managed to fall asleep, only to wake up to a faint "Hello" drifting throughout the sanctuary.

I gathered my things hurriedly and began to dart down the stairs as quietly as possible. Though as I made my way down the steps, I was met with two panicked eyes staring back into my own.

"Scott, for heaven's sake, it is just you," Paul smiled.

'Sorry to startle you, I was just getting some work done.'

Paul glanced at the clothes and various toiletries in my hands.

"I see," He sounded skeptical.

'Yeah, so I will just be on my way.'

As I passed him, he gripped my arm.

"How late were you here, son?"

'I-' I didn't know what to say.

"It is 5:30 in the morning now. Were you here all night?"

Again, I did not know what to say. I finally got caught, and I didn't have any answers for him.

Paul softened his glance and put his hand on my back.

637

"Son," he motioned to the pews in the sanctuary. The two of us found a place on the pew to the right of the doors. "You are not in trouble."

'Okay,' I quivered slightly. I was not sure what he was going to say next.

"I want you to know that Queens Community Church is your home. *We* are your home. I never want you to feel as if you can't spend time here." In a way, I think he sensed I was homeless and in need of a place to lay my head.

After those moments, we chatted for a bit about the next adventure for Windows of Opportunity, and he discussed how he was so proud that I was a part of the community.

"You truly do put the unity in opportunity, Scott," Paul joked.

I helped him set up the sanctuary for some sort of morning event they were having in a few hours, then I was on my way.

I sensed that Paul always knew about the sacrifices I was making on behalf of youth and Windows of Opportunity, yet he never wanted to say anything. I did, however, usually come "home" at night to a cool or warm attic depending on the season, which meant that he must have turned on the air conditioning or heat in the church before he left for the night. I didn't want pity, for that does not help. A helpful space needs to be empowering, and Paul helped give me that space.

His soul knew that I was in need of some silent compassion, and he happily snuck in a few acts of kindness when he could. We all have gifts and a purpose. We all have something to deliver in this world, no matter how big or how small. Each moment in our life acts as a chance to express what we are capable of doing.

This was a commitment of an entirely different kind. This was not a job. This was integrity. This was not a display of morals.

This was my human spirit showing up.

I was going to do what I said I was going to do. I was going to deliver some sort of plan. I was going to make sure I am always aligned with my principles. I was going to speak up for what I stand for. I was going to get support from the universe. I knew that the right team would come. I told myself I would shift the education system and other systems connected to it. I would manifest change in society. I would stick to my guns. The universe is a world of enrollment and it had enrolled me to shift the education system.

I felt that in my soul.

Still, I wondered, how do I create a platform for change while allowing my soul to continue to emerge?

We must empower souls.

I pondered: How do we access other people's power and my own power simultaneously?

What do I stand for?

What do people stand for?

Is that where they find their power?

I would look at myself in the crusted-over church mirror and ask: 'Do you walk the talk or just spout out thoughts?'

I think I did a little bit of both, but I needed to make a stand to forge ahead.

Why was I scared of my own voice? Perhaps because I was always told I was wrong or not made to feel good enough?

I got so upset because I knew deep down my intentions were true, but I did not know how to keep feeling my inherent power. I did not know if anyone would listen to my voice, though hypocritically I taught everyone to have their own.

I needed to go within and listen.

People ridiculed me, including myself. I did not know how to stop listening. When people ridicule me, can I recognize the issues that come up in myself? If people can do this on a larger and less-demeaning scale, then we can overcome and lift ourselves to new heights.

I knew I was not a bad person, though the ghosts of my past made me think I was.

I always fell short. Was that my intended legacy?

Sometimes, I am my own worst enemy.

On those silent July days when the sanctuary was slightly illuminated by the rising sun, I would find myself pacing the pews and talking about my ambitions.

I wanted to be the shift, the devout answer; I wanted the universe to create through my existence.

I had pages and pages of goals for WOO. Among them was the expansion of programs, creating a movement, raising money, running events and conferences, and being in more schools and getting in front of thousands of youth to inspire them.

I saw it clearly at the time and I didn't at the same time. I needed a new lens to see what I wanted to transcend. I did not want to be part of the problem. I did not want the problem to be my identity. I wanted to be the expansion of that thought.

I was so tired. Could I do it all?

There are two different types of tired: tired as in the idea that I am mentally exhausted and weary, and the other idea is the idea of being so tired that I need to let go of the fight. I did not want to let go of the fight when I had not made it to the battlefield yet. Then again, was there a battlefield, or was it just a figment of my imagination pushing me to see something else?

A truly open mind is the rarest thing on this planet. That is the mind I wanted. I wanted to defy logic and break the boundaries that society saw as the norms. This is in leadership, communication, and in love.

I wanted the abnormal as normal. Within that field of comprehension rests the truth of the soul.

What woke me up on the hardest days of my life to do the work that I do?

It was my vision for humanity and the search for a love I knew had to be out there, but I couldn't believe if it was true or not.

Is there such a thing as blind faith or should it be faith with inquiry? Should we continue to go deeper and search for more answers?

I wondered how do I incorporate that into my programs?

My programs are great, but this Project Evolve venture made me feel like there was more. I was linked to the concept and I was building it out, but there was another level here to reach for but I couldn't figure it out yet.

I wondered: Is the relationship between whatever you see: God, the divine, the universe, Allah, at a level of higher consciousness? There could be if you open your mind up and connect in that manner.

If I did not take action at that point, then was I condoning this broken system permeating society? If anything is possible, then nothing is impossible. Right? Or was I fooling myself? I had spent months on this.

I hardly saw the light of day except to see my clients and run my programs.

Nobody saw how depressed I was, for I merely lied and wore a mask.

I was lost. I needed help. I needed a deeper spiritual type of help. I wanted to be there for humanity. I had all these ideas laid out in hundreds of pages and books in front of me in the church.

I had been in there for months just obsessing on building this dream.

I wanted to move beyond my story. I was co-existing with the pain and the loss of my Aunt and every relationship after that.

How do I stop the pain? How do I finish my silent grieving? I kept picking at the scab on my heart, which could not seem to heal.

My life had become my project.

I wanted to break the boundaries of my life and what society settles for. It would be a bigger crime to know you can change a system and not even try… I implored upon the universe: Can you bring me the right support and people to help me?

In the midst of this series of questions that fluttered through my core, I did not realize that the subtle noises behind me were that of another human being.

She stood there in the shadows of the stained-glass windows, just watching me ruminate and create images before my very existence.

"You don't pick up my calls anymore, why?" I turned and saw her.

Morena's hair was shorter, her frame taller, and her voice more confident.

'Oh hey,' I was slightly caught off guard again.

"Hello Scott." She crossed her arms and made her way up the aisle.

The two of us sat on the altar and she began thumbing through all of my notebooks. It was almost as if months had not passed since the last time we saw each other or spoke.

'What are you doing here?' I looked at her quizzically.

"You have vision, you have ideas, and you are hiding from the world. I see it, Scott." She did not sound angry, rather she sounded determined.

I motioned to the papers before me: 'I am leadership. I embody faith. I represent an idea… or are they just masks that I wish were real. I have to stand in my power and allow people to stand in their power. This is Windows of Opportunity.'

Morena looked on in silence, just allowing her eyes to graze over everything.

"There are stories behind every story," She finally said.

'How does that play into this vision and into what I want to inspire on this planet?'

The two of us sat there, mainly in silence, reading through pages and pages of notes I had sprawled out across the floor. A piece of paper with a single quote flew from one of the pages:

"The work which is most likely to become our most durable monument, and to convey some knowledge of us to the most remote posterity, is a work of bare utility; not a shrine, not a fortress, not a palace, but a bridge."
- Donald Langmead

At that moment, I needed that message. I thought to myself what other messages would spring forth from this seemingly perpetual darkness I was entrenched in.

Time would have to fill in the rest of that tale.

∞ ∞ ∞ ∞ ∞ ∞ ∞ ∞

When I woke up the next morning in the attic of the church, I was alone. The floor was cold, which was a nice juxtaposition to the intense humidity floating through the air. I rolled over in my own puddle of sweat, only to find a quote resting on a scrap of paper:

"Until one is committed there is hesitancy, the chance to draw back, always ineffectiveness. Concerning all acts of initiative and creation there is one elementary truth the ignorance of which kills countless ideas and splendid plans: that the moment one definitely commits oneself, then Providence moves too." -
W.H. Murray, The Scottish Himalayan Experience

It really made me think about how long I had spent wallowing in a sea of questions, yet I was devoid of pursuing answers.

I had so much potential, though I found myself trapped in expectations and a fractured reality. The skills, gifts, and talents I had ran rampant through my veins, though my heart was not beating in tune with any of those aspects.

Something told me that I desperately needed a change of scenery: it had been years since the lawsuit was over, yet I felt like its shadow was clinging to my body.

Grace, the woman who I met at United Global Shift in Toronto not long before the brunt of the lawsuit came to its ultimate conclusion, called hoping to chat with me. As the two of us spoke and caught up, she told me to come visit her in Canada. She told me she was living at a place called the Sunshine Coast and that I was welcome to come stay by her as long as I would like.

Those fateful words, "All you have to do is pay for your flight up here, I'll take care of the rest," were what drew me in.

I wanted a sign from the universe, and here it was: a new adventure was placed before me.

I wasn't sure what to expect and went into this whole idea of Grace's without any expectations.

I was so exhausted from the whirlwind of events that took place over the past few months. Between the internal pressures and external stressors plaguing my soul, I figured I had no time to bask in the anxiety I was feeling.

Had I really sat down and thought about it, I would have let my past heartbreaks stop me from wiggling in this experience that was about to happen.

However, there are no coincidences, and I am learning that rapidly. Faith was gone, Alessandra was becoming a fleeting memory, and I had to heal from the shattered situations I was a part of. There is a certain oddity that exists in running from the situation I was in, but maybe God was giving me this moment in order to fully embrace the closure I so desperately needed.

Within a week, my flight was booked, Morena was tasked with watching over Windows of Opportunity, and my mind was set on growing. The type of growth I expected, however, was holistically unknown to me.

After months of running on fear and adrenaline, I ended up passing out on the plane to Canada. It was a detox from society of sorts, for the Sunshine Coast would prove to be a rather isolated region.

∞ ∞ ∞ ∞ ∞ ∞ ∞ ∞

As my feet hit the runway in Vancouver, butterflies spread throughout my stomach. I was so nervous and I didn't really know why.

Once I walked out of the customs area and saw her, Grace's gentle embrace made me feel as if everything would be okay. I wanted to see where she was from and where her incredible spirit came from. The two of us walked around and began to engage in philosophical conversations about life. Grace happily obliged to act as a tour guide, and it was nice to be a visitor of sorts for once.

The two of us ate at a quaint French restaurant, where the aromas of fresh bread and exquisite cuisine flooded the air. It was an elegant change of pace from eating leftover Chinese food from a Styrofoam tray in a church attic.

As the night came to a close on our first day venturing around Vancouver, Grace informed me that I would be staying with a friend of hers during my trip. She explained that a family member of hers would be staying at her house, and her close friend had a spare guest room where I could stay.

At first, I was nervous. I travelled all the way to another country, another coast, and another time zone, and the only familiar face I knew would be a few blocks from where I would be staying.

When the two of us walked up to her friend's house, I saw a series of windchimes swaying in the patient atmosphere. There were faint melodies from the soft metallic clanking, which seemed to wrap around the house that ushered me towards the front door. Grace's high heels clicked against the wooden planks on the porch.

"You coming?" She said, turning to meet my wandering eyes.

'Yeah,' I practically skipped up the steps to this whimsical house.

I took a deep breath as she knocked on the door, for I felt anxious about meeting her friends.

A short-statured man appeared before me, his gray hair askew and his sweater slightly covered in crumbs of some sort.

"Oh dear, Grace," he began to brush himself off. "I am so sorry, I fell asleep on the couch. Please, come in." He stepped aside and allowed both of us to pass.

Grace gave him a big hug as she walked past; it seemed that they were very good pals who were thrilled to see one another.

I looked around his brightly colored living room, which was dimly lit by candles and faint lamps. The man extended his hand and placed his hand on the side of my right arm:

"I'm Sam, welcome to our home," he grinned.

'Our?' I asked quizzically.

"My wife, Hannah, will be home shortly. She is out delivering some goodies to our neighbors," Sam took a seat on the couch and motioned for Grace and I to do the same.

I was skeptical for a moment, but his mannerisms and his spirit were rather open.

"I do not know what Grace has told you," he began to sip from a teacup to his left. "But I am a medium."

'Oh, no,' I was unsure of what to say. 'Grace didn't give me too much information.'

"That's okay," Sam spoke softly. "It gives us a chance to have a more enriching conversation about our souls."

Our souls; it was the way he said it that struck me with a certain sense of nostalgia mixed with serenity. The three of us began to talk about New York City and my life in, as Sam called it, such an urban paradise.

The entire evening was incredibly spiritual, and he even started to talk about how my aunt was my guardian angel.

A general warmth rushed over my soul, for I knew it was the truth.

When a woman with blonde and white streaks in her hair entered through the front door, the energy shifted in the room. It felt as if all of the plants adorning the walls turned to greet her.

"Hello, you must be Scott," the woman dropped her bags on the floor and rushed right over to me. "I'm Hannah."

The woman didn't hesitate a moment, she just threw her arms around me and embraced me. It was as if she sensed the pain within my soul.

The four of us engaged in such lovely conversations about growth and empowerment until Grace fell sound asleep on the couch. She curled into me as if my warm body had a gravitational force over her exhausted frame.

Sam threw a blanket over her and told me to just turn off the lamp beside me before going to bed for the night.

I took a stroll over to the window as Grace's faint breathing lulled my heartbeat into a sense of belonging. The moon glistened as its light struck the water. For once, I felt that I could have a good night's sleep despite the continuous chirping of wind chimes that swayed outside the open window.

My shoes made a muffled clunking noise on the floor, and that was the last thing I remember hearing before my head hit the pillow and I passed out.

∞ ∞ ∞ ∞ ∞ ∞ ∞ ∞

The next morning, I woke up to the smell of blueberry pancakes drifting into the room. Hannah was hunched over a frying pan in the kitchen pushing a metal spatula around to scrape all of the batter from the edges of the Teflon.

"Good morning, how are you?" Hannah didn't even look up from the pan, it was almost as if she sensed my presence.

'Hi,' I groggily made my way over to her and sat on a stool next to the counter.

Hannah plopped the plate in front of me as the scent of pancakes rose to meet my exhausted face.

"Eat," she grinned. "Grace woke up earlier and she said she'll be right back... but first, breakfast."

Hannah edged the plate towards me again.

Though I met Sam and Hannah just the night before, I felt as if they had been a calming presence in my life for years.

After nibbling on the delicious pancakes, Grace re-entered the house and greeted me with a genuine smile. Within minutes, the two of us were out and about on a walking tour of Gibsons, another coastal town filled with smiling faces.

We waltzed through the streets and down to the beach. The two of us eventually ended up eating lunch at a pleasant local seafood place called Smitty's, where lobster and fried clams were fresh and bountiful.

Once we ate, the two of us walked down to the boardwalk where we saw an inscription before us in chalk. It said, "Before I die, I want to..." and people were lining up to respond to the statement with chalk.

Grace wrote three words in front of her toes: "Change the world."

I didn't even hesitate when she passed me the chalk. I wrote, "Make a real difference in our world with a great team around me."

Hours later, Grace dropped me off at Sam and Hannah's house and explained that she had to visit with her current houseguests. Without missing a beat, Hannah wrapped her arm around mine and said that I could go to dinner with her, Sam, and Hannah's younger sister.

They didn't really know me, yet they treated me like family. It was pure unconditional love.

The third day I was there, I woke up to Hannah and Sam leading a peaceful meditation just beyond their back porch. A few neighbors of theirs were sitting with their legs folded in the lush greenery that sat in the middle of their backyard. I looked on with my curiosity peaked, only to be brought into the circle as Sam motioned for me to join them.

That afternoon, Grace and I sat in on a prayer circle experience that Sam and Hannah were hosting. It was unreal. I felt the positive vibrancy in the words from the souls in the circle, as about twenty-five of us sat around. My mind wandered into a deep trance until I saw a white light, the sunrise, and doves fluttering above my head.

Sam later explained to me that it may have been Jesus giving me a blessing, and that the dove was a symbol of inner peace. I loved the energy and spirit emulating from this entire experience.

Maybe this is what I needed to recenter my soul in the context of this universe.

Though I felt myself missing Faith dearly, I tried to control my tears.

Hannah must have sensed my deep sadness, as she pressed a reassuring hand on my shoulder.

"It's okay to let go," Hannah whispered.

'I know,' the tears began streaming down my face. 'I did, and that is why I am crying.'

∞ ∞ ∞ ∞ ∞ ∞ ∞ ∞

The next day as Grace apologized to me for having to leave; I told her that it was totally okay. I had not booked a flight back to the United States, nor did I know how long I was going to stay, but Hannah and Sam assured me I could stay as long as I wanted.

I loved the energy there and something told me not to leave as of yet.

Sam walked me down to the beach, where plenty of people from the town were resting on the sand. As the two of us left our footprints in the sand, he pointed out the Inuk, or Indian sacred rocks, where I would eventually have spiritual, soul-searching conversations about who I was while sitting around the rocks.

People were waving at us and calling out our names: it was your typical small town feel, where almost everyone knew each other's names. Though I was just there for a few days at this point, people were greeting me by my name.

We ended up going kayaking on the Pacific Ocean, and I could swear I was living out the scenes from *The Notebook*.

People looked on as we navigated through the water and made our way towards what was beyond the land we were encircled in.

As we passed the last bit of land we could see, I looked out at the sheer expansiveness of the ocean. The sight of the calm waters and the deep midnight blue ripples beyond Canada made me realize that there is an entire world beyond the horizon. We may not always see what is beyond our shores, but life exists past our perception.

I had to remind myself that.

In the few days I was here, I was learning more about myself, my power, and who I truly am despite being so far from, "home." It was something about the majestic beauty of Canada that seemed to recenter my soul.

Growth is genuinely incredible.

"Hey," Sam shouted as he was drifting through the water.

'Hey,' I smiled back at him.

"Scott, it is okay to struggle," he began. "Just don't live in that struggle for too long."

It was almost as if he could feel the pain leaving my body and floating away.

"Trust the process, just trust the process." Sam turned his kayak around and I could hear the plastic sloshing in the water. I turned my kayak as well and we ventured back to the shore.

The two of us were silent as we retreated to the dock. I spent every moment embracing the sound of the water and the warm sun beaming on my face. Sam began talking to me as we paddled back, but he told me that I should listen and not reply right away.

"Patience," he muttered softly.

We spoke about my Circle of Angels, my Aunt Barbara, and all of the light that encompassed my soul. He encouraged me to love myself and support myself, as the angels were attempting to do the same.

"Your soul is so full of light," Sam's eyes glistened as the sun glazed across them. We spoke about my evolution of faith and love, and how true, divine love was out there.

'Divine love?' I perked up.

"Listen to the water, not the words," he recommended.

Sam seemed to close his eyes and let the water just guide him. He continued to discuss the enlightenment I was about to embark upon and the blessings I would receive shortly.

I had studied a lot of different schools of thought at this point, but divine love was new to me.

As we approached the dock, the two of us were greeted with an eloquent view of Robert's Creek. I could see elaborate swirls and rock formations as we stood on the wooden planks. The swirls spoke to me in a manner that was spiritually awakening. It was as if the universe was trying to talk to me, but I was unaware of what it was saying at the time. Before we stepped onto the kayaks, I don't think I truly appreciated the symbols, swirls, and intricacies before, but I had a new appreciation for them.

It was almost as if I had to travel beyond the beautiful scenery, then return in order to truly cherish what was before me. The vivid colors were soothing to my soul, and I could feel my soul spiraling between the swirls and the spaces between them.

When Sam and I returned to his humble home, we spoke more about divine love. He explained that it was a school of thought as opposed to a religion. The entire concept seemed philosophical and spiritual in nature.

Though Hannah was cooking something enticing in the kitchen, she even chimed in on the conversation: "We have the ability to love one another, to feel one another, to provide for one another, and genuinely raise the bar of our life's true purpose."

I heard each of the words flowing from her mouth, and for once there were a series of statements I could genuinely resonate with.

My mind was exhausted, and though I spoke with God and my angels often, I am not sure I was fully connected to them. I was lost. The pain in my heart radiated to other parts of my body, and I tended to lose myself in the midst of what is and what could be.

I sensed I had a spiritual calling to visit this place.

So many people rely on me for emotional support and comfort, yet what happens when I am holistically unaligned with what I so truly want and need in this universe?

I was suffering. I was in the depths of an intense spiritual pain.

I was in desperate need of salvation.

Has God put me through this as a preparation for what is to come on this next journey?

∞ ∞ ∞ ∞ ∞ ∞ ∞ ∞

The lyrics to "More than Words" by Extreme fluttered through my head:

"Saying I love you
Is not the words
I want to hear from you
It's not that I want you
Not to say, but if you only knew
How easy it would be to show me how you feel
More than words is all you have to do to make it real
Then you wouldn't have to say that you love me
'Cause I'd already know."

Love exists beyond words. The song anchors me to a time when I was leaving a hardware store with Faith, who seemed like she was about to become my girlfriend at that time, and we sang the words to that song in unison.

It seemed like an intense bonding of love. It seemed like an expression of love.

Yet time said otherwise.

"Be patient" hung at the tip of my tongue, almost as if Sam was inside my head and ushering me to a certain train of thoughts.

Though I felt that I was utterly derailed from ever finding love.

My ego was interrupting the bigger picture here.

I woke to another beautiful morning on the Sunshine Coast feeling disconnected; yet rested. What was happening to me?

Everything within my core felt as if it were on fire. I was nervous, nauseous, but I felt that I was at peace for a change.

Hannah was standing in the kitchen watching me flicker my eyelids open.

"You have a special angel assigned to you, her presence is strong," She was looking directly at me.

'Oh, thank you,' I was unsure of what else to say.

Why do I have an angel? Who is my angel? Why was I so special?

Moments later, Sam motioned for me to join him on the porch, to which I automatically drifted towards him.

"Your life will be very different in four years' time," he spoke softly again. It was almost as if he whispered his thoughts into the universe, hoping they would soon come true.

He liked to drop insightful comments in my direction, but somehow, they were a window to my soul.

'Maybe in four years I would be married' was the first thought that popped in my head.

Sam must have known what I was thinking, for he just smiled and averted his glance to the water.

I had slept well, but Faith's memory and "More Than Words" lingered in the forefront of my mind.

Sam invited me to join in a prayer with a number of visitors they were having, to which I happily obliged. Something magical was happening.

Suddenly, I felt filled with love.

Hours later, I found myself, Sam, and three other people walking around in the Soames Woods. I loved walking in nature and having talks about spirituality. It felt natural and quintessential to the growth of my soul.

It became obvious: I had to take care of my soul and build a strong foundation for my emotions before I let my mind crumble.

Divine love, this new school of thought, was the way.

While walking on the trails, I felt as if the trees were parting to let us travel through the landscape.

When we emerged from the woods, more people came to join us in a prayer. The faces of strangers suddenly felt like family, though in an altered sense. We were bonded by mutual thought, not by blood, which represented how devoutly we were committed to growth.

It had always been my soul's mission to help people and raise the spirits of those around me, though I never knew what that looked like until Elyza helped me hone my passion for helping youth.

The experiences I was a part of on the Sunshine Coast were a holistic representation of spiritual growth. Divine Love was a school of thought I was being exposed to, and I was an eager student.

I soon found out that Divine Love was not something automatic, nor was it guaranteed when a person passed from this life to the next.

Apparently, as we pray for our Father's love, we help our loved ones in the next realm. As a result, we then help grow our souls and those around us.

I was blessed to learn this knowledge from such enlightened people. There was no exchange of funds or membership; the only currency that was required was being open-minded.

It is a true community.

∞ ∞ ∞ ∞ ∞ ∞ ∞ ∞

Upon getting out of the shower the next morning, I felt more refreshed than usual. My showers in New York had been quite scattered during the past few months, and I could feel the difference between sloshing a ratty sponge in the sink of the church versus the cool, calming waters of Canada rushing down my spine.

My skin and hair felt different, but no one seemed to notice or comment on it.

I tend to think that most people are not cognizant of their surroundings. At this point, I all but lost track of the time I had spent here so far, but Sam and Hannah continued to welcome my presence in their home.

I had been an active participant while here, but I was taking everything in and absorbing the energy here at the same time.

Back in New York, I was balancing the relationship between Windows of Opportunity, the Queens Community Church, and myself. Oftentimes, this balance did not suffice for my soul or my innate sense of self, for everything happening around me seemed more important than what was going on in my own head.

At this point in my journey, I realized that the small arguments I would have with people in New York were inundated with negative energy and detrimental spirits that encompassed many.

I am sure that upon first glance, this whole experience and school of thought seem to be inundated with hocus pocus, but this is all far beyond that.

Divine Love is a series of questions and thoughts that augment upon each other to create a better sense of our respective souls.

How do we truly give our souls more space to explore developmental thoughts and notions?

How do we become more positive, more loving, and strengthen our souls to overcome difficult situations and live a higher form of existence?

We need a communal place to speak and express ourselves.

Step one of any journey should be to love ourselves. Though I did love who I was, it took me many years to comprehend that I am more than my circumstances.

The past is just a series of moments that surmount to strength.

Though I realized that I deeply regret a lot of what I had caused or experienced in life, I discovered that everything was building to help me become a better man.

I continued to listen to Sam, Hannah, and the community they were building there. With every prayer or soul-searching activity we did, Sam encouraged us to create questions we would ask God. Though we were limited to just five questions, my mind succumbed to my usual inquisitive nature.

My mind was racing.

I began to think about what God would intend for me and my life. How would my personal growth flourish in contrast to the souls around me? Are prayer circles and lightworkers the answer? Can a small group of people impact the world on a large scale?

Does change exist?

Can I be strong enough for this world?

"Scott," Sam murmured. "Just five questions, son."

I had not realized I shut my eyes for what must have been about thirty minutes, so that my thoughts could stir up a series of questions.

The impact of that day is something I would not soon forget. It was a powerful and spiritually deep day that I still process in my mind.

There we were, about twenty different souls, overlooking scenic mountains and the calm waters nearby.

Within my mind I kept asking questions, though I discovered that in order to develop my soul, I had to strip away the ego deep inside of me.

I sensed the shift in energy that my soul was experiencing.

I sensed my Aunt Barbara was with me.

∞ ∞ ∞ ∞ ∞ ∞ ∞ ∞

In the days that followed, Sam spoke about how our planet was in trouble and that our work truly matters.

As I expressed my opinions within the group, I found that seemingly total strangers wanted to hear my story.

While sharing an abbreviated version of what I had endured, most people were stunned or leaning into my discussion; it was almost as if I suddenly became a centre of light.

Maybe I was a beacon of hope.

As I spoke about my past relationships, Sam gripped his fingers around his knees and glared into my eyes.

"Scott, you will find love soon," he sounded solemn, but very reassuring.

Afterwards, I walked around for what seemed like hours. His words rumbled in my mind as an avalanche of unanswered questions. Who was he talking about? Was there truth behind his words?

∞ ∞ ∞ ∞ ∞ ∞ ∞ ∞

Something was bothering me and I was not sure what unbalanced my soul. I figured maybe New York was not the place for me. Maybe I had a life in Canada. Maybe I was just lost.

I wondered, 'Will I ever find my way home?'

∞ ∞ ∞ ∞ ∞ ∞ ∞ ∞

Sam and Hannah continued to lead prayer circles and discuss the innate gifts each soul has within.

I could tell, as we all sat in silence, that something shifted in the depths of my core.

It was time to return to New York.

I booked my flight for the following morning, and promised to keep in touch with Sam, Hannah, and the community on the Sunshine Coast.

On my last day of my trip, there were plenty of moments filled with gratitude, tears, and transformative conversations.

As I made a final walk to the beach by Robert's Creek, I watched the waves ebb and flow. It reminded me of the last line of F. Scott Fitzgerald's *The Great Gatsby*: *"And so we beat on, boats against the current, borne back ceaselessly into the past."* Though in that current state of mind, I knew history was not going to repeat itself.

Sam and Hannah made a delicious breakfast for me and I was on my way to New York.

∞ ∞ ∞ ∞ ∞ ∞ ∞ ∞

Tears filled my eyes as I gazed upon the buildings of New York City from within the airplane. It was mid-August at this point, and I had been in Canada for about three weeks. My heart was heavy, but I knew I had a mission to work towards.

I slammed my eyes shut and hoped for the best: 'Angels,' I wept. 'Please be with me.'

That first night back, it was hard to sleep at the church again. The cold floor showed no mercy towards my soul. Nothing felt right. I was easily slipping back into the daily routine I once had, though deep within I knew that everything was changing. Rearranging my schedule to benefit my new health and higher consciousness-based lifestyle would be a difficult transition period, but I desperately needed it. I know that if I maintain my prayer and meditation practices, I would be able to handle the work and life I was leading.

I felt good.

If I eased into this sort of new transition in my life, everything would be powerful and smooth.

There are spirits and angels working with me, and I felt a sort of cloak of protection reigning over my soul.

I have to keep the faith.

Although I missed being in Canada, and the positivity that embraced me when I was there, I knew that I would return there one day.

The relationship I have with myself trumps any relationship that I was a part of in the past. Until someone extraordinary crosses my path, I refuse to let my soul express itself in a romantic way ever again.

'I am worth it,' lingered on my lips.

As August dwindled down, I packed my schedule with so many counseling appointments and business meetings. Morena was handling the paperwork from the back end of Windows of Opportunity, and the two of us continued to meet and talk about life and my newfound education related to spirituality.

She was very receptive to everything I learned. Morena even seemed genuinely interested in prayer circles, lightworkers, and the entire divine love movement. In a sense, I always knew that Morena was part of a higher school of thought; I just did not realize what she was capable of discussing until we finally dove deep into the recesses of my soul.

As the two of us walked the usual paths of Alley Pond Park in the sweltering heat, Morena looked me in the eye and said her favorite catchphrase: "Maybe what you are searching for is not what you are looking for."

'What does that even mean?' I snapped at her.

Her eyes looked sullen as she turned away from me.

"One day, you will realize it."

'One day?'

"One. Day."

When the two of us made our way to the end of the trail, I discovered Sam and Hannah had emailed me a message. The two of them said that Sam received a powerful message about me. In their respective elaborate way, the two of them were certain that I would soon meet a girl at a school who would be the one for me.

Who would have the audacity to assume this?

At that point, I swore off relationships. I did not want to be seen as so weak and lonely that I would just pursue anyone or toss my fragile heart around.

My heart was permanently removed from my sleeve, and I was keeping it that way. I don't quite understand my feelings sometimes, but the law of attraction and my own soul's growth were worth it.

I was steadfast in acknowledging I would not find love within a school building, especially since I was usually working for after school programs and with youth.

August came to a close with a wealth of knowledge at the tip of my brow: I had to grow Windows of Opportunity's reach, and I was excited to continue running after school programs at different locations.

Despite being surrounded by the usual New York mayhem, things were going well.

∞ ∞ ∞ ∞ ∞ ∞ ∞ ∞

I received a call from Bryan, who had just settled into a new dorm room for his upcoming year at Stony Brook. When his grandfather, Gemma's dad, passed away, he decided to leave his car to Bryan. Though we were grateful for this and thankful for the love that still existed within our family, Matheson men do not seem to have such good luck with cars.

It turned out that Bryan accidentally drove the car into the brick wall of a deli. Fortunately, no one was injured, but the car needed quite a lot of repairs.

As I sat in the autobody shop watching the mechanics work on the car, I began thinking about my parents. Though I had a very strained relationship with them as a kid, I thought it was about time I officially buried the hatchet and released the pain I endured from my soul.

I love my parents. I do forgive them for everything I went through. Forgiveness is not about excusing the act. Forgiveness is a gift for the soul: it gave me the permission to move forward towards a solid, healthy place in my life.

I let go of the pain knowing that in the experiences they granted me, they reacted from their own innate pain. They had a limited comprehension of love and the way they displayed it.

There was a limited comprehension of unconditional love. Yet in my mature and wiser years, I developed an understanding of loving humanity.

I do not hold them responsible for the moments we experienced together.

I loved my parents very much, and this moment, where I watched Bryan's car transforming before my eyes, I discovered that love for a child manifests in many ways.

However, youth need the most optimal experience possible.

I only hope to give Bryan the love and support he deserves.

While I was still sitting there, I rested my head against the back wall and let my mind drift to a safe haven.

As my phone rang, I picked it up instinctively and without thinking of who it could be.

It just so happened that it was a former elementary school friend of mine, who I kept in touch with on and off throughout the years. She told me that her school's principal was looking for a social worker to run a series of after school leadership programs, and that I should come in right away for the interview.

The next day, I found myself sitting in the empty halls of Lincoln Memorial High School. All I knew about the school was that it could be a place where I could expand my leadership programs on a larger scale.

Lincoln Memorial was doing some sort of education initiative called Social Emotional Learning, which seemed right up my alley. Still, I was not sure if I wanted to stop working for the other schools I was a part of. After all, I had been with those schools for years.

Then a familiar voice emerged from the principal's office. She gazed at my long blonde locks, seemingly unfazed by my black jeans and dark gray t-shirt.

"Hey, I recognize you," she started.

I turned and looked at her. She did look familiar, but I was working with so many people at this point, I did not know where I knew her from.

I rose and shook her hand.

"I'm Shirley," she smiled and I felt the energy in my soul shift.

'Hi, it's nice to meet you,' I grinned back at her, thinking that maybe this was the start of a new chapter in my life and Windows of Opportunity's legacy.

"I remember you," she shouted joyfully. "You broke up the fight at Musicapalooza years ago... my son was the drummer of the band."

Then it hit me: I did know her. I did remember who she was.

The two of us spoke for a few minutes, catching up about what happened since that fateful night, and she blurted out the two words that I never thought would be uttered to me in a school system ever again: "You're hired!"

Without hesitation, I apologized to her and said that I was not interested in being an employee, only in expanding WOO. I would be more than happy to provide her with programs created by Windows of Opportunity. Her face dropped instantly as desperation filled her eyes.

After everything that happened with the lawsuit, I made a personal vow to myself never to work as an individual school employee ever again. Yet here I was, standing in the office of a school principal, being offered a job.

"Please," Shirley begged. "I promise that we are a good school."

I saw those eyes before: the glance of someone ambitious who just wants to make a difference in the world.

"You can trust us." Her words stuck out in my mind.

Everything deep within me felt as if I could not go against the maltreatment the system brought to me years ago. Still, I was slowly becoming the man who was working past misunderstanding and misjudgment.

Something deep within me called upon me to take a chance.

She appeared passionate about shifting the system... if she was willing to take a chance on me, and carte blanche on creating something to impact youth in an extremely positive way, what was I waiting for?

The voice within me begged that I take a chance on her.

A brief pause stood between us as I chose to take a leap of faith.

'Ok,' I smiled at her. 'You have a deal. You can have me and Windows of Opportunity.'

She thanked me profusely and the partnership between Social Emotional Learning and Windows of Opportunity began.

In the few days that stood between beginning to work at Lincoln Memorial High School and letting go of the pain within, I was told I needed to take a student safety seminar that was mandated by the state. That Sunday, I walked into the room eager to learn about how to help students from the state's perspective, and I directly shook hands with fate.

My former supervisor, the woman who launched the lawsuit against me, was the woman running the seminar.

Though I was shaking and my heart was pulsating from my chest, I knew this was God's way of testing my strength and faith. Sam's wisdom, "Patience," came to the forefront of my mind.

She recognized me and greeted me warmly, but we did not talk much. I did not tell her where I was going to be working, though I knew that she could figure it out if she wanted.

Spirituality and positivity are muscles. I had been trying to work it out but I struggled deep inside. I wanted to create possibilities.

You can't learn to swim unless you are in the water so I had to jump in and be in action… Lincoln Memorial High could be the best place to take that first step towards something bigger. The day I could forgive without condoning an act against me is the day I would get my life back, for leaders inherently get the job done.

I needed to jump off a cliff, metaphorically speaking, and build my wings on the way down. I knew I had a higher purpose. I was not going to figure it all out in hiding.

The world is numb. What comes from the heart goes to the heart. The world is just putting bandages on issues. We had to go bigger for real change to occur. My license did not make me an expert. A license is just a part of a social system, just like a degree. My experience and my soul gave me the strength to move forward… so forward is where I intended to go.

∞ ∞ ∞ ∞ ∞ ∞ ∞ ∞

On my first day of work at Lincoln Memorial High School, I washed my body in the church's sink with that ratty old sponge. Remnants of a mysterious dream were floating through my head as I prepared myself for whatever was to come next.

I glanced in the mirror, the water droplets cascading from my freshly-shaven face, and watched my eyes brighten with the possibility of something powerful ahead of me.

'If I am going to rock the boat,' I watched my face ease in the mirror. 'Will you sway with me?'

I stand for the fact that youth can change the world: "For youth by youth" had been Windows of Opportunity's mantra for as long as it has been in existence. Youth can make a real difference, and have a powerful positive voice. I stand for programs that are innovative and impactful, filled with empowerment and possibility.

Possibility is the seed we are planting, and watering it with platforms of opportunity.

As I pulled up to the school, I took a deep breath and turned off my car. When the key slid from the ignition, I felt my fear fade away.

This was not just another day... This was the first day of whatever would come next.

CHAPTER 36

Refuse to Sink

~

"If she runs away she fears she won't be followed...
What could be the worse than leaving something behind"

- **Vanessa Carlton, American musician, singer, songwriter, Milford, Pennsylvania**

New beginnings come with their faint scent of resolute hope. As situations present themselves before our very eyes, we find that our experiences have tainted an unwavering part of who we are: our respective souls. We may transform and transcend as time progresses, but nothing truly prepares us for the next chapter. Nothing knocks on our door and says, "Hey, the next part of your life is beginning now."

We just ebb and flow with the tides, floating in the infinitesimal abyss that lingers between who we once were and what we will become. It is a beautiful feeling: embracing the new piece of our puzzle, while recognizing that all of the pieces before us had to be earned along our respective journeys.

Morena's voice persisted from within the depths of my mind: "Make each day count."

For once, I was not counting the seconds on a clock or counting on a relationship to manifest before me. I was making a conscious effort to count on my innate longing to do good in this world...

As it always should have been.

There is a balance that exists between all the light we cannot see and our true soul emerging from the ashes. The plight of miscommunication remains fervent when we do not, even for one moment, stop to look at our surroundings. When we choose to cast aside logic and reason, and replace it with the lies of false supposed prophets, we throw our dignity through the dirt as well as our soul.

Mud and hate should not cast a shadow on who we are and all our souls wish to grow into.

We should not and will not forget those who brought us to where we are today. We must carry the legacy and torch of those whose physical entities perished long before their goals were fulfilled. We must blaze a trail with enough tenacity to say, "You do not scare me and you do not own me."

We must encourage the lost and lonely to find their wholesome, consummate power through the energy they put forth into this world. We must light a candle in honor of those who cannot see through the darkness.

We must thrive through ashes. We must dust the pain off and grow. We must heal ourselves and heal the world.

For one day, and I knew this to be an evident and eventual truth, I was worthy of love.

I just never knew what kind of love, until I found my perpetual equal.

I am rushing too far ahead with the story though, for there is a lot that happened between then and now.

∞ ∞ ∞ ∞ ∞ ∞ ∞ ∞

As the sun climbed over the high school, I watched the gargoyles look sternly upon the landscape. Their eyes were downcast in a way that could strike fear in even the sternest individuals.

When I entered the school, although this was not my first time in the building, I felt as if everything shifted. The world tilted on its axis for a moment and caught me off-balance: This was my new workplace.

Though I would just be working part time after school here, the principal, Shirley, insisted that I meet with the entire staff so that I could feel like part of the blossoming family they were developing there.

I happily obliged, but within my first few minutes there, I realized that I did not know where to go.

Shirley, clad in a crisp jet-black suit, made her way into the hallway and rested her eyes on me: "Scott, I am so happy you are here!"

She sprung forth from the conversation she was engaged in, and made her way over to me instinctively.

"What's new," she put her arm around me as if we were old pals just catching up.

'Nothing,' I smiled, trying to hide the silent anxiety sifting through my soul.

"I forgot," she snapped her fingers. "I have to show you your new office."

'New office?' My puzzled expression caught her off guard.

"Yeah," Shirley grinned as if she were slightly confused. "You have an office here."

An office. My *own* office. It was a pleasant surprise, to say the least.

Never in my life did I instantly get offered a space to call my own. Though I had some semblance of ownership over past places and areas, Shirley had granted me the capacity to express myself within the confines of a school.

665

It was something I did not expect, though it welcomed a plethora of unrequited feelings.

As the two of us walked through the brightly painted hallways adorned with positive messages and images, it felt like I was finally in a high school that was meant for me. When the two of us traveled downstairs and unlocked the door, the dim sunlight cut through the room and rested at my feet. There was a wooden desk, a leather couch, and chairs that reminded me of my old office in my other high school.

Images of the International Beer Club hanging out in the hallways of Jamaica High School danced through my head.

I wondered what Tommy was doing. I wondered what Danielle would have been doing if she had not joined my Circle of Angels. I pondered what my life would have become if I had a Social Worker running programs for youth when I was a student.

I was hopeful that the same guidance counselor who helped me had been helping students for years.

My middle school teacher, who took my friend and I to dinner, came to mind. Where was she now? What happened to all of the souls in my life who shaped my perspective of high school?

Many of the moments from my elementary, middle, and high school years were fading into the sunset, but that did not mean I was not cognizant of their impact on my soul.

"Well," Shirley stood there eagerly waiting for me to say something.

A seemingly long pause hung in the air as I slowly spun around the center of the office.

'It's perfect.' I did not know what else to say. This school felt holistically different from my previous school, and I did not think it was as oppressive of a situation as my own high school experience.

Shirley smiled again, "I'll let you explore in here for a bit. Our staff meeting is in the library in 30 minutes."

The door edged shut behind her as I became acquainted with the energy in the room. It was different. It was unique.

It could have been my home.

After sitting on the couch for what felt like hours, I made my way towards the school's library. Sam's comments seemed to be coming true.

I was in a better place, a clearer space, and somewhere that was genuinely different from where I once was.

There were faces strewn about the library, some seemed familiar with one another, but it seemed like there were a lot of young, brand new teachers.

Shirley was standing at the front of the room, shuffling papers behind a podium, motioning for me to take a seat at one of the tables.

I found a spot near two women who appeared to be meeting for the first time. They seemed friendly enough, and I figured that if the three of us were new to the staff, we would form some sort of conversation based on where we came from and how we got here.

The woman on the left, who was closest to me, seemed to be nervous about her first day on the job. Though she carried herself confidently, the woman kept playing with her fingers and twirling her hair. It is truly amazing how you can discern a person's nervous tendencies if you pay close enough attention.

The woman on her right, who kept pushing her glasses towards the bridge of her nose, was perched with one leg tucked under the other. It was almost as if the leg folded underneath her was keeping her from teetering over and into the woman next to me.

As Shirley began her welcome speech, she explained how a number of new staff members, myself included, would be joining the school this year. After a few moments of giving some basic information about the school, she told all of us to turn to each other, introduce ourselves, and talk about the strangest thing we had on our minds.

The two women and I looked at each other and smiled coyly. I was unsure of what to say and how to start a conversation between the three of us, but I figured that I would take a stab at it.

'Has anyone ever heard of Anna Kendrick?'

The two women looked at me, wide-eyed.

"What?" The woman on my left stopped twirling her hair. The other sat quietly with a blank look on her face.

'So, I was watching this movie called *Pitch Perfect 2* a few months ago, and I saw this actress Anna Kendrick,' the women continued to look at me. 'I know that people always say they are *in love* with a famous person, but I would *love* to meet her. Seriously, I am a huge fan of hers.'

The women giggled and did not know what to say.

I continued: 'The moment I found out there was another *Pitch Perfect* movie; I knew I had to watch it. I don't know what it is, but she seems to have captivated me.'

"Well," the woman on my left began twirling her caramel hair again. "What would you do if you ever met the *one-and-only* Anna Kendrick?"

I was unsure of how to answer, but the three of us started laughing.

"I'm Emma," the woman who was twirling her hair extended her hand.

The woman next to her grinned and shyly extended her hand as well, "I'm Joy."

The three of us continued our conversation, and I shrunk into my new office rather quickly. This dynamic was something I was not accustomed to. Here I was, sitting with a bunch of teachers, nonchalantly talking about my interest in Anna Kendrick and *Pitch Perfect*.

What was wrong with me?

Why was I hooked on talking about love or relationships, though I was set on never getting into another relationship again?

I heard a knock on my office door, believing that Shirley was coming to speak to me about what type of timeline I had to implement my programs.

Emma crept into the doorway with a coy grin on her face. She seemed like she had some sort of purpose for coming into the room, but I was unaware what she would want.

"Hey," she looked at me as if she knew me my whole life.

'Hey, what's up?'

"Um…" it seemed that she was trying to find a lucid explanation for coming into the room. "I was going to ask if you needed to borrow, like, cleaning wipes, or… something."

'No,' I picked up the antibacterial wipes that Shirley left in my room. 'I have enough, thank you.'

"Oh," she seemed disappointed. "Okay."

'Hey,' I caught her attention as she was trying to leave the room. 'Sorry for rambling about Anna Kendrick before.'

"Oh," she began twirling her hair again. "The first day of anything is awkward, right?"

I laughed, 'Yeah, right.'

An awkward pause cut between us.

"Do you mind if I get your phone number?" Emma held her cellphone towards me. "The principal said that you are the Social Worker, and that you would be working part time with us."

'Yeah, sure.' I snatched the phone from her hand and began typing my cell number in.

"I mean," she began searching for words. "If you aren't here and I have a question, I'd want to ask you right away. I can't wait to help the kids."

'Is that why you wanted to be a teacher?'

"For the kids, yeah."

'That's awesome, what are you going to be teaching?'

"Social Studies," she gulped.

'That's good,' I flashed her a smile. 'Every child needs a good teacher, and it seems like you're going to do great.'

"Thanks," she turned bright red and shot her eyes towards the floor.

'You are welcome.' I handed the phone back to her, which she grabbed quickly.

"I appreciate it." She did not know what else to say, and neither did I, so she began turning away.

'Uh,' I tried to think of something cordial to say. 'Good luck with your first day of school tomorrow.'

"Thanks," she eyeballed the couch and my bare walls. "I can't wait to see how you decorate this space."

I looked around at the walls.

'Oh, yeah,' I chuckled. 'I didn't even think of how I was going to decorate.'

"Sorry, I don't mean to be rude," she spoke more confidently now. "I like to paint."

'Really?' I swiveled my chair so my body was facing her. 'What do you paint?'

"Mainly landscapes and stuff, nothing crazy," she tilted her head and shrugged.

'That's really cool,' I was running out of things to say to her, but something seemed to be keeping her in the room.

We locked eyes for a moment, and I could see specks of mocha in her chocolate brown irises.

'You have a story,' I said to her. 'I don't know what it is, but I can tell something exists behind those eyes.'

She blushed again and started moving towards the door.

"I look forward to working with you," she lingered in the doorway for a moment before letting it slam behind her.

Our exchange was odd, but I figured that it was just another example of how I interact with people who are looking for my expertise and insight, without actually getting to know me.

Once the day was over, I retreated to my silver Monte Carlo and drove back to the damp church attic.

∞ ∞ ∞ ∞ ∞ ∞ ∞ ∞

If I were ever to fully explain or express my innate pain and agony, I feel that I would fill a river with my tears. How do you articulately express to someone how much agony your soul is in? How do you fathom expressing your inner voice to another human being? How do you tell someone you are suffering, when you don't even know precisely what you are dealing with?

When does it become clear that you need to reach out for help, even when it appears that no one is listening?

How do you know if someone is listening?

Is there anyone out there who could truly hear me?

Is there anything that would provide salvation to the torment I deal with regularly?

How devoutly tortured is my soul?

When will this suffering cease to be?

When will I stop clawing at the possibility to merely survive each day, and truly get a chance to live?

I had nobody and I had never felt so alone.

There was something wrong with me.

Nothing had been the same since the day I lost Faith.

I had the celestial kingdom at my beck and call.

I had a deeper relationship and faith with God than ever before.

Anna Kendrick seemed so far out of reach, but has characteristics that seemed perfect.

I was sitting in the attic of a church on a Tuesday night bored out of my mind and so very alone.

That is why I stayed busy. I hated that feeling. It was dingy there. The darkness succumbed to the broken crevices of my soul. I was trying to play "home." It was embarrassing.

I put myself in a spiritual refuge. I was closer to a sense of a spiritual vibration like never before, and yet it felt pathetic.

I had to clean myself in a church sink, wash my hair with a plastic cup, and regularly give myself a sponge bath.

Those were the nights that reminded me how sad my life really was.

Faith turned her back on me and loved a guy who said he would never commit to her. She still chose him over me and opted to add salt to the wound. She threw our "friendship" and our relationship away.

The only people I had were people who needed me and sucked as much out of me as possible, which I didn't actually mind because I cared about them deeply. It was God's work I was trying to carry out. At least I mattered in that respect.

Sometimes something inside of me said not to go on... but I could never do that. I still had to persevere.

The faint chime and flickering light from my cell phone made me realize that it had just been a few hours since I left work. Another day would prevail over this one, and maybe I would get some clarity regarding my life, my future, and any prosperity that would conjure up the next puzzle piece to my journey.

When I glanced at the screen, a new number had texted me a few words, which made me chuckle:

"Hi, It's Anna Kendrick."

I looked through my phone and found the letter I wrote to Anna Kendrick the first time I saw her in *Pitch Perfect 2*, but never sent, because I did not want her to think I was one of those lunatics that chase celebrities:

Dear Anna,

Don't worry... Let me start by saying I am not a crazy insane fan and I am sure the chances of you actually reading this is probably zero to none, but if possible, I am hoping the universe pulls on your heart strings, and raises your curiosity enough to read this through… My name is Scott and I am the CEO and Founder of a NY based non-profit agency called Windows of Opportunity.

I do a lot of work in education and have a huge dream of reforming the education system. I am all about giving youth a voice, and a sense of purpose, belonging, and passion to make a difference in the world. I have created many leadership programs and have reached 250,000 youth to date through these programs. Many say I am successful, but I feel like I have not begun to scratch the surface of my potential. Anyways, I feel compelled to write to you and share this story with you. I've been so swamped in my own non-profit agency and mission to impact the world that I guess to be honest, and I'm embarrassed to say, I just discovered who you are today.

I have been pushing an event that supports a youth message that "we are all beautiful" and I needed a break from going out there, speaking to sponsors, helping people, and going full force on these projects. I just came from a big sponsorship meeting and I was mentally exhausted. I could not focus at all.

So I decided to go to the movies, which is often what I will do when I am feeling drained and just want to escape. There was nothing really playing and I was with one of my program directors. She turned to me and said we should see Pitch Perfect 2. My first reaction was "Isn't that some teenie bopper movie or some slapstick comedy?" She laughed at me and said, "You didn't see the first Pitch Perfect?"

Obviously not.

Anyhow, she pushed and pushed and I decided to see that movie against my better wishes. Fast forward, with a huge tub of popcorn on my lap, the second you came on the screen, like I'm sure many men and boys in the world probably feel, I was completely taken in by your energy. Or, at least your character's energy. Not seeing the first one or any of your movies I leaned over and asked my director "Who is that?" She whispered back, "Anna Kendrick." I replied, "Wtf is an Anna Kendrick?"

Shaking her head at me in shame, she was like, "I can't with you." Of course, the rest of the movie I was glued to your energy, and I love music. Being a drummer, and loving all styles of music, I really appreciated your talent, as well as the rest of the cast. I'm a spiritual guy and felt like there was more to who you were on that screen.

672

At first, I was joking around after the movie about how beautiful you were, how the universe was going to make sure we meet, and where the hell have I been that I never heard of you. When I left the movies, I turned around to my program director and said I would do anything to meet you, but I'm sure she's nothing like her character Becca in the movie. When we went back into the church, we did a tremendous amount of work. Later on in the evening I decided to go on YouTube and look up your name. I saw some interviews with you and was completely taken in by how genuine, natural, and real you seem. Apparently, many people feel this way about you, and are instantly attracted to that aura, even if they do not have the emotional maturity to express it. I told my program director I was going to meet you and we were going to become true real friends, and maybe perhaps you would even be interested in the youth that I help and the mission I have in the world. She thought I was crazy and I said based on my spirituality and my faith, I am sure that anything in this world is possible. I explained to her that "stars" are people too, who all have a story and happen to (in most cases) be blessed to do what they love to do... and if I can feel the energy of somebody's personality, then why not try to reach out and strike up a real friendship?

I felt like if anyone would be real enough to handle media and life the way you do (and I can't imagine how difficult it must be at times) that you may be willing to actually sit down with me and see what I'm about. Crazier things have happened in this world and how do you know if you don't ask? I would love the opportunity to speak with you or meet with you about the work I do, and learn more about who you are. I attached my website and information about my vision and you can Google my name and see that I'm not totally insane and that it would be safe to contact me. I now put this long shot into the hands of the universe and I look forward to a possible friendship in the future.

All the best,

Scott

I never sent this letter because I figured I would rather trust the universe. Besides, so many people must contact her. I stood by the affirmation that if it's meant to be, it will happen.

I am a rare genuine soul who would love to meet another rare genuine soul. I once almost went to a book signing that she was appearing at, but I chose the youth program that needed me to present that day. I took that as a sign as it was not the proper time or place.

I guess you never truly know where life will take you; that's probably the most realistic and honest summary about my entire life.

Regardless, this text was clearly someone's effort to be funny.

It was Emma's effort to come up with a witty first text.

I texted her back after I let my mind wander, and the two of us struck up a conversation about trivial things. At least her text was a welcomed distraction from the musty church.

Before I knew it, I had fallen asleep with my phone laced between my fingers. I did not remember passing out, but I knew that I was exhausted and my mind probably ushered in some semblance of a dream-like state while I was texting with Emma.

∞ ∞ ∞ ∞ ∞ ∞ ∞ ∞

In the days that followed, I started to meet the students at Lincoln Memorial High School and started to implement the programs that Windows of Opportunity had to offer. It was a refreshing new start.

With Shirley as both my principal and boss, it was nice to have some freedom to help youth become empowered and finally advocate for themselves.

Emma would always stay after school, watching the kids communicate with one another, and often tried to refer students to me through text messages and little notes she would leave for me.

Her presence was interesting. I could tell she seemed to be flirting with me quite frequently, but I did not want to assume anything. After all, Faith was the last person I truly loved or cared for, and since my soul was shredded by her actions; I could not fathom getting hurt again.

'Never again,' I promised myself.

Then one day, during one of the after-school programs, I was talking to the kids about things that they seemed to fear the most.

Emma sat there, her feet tucked underneath her and a smile adorned across her face, helping me counsel the kids. I even asked her what her fears were, and though she blushed and tried to shy away from responding, I sensed she wanted to spill everything to me right then and there.

The next morning, there was a notecard that was slid under my door: The white envelope simply said:

"To feed your dying hunger of my fears."

The inside read as follows:

Scott,

Don't go all social worker analytical on this but I have some general fears: I am TERRIFIED of drowning. I'm a terrible swimmer. One summer I just jumped in the pool and almost inhaled all the water. I suddenly had to hold my nose. WTF. Once after that I was swimming under water and someone jumped right on a float I was under. I thought that was my moment to drown. I also don't like that you can't see underneath you in ocean water so I never just dive in. I'm slowly taking small risks when we go on the boat and I have to jump in the water to pull the anchor to shore.

I am double terrified of riding a horse. When I was 6 we were camping and I was with my cousins and siblings around horses and I don't know what spooked them but they ran, I fell, and got stepped on in the back by one. My aunt found me and I cried A LOT! I've tried since, two times, getting on a horse. I totally broke down and full-blown cried both times.

I am scared I won't be a mom. Idk why. I can't picture myself old, so Idk. If I can't see raising older kids, like will that mean something will happen to me. Or if it is more I won't be in the era of time where I'd have kids like no longer here on Earth. It is scary. I try not to think about it.

Brings me to dreams of being shot in the back. I have NEVER told anyone but I am constantly scared to death looking over my shoulder.

Recently I have been having fears of divorce. Not linked to just my recent ex, but since I started with my college boyfriend years ago. Maybe 3ish years now. It has been a fear on radar.

Love, Emma

Love. Emma.

The fact that she signed the card with "Love, Emma," scared me. I was not sure what to think.

Who was this woman?

Was Sam right when he said I would meet someone?

No, he couldn't be.

How could he have known?

I felt my stomach churning and turning over and over again.

The nausea brewing in my stomach felt like it was about to burst at any moment.

Emma seemed to be persistent when it came to pursuing me, but what if I was just imagining everything?

I paced the floor of the sanctuary nightly again.

Morena came over to chat with me about relationships and my future in general.

She sat in the middle of one of the pews, gazing up at the stained-glass window undergoing a metamorphosis in the waning sunset.

"So, what exactly are you worried about?" She did not avert her eyes from the image she was glaring at.

'It's Emma,' I started. 'She seems like she is something else. There is something about her. She seems like she could be the one.'

"You've had many *ones* over the years, Scott," she sounded monotone at this point. "What makes you think that she is *the one*?"

I stopped wandering around. 'Are you being condescending?'

"No," she said matter of factly. Morena caught my glance, "I just don't want you to have your heart shattered into bits again."

'So you think that she is not the answer?'

"What exactly is the question here, Scott?"

I didn't know. Maybe she was right: how could I find someone so soon after Faith? Was this God's way of tempting my strength?

'Emma is pursuing me; do I just give in to her?'

"Giving in implies that she is some sort of momentary element you are forcing yourself into."

'She isn't.'

Morena rose and walked up to me, "What makes you believe that?"

Again, I didn't know.

676

She dragged her right pointer finger over my heart in the motion of a cross. "What have you done to protect your soul from any more pain?"

'I don't know.' I moved away from her.

"You crumbled when Faith left, because you made her a part of your foundation. However, you have to be your *own* strength, Scott."

I pivoted and met Morena's eyes.

'I don't know how to let someone in without caving to their every whim. I love with all of my heart.' Tears began welling in my eyes. 'That's all I ever really knew.'

I could see Morena smiling and looking at me with a sense of pride in her eyes.

"You know what you have been through, now you just have to commit yourself to a new mindset."

'How?'

Morena rested her hands on my shoulders, "Only you can answer that."

Emma's texts kept coming in nightly. We would talk about leadership skills for the kids and spoke briefly about her story.

It was clear that Emma was immersed in a wealth of pain: she would talk about how love was complicated for her, and that she loved with her whole heart just like I did.

After the kids would filter out of my office for the night, Emma would hang around and talk with me. I found myself comfortable in her company, to the point where we would talk just about anything and find a way to see the silver lining in every and anything that happened in our respective lives.

A still silence hung in my office as the falling leaves brushed against the window.

'Isn't it weird?' I tried to break up the quiet moment in the room. 'The leaves change into such beautiful colors as they drift from the trees.'

"Well," she started awkwardly. "It is mid-October."

'Yeah.'

Again, there was a resolute silence in the air.

"As a painter, I find that certain colors hold more value in a situation," she shot me an alluring glance.

'Oh,' I wasn't sure what to say.

"If burgundy is the color of love what is the color of this connection we have?"

Emma had looked deep into my eyes and began to move closer to me. I had only known her a few weeks but I could feel my soul shivering.

"I can tell you have a story to tell," she said mockingly, almost echoing what I said to her not long ago. There was a hint of flirtation in her voice.

I smiled at her and said, 'Take a seat then, and I will tell you.'

Emma sat down on the leather couch, and I began to tell her about my car accident. With each word that left from my lips, she appeared to hang on every single syllable.

In the days that followed, I found myself writing in journals, *our journals*, to mutually discuss our stories.

I have always been amazed by the fact that every single thing I have read has been made up of the same 26 letters, but just arranged differently. Every time the letters are weaved together, emotions burst from them like lava from a volcano. The words combined seep into my soul, grasp it, and speak to it. The words speak to me as if I were learning a new language: slowly, yet patiently.

Each time I read what she writes about me and how she sees me; peace reverberates through my entire body. The words crash into my skin and latch onto my soul with such a pristine gentleness. The cracks of my soul become filled with her thoughts and her ramblings, and she didn't even notice how much she had struck me.

She didn't realize how much she had changed me.

I was at the mercy of how she rotated her wrist, with her fingers firmly grasped along the pen, and brushing my story onto the page. My life was her masterpiece and her artwork; yet somehow through writing about my life and my experiences, she faded behind the words and raised me onto a pedestal.

She ambitiously floated in my shadow and glanced at me with such wonder, almost like a child on Christmas morning. She told me that my presence was a gift, but I was afraid that if she continued to pull the wrapping paper layer by layer, she would realize that this gift, my soul, had been damaged for a long time. Still, knowing her, she would pull out glue, tape, bandages, and whatever else she carried with her and would whisper, "It's okay, I can help you fix it."

678

∞ ∞ ∞ ∞ ∞ ∞ ∞ ∞

'Morena, I think this may actually be real,' I muttered to her as I paced past her in the sanctuary.

"Then if you think it is real, it is real," She smiled at me and I felt the weight of my past slowly edging off of my shoulders.

'How do I know if she is or is not the one unless I go for it?'

"Go for what?"

'Ask her out, I don't know.'

"You," Morena chuckled. "You are actually going to ask her out?"

'Yes,' I yelped. I think she may really like me; maybe it is more than that.

"Then," Morena patted me on the shoulder with her fingers catching slightly in my cotton shirt. "Go find out your truth."

I had to. I just had to.

It was about time I started living, not just surviving.

During this time, Faith also chose to re-appear in my life. She texted me, and asked if the two of us could get together. I figured that with this new chapter of my life starting to open up, I would try to reconcile the loose ends of the relationship that broke my heart into pieces.

If she had contacted me any other night but October 24, 2015, I would not have been able to meet with her.

I figured: 'Is this the universe lining up, or am I just overanalyzing everything?'

In usual fashion, and reminiscent of days far in the past, Faith asked to go to a cultural restaurant. It was only when I was with her that I would try new things and experience life differently.

We met at the Peruvian restaurant not far from the church, and spent the next two to three hours just talking, sharing, and laughing, as if we had not missed a beat. We talked about our break up and mutually apologized to one another.

When I brought up the other guy she was seeing, Faith began to cry.

Instinctively, I grabbed her hand, but I knew that I was not going to make the same mistake. Though my feelings for her were still there, and I mean, how could they not be considering all we had gone through over the years, I knew my life was on a different path.

The way she expressed herself and her beauty were exquisite, but despite how much she missed me, and how much I did miss her, I knew that there was a lot of our story that was greatly rooted in absolute pain.

I did not want to suffer anymore.

I knew, from just a few moments of looking into Faith's eyes, that Emma had potential.

Upon driving Faith home, we gave each other a hug that was real and powerful. She wanted a father figure in her kids' life and she was confident in sharing that with me.

Still, God put Emma in my life, and though she constantly brought up her ex that she seemed to have left permanently, I was interested in her.

Something in Emma's soul ignited a fire within me. It felt so real.

Faith re-entering my life made no sense at all, but I figured that there had to be a story behind the story there.

The next morning when I woke up, I participated in my ritualistic tendencies before work. I twiddled with my hair nervously all throughout counseling sessions with the students at Lincoln Memorial.

I knew Emma would be gracing my presence shortly after the kids' departure, so I puttered around the office cleaning up what I could.

When she finally walked in the door, she was wearing black heels that clicked slightly as she entered the room.

The second I laid my eyes on her, and from that moment on, I knew my destiny had been fulfilled.

Emma handed me the journal, ready for me to read the beautiful words she wrote down for my eyes only, and our hands brushed against one another's.

Without hesitation, the two of us felt something in that touch.

As our eyes shut slowly and our lips grazed each other's, I discovered that there was a part of my soul that could still love.

Upon stepping back and meeting her gaze, she looked different than she had before. I had never realized how deep her eyes were. Like roses, her cheeks were in full bloom.

From the moment our lips met, I had not stopped thinking of her. In seconds, four to be exact, two worlds collided, but did not crash. Two walks of life found the same path for a change. It was magical, but only because for once it just seemed so natural.

A small part of ourselves became vulnerable, and for a moment we said everything we ever wanted to say without using words. The sensation is something that can never be duplicated or recreated.

A flicker of light from a singular burned down candle in the darkness of the night.

The oil in a lantern that had not been discovered for years.

A life preserver thrown in the exact moment I fell overboard.

A strong bandage that managed to miraculously connect the fibers of a shattered heart.

A sign that there is an ounce of hope left in the world, as long as you realize that what you are searching for isn't always what you are looking for.

Emma was an absolute pain in the ass, but for some reason, which I didn't know, she listened to me. She listened to me on a level I could never fathom nor comprehend. She flew into my life like a wrecking ball, but rather than plow down every fiber of my being, she rested her pale hand on my heaving frame and softly whispered, "It'll all be okay."

Then suddenly, it was. Just like that, just because she uttered those four words.

∞ ∞ ∞ ∞ ∞ ∞ ∞ ∞

As November rolled around, I found myself eagerly waking up at 5:15 each morning in order to read a text message from Emma. Each day, we would take turns writing in one of our countless journals about whatever was on our minds.

Her words were slowly softening the hardened shell that had melted around my soul. It was as if she was sent to me because the universe wanted me to finally experience true love.

Love. There I was, I had just met her, and suddenly I was proclaiming my love for her.

Each day was more magical than the next and in a way I could never have imagined or expected. The past two weeks brought me to new heights, and it was her soul that granted my soul the wings to fly again. I could finally push past the limits of a difficult story and soar to new expressions. It was the reigniting of an ember that supposedly burned out long ago.

Like waves crashing slowly and gently against the rocks of some random shore under a cool, summer's night, the peaceful desire and yearning for true love never gets old… specifically with her.

I saw her in every girl's eyes, she was in the fresh air that I inhaled each brisk night, and her presence existed in all of the spiritual moments the universe bestowed upon me.

Her essence was all around me.

We continued to chat regularly, which led to late nights and early mornings inundated with what we perceived to be true love blossoming in the late fall air.

After one night of running a leadership program at the school, one of the students did not seem to want to go home. Emma sat in the room and watched me counsel the student one-on-one.

In the moments that passed, I felt all of my energy focusing on the student, and I almost forgot that Emma was perched upon a chair and embracing the scene unfolding before her.

I forgot what I told this student and over the years I realized that the advice I gave students seemed to seep out of my mouth without hesitation. Yet in all of those moments, I felt as if the words that I spoke were not from my soul, rather they were from a place of higher consciousness.

Students and those around me would listen intently, and I could tell when the advice I was giving them reached a special part of their soul. At that moment, with Emma watching me and embracing every word I spoke, I was petrified to know what was going through her mind. All I knew was that she was listening, and it was in a way that transcended any semblance of focus that anyone had ever bestowed upon me.

Once the student left and we were alone together, Emma smiled modestly and stood up.

"Would you mind walking me to my car?" Emma blinked repeatedly and grasped at her bag, which almost slipped off of her shoulder.

'Yeah, of course,' I said.

"Thanks."

The two of us walked in silence until we reached the employee lot. She kept kneading her hair as we moved forward in the night, and I could see the twinkle in her eyes shine almost as bright as the stars above.

When we got to her car, she paused for a moment by the door handle and sighed deeply.

'Are you okay?' I was genuinely concerned at this point.

"Yeah," she let out another exasperated sigh.

'You don't sound like you are okay,' I moved against her car and stood perpendicular to her.

We stood in silence, as she seemed to keep taking deep breaths to calm herself down. I didn't understand what Emma was doing at the moment, but time was about to set our story on a different path.

The cool evening descended upon us, which led her to toss her bags in her car, shift her eyes towards me, and as her car door slammed shut, she asked if we could go sit in my car.

'Sure,' I responded. I was getting quite cold as well, but I did not know what Emma intended in those fateful moments.

Little did I know, this conversation was about to define our mutual path into whatever was coming next.

As the two of us leapt in my Monte Carlo and the engine began to purr slightly, I caught tears welling in her eyes.

'What's wrong?'

"Nothing, nothing."

Emma pulled her sleeves over the palms of her hands and looked me in the eyes.

"How do you do it?" Her voice started to crack.

'Do what?'

"You have been through so much, and you keep going, how?"

I reached out my hand towards hers and intertwined our fingers.

'Because I always try to keep the faith.'

"I refuse to sink," Emma said confidently.

Her words cut through me like fragile glass.

'What?' She caught me slightly off guard. I always assured myself that I *refused to sink* and, after years upon years of whispering this mantra to myself, those words managed to escape the lips of another human being.

What were the odds?

"I refuse to sink, it is something I have always believed in," she began. "I really like anchors: the imagery they depict, the symbolism, they are truly beautiful. They remind me to stay anchored to who I am."

Her description was beautiful, and suddenly anchors became one of my favorite symbols, too. Well, of course the infinity sign is tethered to my soul in many ways, but the anchor became a holistically unique part of who I am.

We spoke for a bit about anchors and infinity signs, until the conversation came to an awkward standstill.

"I-" her voice was strained again. "I'm sorry."

'Why are you apologizing?' I whispered.

"I don't want to-," she began tearing up again. "I don't want to be the one who breaks your heart."

'Emma,' I drew her in closer to me. 'You could never break my heart.'

Her tears dripped onto my leather jacket and rolled down into my lap.

"I think I love you," she murmured into my chest.

Emma glanced up and met my gaze.

'I love you, too.'

She kissed me in a way that was indescribable, and our first night where our bodies physically coalesced into one commenced. The touch of her skin felt so natural, but I found myself clumsily moving around her while trying to savor the moment.

The two of us danced within the confines of the car as if we were unsure of how long the moment would last. With each tumultuous twist, I found myself yearning for our skin to touch for longer periods of time.

From that sudden passionate encounter, and from the connection I felt from just existing in her presence, I could tell our connection was a bond that would not break.

The windows began to fog and her passionate moans became more fervent. As my gentle kisses edged along every one of her curves, I could feel her writhing in the heat of the moment, as our connection grew deeper and deeper.

I slid my hand between her legs and she pulled me closer to her. My fingers moved slowly, but with devout purpose, which sent her into a frenzy of pleasurable commentary.

As the moments flashed before our eyes, I realized that this situation would manifest itself over and over again throughout the weeks that followed. Frankly, I was delicately satisfied by watching her pleased face melt in the heat of our passionate embrace.

It made me feel that despite my earlier incidents with Gemma, and situations with Starr while I was in Texas, I did have the capability of pleasing someone and in such a physical manner.

Though I was still wrought with nerves, the two of us smiled at one another when we finally collapsed on the folded-down seats of my car. As Emma rolled towards me with a breathy, "Hey" dripping along with the beads of sweat on her supple skin, I savored our first intimate moment.

'Was that what you wanted?' I was genuinely curious how long she was holding that in. Did she want this to happen?

Emma reached out and brushed the fingers on her right hand along my face.

"You can do that to me *any* time," the wide grin spread between her cheeks.

I felt that her heart was eternally woven into the fabric of my soul's tapestry.

Our first moment was not perfect, but it was ours.

And that is exactly what I wanted it to be: ours.

∞ ∞ ∞ ∞ ∞ ∞ ∞ ∞

Eventually our rendezvous led us to new heights. When I came into work, I could feel her watching me walk down the hallway to my office after school. It got to the point where she would send me flirtatious text messages about a special skirt or heels she wore just in my honor.

Sheepishly, I always replied that I could not wait to take whatever she was wearing off of her later that night.

Though it could be mistaken that the physical love we explored together was what held us together for so long, it was much more than that.

We were ensnared in a passionate embrace whenever others were not around, but our conversations were what drew me into loving her more than I could imagine.

Day by day, I realized that we are caught in the balance of a deep-rooted connection and comfortable space. We are sewn into the seams of alignment and individualism. Yet with each turn of the needle and thread, we simultaneously become cohesive independent souls on their respective and collaborative journeys.

By themselves, a needle and thread are useful in their own right, but when they are together, absolute magic is created. Two souls weave through one another to create a symbiotic medium: a synthesis of the perfect notes being played in undeniable harmony. Time weaves its own legacy through the experiences we create in developing our own reality. It feels like just yesterday you were standing next to me, us talking about the gift that is the future that could be created.

Though we have the perfect pitch, it was clear we had two different songs that played in our lives. My beat does not match your march, yet somehow it all works... even if it just comes in bursts or a little bit of time here and there.

Regardless of anything that happens in life, I came to the realization that communication is key: you can sing and I can drum and though we are vastly different, we need each other to create beautiful music.

Until the day comes where you learn to play your instruments in tandem with another's innate ability to create sweet music: you play your melody, and I'll play mine.

Thoughts like those drifted through my mind as I watched her move through the school merely glaring at my presence, and I quickly acknowledged that she would hide our relationship from the world... at the time, I just did not understand why.

Then I went away to Canada for the weekend.

∞ ∞ ∞ ∞ ∞ ∞ ∞ ∞

I always had that innate fear that I would hear "Goodbye to Romance" again, and see the girl of my dreams in the arms of another man. Each time I left for too long, even just a few days, I would sense a shift in my relationships when I returned to whatever I considered home.

Still, you can't shatter something that is already broken into fractions of whatever it once was. I pray that those who try understanding that when someone looks into a fire and smiles, they're not someone who you should dare mess with.

Standing in front of the mirror, I saw a panicked version of myself that brought me back to my childhood.

686

'I would say that I could see pain and suffering in your eyes, but you won't even look at me anymore,' my voice cracked as tears rolled down my cheeks.

'No,' I told myself. 'This is not middle school or high school anymore.'

I don't believe in the existence of hell in terms of the mythological story we conjure up as human beings. The concept exists in the torments of our minds and as a result of the pain we experience.

Losing Emma at the time could be the closest thing to the fiery, eternal damnation of hell that existed in the confines of my mind.

It would be a manifestation of the ultimate pain.

The thing about a six-hour flight to the Sunshine Coast is that it leaves you with plenty of time to ruminate about whatever is on your mind. Emma spent weeks before Thanksgiving acting sweet and spiritual, but something was missing. I felt I was not privy to every inch of her story, though I saw how gorgeous she was in the pages of our countless journals.

The two of us concealed our strong feelings for each other in a series of brick red, leather bound journals we called "The Vault." We wrote back and forth with the intent to express ourselves without inhibitions. Her letters stung an intricate part of my soul, for I knew that she was always hiding a part of who she was from the outside world:

Scott,

I feel like these pages are going to be finished before you know it! Today was a bad itching day for me. I have like... itch "hot spots." Today my inner thighs are beat red and I cannot stop. Other hotspots are my shins and my armpits. Ekkkk, I cannot believe I just said that! I am so embarrassed!

Why is it so easy to speak to you? That makes me nervous.

I truly, honestly was in so much physical pain from the scratching I did there that they were burning all day. I couldn't put them down to rest against my body. I should have seriously called out of work. You know I felt badly about our afternoon and I did not realize until you first said it that maybe I wasn't ready for it. Maybe I'm not ready for any of this. I cannot handle my emotions around you and I need to back off and hide at times. I scratched Monday night, so maybe, this is all stress related and it was in the back of my head?

I'm really not sure.

Consciously, that was not my reason, but subconsciously you could have been right. Any hunches about why I cannot stop scratching my thighs today? This is all so confusing. Ew, My handwriting up top looks different than the body. That annoys me. I texted you a few minutes ago "surprise" because you thought we were done for the night. Right now, I am sitting in bed with two dogs curled into tight balls huddled against the sheets. I have the drop-down attic stairs in my room that something must've bent because it's slightly cracked open and my room is an icebox. I still need to pack for this upcoming weekend but figured I would write you first. Also, sidenote, I always want to ask how your day went but you have a job with a lot of confidentiality and I never want to come across prying and putting you in an uncomfortable place.

As much as I do make you tell me some things, I hope you know they are all safe with me. As much as some of it is interesting to hear, I want you to be able to tell me as a release off of your chest. I feel like you carry so much weight. But like you said we are a team and I think that's how we function best. I was hoping I would hear from you before bed and my phone just beeped. Let's see what you said!

Emma

I do wonder what was going through her mind at the time.

Though I wholeheartedly thought I belonged to her, Emma was caught between a promise she made to herself and an expectation she never thought would appear.

The thought of sleeping next to Emma and being in her arms kept me tethered to New York, although Sam, Hannah, and their neighbors on the Sunshine Coast were calling upon me to delve deeper into the concept of higher consciousness love.

Upon texting Emma, and waiting for her to respond, I felt a tinge of Audrey's situation fluttering through my mind. Would I return to find Emma in the arms of another? Would I be ensnared in another situation where I lost the love I hoped I could have?

When she would finally reply later that evening, she was frigid and distant.

In one of our letters, Emma and I had talked about marriage. We talked about kids. I conjured up images of a Cinderella story romance permeating our journey.

There I sat, in the middle of the most beautiful place on this Earth, with my head in my hands and fearful of what was going through Emma's head. Our conversations went from deep and exhilarating, to glaring at my phone and wondering when she would text back.

She had to still love me... she had to...

Though we were thousands of miles apart, her voice on the other end of the phone assured me that we were, indeed, still in love.

"Scott," she broke out into innocent tears. "I love you. It will always be us."

'I know. I love you too.'

She had to be the one. She needed to be my one, special love. I felt it in my bones and in my soul.

During my flight back to New York, my mind was racing as I thought of the perfect thing to say to Emma when I saw her.

Would I walk in, wrap my arms around her, and profess my undying love for her?

Would she fall into my chest and cuddle with me throughout the night?

Regardless, she said it would always be us. That's how it would be.

∞ ∞ ∞ ∞ ∞ ∞ ∞ ∞

Upon my return, I watched the rain cascade down the basement window to my office. It had been hours since my feet touched the ground in New York, yet something seemed horribly wrong.

Emma was at work, but dodging my presence and text messages.

I feared the worst, but then again it was Emma I was dealing with.

She loved me. She said it countless times. Our words and shared moments had to mean something.

Together was our favorite place to be.

After I finished counseling students for the night, she stood in my doorway and let the phrase "We need to talk" jab daggers into my chest.

The two of us walked in silence to the parking lot, where just days prior we were ensnared in a seemingly loving embrace.

Her energy was holistically unaligned with mine. I could not pinpoint exactly why I felt the two of us needed to re-connect on many levels, but there was something in her eyes that was not there before... a certain lingering sensation. Emma appeared to have a yearning feeling to speak her mind, though each time the thought would materialize in her head, her lips would push her words further into the pit of her stomach.

As the rain washed over our conversation, I felt a stoic cleansing of my soul and spirit in one fatal swoop. When the two of us approached her car, I saw her take a deep breath and shift her gaze from mine.

'What's wrong?' I placed my hand on her shoulder, and she ripped away from me instantaneously.

"Nothing," yet I heard the tears mingling with her voice.

'Please,' I moved towards her again. This time she did not turn away.

Our lips were just seconds away from one another's, yet neither of us moved closer to soothing our souls.

"I'm confused," she whispered into the unsettling physical space between us.

'About what?'

"About us." Emma motioned towards both of us and stepped back.

The rain grew more rampant and pulled her mascara further down the edges of her face. Even with the water washing over us, she was still as beautiful as ever.

We were the epicenter of an image from a romance novel, though the scene was about to transform into a tragedy.

"It's my ex," the long pause she took between her thoughts sent my soul into a frenzy. My heart rate skyrocketed far above the clouds as her voice shook.

"It..." she trailed off for a moment, almost as if she was reminiscing about better days in an effort to keep herself from breaking down. "It's Greg; he wants to propose to me. He misses me and I think I miss him too."

Her words shot through my soul.

I was shattered. My mind diverged from my body as I felt everything in my system start to shut down.

It was "Goodbye to Romance."

The rain began pouring down as she wept and got into her car.

I could not help but cry at the sight of her leaving. Was this for good? Was our story coming to an end just as soon as it had begun?

The hollowed sensation in my soul rang throughout the empty parking lot as she drove off and left me standing there alone. I learned that tears and blinding rainstorms go together so well: once the raindrops mix with teardrops, all of the pain appears to wash away.

She shattered every piece of wholesomeness I had left in my body.

That upcoming Thanksgiving weekend, Greg would whisk her away and hinted he was going to propose once and for all. Months ago, before we met, she gave him a ring and said, "I will leave it in your hands."

She signed away her heart before I had a chance to even meet her, though her soul was screaming, "I didn't know it was you I was waiting for."

I watched the raindrops roll down my front windshield as my heavy heart rested against the driver's seat of my car.

> *"Goodbye to romance,*
> *Goodbye to friends and to you*
> *Goodbye to all the past*
> *I guess we'll meet, we'll meet in the end."*

There was a shift occurring within me that was both spiritual and devastating in nature.

I needed her like I needed oxygen to survive, but now I had to breathe on my own. She was getting her fairytale ending and I was met with another roadblock.

Why me?

Just… Why me?

∞ ∞ ∞ ∞ ∞ ∞ ∞ ∞

I was never into following the rules, or abiding by standards or labels and whatnot. Still, I felt that Emma and I were a couple. Everything seemed so real and powerful, yet the moment she said that her ex was back, I could not handle it.

Emma had her heart set on keeping our relationship a secret at Lincoln Memorial High School, for she figured that no one would accept us. She always said that our reputations and careers came first. I understood that.

Still, I felt empty inside.

It made me feel as if she truly didn't want me.

I came so far and I was beginning to see just how far I could go. After longing for that "power couple" relationship for what seemed like my entire life, Emma appeared to be the other half of me.

I began to wonder why God put me in such a powerful situation, especially when he was going to pull her away from me.

Would God be mad at me if I got on my hands and knees and begged for her to come back?

Would God get mad?

Would I still be able to move forward if I didn't have Emma coexisting with me?

Why else would God send her to me?

It was Emma who appeared to be the equivalent to any definition of happiness in my soul. Our souls are constantly being developed whether we realize it or not, yet God had to have a complete and consummate love for us whether we wanted more of it or not.

In the process of all of this, Eve would send me text messages about the church and what needed to be done there. She tried to start an argument with me, though the senseless drama paled in comparison to what I was dealing with when it came to Emma.

I felt safe within the walls of the church, and I felt even safer with Emma by my side.

She was the best person who could walk into my life, yet it seemed that she was running from me. Our connection was a matter of balance, and I needed to re-evaluate what it meant having her in my life.

During one of my nightly meltdowns at the church while Emma had fallen off of the radar, Morena came to help me process what was going on.

As I paced the sanctuary floors, leaving a murmured creak from the floorboards below, I felt my body heaving with each repulsive tear that dropped from my eyes.

Morena sat there, humming a melody I didn't really recognize, occasionally pausing to take a deep, long breath.

'What are you doing?' With my voice cracking, I sat beside her.

"Everytime I hum the melody to 'You are my Sunshine,' I always take an extra pause between certain lines."

'Why?' I sat back. 'And why are you humming *that* song?'

"We all need a bit of sunshine sometimes." Morena smiled at me.

692

'So why all the pauses?' I wiped my tears.

"It's called a caesura," she continued to hum.

'A cesarean?'

"No, silly, it is a timely pause," she started. "It is kinda like a strategic silence."

'Okay,' I remarked.

"Maybe you and Emma need this strategic silence to find out who you are."

I heard her. I understood her and suddenly, everything made sense.

∞ ∞ ∞ ∞ ∞ ∞ ∞ ∞

As a creature of habit, I spent Thanksgiving weekend soulfully alone. I watched the dust in the sanctuary settle with a sort of delicate curiosity. As the rock band Kansas said, *"Are we but dust in the wind?"*

As Outlet and I met for band practice, I felt my drumming was distant. My soul was elsewhere and all I wanted was her in my arms. I wanted Emma beside me. Elyza asked me if I was okay, and though my emotions were jumbled and I desperately needed to confess my love for Emma, all I could muster up was, 'I'm fine.'

Fine drowning in my own sorrows, I guess.

In the days that followed, Emma returned from her short trip with Greg and made her way back down to my office.

"Hey," she mumbled as she walked in the room.

'Hey.' I gripped the bottoms of my sleeves and crossed my legs at my ankles.

We looked at one another for a moment until she finally spoke: "I missed you."

Emma rushed forward and kissed me on the lips. I wasn't sure how to respond, but her touch felt so right.

The two of us sat down and just started talking. Although I still felt she was holding back, she confessed that she did truly, madly, and deeply care about me.

"Like I said," Emma grasped my hand. "It will always be us."

And so that's how things were: we were "us" again.

Our afternoon meetings at Kissena Park in Queens and early morning text messages continued on. We would delve deeper into what made each other's souls grow and expand in ways neither of us ever thought were imaginable.

Together, we were a force to be reckoned with. Individually, we were becoming professionals with a penchant for helping youth achieve their goals.

Every moment we spent together was a journey filled with love, excitement, and a devout yearning for whatever would come next.

∞ ∞ ∞ ∞ ∞ ∞ ∞ ∞

Though Emma did consider herself to be spiritual, once I went to a spiritual guide to help me sort through my feelings for her, she did not want to know what the guide said. Morena, on the other hand, encouraged me to read what this spiritual guide told me out loud.

As Morena said, "Speak what you wish for into the universe, you do not know who is listening."

I read the transcript of what was told to me to Morena.

The notes read as follows:

'You must tell Emma what you want.

She needs that. If you are not honest with her, she will turn away. It is a lot for you Scott to say you love yourself, but if you honestly show that, Emma will come around and choose you. Yes, she has not told you yet but she is going to be struggling over a choice.

You are being too patient. If you show her less patience, then you will get more from her. The issue from your soul is you do not want to pressure her.

God has brought you both together for a reason and wishes you to be together.

Your Aunt is here and approves with her but has a warning. She may have to take a step with another soul first so that she can get her power back. She knows that you do not understand that at this time but you will in the future. Emma is very interested in taking the next step with you but is also very scared.

If you are less patient, she will love herself more. If you give in easy, she will get comfortable and not make the moves in her best interest.

Emma has to face her fears.

694

She will be receiving an offer that will be hard for her to say no to in order to have a better life with you Scott. Emma is scared and needs to work with her inner anger and fears to finish something karmic. This is something karmic with another soul, another relationship in her life.

She has to get angry at that soul, but in many ways is not able to get to the root of that. This relationship has something to do with what she is angry with. She is turning a blind eye based on fear. This relationship is acting a certain way towards her.

This is freewill.

Emma can be another way but she may choose to be a certain way with him. This is up to her. This relationship is invading her boundaries but she must see that. Emma loves you Scott for the new boundaries and borders you have created for her. You let her be her and this is something she deeply desires and fears judgment on. Emma's spirit matches your spirit when you hold this space of truth for her, and this is the energy and connection you feel. This can easily turn though. You are both creating what humans call "falling in love" but at this time you are both too scared to admit it.

What is going on here is divinely driven.

Stop being scared, Scott. Emma will love you more when she discovers the truth about your past. Your whole past. Emma sees the world as a mathematical equation. If you do not give her all the factors, her equation will compute the wrong answer, but she will not know it is the wrong answer. This will be up to you, Scott, to present to her.

If you present the right equation, Emma will feel more confident in you as a couple. If you present the wrong equation, you risk losing her forever, and her never knowing the genuine truth of your soul.

Let this be your warning.

Your past Scott will allow her inner light to shine more. In knowing your whole story, she will know that after all was said and done you chose her. If freewill doesn't bring you to this loving conclusion there will be darkness for many years, and then hope again.

This will be a big fear for you to face Scott. This will be tough. Let your love for Emma guide you to the right choices. The word "competition" keeps coming up. Emma feels she will not have to compete. She has a difficult time with the fear in her mind, and she has not learned to come from her soul yet. She does know that your love for her is pure; she just cannot comprehend why.

More is coming and she will feel more engaged with you as the months unfurl. Communication is key. If you share with her this reading, her soul will smile.

Emma likes when you make her smile, Scott. Even when she tries to hide it.

Emma really cares about you a lot. God brought her to you based on the law of attraction. We angels are answering your prayers. The masculine side of you attracted her. Fathering patterns brought Emma to you.

Emma helps you to learn how to love yourself more.

This is your journey.

This other relationship that will challenge you makes you feel alone and disconnected from your God force. You do not need to be jealous of any other soul.

If she does not choose you, this is okay.

Your journey shall continue.

You will always have to work on yourself. Growth is endless. You do not need to fear the outcome. There is no time limit.

Emma will take all the time she needs to work on this karmic necessity and will realize in her own time, not human time, that she still has the option to choose you. This can be weeks, months, and maybe years.

Your choices may change by the time she realizes, but this cannot be seen at this time. Freewill impacts many infinite possibilities.

Yet, no matter what, the love shall remain. Maybe silent, but constantly true, and rarely rearing its head. Your being is allowing the space for Emma to love herself more, but if you push too hard she will be forced to face herself too fast and will leave you.

She must be empowered to go at her own pace.

Something is coming up about her father. There is something about the way he pushes into her life. Her brothers are not going to like you at first. You are a threat to the family balance. They will give you a hard time. Emma knows this. She is a fish out of water there and often feels trapped. Emma does not want you to know yet or she has not faced it yet, however, she loves her family very much. Family is an important value to her.

You have jealousy in your heart Scott. This will be your downfall if you do not resolve. We must look at this. It has to do with loving yourself. There is a lot of love there with Emma. I know this scares you as well. Emma and yourself are very well suited in the male/female balance. There is love here. The angels approve of this relationship.

Your jealousy Scott has to do with your masculine pattern issues. Your father figure was not good. The imprint from your dad is causing your jealousy. The answers to resolve this will be in your alone time and what you choose to do with it.

Prayer and meditation are important.

Emma and you will have balance and be together according to the angels, but this may take some time. They are saying this is a message from God... "in time" is the important phrase to focus on. Do not act according to this knowledge and reading. You are to both be yourselves and follow your own path and guidance.

This is the journey.

When and if this is meant to be, the unfolding of this union will help you each to grow individually as you go through this experience. There is a magnetic and physical attraction between Emma and Scott. Scott, you should not have low self esteem.

Emma thinks you are good looking and loves your personality. You prayed her into existence.

Your aunt is here and has a message for you. She says she wants you to have more fun. She said she wants to see you married. It is time. She wants you to recognize that your masculinity is priceless.

She wants you to take that step with Emma and not be scared. She said that you should stop and change the way you think of yourself as a man and your self-image. She said you have charisma and you are desirable. She said that she could tell Emma desires you and that you are lucky that you found her. She approves of Emma.

She wants you to know that you as well are good enough for her and Emma is lucky to have you. She said that you deserve love and you deserve contact.

The word "complacency" is coming up. She said stop being complacent. She said fix your shit and stop stalling. She said be more active and stop worrying.

Your aunt loves you. She said Emma loves you. Your aunt sees how Emma makes you feel.

She is saying if you pressure her she will be into you more. The more masculine you are the more she will be into you. Your aunt keeps saying over and over that she approves of Emma. Emma is curious, loving and will bring you peace of mind.

Emma needs to feel better about herself. Scott, you need to speak to yourself in a more blissful way. You are not seeing the value in yourself. Your "one on one" relationship with yourself must improve.

Your aunt says she loves you and is always with you.

"Complacency" is coming up again. She is not happy with your living arrangements. She fears you are going to get sick. She wants you to love yourself and wants you to want more for yourself.

If you choose the right path you will have what you want. Your aunt sees you working hard but wants you to think differently about what you are doing. It is okay to plan around Emma and a future with her. She said, "build a nest and she will come." The nest she sees increases her fear and dampens the truth in her soul from coming out.

Emma wants security and safety.

She sees that you put others before yourself too much. Your aunt is asking you to be curious about this and think about it. Your aunt has only one disapproval of you.

You are serving too much. Your aunt sees your fear that you do not want to have regret. God saves the world, not you. God wants you to be happy and have fun. God wants Emma to be happy. You are both a gift to many people and many people on this planet are gifts yet to be discovered.

This is your ego Scott. You do not have to do as much as you think.

You are a gift to so many Scott and without you they would be more lost and bumping around more but this is okay. Your aunt says she has nothing to do with bringing Emma to you. She said that was God but she likes Emma a lot.

She likes that Emma makes you happy and she likes seeing you happy.

Your aunt sees that you are exhausted and asks that you take care of yourself. She is concerned about your health. Your aunt says she will help you in your future life. Just ask and speak to her. She is hoping that your life is about to get really good and she is hoping that it is with Emma.

She also knows you are sorry and she forgives you. She has nothing but love for you. She is giving you a hug now and is saying that she knows who you are, what you want and who you are becoming.

Your aunt sees your regrets, and wants you to be more blissful.

She knows God and wants you to know that you are on the right spiritual love path. She is also in the light and on the right path. This reading and asking her for help supports her in taking a step on the right path on her side.

We can help her in prayer by keeping her in our hearts about her transitioning up. She is definitely ascending but will not leave you. The Circle of Angels are real and are from the creator. She can see that now.

Communication is always key.

Your aunt says love yourself, give lots of hugs, love yourself, your job is good, but you will need to stay grounded and in time you will need to lean on Emma. She will need to lean on you as well. You will both know in that job when it is time that all you have to count on is each other. You need each other. You heal each other. You cause one another to grow even when you do not realize. You will help many people in this world.

Be honest and straight with her. She will accept you. The future is much bigger than the past. Go get her. Do not give up.'

Morena sat there with her hand propping up her head.

'Well,' I asked her.

"Well, what?"

'What do you think about everything?'

"You want me to sum up everything you just read in a matter of a few words?"

'Yeah,' I started. 'I trust your judgment.'

"Thank you," she crossed her legs and propped herself up against the pew in the sanctuary.

A long silence stood before us. Morena just looked at me with a distinct curiosity, then shifted her head to the right.

'Are you going to say anything?' I sat beside her.

"No," she smiled. "I don't think I will."

'Why?'

"Because you need to listen to your inner voice," she stood up and walked over to one of the stained-glass windows. "You need to make your own decisions, Scott."

'Okay, that's all you got out of that?'

"No," she gently rested her fingers on the glass. "But you need to be the one to carve your own path."

I rolled my eyes and walked over to her. The two of us stood perpendicular to one another while I waited for another response.

"It is time you made your own decisions," her voice grew stern and more purposeful. "The angels will support you, but you need to support yourself above all."

I scoffed at Morena. She was hiding something she just did not want to speak about. I never understood why she would tend to try to wholeheartedly reserve her judgment, even when I would ask her to tell me what was on her mind.

'Tell me,' I rested my body against the wall. 'What are you thinking?'

She sighed and flashed a smile towards me, "Just go within. Listen. Try to hear what that inner voice is telling you."

Yet every time I tried to listen to whatever my heart was saying, I was caught up in believing that Emma and I had a chance.

Our story was far from over. I devoutly believed it had to be the beginning of our story, and so it was.

∞ ∞ ∞ ∞ ∞ ∞ ∞ ∞

On the day of Lincoln Memorial High School's holiday party, I was nervous beyond belief. Emma seemed to be a lot happier than usual, which I hoped was due in part from the rekindling of our relationship.

Outlet was going to be performing at the Queens Community Church later in the evening, and Emma promised that her and Joy would make an appearance at the concert, before attending the holiday party. I wondered if life would be different after tonight or this weekend.

There is a famous saying that things change in a "New York minute," and I realized that my life would soon embody that phrase quite well.

Emma was wearing a black dress at work, which she looked utterly exquisite in, and her mere presence took my breath away. I always wanted it to be like that. I always wanted to bask in the glory that was her vibrant love.

As the hours marched on, I was anxious to be in the same room as Emma and get to experience her seeing me pursue my passion: drumming. Music was such a special part of my life for so long, and I was hoping that Emma would sense how important she was to me considering I wanted to share the experience of playing with Outlet with her in the audience.

Whether it's the words Emma wrote in "The Vault" or just sitting across from Emma, everything she did during those pivotal weeks of our relationship was sheer magic. I felt that I was experiencing an entirely different mindset be it spiritual or just in terms of insight.

Every breath I took was in honor of the love I shared with Emma. Each moment that passed made me think of the future we could have together.

With each beat of the drum that was located on the altar of the sanctuary, I could see Emma's smile getting wider and wider. Joy sat with her head resting against Emma, the two of them looked on arm and arm with a beaming sense of pride. Their friendship and compassion towards me, above all, made me feel as if all of my dreams in education were possible.

Both of them were helping me lead the way to a better tomorrow, and at that point I didn't want it any other way.

A day later I was meeting Emma, Joy, and a few people from Lincoln Memorial at a local bar in the area. Although Joy was Emma's best friend, neither of us were comfortable telling Joy about our relationship. Emma stood steadfast when it came to hiding our relationship from everyone. As she said, our reputations and our careers were more important than what the world would see.

At the bar, once Emma had a bit of alcohol in her, the two of us could not keep our hands off of each other. Part of me wanted to say that I really didn't care because I was crazy about her, but I respected who Emma was and what she wanted.

That night, Joy looked on as Emma and I were moving closer and closer at the edge of the bar. Joy recognized how Emma's eyes were glistening each time they shifted towards me, and part of me did not care what she thought.

Part of me did not care what anyone thought of us.

Part of me thought that Emma's seemingly newfound liberation meant that she was coming to terms with the fact that our relationship was real. In my eyes, it didn't really matter what people were going to say.

Feelings are feelings, and our connection was proof that reality can be just as satisfying as fantasy.

In Emma's drunken stupor, she began to caress my back and smile intently as she continued sipping on her drink.

"I don't get it," she whispered in my ear. "Why now?"

'What do you mean why now?' Joy shifted her eyes away from Emma and I.

"Why now?" Emma moved closer to me and started to giggle.

I smiled at Joy and she rolled her eyes.

I mouthed the word 'What?' to Joy, but she turned away.

In those moments with Emma resting against me, I realized that you could plan and plan as much as you want, but you never know when something or someone life-changing will appear.

As I watched her saunter away to the bathroom with Joy attached to her arm, part of me thought that maybe I should just leave. At that very moment, I wondered if I should just walk away and let Emma have a life that she planned out for herself.

Though I knew in my soul that we were meant for each other, something from deep within me said that Emma needed to make her own decisions. I made millions of decisions in my life that just never felt right, yet I followed them anyway because I didn't think happiness had any other definition.

But then there was Emma… and everything seemed to make sense.

I believed that years of fake smiles and just getting by finally had a purpose: to find her.

I thought I knew who I was and what I wanted in life, and once I found her; I figured that I could never let her go. I came to the irreconcilable conclusion that somehow and, in some way, Emma would manage to slip through my fingertips. Still, I vowed to hang onto her as long as I could.

When Joy and Emma came back from the bathroom, Emma fell into my arms accidentally and yelped loud enough for everyone in the bar to hear. As the eyes of our co-workers shot directly in our path, Emma jumped backwards and fell into Joy.

Joy appeared to be startled, but she did not take her eyes off of me.

"What the hell, Scott?" Emma beamed her inebriated eyes in my direction.

'What?'

"Do *not* grab me. That is inappropriate!" Emma seemed to be incredibly bothered by my presence.

'You fell into me and I-' Everyone was watching us intently and some were even giggling. I figured that this would be the very moment when our secret relationship was about to spring forth from the shadows and into the light.

Instead, Emma was sobering up and realized that she, in her eyes, just made it obvious that we were together.

And that was something she did not want.

The two of us argued as we made our way through the crowd and onto the rooftop of the bar. The lights from the street below glimmered with the hope that this brisk December night in Queens would turn to a romantic evening between Emma and I. However, as we continued to bicker, that idea seemed as if it were fleeting.

Joy followed us upstairs and stood in the doorway as the two of us sat at the wooden tables nearby. We barely noticed her for she was doing her best to seem invisible. The fabric awning whipped in the gentle breeze above us.

"You need to understand where I am coming from," Emma shouted at me.

'I do,' I yelled back. 'I understand you more than you know.'

Despite reaching out my hand to comfort her, she was still aggravated.

"No," she screamed. "No, you don't!"

'Hey,' I shouted back.

Joy began to recede into the staircase, though I could see her head peering over the window.

Emma strained to speak her mind: "You don't *get* me."

'I get your soul,' I extended my hand to Emma again, but this time she rushed towards me and kissed me.

The two of us embraced in that picturesque scene on the rooftop for a few moments, which made me feel as if nothing else mattered in this world.

As we looked into each other's eyes and made our way hand in hand down the steps, Joy reached out and tapped me on the shoulder. I released Emma's hand as she made her way back down to the party.

"I never want to be a third wheel to you two ever again," Joy spoke sternly and followed Emma downstairs before I could even respond.

Hours later, Emma and I decided to rent a hotel room and allow the rest of the night to unravel before us as the ribbons of time eloquently made their way down our merging pathways through life.

The intimacy the two of us shared could not even be expressed in words.

Emma and I shared our fears, our hopes, and our ambitions for the future. I caught her scratching at her thighs and we spoke about how nervous she was to finally be in a bed with me.

"Do you want to feel them?" Emma asked awkwardly.

'What?'

"The scratches," she pointed at the gentle scars on her skin.

Instinctively I wrapped my fingers around her insecurities in hopes of making her see just how beautiful she was, both inside and out.

It was an intricate moment in time, almost as if the two of us were in a movie.

Emma was vulnerable and allowed me to fall in love with every touch of her supple skin: her perceived imperfections were exquisite from my point of view.

Letting someone into your world is difficult, whether you are intoxicated or sober, and I knew that first hand. It spoke volumes about our relationship and where we were going.

I loved every inch of her body, and there was nothing she could say or do to tell me otherwise. The intermingling of our hands and the sinuous peace that appeared as she smiled with her head on my chest granted me with the notion that life was and would forever be composed of our love's sweet music.

Yet the first line in a song about our love seemed to scream out, *"I should walk away from you forever…"*

And that would have seemed to be another sign that something was so wrong in thinking we were so right, though I could not fight the feelings that arose when her hair brushed against my bare chest.

∞ ∞ ∞ ∞ ∞ ∞ ∞ ∞

'I don't know what it is, but I feel like I am going to screw up.' I looked in Morena's eyes and she seemed to change her demeanor.

Morena knew that I loved Emma deeply, but she seemed to fall short when it came to the words of wisdom that would usually be so natural for Morena to conjure up.

"If you feel like you are going to screw up," she began. "Then you are willing that into the universe."

'But,' I rested my forehead on the pew in front of me. 'I am terrified of losing her.'

The sanctuary provided us with the comfort of talking about practically anything, though I knew that God was granting us the elegant space to express ourselves.

A resounding silence echoed through the room.

'Morena,' I whipped my head towards her. 'Speak to me. Tell me what to do. I need help.'

"I know," she smiled. "I just want you to finally make a decision that will be yours and yours alone."

No one ever wanted that for me before.

'Thank you,' my impatience simmered in the dust particles that spread throughout the room.

"Ask yourself why you love Emma," Morena started. "Why do you want to choose her?"

'Because,' tears welled in my eyes. I took a deep breath and exhaled in such a resilient manner. 'Because I want her to be my everything. I do not want to imagine my life without her. I do not want to be alone.'

Morena grinned and stood up. She smoothed out her pants and stretched slightly as she stepped towards the altar. As the sole beam of sunlight wrapped itself around her shadow, her glance took on a more devout meaning.

"If you truly, deeply believe she could be your everything," Morena's voice took on a stern tone. "Then you need to do everything in your power to grow your own soul."

'What?'

"You need to make sure that the image that looks back at you in the mirror is someone you are comfortable with. Be comfortable with your skin, and then you'll be comfortable within."

'I hear you.'

The two of us stood there, looking at each other, just smiling.

'I'm working on loving myself, honestly.'

"Keep working at it, Scott," she began walking down the aisle, brushing past me slightly as she left. "Everything is going to be okay."

Something within me felt ready. A sense of purpose was growing from the depths of my soul: Emma and I could be the ultimate power couple. There would never be a love like ours and I had never experienced what the two of us were going through.

I thought possibly I had finally found the one.

Days later at work, I was building up the courage to speak to Emma about potentially taking our relationship to the next level. I knew in my heart that Greg could never be the soulmate she was looking for, and that I loved her more than he ever could.

When I woke up in the morning, it felt as if the air became less dense overnight. I could finally breathe fresh air without worrying about what would happen next.

For all intents and purposes, Emma was my future.

As I walked into work later that afternoon, there was an extra pep in my step. I could not wait to counsel the students and speak to Emma about my future… well, our future.

The minutes passed before me and the next thing I knew, I was nervously staring into the mirror at my reflection. Morena's words floated through my head, but they paled in comparison to the majestic eloquence that was Emma's abrupt entrance into the room.

When I leaned forward to kiss her, she put her hand up and crinkled her face.

"Who is Bryan?" Her tone was partially furious and partially spiteful.

I never told her about Bryan, for I didn't share with her every aspect of my past. Our relationship was moving so fast that I did not think to tell her. It is not that I was ashamed of my son or my experiences, but parts of my private life simply did not come up.

Bryan is the most important person in my life, but maybe I had this subconscious weird feeling that she would not accept that I have a son. In hindsight, I realize it is a very poor excuse because lying is never a good thing in any relationship.

Still, I do not think that I was ever outright lying.

I wanted to find the right words to tell her how complicated my past was, but I struggled inside.

I loved her, though I did not know how to balance the deep pain from my past relationships and the emotions I felt each time I thought of Emma.

The two of us sat on the couch and she expressed how angry she was with me, although she said she loved me so. I apologized immensely for hiding part of my life from her, but she said that we would be okay.

We walked back towards the parking lot and began listening to music while sitting in my Monte Carlo. Emma ran her fingers along the leather passenger seat looking to find something to say.

"Empty Apartment" from Yellowcard came on the radio, which made Emma's eyes well up with tears. It seemed that she was lost in the lyrics to the song:

> *"Call me out*
> *You stayed inside*
> *One you love*
> *Is where you hide*
> *Shot me down*
> *As I flew by*
> *Crash and burn*
> *I think sometimes*
> *You forget where the heart is."*

I looked over at her and brushed my fingers along her cheek. She leaned over and fell into my arms instinctively.

Deep down, she knew I loved her and I knew that she loved me.

"It will always be us," floated from her lips and directly to my heart.

Nothing could stop us.

∞ ∞ ∞ ∞ ∞ ∞ ∞ ∞

Joy texted me as the weekend rolled around.

She said that her and Emma were definitely excited to see Outlet play later that night, though Emma told me privately that she was thinking of staying home that night.

The band was performing at a local bar in Queens and I was thrilled to get behind the drums again. I had begged the band to learn to play "Empty Apartment," which I discovered was Emma's favorite song.

Though as the night closed in upon us, and Emma and Joy looked on with excitement in their eyes, I discovered that I created a door for Emma to escape from.

As the band played "Empty Apartment," Emma's face instantly went sour. Little did I know that her favorite song harnessed such a tragic memory for her.

That was the second strike in less than 24 hours.

I was not doing too well.

Emma stormed off and Joy watched the love drain from my eyes as she walked away.

"It'll be okay," Joy smiled and placed her hand on my shoulder. "It will all be okay."

∞ ∞ ∞ ∞ ∞ ∞ ∞ ∞

The following day I went to Alley Pond Park and wrote Emma a five-page letter. I did a lot of soul searching: Why did I hold back parts of my life from her? Who am I? Why would I hide myself from someone who meant so much to me?

Emma did say she never wanted to lose me, so why was I so afraid?

I watched a squirrel dive in and out of a dead pile of leaves then scurry up a tree. It reminded me of the life Emma and I were creating. We were playing in the leaves in such a joyous manner, and neither one of us wanted to climb up the tree just yet. Though if we dug our nails into the tree and climbed together, would we find what existed beyond the surface?

When I returned to work that Monday, there was a note on my desk:

Scott,

Sorry this world can suck sometimes but it could be worse - Anna Kendrick could be dead and octagons could be declassified as a shape.

Love,
Emma

Octagon was our code word. It came about one night when she was drunk and trying to make a shape out of her hand gestures. It was a silly moment that stuck and became our inside joke, our code word, our everything. There was even an octagon building near our job that we would make jokes about.

She was struggling. I was struggling. I had to let go.

Greg was back in the picture and she was wholeheartedly torn: she had to choose one of us, and I was fearful that it would take her too long for her to realize that she should choose me. I guess that idea is selfish in a sense, because no one should ever feel pressured to choose between two people.

Still, I loved her so much. She knew that. It was a deep-rooted truth that lingered in her soul.

In the days that followed, I was working with the students at Lincoln Memorial on a puzzle piece-shaped project we were hanging on the walls. Every person in the school had to add a positive message on the puzzle piece in order to spread some semblance of joy around the school.

One puzzle piece struck me with such a sense of profound love:

"Dear Scott,
Thank you for giving me the power to challenge my independence.
Love, Emma"

I was not crazy. She loved me.

Emma ended up giving me two beautiful paintings she created, along with a magnificent sketch of an infinity sign and an anchor, which had an inscription that said, "Refuse to Sink" on the right side.

The first painting was an image of her silhouette adorned with the lyrics to one of her favorite songs, "Rinse" by Vanessa Carlton:

"...If she runs away she fears she won't be followed.
What could be worse than leaving something behind?"

The second painting was an image of a Christmas tree in front of a cross, for she knew how spiritual I was and how much I loved Christmas.

I wanted nothing more than to do something special with the sketch she gave me, so I chose to carve her image into my soul forever: it became the forearm tattoo that runs through my veins day in and day out.

The anchor and infinity sign wholeheartedly represent who I am and what I stand for: I refuse to sink.

And as the tattoo needle burned her artwork into my skin, I knew I never would sink. When she saw her artwork adorned on my body, her facial expression was a mixture of shock, awe, and elation. At the time, I just couldn't tell what she felt more.

In the days leading up to the school's weeklong winter break, a sense of trepidation lurked in my mind again.

I left the notebook, "The Vault," in Emma's mailbox at work and she left me with this last entry of the year before we left the building:

Dear Scott,

With 4 minutes left to this night, I do not really know what I want to write about. I feel guilty holding this book for so long because so much has happened and been said that there is a gap in our entries… in our story.

Today was a long day and I wasn't exactly the nicest person to you. You didn't deserve it but subconsciously I think I was mad at you. So so so much has unfolded and with every word, as much as I can expect it, they are still unexpected. Waves keep breaking and I am taking them each time to stay afloat. I had a large agenda today and reflecting back I think that thinking about the day, all I was dealing with, keeping up with "us" was not on the agenda.

It was too much.

I wanted to push it all out of my head today and not deal with it. Do not get me wrong. Some amazing things have happened between us and I really do treasure you, but wow, when I take a breath I am blown away on how I can still be a functioning human. I got thrown into this ring of love, taking punch after punch to my soul, and trying to stay ahead calm and cool, and it just all caught up to me today.

I needed to push you away.

Also, after the tattoo yesterday… I know I did this for you…. And for us, but it hit me hard…. You got this grand permanent ink on your body and what if days later I am faced with this ring… how do I say no to that? Maybe I am feeling guilt.

Now I am feeling should I have not drawn it?

Should I have not given you this for Christmas?

Yet, I did and I was determined to give it to you. I wanted you to have this. I wanted this on you. I wanted on some level for us to be permanent. All I wanted in that moment was to surprise you and make you smile as you make me smile always. I wanted you to have this before I left for my weekend. I wanted you to have this piece of us to hold and to treasure. What does that say about me? It is all confusing. So confusing.

It scares me and it is sitting in my throat.

Please please do not freak out and lose it. Maybe I just need to write this out so we can talk through it. I do not want to hide these feelings from you and maybe writing it out will make me feel better.

I do not want to say anything else to upset you. I really do care for you. It is my turn to have a bad day.

This may be the last entry from me before the break. RELAX! I am so excited to come back to reading all your entries. I love when you write. It makes my cheeks hurt from smiling so much!

Everything will be fine!

ALWAYS remember that.

Does the earth stop moving? No. So why should we? Take deep breaths and treasure the moments, don't count them. Wasteful habits are horrid. Even though I do not have anything imprinted on me, you have left marks on my soul that will never go away.

This is not a one-way street.

We will talk a bunch I am sure of it, but when I am up in the woods, talk to me here. Each entry is like a surprise and I love surprises. It has definitely been an incredibly crazy adventurous and emotional end to the year but it has all been something I know I am tremendously grateful for.

Just remember, whenever you are having bad thoughts, picture my hurting cheeks smiling, my "ughing" and saying "its finnnnne Scott." Okay? Ok. Great!

You got this.

Please forgive me. It will all be fine.

We will be fine. Write me back. I like when you write.

I love you.

Always,

Emma

Despite acknowledging that Greg could propose to her over the break, I wrote back. I was supportive and loving. I told her I would take things slow, give her space, and just be there for her.

For Christmas I gave her two charms on a bracelet: the anchor and infinity sign looked beautiful in silver.

She placed it on her ankle and wore it with such pride in our love.

She struggled for days and we texted on and off, but we were never apart.

We continued to call each other; the journals and adoring words were exchanged.

We were on borrowed time, but I did not want to give her up just yet.

∞ ∞ ∞ ∞ ∞ ∞ ∞ ∞

I gazed out into the darkness of the sanctuary. My chest felt heavy as my heaving sighs and sweat-drenched forehead registered some semblance of balance while scurrying to my feet. The curtains rustled in the wind that burst into the room. I don't remember leaving the window open, but I must have, because I was the only one there.

Remnants of Emma's hair lay strewn across the floor as I teetered over to slam the window. If I hadn't known any better, I would think that she had just got up to use the bathroom and in her infinite wisdom, opened the window on one of the coldest nights of the winter season. Though I knew deep in my heart that she was not there and I had to have been the one to crack open the window. I was all alone; it couldn't have been anyone else.

A sudden creaking noise drew my attention to the corner of the room, only to be met with the silhouette of my robust figure being cast on the glimmering wall. It took looking in the reflection of the shadow that I realized I gained some weight. It was a harsh reality that only sunk me deeper into a depressed state. The door swung open and I was startled by the figure of a small woman standing in the shadows.

"Scott, what are you doing out of bed," the voice whispered, "You'll wake the baby."

I rushed closer to the figure, 'Baby,' I gasped, 'What baby?'

The window burst open and I heard loud screams. I actually woke up this time, my head resting against the car window. As I watched my breath collect in the form of fog on the window, I realized that Emma would always be with me in my dreams, even if she did physically leave me.

Each day that passed, Morena watched me putter around the sanctuary. I think both of us expected that Emma would call at any moment saying she was engaged.

One night, Morena found me passed out on a pew with my phone still on. Emma and I had passed out on each other while we were on an intense call together.

On Christmas Day, I went to the school and sat in an exterior doorway with just a lawn separating me, and the windows to her classroom. I had nowhere to be and nobody wanted to see me. Bryan was in Florida and I just wanted to be near Emma.

I sat there in the snow for over an hour and cried.

It felt like a bad 80s romance movie, or that scene in *The Notebook* where Allie was proposed to, though she had the image of Noah in her head.

I wondered if I could be her Noah.

Then it hit me: I could not experience a painful love like Faith's ever again.

This was exactly why I didn't want a relationship.

My head smashed down into the snow as I heaved and felt nauseous.

"What are you doing to yourself?" Morena stood before me; her tracks traced her purposeful steps in the snow.

'What are you doing here? How did you find me?' I wiped my tears.

"I know you well enough by now, Scott." She sat beside me, and the two of us shivered in the snow for a while just watching Emma's classroom windows.

It was there, with the pristine snow falling before us, and our bodies shivering, that I realized that Morena was not as she appeared. I spent years upon years asking the universe questions, but she seemed to have the answers. Maybe that fateful day when we met in the coffee shop the universe was telling us that we were destined for more than just the trivial day-to-day nonsense that pandered before us.

"If you want the love you deserve," Morena put her frigid hand on my shoulder. "Then you need to go within."

A solitary tear rolled down my cheek.

'I know, Morena,' I let out a deep sigh. 'I know.'

Minutes later she stood up and extended a hand towards me.

"Let's get you out of this cold," Morena hoisted me up and we walked to the nearest coffee shop to warm up.

Emma ended up calling the day after Christmas while I was on a five-mile walk. She was upset that Greg did not propose to her and her sadness confused me. I was supportive, but I was secretly devastated: there I was, loving her and appreciating her, but she did not honor my role in her life at the time.

She admitted that she felt guilty, but I reassured her that I was there for her. I would comfort her soul and I would help her work through her emotions. I also told her that if he were playing games with her heart, I would step in.

Her voice suddenly took on a stark contrast to what I expected would happen.

Emma told me she was uncomfortable and a fight ensued.

"I have to go. Greg is coming now." Her curt tone left me with a sour taste in my mouth.

The two of us didn't speak again until the New Year started, but it gave me the strength to start writing some of my story down. I firmly believed that every great love started with a great story, but I just didn't realize the gravity that this relationship would have and weigh upon my soul at the time.

As I rummaged through my private journal and the papers in my bag at the time, I stumbled across the card Emma gave me for Christmas:

Scott,

"You have a special place in my heart. As I thank God for all the blessings He gives, I'm thanking Him especially for you because you <u>mean so much to me</u>, and I'm so glad you're part of my life! We have shared together the blessings of God." Philippians 1:7

I hope you like this card and know I went a "little bit" out of my comfort zone for it. It was the first one I spotted, and when I picked it up, it just seemed so "Scott." What I write here is all separate from the vault and I just want you to know that over these next days, I'll miss you. I'll also be wishing for you to have the best Christmas and New Years. You're an amazing guy who deserves it. Looking back on this year and more so the past few months, you taught me a lot about myself and just been the first person to walk into my life that I can share this way with. You get <u>ALL</u> of me. Yes, it is rare. This journey we take moment by moment, <u>uncounted</u>, that is key. Each day is a gift, and blessing, and life is life with its own rules and ways. Right now, it's chosen for US to be here at these crossroads. Let life happen. Everything is fine always and thank you for the most precious gift this year I could receive. Have a wonderful Christmas, and a Happy New Year.

Love "Always,"
Emma

P.S. Breathe!

I threw everything back in my bag and dashed out the door to the church. I had to go to the bridge.

Red and blue flashing lights in my rear-view mirror were a poignant ending to this day. It had been days since I last heard from Emma, and I was beginning to think that bottling up everything from today meant that I would burst momentarily.

In the hustle and bustle of the chaos around me, I felt sick to my stomach. Maybe it was a bad day, but it certainly was not a bad life. Though she will never realize how much those words in her card meant to me after everything, I pray she felt the extra positivity I sent to her that night in my dreams.

∞ ∞ ∞ ∞ ∞ ∞ ∞ ∞

When the two of us were in flow and in our prime, we were working together and splitting up counseling meetings with students. Anytime Joy needed help, the two of us supported her and friends and beacons of infinitesimal hope. For all intents and purposes, Greg did not exist.

Our conversations consisted of philosophical questions like "Where do you go when you die?" and Emma would sit in the church with me for hours talking about her spirituality. The two of us would lay on the mattress I had in the attic of the church, which was situated above the sanctuary. We would talk for hours upon hours and our conversations never seemed like they would have a concrete ending.

Leading up to her birthday in late January, the two of us were in the midst of a rollercoaster of emotions. Emma continued to flip flop between pursuing the life she created for herself with Greg and the relationship she had with me.

She continued leaving cute things on my desk like homemade pies and cards, which usually sounded endearing, like this one:

Dear Scott,

You asked me once about my standards and I said that they have only gotten higher, so let me name some and just say you can take a breath because you over achieved them all:
- *HAS to make me laugh*
- *HAS to know and do what I want/need without asking (because I am a girl, duh!)*
- *CANNOT be afraid of my extreme weirdness moments but can join me and be just as weird.*
- *Understand how hard I work (physical job)*
- *Understand that deep down at my core I am a people pleaser that does anything and anything for someone.*
- *Shows me appreciation and affection.*

Of course, a girl like me has more than six, but those are the tops. I do not want to kill you with expectations. You are doing great!

Love Always,
Emma

I would spend hours looking at the paintings she made me and reading her words. Her presence and how she loved me seemed so real, but I could not fully fathom how she was ensnared between two seemingly different relationships: one with me, and one with Greg.

When her birthday finally rolled around, I watched her favorite movie, *Galaxy Quest*, alone in the church. As a blizzard roared around the edges of the building, she called and told me she was devastated that everyone decided to stay home and forego her birthday party plans.

It was clear that she was in pain, and there were a lot of romantic exchanges between the two of us, but Greg was on the forefront of her mind. I gave her plenty of my own philosophy on true love, her soul, and how she should embrace her inner power. Emma appeared to hear what I was telling her, but she seemed hesitant in terms of embracing my words in her own soul.

That weekend, the two of us met at a hotel and we celebrated her birthday with much less pomp and circumstance, but with the utmost love I had in my heart. Hours passed by and she ended up having to leave earlier than expected, so I left her to gather her thoughts and allow myself the space to think about our relationship.

I stood trapped between reality and our passionate love dwindling in the setting sun. As I leaned on the railing to the church, glaring out at the majestic colors fading into the horizon, the moon was a reminder that all things, including the end of a day, were beautiful.

Leaving Emma in the bed, wrapped in the sheets and too pristine for this world, I came to the stark realization that true love can wear a person out. Flashes of our love danced in front of my eyes as I sincerely missed her hands intertwined between mine.

Just a mere thirty minutes had passed since I last kissed her forehead. Just a miniscule hour ago, we were skin to skin. Our hearts beat rapidly and as one. Our souls collided in the most humanistic and ravishing ways.

We were infinite. We were doused in each other's sweat and adoration. We reached the peak in any physical relationship, and we dropped to the sheets knowing the effect we had on each other: passionate love is passionate love. A deep, sensual love exists in those who have collided skin before… it was an accident that carried so much merit. It was a cataclysmic event where you are holistically vulnerable.

As images of her body rocking close to mine danced away in the night sky, I dragged my exhausted frame into the church. Still, I knew full and well that I had to resist the urge to run back to her. I had to force myself to linger in the melodic chimes of the church building, for if I went back to Emma now, the odds of one of us passing out would be probable.

I eagerly and impatiently waited for the next moment I could cling to her body. I yearned to be in her arms again… holding her gently and caressing her supple skin…

Yet I knew I had to wait for tomorrow…

But tomorrow was just one day away…

She continued to leave little notes on my desk, while I texted her my thoughts. Emma was worried that people may notice me walking in and out of her classroom, so I stopped leaving things for her where someone may stumble across them.

She would tell me in texts that she loved me and that it would "always be us." Emma said we would get through this and that she missed me.

In the dwindling days before February began, the two of us had one of our rendezvous in Kissena Park. We would meet far from the building so that no one would see us together.

I would pull into the parking lot of the park and watch her leave her car. Sitting back in the driver's seat of my Monte Carlo, I could see the outline of her silhouette appear more defined. A gentle gust of wind grasped her hair and whipped it forward each time she leaned back. Her eyes were far shallower now than they had ever been, and her lips were far too dry for a kiss.

As she got into the car, she leaned into my chest and began to cry openly. As the snow flurried down upon the windshield, our intertwined bodies merged in the symphony that surrounded us. The flakes cascading down the car emulated the sweat that beaded down our foreheads.

We were flooded by both the intense passion enveloping our bodies and the snowfall that began to encompass the car. The gentle fog sealed us away in our compassionate love as the lyrics to "Keep on Loving You" by REO Speedwagon wrapped around our skin. Our heated embrace and sweet whispers were exchanged over and over again. Two hearts beat as one, a rhythmic entity that refused to part ways.

And despite threats of Greg's engagement, I sensed that she would end up choosing me.

After we cleaned up from our afternoon delight, she told me about how she prayed for me each and every night. Emma had a ritualistic nature to her, as she called them, "bedtime prayers," that ushered her into a tranquil night of sleep. She told me that I was consistently on her mind, especially before she went to bed.

Our nightly texts continued, but our daytime fights were running rampant through my soul. I started feeling an aching sensation in my core, but I knew I did not know how to process losing and loving Emma all at once.

My greatest fears were being actualized, but I was clinging to some semblance of her love.

Then in the midst of everything, Bryan told me he was going to move to Florida to be closer to his mother. I was crushed, but I knew that he was free to live his life how he pleased. Bryan told me that he was miserable and had to try something new. Emma was supportive throughout my emotional turmoil, and she assured me she would be with me throughout this difficult time.

I found a purple envelope with a peacock on it that said, "A thank you for being you" on it. Emma must have left it on the passenger seat of my car at some point. It read:

Dear Scott,

Simply saying "Thank You" couldn't begin to cover the gratitude I have towards you. Not only have you shown me so much but you've let me be the inside me on the outside. Thank you for that connection. Thank you for always being there. Thank you for coming back after I left. Thank you for making endless time for me. For making me feel unique, one of a kind, and special. You have such an influence on me as well as others and you do not hear appreciation enough. You are an amazing magical soul. Thank you for allowing the world, and especially myself to see that.

> *Love Always,*
> *Emma*

This would be one of the last notes she would leave for me. The last one was a vertical infinity sign that was superimposed over an anchor. At the bottom she inscribed, "I love you" in big, bold letters.

She did love me. I was sure of it. Sometimes she was scared to say, "I love you," so she would tell me that she "liked me a little bit." "A little bit" became our inside joke and our way of saying we loved each other without actually saying it.

The two of us joined Joy and a handful of other co-workers at one of the local bars for a few drinks after work. Although my drinking days were in the distant past, I liked socializing with everyone.

No one suspected anything between me and Emma, except for Joy, though Emma and I were comfortable enough knowing that Joy would never say anything to anyone.

The bar was packed with idle chatter and clinking glasses, but Emma was the only person I was focused on. She was swallowing alcohol almost as fast as she was breathing in air; I could tell she was nervous. I didn't understand why at the time.

Soon after she finished guzzling down what appeared to be her fourth drink in less than a few hours, Greg showed up.

I wanted to walk up to him and address him, man to man. The chill crept up my spine and split itself down the center of my core. A solitary thought whipped through my mind: Do you kiss her goodnight just as easily as you shatter every fiber of my existence?

The two of them got into a heated argument and they left together. Emma walked right past me without saying anything. She was being nasty on purpose and I never saw that side of her before.

I was crushed. What did I do?

Upon walking out the back door of the bar, I didn't hear Joy follow me into the bitter cold. I threw myself onto the floor sobbing hysterically, almost throwing up in the process, and tried everything in my power to prevent my wailing from disturbing the people who lived in the nearby houses.

Joy bent down and hoisted me from the floor with such sincerity.

"Do you want to go talk somewhere?" Joy's concern was adorned across her face.

'Yeah,' I swallowed. 'Yeah I would really like that.'

This was the first night that triggered a deep-rooted friendship with Joy. We spoke about our lives and I poured my heart out to her without any guilt.

I began to hang out with Joy to make Emma incredibly jealous. It was absurd that Emma did not treat me with the same respect that Joy bestowed upon me. This eventually led to "The Vault" slamming shut for the rest of eternity.

Joy started to pull away from Emma as she coached me on how to get back with her. As Emma's demeanor and nastiness began to rise to the surface, I could see Joy getting crushed by the dissolving bond that was once sturdy and true. Joy and I would reminisce about the "old" Emma and I started to tuck away my emotions.

Both Joy and I realized that a concrete line drifted between myself and Emma, but I was resisting it wholeheartedly.

Even in the resolute silence that existed between myself and Emma, and after several weeks of silence and pain, I came to a spiritual crossroad. I had never felt more betrayed or misunderstood by anyone.

Losing Emma was dragging me to my knees.

I saw a family in our future, I saw a life together; I saw so much that we could accomplish, but with Greg's looming proposal, everything was starting to fade.

Nobody knows my true soul and my inner search for God and divine love, but in sharing snapshots and thoughts that fluttered through my head I thought I might have had a glistening moment in time. Who would have thought that another human being, who I admired and respected, would demolish those snapshots?

Morena watched me sit in the sanctuary night after night again.

"Don't try to bury your pain," she would reassure me. "Let it all out. Crying is pain leaving the soul."

I had a nightmare in the true definition of exquisite horror. There was a little girl standing in the center of a long corridor. It looked like the wing of a hospital. There she stood, in a small gown, glaring into the darkness. The fluorescent lights flickered and scattered hospital equipment lay strewn around the floor. The linoleum tiles, though white in reality, were bloodstained almost as bright as the streaks on the walls.

"Come play with me, Scott," the little girl whimpered. Upon turning, a concrete wall lay blocking my return path. The only way to go was forward. I reluctantly followed her. Her blonde hairs spread across her head like static. She could not have been older than 8 or 9... maybe 7.

We walked through the hospital knocking into broken wheelchairs and boxes along the way.

'What happened,' I asked inquisitively.

"They attacked," she said, a sullen tone emulating from her. We stopped walking and I looked down at her.

'Who attacked you?' I bent down and met her glassy eyes.

She shrugged and merely said, "the bad people." Her arm rose suddenly and three people stood at the end of the hallway, dressed in heavy black clothes and covered in blood. The scene shifted to a school hallway, dimly lit, with the three walking down it.

"You're next, Scott... run," a voice echoed down the hall.

I planted my feet firmly and boomed: 'No. I don't run."

The three sets of eyes I didn't recognize locked on my gaze.

'You run, run now,' my voice echoed down the hallway. Their stern faces transformed into fearful ones. They darted down the hall and one tripped in her retreat. I scampered over to pick her up from the floor.

'Here,' I said, 'Take my hand.' I tried pulling her up, but she refused my help. Her hazel eyes sunk into her skull with devout fear stemming from her body.

"I did this to me," she yelled. Her head twisted into the pit of her elbow and she retreated further back. "I'm sorry" were the last audible words that she muttered before bursting into mere ash.

"Save them, Scott," boomed from somewhere. "Save them now."

Then I woke up as a bright light ascended over me. Morena looked at me with a tinge of panic in her eye.

"Are you okay?" She was sifting through papers.

I didn't have to lie to her and say that I was fine; Morena knew that I was struggling and she continued to reassure me that everything was going to be okay.

∞ ∞ ∞ ∞ ∞ ∞ ∞ ∞

The frigid wind whisked through my hair with intense violence. The air was still, but turbulent enough to catch whomever was in its path in a whirl, a twirl, and an instinctive squint.

Looking down at my watch, the numbers read 2:22 A.M. A sigh pulled my breath in front of my face, as my shivering kept me awake and from feeling fundamentally alone on that dimly lit street.

The little dance I did to warm me up did not prevail. My shivering was unending. 'Where is he, where is he,' managed to leak from my frostbitten lips.

Time kept progressing under that streetlight in the harsh darkness of that bitter morning.

I stood impatiently waiting for something. Anything. A sign.

I had been summoned here under the pretense that a sign would materialize. Something would happen, and that something would be clear.

Faint music could be heard from a car radio in the distance. Could this be it? The sign?

No, it is just a passing motorist.

Great, 2:48 A.M.

Another few minutes ushered themselves through the floating garbage in the street. The wind showed mercy to not a thing, nor a soul, in the morning air.

Footsteps echoed in the air. A faint memory of someone who should have been standing there with me, yet somehow dissipated into the atmosphere.

The feeling was rather haunting. It was a terse reminder of how we spend so much time trying to please others, yet falter in actually trying to do what is best for ourselves.

I would say it is sickening, but it is yet another part of being a wholesome soul... or at least something to that extent.

Dancing with my shadow in the streetlight, I saw another figure moving slowly in the dark. I relaxed my back against the streetlight's post, hoping this was the foretold sign.

3:03 A.M.

The figure slowly dragged its frame closer and closer, without a hint of personality lurking underneath its hood.

Pensively, I squinted at the sight of what was nearing my aura. I could not read the person's intentions.

The click of their shoes meeting the pavement grew louder.

3:04 A.M.

As the person approached me, their dark hood waved in the wind. The suspense of who this figure was grew. I was struck by silence.

The dark hood stood inches from my face without showing its face. All that was visible was a shadowy chin, cast upon by the overhead light.

3:05 A.M.

A frigid peep lurched from my mouth. 'What do you want? Why am I here?'

A stern voice crept from under the hood. It shook me to my core as I heard it echo through my soul.

"You wanted answers, well here I am," the hood flew back, revealing her pristine face. A face that had melted somewhere into my past many many moments ago. Wrinkles pooled themselves at the edges of her eyes, as they met my gaze with a harsh tone.

"Well," fell from her lips, almost as if she were impatiently waiting for some sort of response.

A surprised look must have been the first thing she expected, because she was unfazed by the cold. She was locked onto my gaze.

"Say something Scott, no one knows I am here, just say it," she clattered her teeth.

'Hello Emma,' 3:06 A.M.

Emma and I rekindled some romantic moments in Kissena Park in the privacy of our cars, but she would ignore me at work. I was no longer permitted near her or her classroom when the two of us were in the building.

As my eyes fluttered open, I could feel last night on my skin. The words clung to my body like the sticky residue from an old movie theatre's floor. Switching masks had become a painful reminder that not a single person saw 100% of the pain I am in. As each mask was removed and laid on the floor, I couldn't help looking at the scattered existence of what once was and what could never be.

We would have long winded fights on the phone. It grew ugly but she assured me that we were still us, and we were still together.

Being considered a passenger in your own life is fundamentally depressing. With each step, each movement, your strings are being pulled left and right with no control. It burns to the core and cuts way deeper than anyone could fathom.

Knowing all this, I stood in front of the mirror gazing at the image of a fractured man. Looking into his eyes and watching life slowly drain from them was painful. Almost as if he knows what he is doing, yet he can't control himself. He doesn't know what the truth is, so he feeds into his own misery because he became devoid of emotion a long time ago. However, he's trying to find the pieces of his heart in the shadows of what once was and what was never meant to be.

In being everyone's rock, he's chipped away at his values and core beliefs until nothing but silenced echoes remain. He is lost in emotion and caught between doing what is right for him and what his heart is trying to whisper to him in the balance of dawn and dusk.

His joy disappeared the day it was created. His life became a puzzle with the right shapes but the wrong pieces. Now he is more isolated than ever, for he is an island and desolated the water encompassing him.

Who would be brave enough to risk treacherous waters in order to try to reach him?

In the midst of my downward spiral, I figured that the image of being half of a power couple was fleeting, and then I got some reassurance from the universe that there was hope. There was an ounce of yearning and an ounce of ambition left within me.

With a single phone call, I thought my life was about to turn around again… I just didn't know whether to take a step towards the light.

For even in the depths of what seemed to be my soul's darkest chapter, a solitary beam of light beckoned towards me.

"Hello Scott," the sultry voice at the other end of the phone was so familiar. "I miss you."

With trepidation in my voice, I replied instinctively: 'I miss you, too, Faith.'

CHAPTER 37

Keep the Faith

~

"I'll do what I got to, the truth is you could slit my throat, and with my one last gasping breath, I'd apologize for bleeding on your shirt"

- Taking Back Sunday, American Rock Band, Long Island, New York

Fractured fairy tales laid open in front of me: their textured words emulating from empty pages of a love that never was. All that remained was the sinking feeling that the words dripping off my diaries were that of a mistaken goddess.

Her words, though once airy and gorgeous elements of all that was pure in this world, echoed the halls that stung from her loneliness.

And there I was, a knight without armor or a white horse, standing at the edge of tomorrow… hoping that one day, some way, somehow… she would realize that she could come down from the tower all on her own.

She would need saving… but she only needed saving from her own soul.

And that is the hardest fairy tale to tell after all: what do you do when you are the heroine masked by the darkness that you allowed to consume your soul? What do you build when your castle was merely made out of sand?

You cannot wash away the shame and pain that is your personality, but you have a chance to show a little bit of compassion and consideration for yourself.

The bitter cold pushed against me as the alarm clock blared its usual scream. The weight of the frigid air heavily compressed my chest as I waited for the tears to subside.

Another day.

I slid out from under the shelter of the blankets and gazed up at the moon peering through the window. It looked lonely. I knew that exact same feeling.

Scurrying into the bathroom, I felt my toes wrap around each frosted over floorboard. Upon flipping the lights on, I glared into the mirror and saw someone I did not recognize: it looked like a version of me, but one that very scarcely resembled what I thought I had become.

This second version of me reached through the mirror with the fervor of rage visibly running through their veins.

"It's coming," the mirror image blurted out, almost sing songy. It grasped my neck and ripped me against the glass.

With its frosted fingers around my neck, its horrid breath graced my ear, "It's coming. Be ready."

Glancing down at my body, I saw blood rushing from my shoulder mercilessly. A gunshot wound of some sort materialized on the surface of my skin. The reflection laughed maniacally and transformed into a person whom I had seen many times: a vivid image of my past manifesting inches from my face.

"Face your demons. Now." were the last words thrusted into the cold air before the image disappeared.

My eyes slammed shut and flew open between my rapidly beating heart. The illuminated digits on the clock read 3:14 A.M.

3:14 A.M. 3:15 A.M. 3:16 A.M. Time stands still for no one. Time relinquishes no control. Yet through the pangs of a heavily beating heart, there is solace in knowing strength overpowers malice every. Single. Time.

Last night began playing over in my mind like an old film. The reel was getting snagged in the machine, but the images cast on the wall haunted me so.

I grabbed my ratty old towel and started the cold water in the small church sink. The grime and mold on the walls appeared to scowl at the sad excuse of a man cleaning himself up in the miniscule bathroom.

Desperately and diligently, I was doing everything in my power to care for the building and save money so that one day, Windows of Opportunity would have a home within the walls of the Queens Community Church.

Still, Eve treated me as if I was under her merciless thumb.

We argued almost as much as I was arguing with Emma. Except with Eve, the hounding did not stop. She was wholeheartedly unaware that I was practically living in the church, though she knew I was sleeping in my car a few nights a week.

Emma wanted to have the white-picket fence and cute little house in the suburbs, and I was praying that one day I could provide that for her.

In this tumultuous time in my life, Morena came to the church bright and early to help me through my suffering.

She waltzed into the basement where I was washing my hair and brought me a fresh cup of coffee.

"You ready to get to work?" She passed me the cup and smiled.

As I grasped it from her, I looked up and asked if we could sit in the sanctuary for a bit.

The two of us made our way up the paint-chipped steps and through the glass doors. I could tell there was an energy shift the moment I walked in, for Morena and I stopped in our tracks.

I turned to her for a moment: 'Can we just talk?'

"I thought you would never ask," she replied, motioning to the seventh pew to our right. I usually sat there and had philosophical talks with God. In addition, my favorite stained-glass window was diagonal that pew.

I read her Psalm 42:5:

"Why am I so depressed? Why is this turmoil within me? Put your hope in God, for I still praise Him, my Savior and my God."

The two of us sat in silence for a moment, taking in the meaning of the words that I just said. I cut the silence between us with a realization:

'I wrote a lot during the years and most of my journals capture my daily life, love, or challenging aspects of my life. I don't know what is going on, but I feel like God is responding to what I have asked for.'

"Why do you think that," Morena asked.

'It's a song, it's a conversation, it's a movie, or a random moment,' I started. 'I just feel this overwhelming sense of faith growing within me. I just... I feel everything is happening for a reason.'

"Well, your life has been a test of faith through and through."

'You got that right.'

We let the silence boil over for a few more moments.

'The church seems like a gift from God, right?'

"What do you mean?"

'It's like God brought me a window of opportunity in allowing Windows of Opportunity to thrive here. We can truly make this place something special.'

"We can," Morena looked at me wistfully. "We can."

∞ ∞ ∞ ∞ ∞ ∞ ∞ ∞

February 2016 was a particularly bitter month for many reasons: Emma and I were caught in a tumultuous love story, where I didn't know if I was losing her or not, and I was running myself into the ground to keep the youth of Queens engaged in leadership programs.

Paul and Eve were beyond happy to have youth fill the halls of Queens Community Church, which meant that I was at the church well past

10:00 in the evening on school nights and often cleaned the community room in the basement.

After all, I was sleeping in the musty attic on a mattress I kept on the floor.

During the middle of a terrible snowstorm one weekend, Eve still insisted that a group that rented the church was still going to host an event in the community room. A gang of rowdy people showed up and ended up trying to attack me while I was attempting to break up a fight. A bunch of people spilled out onto the lawn of the church and they were trying to bring in drugs and alcohol.

Someone pulled a knife on me and before I knew it, I was trifling through terrible flashbacks of my time in Texas.

A rock flew through the church window and my hope of having a quiet night in during the storm was shattered.

Over a hundred people had to be thrown out of the church and Eve didn't care. We argued about having boisterous events late at night, but Paul told me the argument was not worth it.

"Let her be," Paul assured me. "Just let her be."

Morena and I continued our daily spiritual talks throughout the month, and though Emma was texting me, Faith was calling me consistently.

At this point I had been hurt, I was weak, I was in need of some serious soul nourishing moments. The sanctuary and the cross at Queens Community Church were peaceful and granted me with no clear direction in terms of what to do or say with regard to Emma and Faith.

"What does your heart say?" Morena asked me.

'It doesn't,' I would reply. 'It just doesn't want to say anything.'

I texted Emma and told her about my talks with God in the sanctuary. I didn't want her knowing I was speaking with Joy or Morena at that point, but I wanted her to know that I was doing some soul searching.

"Lighten up on the God stuff," was the only response Emma left me with.

I didn't know what else to say, but all I knew was that my soul was crying out.

When it came to Emma, it became difficult to determine where the illusion of our relationship seemed to end and when our reality cut in.

Love comes in all shapes and sizes, and I suspect many often misunderstand love. Love can be in the beginning of a smile or a silent exchange between two people that nobody else comprehends. Real love is a friendship that has caught on fire and still has faint embers burning after the test of time.

No matter how deep the test, and how much water has been tossed on the flame, you cannot extinguish it.

It can be a quiet understanding, a mutual confidence, or the sharing and the forgiving of past expressions. Every moment we experience is an opportunity to learn, and even through mistakes or choices, real love cannot, and will not die.

Love is a quiet truth in your soul that burns through good and bad times, no matter how the exterior of your life is perceived by yourself and others. Love never truly admits defeat to our human desires for perfection and makes allowances for human weaknesses.

It is not a fairytale. It is not a story you have to dive in with the hope of a specific ending. It should not be forced into the idealistic vision we were taught growing up. Love can be facing challenges together, overcoming those obstacles, and never letting go knowing it is real in your soul.

It can be a passion of different sorts: creating together, supporting one another, reaching out when needed, and just knowing you have someone to lean on. It doesn't have to be more than that realization but isn't that everything?

Love is an undeniable energy that should not be a label and recognized as such. Allow yourself to be loved by the people who truly love you, the people who want to give you their heart, and who will never sway from that.

Morena told me, "Don't be blinded by society's definition of love or pushing people into a box, because we want someone to love us so badly."

Despite the quiet embers true, real, rare love can look you in the eyes, set your soul ablaze, allowing you to reach down and ignite the night like a phoenix. It is the process of supporting your soul's growth and enjoying the enlightening moments that present themselves on your doorstep.

By those criteria, I was not sure if Emma or Faith fit that bill.

Morena took me to a coffee shop to clear my head, where we ruminated about life's most pervasive questions and ideas.

I placed down my coffee cup and turned to Morena with a plethora of questions: 'Why does clarity find us when we are picking up the missing pieces of the soul we once believed was whole? Trapped between the tragedy that was a love painted gold and placated as a trophy and one that devoutly hangs in the balance of the contrasted state of why did she pursue him and why didn't she love me?'

Morena read my face blatantly. She could see me caught up in the net that was Faith's love hoisting me from the ocean and smashing me onto the shore.

'Do I go after Emma or do I choose Faith?'

Morena's eyes were fixated on something in the distance. She was not spiritually involved in our conversation. I turned to see what or whom she was staring at and my eyes locked with Faith's. When I turned back around to speak to Morena, a sole white napkin sat in her place.

"Scott, I thought I would find you here," Faith stood beside me in the coffee shop. Morena disappeared without a trace and Faith treated her presence as if it were a dream.

My mind went wild thinking about how Morena could disappear so quickly… but Faith's abrupt kiss on my cheek brought my attention directly into wanting to feel her lips pressed against mine with each passing second.

Faith was in, Emma was no more.

Or so I thought.

I felt my mind shutting down with each passing moment, for I never thought Faith would walk back into my life like a hurricane.

∞ ∞ ∞ ∞ ∞ ∞ ∞ ∞

Just when I thought Faith was about to re-enter my life as the other half of my power couple, I was struck by feelings of utter confusion. As I arrived at the church, I found Emma sitting on the steps leading up to the entrance.

"Hey," tears were streaming down her face. "Can we talk?"

I let Emma come into the church and the two of us sat for a bit and spoke.

She cried on my shoulder wondering why Greg wouldn't propose to her yet. It was a universal juxtaposition of sorts: there I was, the man who would do absolutely anything for her, helping her through an emotionally difficult time for her.

When you see or experience so much hurt in the world, you start to question the notion of love. Then when you finally experience it for yourself, you see what all the fuss is about. You can't imagine not having that person in your life, and you feel like the luckiest person in the world. You would do anything to make them feel the same way about you.

There is a difference between feeling like the luckiest person in the world, and actually being the luckiest person in the world.

Emma wore a mask adorned with her crooked smile and my leather heart, which she beat mercilessly until I bled acidic tears. They dropped as I screamed in agonizing pain, for when she asked me how I was feeling in that moment, the only words I could muster up were: 'I'm fine.'

Greg appeared to be stringing her along while I was more than ready to love Emma the way she needed to be loved.

How come the most beautiful souls on this planet are the ones who seem to get hurt the deepest? Why does one human being get away with damaging someone's soul, especially one that is so uniquely precious? Does he get away with doing this to her?

The pain in my heart was so difficult to mask. I had never experienced the magnitude of that feeling before. You had someone, a literal angel on earth, who was so powerful in spirit and had rare strong values, with whom I connected with like no one I had ever connected with. I was so ashamed that in my erratic emotions of loving this blessing you provided me, that I was blind to the pain she was in, and in turn hurt her myself by my constant wanting to "win her."

Life isn't a contest and neither is love, and even if she could not see it, all I wanted was her true happiness, if she could recognize the reality of "truth."

Did I even know what the truth was? I thought I knew, but I was so angry at my actions of being a selfish man. She was just so rare that I took my wall down in overwhelming excitement and put my blinders on to all else.

After Faith, I swore I was done. I missed Emma when she was with Greg more than words could begin to describe.

How do you show someone that you are deeply genuine, who lost trust in you? Did she lose trust in me? Was our energy just off? But she continued to come to me for support.

She didn't get the spiritual connection but she responded to it… and then ran away from it.

There was not a bad bone in my body, and how could she realize that I was not like anyone who had ever hurt her before?

I saw the world differently. I still see love differently.

How do you show someone that their soul and energy is the greatest feeling you have ever felt, and that all you wanted for them was to truly be happy – no matter what that looked like or whom that was with?

How do you say to someone I want you back, when you were never even technically with them in the first place?

Physical and emotional love unknown to the world does not exist in the reality we call the sands of time, or does it? How do you show someone that your words were true when you told them "you saved my life?" How do you show someone you unconditionally love them with no desired outcome and that you respect them and do not have an ulterior motive?

There was this constant gnawing slow pain in my chest that would not go away. I simply couldn't imagine my life or a world without her. I saw her struggle with me, and with life.

When she left, I found myself in the sanctuary saying, 'God, please help her. I ask you that any blessings you have stored for me, please trade them in and hand them to her. I do not need to be with her ultimately.'

I wanted her and I loved her, but truth be told in the silence of this church, I wanted her to stay with Greg if that's where her heart was. If someone truly wants to be with you, their heart will be there and show up. If not, they will stay with where their heart truly feels like home. It is that simple.

If she couldn't see my love and energy, though she acted on the energy subconsciously, then I wanted her to be where she was.

That was her truth in the universe, even if it was not mine.

I figured it would crush me to see her married and build a family, but if she wanted my shoulder and unconditional love, I would give it to her. I figured I would do so gladly and without showing her any pain I may have had in my soul.

She had been tested and she would rise above it all, I had no doubt in my mind. I would help her from whatever position she allowed me to help her, but I prayed she would come to me eventually and let me in.

I wanted to be her real friend. I wanted to show her what she was truly worth. I wanted to grow with her and make sure she knew how much she mattered. Instead of pursuing what "I want," which only perpetuates the cycle of selfishness and a message that I do not have energetically, I could only provide her with what she wanted.

It was truly not about me.

It never was.

Before I went to sleep, I let my mind wander. When I shut my eyes and reopened them, I was standing at the bridge, watching her lean over a bucket filled with flames and ash. She was kindling a small fire.

'Emma,' I called out. 'What are you doing?'

She tilted her head slightly and met my gaze. She didn't look well. We stood glaring at one another.

'Emma,' I shouted desperately. She remained silent. The fire raged on in the bucket. She moved towards me and handed me the pen I keep in my pocket.

"Tell me the truth," she murmured. I stood gazing at her in astonishment for a moment.

'What truth?' I whispered. We stood there for a moment longer and watched each other's every move.

Then someone I didn't know handed me a pen and paper. They told me to write a letter to my past self. So, I did:

"Dearly Beloved,

You weep for a heart that was never meant to break. You shatter bits of your soul so others could be rebuilt. You are the definition of an empath. You embody the spirit of those whose journeys were cut short. You bend and break, but don't you ever waver. Don't give in, not for one moment, to the voices in your head. Burn your demons and inhale the smell of your soul being reduced to ash. Find the goodness. Find the happiness. Feel the wind break through your skeleton, renewing all that once was and all that can be more powerful. Exhale the stress, the agony, the pain, the suffering. You were not born to be a minute. You're an infinite amount of time. You are a living legacy. You need to wake up. Please wake up. I can push at your heartstrings and head for so long. You are sleeping. Please remember to wake up. You have fight within you. Do not succumb and fall into the darkness. A beautiful soul is often beaten, but just bruised. Get up. Wake up. Wake. Up. Now. I am sorry you are here at this point, but I am overjoyed that you can have the satisfaction of growing again. You are a seed; you have been planted. Blossom. Not into a flower, no, something bigger than your imagination. See yourself from my eyes. You say you aren't that person. You say I am better. You are blind. Open your eyes. Wake up. I will always be on either side. Live. I got to see what your life becomes. Cling to hope. You have your faith. Do not falter. You are a beautiful soul, just wake up."

∞ ∞ ∞ ∞ ∞ ∞ ∞ ∞

Upon waking up the next day, I got the answers my soul was trying so hard to tell. A story fluttered within a story. A name trapped within a name:

Faith in love and a future wholeheartedly existed within her, within Faith, within the words we could not say to one another.

I felt as if I was cheating on Emma, but I knew she had made her decision. She didn't want me. She didn't want me…

The phone trilled and I jumped up…

3 Missed Calls: Emma

1 New Voicemail

Dare I listen? Dare I hear her smashing my heart to bits? No, I couldn't. I wouldn't. I couldn't face the hurt or the pain. I was not the one.

Incoming Call: Emma.

Do I answer it? Do I go for it?

No, no, no, no… I couldn't do this. I made my choice. Stay true to your faith.

'Stay true to your faith,' I told myself. Though I knew in my heart that Emma was the one for me.

Images of months past flickered innocently across my line of sight. The feel of her skin against mine lingered between my fingers, as a reminder that what once was is just a pleasant memory ruminating in my mind.

The connection between two souls can be severed. A bond of togetherness can simultaneously collapse with the fluttering of false eyelashes and genuine beauty.

I wondered if she, too, looked up at the sky and reminisced about our hands and minds intertwined on that luxurious park bench we called home. I wonder if my name floated through her brain waves on a daily basis. For in my own mind, I still felt the ebb and flow of her hips crashing through my mind. I sensed my mouth forming her name on my lips, but the crisp air caught the words before they slid out of my cracked lips.

Her energy gave me the intensity and the hydration that no other soul could ever manifest.

And for her presence, I would forever be grateful.

But I know when it is time to let the universe consume a connection, for when one bridge collapses, another will be built in its place. Though she was fundamentally irreplaceable, I knew in my heart, another beautiful soul would fill the void she left within me.

For Faith may be strong; but my personal faith is much stronger.

I think Ella Wheeler Wilcox said it best:

"Lean on thyself until thy strength is tried; Then ask for God's help; it will not be denied. Use thy own sight to see the way to go; When darkness falls, ask God the path to show."

My path was not complete darkness, but I was spiritually searching for strength. I had entered a transitional period I found myself lost in, not expecting to be in, and felt the pain of all my scars.

I was scared and found strength in the idealism I had set myself up to be. Many people count on me and there is a reason for that. I have been given a gift. My difficulty was in sharing that gift when I felt so hurt and hypocritical inside.

I prayed every night in the church for wisdom. I did not want to pray for strength, as I did not want to face any more tests of strength.

My past and my history have made me strong.

I wanted to release my worries and exhaustion to a higher power, so I could have the unconditional love and positive energy to share with humanity. This was where my journey led me and where I was stuck.

The phone rang and I found myself begging for Emma's name to be the one looking back up at me.

It ended up being Faith who was calling and who wanted to meet up. At a loss for words and in the midst of utter confusion, I obliged.

Faith and I agreed to meet at a new restaurant in the neighborhood. I didn't consider it a date, but I told Emma where I was going and who I was meeting.

Although she was pissed and incredibly jealous, I had a feeling Emma was not going to do anything about it. Deep down inside she had to know I loved her, and I was trying desperately not to make her choose between Greg or me.

It was my devout and firm belief that Emma needed to choose herself above anyone else. For though I hoped she would choose me over Greg, something told me she was not going to choose herself.

On my way to see Faith I realized that I could feel so lost at times. My only comfort was knowing that I was exploring my faith and growing spiritually. You can be on one path at one point, and be on a totally different one in mere minutes. That is the beauty of life, I guess… times change and people change as well.

We all just need to ensure that we are all changing for the right reasons.

Faith and I met up, but as soon as we sat down, she had to rush home. It was almost as if the universe did not want us to meet. I texted Emma to tell her what was happening, and she almost sounded relieved.

In a way, I knew that our love would triumph over anything her and Greg had, for I believed that Emma knew her own soul at the time.

When I returned to the church, I spoke with the angels and the universe. Morena came by for a while and we spoke about both Faith and Emma.

"Why do you think you are so torn?" Morena ran her fingernails along the pew.

'I don't know,' I rested my head on the wall next to my favorite stained-glass window. 'I mean I have a history with both of them and I love both of them in different ways.'

There comes a point when you suddenly realize you're in a moment that would normally debilitate you, and you find yourself automatically turning the situation over to faith. When you're feeling every moment of letting go and letting God, there is a sense of peace.

I knew my faith was getting stronger. I remained alone with my thoughts and misunderstood by many, but it was okay. I learned that someone you used to easily speak to and express love towards could become the hardest person to speak to, and someone you desperately want to scream the words of love to may not have anything to say.

A momentary smile and a quick and embrace could mean the world to someone. God is at work in both scenarios. I didn't quite understand the methodology and though I tried to figure it out, I trusted God, and the mantra "what shall be shall be."

Sometimes emotionally removing yourself from something you want so badly helps you to see things from a perspective you were not aware lies within you, and herein lies personal growth.

To love someone enough to let them go, to love someone enough to have space and time to learn their own soul and power, to love humanity and dedicate my existence to making a difference on our planet, is powerful. There was a powerful love present. I was excited to watch and feel it unfold. I was aware of it, and I stood for it, eternally grateful.

I started allowing Emma and Faith's respective images to pass through my mind. Morena sat before me watching everything register in my hollow expression.

The fond memories I had with Faith floated to the surface. I felt a warm sensation reminiscing about long, spiritual talks with Faith. Her hair brushing against my skin while we spoke of ideas that seemed so much bigger than us. Her kids came to mind. I could feel the gravel beneath my feet from the long walks we took in the park. I smelt the cultural cuisine we would have.

Despite the beautiful memories that reminded me of why Faith seemed like the one, I could not shake the pure, unconditional love I had for Emma. I would not dare sever the connection I had with her. The sacred "vault" we kept together and our scribblings transcended the definition of what love is. We poured our souls into every conversation we had and each day seemed like a poignant fairy tale. If God had answered my prayers years ago, I would have never had the relationship I created with Emma.

I must trust in the process and keep the faith. I must refuse to sink, as I had always wholeheartedly believed, and as Emma endearingly says.

One day this journey and this stage would make sense, and until then I needed to be the best human being I could be.

Morena seemed to gaze into my soul as she smiled.

"So, you know what you must do," she spoke as if she was asking a question, though with slight hesitation.

'Yes,' I replied.

I stood up from the pew and left the sanctuary. When I turned around, Morena had disappeared. It was a pervasive thought in my mind that she was almost an apparition of sorts. Whenever I needed Morena, she appeared before me and seemed to know what to do or say, though I must admit she was holistically a ghost in the body of a human being... or at least that's what I thought for the time being.

I called Faith who surprisingly picked up the phone within moments.

"Hey," her sultry voice made it sound like she was reaching through the receiver and caressing my cheek. "I miss you, when are we meeting for dinner?"

'Hey,' was all I could get out of my mouth.

"What's wrong?"

'Nothing,' I knew she would sense that something was up, and she did. We spoke for a while longer, and I ended up meeting with Faith that night for a quick bite to eat.

When we sat down, Emma was the only one who I wanted sitting across from me. Although Faith said that she finally made up her mind and realized she wanted to be with me, it was like we could never get the timing right.

I always wanted her when she did not want me and vice versa. We were on a carousel of emotions, constantly getting on and off of the colorful wooden animals we chose to sit upon, but at the end of the day we were just going in circles.

It was time to get off of the carousel and just enjoy the carnival of life.

'No,' I told Faith.

"No?" She dropped her fork in the most dramatic way.

'I am with someone now,' I began. 'She's the one.'

I smiled, waiting for a response from Faith, who looked at me in awe.

"Well, I didn't think about that," she chuckled. Faith stood up and hugged me, "She must be something awful special."

'She is,' I put my hand on her back and gave her a reassuring pat.

"Goodbye for now, Scott," she began walking away. "Until next time."

Faith took our conversation in stride. She appeared to understand my soul, as I understood hers. I think it was the first time in years we spoke the same language without having to interpret each other's words or actions.

I was incredibly thankful for her understanding.

For all intents and purposes, Emma was the one I wanted to spend my life with, and I knew I would stop at nothing to make her mine.

This is how it was going to be.

∞ ∞ ∞ ∞ ∞ ∞ ∞ ∞

Now that I had made my mind up, I chose to keep my decision between Morena, God, and myself. No one else really knew how much I adored Emma at this point, and I wanted to keep my next move a secret.

I loved Emma. Nothing and no one would stand in my way of confessing my unconditional love for her. She knew, deep down inside, that I loved her more than anything else in the world. Oftentimes, I convinced myself that I loved Emma more than I loved my own soul.

My nightly ritual of pacing the sanctuary re-ignited a flame in me. At the time it seemed to feel like there were rocks churning around in my abdomen; this should have been one of the first signs that something else was manifesting inside of me.

I continued to see Emma in the halls at work, but I was careful not to approach her and make it obvious to others that my eyes utterly adored every inch of her body and her soul.

Emma would occasionally flash me a coy smile while we were at Lincoln Memorial, but our relationship was contained to rendezvous in the park and long phone conversations after work.

On the morning my life was about to shift forever, I did not suspect anything was wrong. Emma and I had a lengthy phone conversation about some trivial matters, though by the end of the conversation we were both consumed in a flurry of "I love you's" and "I am grateful for you's."

I never would have hung up the phone if I knew what was coming next.

Morena and I were spending a quiet evening organizing papers for Windows of Opportunity, as we were in the midst of structuring one of our programs for the kids.

Laughter and spiritual conversations flooded the air that night in the church, until a chime from my phone brought our frivolity to an abrupt halt.

I remember looking over at my phone and seeing the message from her. I was excited that although Emma was with her family and busy doing her ritualistic weekend activities, she would still be sweet enough to find the time to text me.

After looking at my phone, I fell to the floor so tragically that Morena leapt across the table thinking that I was having a severe heart attack. To me, it was worse: my entire soul shattered.

As I cried and clutched my abdomen in pain, Morena picked up my phone.

Her face dropped almost as fast as the tears rolled down from my eyes.

"Scott, I-" Morena's words drowned in the sorrows I quickly succumbed to.

I had hoped that what I read was just a misunderstanding, until I took my phone from Morena's hand and re-read the text message from Emma:

"Scott,
There is no right way to tell you or a good way, but today Greg asked me to marry him and I said yes.
It's just another day. Breathe.
Love "Always,"
Emma"

CHAPTER 38

Always Just Another Day

~

"You're not listening now. Can't you see
something's missing?
You forget where the heart is."

- Yellowcard, American Rock Band,
Jacksonville, Florida

The sensation of reality slammed into my head. Emma had chosen Greg and I was at a loss for words.

Two days after her engagement, Emma left this note on my desk:

Scott,

I feel like I don't know where to begin. All I have playing over and over in my head is how this was already such a hard time for you, especially with Bryan. I figured you got my message and it was one of your worst nightmares coming true. With that said I've wanted to give you space. I know you are hurting and I'm going to hold back from saying much more because the last thing I want to do is add more hurt. I want to be there for you like you've been for me but I also know you might not want me to. So the ball lies in your court. Just remember the conversations we've had before about when this moment came. It's just another day...

Love,

Emma

Is it really just another day?

Maybe it was time to emerge from sadness into a state of higher consciousness where "another day" represents a chance to spiritually awaken from who I once was. There is a realm of possibilities and new perspectives, although I knew I needed to pull the dagger from my back, which was laced with Emma's words and her fleeting love.

We are all angelic beings masked by our human attributes. You can recognize those who are moving towards enlightenment when you yourself open up your very own eyes.

The moment I laid eyes on Emma, I knew I had found one. The moment I saw Emma, our intermingled lives flickered through my mind. In seconds, I was struck by a pull so indescribable that gravity itself was nonexistent compared to our energy.

Souls' crashing into each other is the greatest feeling in the universe. When your soul burns with passion, and your faith is operating on overload, life seems to shift. The positive shift and vibration is almost overwhelming, but the most devout and unwavering feeling of awareness ever experienced.

It's so important as we build our futures, implement our strategies, and search for our dreams, that we go deeper than we could ever fathom.

It was crucial to believe in a path beyond the physical eye and pass the point of should, could, and would.

It was painful, but I had to accept living life in the exorbitant now, patiently waiting for us to succumb to what is and not what should be.

There is a light that shines bright, not only from inside our souls but upon us from above. There is an energy that could fill your half full cup to the brim with unconditional love and overflow it with joyous life experiences. Think it, see it, and live it. For after all, we deserve to live a life of enlightenment.

I had to awaken the voice within, because it is not just another day anymore.

The "one" who I thought would never destroy me ended up being the "one" who would shatter my soul and shred me to pieces. There was never a love like ours before, and clearly this love never would be.

Was it ever love to begin with?

Music seemed to be the only thing that would fill the cracks of what once was. I figured that the lyrics would take the place of the words she left in her last entry in "The Vault," which was melting off of the pages due to my incessant crying.

Oddly enough, the first song to shuffle on was "You're No Match" from Bayside:

> *"You are the monster I was scared you'd be*
> *And now you're blaming it on your surroundings*
> *And your horns came out so gradually*
> *But honey, you're no match for me."*

The song reminded me of my connection with the band. The lead singer of Bayside was a former student of Elyza's, and over the years we ended up becoming good friends. The band was incredibly popular in the underground music scene in New York, and after they made it big the only show the band actually performed in Bayside was due to the Musicapalooza event I coordinated.

The next morning after their performance, I was walking through the parking lot and heard the principal blasting Bayside's album from his car. The two of us made eye contact and he gave me a thumbs up.

He cracked his window and said, "This is good, I am glad we had them here."

They are truly amazing musicians who deserve to be admired with the likes of Bon Jovi, and I am not just saying that because I know the band members personally. Each of them truly connected with their fans at shows. Bayside became one of those bands that you genuinely admired because of their musicality, their lyrics, and just how thrilling they were to listen to or see live.

Bayside's songs have a true, devout message. Their lyrics have something powerful to say.

I was devastated the day their drummer passed away, and I carry and cherish his memory with me day after day.

The band is resilient and unwavering in their commitment to music and their fans. Their message to the world is inspiring. Words that they pieced together illustrate the melody people never realized they needed in their souls.

One day they will gain the notoriety they deserve.

As I listened to more music seeping through the speakers, these tears tasted familiar and these songs sounded the same. I was stuck in a music box, except I was the ironic ballerina spinning on the spindle, waiting for the lid to slam down hard and the music to stop.

∞ ∞ ∞ ∞ ∞ ∞ ∞ ∞

Dawn was creeping through the wind. Fresh beams of light were reaching out and caressing my face ever so gently as to lull me back to sleep.

Too late, I was already awake. I hadn't slept all night. All I could do was think of her. I imagined her rolling over in bed, her amber eyes flashing open slowly to greet the new day. Locks of her luscious brunette hair dance over her pillow and land on her pure face.

"Good morning," she says groggily. Only it isn't to me: it's to Greg.

I wondered if her fiancé cherished her as much as I do? I wondered if he shivered as I once did, as she tenderly presents her kisses. I wondered if she left him adorable notes on crinkled pieces of paper. I wondered if he looks at her in awe as I have done. I could not help but ask: Does he take her for granted as much as I had?

There is that old saying, "All good things come to an end," and I consider the notion all the time. Then again, were we ever a "thing," or just two lost souls floating in the ocean? Or was she just looking for a temporary shelter from her soul's pain.

Turning the page on a chapter that was barely written is echoic of the inner turmoil that flooded my soul for years. A single page blank in the greater landscape of the epic saga that is my life.

Looking skyward, I felt the sunlight embrace my skin with each breath I exhaled. Our story lay cemented into pages at my feet: an entire love story whittled down to ash in moments. The match hung shakily in my hand, about to take its final descent.

Memories flickering past me reminded me how love was a temporary flame. We burn out eventually. We go up in smoke with the dissipation of the flame. We turn and we catch fire.

We were everything and nothing in the passing remnants of a solitary day.

And we were bright.

And we were everything love needed to be at that time.

But we were a lesson: hearts cease, but they beat on eventually.

And with the drop of the match, I could feel her wrapped in the arms of another just miles away.

Everything. Gone.

The ashes danced towards the sky in the most majestic way imaginable.

And our souls lay scattered in the bucket, doused in the tears from years past, yet burning vigorously as a means of sealing our fate forever and a day. Yet again, "just another day" rocked through my mind and pushed any semblance of love far from the depth of my own, decimated soul.

I was a mess without her, but it felt like my soul wanted absolutely nothing to do with her. How do you manage to miss someone terribly while still acknowledging that person shredded your heart?

After everything we went through, part of me could not believe that she still said yes to Greg and must now live with the story she perpetuated each and every day.

I spent over an hour and a half after school counseling a student who recognized that the two of us loved each other. She sat there in my office while I had to calm her down and explain to her that it was okay that we were not getting married.

Still, the student turned around and said, "I don't get it. You are both the definition of true love! I see it when you look at each other."

Deep inside I wanted to tell the girl that although she saw it, you were eclipsed by the shiny diamond ring precariously sitting on your fragile hand.

Emma's happiness and my stinging agony were slammed in my face every single second while I was at work. It got to the point where I didn't even want to work there anymore.

Just a week prior, Emma painted my soul with ornate words of grandeur, claiming that I was her soul mate. Then in one fatal swoop, with four words symbolizing a humanistic commitment, Emma started to nonchalantly talk about how her and Greg would grow old together.

I am happy she found the love she wanted to connect with at the time, but I knew in my soul our relationship was bonded on a deeper level.

Greg's love was a thrill.

Emma began to ignore me in the hallways. Our moments and glances faded into the illusory distance.

Her voice, her life, and her dreams began to beat my soul to the senseless point where it seemed as if there was no return.

I wanted to talk to her. I wanted to tell her how much I loved her, but it did not seem to matter and she did not seem to care. Reality seemed to dictate that the two of us were not true love. The way she kicked me aside made it appear as if we were a total farce.

It appeared that I was all that Emma needed for the time being, so she could fill the void of loneliness until Greg chose to stand up to her expectations. Emma needed a story to tell and she was setting the stage: she got the boy, she got the ring, and she was on the verge of getting the white picket fence she so desperately yearned for.

But where was the love?

There was no room for a man who bared his entire soul in hopes that Emma would see just how much of a treasure she truly was.

The moment the ring slid onto her finger, the circle was complete: the love they had fit into that continuous flow. Meanwhile, I existed outside the ultimatum she put forth months before I even had a chance to deeply adore who she was.

Though weeks prior she proclaimed that I was hers and she was mine, there was an asterisk on Emma's love. The disclaimer read, "I will love you, until Greg gives me a ring."

The truth was that she wanted the commitment from Greg. I was nothing.

I wonder if she even thought of me when he put the ring on her finger. Devastated was an understatement at that point, and I couldn't even show it to anyone. Within weeks, I lost Emma and I lost Bryan... and I lost myself.

I was numb with the exquisite exception of the uncontrollable moments when a few solitary tears would slide down my cheek.

The walls went back up.

Who cares about feelings?

Who cares about love?

I was hurt so many times, and despite my better judgment telling me to resist... I risked everything. I risked my soul and my sanity...

And despite it all, I was left with one conclusion: just settle.

I found myself sitting at the bridge for hours upon hours, brushing my fingers against the peeling pine-green paint on the bench where Emma and I once sat together. I longed for the days when we were truly us. Though our meetings in Kissena Park were sensual in nature, I was craving a day where Emma and I could meet there again and just talk.

Without her in my life, I felt that my reality, all of my hopes, and every single one of my dreams were gone.

It took so much effort to walk into work each day and put a fake smile on.

How could it be just another day, considering she was no longer in it?

How could an engagement be whittled down to three words: just another day?

Emma was craving true love and it appeared that I was not the flavor of the week. It made me feel like our few months of passion and promises were an absolute lie.

How did this happen? How did I get here?

Why would the universe put someone so perfect in front of me, just to have her rip my soul to shreds?

∞ ∞ ∞ ∞ ∞ ∞ ∞ ∞

I found myself roaming through Alley Pond Park once again.

The sunlight cut through the trees and ceased on its journey through the woods to rest on my face. I could not help but let the tears rush down my face with the fervor of a coursing river: I truly missed Emma.

Morena sat pensively in the shallow dirt by my feet, gazing up at the shell of a man heaving and filling his head with grandeur of a once beautiful, passionate love that was shredded to its core.

All because of Emma.

All because she did not love herself as much as I could ever love someone so toxically beautiful.

And there I was crying again to mourn the soul of a woman who never died, but rather killed her chance of a beautiful relationship smothered in true, impartial divine love. She killed us with a slender knife to the heart.

Yet, all this time later, there we were, sitting in the woods discussing her lost soul.

And my fleeting hope sewn together by the sliver of hope screaming, "you have a chance."

What chance? What chance if she is not willing to accept our love? Our bond?

I would die for her, while she would just let me drown in the misery that is her absence.

Through strife and tears, I could see Morena's face slowly forming a more compassionate demeanor. The devout pain was burning a gaping hole in my soul... and all she could do was look on and watch me shrivel and fold into itself.

A devastating scene grew more contrastive to the silent trees bending into our conversation to hold me back from falling into a pit of despair and tragedy mounting on the edge of the rotted log I perched myself upon.

I was drowning in tears. Scoffing off any positive energy that inched closer to my frame: Morena's frozen hand reaching out to pull me out of the shattered existence before her.

I could not reach out for her. Emma's absence clasped around me and ripped me further into an ocean of this depressive state.

Morena stood before me, and I could see her smile tear through my shallow tears.

"Scott, it will be okay, don't let go," Morena wrapped her tired body around mine. She clung to my tears, absorbing them as her own as to shield me from the pain and agony that crashed down onto the dirt before us. Heavy drops of emotion spewed from every ounce of my soul and split the air in a matter of seconds. I could not hold in the pain any longer. The pressure mounted.

I needed Emma more than I needed anything in the world... but she was too blind to see that.

There was a quote I read somewhere, I am certain it was from Yann Martel's *Life of Pi*: "*You cannot know the strength of your faith until it has been tested.*"

If I only knew the truth in those words when I met Emma, I am unsure what I would have done. I tended to let my mind drift to a realm where Emma chose me over Greg. I wondered what it would have looked like if I was hers.

Questions fluttered through my mind: Would we have had the white picket fence? Would the two of us be everything she wanted in a relationship? Or was she assuming that I could never give her what she wanted?

The truth is you never really know what the next moment holds.

You can have your whole future planned out, and it can finally make sense, and then all of a sudden it evaporates in between the seemingly innocent tears you shed. You could have a love that is an absolute blessing, only to discover their love is being bestowed upon another person.

You could be an inspiration to so many lives yet hate the person you have become.

Morena interrupted my spiritual derailment of sorts to release me from her grasp. She walked towards one of the trees and brushed her fingers along the rugged bark.

"Tell me," she began. "You can hear the whispers of the universe and know that the truth in your heart is real, and yet you are still scared."

I looked over at her and allowed a teardrop to cut between my bashful smirk.

'The truth is I would give it all up if the trade off would mean she would find her true inner power that she hides from the universe.'

"It is more than that," Morena's eyes shifted towards me. "You know that."

'Do I?'

"Listen to the voice from deep within your soul, Scott. What does it say?"

I sat silently for a few moments.

'You can be in the same room with the person you are spiritually devoted to, yet as she talks about another man she loves, hear everything inside you scream. She is just impressing society's demands. She has to be.'

Morena rolled her eyes and plopped beside me.

"It is more than that."

'I fall asleep in the sanctuary sometimes with her as the last thing on my mind.'

"Maybe the stars just don't align for your souls."

'But she was the one who initiated the relationship!'

"And?" Morena gripped the edges of the rocks we were sitting on.

'And shouldn't that mean something?'

"It does," she paused. "Maybe what you are searching for is not what you are looking for."

'I am looking for her,' I felt my ears burning up. 'I know she is the one for me. With one smile, one hug, one look with those eyes of hers… all my pain goes away.'

"Is that your pain dissipating, or your soul?"

'Morena, what does that even mean?'

"Think about it," she stood up and brushed the dirt from her hands.

'Maybe my *greatness* and *worthiness* is all in my mind.'

Morena sighed, "Why do you instantly jump to the conclusion that you are not worth it?"

I looked at her blankly for a moment.

"The truth is judgment and society will tear you to shreds if you let it. If you do not trust in true love, you can't overcome the maliciousness that others may cast upon you."

We glared at each other with empathetic eyes.

'I am mad at her.'

"Good," Morena said. "Why?"

'Because I am so scared of losing her.'

"What does 'losing' mean?"

Morena was right; I didn't know what it *really* meant. I could not fathom what loss even looked like in that moment, for Emma was truly just a call or text away.

'No one would defend their love for me, they would rather walk away.'

"Did she truly walk away?"

'Um, yes?'

"Maybe you are just looking at things the wrong way."

'Well if you are going to be that insightful,' I quipped. 'Then where should I look?'

Morena put her hand on my chest and gazed up at me. When our glances met, it was like I could see the entire universe sprinkled throughout her eyes.

"Within yourself," she replied.

Every great hero has a phenomenal love story to catalogue the reward for their perils. Emma was the love I needed to change the world.

I felt it wholeheartedly. Though it dawned on me: what if I wanted love so bad, but I was looking in all the wrong places? How would I know?

'Morena,' the two of us turned and started walking away in unison. 'I searched my entire lifetime for love, and she has to be the one. I am tired of searching. I miss her. I dream about her. I love her.'

She did not respond.

'The next time she falls into my arms, I will treasure her more. I will show her that I love her because we just make sense.'

The two of us got to the edge of Alley Pond Park and I found myself alone again.

It was becoming a natural occurrence at this point.

∞ ∞ ∞ ∞ ∞ ∞ ∞ ∞

There is nothing like a rainy morning in the spring. As I was laying on the mattress in the attic of the church, listening to the rain pelt the roof, I felt the ghost of her cuddling into my arms. I wondered if she missed our cuddling sessions where we curled into each other and felt the warmth of love.

I couldn't get out of bed. I was debilitated by my loneliness and what I took for granted for so long.

My pain was my punishment and it cut through me with such tenacity.

I was stuck inside my own love story, yet the rest of the tale was stuck between the pages of someone else's journey.

I went into work with my head hung low, only to find her waiting in my doorway as my students were coming in.

"Hey," Emma spoke coyly, though I could see the light reflect from her engagement ring.

'Hi.' I wasn't sure if I could hold my tears back in front of the kids. I tried to forget her and move on, but then I felt her love spilling over from my soul. Then almost poetically, I looked up and there she was.

Emma sat down and started to counsel students with me. I almost wanted to run up to her and kiss her on the spot, just to see if she was truly real.

When the students left hours later, she reached up and touched my face as a breathy, "Hey," escaped her lips.

Touching her was getting easier. Kissing her hand evoked a genuine smile.

Embracing her made every ounce of pain instantly disappear.

I was under a spell, knowing in the recesses of my mind that ruin was about to be the road to transformation.

My soul shivered out of fear: I was petrified that she would have wanted to stay with him and I would be hurt forever.

I found my heart of gold.

She makes me want to be a better man. It's loving her that drove me to push my body, mind, and soul to a greater awareness.

Now I stayed in the moment.

I refused to pressure her. She chose him and he has the financial resources they need. I couldn't compete with that. Still, though I loved her from afar, she became a permanent part of my soul.

How do you let go when you don't want to?

I was so confused. The situation seemed like we would never be together again, but then she reaches out to me in her own quiet way and it feels like we are the true love I believed in.

Prayers hung against the back of my lips. I hoped she could admit she was fighting her feelings, so I would have at least known that our love was real and that I was not insane.

I wondered why I kept falling harder for her.

With her in my arms, pressed against my chest, I wondered: Why am I afraid to lose you when you are not even mine?

I saw a story in her eyes, but I must have been reading the wrong book.

"I missed you," she murmured those sweet words in my ear without remorse.

Instinctively, I leaned towards her and pressed my lips against hers. She reciprocated the kiss, which made me feel that something was happening between us again.

The two of us sat and she cried on my shoulder. I tried to sit in silence just for the sake of being. My mind was on the verge of bursting, but I had to just be. I had to just exist.

I was so lost without her. Just having her with me for a few moments meant the world to me.

As tears streamed down her face and I embraced her, I tried to rise above the pain of nursing a shattered heart.

I would have shattered my own heart into teensy bits, if only it meant giving Emma the pieces that would make her whole again.

Her phone rang and she scrambled to pick it up, almost as if I was not mere inches in front of her. Emma and Greg were bickering back and forth about something I struggled to hear.

Within moments, Emma apologized to me and rushed out of the room almost as quickly as she seemed to enter my life. While standing alone in my office once again, I realized that I had to stop teetering between wanting her love and genuinely loving myself. Although it is honestly easier to speak something into existence than to physically will yourself to do something.

The worst crime I have committed against myself was to expect someone to love me the way I loved them. I had hoped she would feel that same jolt of energy I felt when I saw her smile.

I prayed she would hang on each word I would say. I aspired to be her everything, and not just her something.

I think I had said this time and time again, but I truly meant the words: I would rip my heart from my chest, slam it against the ground, and pick up the shattered pieces and give them over to her. Maybe that was my problem: I would sooner break myself further and further into a pit of despair so that she could become whole again.

Maybe that has been my problem all along. Shattering my very core and my dreams seemed like the right thing to do, since she seemed to replace any aspiration I could ever imagine.

So that's my problem... I would rather break down than see her suffer, but she is not worthy of my love. She should stand in the shadows while I claw my way back into the sun. Let her feel my pain rush over her like the wave of agony she thrust upon me. Let her feel her blood boil when she reads this. Let her see how painful it is to look at yourself in the mirror and beg yourself to be okay again.

Maybe it was time I stood firmly rooted in the ground...

Maybe it was time I grew...

Maybe it was time I stopped discounting myself...

Maybe it was time I rose from the ashes and truly "keep the faith..."

Although I was speaking such a devout series of truths to myself in the quiet solace of the office, something was physically preventing me from living out these truths.

I promptly ran home to the silence of the sanctuary so that I could speak to God and the universe. The whispers I released into the universe were of a purposeful nature: I believed that if I truly proved I believed in my faith, I would be able to attract Emma back into my life.

As the night sky enclosed upon the stained-glass windows, I felt a sense that something was shifting. My mind was filled with intentions for my future, though I felt that it went beyond the typical "power couple" idea I always considered.

I felt my spirit was being renewed over time and I was thankful for that miracle.

However, with such a great blessing, namely a growing sense of being and self, I felt more burdened as I absorbed the pain of those around me. Countless youth were being belittled or disregarded for their respective passions and interests, people in my life were suffering from battles they could not even articulate, and in general, I felt that Emma was the epitome of what happens when you love someone and can't outwardly pursue that love.

Asking God and the universe to heal the souls of those in pain seemed to be the only thing I could do in those moments. I needed help with people on my team. The intricate and hidden pain within their souls is hindering them from moving to a state of higher consciousness.

I recognized that I was also stuck, but I knew I could rise above. I just needed to see what I was capable of. I needed to remind myself of how strong I was and what path I was on.

In a sense, I did not know what I wanted other than divine love.

I wanted to be outstanding. I wanted to develop and design programs for youth. All of my life lessons, celebrations, and challenges were preparing me for the moments ahead.

The next inspirational chapter of my life was on the verge of appearing; I just hoped that the one narrating those chapters would be Emma. Her voice and her presence was all I truly wanted in my life. Although Bryan was my source of true happiness, his departure to Florida provided me with less of a daily reminder that love was close.

Emma's sudden exit and engagement was a blow to my ego, though I had to know in some respect that love had to be a feeling beyond just the human ego. Everyone has their own gifts and talents, and mine seemed to be providing love and inspiring others to see how they could pursue their passions.

There is so much potential and insight brewing in the minds of people in this universe, and I hoped that Emma would see that as well. I prayed Emma would discover that for herself and come back to me at that moment.

Just as I sent God a prayer and yearned for Emma to feel her innate power, I heard my phone's vibrations echo through the sanctuary.

A solitary text message was glaring up at me. Emma sent one statement: "I don't want to lose your friendship, but Greg is very special to me."

I felt my spine go up in flames. I sensed the hairs on the back of my neck stand at attention. All of my prayers and ambitions appeared to melt away.

Emma used the term, "friendship," as if that was all we were. Oftentimes she made it seem like so much more than that, both emotionally and physically. I had years upon years of a connection with Faith, yet I was willing to throw it all away just for Emma. I could tell she was worried about Greg getting jealous of what Emma and I had.

In my mind, it did not change the truth I knew about us, or what we felt. However, in her fear-laced words I sensed that everything between us seemed to be a lie. Yet before she had that ring on her finger, her messages never harbored that tone.

Time and time again, she said it would always be us. Though once one of "us" had a ring on their finger, I guess our memories were erased.

Once upon a time, as most fairytales begin, I was Emma's "rock" and "soul mate," though those words crumbled as soon as Greg sealed their love with a ring. How poignant: she ended up with the charming prince in a story she wrote long before my character crashed through her happily ever after.

I wondered what happened in her mind when she would roll her eyes at him and saw what she created.

Part of me was glad it was Greg who she chose instead of me. She caused me so much pain in teetering between her self-developed games of, "Whom do I want more?"

It dawned on me that I became a secret because I did not fit in the quintessential picture she wished to place in her frame. My mind plummeted into a realm of "what ifs" and broken promises. What if the words I spoke to her were not real? What if the love I showed to her was all a dream?

I loved Emma wholeheartedly, yet she denied our existence with her perturbed notion that I was "just a friend." Months of loving her came to a screeching halt, for the second she sent that text shattered what was left of me.

As tears dripped down my cheeks, I was practically paralyzed by the many thoughts left unsaid. I wondered if she was just living a lie; honesty was not her strongpoint, as she had an entire life planned before we met. Part of me hoped Emma just forgot to tell me about the life she had planned, but how do you hide so much of your soul from someone who you supposedly love?

The painting, the silhouette of her shadow, hours upon hours of our texts, the vault, was it real? How do we even perceive reality in its most reverent form? I considered it to be a deep connection.

However, what is a deep connection?

Is it defined by the euphoria a person feels the moment they rest their eyes upon another soul?

For if that were so, then the definition of euphoria would be up to the person caught up in that sensation. Greg might feel euphoria when he looks at her, but does she mirror that feeling?

Does she paint him her soul as she did for me?

Even if she did, would he receive it the same way my soul did?

The unanswered questions in the shadows clung to the desperate parts of my soul. My tortured soul was plagued with loneliness, and I assumed that was how it was going to be for years upon years to come.

I felt cast aside.

I felt used.

My heart was just a tattered rag doll at her disposal.

I wondered if she would flinch when she looked into my eyes each day at work, for she would be the one who made me take down my walls, only to destroy any and everything I had left within me.

As I made my way out of the sanctuary and onto the mattress where we once held each other, I saw an old copy of Nicholas Sparks' *The Notebook* sitting on the floor. Its pages were torn, just like my soul, and it was a pitiful reminder that like Noah and Allie, Emma and I would just be "friends."

∞ ∞ ∞ ∞ ∞ ∞ ∞ ∞

The storms and rough tides that plague our waters are echoic of our innate existence. We are an ocean of opportunities encased in a heart, mind, body, soul, and spirit, though sometimes the facets that make us whole are not as we make them out to be.

Other souls touch the fundamental parts of our being. Other people can raise our spirits. We can bestow empowerment on ourselves and on those who are around us.

We are the leaders of our lives, and it was my belief we started to act with that strength brewing deep within us… yet in those moments of mourning what I thought I had with Emma, heartbreak and notions I could have had a divine love with her masked my true energy in this universe.

Despite all of the apparent blessings around me, I often felt lost more than ever. I was intellectual and passionate enough to comprehend that all of this would make sense one day, though I did not know how long I would have to battle my way through the trenches.

I was praying for a sign in the attic of that church. I was praying for someone to come rescue me.

Something had to be out there, and I was sure of it.

A murmured thud snapped me out of my trance-like state.

Footsteps began to make their way up the steps and just behind the door. I did not know what was about to happen, but I figured that since I was asking the universe for a sign, whatever was about to make its way into the room would create a massive shift in my soul.

The door creaked open and I was met with a familiar face and a smile. It figures, when I usually ask the universe for a sign, it does deliver. No matter what was about to happen, I sensed that it would be just what I needed.

Morena's face appeared in the door and my heart sank a little. I was hoping that Emma would be the one standing in the doorway, but I guess it was not meant to be at that moment.

"You wanted a sign," Morena moved slowly across the room. "Here I am."

'*You* aren't what I expected,' I rolled over on the mattress and pulled the blanket over my head.

"I may not be what you expected, but I am what you have." She plopped down on the mattress and looked at the mirror across the room. It was difficult to make out her reflection, which is why sometimes I figured she wasn't real. Morena also always seemed to show up just when I was asking the universe for a sign.

Yet in some twisted way, she seemed to be the sign. It was strange.

"Scott," she spoke softly. "You can't do this to yourself."

'Do what?'

"Beat yourself up over Emma."

'I am not-'

"You are," she cut me off. "You are, don't lie."

I sat up and whipped my head around, 'Okay, so what if I am?'

"You are so focused on divine love and Emma, but what do you *really* want Scott?" She stood up and walked to the edge of the room. "What do *you* want?"

'I want love,' I shouted. At this point I was exhausted beyond belief. Tears started streaming down my face again, 'I just want love.'

"Think beyond that," Morena turned back around. "You have a company and you have a vision... yet you are stuck on her. Why?"

'It is more than that, Morena.'

"Then tell me, tell me what it is."

'I want to give people jobs and reach youth around the world. However, there's one problem-'

Morena cut me off again, "Think beyond divine love for Emma for a moment."

'Something is not right with the pieces of this puzzle. They are being forced together and not clicking naturally. Someone is always upset, angry, or sick, and it's not just a momentary thing.'

"What do you mean?"

'There's always something going on with Eve and the church, my program directors are going through so much, and this lonely, broken heart is a mess.'

Morena's face was partially obscured by the faint darkness in the room. It reminded me of the first time we met when she was covered in bruises. So much had changed since then, I sensed the fire burning within her soul, yet I barely knew her real story.

'How do you mend a broken heart? You must know.'

A lingering silence hung in the air.

"Love is lost when one does not understand the balance that must exist. It is like yin and yang. Sometimes there is light, sometimes there is darkness, but the most empowering creations happen when we are aware of the strength and beauty within us."

I laughed slightly, 'That is very profound.'

"I have my moments," she smirked.

'I have had the most incredible love and moments that have been etched in my soul for eternity, yet why did those moments get destroyed?'

"It's not the memories and moments that get destroyed; it is our expectation that things will be the same forever. People grow, people change, we change," She moved closer. "Our souls grow, and that is what makes them beautiful."

'That makes sense.'

"At the end of the day, the most beautiful souls are the ones who grow and acknowledge the true gift they are to the universe."

'Doesn't that contradict who we innately are?'

"How so?"

763

'If we see ourselves as a gift, isn't that conceited?'

"You need to own your soul. You need to empower yourself and others… it is who you innately are."

I saw Emma's pain, the walls she put up, her strength, her courage, her heart, her spirituality, and her beauty. The divine love concept embodies her almost perfectly. The possibilities with her seemed endless, yet I was clinging to the love I thought we shared.

Everything within my beautiful soul said that she could be the other half of my power couple. Everything. I could not fathom how Greg could see her. It boggled my mind that Emma could show up for him the way she showed up for me.

I watched Morena drift about the room and fade into the shadows.

As I closed my eyes from sheer exhaustion, I could sense her spirit crawling up my spine. I knew that somewhere else in the universe she had to come across a memory of us. She would have to look at herself in the mirror and try to deny what we had because she could not fathom the guilt: she had me and she had Greg, and she had to choose.

Nothing that she did or said could prove that she could deny the guilt coursing through her veins. Emma did not see the light shining within her, and I sensed that I loved her more that she could even handle.

I was not overromanticizing us.

When two souls collide, as ours once did, the flame never truly goes out. Even in the wake of destruction and in the ashes succumbing my tattered heart, there was a glimmer of hope.

With my last cognizant thoughts, I realized that though I was hurt, it meant that I could still feel.

Our story was not over yet.

Once souls like ours are anchored together, the ship we commandeered together could never sink, even if it was stationed at someone else's port.

∞ ∞ ∞ ∞ ∞ ∞ ∞ ∞

It was an emotionally challenging month, but I figured I was doing okay. I did not know if it was because of my continual spiritual search, however I felt like I was getting stronger.

I was completely helpless, yet full of confidence; I was a walking juxtaposition. I was drowning in the depths of insecurity, though I felt I could do something... anything. The idea of letting go may not be as simple as flicking a switch on or off, rather it was a journey between growing my own faith and shifting elements of internal personal growth. I never could have imagined the tearing apart of my heart and soul as I had experienced during the past few months, but I felt in my heart that we were real.

There was an overwhelming sense of self-doubt and giving up on love, but I had been blessed with love throughout my life. I felt I still had a lot to learn, but I also had a sense that Emma would return.

My pain and sadness were carved into my soul though in some customs and cultures, cracked porcelain was filled with gold to keep broken treasures together.

In a sense, I hoped that I was a broken treasure. I prayed someone would see me as a precious gift.

Trust was becoming a fragile currency, and my love was running out. I prayed for a partner to help me on this journey through life, and little did I know I was perceiving partnerships all wrong at the time.

In the initial weeks of the tears I shed in honor of Emma's love, she would occasionally text me as an indirect reminder that she loved me, but she could not fathom "us." We went from texting every single day, to once a week, to once in a while.

Then the texts seemed to stop. I watched her parade around work, flashing her engagement ring to anyone who would catch a glimpse of it.

In praying for love to return however, I was greeted with a pleasant surprise: Bryan decided to come home from Florida and chose to stay in New York for good this time.

When I went to go pick him up at the airport, I sat in my Monte Carlo and watched raindrops slightly drip down the window. I missed Emma, I truly did. The longing I had for her became a constant pain in my chest.

I shut my eyes for a moment, mourning her disappearance, when my heart suddenly filled with glee.

"Pop?" Bryan's voice provided me with the most love I felt in a long time.

'Son, you've come home.'

He jumped in the car and we embraced quickly. The tears that fell from our eyes were a reminder that we were the definition of unconditional and true love, and we were all we needed.

Bryan began to tell me about how challenging of a time he had in Florida, and asked if we could listen to some music.

The two of us were driving down the highway blasting Bayside's "Head on a Plate:"

> *"With tied wrists we're under their control,*
> *With fists clenched, we're taking on the world.*
> *I write down words with cathartic intentions.*
> *But they spawn revolutions of minds."*

Everything felt natural, everything felt phenomenal, and for a few moments, everything was perfect because my son was home.

∞ ∞ ∞ ∞ ∞ ∞ ∞ ∞

Forgiveness and acceptance seemed to be a theme that spring. Though I was just shy of begging Emma to come back into my life, Faith was contacting me non-stop to talk as friends.

I trusted in God and the universe, so I chose to see what Faith wanted.

The two of us met at a cute café on a busy New York City corner. It was once a popular Italian restaurant, which was turned into an Irish pub that served breakfast early in the morning.

Our small table rested against the tall glass windows. The sunlight beamed towards us and I could not help but admire Faith's exquisite beauty. It was difficult to be around her energy, but I knew that she just wanted a friendship.

"I can't say that I love you anymore," Faith started the conversation. "It's a sign of weakness in me. I have to grow and connect to the universe."

I looked at her over my cup of coffee.

"We are like transmitters trying to find the right tune, so that we can finally realize our power and purpose."

She sounded a lot more aligned with my thoughts and beliefs. What really engaged me was listening to her share what was going on within her soul. It was honorable to see her spiritual expansion happening before my eyes. It made me feel as if I was her sounding board and she was my partner, but in fact, she wasn't.

Though I felt like I was tempted to fall back in love with her, something told me to back off.

Something told me that she was a part of the larger picture, though I was still trying to figure out what that picture was.

The two of us joked about how long we had known each other and how we were both a blessing and a curse. I did not see her as the spiritual love I thought we once were, but that was totally okay. We went through so much, but despite going to hell and back, we were right in front of each other once again.

It is amazing how everything seems to come full circle.

After the two of us spoke about everything, including my fears surrounding Emma, she seemed to echo what Morena told me. Faith's spirituality was growing, and I was proud of who she was becoming. We explored our respective fears and ambitions, and I told her I wanted to do so much more in this universe.

"Then do it," her accent brought a certain thrill to my soul. It was almost as if she knew just what to say to push at my ambitions.

As we left and I was rushing across town to meet Morena, I turned to Faith and put my hand on her shoulder.

'Sometimes it is okay to face your fears, so from me to you: I love you, my dear friend.'

Faith looked at me and smiled: "I love you too… so much. Thank you for listening."

I darted across town and saw Morena sitting on a bench.

'Mo,' I shouted to her.

"Hey," she shut a notebook she was scribbling in.

'What's that?'

"Oh," she pushed her hair behind her ear. "It's my journal. I write ideas in it."

'I never noticed it before.'

"Oh, I'm always writing in it. If I don't have a thought rumbling around in my head, then I am at a loss."

'Can I see?' She passed me her notebook and I opened it somewhat cautiously. Her hopes and dreams were caught between these pages. I flipped through her scribblings until a drawing caught my eye. 'What's that?'

She leaned over and looked at where I was pointing.

"Oh," she grinned and pulled her head further into her chest. "It's the White House."

'The White House?'

"Yeah, you know like in Washington, D.C.?" She looked over at me, almost waiting for a response.

'That's cool.' I was curious. 'Why are you drawing the White House?'

"Um…" she didn't seem to know what to say. "I always wanted to go to Washington, D.C. and see the White House and all the buildings there. I just never got a chance to go."

Something ignited within me at that point. I think this was the first moment that D.C. truly came to mind.

'We should have a leadership program there,' our eyes locked for a moment.

Morena was quiet, but something was churning in her head… I could see it.

"We should," she smiled from ear to ear and grabbed her notebook back. "I think we should build out those curriculums you have. You truly have something exciting."

'That sounds good, but what would we do with them?'

"Oh," she seemed to be holding something back, but I didn't question it.

The two of us stood up from the bench and we started to walk down the sidewalk.

"I am sure you'll find *something*, Scott."

It was almost like she had all of the answers, but did not want to share. It was like she was holding the best kept secret within her mind, and at the time I think she wanted me to see just how empowered I could become.

I spent years inspiring and empowering so many people, little did I know I could do so much more than working in one school. At the time I was thinking of the bigger picture, but I was ensnared in a web of wanting to find the other half of my power couple. I did not see what I had within my own soul.

Time would tell the rest of my story.

∞ ∞ ∞ ∞ ∞ ∞ ∞ ∞

As summer closed in on the leadership programs within the high school, Emma's presence was about to fade into the summer. I was partially terrified; because I did not know what she would do in the months we were apart.

Would she think of me?

Would she call me or text me?

So many thoughts clogged my head and distracted me from what was truly important, though Emma was for all intents and purposes who I wanted to be "my everything."

When the bell rang and all of the students filtered into my room, she was standing behind a few of them. I was unsure of what to say to her, nor did I know what I wanted to say.

"Have a good summer, Ms. Paige," one of the students said to her.

'Yeah,' a somber tone overtook my voice. 'Have a great summer.'

She looked at me and smiled slightly, but she did not say anything. I lost her for good, I was sure of it.

Days later would be her engagement party, and I did not know how she would stand there in a short white dress and pretend she was so just and pure.

Then again all of this sounds judgmental, but it was the story that I told my soul. Part of me thinks that I had to tell this story at the time in order to justify why she ran away from me. She flew right into his arms.

I was not invited to the party, so Morena asked if we could spend the day working on the curriculums. Naturally, I obliged.

That late afternoon, Morena and I were working in the office at Queens Community Church and I was deeply sad. Then my phone chimed and I looked over to see a text message from Emma on the screen.

"Can we talk?"

Emma wanted to speak to me.

I figured that something was wrong; I felt it in my core.

I excused myself and ran outside to speak to her. Emma told me that her and Greg got into a huge fight, and she asked for my advice.

Emma wanted *my* advice about *her* relationship with *Greg*.

I wanted to vomit. I wanted to run away and never look back. I felt sick.

We spoke for a while until I asked the question that I longed to hear the answer to.

'Do you miss me?' I held back the tears.

"A little bit," she said softly. "I have to go. Thanks, bye."

The line went dead and I retreated back into the church.

As the door slammed shut, I could feel my heart drop into the pit of my stomach. The love I felt for her was in its purest form. She was anything and everything I could have hoped for. She was the embodiment of divine love and the retribution for years of my soul's torment.

Then, in moments, she slid through my fingers. No warning. No sirens or flares.

Gone.

I had never figured it would become this sort of fractured fairytale. I painted this image in my head of what our life would grow into: her dream of having the house with the white picket fence in a quiet suburban town, her dog zooming around the backyard, the kids playing in the kitchen while their mother baked cupcakes... the perfect family.

Yeah, maybe the perfect family... but not our family. Not mine and Emma's family.

Greg's family. Greg's house. Greg's yard. Greg's fence. His grass, his trees, his kids... my wife. My love. My divine love and my soulmate.

Emma.

Now she is just a distant memory.

A faded carving in a tree: S + E forever.

I guess forever ended weeks ago.

And all she left me with was "Breathe, it is just another day."

Emma, when you look at me, I often wonder what you see. Do you see a hopeless shell of someone who once was? Do you see a pliable existence bent by a single gust of wind? Do you turn your back and brush off all of the love that could have existed between us.

Oh... wait... *could have.*

I stood there in the darkness, peering out the window where I once glared out of when I was moments away from one of our passionate nights and wrote what came to mind:

If I called out your name in the darkness, would you come running towards me? Would you know just where to find me just by hearing your name? Would my soul beckon you back to the place where you belong, with me, or would these mindless noises tell me I am wrong?

I stared at it for moments before I crumpled up the paper and threw it furiously against the wall.

She wasn't coming home to where she belonged. She was not going to fall into my arms ever again.

Days must have passed by during my depressed state. My hand became caught in the rough stubble that had formed across my face as I waited for her call. Something inside me knew she would never call me engorged with lust ever again, but oh did I pray for the phone to ring.

My Circle of Angels must have heard me, for within an instant my phone began to buzz. The blue and white glow from the phone shouted the name I did not want to see: Morena. Of course, she has a habit of falling into my life at just the wrong moment, but then again, the Circle of Angels keeps tossing her into me nonsensically, almost as if bowling pins were persistently chasing after a bowling ball.

The dreams of Emma and I continued throughout the rest of July and August. I did not know if my soul was detoxing or what, but my subconscious seemed to crave Emma. The two constants, other than Emma, in each of my dreams were Morena's notebook and Morena's voice. Before I woke up each morning, Morena would say, "It's time to wake up."

And there I was, sitting up on the mattress by myself, covered in sweat: slightly confused and wholeheartedly missing Emma.

∞ ∞ ∞ ∞ ∞ ∞ ∞ ∞

When I went back to school in September, Emma and I were walking in the hallway in different directions. We were alone, but we were together.

It was a strange, yet comforting feeling to see her again.

The two of us stopped in the hallway and she looked up at me. I could tell she was reading my energy and she smiled.

Emma giggled a bit: "Still?"

'Still?' I replied. 'I haven't stopped.'

She blushed and rubbed her shoulder.

'Still?'

She began to walk down the hallway. I heard her whisper a faint "Always" as she went into her classroom and slammed the door.

The day flew by and the night was filled with dreams of Emma kissing my lips again. I woke up to find that once again I was alone in the church attic, with a throbbing pain pushing against my lower back.

I drove to the parking lot of Lincoln Memorial High School and watched the rain begin to twist through the sky.

I could hear a solitary heartbeat overhead. It was as if I was walking in another's shoes, wandering this planet as an addendum to someone else's story. My misshapen hair flopped to the side and I dragged myself out of the car and into the pouring rain.

No one can tell you are crying when raindrops grace your cheeks with the same intentions: to cleanse.

My eyes were glazed over and it felt as if I was trouncing around in a daze. I could not feel, rather I could not feel because I had been so numb to her touch for the longest time. The very thought of her pressing against me again made me yearn for yesterday, or maybe the day before, or possibly years before that. Time has melted away since we last had a heart-to-heart conversation, and I so desperately wanted to burst into her room and apologize profusely.

I wanted to get on my hands and knees and bow down to her essence and her soul.

Yet upon walking into the school, rounding the corner, and catching a glimpse of her beautiful brown eyes, I realized that I had to swallow my pain and be patient. Maybe she would not communicate with my soul today, tomorrow, or the next day... but someday.

Just someday.

I caught my breath becoming more and more labored: I was having a full-blown anxiety attack. It was my fourth one that week, and they seemed to come throughout the day at this point.

At night I would wake up discombobulated and I did not know where I was at certain points. Emma's presence, or lack thereof, was beginning to plague my thoughts.

Emma would always visit my dreams.

Night after night I would find myself standing in the doorway to our first hotel room. I could see her silhouette resting patiently in the bed. Her body was tangled in the pure white sheets that reflected every innocent thing about her soul. She was in an incoherent state of peace and tranquility: one she would never experience while being wide-awake.

Then Morena's notebook would appear and I would hear her telling me to wake up.

'You haunt my dreams,' I would tease Morena.

"You're haunting," she would quip sarcastically.

We find symbols when we manifest them. We seek out validation from the mundane and create our own reality. Respectively, if we truly look within, we are all creatures of habit and habitat. If you want a reality, find it. Create it.

Emma always said she fears being a parent. She fears loss and solitude beyond her control.

Everything inside of me pleaded with my soul: Do not allow the wound to fester.

"Look deep within the recesses of your mind," Morena told me. "The key is there. In reality you have much more value than you believe."

'I don't know what I'm supposed to do haunted by the ghost of Emma,' I told her.

It was the essence and the presence: her adorous infatuation with pulling the leash just far enough for the dog to snap back methodically.

A cruel intention was anchoring and weighing on my soul.

A saying and sensation were brewing within me: "Toss the ropes but drop the anchor: if the weight is held, the roots are set. If not, sail on. Another lighthouse beckons with its glow."

If only I knew where the light was, I wonder if my soul would have been this tortured for years upon years.

In late October, almost a full year since Emma and I started on our spiritually shifting, yet tumultuous relationship, a glimmer of hope presented itself before me. As I was packing up to leave one night, one of my students rushed downstairs to my office to proclaim that Emma was still in her classroom.

Something about it did not seem right.

Part of my soul was frozen in its tracks, wondering why, after so many months of beating myself up over the lack of her presence, someone would rush into my room and proclaim she was still in her room.

Something within me said to trust in the universe and take the leap of faith.

I walked up to her room, where she was sitting with a restless look on her face, and offered her a hand.

'Are you okay?'

We gazed at each other in a moment that could rival even the most romantic scene in a movie. I felt it: our love was real.

"You know," Emma said matter of factly. "You know my rule about us at work."

Her comment caught me off guard. I did not understand what she was getting at exactly.

'You look like you need a shoulder to cry on.'

"I need a *lot* more than a shoulder," I heard her voice breaking.

'Do you want to go get some coffee or something?'

"That would be great."

The two of us walked out the door, went our separate ways, and met up at a place fifteen minutes away from the school.

"Greg and I keep fighting," were the first words she spoke when she sat down.

'You can talk about it if you want.'

She laughed, "That's why I am here."

I sipped my coffee. 'Is that the only reason why?'

Emma glared at me with her chocolate brown eyes. "You know it will *always* be us." She reached out and grabbed my hand. As I maneuvered my fingers between hers, something felt different.

"You okay?" She looked concerned.

I sensed that the pain and agony stirring within me were ensnared in the conflicting feelings I had for her: I loved her, but she hurt me so much.

How do you look into the eyes of someone you were once so vulnerable with, someone who you were once so in love with, and allow yourself to say those three words?

'I am fine.'

We continued to talk about her and Greg, ignoring the fact that our relationship was once so much more than spiritual pillowtalk. We were the embodiment of love.

At least I thought we were at the time.

As I walked her to her car and wished her a goodnight, she looked at my lips and spoke softly, "Scott?"

'Yeah,' I put my hands in my pockets.

"Thanks."

She got into her car and slammed the door.

I began walking down the block, crumpling leaves on my way to my car, when a homeless man approached me. I don't know if he was really homeless, but he was definitely poor and in shambles.

Though I thought he was going to ask me for some spare change, he merely said, "Buddy, try smiling... you may actually start to have fun."

It made me laugh and, in that moment, I realized how sad I was. The energy I was putting out must have been incredibly desolate.

Faking it gets hard sometimes.

Why I allowed her to anchor my soul this way is unknown to me, but I must raise the weight and sail on.

This was just a case of two ships passing and briefly touching... yet it's an ocean I want to swim in. Is there anything wrong with that?

I miss watching our natural flow.

It led to paradise, yet now I am drowning.

I refuse to sink with or without the anchor.

I have a huge future and I had to begin acting like it.

The voice within me said that I should just sacrifice true love once and for all. Did I really need love if I knew I was destined for much more than the physical?

My innate existence had to be of a metaphysical nature. Why would I continue to survive through all of these trials and tribulations?

However, my soul kept saying do not let go.

When I got into my car and thrusted the key into the ignition, the radio hummed with the melodic tune of "Patience" by Guns N' Roses:

> *"Said 'woman take it slow, and it'll work itself out fine'*
> *All we need is just a little patience"*

Stacey was with me. I sensed it.

Maybe at the time I did just need a little bit more patience, though I was too blind to that notion.

Emma's love, or lack thereof, was extremely loud and incredibly close. Still, I was wading in the waters of chance: Maybe, just maybe, she did love me.

When I got back to the church, I felt exhausted. For some strange reason, Eve and Paul were standing out front arguing loudly about something.

As I got out of the car and slammed the door, Eve whipped her head around towards me.

"*What* are you doing here?" she hollered.

'Oh hi,' I said quietly. 'I-'

Paul cut me off: "Eve, Windows' office is here. Let the man be."

"Fine," she snapped sarcastically. "Fine by me. People come and go as they please."

She retreated into their car without saying anything else, and Paul apologized to me for the scene.

'Is everything okay?' I asked innocently, knowing that something strange happened.

"No, but it will be my son." Paul put a reassuring hand on my shoulder and smiled.

'Okay, well if you need anything, just call.'

"One day," he wrapped his hand around my shoulder. "One day this building will be yours and it will truly bless this community. I know it."

Eve rolled the window down and shouted for Paul to get into the car. He wished me a blessed night and scurried away.

I did not know what to think about the conversation, but maybe that was what I needed to be patient for: Windows of Opportunity might have a true home, and not just an office, at Queens Community Church.

I felt so blessed for everything, for who I was in those moments, for what I knew, for what I felt, and for what I connected to.

The universe has always been incredibly kind to me, and I just didn't really understand why at that point.

Why me?

Why did I have to see the things I had seen and loved as deeply as I did? I did not understand my role.

I knew at the heart of things that people had to be happy and that we are all here to find our innate happiness.

For the most part, I was happy.

When I looked at my life, who I had loved, and who loved me, I knew everyone was teaching me some sort of lesson about myself. I just did not understand what lesson Emma was teaching me as of yet.

My heart was crippled in the unresolved situations I was a part of. Emma and Faith's respective love unearthed my soul, yet I could have a peaceful conversation with Faith. Emma's conversations left me feeling dreary and longing for what we had.

The moments were deafening to my soul and I could barely hear the voice I had within me.

At this point it was midnight and I could not sleep. I jumped into my car and found it almost pathetic that I was sitting there, at 12:30 in the morning, looking at Emma's darkened classroom windows and waiting for the gym to open so I could shower. My mind was wandering. My sacrifices were mounting. My lower back began to ache at the very thought of how much real change I knew I needed to make in my life.

I wondered if anything mattered at all if Emma was not going to share my life.

My voice took on a solemn tone as I whispered Bon Jovi's lyrics into the brisk night sky:

"What do you got, if you ain't got love
Whatever you got, it just ain't enough
You're walkin' the road, but you're goin' nowhere
You're tryin' to find your way home, but there's no one there
Who do you hold, in the dark of night
You wanna give up, but it's worth the fight
You have all the things, that you've been dreamin' of."

I drifted off to sleep feeling grateful for what I had, a roof over my head, even if it was just a car.

∞ ∞ ∞ ∞ ∞ ∞ ∞ ∞

Glass ricocheted as screaming rang out through the room. In those brief moments between the heaving breaths and wallowing, it was almost peaceful. I could not find the appropriate words to materialize any sort of thoughts, so my mind just went blank.

All the memories from the past few months flickered by as if a film was being made about what she meant to me.

But she was gone.

She was a shattered existence of the woman I once knew.

And I was okay with it.

And I was no longer the morose figure dancing just past her line of sight, beckoning her to step closer.

To come closer.

Loneliness was no longer the moniker that would cling mercilessly to the depths of my soul. She was released from the fundamental roots that once ruptured this tree.

I am past tense and he is future perfect. I was the one, but I hope he will be worth it.

She no longer controls every aspect of my gaze. She does not have the privilege to see me soar and fly. She does not have the honor of standing beside me when I genuinely shift this world into a more positive space.

I miss her. I do. Do not, for one split second, believe that this is my whimpering plea to earn her back.

This is my Declaration of Independence. This is my Magna Carta.

I was standing with my eyes closed near a still body of water.

When I opened my eyes, the Washington Monument was directly in front of me.

'Take care of yourself, Emma. I am proud of you.' I whispered as I turned and glared at the Lincoln Memorial. 'I hope you find the solace from our severed love that you so deserve. Rest in peace, or rather, rest in the pieces of our memories that you choose to savor. Rest in the pieces of us.'

Because something is shattered, that does not mean it is broken.

"And now neither are you," A voice echoed throughout the monument.

'What?' I shouted. 'Who is there?'

Morena emerged from the shadows and held out her notebook.

"The question is, are you ready?"

I jolted awake to find the sunlight peeking through the urban cityscape.

I did not know what any of that meant, but I sensed that Morena had to have some sort of answer for me.

Her notebook had to be what was holding all of the answers.

∞ ∞ ∞ ∞ ∞ ∞ ∞ ∞

After I got in and out of the shower quickly, I rushed to the school to start going through some papers I had in the office.

Joy appeared in the doorway and said good morning.

A few students filtered in and out of the room.

I did not really know what I was looking for, but I needed to find an excuse to get closer to Emma again.

"What are you doing?" Joy was standing over me looking at all of the papers scattered on my floor.

'I am looking for something.'

"Okay," she said. She shrugged and grabbed her lunch from the fridge.

'I look a little crazy, don't I?'

"A little bit," she quipped back.

A little bit. She said one of Emma's catchphrases.

I figured I would just walk past Emma's classroom and see what she was up to. Odds are she was teaching, I mean it was the middle of the school day.

When I walked up the stairs, a sense of existential dread washed over me. I noticed that her classroom was empty and she was nowhere to be found. There must have been an assembly or something.

I walked into the room and saw the picture of her and Greg on her desk. The two of them looked nauseatingly in love with one another, though Emma's eyes looked dead compared to the way she once looked at me.

It was pitiful.

My mind drifted to a series of questions, as per usual. All of them were focused on Emma:

If you came into this room right now and whispered the words I longed to hear, would you mean them? Would your soul collide with mine in the most breathtakingly cataclysmic way? Would you linger on my kisses a bit too perfectly?

Would you capture the essence of a love paused in time, only to return to the scene of the crime and steal my heart again?

Would your eyes drag themselves along the outline of my sunken shoulders? Would you caress my skin with the intention of leaving your fingerprints along them in the most delicate of ways?

Would you realize the hurt you caused me in the most shattering of ways? Would you walk on eggshells around my soul for the rest of my life, knowing you damaged the pieces that were already broken?

Would you lay awake watching me rest in your comforting arms? Would you brush the tears you placed on my cheeks? Would you fall into my arms like it was four years ago? Would you cling to my soul because you realized you left me when you needed me the most?

Do you also think about these questions, day in and day out, with the same dragging feeling in your chest? Or do you beat on, ignorant to how much you have hurt me and continue to drive the knife further in my back each moment we are apart?

As I looked at the picture of Emma and Greg again, wisdom filtered into my soul. If I could have spoken to her in those moments, I would have said so much with so little.

'May you never feel the pain you have caused me. May you always be loved twice as much as you ever loved me. May you recognize my face in the crowd when our paths cross again. May you feel my touch against your neck when your back is turned to him, for he may touch you now… but our love will touch you for the rest of your life. And don't you ever dare forget it.'

I left her room and caught a glance of her walking up the hallway.

Our eyes locked in an attempt to remind each other of the days when we were us… and in those solitary, rare moments that arise… I can tell, just with the gaze she bestowed upon me… that she remembered, too.

When I got back into my office, Joy was gone.

I started to pick up my papers from the floor and came across the original infinity sign and anchor tattoo drawing Emma created for me. Instantly, I felt sick.

My fingers traced the infinity sign tattoo on my forearm. The number 88 and the infinity sign have always held such a profound meaning to me.

For as long as I could remember, I was always attracted to the number 8. Eighty-eight was the number on my lacrosse jersey. At some point, I made the mental connection that the number was the same shape as the infinity sign.

To me, infinity meant that life was ongoing, strong, and unbreakable. It was the metaphor for how things should be. It provides power and energy to my soul.

Emma understood what 88 meant to me, both physically and spiritually. Once upon a time she had the desire to get to know me. She connected to my soul and I shared this part of my spirit with her. She explained to me that her favorite symbol was the anchor. To her, it was a constant reminder that she had to "refuse to sink" in life.

Her words echoed through my head as the ghost of who she was to me floated through the room: "I refuse to give up on us, on life, on love, on humanity."

No matter what was going to happen to us in life, she was etched into my soul. Her soul was drawn in ink on my skin, as her love was permanently inscribed in my spirit.

Our fleeting moments were drifting into the distance, so I quickly collected my tears and chose to continue with my day.

As the night fell upon me, I looked at my phone for some semblance of hope. Still, Emma did not text or call. I was holistically alone with my thoughts once again.

Upon returning to the church, I heard rustling in the Windows of Opportunity office. I assumed Morena let herself in to work on something, and I intended to ask her about her journal that kept appearing in my dreams.

Instead of being greeted by Morena, Eve was the one rummaging through the office.

'Hi Eve, how are-' Her eyes narrowed and cut directly through me.

"What are *you* doing here so late?" Eve was not happy.

'I was going to work on some stuff.'

I could not tell Eve that I was home for the night, and that I was about to pass out on my mattress in the attic.

"You are *lying*," she shouted. "You *live* in this church!"

I did not know what to say. Yes, technically I was sleeping at the church and all of my clothes were here, but there was no shower or real place for me to stay here.

'I-' the words I wanted to say were trapped at the tip of my tongue.

"Get out," she screamed. "You can keep your office here, but all of your stuff needs to go. *Now.*"

I wondered if Paul knew. If he realized I was homeless, would he make me leave?

Within 24 hours, I packed everything up. Eve told me that we were going to get reported, though we never were. It had to look like I never stayed there.

Those moments where I had to launch all of my belongings in bags and boxes were insane and sickening. Morena assured me that everything would be okay, and that this was all happening for a reason. At the time, I did not think to ask her about the journal she had just yet.

"It is all a part of your spiritual journey," she said.

Faith offered me a place to stay, but I humbly denied her. I could not impose upon her or her sons, for I thought our friendship was fragile and something I did not want to test.

For me, sleeping in my car meant that it was just another day. My life was filled with just another sacrifice.

I fell asleep, night after night, in the front seat of my car. The faint murmur of my engine reminded me that my heart was still beating and life was still worth living.

One early morning the phrase "It was not just a dream" faded out into a distant echo as I awoke to find a man knocking on my car window. A police officer, neatly dressed and too eager with his flashlight, clanging on my window, stood before me.

I rolled down the window and shielded my eyes from his bitter existence. He looked tired, defeated even, in the rising sun. The shadows dragged along his face with unwavering certainty.

"Sir, are you okay?" He boomed. His eyes pierced into my soul.

'What-' I groggily lowered the heat in the car. The fan burst its hot air before succumbing to the contrastive cold air outside.

"Sir, you were passed out, do you need medical attention?" He beamed the light into my car as his radio murmured at his waist.

I hastily responded with a jumble of words. I drummed up some concoction of 'just tired' and 'I work in the church.' He retreated to his car and left me alone in the dusk that settles right before the sun creeps up the horizon.

I savored the dream I just experienced as I drove off to a coffee shop. I was in a freshly polished pair of shoes. My suit was crisp and dark blue. I was standing on the steps of a grand building... it looked like Washington, D.C., but, no... why would I be there?

Maybe these visions of grandeur are just a manifestation of Morena's wishful thinking... After all, she did say she wanted to go there.

Yet as I glared up at the sun rising over Northern Boulevard, I could see a majestic flag billowing in the morning air. It flattered the hollow parts of my soul. It squeezed my heart and yelled, "Beat on."

As the light turned green and a man violently honked his horn to interrupt my destiny, I inched forward and towards the shop. As I parked my car, the realization hit me...

I just said destiny.

This was not a dream. This was real life intermingling with the hand of reality, hoisting me high above the turmoil flooding my soul.

D.C. was coming... it was speeding like a train bolstered tightly to the tracks: remaining constant and unabashed by the speed and tenacity it so desperately clung to.

This dream would not be derailed... no, no... no. This was reality. This is the reality I would manifest and create.

I just did not know what Washington, D.C. would mean to me at that point.

My life revolved around running leadership programs in a high school and living in a car. It was then I realized that you can be homeless, but you can still have a home in the hearts of those you help heal.

I am awake.

I am in pain.

I should be sleeping, I figured.

What message does the universe want me to give the world?

There were hints, the moonlight peeking in through the darkness, the sounds still heard in the silence, the rustling of tree branches I see through my sunroof, the lyrics in a song, the look in someone else's eyes, a text message, and the vibration felt in closing my eyes and clearing my thoughts.

Morena had to be the key.

Our stories intertwined and it was all for a higher purpose.

I was ready to step into the bigger role… the larger frame.

I knew Morena was part of that puzzle. A huge part. Her strange gift combined with my story and our mutual support could spread messages from the universe in a way that has never been done before.

While Morena and I were at the church one afternoon just before the new year fell upon us, I looked over at her and asked for her journal.

'It is time I know what the scribblings in your book mean.'

She rose from the chair and handed me her book. Her fingers were still wrapped around it.

"Remember," she spoke solemnly. "We complement one another and it isn't a contest. You getting down on yourself cuts off your flow of positive energy. Avoid all of that negative nonsense."

'I'll try.'

"Trying is all SHE could ask for," she released the book.

'SHE?'

Morena seemed to ignore my question: "You are loved and your journey began way before you were manifested into this timeline. You have made what you call mistakes, you have learned, and you have evolved. Each lesson makes you wiser."

'What do I need to do?' I asked, wondering what was happening.

"This world needs higher conscious-thinking leaders. Some will refer to these souls as thought leaders. The next generation will be progressive, but needs spiritual guidance. You are damaging your body and it is the vessel to bring you higher. Do you want to go higher?"

I hesitated and thought of Emma.

'What lesson was she bringing me?' Morena instantly knew what I was talking about.

"You aren't ready." She pulled the book from my grasp and tucked it back into her bag.

We did not speak of that journal for quite some time after that incident.

'Why,' I yelled at her. 'Why am I not ready?'

"You aren't," she did not look up from the paper she was reading. "Stop punishing yourself, for you are love. When you are ready, you will know."

We sat in silence for a while and I figured I would just drop it.

Her words echoed in my head, "When you are ready, you will know."

∞ ∞ ∞ ∞ ∞ ∞ ∞ ∞

An unspecified longing for Emma's presence haunted me daily at work. To make matters worse I began to work at Lincoln Memorial High School full-time, which meant that I had to see Emma trounce around for an entire school day.

While on my way to a meeting one morning, I rushed out of my office and there she was. Emma stood before me in fuchsia pants and beige platform shoes. That odd walk that she has made me melt. She looked beautiful and her energy consumed the hallway.

No one else was there. Nothing was between us.

She had her back towards me and was walking away from me. The only sound gracing the hallways was the pitter-patter of her shoes.

I wanted to call out her name.

I wanted her to see the pain in my eyes.

Yet the only thing that escaped my lips was a breathy sigh, it was the residue of months of love and affection whittled down to the fact that she still took my breath away. She had no idea I was there. She could no longer feel my presence like once upon a time.

Emma slid into a classroom and vanished from the physical space between us.

Sadness consumed me, and I realized that was the first time I actually saw her all week. Why did her existence have to be one of the last images I had to see before the end of the year? 2016 had been a violently sickening experience in my soul.

It was almost a poignant metaphor that she slipped into the abyss.

I had to pause for a moment and ask myself: What is wrong with me?

My emotions flooded my throat and I was trying desperately not to lose it.

Damn you, Emma.

The night we were in the hotel room pulsated in my mind. Her apparition was a painstaking one.

It was almost as if she was directly in front of me on the hotel bed, *our hotel bed*, in my mind. The rustling curtains and the dimly shivering red letters from the hotel's sign shimmered at the back of my eyelids.

Sitting across from Emma in the vision I had in my head brought me such sorrow. I realized that selflessness had a name, a concrete voice, and a shattered heart.

I had an epiphany: I was so much stronger for going through hell and back, and back and forth, countless times. The pendulum has to swing at some point: gravity has a funny way of drawing us back to where we are meant to be just before we tip over the edge and crash.

"Say something," Emma's ghost spoke to me.

My eyes filled with tears as I reached out to stroke her face.

'You were an accident, you were a coincidence, and you were the best I never had,' my words were shattering as they escaped my mouth.

'You were the best I always wanted and always deserved, but I knew that a soul as gentle as mine could never feel true and honest comfort. There's that old adage: forged in flames, a soul set on fire, or something like that, I don't know.'

The room grew warm and as I pivoted to see what was illuminating her face, a fire ensnared the room.

Beauty can come out of ashes. I am the living, breathing, agonizing truth clawing my way up from rock bottom. I may burn myself into despair trying to light another's fire, but that will not stop me from glowing bright before burning myself out.

Her voice grew louder as the flames climbed up the walls: "I will be your flame, I will be your burning passion, I will be whatever light you need… well, could be or could have been."

Emma disappeared and my daydream brought me back to the dingy, crackling paint. The school was brighter than I had realized.

A star shines brightest before it burns out… right? Emma was an accident, a coincidence, and was the best I never had… but I will always be thankful for her. Despite the pain and whether she would ever really catch my silent glow emulating from the shadows or not, I figured I would always be that faint flicker she saw in her peripheral vision. However, it became a sick reality that I would never be in front of her again.

And that is the hardest truth of them all, and the hardest one I had to swallow in those desolate, passing seconds.

When I returned to the church that night, just to churn some work out before the darkness fell upon me, I pulled up the application on my phone that we used to use to text each other. She was always petrified of texting back and forth with me, for she did not want anyone to grab her phone and see it, so we used a special texting app to keep our conversations a thrilling secret.

This should have been the first sign that something was wrong.

Who was she hiding from?

Oh, yeah, I guess Greg.

After a while she stopped responding on the app, which must have been her definition of "pulling the plug."

I kept writing to her, but I assume that she never saw the messages, for she never responded there after some point. I don't really remember when that was.

Morena appeared in the shadows. I caught a glimpse of the side of her face in the reflected light from my phone: "What are you doing?"

'Nothing,' I tucked my phone back in my pocket. 'Nothing, nothing.'

"You are still hooked on her," she locked eyes with me.

'No.'

"You are lying to yourself. You are not lying to me. I know your truth."

I felt a sharp pain in my lower back again… Emma still had control over me, even though I knew I had to let her go in order for my soul to grow.

If only…

If only I could let go then.

∞ ∞ ∞ ∞ ∞ ∞ ∞ ∞

January 2017.
February 2017.
March 2017.
April 2017.

787

May 2017.

June 2017.

The days were filled with leading students and organizing conferences, empowering and counseling students, running events that displayed great attendance, and staying ahead of the curve, yet regardless of what I did, Emma's curves were all that I wanted to see.

Even the lyrics to Bon Jovi's "Novocaine" could not dull the pain in my chest:

> *"I guess there'll be no happy endings*
> *When 'once upon' is doing time*
> *There's a different kind of meaning now*
> *To livin' on a prayer*
> *Some don't seem to notice*
> *And the rest don't seem to care."*

It was oddly damp and frigid for a summer day in June, but I did not seem to truly care. Once it started to downpour, all sense left my mind.

I sat there frozen.

It was happening again.

The windows fogged up but through the pelting rain, my eyes were affixed on the memory playing over and over again. Ghosts echoed through the stereo: "Goodbye to Romance."

A love lost revitalized in the lyrics of a song from long ago.

The ghost of Emma appeared in the parking lot.

"He hinted he is going to propose to me," reverberated in my soul. "He misses me and I think I miss him too. I'm sorry."

"I don't know if I am going to say yes."

I should have walked away then.

I should have run.

Instead, I braced for impact.

Getting out of the car did nothing to soothe my soul.

Wiping the rain from my eyes that I could feel were mixed with my salty tears, I recalled planting my soul firmly within her hands.

'This is going to be a long ride, but I will wait.'

I shook my head to try and erase the memory. The rain was pounding hard just as it was that same dreadful November day.

Guns n' Roses poetically seeped into my soul. Thoughts of missing Stacey added to the moment.

> *"Nothin' lasts forever*
> *And we both know hearts can change*
> *And it's hard to hold a candle*
> *In the cold November rain"*

It is the same lot. It is in the same spot. It is the same type of rain.

And my heart is still shredded, just the same.

I finally peeled myself from that spot and forced myself to walk into the building.

The same tears flowed from my eyes; will she ever know how much I still love her?

Did it even matter anymore?

I needed to wipe my eyes and dry off before I began my day. I walked into the building, the play by play of days past running through my mind.

I did not think she would ever know how much this still pained me daily and how much I would have done anything for her to know what was going on in my soul.

"Hey… hi…" I didn't realize I was looking down at my feet in shame and was lost in the memory of Emma when I heard that familiar voice.

I looked up.

Emma's huge beautiful eyes locked on to mine.

It took a matter of three seconds for her to download all I was feeling at that moment and know exactly where I was at.

She smiled and said, "It will be okay."

I didn't have to say a word.

She knew.

I went into the app where we used to text one another and sent her a message:

Dear Emma,

I haven't written on here in a long time, though there were so many times I wanted to. Today was the last day of the year and there were so many things I wanted to say to you. I am just hoping you are well... that you have a great summer... and that one day our friendship will find its way back to one another. Please take care of you. Keep the faith...

Always,
Scott

The summer would greet me with a downward spiral lodged between prayers and a broken heart. Two people who were affiliated with Windows of Opportunity committed suicide.

A friend of mine died of cancer.

I was begging God that Emma's friendship would reappear in my life, yet I was met with utter silence in the dark shadows of the sanctuary.

Morena continued to work with me each day on building Windows of Opportunity, sitting in silence and denying me the chance to see the journal she so highly coveted.

A wave of existential dread washed over me, knowing I would have to face her sneering once again. Emma's wedding was within the coming months, and I had run out of options. Visions and sounds swirled between my ears, simulating the harsh reality that this was no nightmare: this was my life. This is what it had to be.

I had no tears left to cry for her, yet I was nursing the harsh hole brewing within my core. Only the tears that reminded me of her shattered soul dripped from the edges of my eyes.

Out of habit, I continued to write to her on Viber, our secret texting app:

Em,

28 days. You must be in that last-minute tunnel vision exciting anxiety. I truly hope you are well and soaking in the moments. So much I wish I could talk to you about. Sending you positive love and prayers.

Always,
S

I reminded myself that she made her choices, and I had to make mine, and her choices were a stark contrast to all of our combined hopes and dreams. I once thought that it would always be Scott and Emma, but now I found myself in a place where her touch is a fond memory.

There were moments in the sanctuary where I prayed for her to return, then promptly texted her in hopes that she would remember me.

Dear Emma,

19 days. You must be sooo thrilled! Hope all is coming together for your wedding. Just left a concert and so many lyrics... well, so many songs I think you would have enjoyed. Wishing you the best!

Love Always,
S

Still, there was silence.

Days passed by rapidly, yet I continued to hold out for her to be my hero. I wished devoutly that she would come back to my arms.

Desperation hung in my texts to her:

Emma,

5 days to go. You must be excited. Hope you're doing well!!

Love Always,
S

Emma still did not check our secret texts. The scripture of our love lay dormant in her phone, though she had no clue I was still waiting for her.

She chose her path and I chose mine. At that moment I figured it is a shame that our roads may never cross, but maybe it is just meant to be that way.

Day after day at work, once school started back up again for the year, I was petrified of what was to come. She would run off and marry Greg, and I would still be sitting in the sanctuary, night after night, with pieces of my shattered heart grasped loosely between my fingertips.

As a last-ditch effort, I figured I would lay everything out on the table.

I sent her one last text as I sat in the sanctuary, tears flowing from my eyes, thinking she would read it and find me:

Dear Emma,

Night before... sitting in the church and praying something guides you here. I keep sending you messages here hoping the universe will intervene and cause you to download the app again because I really miss the friendship and connection part of our relationship. Would love one more conversation and to send you positive vibes of support and to know if you're ok and what you are thinking. I know it will be magical for you. Congratulations! Xoxo

Always,
Scott

After I hit send, I hung my head in utter disgrace.

She was not coming.

She did not care anymore.

I wondered if she ever cared.

I dragged my body out of the church and into the driver's seat of my car. My bed for the night used to be where Emma and I made one of our first daring memories.

As my eyes slammed shut, I imagined she was in the driver's seat next to me, though as I reached my hand out to grab for her, Emma was probably in bed with her soon-to-be husband.

∞ ∞ ∞ ∞ ∞ ∞ ∞ ∞

Dread hung over me as if it were I who was on a hanger, and not the jacket in front of me. I slid the coat off of the hanger and draped it over my back: this would be the only warm hug I would receive that day.

Not a single person I would see would know that.

Nor would anyone who interacted with me understand how you could be surrounded by people, yet fundamentally alone.

Loneliness is that sharp knife that people warn you about: do not use it unless you really have to.

But what if you grab it by mistake?

I felt that with each step forward, I got two steps further from reality. I had been six steps closer to the edge with each passing moment. With each passing second.

Yet something always drew me back.

A light. A beam pushing me into a realm I just did not understand.

I felt like I died every solitary night since she left me. Every movement from the second hand ticked closer to the end of Emma's fateful, adoring glance...

Or to the start of something bigger.

I kept a countdown in the back of my mind leading up to her wedding. Her white, perfectly laced gown would never run through my fingertips that fateful fall day.

On the exact day of her wedding, I woke with a sense of longing on my chest. Something or someone was pulling me towards them in a manner I could not articulately describe in concrete words.

The passenger seat was empty next to me. The blankets coddled me in their everlasting warmth: comfort wrapped me in its confines. Yet I wanted more. We develop comfort when we think we are in a stable space. We push ourselves into this comatose state of, "No, everything is fine."

But it isn't. Nothing is fine when you are missing a crucial piece of your spirit.

Fine is an illusion, existing merely to convince us that we are not settling. But then aren't we? Are we not clinging to the past as a means of comfort? As a means of lying to ourselves that we can't reach our full potential because we do not or cannot face the treacherous path to earning everything greater than our hearts could imagine?

It is all there. It is all out there.

It just takes a moment: a wince, a flinch, a smile, the upward roll of another's eyes... to simply see everything we never knew we could fathom or define...

We push on. We persevere. We launch our rockets into the sky and enter an entirely new atmosphere.

We become the stars, and if we are lost, we are shooting stars that illuminate the right of the night's beauty.

We harbor the generosity to love ourselves; we just need to release the pain within in order to do so.

It is time to let go.

I found myself driving towards the church and praying that something would guide her there. I would have loved one more conversation with her before everything came to a screeching halt.

I looked down at my watch and prayed one last time.

I hoped for one last *"Thinking of you"* text or something that would show she was still there.

Nothing.

Naturally, I decided to go to where I felt most at home: the bridge.

It had been quite some time since I last approached the bench, our bench, by the bridge. The wooden planks looked almost bleaker and drearier now, maybe because it was almost winter, but in reality, it could be the semblance of memories and her perfume that hung in the air. Regardless, everything here was gray and tiresome.

Upon approaching the fence, I felt the wind whisk around my body. The voices of nearby children contrasted the bleak image being painted in the bitter aroma that clung to the scene. I turned to see where their laughter was emulating from, but all I could find were playground swings drifting in the air.

Beyond the fence, the water calmly ebbed and flowed with the fervor of a gentle breeze. It seemed that no matter where you looked: the water, the bench, the playground, everything was still.

But not the bridge.

The bridge contrasted the entire scene. With its expansive length that appropriately framed the drab winter scene, it beckoned me to sit for a moment. To take in the entire scene. To bask in the emotional glory that awaits me.

The twinkling lights from atop the bridge were breathtaking. So I inhaled deeply, sat upon the old bench, and invited my eyes to drift shut.

Within moments, the cold winter air dissipated and memories of what felt like yesterday shifted into the scene.

A haze of lights flickered across my sealed eyelids, and a familiar voice sat upon my ear: "Scott, isn't it beautiful."

It was Emma.

My eyes jetted open at once, and she was sitting in my presence once again. I could hear my heart beating from within my ribcage.

"Isn't it a little bit chilly," she questioned, wrapping her arm around mine almost naturally. Her head rested on my shoulder as her weight shifted against me.

In disbelief of being next to her, I asked her why she was there. She looked at me quizzically for a moment.

"I'm here to say goodbye," she murmured. Instinctively, I responded: 'I know.'

"You know," she quipped back.

'Yeah,' a sigh released from my body.

"Okay then," she said almost happily. I could sense a tinge of hesitation on her lips. She stood robotically and walked toward the fence. Her hair whipped in the sudden wind that filled the air.

"Ok Scott, remember what I said," she seemed almost stoic in nature.

'What's that?' The wind picked up and my eyelids began drooping. They slammed shut almost signifying her chapter was just about over.

Her voice trailed off and I felt a hand fold within mine. A new voice, pristine in nature, relaxed itself within my ear.

"Scott, you know you must keep moving forward," the hand clutched mine tighter. Upon opening my eyes, Faith sat pensively against my arm. Almost hurriedly she said, "You have to do what your soul calls upon you to do."

My eyes ripped shut again. The water became more turbulent and rancid. Another voice faded in as the wind picked up.

"Scott, focus on me, it will all be okay," Joy's voice faded in as Faith's dropped into the background. My eyes were greeted with a colorful fall scene: leaves cascading in the wind. Vibrant yellows, succulent oranges, deep reds: the scene was picturesque. The bridge was illuminated in the late autumn sky.

A genuine grin spread across her face. Through a smile and wispy hairs flowing across her face, she gave me a sweet kiss on the cheek. "Seasons change," she began, "and so will you. Never forget your roots."

My eyes shut violently as the cold air pushed against me. Another voice faded into the setting. Warmth encompassed my frame. Upon opening my eyes, I saw a figure standing in front of me: her back towards me with her brown locks floating in the dry air.

"Hey smartass, why don't you just shut your eyes and meditate? That is why you're here."

Morena.

'Do you always have to be this-' the words were cut short as they flowed from my mouth.

"Blunt? Sadly, yeah, I do," she grinned and turned towards me. She sauntered next to me and plopped down. "What's up?" She placed her elbow on my shoulder and rested her head in her hand.

A smirk crawled across my face.

'Nothing,' I nonchalantly responded.

She began sniffing the air passive aggressively. "I smell," she began, whiffing again, "Bullshit," she pronounced confidently.

My eyes shut as I laughed, but when I opened them, she was gone. A sole hand lay on my shoulder as a ray of light shone down on me.

Aunt Barbara.

"Hey cookie," she spoke sweetly. I could not contain my happiness. I stood up and lunged at her, embracing her joyfully.

'Thank you, thank you, thank you,' tears sprung from my eyes and froze as soon as they manifested at the edges of my tear ducts.

She stood there, gleefully holding my shoulders, on the verge of tears herself.

"My baby, you always will be," clung to her lips as a light encircled us both. "It is time you realize how important you are to this world. Be the light, Scott, shine," were the last words she said before she evaporated before my very eyes.

'Aunt Barbara, this is in your honor,' flew from my lips as the cold air re-attached itself to my face. I could hear the water flooding against the retaining wall.

The light glowed deeper as I re-opened my eyes to greet the bitter air.

She was gone. They all were, or at least from this stark winter scene. All that remained was a distant memory of words digging deep into my ears.

Look into my soul. Okay. I can do this.

The stale air, though once hurtful to the touch, reminded me I was alive. The American flag across the water waved valiantly to the pace of the wind and my heartbeat.

I was alive.

The bridge burned brighter. The water was clearer. The ebb and flow moved rhythmically.

.I was reborn.

I have another chance.

For the world, for the kids, for Aunt Barbara, for the angels, for Morena, for all those past and present.

For the future.

My breath materialized as I exhaled, leaving its mark on the painting that illustrated my past, present, and my future.

A sole man stood gazing out at the bridge: me. My passion, ambition, and resiliency miles from the American flag, but realizing it was my symbol of hope. This country's symbol of unity.

All I have to do is bridge the gap between love and misunderstanding. Between tenacity and diligent strength.

Between divine love and faith.

This may seem to be no easy task, but I will make it happen. I have to. For me, for every window of opportunity I can construct.

To empower and encourage tomorrow's leaders.

Anything can be right in front of your eyes: even a bridge between two beautiful souls finding themselves for the first time.

For my rebirth, for the world's rebirth.

This is the start of a whole new story.

Now... to lift the pen higher than it has ever gone before.

To bridge the gap between eternal light and misunderstood darkness.

'Just keep the faith,' faded from my mouth into the brisk winter air.

The bridge peered over my shoulder as I left the park, wondering what emotional and spiritual journey transpired in front of it just moments ago.

She haunts me.

Emma wholeheartedly haunts me.

She gave me the chance to see the beauty within my own soul after years and years of being at a loss for divine love. Emma handed me the mirror to see the best version of myself.

Then she left.

She left in the prime of our devout bond. Emma left a gaping hole in the man I was becoming. The team we were becoming. She knew how much I loved her. I would die for her to look my way. Still, she hid her true feelings and everything she could be.

She broke the foundational elements of a man who was already praying for somebody to love. And she just walked into my life like a hurricane.

Then she blew through my soul and took everything with her.

And she won't let it go.

And she can't let it fester inside of her... our love, that is. She walks this Earth day by day silently moaning to herself about her life, ambitions, and Greg, yet Emma is blind to the fact that while she whittles away her energy on a man who loves her to the best of his abilities, I still loved her. I am rambling. I know I am.

But there was something that drew me to her soul. Something that drew me into the inseparable beauty that she has within her.

We always want what we can't have and we always hope for what's next, but what about what's in the past? What about what we inherently believe will feed our souls? What about divine love? What about our resolute promises that we exchanged in the joining of our lips?

What about me?

As I continued to look down at my watch, I assumed that the vows had already been exchanged and that Emma and Greg were embarking on their coveted relationship as Mr. and Mrs. Whatever-his-last-name-is.

∞ ∞ ∞ ∞ ∞ ∞ ∞ ∞

I did not see Emma for about a week, and during that time I found myself needing to take shelter from the cold weather that was burdening New York.

I missed Emma, I really did, so I went to where we once slept cuddled up against each other: our hotel.

The warm radiator buzzed as I wrapped myself in the crisp sheets. I was homeless, but between these sheets I felt closer to home: I felt closer to her.

Static from the television illuminated the room as a reminder that I was fundamentally alone. My body lurched towards the floor, as I allowed my feet to drop onto the solid wood.

My toes gripped the cold floor, clinging to a little bit of hope that lingered in the air. Looking around, I felt the world get heavier almost instantaneously: she was gone. It was true. It was over.

Out of habit, I messaged her on our secret app again:

Dear Emma,

I wish we were still talking because you would never guess in a million years where I am tonight. The universe is crazy how it works.

Always,
Scott

While lying in our bed, I came to realize that begging for affection has to be one of the saddest things in this entire universe. To have to ask someone for a hug is utterly repulsive.

Have human beings forgotten how to be there for one another?

Have we fallen so far from grace that we forget how to treat one another?

It rattles me to my core.

How do you, as a breathing human being, resist the ability to make someone genuinely happy by just smiling at them? It makes me want to run up to someone, grip their shoulders, and scream, "Look at me, damnit, I am suffering."

She wouldn't bother acknowledging my presence still. To her, I am transparent. To her, I am a ghost of a life past.

That's okay, though. Let her lose out on having someone amazing in her life. Her loss, honestly. Though if one day she did come back into my life in some way, shape, or form, I know I would show her devout kindness. That is just who I am in the universe: the one who heals and the one who accepts flaws.

I was blasting "Unwell" from Matchbox Twenty from my phone. The music radiated through my fingers. I was still trying to process everything.

I'm not crazy; I'm just a little unwell
I know right now you can't tell
But stay awhile and maybe then you'll see
A different side of me

Losing a dear friend without saying goodbye is painful… and she is still there, just miserable and broken because someone else decided her fate.

I was told I had a hero complex, and in a sense I did. I still do. I never had anyone rescue me, and so I went around making up for that.

I made up for the people that couldn't save me.

I saved others. I struggled to save myself.

Those around me barely realized what was going on.

Did they see the papier- mâché skeleton I had?

I was a mere shell of who I used to be, but I am damn sure this shell is a thousand times stronger than I expected.

I was trying not to drown. I was swimming as hard as I could.

I was diving face first into an inaudible scream.

I ended up in the right place at the wrong time.

Maybe it wasn't the wrong time… maybe I was just walking into a shitstorm with the ultimate bucket.

I begged, 'Please universe, please stand by me. Please show me the way. Even if you aren't a guiding light, be a hand to hold when the sharpest words try to cut me down. How can I fit in on Earth when I was born to be a consolation?'

Yet the desolation continued to leave my soul dripping with pieces of the man I once was, and the man I was yet to become.

∞ ∞ ∞ ∞ ∞ ∞ ∞ ∞

On the verge of the New Year, I seemed to be losing even more of a grip on the vision I had for my life and for Windows of Opportunity. Day after day I was tucked away in my office at work, watching the door intently to see if Emma would walk in and remind me that it would "always be us."

Morena continued to remind me that I had to focus on my future, but for all intents and purposes, Emma seemed like she would be my future.

Working on the curriculums and leadership programs was fulfilling, but I still felt like I was leaning towards being "half-empty" instead of feeling "half-full."

At night and on the weekends, I felt myself doing anything I could to occupy myself from thinking of the memories I made with Emma.

Sure, I went on some dates here and there, but no one else made me as happy as I was when I was with Emma.

One evening as a light snowfall cascaded along the roof of the church, I stood looking out at my jet-black Dodge Charger. I felt terrible replacing the Monte Carlo, but after the air conditioning and heating systems gave out, it was necessary. After all if I was going to be sleeping in my car, I figured I might as well be comfortable.

As I was glaring off into the distance, Paul drove up to the church and got out of the car.

He seemed excited to see me, "Hey, Scott!"

'Hey brother, what's going on?'

"Nothing much," he began rubbing his hands together. "It feels like it is just getting colder and colder."

'Yeah,' I stuffed my hands in my pockets. 'It is freezing.'

"Let's go inside," Paul held the door open for me and we walked in.

As the two of us stomped the light dusting of snow off of our shoes in the doorway, we chatted about the high school and the programs I was creating.

"You know," he said as we walked into the sanctuary. "You have a big heart and a lot of great ideas."

'Thanks, I try.'

"It's astonishing how you just keep building new things, how do you do it?"

'It's my team,' my voice became solemn. 'My team sparks passion in these programs.'

"Passion," he laughed. "It's passion, it's promise, it's so much more than that. It's doing things for the right reasons."

'I've always been about all of that.'

"I know, son." Paul wrapped his arm around my shoulders. "And I am grateful you came to Queens Community Church."

'I am grateful, too, Paul.'

We locked eyes and I felt that something more powerful than us was building.

The two of us continued to talk about programs and initiatives we hoped the church could host. Over the years, Windows of Opportunity's various leadership programs found a home in the church, and sharing the space was the utmost example of how giving and loving people can be.

Queens Community Church embodied the essence of connectedness. Paul was sure to include Windows' programs in any conversation he had related to the church, and that helped to grow our impact on many different levels.

After a long conversation, the two of us walked out the door and back into the cold air.

As he slammed the door and locked it for the night, he laughed softly.

'Thank you, Paul.'

"No, thank you, Scott."

'For what?'

"You have given this community a beacon of hope. I am a better person for knowing you."

'Same here, Paul.'

We stared at each other with the innate sense that both of us played a larger role in each other's lives than we thought.

"By the way," he said inquisitively. "What was it you were thanking me for?"

'I am just thankful for you.'

Paul grinned again. The snow was falling more fervently upon us.

"One day this church will be Windows' permanent home, not just a small office and an attic. I promise you this."

We spoke for a bit longer until the two of us decided it was getting too late and too cold to stand outside.

"I'm going to get home, are you going to be okay?"

'Yeah, I think so.'

"Keep the faith, Scott."

Paul got into his car and before he drove off, I whispered 'Yeah, keep the faith.'

Naturally, I would always keep the faith. The phrase has always been a part of my soul, and is something I strongly live by.

No matter what, I could never go against the voice in my soul. Though sometimes I have had trouble listening to what the voice was trying to tell me, I learned that it often takes time to comprehend what your soul's purpose is.

Even when you think you know who you are and what you are destined for, the universe has a way of showing you another path is out there.

As I left the church and drove off in the car, I felt a humbled sense of relief: Windows of Opportunity would finally have a real home. With an entire building, we could host about any program imaginable.

Finally, everything seemed to be coming together despite Emma's absence.

Then days later as I was sitting in the sanctuary praying for clarity, I got the phone call that would change my path yet again.

In the middle of the night, Paul passed away.

∞ ∞ ∞ ∞ ∞ ∞ ∞ ∞

To say I was devastated to hear about Paul's passing is an utter understatement. After years of seeing his positive presence at the church, now I was left with the stark reality that he would never walk through the sanctuary doors again.

It was a bitter truth that I did not want to swallow.

In the weeks after his passing, I found myself praying even harder than before. Losing Emma was a nightmare, but losing such a kind soul was something I could not fathom.

Life was tilted on its axis and I desperately needed gravity to kick in.

When I returned to work the following week, Emma was standing nearby and I instinctively walked over to her. Though she was with a number of different teachers at the time, I hoped that my presence would not seem suspicious. Above all, I missed the spiritual friendship the two of us had, and I had hoped she would sense my sadness and attempt to connect to me.

Instead, she dismissed me and was angry that I would dare walk up to her while other people were around. I sent her a text message on our secret app in hopes she would understand I was not out to get her, although I did miss our connection:

Dear Emma,

I feel horrible and embarrassed that I put myself out on the line to try and reignite this friendship. Your actions and your curt words, and then lack of response to my last text on friendship, really hurt more deeply than any words can describe. There's so much I wanted to share with you about my life. So much I know I missed in yours. I truly cared about this friendship and needed it. 4 suicides and 1 friend passed in the last 6 months leaving me distraught and changed.... but mourning the loss of you has been the worst of all.

I know you will never see this but this is my last message. My last attempt to reach you as your soul is long gone. I will no longer be a bother. I'm happy for you and your support system. I wish you the best always. Thank you for the brief moments of whatever it was we had - even if it wasn't real. Take care and God Bless.

Scott

Sometimes words and actions burden us more than we realize. Sometimes it's not "just another day." Years of "friendship" should be silently celebrated with "rainbows, butterflies, and compromise."

In the months that followed, I continued to spiral and transform into a man I did not recognize.

I could not shake the fact that Emma was resistant towards my presence. Day in and day out I wanted to spill my heart to her, but I was shattered.

Everything within me screamed that Emma was a part of my long-term vision.

The Titanic was wholeheartedly human error in guidance, not in structure. You can have the foundation but if the leadership and vision is off, the ship will still sink. No matter how much you refuse to.

I was shrouded in resiliency. In the fundamental respect that laid within having to face each day with a shattered soul and a heart held together by mere shreds. Torn apart did not appropriately describe how I felt in that moment.

There was a gaping hole in the center of my body where bits and pieces of me used to live. I was wholly unwhole and had been desolated to the point of no return. The look in her eyes was blank and shallow, almost as if she was a ghost of what she once was. Having to see her each day, knowing that she had forgotten us in the naturalistic sense, made me want to crawl into a hole and rot there for the rest of eternity.

But why should I? It was true. She destroyed every last fiber of my being with the exception of one: my willingness to stay strong in the face of adversity. Strength is all I had left. The eagerness to fight for a better tomorrow courses through my veins. I am bathed in the blood of try and try again. It took all the strength within me to fall for her, and it took all of the remaining power within me to get back up.

I will survive; I knew I had to. Not everyone in this universe is entitled to the experience that is me. Some are not even granted the authority to be in my presence. No, I am not going on an ego-filled adventure, because there was nothing left.

There was no foundation to stand on, and there is also no solitary soul that would or should ever experience the heart-wrenching grip of despair that she clasped me in. Emma destroyed me. Emma took me and stabbed a knife in my chest without getting close enough to touch me… but she did touch my soul. Once upon a time…

Morena kept texting and calling me, and I asked myself what for.

I don't get her. I can't fathom why she exists in my life or how she even got there. The further I push her away, the quicker she rips herself back in. She went through her own sick and twisted hell, but for some odd reason, she enjoys my company. Morena said she waits to hear from me, almost as if I am the pieces of her that are missing. It was almost as if Morena and I needed each other to be whole in the sense of having some peace.

She is repulsive in the sense that she is resilient and will stand her ground even when she is burned and reduced to mere shreds. Her fight is more devout than her fear, and I wonder just how much do you have to break a person down to push her to that. Morena tells me she is cold and calculated, but it is just a thinly veiled crimson blanket that whispers, "I have an elastic heart, and I am not afraid to let it care again and again." Does she see who I am? Can she fathom my pain? I know she is wrapped up with her own agony and crumbled bits. Still, looking at her tenacity and her wounds do nothing to heal mine.

Morena was calling again. She was bound to leave some motivational message on my phone.

I told her to run, yet she continuously wrapped her hands around my shaken frame and said, "Try me." I tell Emma to come, and she runs faster than ever. Souls are a tricky thing.

I was beginning to think that Morena is not real. She is the working definition of an Earth Angel. She crushes every standard and stereotype she wants, and does whatever she pleases.

She is dangerous, as am I, and I knew that this lethal, peaceful combination will lead us to a higher power one day.

One day or day one. I guess I decide…. With a heavy heart, that is. A bitter chill crept up my spine and through my shallow exterior. I rolled to my right and saw my bag resting next to me on the seat. Another night in my car felt like the beginning to a crude joke.

Only it was just the reality that was my life. Loneliness became a common thread between myself and the plastic bag tumbling down the street in the wind. A brisk gust of air filled my car as I stepped out into the morning sun. This time, I slept only 4 hours during the night. That became my new record, honestly. I didn't think it was possible to find utter peace in sleeping in a car, yet the still air freezes time and space overnight.

They say pain is inevitable, but suffering is optional… so why suffer through when I could have just faced reality: the positivity I exude and the joy I bring to others keeps me warm. It is a devout and refreshing reality, even though my kindred spirit would have loved to have a warm bed, a warm soul is far more worth it.

From where I was parked, my car was overlooking the v-formation of the birds above signal that this frosty air would not cease anytime soon. For me, that was just an honest reality. It doesn't matter who in this world you are, what matters is how you treat each other when you have nothing to gain. The birds fly together to find warmth, but do they know each other's hopes and ambitions? Would that alter their consciousness? I mean… do birds have a consciousness? They must if they fly like that. They must. I certainly do, yet most days I fly alone.

I flew towards the cold, the seasonal changes, the pain. It is a bitter reality that we all must face. Sacrifices have to be made for the greater good… no matter what the cost is. It is more expensive to be as cold as the morning air than to give yourself to the world. You may lose sleep, shelter, salvation, and bits of your soul in the process, but it is far more worth it to see the birds flutter their wings in perfect balance and harmony as a team… even if it means the cost is living in your car and watching this regulatory celebration of togetherness from the comfort of resting your tired body against the hood of your home sweet home… or rather, car sweet car.

The beckoning sun evacuated any sense of pain I felt clinging to my soul. In loss, there is a realization that there is still life. Pain reminds us that we still feel. We still have time to change what tries to settle within us.

Time is, in essence, a reflection of what we choose to manifest and how we choose to impact this world. We spend an inordinate amount of time consuming negative energy around us, yet are blind to the effect it causes on our body. We wrap our souls in papier- mâché shields, claiming that we can hide our scars and sicknesses from the world. Yet the swords, others' words or actions, may not always cause immunity our hearts need to survive. Hatred, in and of itself, is an illness. Vile hostility is a disease we have yet to find a cure for. However, higher consciousness and growth can remedy the hurt consuming our souls.

The moment we realize that the words and pain of others is a prejudicial reflection of their experiences, and choose to abide by that philosophy, is the moment we open our minds to new perspectives. It is not always in our best interest to consistently expose ourselves to certain situations. However, when they arise, oftentimes we must manifest a cloak of protection built on the foundation of the goodness in our souls. We can all embody higher consciousness if we choose to do so. Adversely, we can develop a strong sense of desolation if we so decide that hatred is a better fit for us.

Still, why would you spend your time harboring such sincere feelings of negativity? Don't you owe it to yourself to feel unburdened? Would you rather be weightless or consumed?

It is our inherent responsibility to ourselves, and our society to be positive: to light the darkness with the etchings of our kindness and genuine love for one another.

Be authentically aware of what you put forth into this world. Be cognizant of how to make the world a much better place with you in it. Solitude is reserved for those developing their souls and concocting an understanding of how to become more spiritually informed individuals.

It is time to harness the knowledge we feel so deeply, yet need to translate into a language we can comprehend. We are the world and we are the universe; it is time we begin to act that way.

Though I knew all of these truths were manifesting, I was not ready to face what my future held. Sometimes we need to progress further than we ever imagined in order to build up the courage we inherently need to go forward.

∞ ∞ ∞ ∞ ∞ ∞ ∞ ∞

Nightly, I would succumb to my fantasies. It was like Emma was haunting me, yet I did not mind. It seemed as if anytime I found the strength to walk away, her presence continued seeping into my soul.

Each time I forced myself to walk down another corridor or stairwell in order to avoid her path, I still caught a glimpse of her classroom or her glance seemingly lingering a bit too long.

We were like two tormented ships passing in the night. The moments were beginning to feel inevitable.

I still tried to remain focused. I was persistent in staying in my element. My team continued to work with me and help build the vision I had for Windows of Opportunity, though the missing piece of my puzzle was centralized in my soul.

Negativity about the casual work-related drama seeped negative vibes through the souls of those in the school, but outside of school my team was cutting through the pessimism with a glorious knack for reform and spiritual grounding.

As my eyes would flutter closed each night, Emma would press her body against mine and sensually whisper in my ear: "I see you and I know you are doing this all for me."

My heart raced as she placed her hands on my lower back.

I felt her breath on my neck as she moved closer to me. We were drawn into the exquisite moment together.

Our lips locked with the fervor of a passionate reconciliation. It was akin to the fire a drug addict feels when he cannot get clean, and finally has that first hit in ages.

Her love filled up my veins.

My heartbeat constricted and pounded against my rib cage.

Why did she keep coming back like this?

Why did she consistently show up how she did?

I wondered if it was God's way of testing me. I wondered if it was a sanctioned rite to truly embody the mantra, "Keep the faith."

Confusion filled my throat. I was lost, discombobulated, and my eyes needed to readjust because I could not believe what was happening before my very eyes.

What was I missing?

What did I not understand?

As my eyes fluttered open in the stale morning air, I came to the exquisite horror that it was just a dream. Her gentle touch, her glances, her hand reaching out for mine: it was all just a dream. The stark reality was that she would never see me or feel me the way I visualize her.

She lived in the catacombs of her own reality, lurking in the basement of positive thought, preying on the energies surrounding her. She had a habit of wrapping her fingers so tightly around the mindset of others in this realistic realm, but is this all truly real? Is she living in the moments that pass before her, or is she trapped in the false clutches of her own past? Does she see her future? Does she want to see her future?

It may be that she possesses the lips of a mistaken goddess: her whisperings hold no merit to the prison bars she clings upon. She is trapped in her own mind, busy convincing the world that her life, the one she forces, is what it appears to be.

It is a harsh reality: we try manifesting false prophets through the flesh entities we project into our lives. However, in playing God and trying to influence the balance between what is meant to be and what we so wistfully hope life will be, we are oblivious to the mounting energy we put forth in the world.

You could spend days, months, or years building bridges between what you anticipate and what you push another soul into, but if you build that bridge on the foundation that "this is the life I want" and "I did this for us," your false words will only bolster and crumble when the water floods. The true test of a bridge comes when we try so diligently to balance weight on its beams. When we make an effort to cross the boundaries put in place, how will your words hold up against your actions? Will you stand or will you fall?

Will you bear the weight of your actions? Will you hold firm to your truth or your fantasy?

The illusion of time marches forward as you emulate the sensations of weary eyes casting downward over your true soul. She ran from me because she knew she could not hide her true self from my prescriptive soul. I am the truth serum, the drug you asphyxiate yourself with to feel life. You want to feel alive, but you occupy your time with the world you create and force upon other souls to try to make them feel.

Try.

Yet I could not help but ponder what I would say to Emma: when you show your true colors and bleed into the sky and its rising sun... will your bridge still be there?

Will he still be there...

Or will I?

I continued to whisper to the image I had of Emma deep within my mind: 'I'll see you in my dreams, while you will see me in your reality. I am the ghost of the life you could have lived. While you are too scared to own your soul... know your words, your actions, and your demons are brewing and conjuring in the light of day. For when you close your eyes to escape from the world you perpetrated, there will come a day that you will open your eyes and maybe... just maybe... the reflection before you could just be your own.'

By morning, she would always disappear from my life. However as the universe would have it, I would see her at work and watch her flash a smile in my direction.

I consistently wondered what was going on behind those chocolate brown eyes of hers.

Still, I was left without a clear response from her: it seemed she was teetering between trying to rekindle a friendship or sorts while resisting whatever story she was telling in her own head.

The cycle would repeat each and every night.

I was convinced my earthly soul was speaking a language that was difficult to interpret: I wondered if I was romanticizing Emma and our potential friendship.

The universe seemed to be utterly silent though I begged for it to answer the same question time and time again: Why did Emma have to leave when she did?

Day in and day out, I would cry myself to sleep after eating my feelings. The car would reek of junk food and I knew I was destroying my body, but part of me did not really care in those desolate moments.

As the weather grew warmer, I would find myself making solo trips to the bridge in order to clear my head. Each time I would bring junk food with me to quell the bitter taste of Emma's lack of compassion.

With an incredibly harsh day in my rear-view mirror, I rushed to grab the greasiest bucket of chicken possible before running to the bridge. As I made my way to the fast food place, I saw Emma's truck parked out in front and panicked.

I rushed to the bridge with tears obscuring my vision, and praying she did not see me.

When I arrived I didn't even lock my car, I just ran down the path and to the pine green benches by the fence.

I froze in fear upon seeing a woman sitting at the bench with a bucket of chicken. Her brown hair was flowing in the wind, and for a moment I was convinced Emma came to answer my prayers.

As the woman turned and placed her arm on the bench, she shook the chicken and smiled: it was Morena, of course.

She grinned and happily shouted, "What took you so long?"

Morena serenaded me with the heaviest melody ever: "If I truly want to admit that I've committed wrongs against myself, then fine, I'd admit that having to deeply love someone who carries so much pain and sorrow in the crevices of their soul, and not being able to help them save themselves, is the worst and most sincere crime ever."

'Mo, I-' as I tried to find the words, I felt them trailing off into the serenity of the sky.

She stood with her hair flowing in the wind. Locks of her hair mimicked the waves of the river as they crashed upon the shore. The bridge was being caressed by the crisp beams of sunlight that gently floated down to Earth.

My heart sank into the recess of my gut in that moment.

As she turned away while brushing against my shoulder, she gazed at me in that stark moonlight, and I could feel the years of pain and agony emulating from her body. Her brokenness was something so dangerously beautiful and painstakingly cautious.

Broken was her state of mind, her heart's circumstance, and her body's only comfort. All she ever knew was pain, but she glued herself together enough to show me her soft side that had been buried for far too long.

Like a priceless porcelain china doll teetering precariously on a shelf, she was daring herself to collapse regularly. Today was the day she tipped and cracked, but she caught herself just before the fall as she always does.

Nearing closer to my shoulder, she murmured, "Quit your agony and just be your own hero for a change. You don't need to save the world, you just need to save yourself."

Tears welled up in my eyes and I clasped them shut to prevent her from seeing how much those words affected me within seconds. When I had opened my eyes to show her how vulnerable I really was, she seemed to vanish into the setting sun.

Still, I felt her words coursing through my veins and assuring me that tears are part of weakness leaving the body.

I have spent my entire life saving everyone around me and picking up the pieces of their shattered hearts, but what about my own?

'Why can't I-' tears were preventing me from spilling the words out of my mouth.

Softly and with much trepidation, Morena whispered, "Why can't you what?"

The words rumbled as they left my mouth: 'Why can't I hate her?'

A long pause stood between the two of us on that bench as Morena forced herself to say the words she was slightly unsure of: "Because you can't hate what you created."

I stood up and started to run away from where we were sitting.

"What are you running from?"

'You, it's you. I am running from you.'

"Why, why run?"

'Because you aren't real. You can't be real.'

"Why not?"

I stopped in my tracks and looked right at her: 'Because you just seem to know. How do you know?'

"How do I know what?"

The wind whipped between us to fill out solemn silence.

"Why can't you just trust in the universe?"

'I don't know,' I began to cry. 'God, what are you trying to tell me?'

"Our hearts beat on," Morena started. "We all find a way."

Nothing prevented me from crying on Morena's shoulder.

'Please,' I wrapped my hands around her shoulders. 'Help me.'

She put her hands over mine and said, "Then let me."

I had to keep the faith. I had to see there was a vision much brighter than the one I was living through at that moment.

There had to be more.

∞ ∞ ∞ ∞ ∞ ∞ ∞ ∞

The cruel summer continued with my soul being wrought by Emma's absence. I looked at her social media pages over and over again, hoping I would see a sentimental secret message meant for me.

Still, nothing appeared.

The kids at school seemed to be more in tune with my energy come September. The new school year was keeping me inspired and engaged with what future I could have.

The higher calling I was looking for had to be there somewhere in the world, I figured, but my head was still clouded with anticipatory hope for Emma's love or friendship.

As I wandered to the corner deli one day, my head was in a thousand different places. I was examining my surroundings in hopes that Emma would appear out of nowhere, but instead I saw two large boys harassing one of my leadership students. I approached them with caution, but I kept my head held high.

Something seemed off.

'Hey Larissa,' I started. 'Everything okay?'

One of the guys pushed her to the ground and glared at me.

"Can I *fucking* help you bud? I'm with my girlfriend here." His eyes pierced through me.

My inner hero reached out to Larissa.

'Get up,' I gripped her hand. 'We are going back to school.'

With fear flooding over her, she jumped up and ran towards my arms. The two guys surrounded me and looked as if they were going to beat me up. I threw Larissa behind me and the two guys began to verbally belittle me.

I had all of the strength within me to stand up to them when a student needed me. I had the courage to save her when I could barely save myself.

After I grabbed Larissa's hand and the two of us walked back to the building, she began to sob violently as she admitted what I feared: they were about to assault her. There was so much tension in her soul that I could feel it dripping off of her. Larissa's energy was all over the place, though she was grounded in innate fear.

Even though I did not know whether those guys were armed with weapons or not, I knew I had to help her. I knew I needed to step in and do what was right.

Then it hit me: I had to truly stand up and do right by my soul.

After work, I rushed to the church and told Morena that we truly had to kick it into high gear. She looked me in the eyes and smiled.

Morena began rummaging through her bag and asked if I was truly ready to step into my power. I did not know exactly what to say, so I looked at her and grinned.

She pulled her notebook out of her bag and passed it to me.

"Take a look at your future," she smiled at me and I smiled back.

I was still a work in progress, but I needed to truly step into whatever was next. Everyone is always a work in progress, and forward is forward. It was about time I acknowledged that I had to move forward with or without Emma by my side at that moment.

As I opened her journal, the number "1600" was written on almost every single page.

'What is sixteen-zero-zero?'

"It's sixteen-hundred," She scooted next to me.

'Sixteen-hundred, what?'

She stood up and walked away while calling back to me, "You'll see in due time."

Her journal was adorned with curriculum ideas and scribblings I did not understand. Images of buildings were sketched at the center of most pages, and a common theme was the word, "systems."

I sat there and read through her words for hours. They did not make total coherent sense, but I was getting the gist: all of her ideas centered around Washington, D.C., and it seemed like something there called to her.

As I read through everything, D.C. seemed to call to me as well.

Morena watched as my eyes registered the epiphany in my soul: it was time I aimed for true higher consciousness and a realm of higher thinking.

The two of us got to work and began moving various documents around Windows' office.

Instinctively, I wrote to Emma:

Dear Emma,

I'm still having a hard time. It's so crazy. I shouldn't be so lost and hurting after 3 years but I can't help it. I wish you were around to talk it through like we used to. I can't shake you, and I guess I don't want to. I miss your friendship more than anything. We were unstoppable. October 18th is our anniversary. I've been good and strong - so many great things going on that I wish I could share with you and trust you with again. I want that back more than anything. I know you have your new life and I hope you are well. Wishing you love and success from afar.

Always,
Scott

As that fateful "anniversary" of ours rolled around, I took a leap of faith and went into Emma's classroom early in the morning. Before I even knocked on the door, I stood there admiring her soul's beauty.

She was sitting there, cloaked in innocence, dragging her pen along the metal rings of a notebook. At the time, I wished I could take a picture of her and frame it forever. I wished I could preserve her pristine and sweet existence, so that years later I could return to that moment when I needed a moment of peace such as this.

The moment she looked up I felt my nostrils flare and my breathing grow more labored. A subtle sense of panic set in.

"Hey," Emma said nonchalantly.

'Hi Emma.'

"What are you doing here so early?"

She seemed to forget the days when I would come to the school early, just to leave a sweet note on her desk or drop off our journal, The Vault, in her mailbox.

Part of me wanted to run from the room and bury myself in my office.

Part of me was on the verge of tears as a rush of our memories flooded to the edges of my eyes.

'Happy Anniversary,' I blurted it out and instantly felt my heart drop.

I could tell Emma was shaken by what I said; yet she managed to crack a smile.

"Happy Fourth Anniversary, Scott," she cast her eyes downward to her ring.

'Emma, it's only been three years… well, it would have been.'

"No," she quipped. "It's been four."

'Three.'

"No, four." She looked back down at the notebook and continued to run the pen along the side of it.

Considering how much our relationship, or lack thereof, tore me apart, it was shocking that she even remembered our "anniversary." On top of that, I did not know what to make of the fact that she didn't even remember we would have only been together for three years, not four.

I had a cordial conversation with her about a few students before rushing from the room. It amazed me that she was so far from the woman who I first fell in love with, yet she was merely inches away from me each day at work.

I missed her, yet I wondered at the time if I even crossed her mind.

The day flew by and by nightfall, I was immersed in a dream that was far from familiar.

Emma and I were cuddling, hugging, and being romantic, but then she pulled away from me and stood up.

"I'm not in love with you anymore," she told me.

'Why didn't you just outright say so?' I stood to meet her gaze.

She did not reply and I began to walk away.

I could hear her voice calling out for me, but I just appeared to ignore her.

Before I woke up, I remember looking her in the eyes and saying, 'I know this is just a dream. I will always, *always* love you… but I will be okay without you.'

I woke up without tears in my eyes for a change as I felt the winds of change brushing over me.

Her presence was edging further and further from my purview, and I was not too sure what sort of sign the universe was trying to tell me. My soul needed a clearer translation of the message being told, yet I needed a much clearer understanding of the language being presented.

At the time I was blind and deaf to what was before me, for the best was yet to come.

∞ ∞ ∞ ∞ ∞ ∞ ∞ ∞

Days away from her first wedding anniversary, the holiday party for Lincoln Memorial High School was being held at a local bar. Naturally I felt I had to go, for I felt I was practically obligated to go celebrate the holidays with the people I saw each day.

Upon parking my car and trudging through the bitter cold, I found myself alone at the bar sipping a ginger ale.

In the thickness of a dark, lonely night, a small distant light illuminated the corners of the windowpane ever so slightly. Staring through the fog that hovered both inside my mind, and outside the tempered glass, I thought to myself: 'I'm glad she found her wings finally, but I didn't think she would actually fly away.'

The ice cube pushed against my upper lip, creating such a harsh reality: the last person to kiss my lips was Emma.

It had been a year since she chose Greg, and though her lips were graced with his lips each night, I still longed for her kisses on my skin.

I thought that nothing else could hurt me in those fatal moments.

I would have bet my life on her. I would have bet my life that she was more than the impressions society placed upon her. The problem was that she would let me die…

And I would have died for her even after everything she put me through.

People from work started to filter into the bar in groups, with Emma finally arriving with some of her buddies. The other teachers looked on as I nursed my drink, with a handful of them eventually making their way over to me.

She always told me that I looked good in red, so I wore a crimson, button-down shirt in hopes that Emma would notice me.

Her eyes bolted towards me and the small crowd of teachers around me, but Emma was resilient. She tried her best to stay away from me, but a combination of alcohol infiltrating her system and country music blaring throughout the bar drew her closer.

The moment Luke Combs' "Hurricane" graced the speakers; I sensed her impending appearance on my shoulder for the night.

She glared at me, almost as if the lyrics called her closer to what we once were:

"Hadn't had a go.od time
Since you know when
Got talked into goin' out
With hopes you were stayin' in
I was feeling like myself for the first time
In a long time
'Till I bumped into some of your friends
Over there talkin' to mine
Then you rolled in with your hair in the wind
Baby without warning
I was doin' alright but just your sight
Had my heart stormin'
The moon went hiding
Stars quit shining
Rain was driving
Thunder 'n lightning
You wrecked my whole world when you came
And hit me like a hurricane."

She was pounding back drinks and staring right at me.

Her fingers frosted with chipped nail polish slid across the counter. The damp wood dragged itself along her gentle touch. Her hand jumped from the bar to my hand as she launched herself forward at me in some drunken, involuntary state. It was almost as she longed to grasp my body. Three years of adoration and lonely nights longing to touch each other flew through her fingertips and through the very arm where her heart was etched in forever and ever. Her eyes anchored to my soul and plunged me into her enticing aura.

She was intoxicated beyond all belief, but even in that state, her soul knew that her body had to pursue every fiber in my body that longed for her dignified touch.

A cupcake rested poignantly in her hand.

"Scott," Emma began slurring her words as she bellowed loudly, "Eat my cupcake, I know you *love* my baking." There was an extra emphasis on the "love" that taunted my lips to press firmly against hers. Emma forced the cupcake into my palm as her lingering gaze was pushing into the depths of my soul.

Three years. I wanted her so badly I was ready to drop her cupcake onto the bar, grasp her in my arms, hold her head inches from mine and... and...

I realized at that moment I had to snap out of it! Three years is three years... and she was drunk... and she was beyond the point of remembering these moments...

...But she was talking to me.

She stumbled backwards into the party to converse with her other co-workers. They were stunned to lay their judgmental eyes upon me. My leather jacket nearly dripped from my body with the sheer amount of hot sweat Emma had forced me to develop.

'Ugh,' I thought, 'She isn't coming back over now.'

While fixing my hair in the reflection beyond the bar, I caught her glance fixated on the back of my head.

'Shit.' I whipped my head around.

She had a velvet cherry in her mouth, just hanging from her fingertips and calling her mouth home, even for a moment.

Her eyes screamed, "Come here, now." Though I had a feeling I was misreading her glances.

About 20 minutes passed and my eyes darted to hers for what felt like the thousandth time in seconds. A slender pointer finger beckoned me closer as she pulled apart from her friends. The heat grew between us as a fire burned within me.

Years turned to seconds as she stumbled into my arms and our eyes locked in a passionate, ornate web. I wanted to be tangled in between her legs so badly, my feet hurt from the pressure I felt in resisting the urge to ram her body against mine and start shredding her clothes off with my bare teeth.

Where was my mind going?

She stood before me as years of thoughtful conversation and her once innocent kisses flowed in my brain. Every time I blinked, I expected her to fade somewhere into the recesses of my mind.

Yet this was not a dream.

This was not an apparition materializing in front of me to act as a silent reminder of a past soulful relationship.

No, she was here. She was real.

Our respective journeys from the past few years led us on separate paths...

And yet on this very night, our paths intersected.

I melted into the very words she spoke. I dove head first into the ocean of memories before us... and we began reminiscing.

This could not, in a billion lifetimes, have been more perfect or real, I figured.

Her brown eyes darted around the room, though they always found their way to refocus on my inner light. My soul felt like it was about to burst from my body in a fit of pure, unfiltered higher consciousness: I wished this moment on myself. I persuaded the universe to grant me this moment. I begged on my hands and knees with tears splattering in the midst of the shedding of my soul.

All of the universe's innate magic whittled down to this very second. And this one.

And the ones that followed.

I was asphyxiated by the scent of her beauty. She was intoxicated beyond all realistic definitions because she was fixated on finding answers to her questions at the bottom of glasses upon glasses of beer and hard liquor.

"Scott," she bellowed, "I can't believe you made it!" Her body was moving cyclically, almost in the form of an infinity sign, but that would have been too perfect and too coincidental to be true.

If only she would have fallen forward a bit more in her intoxicated state, she would have melted into my arms and we would have been spiritually intertwined forever... but she was miles away although she was inches in front of me: I was afraid I would be undying and unwavering in the pursuit of touching those fateful, effervescent lips for at least one last time.

Emma continued talking to me as I began to absorb the positive energy the universe bestowed upon me: here I was, in a bar of all places, with the opportunity to turn the page in what could be the greatest chapter in my life to date.

She kept rambling, but all I could hear her say was "Scott, you have hope."

Emma smiled as the speakers in the background of the crowded bar played Queen's "Another One Bites the Dust:"

> *"Are you ready,*
> *Hey, are you ready for this?*
> *Are you hanging on the edge of your seat?*
> *Out of the doorway the bullets rip to the sound of the beat...*
> *Another one bites the dust."*

I felt the driving rhythm give me courage.

She was three sheets to the wind and I felt guilty saying I would want her this drunk nightly if it meant that she would connect and open to me like this all the time.

The two of us stood there in spiritual solitude, almost as if our souls were talking in a manner that synthesized all of our emotions.

"What's *really* going on in that head of yours, Scott Matheson?" She was sliding all over the place and I kept reaching out to hold her up.

'Nothing.' I wanted so badly to profess my love to her, but I figured she was so far gone and we were in public with all of our co-workers. I couldn't betray her image, although her drunken stupor was not helping her.

"Tell me, *everything!*"

'Maybe you should sit down.'

"No," she screamed. "Talk to me."

I took a small leap of faith: 'I can't speak to you anymore, no matter how many times I have wanted to.'

"Yes, you can!" She grabbed my hand.

Everyone turned to look at us. Emma's intoxicated banter was causing a scene.

'I can't,' I whispered. 'You left me. You pushed me away. I have wanted to call you so many times. I couldn't.'

"No," she whispered back.

Then I said it: 'You getting married sucked, and I felt like I lost my best friend.'

"You didn't lose your best friend, I'm right here."

'I have missed you. Do you miss me at all? Our late-night talks and texts?'

"Yes," she began to walk away and I followed her. "Of course, I do."

The two of us stumbled out the side door of the bar and onto the sidewalk.

I caught her before she fell into the gutter and pulled her close. She looked up at me and I kissed her cheek. As the two of us held one another in the frosted air, my mouth edged towards her ear as I whispered, 'I love you.'

"I *know*," she replied quickly. Emma rubbed her hand in a circular motion before releasing from my grasp.

She said I love you a million times without spilling a syllable of it.

I told her what her soul meant to me and how much light she had inside her. The tears that welled up in her eyes told me she hadn't connected to that level of love in awhile. I told her if her nephew and her future kids mean so much to her that the best thing she could do for them is to step into her power and be the role model she was meant to be.

'You have to be the best version of yourself,' I told her.

"You only know my fears," she retorted.

'Yeah, but-' she cut me off.

"You know me, but you don't *know* me," Emma shouted. I followed her back into the bar.

Everyone's eyes turned towards us, and she seemed to panic. The two of us moved back towards the barstools and she knocked into one of them before shooting glances at everyone in the room.

Emma grew hostile upon realizing everyone was looking at her: "You don't get it, do you?"

'Get what?'

"It. *All* of *it*."

'What do you mean?'

Our co-workers looked away, almost as if they were trying to avoid the awkward scene.

"Greg won," she shouted

'Won what?'

"He won. He won me. That's it; you've lost. Get out of here."

Her mood swing shot right through my core: we went from being cordial to a sudden and total dismissal of who I once was to her.

I felt an utter sense of betrayal.

She didn't want me.

Apparently everything was a competition, and my love just was not enough.

At that moment, I was not enough.

The fractured glass representative of my heart was strewn about the floor as I replayed my night in painstakingly slow movements. My heartbeat was the only thing I could hear in the piercing silence. Years upon years of memories flushed down the drain with the dreadful epiphany that anger and violence sometimes run fervently and rampant.

Grief and mourning are not silent reservations for the dearly departed. No.

Rather they are exquisitely inclusive of those whose love ran out miles before the daggers of emotion pierce through your heart. A tattered soul lies where a field of dreams once existed as lush and bountiful. A broken heart was smashed to bits, mixed with equal parts hurt and unyielding torment. A mind flooded with reeling thoughts and chaotic, melodic confusion. Through it all, a smile and three words held up the illusion that everything was okay.

Emma stormed off and I saw Greg enter the bar. She wrapped her arm between his and cuddled into him.

Joy looked over at me and asked if I was okay.

Three words, 'I am fine' drowned out the sorrows temporarily while my soul resisted succumbing to agony and sheer desolation. And though the world looks on and sees a smile, the truth occasionally seeps out when the levee breaks.

As the water went rushing down the edges of fading smile-induced wrinkles, all I could do was cling to each facet of hope that remained. There was a lot of hope, too. A lot of pain was persuaded to evacuate the recesses of my mind... for there is always faith, a light and a glimmer of decency in realizing that despite being fractured, the light shines brightest when the broken pieces exist.

Broken is beautiful. Lost is found. Love exists in every language, even if that language is anger.

Fractured just means something has fallen... and fractured means that everything can be mended, though the pieces may take longer to place...

Though the one being mended, the beauty emerging from the ashes will be my own soul for a change.

I loved myself enough to realize, I have earned the right to respect myself enough to stand.

And to walk...

Then to run.

As the hammer dropped through the metaphorical glass, screaming filled the room. Every echo and reverberation dove deeper into my consciousness.

Yet life kept on occurring.

Everyone was in tune to their own adventures and excitement, though the droplets of water cascaded down my lungs and into my heart: dampening the love story that was just a figment of my romanticized imagination... or so Emma thought.

We were a fragile entity. We were delicate roses wilting in the frigid, brisk air. We were damaged upon arrival and shattered with two words:

"Greg won."

The incarceration of our love was a hard pill to swallow. She thought we were nothing. She believed in her lies so much that her pupils did not even respond to the quivering of my upper lip.

Gone.

Done.

"Greg won."

What did he win though?

Was Emma suddenly a trophy?

824

Was she enveloped in a golden arras, clutched in the sentiments of those who adored, but did not touch? Was her ego and confidence so inflated that she ballooned at the very sight of me.

Yet we burst, and not just her bubble of confidence.

Our intertwined hearts drooped to the floor and melted away into the gutters outside of the bar. The river of tears from years and years of heartache evaporated. I had no tears left to cry for her.

I was only imagining that she was all that I fantasized her to be.

I thought she was real.

I thought she would elevate my soul… yet she was just another face in the crowd who devastated her own soul… and in the process, she spray-painted herself gold, masking the crimson traces from the blood of the hearts she mangled.

Oh, dear Emma, if you only recognized that the only heart you would be breaking from here on out would be your own.

One day you would wake up next to Greg and see that his eyes glare into your existence and see a desolated mold of the mess you manifested. One day you will realize that just another day is fragmented in the hearts of those you embraced and ran from… only the most heart-shattering epiphany is that you will always be running from yourself and the messes that you have made.

Always.

You can love someone with all of your heart and soul, but it will never resolve their pain. You can genuinely care for someone in ways they could never fathom, and they will always expect more.

To some, you will never be enough, and that is heartbreaking if you allow that to be your truth. In actuality, if you think about all the pain, hurt, turmoil, and agony you have gone through to appease someone; that is just your perspective.

The thoughts you process and put into fruition will be your reality. What do you want out of your own life?

You may not be their missing puzzle piece.

You may just have been their tale for the time being.

You may have been a set of comfortable arms to embrace them at their worst… and that is all okay.

The best part about life is that there is always something else coming. There is always growth from your experiences, and there is always someone out there looking just for you (though they may not know it yet).

You could be someone's everything. You could be just what someone needs for the time being. It is okay to be a part of someone's growth and journey, but do not forget your own path.

If there was anything I learned from loving Emma, it was "Do not forget to kindle your own light. Do not forget to grow your own soul. You are paramount and primary. You are your own saving grace. Never forget how special you are to yourself, and just how brave you are for saving yourself from a situation that could be harmful to your soul and growth. Love yourself louder than those who try plummeting your existence into absolute desolation. Even if people think they know what is best for you, all in all you are the creator of your own reality."

Someone may love you, but they may just be able to love you as much as they could love. They may not love you how you deserve to be loved. You can't fault someone for loving you less than they can actualize.

You deserve to be treasured, for your soul is a brilliant gem.

You deserve to shine and be seen in your own light.

You deserve everything and anything this universe can offer you, just know you may have to work very hard for it.

This world does not promise anything other than life and death: you choose what you wish to pursue.

You can see your life as a persistent march towards death, or you can choose to live. Death is the tension that motivates you to live to your fullest. You can choose to pursue your passion. You can choose to create your own reality. You can be your savior and the real deal.

Decide what path you want to pursue... then go forth.

If there was anything I could have said to Emma in those moments, I would have said: 'You may have shattered my heart, but that will just be for one day. After everything, you have earned that: one day of my solitude to mourn the beliefs you had bestowed on my soul. You may have desolated bits of my soul and smashed what was left of my compassion, but that will not stop me from being a good person. You will not break me forever and ever. Listen to the lyrics of the songs we have left behind... tell me, do they still speak to your soul?'

And just like that... I didn't feel like crying for her.

I guess I knew the inherent truth all along... I was never enough for her, and I guess I never wanted to be... in the denouement, darling, you were no match for me.

I jumped in my car and sped off into the darkness.

∞ ∞ ∞ ∞ ∞ ∞ ∞ ∞

I barely slept that night. I kept tossing and turning, letting her image seep into my mind and rip me back and forth like a puppeteer. Why did I do this to myself? How could I let one person have so much control over my soul?

Now that I was in too deep, I was afraid that I started sinking too far to the bottom. I figured that I couldn't get out and that I couldn't escape.

I was suspended in a perpetual state of bowing down to her presence, for I thought I was too inadequate to ever be the same.

This was good though, I guessed. I mean, does anyone ever stay the same?

We wake up each day different from the last, and then sunrise, sunset; we rest our heads on a pillow composed of a day's hard-learned truths.

It is how it has to be.

It is how it will always be.

I will always wonder what it would have been like to open my eyes in the morning and rest my gaze on her peaceful existence.

At the time I remember shouting to the universe upon mourning Emma's official exit from my life: 'Do you know how much I loved her? How much I still do?'

If she turned and looked at me and said, "Let's run for it," I would have transformed into a hot air balloon and floated us straight out of the mess we were in.

But at the time she was too fearful of her image, society's perception of her, and how the world wrapped her in a little box, red bow and all.

She is probably reading this right now in a dizzy morning haze, or a dimly lit coffee shop and is thinking, "Wow, you know me so well."

But I don't... Did I ever?

We were just fractured memories of a love that once was. Though day in, day out, I cherished who we once were and who we could have been at the time. We lived in those final seconds before the clock struck midnight; only I never had the right to place my hand on the glass slipper at the time... or did I?

Tell me.

Tell me I was wrong all along.

Whisper in my ear that I am the only one: "You and me, forever and *always*. It will *always* be us."

It wasn't just another day, and it took me seemingly countless lifetimes to get over the passion I thought I saw in her eyes back then.

But my darling I lived a thousand lifetimes before, and I wholeheartedly knew one truth: despite her indifference, our passion, and what could have been us, you, Emma, were no match for me.

Yeah, it is even sad to release those words onto the page now, but she helped me learn, the hard way, that she was indeed no match for me at that time.

I had a lot of spiritual rehabilitation to do before moving forward.

Though forward is forward.

Let that roll around in your head for all of eternity... for I thought she would be slipping through my mind and rolling into another's arms...

For the rest of my life.

But all in all, before I slammed the casket shut on the embodiment of who we were at the time, I could not help but come to an epiphany for Emma:

'You say you refuse to sink, well let that sink in.'

CHAPTER 39

This House is Not For Sale

~

*"Look what they've done to this house of love.
It's too late to turn river to blood. The saviors
come and gone, we're all out of time.
The devil's in the temple and he ain't no
friend of mine."*

**- Bon Jovi, American Rock Band, Sayreville,
New Jersey**

"I wish I could tell you that once you realize what's been irking your soul for so long, you are able to just recover from it," Morena spoke solemnly as she stirred her hot chocolate. "But the truth is, it takes patience to inject tranquility into our souls."

'I hear you, I do,' I continued glaring out the window of the coffee shop. My eyes drifted from each person who passed.

"Maybe what you are searching for out there isn't precisely what you are looking for."

'You always say that, but I never understand what you mean.'

She took a faint sip from her cup. "Maybe it is because you are still looking."

'Okay, whatever.'

Morena smirked and let out a sigh. I placed my palm on the window and began tracing an infinity sign with my fingertip.

"You know," she said. "You don't have to look so sad. This is a happy occasion."

'Why does everyone keep saying I look sad? I've had the mask on. Is it falling off?'

"You forget I know your soul."

'Oh, so what, do you and everyone else know my soul better than *I* do?'

"That's not what I said."

'It is what it is, I guess.'

In hindsight, I did not realize how my innate pain seeped out of my soul in the form of crisp words and an irreverent tone.

"It is what it is, but it is so much more."

'Stop it, Morena,' I snapped at her. 'I just want to run away.'

"Then fine," she stood up. "Run away, but what is that going to do for you?"

'I feel sick,' I grasped at my lower back, attempting to ease the sharp pains I was feeling.

Morena softened her tone. "You need to go within, Scott. You can't keep beating yourself up like this, or something bad is going to happen."

'Something bad did happen,' I stood up. 'I'm alone.'

She cast her eyes downward at my tattered black shoes. "Do you really think that?"

'Is it possible to say no and yes at the same time?'

"Yes," she chuckled a little.

'Then no,' I paused. 'Yes.'

The two of us spoke for a while about my sudden wave of solitude as I continued to nurse the stabbing pain in my lower back.

"If this conversation is making you feel pain," Morena motioned towards my back. "We can stop talking about all of this."

'No,' I continued rubbing my back anyway; blind to the emotional turmoil I was feeding my body. 'I'm okay, seriously.'

The two of us decided to get up and go back to the church. We always had our most spiritual conversations there.

She was quietly gazing out the window at the barren trees, their branches drooping downward in the sullen winter air, as we drove past the back of Alley Pond Park.

The car stopped at a red light and the two of us sighed almost in unison.

I began tapping on the steering wheel to the idle nonsense on the radio. Both of us had so many thoughts in our respective heads, but neither of us could speak upon seeing the wave of desolation that hit Alley Pond Park. The lush greenery was obscured by the change of seasons.

As a matter of fact, I was also obscured by winter's harsh frost, though this was a rather mild month for one of New York's infamously cold seasons. Some years we were blasted with multiple feet of snow, yet in recent years everything seemed to hit us in February, March, and sometimes even April.

Our seasons reflected my inner voice: they were equally delayed for some sort of shift prevented the next wave of weather from manifesting in the sky.

The only difference between the seasons and I was that my voice seemed to have stalled from moving onto the next chapter. My soul was irked by a devout sadness and the injustice I was navigating due to a lack of divine love.

I was not okay, but I was so far from admitting it that I often found myself denying my soul's true intentions.

I needed love. I craved love. Yet, in some odd twist of fate, love did not crave me.

As the two of us pulled up to the church, Eve was standing outside of the building with her cellphone in her hand. The moment Morena saw her; she slunk down in the car to avoid eye contact.

'What are you doing?'

"I don't want anyone to see me."

'Why?'

"Just," she paused. "I'll stay here a while."

At risk of questioning Morena's usually odd behavior, I shut off the engine and got out of the car. The condensation from her breath instantly fogged the bottom corner of the passenger side window.

Eve did not appear to see Morena there, for when I got out of the car, she was rather fixated on me.

Eve snapped at me, "What are you doing here?"

'Hey,' I walked over cautiously. 'I'm just getting some work done for Windows.'

"Oh," she said indifferently. "I thought you were sleeping here again."

'I don't stay here anymore, Eve,' I replied. 'I'm homeless, or did you forget?'

She smirked, "I didn't forget. I was just checking."

Eve wrapped her gloved hands around the door handle and ripped the large wooden door open. The creak from the hinges seemed to have been just as scared of her as the rest of the building was.

Since Paul passed away, the building sat barren almost every day and night. If I did not go visit the church, the only people to occupy the church were a community group that met Tuesday and Thursday nights for a few hours. Eve did not approve of a handful of our youth leadership programs hosting events there, so Windows was at somewhat of a standstill.

As the door slammed behind us, the cold air drifted in to denote the sullen sensation floating about the church.

Paul's presence was certainly missed.

'I'm going to just head downstairs and work on some things,' I cut through the silence between us.

Eve was busy looking at the chipping paint, the cracked walls, and the dust resting upon the office that the ministers used each Sunday morning.

"Alrighty," she snapped.

She made her way up the stairs to her office while I continued my descent into the basement.

Morena was sitting quietly in the room shuffling through papers.

'What?' I was startled by her presence. 'How did you-'

She shushed me and pointed upstairs.

I realized that she was trying to hide from Eve, though I did not understand precisely what she was doing.

'What are you doing' I whispered to her.

"Sometimes it is better to work in silence," she shot back.

'But why?'

"Stand in the shadows, adorned in your scars, until you can stand in the light and be who you are."

'That makes no sense.'

She looked up at me, "Do I ever seem to make sense, Scott?"

The two of us chuckled and I pulled up a chair. Both of us were going over the curriculums until about an hour later I stood up.

"Where are you going?"

'I need some time in the sanctuary... alone, if you don't mind.'

Morena smiled at me and motioned towards the door. I left and drifted past Eve, who seemed to be tucked away in the minister's study.

Sitting in the sanctuary alone, I felt the calm silence rain over me.

God appeared to whisper in my ear in a manner that was much clearer than ever before.

"Those in your life are beautiful in their own way, they are not there to choose one over the other, but rather they guide you in your journey. One is not better than the other, for everyone has different, significant qualities that will elevate your soul into a higher realm. Souls compliment one another, not by the rules of humanity, per se, but by the rules of the universe. We are still learning these rules. They surround the notions of love, but not as love is always defined."

'Love is the fuel of the soul,' I responded into the shadows.

"Ask yourself why you are on this spiritual journey, and you will find your way. You will finally see why you have cried so many tears. You will-"

The door to the sanctuary swung open and Eve was standing there. Her firm voice shook me: "What are you doing?"

'I... I am praying.'

"To whom? To God?"

'To whomever will listen.'

I could see the marks on her face where it seemed many tears had cascaded over the past months. Eve sat down in the last pew and bowed her head. She began to silently pray, and I saw the name, "Paul" escape her lips.

She devoutly missed him and nothing was the same without him.

Eve wasn't even the same without him.

I looked up at the cross and blew it a kiss, 'Until next time.'

As I passed by Eve, I placed a hand on her shoulder and said a silent prayer. No one ever deserves to lose the ones they love. I am far too familiar with that notion.

For although I have not experienced a loss of love in the terms she has, many of those who I adored seemed to stop loving me... and that appeared to be both the harshest of realities and the makings of a grand journey to find what truly speaks to my soul.

The things we see as wars, anger, fighting, having a cold personality, or a lack of commitment are just sentiments of a broken heart.

Souls are often filled with pain and sadness, though it is the process of searching for what innately speaks to us that aids us in the ability to become more than what we seek or seem.

I was desperately trying to fight who I was, but it was the person I was fighting, myself, that I needed to listen to.

Oftentimes I was deaf to what I needed to hear and it constantly hurt me.

My health was deteriorating, but I didn't recognize it. I didn't listen. I was blind to my pain and I was blind to my soul's devout ambitions.

Awareness comes from opening your soul and being knowledgeable of trying to search for yourself. That alone puts you on a closer path to whatever awaits you.

I needed to live in the awe and wonder of what this world was meant to be, not what I perceived it to be.

When I returned to the office Morena was still sitting there, but under the light she took on an entirely new persona. She appeared to be doused in angelic beauty; this is not a comment on her physical attributes, but rather who she was intrinsically.

"What are you looking at," she asked.

I gazed at her for a while and realized that nothing seemed to burden her, but she was consistently connecting to whatever idea or concept spoke to her.

I needed to do that.

I needed to channel my energy before it was too late.

It was a good thing I realized this concept then, for who knows what would have happened if I continued to desolate my soul on the winding, dark path I was on.

As Morena continued writing and flipping through pages upon pages of work, I watched her snatch her journal from her bag.

I don't remember falling asleep, but I do remember waking up and seeing Morena passed out across two chairs with her jacket draped over her.

I had this weird dream that I was driving back from Texas to New York in a 24-foot truck with a car attached to the back. Bryan was about three years old at the time, and I was relieved to finally leave that world behind me.

Once I stood up, the intense pain in my lower back rose to the surface again. It was getting worse and I was ignorant to what it could mean.

I walked into the bathroom and took a look at myself in the mirror.

It was a long, hard look.

How did I let myself get like that?

A wave of sadness and depression washed over me as I scoffed at this shallow existence of mine.

When I walked back into the office, Morena had disappeared. All I saw was her notebook basking in the fluorescent light. I picked it up cautiously and decided I had to have a change in scenery.

I drove upstate in my state of utter sadness. The sunrise eventually climbed over the road, as I felt somber.

My soul was occupied and I felt weird. I was not myself. My sense of dignity also abandoned me.

Morena tried calling me.

My boss Shirley did too.

I chose not to answer them because I wanted to go somewhere and think. I wasn't feeling well and I was not too certain I knew where I was going.

The daze I was in forced me to perpetuate the abandonment I felt deep within.

'Maybe I just won't go back,' I told myself.

That day was not a good day and I prayed for healing. I began breathing deeply and found myself meditating. My mind was filled with gratitude for what I have experienced so far, and I was starting to relish in the notion that my emotional pain had to be causing some of the physical pain.

I was certain my emotions were taking a toll on my body; I had to just listen more intently.

It occurred to me that if my emotional pain caused some of the physical pain, then my ailments could be reversed. Digging deeper within my soul would provide me with the reality I was living in now: I was applying too much stress to my body and rejecting any sense that I was truly more powerful than I currently perceived.

Day after day I was driving around upstate New York basking in the illustrious scenery and growth. I travelled through small towns that were quite the juxtaposition of anything Queens could ever conjure up. My soul was detoxing between the quaint general stores and one-engine firehouses I had the privilege of laying my eyes upon.

As usual a plethora of unanswered questions danced around in my head, but I vowed they would not burden my growth.

No.

Rather, these questions would manifest a new version of me. I would return home focused, strong, and positive. An aura of peace would follow me, and though I would be more empowered, I would no longer be flustered by pain or pestilence.

At that point I was unsure of how long I was avoiding people and my responsibilities back home. It had to be about a week, though I was not entirely sure.

I let the mile marker signs guide me home until I finally saw 150 miles to New York City… then 95 miles… then 60 miles.

My whole life I have always been obsessed with countdowns: Countdowns to music releases, to events, to the end of the school year, and so much more. Moments come and go so fast, yet this was a year I had been inundated with stress. The moments did not appear as savory as they once had been.

I sensed that my childhood had something to do with how obsessive I was over moments and time. Valuable milestones were obscured by countless tragedies and sullen glances.

Soon I would be back at the church and immersed in yet another countdown. After all, the bliss and serenity of nature would become ensnared in the bleak monotony of the day-to-day, which would be contrasted by the love and energy I would put into the world.

I yearned for love, yet I was missing the fundamental elements of what love meant in the grand scheme of life.

As I passed by beautiful lakes and became consumed by the vivid sunset cascading across the sky, the universe's intricate perfection masked my devout sadness.

Everything I was sensing had whittled down to humanistic emotions, though I was picking up on the elements encompassing my soul.

Parts of me were petrified of what countdowns implied: the end of something. Since my Aunt Barbara died at such a young age, and I was edging closer to that number, I was more consumed with fear than what it inherently meant.

I was treating countdowns like some derogatory nuisance, yet they could also be seen as a slow and easy progression: counting could signify possibility and inevitable change.

At about 20 miles to New York City, my body writhed in immense pain. I began sweating and found the safest place to pull over.

My body felt like it was on fire, and not in a good way.

I darted into a dingy bathroom and clasped my back in a state of immense agony.

A clot of blood exited my body, and suddenly I felt better. It was an odd experience, but I assumed that it was a kidney stone.

I was not eating properly or drinking enough water, so I figured I had to start caring for myself a lot better.

On my way out, I grabbed a bottle of water from the vending machine and continued on my way.

∞ ∞ ∞ ∞ ∞ ∞ ∞ ∞

As I drove up to the church, the moonlight encompassed the entire building. In my absence, it did not seem that anyone had even visited the church. Although I was not gone for long, maybe a week and a half at most, the building appeared to remain barren.

To me, it was utterly devastating.

A building of that size could truly be something special for the community. It could be a safe haven for so many people in need. Paul had faith that my programs could bring Queens Community Church to new heights.

However, it was a Friday night and the only living entities filling the church were my tears inundated with past memories.

I went inside to pray for a bit and ended up falling asleep on a pew until 2:30 in the morning.

I think those nights were the hardest to handle mentally. Emotionally and spiritually speaking, I was filled with such harsh loneliness.

Feeling like a hopeless fool began to be the new normal.

No one was looking for me or waiting for me.

I was just left with my own solitude to somewhat keep me company.

As I retreated to my car and drove to a quiet side street to sleep for the night, I was thankful I had a roof over my head. Although I was staying in my car and showering in whatever fast food restaurant's bathroom sink in the morning, I knew that everything was just temporary.

I held out hope that it just had to be.

By Sunday morning, I received a series of bitter text messages from Eve. She said that the church was a mess and that she could not handle any of "this nonsense" in her life anymore.

She began to insult how I ran my music program, and though my program was not in the church at all over the weekend, she blamed her current distaste on Windows of Opportunity.

Arguments ensued between the two of us for years, but it was never this bad. After every fight we had, I did everything in my power to apologize to Eve and Paul. He would always say that it was nothing or just a misunderstanding, yet Eve always saw it as much more than a tart exchange between her and I.

During this latest argument, Paul was not around to allay her discontent.

As her words grew in severity, you could only take "I don't want this in my life anymore" one way: it means that you are unwanted.

Windows of Opportunity was unwanted within the confines of the building.

Eve called me and began to berate me.

She said that I disrespected her and I disrespected Paul's work. I never had an ill intention towards either of them, the members of the church, or Queens Community Church itself.

Enough was enough with the accusations and assumptions.

If someone cannot see the pure intention and passion a person has to build a better life and atmosphere for something, then it is time to leave.

With Emma gone and my hope fleeting, I had to make the challenging decision to uproot Windows of Opportunity from its home.

Eve did not believe me when I said we were going to move Windows of Opportunity out of Queens Community Church. She yelled that I was being selfish and manipulative.

My only selfish intentions were to give the kids I work with a home to continue their memories and their hard work. They had God and faith in the way we administered the program and Eve was taking that away from them. She treated me worse than garbage and left me with no choice but to leave the church.

She said she hated that the kids performed in the music program I held at the church.

Eve screamed over the phone: "The building is not a place for rock and roll, Scott!"

The kids were finding spirituality in a creative manner, but because it was not being enacted by the old school religious ways, she wanted us out.

Although Eve told me that she supported the kids, it was a farce: she would only support them if they would abide by strict views that she appeared to have.

For weeks upon weeks, I argued with her about Windows of Opportunity's place within the church.

'Paul always appreciated us,' I told her.

"Well," she began. "Dragging my husband who is no longer here with us into the conversation shows you are truly disgusting."

The fight continued until Morena walked up to me and mouthed, "Think of your soul, it is not worth it."

My creased face and crinkled nose eased up. I took a few deep breaths as Eve continued to badger me. I decided that I would arrive at the church at the end of Sunday's service to talk with Eve in person.

As I sat with my back against the wooden pew, I closed my eyes and decided to bask in the positive energy from the sanctuary.

There were very few people there, but the families and people who knew one another were sitting clustered together.

I was, once again, one of the odd ones out.

Sitting in my absolute solitude, I could not help but overhear the conversations mingling behind my back.

Some of the members I did not know were talking about Windows of Opportunity and the decimation it was bestowing upon the church.

It was a sinking feeling, realizing you were the topic of conversation and lingering in the mouths of those who had never even seen your face. If they did, they would have known to silence their prejudice.

My presence was an exquisite juxtaposition: here I was, the target of their profanity, sitting a mere few feet from them. Unnoticed and invisible.

Honestly, should I be surprised?

To stand and defend my honor would have meant to force negative energy into the world, yet to sit in silence would mark my complacency.

My voice is not a pawn in another's game. My essence and experience are not invalid because someone else deemed them so.

I stood, my shoulders rising as if they were breaking free from the puppet strings. The marionette has moved on.

I twisted my body in a sort of mechanical way, inching closer and closer to their proverbial conversation. Though the group chittered and chattered away, mocking the experience of someone who was within their purview, I made it my mission to uphold a persistent sense of positivity and sincere humility.

Still, no human or creation on this earth has the right to place someone in a picture frame... especially one whose actions and energy do not fit.

I tapped the woman on the shoulder, gently making my presence known.

'Excuse me,' I spoke in a hushed tone, 'Are you talking about a friend?'

The women stopped, glaring at me as if I had six heads. "No, it is just hearsay, and what is it your business?" The women retorted chuckles and sighs, as if I interrupted their little tea party of malice and diseased hatred.

'Well, if it is hearsay, here I am,' I spread my arms as if to present my aura to dispel their negative comments.

They sat quietly and utterly confused. The invisibility cloak shed itself from my skin.

In those moments between inhaling and exhaling, it dawned on them. The sun rose: I was their topic of conversation.

Their jaws cracked open slightly, their words dripped back into their throats.

'Do not throw stones at glass houses that you have never even laid your eyes upon.'

I pivoted and dropped back into the chair. Their conversations resumed, but they kept cautiously looking at me: praying their judgment would not shatter my own.

The game is no longer a game. It is a life. It is the fulfillment of a legacy...

It is the beginning of a new chapter and a new era.

I did not know where those words came from, but my sudden burst of confidence and strength felt refreshing.

Moments later, Eve came up to me and began to argue with me in hushed tones. People looked on with a mixture of curiosity and guilt on their faces, for they wanted to know what was going on, but no one was willing to stand up and stop what was going on.

After everyone left and people filtered out through the front doors, Eve and a handful of members who I knew receded into the basement of the church. I sat there in the empty sanctuary for a moment, the sun shining up the aisle and resting a solitary beam on the altar, and began to cry hysterically.

'Why, why, why?'

Tears obscured my vision as I looked on at all of the beautiful stained-glass windows. I wondered if it would be the last time I saw those glorious windows.

I tried to listen to God and the angels, hoping that I would find some sort of salvation.

Silence was the only thing that graced my presence.

I felt most connected to my soul and spirituality within the walls of that church, which was such a contrast to what I felt as a child sitting in a temple, yet when I needed guidance most I was left in solitude.

The church became my makeshift home.

I could not tell anyone how much it meant to me, for how could I justify to the world that I was homeless and living out of the building?

All of my money went into keeping Windows of Opportunity alive and well, and if I stopped funding the programs, then who would help the youth of Queens find their inner power?

That night I was not able to sleep. I gazed up at the roof of my car and toyed with the daunting decision I had to make: stay at or leave Queens Community Church.

Overwhelmed by the choices before me, I felt that saving my sanity forced me into a claustrophobic state.

I wanted to cry.

Scream.

Run away.

Go to where I once felt safe, but was now being torn away from.

Thousands upon thousands of my prayers graced those walls, but now the church was becoming just four walls and a roof.

I vowed I would actively work on my soul after Emma's complete dismissal of who I could have been for her, yet I found myself hitting another concrete wall.

Though this one was metaphorical, I felt all of my sacrifices were for naught: the building, Windows of Opportunity's home, was abandoning the partnership we could have created.

It was the neverending story of my life up until that point: everyone and everything ended up leaving to some extent.

Everyone and everything seemed to not want me.

For those who did want me, it was not unconditional, but rather with extreme conditions that humanly could not be met.

I seemed to disappoint many, despite my pure good intentions.

I took verbal beating after verbal beating over the years in order to make sure that there would be a safe space for Windows of Opportunity and youth to grow, yet I was left in the ashes once again. I needed to

842

figure out a whole new plan, but letting go of the church was too strong of a burden to bear.

Naturally, I have always absorbed negative energy, though this situation with the church left me with a gaping hole in my chest.

It was hard to breathe.

It was difficult to sleep.

My soul was decimated prior to this, and Eve's commentary made me feel worse.

The lower back pain I had been dealing with shook at my core again. Regardless, I figured I needed to disregard the pain and fight through. I was certain that what I was on the brink of creating would change the education system for years to come.

I knew in my heart it would shift society over the next twenty or thirty years, and I acknowledged I might not even be around to see everything reach its full potential.

I made a few promises to myself then and there: I cannot accept anyone in my life who will not support that and give me a safe space to be me. I cannot have anyone in my life that does not trust me and love me unconditionally, so that this vision of mine could be obtained.

I needed all of me and I was only a shell.

My cracked outer surface seemed unfixable, and I was petrified that I was going to fall apart at any moment.

I had to heal myself and that meant making some difficult decisions, including the one that kept me up that night.

There was nothing left to say.

My decision was final.

I sighed as tears rolled down the edges of my face. I drifted to sleep with the image of the interior to my car's roof burning into my drooping eyes.

∞ ∞ ∞ ∞ ∞ ∞ ∞ ∞

As I stepped out of my car and into daylight, people were scurrying about and beginning their day. There was no doubt the people who passed me were running through their to do lists in their respective heads.

Everyone was out living their lives.

The morning was such a heavy contrast to the darkness that preceded my days.

I wake up in the comfort of four wheels and a huge secret.

Still, my address did not dictate the world I was creating and inspiring daily.

The mask I wore as a social worker inspired many, but came with great sacrifices.

Regularly, I pushed through delirium in order to embody the transformative soul I had to become. My dreams are an amalgamation of the paths I crossed every day.

By day I kept myself occupied by helping youth in a high school. Then I would meet with different people to create programs for youth.

At night, I parked my car where I could and drifted to sleep.

When I had to use the restroom, which was becoming more frequent, I begged a minimum wage worker at a coffee shop to let me in the bathroom.

I drove around a while longer and brought my car to an abrupt stop when I saw Emma's classroom window.

It was just another night after another.

By day, I would watch people run past me and consider that some of them may be living in their car as well.

The world might never realize it.

What were their stories?

What was my story?

The daylight obscured my dark reality. My daily strengths absorbed my nightly weaknesses.

The journey to find true love masked the broken pieces of my soul: the memories I created with past loves were now gone, but not forgotten.

It broke my heart when I realized a decade of dedication and a sincere appreciation towards Queens Community Church whittled down to a series of volatile text messages from Eve.

It takes a lot to crush someone to their core, but it is possible. I never thought that it would happen at the hands of an individual who claims to be religious, spiritual, and subservient to God and HER ways, but sometimes people genuinely surprise you.

You could have the best intentions for someone or something, yet people would rather misjudge or misunderstand you instead of communicating in a healthy manner.

The act of leaving the church was an act of forgiveness in its utmost form: though I was harboring a broken heart, I felt no malice towards Eve and the members.

We are all on our respective spiritual journeys, and Eve's just so happen to push her to influence my experience. Instead of building a future and a community together, as we had planned, Windows of Opportunity and the Queens Community Church were being forced to part ways at a crucial point in the development of all of our programs. We were deeply doing God's work on a daily basis, and how it can be seen any other way, whether in a fit of rage, mourning, or depression, and stated in any malicious or degrading way, was simply a travesty and the act of a seemingly non-spiritual person who is blinded by misery and in pain.

It was breaking my heart, as I knew some of my programs would now face irreapairable damage, and I also realized that if I continued on swimming in this sea of negative emotions, my soul would also face irrepairable damage.

Throughout our respective periods of spiritual growth, pain may seem like a hindrance to a soul, but it could be a catalyst to help souls grow.

There is a difference between being entitled to your feelings, which we all are, and manipulating the facts to be "right and win an argument." I know God and my angels flow through my veins and guide my spirit. There is nothing I do or decide without speaking to God first; She is with me as these words flow onto the pages you are reading. She agreed that evil was plaguing my soul. I had to sever ties with those who spread negativity or spoke ill of me and my work, in order to protect the youth my team and I consistently empower on a daily basis.

It is disgusting and disrespectful to be subject to anything less than loving and caring feelings, especially when working with a constituent of a church. How can someone preach togetherness and God's words while directing social media posts towards me and my team that say, "You don't get a pat on the back for the SHIT you are supposed to do."

I wondered: Is this the language a Reverend should be using?

In addition, Eve had remarked that "the collar is off" when using vulgar language such as that, and she said that line many times.

This was just one statement, in a collection of many that led up to my heartbreak. If we were able to maintain our partnership, we would

845

have been able to save thousands of lives together. However, I just hoped that those souls would still find a way to stay strong.

Paul always genuinely cared about me, Windows of Opportunity, and our roles at the church. For that I will always be truly grateful. I was in agony over having to leave the church, for I felt like I was losing a part of him in walking away from what he had hoped we would create together.

There was no point in fighting anymore, nor feeding into unhealthy behaviors. I want all of us to find the peace we need to make a difference in this world.

I sat in the sanctuary and I cried there for many nights since I realized I had to leave. I spent my last evenings speaking to God and praying for all of humanity.

I had evolved my relationship with God deeply in that sanctuary. I loved the church building. I love God. I love my faith. I love the work I do. I love myself and God enough to know I could not subject myself to consistent and hurtful badgering.

It was time to go and it was time to grow.

Sleeping seemed near impossible due to my emotions surrounding the church and the persistent pain I was experiencing. Still, I dreamt about the church in its entirety.

I dreamt I went back to the church after what seemed like a few weeks. The entire building was in shambles: it was a pile of stone and dust, which slightly resembled where the rooms once were.

I was alone until I heard voices: two men were trying to pick up the piano as the keys trickled down the rubble. Part of an old drum kit was crushed nearby.

I chose to hide in another part of the destruction, away from the men and the piano. My shelter and salvation were gone, yet I could not do anything about it.

When I woke up, I realized that a music box played "Somewhere Over the Rainbow" over and over in my head. This morning I saw a rainbow halo around the moon. Someone or something is trying to send a message. Call me crazy, but prayer and religion-based songs played all morning on the way to the building. Something wicked this way comes.

We pray on our knees, but resist the willingness to follow through with our atonements when on two feet. We live in verse, only to diminish another's poetry if it does not match our lyrical ear. If "to err is to be human," why do we fixate on flaws and knock each other to the ground, but frown at the sight of someone trying to better themselves?

We were not born this way. We were molded to see this. We need to open our hearts and minds. We need to banish the rain of hatred that tries seeping through the branches and into the roots of our society. It is only natural that we purge ourselves from the disillusionment that we must hate, we must see color in terms of distention and separation, we must see competition, and we must burn our candle at both ends just to make those ends meet. If you are constantly racing to the next goal, the next dream, knocking down the next person to gain notoriety, then consider how much damage this is causing your soul.

Do not place merit on higher consciousness and whatever you deem holy just when you are on your knees. Live the words you seek and preach. Be the shift in light, in prayer, in words, and in actions.

For the universe knows and forgives those who opt to tear down others… but it restores the balance in granting the gifts we so choose to receive. Negativity gets met with the manifestation of those feelings. Positivity is met with its fair share of challenges, but the universe's hand tends kindly towards those who reject hate and ill will.

Born are we of the same consciousness, yet broken down into fundamental components of a global whole. It is our choice then: do we build sandcastles with our words? (Beautiful and eloquent, yet able to be discombobulated with the presence of something as malleable as water) Or do we develop a positive shift through insight, grace, and words integral to building, not breaking?

The perspective we hold is exclusive to our respective experiences, but the question remains: are you on your knees to beg for the universe to look blindly on how you treat others, or are you on your knees as a means of wishful thinking… hoping for the betterment and growth that is being built moment by moment?

I felt as if an entire universe had shifted itself off its axis when I pulled up to the building. Memories of a soul's growth once flooded these four walls, and now I had to say goodbye to them. However, in watching the sun crawl over the trees and houses that lined the street, I realized that so much changed. It was for the better. I spent hours sitting on those

847

steps, wondering if I could ever have a better life, but I was wishing and praying for the wrong things: it is the people who surround you that make your life amazing. The experiences mold you, but buildings cannot do anything for you. Something incredibly stationary can't shake your world and jolt your existence. Sure, buildings give you perspective and shelter, but for how long?

I couldn't help but feel somber about penning the final chapter in the church, especially like this. No matter how holy a place could seem, it still comes down to what you exude from your heart and soul. It comes down to how you spend each moment, each word, each breath, for at the end of the day, when the sun sets and the colors fade to gray, your world can't be at peace if its clouds are blocking your hopes and dreams from shining through. One day I knew I would look back and smile at these days: maybe not tomorrow, or next week, or next year, but one day.

And on that day the sun will rise over four walls filled with memories, and they'll know that they served their purpose. A shroud will be lifted and the walls will serve another gentle, cracked soul. Then an invisible plaque will hang on the altar that says: this house is not for sale, but this house sold its purpose for growth and prosperity many sunrises ago.

The boxes stood before me, representative of a wall between the man I was and the man I could so desperately become. Overcome with intense emotion, I ran from the church panicked and full of misery. My head was spinning and the last thing I could remember before pushing through the church doors was Morena's voice behind me: a cardboard thud emulated as she screamed, "Scott! Wait!"

I got in my car and drove.

I drove further away until the church became the background of a life remembered.

I pulled up to Francis Lewis Park, where Morena was waiting for me against the wooden fence.

'Not now Morena,' I shouted as I pushed past her in an absolute tizzy.

"Not now Morena," she said mockingly, "Well it's gonna be now!"

She rushed after me as my feet leapt off the wooden steps and into the sand. I fell to the floor and she was sure to follow.

Merciless screams escaped my body as I threw myself close to the water that was ebbing and flowing closer to where we sat. The pressures of waiting for Emma to wake up and leaving the church were mounting, and all I could do was cry over what never will be.

Windows of Opportunity could have had a beautiful home within the walls of that church, but the universe had other plans brewing deep from within the cosmic backdrop of this crazy world.

Now the doors were closing, and it felt like the windows were slamming shut… and to add insult to injury, Emma's words were seething into my skin.

"You're thinking of her too, aren't you," Morena's hair flew backwards as the wind began caressing both of our souls.

She knew. She could read me. Emma's words cut like a knife, and losing the church ripped the wound clear open.

"Every day we stray a little bit further from the light that is inside us because we cannot fathom a world where we are the villain in somebody's story," Morena spoke softly.

'I am not the villain, Morena. There is no villain,' I quipped.

"You are right. You are not," she snapped. "In your story, that is. You don't get to control her narrative. You don't get to tell Emma that your intentions were pure and that she needs to believe that as her truth. You don't know exactly what she thinks is right or wrong. All you know is that you are not in her life anymore."

Tears welled in my eyes as I tried collecting some semblance of words to fight the demons within me. A breathy whine escaped my mouth, 'But Morena, I loved her, why doesn't she love me?'

The tears fell from my eyes and splashed onto my cupped hands. Morena bent beside me and whispered, almost in the manner that some fairy godmother would in a children's fantasy story: "Because you remind her of what she could never feel towards another human being. She needs to learn to love herself before she can love another… and that, my dear, is your crime: you loved the pieces of her that she couldn't comprehend. She couldn't appreciate you because she couldn't appreciate herself."

'Morena,' the setting sun brushed my eyelids open, for I just had to see the sky above and show appreciation to the world around me.

"Love yourself Scott, because at the end of the day, you need to learn to love the one person who will walk with you for life," Morena bent down and leaned against me as we watched the sun fade beyond the New York skyline.

"We all learn eventually," she muttered, "We all learn to."

Once the sun disappeared, I felt the urge to return back to the church. I told Morena that I would see her there, and something within her must have forced her to stall a bit... for I pulled up to the dark church all alone.

As it always had been.

I quietly slipped into the back pew in the darkness. All I felt was the thumping of my chest and the creeping sensation of an oncoming asthma attack.

"Help comes to those who ask for it," I heard in my own voice. It was echoing through the empty sanctuary. It was empty and drenched in the darkness, yet filled with light. A long pause followed by a deep sigh.

'Well here I am...asking for help.'

I knew I still loved her, because four years ago, exactly from that day, I laid on the couch downstairs from that very sanctuary, and asked God about her. I prayed and asked if what I was feeling was real, and who is this girl that I just met. She caught my eye and my soul from day one, and four years later I was sitting upstairs in the sanctuary, maybe for the last time, asking God and the angels for help.

I missed her. I was not ashamed to admit it.

Four years later I'm asking the same question. Who is the girl I met four years ago? Was she the real deal?

As I sat in the darkness, I whispered into the vastness: "I trust you father. I trust the universe and my angels. I also know we are the creators of our own reality."

Maybe this is sad, but I desired the following to be my reality: If there was ever a miracle this is what I prayed for, I didn't only want to have her friendship back in a major way, but I also desired to have these beautiful souls get along with one another and collectively feed my spirit, so that I may accomplish the impossible.

I continued my outwardly prayer: 'Thank you, universe, for all my blessings seen and unseen, and please forgive my sins, and my shortcomings. I'm so sorry that I can't shake this depression and that I can't connect to my inner strength and light again. I want to, but knowing I'm a disappointment is impossible to live with. If I can't make the dreams a reality, what is the point of anything?'

I took a deep breath and turned inward.

'I know you blessed me and I see those blessings.'

A door thudding in the darkness made me realize I truly wasn't alone.

'Thank you. Amen.'

"Scott," Morena beckoned, "we have lessons and long-term light in our life. Sometimes people are clear in their role, other times they are not. I-"

It felt as if a message was flourishing through my soul, and I felt Morena's words fading away.

'Something,' I whispered.

"What?" Morena looked somewhat startled.

'Something is coming.'

We stood in absolute silence as she moved closer and closer.

'Time after time I have taken hit after hit. This one was excruciating, personal, deep, shattering, tormenting, and agonizing torture. How do you hand someone your soul, your inner demons, your thoughts, and most importantly your love, while they just take it and ram it heart first into a concrete wall?

'My soul, heart, mind, and spirit were demolished, and I simply couldn't fathom how someone so close became so far. Sometimes you'll want to disappear because the mask you wore was drenched with so many tears that it corroded. The pain succumbs your whole body and shatters you. You can't pick up the pieces and put them together because they stole most of them and refused to give it back. I was holding countless blank keys in my hand that didn't fit in any lock. I could not get into where I wanted because I was permanently locked out.

'My soul believes she completes me. My heart says she is the only one with the key. My body longs for her touch. My head is filled with conflicting emotions. My world lies in ruined disarray.'

"The timeline is speeding up," Morena muttered under her breath.

'I expect nobody to know what it's like to walk in my shoes, and nobody can. This is the scariest crossroads I have been on, and the one I have to show the bravest face,' I glared at Morena's eyes that were immersed in a pool of pristine white light.

It was time.

It was coming.

I retired to my car and allowed my thoughts to melt into a dreamlike state.

My phone rang and jolted me from any semblance of rest I would have.

It turned out to be a representative from a national television show. For weeks, she promised she would interview me and promote Windows of Opportunity, but when we finally spoke, I was devastated yet again.

She said that I did not really have a story to tell and that Windows of Opportunity would not go far.

A lot of people did not have faith in Windows of Opportunity. I was starting to think they were right.

However, time after time I felt I lost myself because someone else was nurturing me, loving me, or encouraging me. This time, I needed to step up and show up, regardless of circumstances.

There were no more excuses left and no more tears left to cry.

Time and time again, I have taught youth that as long as your religion and your faith give you values and morals, then they shouldn't be filled with trepidation when expressing what they believe in.

I always told the youth in my program that nobody has the right to dictate the parameters and boundaries of how they should live their lives. At the end of the day, we are all surrounded by unconditional love as long as we believe in ourselves.

When I was younger, I was told by the religious figures in my life that I was asking too many questions. The community I was a part of was blind to the abuse my sister and I were dealing with at home.

It was a painstaking experience and I did not want the youth in my programs to be judged by their style, their hair color, their relationship preferences, or just about anything.

Our respective relationships with God and the universe transcend different aspects of our lives. This may happen at different times, but regardless of where we are on our individual journeys, the light still resonates within us.

The beliefs we hold near and dear are there for us, even when we do not outwardly see them.

We must listen carefully to the voice within our souls because when we reject our inner light, it could take a lot longer to realize your own self-worth and purpose.

I wish I had realized all of this earlier in my own timeline, though I am thankful for all of my experiences for they all made me the man I am today.

∞ ∞ ∞ ∞ ∞ ∞ ∞ ∞

In the midst of my departure from the life I once knew, I was thankful for the support from my son. At this point in time, Bryan was a part of over half of my life and got a chance to see my growth.

Though Bryan was holistically unaware of my experiences in Texas, he saw what his mother and I did in order to take care of him.

The two of us went to see a movie and as we walked out of the theatre, he put his hand on my shoulder and said, "Pop, I'm proud of you."

It meant everything.

Words carry so much weight to them and can make or break someone. It is phenomenal to see that my growth and progress transcended into my son's actions. The two of us walked down the street to our respective cars, since he was rushing home to his longtime girlfriend.

My son is my world and I wanted nothing other than for him to live a fulfilling life.

I was so happy that he found someone who understands his soul and who makes him genuinely smile.

True love is such a rare treasure and it is a blessing that he was gifted with an exquisite relationship of his own.

The second I got into my car I fell sound asleep.

I dreamt that Morena and I were eating at a diner. The two of us sat there discussing Washington, D.C. and the curriculums.

"You know," Morena started. "With all of your ideas, you should become the next president."

I almost spit my coffee from my mouth.

'The next president? Are you crazy?'

She looked up at me with a smirk plastered on her face.

"Maybe a little, but when you dare to dream is passion truly insanity?"

Before she could say anything else, Eve walked over to us and began screaming at me. She sat down and was trying to explain some sort of story, but it was interlaced with harsh quips and not-so-subtle judgments.

Morena moved next to me and placed her open palm on my shoulder.

"Hey," she whispered. "Did you catch that one? I guess some things never change."

I clenched my fist and Morena wrapped her fingers around my hand.

"Don't let her get to you."

'What should I do?' I turned to Morena. 'Should I go back?'

"Hear her out," Morena motioned to Eve as she continued to ramble. I began to calm down and breathe deeply.

"Maybe what you are searching for, isn't what you are looking for..." Morena's words faded into the recesses of my mind.

When I woke up, I realized it was just a strange dream.

After spending the day with Bryan, I did not understand why my mind suddenly shifted to Eve's presence.

The windshield was fogged over and I was utterly confused.

Why did Morena say president?

Did she mean becoming the President of the United States?

Why was she keen on Washington, D.C.?

Why did Eve appear?

What was going on inside my head?

I pressed down on the brake and shifted my car into reverse. I wrapped my hands around the steering wheel and put on the radio.

Bon Jovi's lyrics boomed from the speakers as I shifted the car into drive.

> *"Look what they've done to this house of love*
> *It's too late to turn river to blood*
> *The saviors come and gone, we're all out of time*
> *The devil's in the temple and he ain't no friend of mine*
> *Look what they've done to this house of love."*

I pulled into the staff parking lot at work and shut my eyes. My mind was mottled by shades of black and white, pictures of people who I had not seen in years, and a podium illuminated by a solid white light.

My eyes slammed shut as the music on the radio dissipated.

∞ ∞ ∞ ∞ ∞ ∞ ∞ ∞

I stood looking down at the people below.

What separated us was a solitary, yet sturdy, glass pane dividing us from ever getting too close and personal. I wonder what it would be like not to have glass divide us.

What would it be like to reach out and touch someone directly in front of you?

To extend your arm and someone be within reach?

Being 48 floors up, I realize it would be humanly impossible to touch another person from behind the window. Yet somehow, I don't think I meant physically touching them in those moments.

What would life be like if we didn't have glass windows that divided us from touching another's soul?

What if we could reach out and hold the ones we love dearly... to actually hold them and not just some superficial meaning of the term hold.

To touch someone and be touched.

To have another human being fully wrap their soul around yours.

Is it possible to fathom someone who was your equal?

Someone who you could be miles apart from, yet feel their every move and twist.

Someone whose very breath would shatter the ground beneath you, then restructure it as they inhale your beauty, then exhale their fears and inhibitions.

I wonder if soulmates or this concept of twin flames are a real thing, or was it made up to justify human nature's inability to compute loneliness?

I extended my hand to touch the glass.

A single fingerprint left its trace on the window, reminding someone that pensive thoughts were developed here. My pain is beauty and tragedy mixed up in one hopeful breath.

Do you see me?

Can you see me?

Would you ever understand me?

Are you out there somewhere in the universe? In the abyss?

I could go on forever asking questions about love and how souls just naturally, or unnaturally, click... but what for? What if I am just doomed to walk this Earth imprinting love and joy on others, but have no one fully grasp each and every fiber of my being... and just understand me.

Is anyone listening?

Can anyone hear me, or am I self-absorbed in the universe's soul?

Can everyone hear me deep inside, but have the inability to understand the words I am saying?

I am but a singular fingerprint on a glass pane: slightly noticeable, constant and unwavering, yet latent until you move closer and acknowledge my existence.

I will forever be your fingerprint, whomever you are out there: a solitary mark on your heart that flows within your blood. A phantom of the love you yearn to have for me, though you do not know I exist... and as your blood circulates through your system, you exhale my soul and I inhale every ounce of you I can.

You have chosen your own path in this lifetime, one without me, one with shortcuts and back alleyways.

Maybe you are out there somewhere rockin this universe.

You didn't try to cling to even an iota of my soul in this time and space reality.

Is that true?

Have you marched on without even an acknowledgement of my presence, or do you whisper for me every night when your head hits the pillow.

Do you know I am here and will we find one another again?

I can either live with that for the rest of my history, or I can move on, or have an undying faith that maybe... just maybe...

Though how could you move forward once your soul knows it has been engulfed in another's flame? A flame that burned strongly from another place and time? There is no remorse or regenerative soul who could see from my eyes, from behind this glass pane on the 48th floor. Yet I so wish there was... Could there ever be another me? Another lost soul rolling around in rubbish, waiting for someone like me. It is a hopeful sense of doubt. You aren't waiting anywhere for me, are you?

You don't exist, yet you do in my mind.

Are you there, universe? It's me, the one you rescued.

Or does life not work that way?

I guess it doesn't.

If you did hear me, you would acknowledge my prayer.

I am closer to you on the 48th floor. I am right near a window.

Can you see me now? Are you listening?

I am rambling now, that is just it. No one knows this is even happening in the outside world. My facial expression is too shallow to

This House is Not For Sale

comprehend, and with everything going on, I just fade like a shadow into the abyss.

As always, I am the clicking pen or foot tapping that serves as background noise until someone focuses in on me. Maybe I am just a dream. Maybe I can push this glass forward and just step out into thin air. Maybe I am a figment of someone else's imagination moving through the darkness, pulled in the direction of lost souls or beating hearts.

Where do I go from here?

Is there anywhere to go?

Is there anyone out there?

My soul so yearns to find you.

A murmur derailed my train of thought: some children laughing in the distant corner and crayons rolling down the hall with a reverberating echo.

The vibration touched my soul.

The room spun abruptly and caught my attention.

Where had the glass gone?

I reached out and placed too much of my body weight on trust and faith. Tumbling out of the window, I felt my inhibitions screaming and fading fast.

With my head as a torpedo, aiming directly for the ground, I found my target.

Come find me.

Please...

My eyes jolted awake and the roof of the car met my startled head.

CHAPTER 40

Carpe Diem

~

"Dear my love, haven't you wanted to be with me? Haven't you longed to be free? I can't keep pretending that I don't even know you...Take my hand. We're leaving here tonight. There's no need to tell anyone. They'd only hold us down... All I want is to give my life only to you. I've dreamt so long I cannot dream anymore. Let's run away, I'll take you there."

- Amy Lee, American singer, songwriter, pianist, Riverside, California

I started to think that maybe the answers to my soul's discomfort were not people. I figured maybe the answers were on a plane that I did not discover or establish yet.

The answers to life's quintessential challenges may not be readily accessible or available at first, but that is what makes the journey through life so fulfilling. Spending time weighing your heart down with the misnomers and false images of another apparition only brings heartache.

It was time to release the pain.

Instinctively, I called up Morena and told her to meet me at Alley Pond Park. Though it was mildly cold outside, I knew that she would still walk with me. It occurred to me that through thick and thin, Morena would always be standing beside me. She may have her quirks and odd tendencies, but she has a genuinely kindred soul.

Though she acted as my spiritual guidance in times of trouble, I knew that she held more empowerment deep within her.

She had a gift, as did I, but both of us were years away from actualizing all of that potential in the universe.

As I pulled up to Alley Pond Park, I saw Morena sitting at the rustic picnic table where I last saw my Aunt Barbara. When Morena turned around to meet my gaze, I could have sworn that the smile adorned across her face belonged to the woman who gave me so much hope.

Aunt Barbara helped to shape the man I am today.

She instilled in me the fortitude I needed to keep my soul intact.

For her, and for the rest of the people in my Circle of Angels, I am grateful. I will forever harbor a sense of gratitude for those who perished and watch over me, and a sense of respect for those who are my earth angels.

"What's going on, kiddo?" Morena pulled her sleeves over her hands and shifted her body so that we were parallel one another.

'Can we go for a walk?'

"Sure," she reached for my hand and stood up.

Both of us began walking up the path and through the slightly blooming trees that appeared to bend towards us.

The two of us walked in silence until she suddenly looked up at me.

'What is it?'

She paused for a moment and looked at the trail ahead.

"Why did we come here?"

'I just needed to breathe some fresh air.'

The pain in my lower back was getting worse, but I kept pushing forward.

Maybe that was my real fatal mistake: not listening to my body.

"Okay," Morena smiled as the two of us continued walking.

'I think it's time.'

"What time?"

'I am fully giving my soul to the universe.'

Morena chuckled, "Your soul is a part of the universe, silly."

'No,' I started. 'I mean truly letting go and letting God handle everything.'

"The universe has looked very kindly on you, Scott."

'I know, I know.'

"Do you know?" Morena stopped and I halted as well.

'I think so... I mean, I thought so for the longest time. Then-'

She stopped me and wrapped her chilled fingers around my arm, which covered the infinity symbol tattoo on my forearm.

"Do not give into another soul, Scott. Find your own soul."

I looked at her quizzically. 'I know,' I said. 'I just said I am letting go and letting God-'

She started to talk over me as if she was discharging a prophecy from her lips: "In the mountains, through the prairies, through the oceans white with foam. God blessed America, and has also blessed you. You have a gift. You have a light. Do not obscure it. Let it shine and those who don't want to bask in its glow can seek solace elsewhere. Their loss. Your gain. You physically are in another realm; emotionally, mentally, spiritually... you are elsewhere. They are here, in a land they do not yet understand or grasp."

I looked over at her, as the sun seemed to cut directly through the trees in search of her.

'Who are *they*, Morena?'

She spoke softly, "Give it time, for the sun will shine."

The two of us stopped as we reached the steep part of the path. In this part of the park, it always seemed like this crackling paved set of steps was our humanistic way of immersing man-made creations in nature. I had a hard time breathing and quickly began to hyperventilate.

'I can't do this,' I leaned against the wooden fence that lined the path.

"You can't do what?"

'I can't keep going on like this.'

Morena sat down in the dirt and began to run her fingers through the earth. "What is it you always say," she began. "Keep the faith?"

She looked up at me and smiled.

'How do I release this pain burdening my chest?' I pounded my fist against the center of my rib cage a few times as tears began streaming from my eyes.

"Music always speaks to your soul, correct?"

I stopped crying for a moment, 'What does that have to do with anything?'

Morena began to hum a familiar tune as she closed her eyes. The wind picked up and whisked her hair in front of her face. My own hair fluttered in the sudden breeze as I lifted my head towards the sky.

Her voice became more angelic and took on a spiritual tone.

"We've got to hold on, to what we've got,"

She paused and tilted her head to the sky.

"Does it really make a difference if we make it or not?"

She sounded like she was singing Bon Jovi's "Livin' on a Prayer," but it came across as if she was chanting a prayer.

"We've got each other, and that's a lot."

'Morena-'

She continued as the trees began to sway:

"We'll give it a shot."

My eyes dropped to where she was sitting, and suddenly I didn't feel like crying anymore.

*"Ooooh, we're halfway there.
Ooooh, we're living on a prayer…"*

She extended her hand and opened her eyes. Morena's irises appeared to glow in the bursts of sunlight that were cutting through the trees.

Although it seemed that she was physically in front of me, it appeared that Morena was translucent. She was not a part of a linear timeline; rather she was a manifestation of exponential opportunities in this universe.

Her voice faded back in again:

"Take my hand, we'll make it, I swear."

The two of us in unison sang,

'Whoa, living on a prayer.'

In those moments, it felt like everything made sense. It seemed as if all of my hardships and turmoil were supposed to be a part of my soul's experience. It appeared to me that my definitions of divine love and being a power couple were taking on an entirely new meaning.

The soul who I was most compatible with would have to be as spiritual and as sincere as I was. The other half of my power couple would need to be insightful, diligent, and able to transcend any challenge with grace and poise.

Until that moment arrived, I would not settle for less.

I would not settle for someone who did not match my vision and values. Although I was steadfast when it came to my ambitions, I was not going to completely shut out someone who was complimentary to the positive energy I planned on immersing myself in.

I knew there were people out there who also had a fire burning deep within their respective souls, I just needed help finding them. The journey I was on had to intersect with others who were finding or found themselves. It was becoming clearer and clearer.

Morena and I continued walking the path and talking about different concepts for education reform. It was almost like I was looking into a mirror: she understood me on a spiritual level that made it appear she was a figment of my imagination.

For all intents and purposes, Morena was a different version of myself, and my soul.

The wind had simmered down and it was just the two of us walking around at this point. We wandered past the pond, a group of children laughing and kicking a soccer ball around, and a quaint shack that served as a storage area for the park.

Morena darted into the playground area and leapt onto the swings. The creaking metal winced at her every whim.

As she moved like a pendulum back and forth, I instinctively watched her.

'What are you doing?'

"Well, what does it look like I am doing?"

'I don't know, Morena.'

She paused and smiled for a moment, "I'm living."

Morena threw her head towards the swing and I jumped on.

The two of us swung in unison with the Earth's gravitational pull. We were giggling as if we were like little children again.

Finally, after what felt like half an hour, I turned to Morena and watched her hair whip in front of her jubilant face.

'Hey,' I spoke softly, yet loud enough for her to hear.

"Hey!"

The two of us looked at each other for a moment again while basking in the sounds of nature.

"How do you feel?"

'Alive,' I shouted. 'But I feel alone.'

"Hey Scott," she placed her feet on the ground and I stopped swinging. She looked over at me as a gentle breeze caught her hair.

"You are never alone. No one ever truly is, you know that."

'Do I, now?'

"And besides," Morena started. Her voice became more sing-songy:

> *"I see everything you can be*
> *I see the beauty that you can't see*
> *On the nights you feel outnumbered*
> *Baby, I'll be out there somewhere."*

"That is breathtakingly beautiful, did you write that?"

She stood up from the swing and started walking to the gate. I watched her take a deep breath as she basked in the glory of the fresh air.

"Dermot Kennedy sings it, its called 'Outnumbered' and I heard it on the way here."

'It's beautiful.'

She whipped her head in my direction to watch the words register in my soul.

'You know,' I walked over to her. 'I hadn't been on the swings since I was a kid.'

Morena laced her fingers in the chain-link fence.

"You didn't exactly have a childhood."

'No,' I placed my finger between the chain-link fence as well. 'But I accept that my childhood wasn't easy.'

"Neither was Rebecca's"

'No,' I ran my left hand along the black paint. 'Not at all.'

"When she calls you, answer it."

'What?'

"There will come a time when she calls you," she said. "Be there for her."

'I will,' I assured. At the time, I was holistically unaware of what was about to happen to my family.

I had been so far removed from my parents and my sisters' lives, that when Rebecca called days later to tell me what was going on with my mother and father, part of me needed to register the words she was saying.

The two of us chatted for a while about what was going on in our respective lives, until Rebecca suddenly adorned a solemn tone.

"Scott, dad is really sick."

With a tinge of concern in my voice, I asked 'How sick is he?'

"Well," she began. "Not as bad as mom is."

'What's wrong with mom?'

It had really been years since I had an in-depth conversation with my parents. Though I knew my parents divorced and my father started a family with his new wife, I always had the feeling my parents were not too enthralled with my organization and my life. Bryan maintained a relationship with his grandparents and my parents and I were cordial to one another when we were together, but we very rarely spoke.

"Uh," Rebecca cleared her throat. "Mom has Alzheimer's. She doesn't really remember too much anymore."

I felt terrible for my mother, for I knew deep down inside she was a tortured soul who needed to be understood. However, in this irreversible state, my mother didn't remember what she did to my sister or me in our youth.

It was like she pushed the reset button, though our scars still remained.

With nowhere to live and my sister in need of help, I moved in with my mother and slept on her couch for quite some time.

Our relationship transcended into a different light, for she was so far removed from the woman she was in my childhood.

The first time I walked up the stairs and back into the house where I was thrown out of, my mother greeted me at the door jovially.

"Scott," she gleamed with excitement. "I'm glad you're home. Did you bring the milk?"

'Uh,' I didn't even know she wanted me to bring milk. 'No, mom, I forgot.'

My mother looked at me with a sense of wonder. "Forgot what?"

Rebecca appeared from behind her and shrugged as she smiled.

"Mom," she put her hands on our mother's shoulders. "Go back inside and sit down."

"Okay," my mother said. This was the first time I didn't see her stubborn demeanor emerge from nowhere. She retreated into the dismal living room adorned with old family photos.

'What's wrong with mom?'

Rebecca whispered, "Like I said, her memory is practically gone."

'I didn't think you meant *gone* gone.'

Our mother plopped down in the cocoa-colored recliner and glared at the static image on the television screen.

"This is my favorite part," she shouted as she pointed at the screen.

'Oh,' I remarked. 'That's great, ma.'

I turned around to look at my sister who was clearly holding back tears.

Rebecca and I sat at the table and talked for a bit until she had to go off to work. I brought a bag of my clean clothes in from the car and placed them on the floor next to my mother's couch.

It was a faded sunflower-colored sofa that seemed to have been there for well over a decade.

The sofa, and all of the other furniture in the room, appeared to be as weathered and tattered as my mother was.

She kept rocking on the recliner and humming various unrecognizable tunes to herself. I looked on in amazement, for the two of us were able to be in the same room despite our horrid past.

I guess it helped that only one of us remembered what life used to be.

Her clothes were baggy and desolate. Though she was clean and her hair was neatly tied back, her sweatpants and large t-shirt were not a sight I was accustomed to. Although she was not stylish in the sense of models strutting on a runway, my mother was always well kempt.

Whenever we went to temple, she wore neatly pressed clothes that embodied the matriarch image she put forth. In her current state however, she appeared to be completely unwound.

It was almost as if the ribbons of time she once clasped firmly in her hands were tangled and in ruins on the floor.

As I watched her peacefully rock back and forth in the chair, I discovered that her entire life was now removed from her recollection.

She turned and caught my glance as small tears began to run down the edges of my cheeks.

"Oh hello," she said with a grin. "Are you comfortable there?"

'Yes,' I replied. 'I am, thank you.'

I turned and looked up at the pictures hanging on the wall. She spun her head around to see what caught my eye.

"Oh," she pointed to the picture of me in my scouting uniform. "Are you looking at my son?"

'What?'

"My son." She pointed up at the picture and smiled, "He's such a good boy; he should be home any minute now."

I looked on at her in amazement.

She didn't know who I was.

It was almost as if years and years of my abuse and maltreatment faded into the sunset because she could not remember what happened. There I sat, in the house where I was destroyed as a child, watching my mother's soul finally exist within inhibitions.

It seemed the woman I knew was gone forever.

My mother rambled on about various different things and would often stare off into the distance. It was disheartening and it was something difficult to swallow.

Seeing her mind deteriorate was painstaking, yet my soul just wanted to weep openly for the memories that trickled from my mind.

The abuse was harsh and painful, yet here I was, sitting perpendicular to the woman who tried to destroy me. Although I hoped that I would eventually hear my mother say precisely why she did what she chose to do to me, the moments were fleeting.

Even if I did confront my mother regarding how she treated me, she would not have understood what was going on. Her life was dramatically different from the woman who raised my sisters and me. My mother's thoughts were compiled of what she could manifest based on her current perceptions.

She looked at me with innocence in her eyes, for she saw me as a man who was helping her, not the one she belittled and bruised in the spiritual sense.

I had to excuse myself after a while and I told her I was going out to get some air.

I hopped in the car and rested my head on the steering wheel.

That night's anxiety attack was the worst I had ever experienced. Usually I can talk myself out of it, but I knew the moment I left the house that it would be a matter of minutes until I just snapped.

I wasn't wrong.

I felt the pangs of pain shooting up my spine. I felt my core fill with magma just before I erupted. The lava flowed through my veins with rigor and persistence. I was gone.

I had been gone for a long time.

I let go and I kept moving forward.

The car and I were out of sync, but I kept driving.

Something inside of me said, "Don't stop, you can make it. You can fight through this." And so, I did.

I was on fire.

I was beyond the point of no return.

I opened my mouth but instead of screams, there was just silence. Even my voice couldn't muster up any comprehension of what was going on. I went into lockout mode with the door swung wide open. Pieces of my shattered existence crumbled before my eyes, and I was picking up my own pieces while more kept crashing down.

Tears gushing from my eyes reminded me I was still alive. I could still feel. Not everything broke down.

There is that Elton John song, "Someone Save My Life Tonight" or something like that... and I didn't need someone... I needed myself.

I pushed myself into the anxiety attack, and I mustered all the strength within to pull myself out.

My mother was not the person who she once was. She was a shell of the person who helped create me.

It dawned on me that if she was able to release the negative energy she once harbored, even though it was due to her deteriorating mental state, and live, then I could do the same.

It was a debilitating and liberating epiphany all at once.

I crashed and rose up all at once.

I shattered and put pieces together instantaneously.

I was my own worst enemy and my hero between heartbeats.

I was prouder of myself than anything or any accomplishment in my life, for I truly saved myself.

I did.

Shattered pieces and all, I was still a hero. I picked myself up and dusted myself off while momentarily dragging myself through the dirt. I had not been okay for a while, but somehow beauty rose out of ashes.

Resiliency was my first name, followed by Not Today and Get Back Up, You're not KO'ed yet.

The angels helped guide me home, whispering all along the way. They sat up above making sure I lived to see tomorrow. And when I walked in the door and caught my glance in the mirror, I did not see faded tears and flushed cheeks. I saw a warrior. I saw a cracked halo. I saw who I was and who I could be. I saw that clinging by a thread meant I was still holding on and tight.

The fight didn't end when my tears started. The river was just flowing in such an uninhibited manner at that point. Yet, I refused to drown. I refused to succumb to the water seeping into the cracks of this boat. I didn't need a life preserver because I can float on my own.

I knew in my heart I would need to stand my ground. I was more powerful than ever. My dreams were just beyond my hand's grasp. And come hell or high water or sleet or rain or ashes… I knew I would not falter.

I was anxiety manifested into hope, and I was not ashamed to step into the light anymore.

I closed my eyes and whispered what I knew the universe was compelling me to say: 'Look out world, for here. I. Come.'

∞ ∞ ∞ ∞ ∞ ∞ ∞ ∞

It was a strange sensation: I wasn't homeless anymore, but I was living with the woman who re-shaped who I could have been if I did not have such a traumatic childhood.

The universe seemed to be working its magic: here I was, back in the house I was thrown out of decades ago, yet the same woman who led to my homelessness is now embodying another consciousness. In this odd twist of events, she was now welcoming me into her home.

It was almost as if my experiences were an infinite loop: every moment would eventually come full circle.

Morena and I continued to build Windows of Opportunity, and she would consistently check in on my mother and me while we worked out of the basement of the house.

My mother would offer snacks while Morena and I were sitting at the table working. It was almost like she was reverting back to my childhood, most likely assuming that I was on a playdate, although the two of us were in the process of changing the world at a dingy kitchen table in College Point.

One day Morena and I heard a knock at the front door. A large letter came in the mail for me and I was unsure of what to think of it.

Morena smiled and prompted me to open it right away.

The letter was addressed to me and had Lincoln Memorial High School's name on it as well.

Upon opening it, I came to the realization that an anonymous person wrote a recommendation letter for the Social Worker of the Year Award for the entire school system.

And by some chance, I won the award.

'How could this happen?' I looked over at Morena partially stunned.

"I don't know," she replied. "Maybe someone saw all of your philanthropic work with youth at Lincoln, and realized that you deserve this."

She winked at me and I had a feeling that somehow she was behind it. Morena never did confess it was her, but deep down inside my soul knew the truth.

'I don't deserve it, Morena.' I dropped the envelope down. 'What have I really done?'

"Maybe it's not all about what you have done, but what the kids created."

'What?'

"I can't tell you how many kids you have saved because of your programs. You may not see it, but deep within you I know it is clear."

I dropped the pen I was holding onto the table in a dramatic fashion.

'What is clear? What did I even do?'

Morena's tone grew more solemn. "You created a literal window of opportunity for these kids: programs, friendships, experiences. Without you, where would they even be?"

I looked up at her. 'I don't even know.'

She glanced at me and smiled. "Think of your dreams," Morena motioned to everything on the table. "What do you want your legacy to be?"

I smiled and thought of my dreams: to find divine love, to expand Windows of Opportunity, to reform educational experiences, to create leaders... the list could have gone on and on.

'There's a lot I want to do.'

Morena placed her fingertips on the envelope and slid it closer to me.

"This is *your* window of opportunity. Take it."

∞ ∞ ∞ ∞ ∞ ∞ ∞ ∞

Within two weeks' time, I was standing outside a banquet hall in the middle of Brooklyn. I brought Morena with me, though she made it clear that this was my night to shine.

The two of us stood outside of the building glancing at cars passing by. I wore a midnight blue button-down shirt and sleek dress pants. I was not sure what the night would entail, but I figured that I needed to dress classy for the event.

Morena could tell I was shaking as we walked closer and closer to the door.

I continued to run my fingers down the front of my hair until she finally pulled me aside.

"Stop," she held her hand in front of me.

'What?' I started fidgeting with my shirt slightly.

"You have to confess something." She motioned for me to stand in front of the mirror.

'I don't understand.'

"Do you ever?"

'No,' I chuckled.

"What do you have to say to yourself?" She pushed me in front of the glass panes surrounding the building and motioned to my reflection.

'Nothing?'

"No," she boomed. "You are earning Social Worker of the Year for a reason. Everyone else can see why, but why can't you?"

'I'm not worthy of it.'

"You preach self-worth like it is gospel, yet when it comes to you, you are silent." She motioned to my reflection again.

'Morena, I-' I turned to her as she placed the palms of her hands towards the sky.

"Place your hands face down and shut your eyes, don't ask questions."

I looked at her and raised an eyebrow, but there was no time to ask questions since the event would be starting soon.

When I slapped my hands on top of hers, it felt like we were transported to another place. A hallowed ringing circulated around in my ears and I suddenly felt at peace. It felt like a pristine white light was glistening overhead.

"Now listen," Morena spoke softly. "What does your soul say?"

I paused a moment, but all I could discern was the resolute silence.

'I don't hear anything.'

"No," she said again. "You aren't listening. What does your soul say?"

I tried to clear my mind, but images of heartbreak and pain flooded my mind. As I started to shake, Morena grabbed my hands tighter.

"Breathe deeper, then say something… anything."

As her words trailed off, I opened my mouth and words finally came out:

'All along, I had been trying to fill in the cracks of my soul with people who were endlessly suspended in hollow emotions. I had hoped they would heal me because I had no idea how to heal myself. I developed a learned helplessness from someone else's instruction manual, because I was too afraid to find my own voice.

'The more I read into another person's set of standards, I realized I didn't fit. I was never going to fit. I could roll through countless sheets and mattresses, over tables and torn couches, but I knew I would never be able to rest until I found the one who I could spend the rest of my life loving and caring for. I needed a sign that there was an ounce of hope left in the world, as long as I could see that what I was searching for isn't always what I was looking for.

'I was searching for the answers to my struggle and hardships in the sunken eyes of broken hearts, and I was always willing to destroy myself and hand the shattered pieces of my heart to someone else so they could pick and choose from my broken pieces… so they could mend themselves while I deteriorated. Not a single person accepted all of me for who I was and who I could be, and I had always settled for less than what I ever deserved.

'There is a certain sensation of loneliness you get when you realized that you've been mistreating the one you've loved all along. The one person you are always with, always thinking about, and the one person you should always do what is best for: that person is yourself.

'In hindsight, I see that so much of what I have done may have been hurting other people, but most of all I was damaging my soul. At many points in my life, I gave up on myself. I looked to other people and said, "Heal me, fix me, fill in the loneliness." Only I was never alone, because I was there for myself.

'I saw the good and the bad times. I saw the suffering and the innate pleasures. I watched pain try to swallow me whole, but I always stood with my soul firmly rooted in the ground. As a tall oak tree towers over the rest, I too have seen the rain, the heartache, and the catastrophe try to burden me. Only I knew deep down inside that nothing could move me or shake me.

'I will always grow from the pain and fight the good fight: not with my fists, but with my words and my soul that has been to and through hell and back.

'Still, I am the tree.

'Still, I have and will overcome adversity.

'And as long as I live and breathe that is my mission: to share my positivity and light with the world… no matter how many try to extinguish my flame.

'I was the answer all along; I was just asking the wrong questions. I am the who, the what, the when, the why, and I believed that those women were my "how." All along, I was the answer to my own soul's questions.

'It just took me years to realize that I had the light within me all along.'

A stale pause filled the air as I waited to see what would happen now that I exposed my soul, my true soul. I shifted my gaze to meet Morena's eyes, which were overflowing with tears. I could see the weight of twenty years fall off her shoulders and crash to the floor. I wrapped my arm around her shoulders and pulled her closer to me. Morena's hands floated to my chest as she rested her forehead above my heart. We were completely parallel to one another, and our hearts and emotions were aligned in that moment.

As her tears dripped cautiously, a calm smirk grew on my face as she wept.

'You do understand,' I began. 'That my soul is finally shedding deep-rooted pain. I am growing.'

She began sobbing even more, and despite her intense tears she did not wince once.

'Why are you crying,' I asked.

"Because after all this time, you woke up."

The last particle of sand in the hourglass dropped at the exact moment her last tear fell. Years of ambitions, hopes, and dreams flowed through my mind. The answers were within me; I just had to listen.

We started walking into the building. Our hands swayed like a pendulum keeping perfect time with the universe. For once, I felt true and honest relief. The world became balanced perfectly under my feet. This was an innate love that superseded Elyza, Gemma, Emma, Faith, Olga, and all of the other souls in between. This was true love, and I could finally admit that the relationship was between me, myself, and I. It's true, they were all beautiful souls in their own way: they helped me piece together the puzzle of who I really became, and they brought me along their own paths before dropping me in a sea of loneliness and forcing me to swim to the safest parcel of land. Each time, I was cast back out into the ocean again, only to have someone else hoist me above water before I grew tired and drowned. Then the cycle would repeat over and over again…

Until now.

Once we walked up to the doors, we were thrust into a large crowd that seemed to have hundreds of people gathered around to see the man of honor enter the room. For once, that man was me.

A shorter man in a crisp black tuxedo zoomed to my side, tugging me down a spiral staircase and into a sea of jovial faces. A cacophony of voices filled the air as I was getting rushed from person to person by some man I had never met. Morena faded somewhere into the background as I lost sight of where she was being relocated to. I could not grab her hand and pull her back in.

"Scott," a mysterious man shouted, "Congratulations! I am so proud of all you accomplished." A symphony of formally dressed men and women were patting me on the back and uttering some form of "Congratulations" as I made my way through the room. I felt heavily underdressed.

As people flew up to me, all I could do was smile and pray that everything would be okay. At one point during my confusion and acceptance congratulatory comments, Morena appeared in front of me, almost masquerading as a stranger for a moment, to pat me on the shoulder and murmur, "This is your moment, go!"

She grinned from ear to ear as I walked past her.

As I went up to accept the award, I turned to Morena who was beaming with pride and purpose. She was standing in the shadows of the bright chandeliers suspended from the ceiling.

Her gaze was unlike anything I had seen before.

Later on, I realized that Morena's stare was not new; rather, I was a renewed soul.

I was finally able to see things through a different set of eyes. My new perspective and I received the award and stepped off stage. Others gathered to obtain their respective awards, so I moved towards the back of the room to find Morena. It was no surprise at all that she seemed to have just disappeared out of thin air.

Though I lingered there for a while to socialize, the questions filling my head were of a higher philosophical nature for a change.

I always considered my thoughts to be insightful and rather bold, but my ambitions were sounding more attainable: education reform was possible, finding my other half was possible, and remaining positive would prove beneficial for Windows of Opportunity.

Despite being in such a jovial state, my lower back continued to throb rapidly.

In hindsight, I realized that this moment must have been my final warning.

In due time I left the banquet hall and found myself resting complacently on the bench outside. My reflection even took on a new persona as I smiled at myself.

When I bowed my head to give thanks to the universe and all of the positive forces brewing within me, I started to murmur to myself:

'God, say your prayers for the lost and lonely. Say your prayers for those battling a war within themselves, yet fighting each day. Say your prayers for those who remain speechless, though there is much left unsaid. Say your prayers for those dying, for those who are deceased. Say a prayer for all of those about to be at peace.'

When I reopened my eyes, Morena was standing directly in front of me. She held out her hand and pulled me off of the bench.

"Congratulations, Mr. Social Worker of the Year," she smiled.

'Thanks,' I replied. As I straightened out my back, I felt the throbbing pain radiate up my spine. My hand instinctively felt out the pain.

"Maybe you should go to a doctor for that?"

'No,' I assured her. 'No, no, I am fine.'

She glanced at me and tilted her head sideways. "Okay then."

'Come on,' I led us down the street. 'Let's go to the diner and talk about future plans.'

The two of us wandered to my car and as I got into the driver's seat, the one question in my mind was: 'What's next?'

Morena picked up my award and ran her fingers along the edge of the wooden plaque.

As she admired it, I felt that she was the one who helped me see what I could manifest and create.

She looked over at me and remarked, "You're going to have to put this in a real important place."

We both laughed for a moment and I felt that both of our souls were suddenly elevated. Although Morena seemed like she was not real, and at times appeared to be a figment of my imagination with regard to how quickly she vanished into the shadows, like tonight, I accepted that some of life's mysteries are just meant to be that way.

∞ ∞ ∞ ∞ ∞ ∞ ∞ ∞

After a night of walking by the Brooklyn Bridge and grabbing a bite to eat, I didn't remember precisely how I got home.

When I woke up, I saw Morena in my mother's kitchen making both of us breakfast. The sheet clung to my body as the warmth of the sun slid through the window.

'What happened last night,' I looked at Morena quizzically. I reached for the teacup and sipped gently.

"You finally woke up," she remarked.

Tea shot from my mouth as a smile formed on her exhausted face. A breathy chuckle and sigh escaped her mouth.

Morena looked like she was holding something back. Something huge.

'What are you thinking, Mo?'

"It's nothing important," she broke her steady gaze as her eyes darted to the window.

'Seriously. What?'

"I said it was nothing."

'Mo-'

We paused and she twisted her body towards mine. A sentence fluttered through her teeth and slammed me right in the chest: "What do you want Scott? What do you really, really want?"

We sat parallel to each other on the couch, mirroring a semblance of urgency and compassion.

877

Every waking thought led to this moment. To this second. To this ounce of hope dwindling in the shadows. Maybe my dreams were foreshadowing something major. Maybe all of these years of questions and ambitions were leading to something completely outrageous and exciting.

"What?" Morena tilted her head and stirred her cup of hot cocoa that was sitting on the table.

'Mo,' I remarked. 'I want to be president.'

"That's a pretty bold statement, Scott." She did not sound surprised.

'I know, but we have so many thoughts about leadership, why not take it to the next level?'

The two of us began to talk about the leadership concepts Windows of Opportunity has been preaching for years. Our insight was our gospel and leadership was our religion.

It is clear that children show us the dysfunction of America. They are the next generation of leaders and revolutionary thinkers who could truly set a new standard for themselves and the universe.

We are doing revolutionary, missionary work. We are the ones we are waiting for. We are the frontlines and the ones who are going to determine what our nation will become. We have to have the hard conversations that may cause plenty of debates, but our words are necessary in order to create monumental changes within our society.

'I need our community to have my back so I can have theirs,' I told Morena.

"Well," she started. "Let's fight for a higher cause and the universe will work itself out. Speak about truth to power."

I reached over to my bag and started to pull out our curriculums and empty notebooks.

'It is time to fight for our planet. To fight back for it. We must fight for our lives. Our individual lives so we can find our individual light. Life loves us. The Universe loves us. So many souls love us. In that exchange of love, we can love the planet back.

Love must be reciprocated.'

Every breath we take, every smidge of food we put into our bodies, enables an infinite amount of opportunities for ourselves and for our planet to thrive. Mutual energy that creates an existence that propels a connection that supports growth, peace, love, and harmony. Together that love storm can accomplish anything, can fight anything, and can transform that energy into everything in this universe.

When you dream of a flame you hope to manifest in the universe, it is possible to make a political vision come true. It could transform the planet.

We are here.

From the birth of this vision, an exponential development of positivity and light will emulate throughout the world.

People do not understand the special vision that exists in society until they live it themselves. They must experience the power deep within them, although there could be moments where they can be brought to their knees.

However, our lives are composed of moments: some beautiful and some that need to be flushed out.

Make every moment count.

Make every second matter.

Every solitary instance is a chance to live.

Frederick Douglass said, *"Education makes you unfit to be a slave."* Currently, we are slaves to the economy, slaves due to a lack of spiritualism, and slaves to a complex world.

We must rise above and build: the pipeline from education to leadership is here. Upon soul-searching and discovering what exists within you, you can find your empowerment as well.

"The time to stand for a higher consciousness is now," Morena's words cut through my train of thought.

'We must close the gap of negative attitudes,' I replied.

My mother wandered through the kitchen and sat down in front of the newspaper.

"Scott," she clamored. "Did you eat breakfast? I made breakfast!"

I was reminded of her mental state and how fragile our souls innately are. Her experience created negative manifestations in my life, but that did not mean I was going to deny myself a beautiful life to be lived.

At that moment, I realized we are all living proof that it is not just another day. Today, every day, is the day to become something or someone positive: individually, we are beautiful creations, and together we can all become a force to be reckoned with.

We must rise up.

Social emotional learning was just a concept, but it is inherent in our souls. We all have it brewing inside us, and we must tap into that energy.

It is not just about education reform, it is about transforming the world.

All of us have potential to learn.

Teachers do not *teach* a subject for a living, they *teach* children.

We can all be teachers of society.

We need curriculums that speak directly to youth; the curriculum has to connect to youth in living color. Their life must be in the heart of the issue. They must see themselves in the work they do. It must be culturally competent and relevant.

Learning must be relevant and responsive to our youth.

Youth are brilliant, but they need the environment to thrive. You need credibility to connect to youth. You must earn it. It doesn't come with a title. You must engage. You must be real. You must bring equity to your classroom and into your life.

You must meet people where they are.

You meet them where they are and pour your soul into their moment, then they will evolve: they will peel back their layers of pain as they realize they are extraordinary. They are impacted by society and situations.

How do we blame them for that? Adults are the same.

We have to close the gap between empowerment and hopelessness; that's how youth, and ultimately society, achieve greatness and excellence.

At this point, Morena and I had all of our papers across the table and were mapping out our framework for education.

It's not about the test grades, it's about whether youth want "it" or not. That "it" can be absolutely anything. The passion burning inside of us for what we wish to create and manifest; that's where the change happens for all of us.

It's in the desire, not the actual grades, it happens as a by-product of soul connections and wanting to enact change.

Live these ideas and the data will come.

"Let's build this framework and it will happen," Morena remarked.

Get excited about connection and learning, and if it means something to you, then you will see change.

With excitement brewing in my veins, I gleefully shouted: 'We must be excited for the future in order for transformation to happen now.'

She folded her left leg under her body and leaned closer to the papers as she said, "We must stand on the shoulders of real history. We have to carry the greatness of our country and educators, within schools and within society; they must have the will to be amazing at their craft. It must be about the vision."

Are you a superstar?

Do you want to be a superstar?

You have to be the best version of yourself every single day, second to none.

It's not an ego trip; rather it is a mindset.

The world becomes better because of how we lead.

What mission do you have in life?

What is your mission statement?

This isn't a job. It's not a career.

This is a spiritual mission.

How are you responding to the universe?

What is your role in it?

Do you realize that you matter? For you truly, truly do.

We all do and we are all here.

We have a responsibility to lift one another up, now and always.

Staring off into the distance, you'll see the path in the darkness. You'll see whatever and whoever you need to be or see in that moment.

God gives you whatever you could handle and people don't get that. They think: Why can't I win something nice for once or have something nice for once? You can't get it because you are so much better than that.

You are given what you can handle.

Why can't I have something once that says here: you can handle it? It won't be what you truly deserve... it is like a scrap drawing versus the Mona Lisa or something.

Get what you deserve. Earn it.

While flushing all of this out with Morena, she remarked, "I know you wish you had something decent, someone decent, but it is not a competition."

I had to start truly transcending the man I was. I had to strengthen the bond I had with those who helped me develop.

Naturally, I called Faith and asked her if she would meet up with me as friends.

∞ ∞ ∞ ∞ ∞ ∞ ∞ ∞

The two of us met at a restaurant close to where I worked for a quick bite to eat. Faith seemed genuinely happy to meet me, and we discussed our spiritual friendship.

"The bond we have as friends is truly unique," Faith smiled.

'It's higher consciousness,' I remarked.

"Higher consciousness," she repeated. "I like it."

We had a fulfilling conversation about her new relationships, her children, and all of her plans for her blossoming cleaning business.

'I am so proud that you have been able to grow so much in such a short time.'

"Short time? It's been years and years."

We both grinned at each other sincerely.

'It has been, and we have respectively grown so much over the years.'

"I agree," Faith seemed as if a weight was lifted off of her shoulders. "I agree."

As we walked down the bustling city street, my eye caught a glimpse of curtains rustling in the wind. Faith's words began fading at that point and I felt a tinge of the past over my shoulder. The burden of a past love clung to my spine with such a strong gravitational force.

A scene was materializing over my shoulders: four years ago flooded my mind as I watched the ghosts of a misplaced love echo through the wind. Memories melted into reality as I distanced myself from Faith. I was captured by the naturalistic sway of the billowing curtains.

Two pristine drapes whipped around the French doors of a bar: a scene so familiar to a former version of the man I could have become. Breaking away from Faith, I saw an empty table along the back of a bar. A solitary photograph etched in time reminded me of an era when Emma and I were at that very table. The landscape painted itself before me: her co-workers mingling and moving along while we sat engulfed in each other's exquisite beauty. Her smile and laughter were almost a solid reality, yet I knew that in this present timeline, she was gone.

She was a mere apparition clinging to what is left of my shattered feelings towards her. My heart sunk as I saw our scene play out before me... her twirling her hair and leaning into my every whim. The scene was a magical reminder of who she once was and who she never could become.

In a sense, this was her living funeral: the empty table in the present-day image before me was a solemn reminder that she put the nail in her own coffin. Miraculously, she even buried herself: she was that stern in her rejection of our love ever manifesting into more than just a six-month speck on the saga that would be her life.

She meant so much more to me than I did to her. Yet in realizing all of this, the stinging loneliness that once filled my heart when I saw a place where we once stood became enriched with utter hope and devout blessings: it is night and day compared to where my soul now rests its head.

Faith's words grew louder as I re-entered this atmosphere.

"And so I said that all you need to do is just try harder..." her words carried no merit to the expansion of my soul at that moment.

Her words, like dust, settled somewhere in the vacant recess of my mind. I could not process Faith's ramblings while engaging in such a powerful memory. Though in some juxtaposed revelation, it was me who chose Faith over Emma, then decided to go back to Emma, then ran to the arms of Faith and found a stern friendship... and here I am again on this merry-go-round of fleeting adoration: I find myself trapped in the memory of mine and Emma's first passionate evening together...

But that is just what it is: a memory casting its shadows four years too late. That is when I realized saying goodbye was okay.

Saying adios y vaya con dios to Faith would not be in vain. Saying it is just another day would fade into the gossamer corners of my mind. Today would not be just another day.

Today would be the day: the day I discovered that like our love, like the empty table in the bar, memories would fade into the sunset or dance majestically into the wind. Memories would sink into a realm where we could say, "We were here, we made these memories."

And all at once, a rush washed over me: the closure I deserved wrapped itself around my once heaving frame.

The tears dried. The sullen sensation no longer weighed heavy on my soul.

"And what is the deal with lotion anyway, I mean, how many different bottles can advertise silky smooth skin..." Faith's words knocked at my mind, but I would not let them in.

'It is okay,' I whispered just beyond comprehension.

Glaring into the bar I could see Emma's frame fade away. I could sense the past versions of our souls pulling apart and being just that: the past.

The present is now; the future is coming.

There would be no more pain or tears of prevalent sadness flooding my eyes due to a sense of departed longing.

No.

I had everything and anything I needed before me. My eyes finally had the appropriate lens to visualize all I had all along: the strength and love within.

I had the greatest love of all before me. I had the passion, ambition, and stamina at my fingertips.

In that epiphany laced moment, I came to a revelation that-

"Are you even listening, Scott?" Faith tapped her foot in a manner that snapped me back into reality.

"Scott," she quipped, "What is with you?"

A waitress dragged her cloth along the empty table in the bar. The wind died down and dropped the curtains to their resting place.

'What,' I was confused where the last 10 minutes went.

"Scott, you need to listen and pay attention more."

Faith marched forward in her driven state of mind. She ignored my momentary pause outside the bar, for she did not know what reality had just materialized before her...

I was a growing soul with the same respect as the lives that graced my presence.

I walked us back to the car as the street faded to a distant sunset caught in the balance of yesterday and tomorrow.

∞ ∞ ∞ ∞ ∞ ∞ ∞ ∞

Morena and I continued to work in the fading hours of the day. We were working tirelessly on building the framework that we often worked past the moments when dew would form just outside the window.

I continued to feel my lower back pain get worse, but I figured that I had to take care of the framework and the future before whatever was ailing me.

The two of us began talking about my past.

We looked at all of my experiences in terms of moments of growth.

'I still believe in divine love,' I told Morena.

"Oh yeah," she smirked. "Well, what is love anyway?"

I turned to her and felt a wave of insight wash over me:

'Love is a drastically dangerous weapon. One moment you think you are enamored by the soul before you, dripping passion and beauty in its most raw form. The next moment, that love you feel stabs you in the back through silent pangs of sunlight that creeps over the daybreak.'

"How insightful," she remarked.

'It is a sinking, devastating feeling... but somehow you lurch forward and try your hardest to keep loving despite having a broken heart. Then you meet another soul you truly connect with. You find someone whose eyes beckon you to bridge the gap between everything you have been through and what you realize you had to deal with in order to get here. You find home within their very soul and comfort in their tender arms. Then it happens again: fate rears its head and twists your soul into a wrought pit of desolation: the love leaves you. Once again, you are homeless.'

Morena dropped the papers in front of her and appeared to be moved by my words.

'You are saddened by the love you thought you had, but lost. Everything and anything seems impossible because the one you thought you adored was a fallacy of epic proportions. You walk the streets alone and seemingly hopeless until you prepare yourself to repeat the cycle again: find love, fall in love... and crash. Crash and burn so deeply and so violently at the feet of someone you thought you loved dearly... and you adorn a mask once again, teardrops straining to inch from your eyelids between moments of desperation: Does anyone love me? Am I ever going to be enough for anyone? Then you look up into the eyes of something or someone who you think could be your home... knowing full and well that you are just steps away from the night crawling into your skin and sucking your heart dry. It is painstaking agony, the act of love. Then one day the mask finally shatters on the floor and you have to face your own reflection in the raindrops before you... what do you do? Well, what... tell me.'

Morena glared into my tear-filled eyes: "You move, and you make a new home. Your real home eventually shows itself in how it genuinely puts your mind at ease. You don't have to run anymore... because you succumb to the comforts of a true soul."

'When,' I shouted at her, 'When does that happen!'

"You'll know," she whispered, "You will know."

We continued to shuffle through papers, until she found something about a peace conference within her pile.

"Hey," she held up the flier. "What's this?"

'Oh,' I looked up and snatched the paper from her hand. 'It's some conference they run every year.'

She looked intrigued. "Who are they?"

'The professional meditation organization I worked with years ago. They were there when I started looking into financial grants for Windows of Opportunity years ago.'

"We should go," Morena said nonchalantly.

'Go? It's always at some rather out-there place.'

"Well, let me look it up," she opened up her computer. "Where is it this year?"

'Who knows, we have work to do.' I continued to shuffle through papers.

She squinted at the screen. "It's on Martha's Vineyard."

'Where's that?'

"Massachusetts," she quipped back. "It is beautiful there."

'Great,' I replied. 'We have work to do. What would we even do at a peace conference?'

"It is a different perspective that we may need for our programs," she paused for a moment to wait for my response. "Come on, Scott. It's a few weeks away and we can talk about the framework there!"

'I don't know, Morena, how do we even get to Martha's Vineyard.'?

She shifted the computer and already had a map in front of us.

"We can take a train and a few buses and a ferry-"

I cut her off. 'Great, we go on some grand amalgamation transportation journey.'

"Ha. That rhymes," she chuckled. "Or we drive up."

'Drive? Why are you so keen on going?'

She seemed to look for a reason. "Because."

'Oh, because, that's a great reason!'

"Just," she seemed frustrated. "Let's go."

Since she was so steadfast in having us go to the conference, I told her that we could go as long as we brought the framework with us. Morena agreed with a devious smile and I squinted at the sight of her sudden jubilation.

'What's that look?'

"Nothing," she spoke nonchalantly. "Absolutely nothing."

Little did I know, Morena must have known what was waiting for me at the conference.

∞ ∞ ∞ ∞ ∞ ∞ ∞ ∞

Days passed and before I could even blink, we were five hours into a road trip to the state of Massachusetts.

Morena sat quietly on the way up, glaring out the window at the lush greenery on the highway. Spring was in full effect and she did not seem to want to miss a moment of its beauty.

We talked about the framework here and there, but she appeared to want to just bask in the glory that was nature. After all, nature is a stunning part of our lives. We must appreciate and give our thanks to what the universe has bestowed upon this planet, for it was created without our afflictions and long before humans materialized on the planet.

The ferry to Martha's Vineyard required that we store the car at a commuter lot in Woods Hole, Massachusetts. It was a quaint town that boasted its oceanic center and delicious food.

On the ferry over, Morena disappeared into the crowd on the boat. I figured that she was enjoying the wind rushing through her hair on the top deck of the boat.

I sat with my arms leaning on the railing, gazing out into the Atlantic Ocean.

The chapter that was the church slammed shut, and all that remained was the hope that the peace conference I would be attending in just a few days on Martha's Vineyard would provide some semblance of transformational guidance.

Things just had to go up from here.

They have to.

When we arrived on the island of Martha's Vineyard, the building where the peace conference was seemed a lot closer than I imagined it would be. It was a beautiful building with ornate architecture and such a breathtaking view.

People were walking around and socializing, and before we all knew it, leaders from around the globe managed to find each other on this stunning island.

Hours were passing before us, but time stood still in the room where peaceful meditative activities were transcending the hearts, minds, and souls of the people there.

As we all spoke in small groups, I looked across the room at someone who seemed captivated by my presence.

Her whimsical nature captured every last crevice of my soul. A sense of belonging filled every broken piece of me in a manner I never truly fathomed before this moment. Her hair swayed rhythmically to every passing heartbeat that radiated through my core. She had a smile that only angels could concoct with their harmonious ways. She was not real. She could not be.

This angelic figure had to be yet another figment of my imagination manifesting before my very weary eyes.

The figure glanced at me and my heart melted. My soul erupted in a melodic sigh of "at last," for I realized that this beauty before me was real.

She existed.

She was not a figment of any imagination or any realm: she was grace, poise, and elegance wrapped up in a solitary human being.

She was what I had been looking for, not searching for.

My mind was confused beyond any comprehensible notion, for her energy could never be duplicated or felt the same, synergistic way ever again. With the curling motion of her pointer finger, I shot across the room as if I were on a string, tied mercilessly to her heartstrings.

"I have been trying to get you close to me all day," she spoke in breathy, hushed tones.

I sat motionless. I could feel the presence of the universe around me, smiling: her resolute grin... reminding me that I had a life left to live. Her aura escalated and permeated the room.

"I'm Layne, and you are?" A sense of anticipation hung on her lips as she leaned in closer to my gravitational energy.

'Scott,' a smile crept along my face, 'I'm Scott.'

My life would never be the same.

CHAPTER 41

You Gave Me Her

~

"Take your time, don't live too fast. Troubles will come and they will pass. You'll find a woman and you'll find love. And don't forget that there is a someone up above... All that you need now is in your soul... Don't you worry. You'll find yourself. Follow your heart. And nothing else. And be a simple kind of man. Be something you love and understand."

- Lynyrd Skynyrd, Southern Rock Band, Jacksonville, Florida

Within an instant, our souls collided.

When I looked into her jade eyes, it was as if the entire universe grabbed me by the shoulders and said, "Stop searching, because she is the one."

No one else mattered.

Nothing else mattered.

The years upon years of misery and impatience were symbols that someone greater than I could have ever imagined would walk into my life. Her presence was strong enough to entice me from across a crowded room of people. It was an energy and a vibrancy that no other human being had ever provided me.

In an instant, everything suddenly made sense. I finally had an answer to all of the questions that were once lingering in my soul. I had a finite sense that there are people out in the world whose souls can burn just as bright and in tandem with yours. The sun's bright potential would not shine with nearly enough fortitude now, for her undying beauty and brilliance eclipses utterly anything that could be produced in the universe.

Every solitary question that once flooded my head manifested into a sign. Her aura was not one to be trifled with or touched, for it was the penultimate experience to compliment a soul who was in the process of developing the most optimal form of higher consciousness.

Each breath that flowed from her mouth was significant; for it meant that she was bound to move a step closer to breathing life into the world's consummate healing aura. As the two of us spoke for the first physical time in this realm, it seemed as if we had met a thousand times before. The passion and energy from both of us combined was reminiscent of lifetimes of budding, building, and blooming into the most decadent roses to grace this universe.

When we looked at each other, it seemed like the two of us were rekindling an old flame that existed throughout the permeable course of history. In this lifetime, however, it just took a little bit longer for the two of us to find each other. Still, we were the chosen ones. We were expected to converge upon each other at a specific point in time: the moment when both of our souls were undeniably ready to enact change in this universe.

The progressive, passionate, and monumental changes were about to grace this world with the necessary amount of energy to substantiate comprehensible action within the universe.

Combined, we would light up the world.

Together, we could construct previously unimaginable enlightenment for ourselves, and the respective souls in this universe.

For years upon years, I was asking all of the questions that would lead me to her.

Days would pass in my own world; my soul would wallow in enough agony and challenges that would shape the man I would become. Everything in the world had to be just right. Everything had to be just perfect so that once the two of us rightfully found one another, we would be able to spark the revolutionary shifts needed to elevate our planet.

We had to respectively evolve before the two of us could revolutionize the universe cosmically manifesting before us. Individually, we had to align our souls so that once our respective souls met again, this time we would get it right. This time we would take the innate experiences from centuries of walking this Earth in order to create. Moments that would develop our pioneering sensibilities had to come before us, so that we could utilize the aftermath to grow this universe.

It was a matter of finding the appropriate sensations: two people needed to endure and overcome aspects of their respective journeys, so that the world would be able to heal.

We healed so that we could harbor the strength to inspire positivity and purpose.

Although my soul was suddenly soothed in her presence, it burned with the fervor to comprehend that I finally found the one.

I finally found her.

"You have a story to tell, I am sure of it," Layne spoke in a manner that enticed me. I always stood behind the philosophy that everyone has a story behind their story, and here she was: asking me about who I was.

I wanted to hear about her story. I wanted to know each and every aspect of who she was: Where did she come from? How did she find me at the right moment? Why did it take her so long to discover me?

I guess the last question is, in a sense, a moot point. She was traveling on her own journey so that once the timing was right; we would know that we found each other.

And we should never let go.

My mind faded back into the conversation.

893

'My story? What about yours?'

Picturesque memories of her life seemed to flash before my eyes. She began to tell me bits and pieces of who she was and what she was building.

"I am a writer," she pulled a notebook from her bag and dropped it on the table. "It's always been my dream to get published, but I haven't gone anywhere."

'Why not?'

Layne shrugged, "I think I have good ideas, but I have a feeling it isn't my time yet. I came here today to meet my favorite author, he was supposed to be here at this conference, but he cancelled at the last minute. That's just my luck."

My heart was palpitating, but it was not out of panic: it was a sense of sheer admiration. She would be the window of opportunity that beckoned my soul to reach its utmost level of higher love.

"Where do you come from?"

'New York.'

"That's exciting," she leaned towards me and grabbed my hand. "I have always wanted to see New York. Tell me, is it as wonderful as they say it is?"

I looked down at our adjoined hands, which tingled with promise. 'It's magical.'

As I glanced up at her, we locked eyes and practically said, "I know you," but without our words.

Our souls were speaking to one another in a manner that transcended all of the idle chatter dancing about the room.

The energy between us beckoned me to dig deeper into the seemingly instant connection we appeared to have.

"I am from Martha's Vineyard."

'That's exciting.'

"That's exciting? It's a rather small place."

'It is beautiful,' we locked eyes again. I paused. 'The island.'

"We are a few hundred miles from New York, you know."

'Oh yeah, the drive up here was beautiful.'

"I am sure of it. I heard the foliage along the highway is gorgeous."

Though it seemed like we were engaging in somewhat nonchalant chitchat, every word she spoke carried a purpose. She did not waste her breath on anything that did not carry the weight of her passion.

'This author that you were following here, is he someone I may know of?'

"I don't think so. He was a local here on Martha's Vineyard for years until his books became incredibly popular. I was hoping that I could talk to him and see how he managed to get his writing out there for the world to see."

'That's exciting.'

A breathy laugh escaped her lips. "Do you think everything I say is exciting?"

Instinctively, my soul responded: 'Yes.'

We both chuckled and leaned closer to each other. Eyes around the room seemed to be entranced by our energy.

"I hope I am not being too forward in saying this, but it feels like I have known you forever, Scott Matheson."

'It feels like I have known you forever too, Layne-' I struggled to search my mind for her last name.

"Don't worry," she smiled. "We didn't exchange last names, I read your name badge."

'Oh,' I laughed. 'I wasn't worrying.'

"I know." A pause allowed us to collect our respective thoughts before we dove deeper into who we were.

Individually, the two of us were attempting to restructure systems; she aimed to write about shifting systems and what the world was truly about below the surface. I shared I was working on education while she explained she wanted to overhaul every system imaginable through her words and insight.

"Surprisingly, I did not consider the education system," she began. "I am largely self-taught. I needed to get a full-time job to support my father and my younger sister. I would buy old textbooks from college bookstores and teach myself. I would sit and rewrite the pages for days in between serving tables at an Italian restaurant."

'You are self-taught? That does not surprise me.'

We smiled again. Being innately happy was not difficult to do around her. Actually, it was an invigorating feeling. She was indifferent to the past I endured. Rather, she made an effort to learn about my experiences.

"I want to know all about you."

'What's there to know?'

"Everything."

'Everything?'

The two of us were tasked with presenting our thoughts about peacefulness. The activity required that we write out our ideas on a massive piece of chart paper and talk about it with other people in the room.

As the two of us discussed our insight, all eyes were on us.

The flow of energy between us took on a synergistic light: it was almost as if we always collaborated on projects together.

Once the two of us moved off to the side of the room, I felt my cell phone vibrate in my pocket.

'I don't know how much time you have.'

"Time is irrelevant when you create a soul connection."

She felt it too.

My cell phone vibrated in my pocket again.

I was trying to stay consumed by her energy, but the third phone call piqued my interest.

Rebecca was calling and needed me to come home. Our mother was throwing a tantrum and she didn't know what to do.

For some reason, the universe was pulling me away from Layne for a temporary interlude. However, our intricate melody had just begun.

I found myself missing her presence the moment we physically stepped away from each other.

"Until we meet again, Scott Matheson."

Her eyes clung to me until I left the room.

I walked outside and found Morena alone with her thoughts.

'What are you doing?'

She looked up. "What?"

'You missed her!'

"Her who?"

'Layne.'

"Is she the woman who was watching you from across the room practically all day?"

'You saw her looking at me? Why didn't you say anything?'

"I don't know. I didn't want to interfere."

'With what?'

She quipped back, "What?"

'Why are you so weird?'

"It is who I am." She extended her arms and plopped down on the curb next to a stunning patch of sunflowers.

I bent down next to her and told her about my mother and how we reluctantly had to leave.

The two of us walked back to the dock to catch the ferry.

A familiar voice cut through the crowd.

"Scott!"

I pivoted to see Layne dashing up the path.

'Hey stranger, I haven't seen you in so long.'

She chuckled and put her hand on my shoulder as she adjusted her high heels.

'I want you to meet-' I turned around to introduce Morena, but she had vanished.

How typical.

"Meet who?" She looked past my shoulder at the apparition of the woman who managed to be more mysterious than the woman before me.

'Nevermind, I guess.'

"Okay," she looked up at me. "Sorry to chase after you. I didn't give you my business card."

It was a stunning picture of her with her information plastered along the edges of the card. I handed her my card in return.

'It's a bit lackluster, but you can't really compete with such a perfect picture.'

She giggled. "You're too kind."

We parted ways and I heard her heels click as she receded from the wooden planks of the dock.

I found Morena sitting against the railing of the boat looking out into the water.

'Why do you keep disappearing like that?'

"Some things are better unseen than seen."

I rolled my eyes as the ferry's horn sounded in anticipation of our departure.

Once we made it back to the car, we had a grueling five-hour car ride back to New York. The entire time, I could not stop thinking of

Layne. Something drew my soul to hers, and I was destined to find out what it was.

∞ ∞ ∞ ∞ ∞ ∞ ∞ ∞

Walking out of the car, I felt a finite sense of peace. I think it was peace of mind, yet when I crawled onto the couch and shut my eyes, all I could see was a silhouette of her figure laying next to mine.

Was she really there?

Did she exist?

I reached out to grasp her but realized her image was a farce.

She faded into the darkness like she did hours earlier. I could not make sense of Layne, even in the slightest bit.

With my mother out cold for the time being, I got dressed again and left.

I started driving around as thoughts of the past weekend pounded through my mind. I needed to think. I was utterly confused and conflicted and I did not know which way to turn.

I drove aimlessly as questions flooded my mind. Global leadership, the planet, purpose, and profit were on the forefront of my every move.

My car squealed as it approached Francis Lewis Park. I had to get some clarity since I was fearful of falling back into the same dreaded routine. This time, I did not want my heart shattered to pieces. After all, it was already decimated more times than I could count.

The bridge was illuminated in its sparkling blue, yellow, and red lights. A calming sensation washed over my body as I perched myself upon the dimly lit benches. As I inhaled and exhaled repeatedly, I began to whisper my gratitude into the universe. Everything and anything I could be grateful for escaped my pursed lips.

I was not sure exactly what happened, but I needed to just talk.

My connection with the universe appeared to have brought me to the conference and welcomed Layne into my life at a quintessential moment.

When I actually sat down and thought about it, it was a combination of the universe and Morena who brought me to that conference. She was the one who pushed for us to go there.

It is yet another example of why she seemed too good to be real. Morena is number one on my gratitude list; without her unconditional and insane compassion for who I am, I doubt I would have made it this far in life.

"Some things are better unseen than seen;" Morena's words rang throughout my head.

There is power in alignment. There is a certain intrigue in seeing someone from across a crowded room and suddenly recognizing their soul.

The lyrics to Bayside's "Landing Feet First" began making sense to me:

"I hope you weren't waiting long
I hope this night makes up for time lost
Feels like I met you years ago
And we're picking up right where we left off."

The sensation was truly uncanny.

We made each other laugh in a manner that was both infectious and made my soul smile. Parts of me wanted to write to her and say:

"From the moment I laid eyes on you, I haven't stopped thinking about you. Your face, your eyes, your beautiful heart. You inspired a light to shine within me, when I didn't think it was ever possible to see that light shine again. Only it isn't just shining... it is gleaming. It is beaming. It is brighter than I had ever imagined. It is all because of you.

When our eyes met, my soul's prayers were finally answered. With every word that flowed out of my mouth, you became the rhyme and the reason. My entire world was in alignment for the first time in my entire life. I had gone through fire and fury just to find you. I would survive through all of my struggles and sacrifices an infinite number of times if it just meant to see you smile at the end of my journey through it all.

You came in just when I was losing hope and faith. You are a miracle embodied in perfect harmony... yet you are miles away."

I deleted the message from my phone upon reading it over again. After the intense pain I went through with Emma, I could not fathom feeling such desolation again.

I had to wait.

Out of necessity, I needed to ensure my soul would not be smashed to bits once again. Adversely, her soul could not be harmed either.

She is too precious of a beautiful being to endure absolutely anything I experienced. Then again, I didn't fully know her past at that point: she could have been living a similar timeline to mine, and as a result, we found each other.

I thanked the Circle of Angels for the blessings bestowed upon me and stood up. My drive home to College Point was oddly soothing, and by the time I made it into the house, the sunrise painted the sky with vivid and monochromatic hues.

A new day had come, literally.

∞ ∞ ∞ ∞ ∞ ∞ ∞ ∞

I must have passed out on the couch, for although it seemed like I blinked, I imagined Morena was driving along a cobblestone-paved road somewhere in Massachusetts.

Angels were circling our car, singing something while floating around us. Morena stopped for a moment and opened the window. An angel reached in and grabbed my face, and told Morena to drive.

It started raining and Layne got into the car. We had to go find someone and bring them somewhere. We drove for a while talking about random things, until Layne turned to Morena and said, "Does he know?"

I responded, "Does he know what?" I glanced at Morena and then looked into Layne's eyes.

She whispered, "Your secret is safe with me" and winked.

I didn't know what she meant by that. The radio came on and the angels started circling the car faster. They kept saying, "wake up, wake up, wake up."

So, I did.

∞ ∞ ∞ ∞ ∞ ∞ ∞ ∞

The moment Rebecca came in from work, I rushed to Alley Pond Park.

For a while I sat with my back against the fence glaring out into the lush greenery in front of me. I tried imagining what life would have been if my aunt hadn't left me.

How do you go from being on top of the world to being cut down within a simultaneous swoop?

It is painstaking. It is agonizing to lose someone… yet it is virtually healing. Through loss, an angel is gained. Through sacrifice comes unwavering liberation. Between the pangs of our rapidly beating hearts, there is peace.

There is a moment to begin again - a split second to reflect on the air you consume and the negativity you dispel.

It is a feeling far beyond gratitude: you are built up and broken so you may grow again.

Glow sticks are merely chemical-filled tubes until they are snapped and shaken. Once broken, they are not destroyed, for rather they are given the opportunity to provide a soft light. The neon coloration fills the air with hope and promise that you, too, can be broken and shine even brighter than anyone could imagine. That is the beauty of pain: as we rebound, we develop our renewed foundation.

We lay the bricks and reconstruct our souls.

We have the power to shift the universe based on how we lose and how we enhance each other's spiritual journey.

After all, the beauty of life can be found in the darkest corners of the world: it is just a matter of creating your own light to obscure the past and illuminate the present.

Morena appeared at the picnic bench in the blink of an eye. I didn't even see her arrive or walk over.

"Why are you sitting on the ground, Scott?"

'I don't know.'

"You are deep in thought; you are downloading some sort of message… I see it. I feel it."

'I don't know how to tap into this part of my soul,' I told her. 'All I know is a layer has been ripped wide open; exposing my awareness to a realm of my soul I wasn't aware existed. The alignment, the energy, the connection, was beyond real.'

Morena looked at me and rolled her eyes.

'What?'

"I despise that the limited words of our English language cannot capture the right sensation."

'I guess you're right,' I stood up and leaned against the fence. 'It was magical, compassionate, synergistic. It was like two lost souls found each other and instantly went back to work together.'

"From what you are saying, it seems like she echoed that sentiment."

'You know,' the two of us started walking up the path. 'I trust the universe. It brought me her.'

I could not help but wonder if my mind was playing tricks on me:

Did I imagine all of this?

What was I missing?

I felt lost.

It seemed like I was on the verge of feeling love again, but how was it possible to find such a rare soul like the one I found in Layne?

This was not an accident.

It felt good to be genuinely and holistically happy for a change. Though I was in the process of growing my soul, and I knew that a person alone does not make you happy, something about her was mesmerizing.

In the days that followed, Layne did not text me. She appeared to have been too busy creating something powerful, which, in hindsight, was phenomenal.

When Layne puts her mind to something, her soul and heart follow in such an exponentially groundbreaking way.

Morena and I ruminated on the connection I had with Layne.

"I see it, I saw her. She acknowledges your soul," Morena spoke as if she was speaking a prophecy.

'Have you ever traveled somewhere and never wanted to return? That is what life feels without her now.'

Morena tilted her head and chuckled.

'What?'

"Patience, dearie. Have patience."

As the dull, mundane normalcy seeped into my day, it appeared that life without Layne was beckoning me to re-think my daily habits.

I would go to work, help the youth develop insight into the world around them, then retreat to my mother's house where Morena and I would collaborate on shifting the education system.

Each night I would dream of the woman who resurrected parts of me that I never knew existed.

In this dream, I sat in the car next to Bryan. He was trying to say something to me, but I abruptly silenced him. I knew the two of us should have sped away from the scene, but a storm was encircling us.

It was too intense and visceral not to watch it.

We were right in its path.

As a cyclone crept inches closer to my car, I turned to see if we could outrun it. It was a total loss.

The storm ripped through the car and I could feel my entire body convulsing. The vibrations were beautiful, yet tragic at the same time.

I wondered what was happening to my body, both in the physical and emotional senses.

I woke suddenly from the nightmare, only to realize that I was suspended in time. The night air hung my soul out to dry, and I wasn't able to process what had just happened, what I felt, and what was real.

Looking to my right, I saw the wallpaper peeling as it always does. To my left, a faint ghost of who I was merely 10 days ago.

Everything seemed so raw.

My lips were arid and stiff.

I grasped at the water on the table and toppled it over in my nauseated state. The clinking noises startled me and I jumped up.

The neon glow from the clock burst forward 3:15 A.M.

One more hour of sleep… would it be sleep?

Would I just toss and turn while thinking of her?

This loss could be the end.

Yeah, I get it; I was being dramatic.

I was not speaking about the death of me; I mean the death of my soul. She was extremely close and she was right there.

How do you go from lost to found to lost again?

How did she manage, like water, to slip through my fingers?

Maybe she is just as fluid as I am: having to constantly change with the ebb and flow of the tide.

Maybe she, like Morena, is just a ghost of a manifestation of my hopes, dreams, and fear wrapped up in one. Yet, Morena said she saw her… do ghosts see ghosts?

Layne is real, and I didn't know how or why, but I was drawn to her existence. She was the Massachusetts version of me.

903

At the time I wondered: Does she remember I exist?

Does she lay awake at 3:15 A.M. thinking of me, too?

"Once changed, never the same," rattles around in my head, bouncing between my eyes like a basketball... and the weight feels just as severe.

I prayed to the universe: 'Layne, if you can feel this vibration reverberating through your body, hear my prayer: Come home. Come back to me.'

My eyes drooped again and my head hit the pillow with a resounding thud.

There is a theory that each and every fiber that exists on this planet is a manifestation of stardust. We are inherently magic creatures, built with the intention of spreading our light into the hearts of others who we encounter.

Sometimes, the combination of two souls creates a supernova: a star that suddenly increases in its brightness because it has been impacted by an explosion of some sort.

What was once dark becomes illuminated by the creation of something majestic in nature. We have the inherent power to create that magic and have it radiate into the souls of billions of people on this planet.

Our vision can develop the space necessary to shine brighter than anything anyone could have ever imagined.

We can provide clarity to the blind ambitions that exist out in this world, and could help these ambitions become quintessential stars that ignite a passion bright enough to light up the sky.

I wondered: How can I unsee what I have now seen? How can I unknow what I now know is the truth within my soul?

∞ ∞ ∞ ∞ ∞ ∞ ∞ ∞

Later that evening, I sat on the bench in Alley Pond Park for a while. I kept looking at my watch. I sat tapping my fingers nervously on my knee. I convinced myself she had to show up. She had to. I shut my eyes for a moment and she appeared.

"Hello Scott," broke the still silence in the park.

'I didn't know if you would get the message,' I said, looking deep into her eyes. They were a soft hazel. She smiled and extended her hand.

"You want to talk, let's talk." Aunt Barbara held my hand and hoisted me up.

We walked down the trails in the rainy weather, leaves crunching beneath our feet.

"Now is not the time to take life for granted," she said wistfully.

'I know,' I responded, 'I need your help.'

She smiled and laughed a little. "You, of all people, need my help. That is why you called me?"

'I need all of the angels, please, please please,' my cries became more desperate.

She patted my back and we kept walking. "You will be okay, my son."

I denied that to an extent and she laughed.

We kept walking on the path.

I asked why I was going through so much confusion, and she responded, "Because this is your experience."

A man stood there, in the park, looking at me with tears in his eyes. I didn't know who he was. He put his arm around me in unison with Aunt Barbara.

He explained that I didn't know him, but he knew me well. He said that I was an investment and quite a tough cookie to convince.

We spoke for a while longer, and he told me that he needed me to stay strong and listen to the universe.

Aunt Barbara nodded in agreement.

Then she said, "How is she?"

'She who,' I responded.

"Judy, how is my baby sister?"

I thought that she was older than my aunt, but I guess not. I responded that she had her good days and bad days, but I think she is okay.

Aunt Barbara smiled.

We spoke a while longer about what I can do to keep the people I cared about safe.

She told me, "Go the distance and go to a doctor before it is too late."

'Too late for what?'

"Goodbye my sweet boy."

I shouted after her as she began receding: 'Too late for what?"

When I turned around, my backpack was on my shoulder and a bicycle was resting next to me. As I put my hands on it, I looked up and saw a sign: Route 118.

Though I was confused, I seemed more exhausted and delirious.

I didn't really know where I was going, but I was trying to find my way home. I rode the bicycle until I came to a dirt road that led towards the woods. It was not picturesque. However, the dirt was solid enough to walk on.

As I looked down the road, someone ran into me and stole my bicycle, my backpack, and for some odd reason, my passport. It seemed like I was in the middle of England.

I walked back out of the trail towards the main road. The people walking around appeared to be robotic and unnatural.

Then my parents suddenly appeared.

'Mom? Dad?'

"We came to rescue you," my father said. My mother was clutching his arm anxiously.

"We were concerned about you, darling," my mother reached out to touch my cheek.

'I'm fine, I don't need you.' I pushed past them and tried moving forward.

"Son," my father rushed after me. "You have to protect yourself."

'I'll be fine.'

"You're going to die if you don't take care of yourself," my mother shouted.

'Leave me alone!'

When I turned around, they were gone. I didn't understand what my mother was talking about.

'This is just a bad dream, it has to be,' I spun around and saw Morena standing by a coursing river.

As I approached her, she turned and handed me her notebook.

'Why are you giving this to me now? What else is in it?' I took it from her cautiously.

She looked me in the eyes and hugged me tight. Morena whispered in my ear: "Keep the faith, Scott."

When I pulled away from her, I was alone again.

I didn't want to lose my backpack, my identity, then end up lost in the woods in a foreign land.

I didn't want my parents to come rescue me.

'I'm not ready,' I told myself.

My eyes jolted open and I felt like I had to go to the bathroom. As I watched the blood pool in the toilet, I knew that something was terribly wrong.

When I told Morena what happened, she appeared to hold back tears.

'I am going to go to the doctor in a few hours,' my tone was solemn and I couldn't ascertain what she was thinking.

"Here," she passed me her notebook from her bag. "Read this when you are settled in the waiting room."

When I arrived at the doctor in the afternoon, I was not sure what to say. My mind was racing and I felt like my heart was about to burst from my chest. It was not normal to urinate blood, but then again, my life was never normal.

I crossed my ankles and put the clipboard filled with medical forms on the chair next to me.

Morena bookmarked a spot towards the middle of the book, which read:

"We have the power to create the life we want to live: it all comes down to the opportunities we choose to align ourselves with. There will always be obstacles thrust in our path and there will always be distractions. We will consistently feel as if life is flying by and we are too busy to accomplish everything we would like to in a time frame that would be ideal for us.

However, do not assume that you have no time for something or someone: it is just a matter of realigning your priorities. What is most important to you? If you can logically define what you want or need then stop stalling and go get it. Stop waiting around for the day for things to just appear in front of you. Surround yourself with people who will help get you closer to your dreams.

You can fantasize about what you want, but if you just keep thinking about it and refuse to do anything to get it, then that is your loss.

Yoda says, "Do or do not, there is no try." Either you give it your all, or you allow yourself to fall. Hard work and unwavering dedication are necessary in order to achieve. Hold firm to your values and beliefs.

Once the path begins to get treacherous and more difficult, then you know you have something worth pursuing, something worth fighting for.

Do not lose sight of your mission, your vision, and your overall goal.

Never settle for something second rate or minor, when you know you are born to make a major shift in this universe.

Exude positivity and actually practice what you preach.

Life is most difficult for those who can handle clinging tightly to their hopes and dreams. Go for it, you do not know what will happen until you take a chance.

What are you waiting for?"

I shut the book just as my name was called to see the doctor.

∞ ∞ ∞ ∞ ∞ ∞ ∞ ∞

"So, what did the doctor say?" Morena looked up from her lasagna, but she kept dragging her fork along the plate.

'He told me that I would get the blood test results in a few days.

"Oh," she dropped her eyes towards the plate. "Okay."

'Hey, your entry was really powerful. I didn't read anything else, but what else am I allowed to read?'

She took the notebook from me and shuffled through it for a bit.

"Here," she passed it back to me. "Read page 88. I wrote it from your perspective. It is what I sense you feel about Layne."

I took it from her and squinted to read her words:

'Unconditional love is the most exhilarating feeling in the world. To have someone look at you and see the real you is a blessing. I can't describe it, but a weight is lifted off my shoulders. I float; I fly. You are my wings. No matter what, those moments elevate me. Excite me. Your glances remind me why I do what I do... most of the time it is because that look in your eyes makes me melt.'

I looked up at Morena, who was sitting on her folded legs to get a better glimpse at how far down I was reading.

I continued to read:

'Your warmth and my frigid exterior make me breathe again. It is a balance. I could never replace that feeling. It is beautiful in every sense of the word. No matter what, I know you see the real me for who I am. You see more of me than anyone. For that I am truly grateful. I love you for when you speak about your past and future, because you show how much you have grown. You show me life's greatest blessings. You make me a better person. Romance novels and movies are drastic exaggerations of love, but you my dear are real. Real in every fiber of everything you do.

'You are more than an angel. People are intimidated by what they don't know. You know me and yet you are drawn in closer.

How?

Why?

What makes you remove all bias and see a tattered, crushed soul?

'Sometimes, when you aren't looking, I glance at you to take in the breathtaking wonder that is your energy. I respect that energy. I respect your will, your tenacity, and your idealism. I love every inch of every part of you. You are destined for greatness.

'You are the sun, the stars, the whole galaxy and universe in one. You light up the darkness and I light up yours, and I am grateful we shine bright together.

'Nothing can replace the way I feel when I cross your mind. I feel you thinking about me. I yearn to be a thought in your existence.'

Morena cleared her throat and read the final line, which was further down on the page than the rest of her writing:

"I am but a mere shadow in the glory that is you, for my light shines so you can see the way."

I wiped the tears from my eyes.

'Wow Morena, that's breathtaking.'

She took the notebook from my hands. "Thank you."

Morena sat back down and tucked her coy smile into her right shoulder.

This was the first year I prayed with the intent to manifest holistic positivity.

I prayed that there is no pain; I prayed that there is peace. I prayed that there is wisdom and I prayed there is faith. I prayed that there is hope and joy and laughter everywhere.

I prayed for a better present, for each day is a gift. I prayed we would find solutions to the world's concerns.

I prayed to empower. I prayed to encourage leaders. I prayed to become a better person. I prayed I could overcome anything. I prayed I could become stronger. I prayed for the beauty that is family. I prayed to create a world where our children could be proud of the strides we make as a nation each day.

I prayed for justice. I prayed for peace. I prayed for humanity, civility, honor, light, stamina, resiliency, and beyond.

I prayed that the world would heal. I prayed. I prayed not in a church or a temple or a mosque, but I prayed in a school, out of a school, and someday, we will pray together as one.

Amen.

On living and loving, there are so many thoughts that came to mind. Love is not defined by words; it is defined by actions. I have all too often heard someone say, "love you," in passing to someone, but it seems that "love you" has just become a superficial utterance that people toss around like a ball during recess: people don't really use it to show devotion to one another, and then they reminisce about the "good ol' days" at recess when they used to run around.

Recess is a beautiful thing, sure, but you always have to go back into school.

In hindsight, are kids thinking about whether or not they utilized every moment from recess to the best of their abilities? I doubt it, because self-reflection is something that is developed over the course of a lifetime… and not just in the elementary school years. I think about recess in the context of love: did I cherish every moment of it? Did I really take it all in: every smile, every laugh, every movement and sensation? Or did I, too, take it for granted, like recess?

I wondered if I could go back in time, would I change everything… I say I wouldn't, because I see myself now and genuinely smile at everything I have become. Sometimes, I can't help but look back at all the different someone's I have become: a mask here, a mask there, a glimmer of the real me shining through for a moment. I chose this path, regardless. There is no one to blame but myself, in all honesty. We love in every language as we go throughout life, and that echoes what I wrote long ago: "If you love in every language, at some point your music will be loud enough for someone to hear."

But did I hear it? Now I do.

I realize that the person that has come in second place is myself. Everyone else has heard my love first and foremost. People have experienced my love and my life, as I have over the years, but I think, while I am sitting alone in someone else's living room, that I need to love myself way more.

I am older now. I am here now. I am committing my love to fighting for the greater good. Unwavering. This moment on. That's it. I love myself through helping others. So what if I am in second place?

I think of all of the seconds that brought me to this moment: the moment I shed my second skin and just flow into myself. Face the music. Face the facts. Face everything as I always have, but face it with another's hand in mine.

About 7 hours remained on that day.

I stood there, about to shed a layer.

I knew this is what I must do and had to do for the betterment of my life. There was no turning back, for everything is "if it is meant to be, it will be."

And so it goes... and so it will be...

And I'm not alone.

Never. Again.

∞ ∞ ∞ ∞ ∞ ∞ ∞ ∞

My perspective on life changed after I left the church, and before then I wasn't counting my blessings, though I began to start appreciating them. All of them. Every ounce of me and within every second that passed, I began cherishing life. It was another chance, another opportunity, and another mark on the timeline to become a stronger person.

Strength has no limits, but tolerance for negativity does.

We have been given a beautiful gift: 365 new days, with 365 new chances to blossom, to pursue our ambitions, and to create opportunities from the ashes of fireworks that light up the sky. In times of celebration, fireworks dust the sky with their aura of beauty. Thousands of chemicals are compounded into tubes, and forced to burst miles above where they were placed. Under pressure and in absolute duress, the fireworks created a magical glimmer that brought joy and hope to billions of people across the globe. With the forthcoming 365 days, it is possible to carry on the light that you saw when the 365 days started.

Manifest that light within your own soul.

Convert the thousands of chemicals that burst in the sky and reflected in your eyes into love, passion, beauty, empathy, hope... and transform it into whatever you needed to be or hear this past year. Grow. Blossom. Burst and let your energy seep into the eyes of those around you. Let them gaze upon your inner power and your beauty. Fireworks are built to explode once and drift away, but you are different. Be the magical, beautiful, out of the box soul that you are. Be passionate about what sets your soul aflame.

Seize the day and seize every single opportunity that brings you to the next level. Shine daily with the warmth and compassion that radiates from you. You have to let your positive vibes grace this world.

No matter what obstacles you face, no matter what setbacks may fall in front of you, allow passion to be the center of everything you do. Let every window of opportunity become wide open... and let it stay that way.

Delve deep into the recesses of your mind. Find peace and devout bliss in the seconds that pass. There is much to overcome and disavow. You must pull all the strength from within you. Find your balance. Seek solace in who you are and your experiences. you have the cloak of protection, yes, but there needs to be something else: a mental protection or a calming of sorts.

My train of thought halted abruptly when the phone rang. The results came back from my doctor, and they needed to bring me in to do a series of tests and scans.

Something was not right in my system.

In order to bring my soul some solace and tranquility, I decided that I was just going to watch a movie.

My mother had fallen asleep for the night and the lumpy couch was calling my name. After rattling the remote around in my hand for a while, I stopped on a documentary-type filmed based on the United States government. *Vice* was a film I wanted to see for quite some time, and it just so happened that on the night rambunctious thoughts were rumbling through my head, the movie appeared before me.

Two hours flashed before my eyes, filling my head with grandeurs of sly actions and deceiving notions.

I sat there frozen, gazing at the credits as they rolled past the top of the screen. I did not know precisely what to feel or think, but my aunt's image came to the forefront of my mind.

Purpose filled my soul.

The movie itself covered the story of Former Vice President Dick Cheney, but it detailed the underlying message that crime penetrated the very foundation of our nation.

I felt the weight of society's wrongs and a broken promise that burdened America's soul: it was revealed that we went to war on false premises and pretenses.

This prolonged my devotion to pursue a higher vision: leadership is all about exemplifying passion. Leadership requires that someone stand for strong morals and a progressive vision. If someone does not stick to the ethical and moral code that is sworn upon, then what does that one person genuinely stand for?

We cannot turn our heads from the truth.

We each harbor a respective responsibility to our souls.

We must be vigilant when it comes to being grounded in our ethics and morals.

The world looked and felt different after seeing that documentary. I was angry. I was hurt. I was disgusted.

I vowed to be a voice for those who could not defend themselves, for those who perished long before their time, for all of the souls who passed on or related to September 11, 2001.

For my aunt.

All of this was on my mind as I returned to the hospital days later to discover what was happening with my body.

The doctor called and said I needed to meet him immediately.

I sat in the hospital waiting room with my thoughts consuming the energy in my core.

Glaring at the painting across from me, I realized how I had never actually seen it before. I sat across it many times: with each child I had to escort to this hospital, here was where I sat: across from the nature scene. The painting echoed my inner feelings at once: the dead tree drawing attention to the forefront of the painting, my soul dead and desolated from years of presupposed divine love that just was not what it seemed to be.

Yet now, that dead tree was more alive than ever. The brown embers cascaded along the tree as gently as a simple waterfall on brisk April morning in the park. The painting gave its full display of nature and showed how nurturing passion could bring about such genuine beauty in the world.

I was the painting, and the painting was me.

The lush greenery behind the rich chocolate tree was brighter than ever. I could feel the moss brushing through my fingers. I could taste the early dew that formed on the grass. The mountains majestically beckoned me to join them in the tranquil scenery.

Tears streamed from the edges of my soul as I took in each breath appreciating this hospital's choice of scenery. The immense joy it brought me, despite my pain, reminded me that each and every gift on this planet was part of the present: a glorious reminder that starting over and beginning again were peaceful acts: I would heal. I would be okay.

As the sun rose over those pristine forest mountains, I too would rise again. I too would sing from the top of those mountains, just as beautifully as the birds that graced the branches of the tree.

Life was beginning for the hundredth time in my life, yet this time was vastly different than I could have imagined. I was within the painting and within the boundaries of my newborn soul simultaneously.

I was alive. I am alive. All the pieces of the puzzle make sense now: despite strife and struggle, the consequence was being born again in the context of an old soul in a new perspective.

No matter what, and no matter who graced my presence, nothing could alter my perspective of the once deceased tree that was resurrected from the charity and clarity of my glance. Now, I was that painting. I had to carry on the elegance of the painting, and let others see the conviction that was being torn and tattered, yet strikingly gorgeous all at once.

When I went and spoke to the doctor, he told me what I desperately feared:

I had Stage 1 Bladder Cancer.

The doctor's demeanor shifted from professional to utterly grotesque in nature. I felt like I was being examined like a laboratory specimen: in his eyes, it appeared that I was devoid of human emotions.

"You'll die if you don't handle this," hung on his lips.

In order to potentially salvage what was left of my bladder, he said we needed to operate immediately and there were no guarantees I would ever be the same.

A tinge of numbness crept up my spine.

Tears streamed from my eyes without remorse, for it felt like this was the last chance I had to cry before succumbing to whatever news he would bestow upon me next.

I just found Layne. I was only at the cusp of understanding what sort of energy we had growing between us.

The doctor's words bled through my ears: his thoughts were fluid, but my mind could not compute the very implications he was making.

"That's life, kid, what could I tell you," the syllables from his words dripped from his mouth without repentance.

It appeared that this was going to be my final confession: I was apparently dying, and fast.

In shock and without a clear thought in my mind, Morena left a message on my phone:

"You'll be okay. You'll thrive and live and survive like you always dreamed. This is just a mere obstacle that is hindering you from moving physically, but that does not mean you cannot move emotionally, spiritually, and mindfully. Your body is healing, your soul is aflame, you're going to embark on a journey and most of all, you will be okay. Choose positivity over strife, and choose living over just a life.

Please be patient. Trust the process. Soon you'll be okay.

Soon is just a few moments away.

Please, please believe that."

Something was wrapped around me, but only in the metaphorical sense. I felt a tinge of sadness flood throughout the inner crevices of my soul.

The phone rang and shattered my thought bubble. Morena's voice was a sullen, yet stern reminder of life happening outside these four walls. Her words were burning into my brain as she tenderly tried to reassure me that I would get better.

Deep down inside, I knew I would.

The surgery I would need to have would take place within a few days.

I could hear her searching for words. Trying to find a sliver of positivity to tell me something that would make me happy or better. She could not piece anything together and the noise in the background pinged for her to return. There was sorrow in her voice, yet she was still trying to masquerade as being energetic and positive.

I could only hope she understood what was going on within my soul. Yeah, only hope.

As the phone call ended fear consumed my soul, but I was trying to raise my state of consciousness. This was my final shot: all of the warning signs must have been there for years, but I was not listening.

The negativity, the pain, and the detrimental habits I had would prove to be my downfall… that is, if I gave into them.

It was time to live the fullest life possible.

It was time I rose up and owned who I was as both a leader and a human being.

My health had to be most important. The rest, including personal love, sex, laughter, fun, money, and incredible living, were all just additional benefits I could thank the universe for. They were blessings in their own respect, but they were no longer priorities.

∞ ∞ ∞ ∞ ∞ ∞ ∞ ∞

Relationships had always been such a crux in my life's story. I am a father, a lover, a spiritual friend, part of soul connections, and take on so many roles in my life. When I really sit down and think about it, my life consists of countless connections I have made. However, when it comes down to it, the strongest bond and connection that needs to be made is the one with yourself.

I had a hard time understanding that.

It was difficult to even see this while enduring such agony from dealing with the cancer diagnosis.

Then Layne finally texted me.

She apologized that she had been so distant, especially since our connection at the conference.

I felt an overwhelming sense of healing flourish over me.

Positive, inspirational videos that she sent ushered me into my doctor's appointment later that day. Nervousness and anxiety were clinging to my body, for the unknown aspects of my diagnosis were abundant.

"Barbara," the medical assistant popped her head from behind the desk. I looked around and saw someone stand up and walk across the room.

"It is a sign that everything will be okay, Scott."

'Morena?'

She smiled at me, "Do you think I would not be here for you?"

'No, I just-' I grinned. 'Thank you.'

Her presence was usually sporadic and spontaneous, and somehow, she knew just when to appear.

"Come on," she handed me her notebook. "Read a little something in there."

I flipped through the pages, yet nothing caught my eye at the moment. I just wanted to talk. I wanted to be present to my soul's growth and the negativity that would soon leave my body.

A mesh, tan tarp rose and fell from the top of the roof and draped over the office window. As it drooped down, the sun would beam directly through it and appear to burst as the tarp and sunlight met.

It was a sign from the universe that even when barricades try to obscure our path, the light still shines through.

The doctor explained that the surgery would require that he operate cautiously. He said that there are different layers in the bladder, which consist of tissues and muscle.

The procedure would take place the next morning.

The first surgery I had was to remove an orange-sized tumor. By some miracle, the cancer did not reach the muscle. I was told I had a 40% chance that the tumor could come back, and that the next few weeks would involve more surgeries to inspect my bladder.

Not to get too technical, but the tumor I had within my body appeared to be calcified and did not spread far into my system; it enveloped the tumor and prevented it from spreading into the more vital part of the organ. We spoke about treatments, other options, and what my life would look like, but it all seemed incredibly overwhelming.

As I woke up from the surgery, I discovered that a catheter was placed inside my body. The clear, dense plastic bag clung to my leg by Velcro straps in order to ensure that I could retain my mobility and prevent incontinence.

The doctor assured me that the surgery was a success, and that I would be moving around later that night.

However, my intuition was screaming at me.

Despite the doctor's seemingly encouraging words, I was in tremendous pain.

Two days later he removed the catheter prematurely, which began the spiraling nightmare my life would become over the course of the following weeks.

While staying at my mom's three days after my first surgery, I had to rush to the Emergency Room at 1:30 in the morning. The immense pain overpowered my body.

Death appeared to be knocking at my door, but I refused to answer it.

Shame and embarrassment would wash over me, as I had to explain to nurses that I had kidney issues and bladder cancer.

In my spiritual solitude, I watched the fluorescent lighting and lime green walls slightly fade to black as a catheter had to be jammed into my private parts.

Though there was immediate relief once the nurses did that, nothing stopped me from feeling wholeheartedly defeated.

Texas embarrassment all of a sudden flooded my memories.

A piercing sound reverberated in my mind.

Not a single person was here to fill the loneliness deep within me.

While caught between a battle encompassing my physical and emotional well being, questions began to consume my every whim: Where was Morena when I needed her most? Why does she appear at certain poignant moments, yet as I lay in a hospital bed, she is nowhere to be found?

My hand hovered over her number in my cell phone before my eyes flickered shut and I drifted into a hazy dream-like state.

A woman's presence lingered next to me.

"Don't show them what you are made of, show them it is their loss that they will never get to fathom what you are made of," were the words whispered in my ear when I opened my eyes.

I laid relaxed on the floor and started counting the ceiling tiles above me. 44. I wonder how they got all of them so high up; I guess somebody had a really big ladder.

Resting my body against the linoleum, I felt peace. She stood over me, looking down at my peaceful demeanor despite everything going on.

"Do you have any questions?... Why you are here, perhaps?" her voice was trailing off a bit. "Answer me," was on the cusp of her lips.

'No,' came flowing from my mouth, a smile forming peacefully.

"No? No... you are content with not knowing where you are," she started walking across the room, almost floating. The fluorescent lights were dimming.

A wider grin was growing across my face. Her presence was fading.

'I forgive you for what you did,' sprung from my mouth with absolute purpose. She was glancing nervously in the direction of the door.

"You can't forgive me. I don't accept your apology," though crossing her arms, she kept moving steadily towards the door.

'I am not apologizing for your behavior or how you have treated me. No, I am merely saying that I forgive you for harboring hatred and jealousy throughout your body: from the crevices of your fingers to the depths of your soul. It is time you forgive yourself for what you have done,' sitting up, I could see the tears welling in her eyes.

"You don't..." her voice was breaking, "you don't know me. You can't judge me." She was starting to crumble.

'I am not judging you,' I spoke calmly, 'I am freeing myself from your grasp. You don't dictate my worth. I am the manifestation of positive energy, you must find yourself.'

She was drifting closer to the door, and was hanging in the doorway for a moment.

"Why are you freeing me," she was whimpering.

Glaring at her as the light from the doorway consumed her, I was genuinely smiling, 'don't mistake my kindness for weakness,' I was standing now, inching closer to her, 'Forgiveness is about liberating my own soul. It is time you tried to do the same, or you could fall forever.'

It was the remnants of my mother's memory planted somewhere in the recesses of my mind.

A series of cries echoed as she was falling down the long tunnel from the doorway. I didn't hear her hit the bottom, so I knew there was still hope for her to find peace... she may have buried herself exponentially, but she still could save the sliver of her that existed between the darkest hours of the night.

At some point during the night, I returned home to my mother's couch and passed out. The catheter was still hanging on my body, wrapped around my leg, obscured by my denim jeans.

I woke up when I heard the alarm clock gently reminding me of the job I had to do. I had a mission to pursue.

I returned to Lincoln Memorial High School masking the deep-rooted pain I was feeling both in the spiritual and physical senses.

As I was about to walk into the building, I was trying so desperately to capture my emotions.

I was not in a good headspace, but I showed up to work anyway.

I meditated, I prayed, and I felt that I was in alignment with the universe.

Though negative energy seemed to be around me, I tried to dispel it.

As the day continued, I had the overwhelming sense that I did not have the strength to go to work that day.

My body was crying out for rest, but I refused to listen.

After dragging my body to the car and dropping onto the driver's seat, I began to weep openly. Everything that I endured during the day manifested into the merciless tears that dripped from my eyes.

I did not want anyone to know the true desolate pain I was in.

Then, as if the universe willed her to reach out at that very moment, Layne decided to call me.

She was positive and spiritually engaging, although she had no idea what was just going through my mind.

Layne, though she just began to talk with me about her projects and what she was creating, began to speak to me about our respective personal lives.

"Will you be able to come back to Martha's Vineyard soon," she sounded very anticipatory.

Without flinching, I was drawn to my soul's every whim.

My soul was steadfast in wanting to be closer to her.

Although the words 'I have cancer' were on the tip of my tongue, I feared that if I told her the truth, she would have told me not to come.

I took a deep breath and felt my tongue dance behind my teeth.

'I can come see you next weekend,' a sigh of relief expelled from my system. I was going to get a chance to be in her presence.

"Really," she exclaimed.

'Really,' I confirmed.

Her genuine smile could be felt through the phone.

The rest of our conversation consisted of deep diving our respective worlds and thoughts. It was oddly refreshing and a soulfully stimulating experience.

No matter what, I was going to do whatever it took to get to her.

However, the universe had other plans.

It turns out my dances through the Emergency Room would be to the tune of a horrific lullaby: my soul was dormant in the midst of my emotional turmoil.

Just before I was about to drive up to Massachusetts, I was rushed to the Emergency Room twice in one night.

During my first trip there, another catheter was attached to me. I was determined to pull through and be strong. After leaving the hospital, I texted her and said I would see her soon.

As I sat and watched television, a solid feeling inundated my core. I discovered I could not urinate and the burning sensation within me remained constant.

Nothing was filtering into the bag, and it turns out the catheter burst within my body. Though the pain was excruciating, I held onto the sliver of hope dangling on a thread: there was still the possibility I would see Layne in a matter of hours.

When I returned to the Emergency Room, the nurses and doctors worked tediously to irrigate my bladder. Crimson clots flooded a bucket as I cried in immense pain.

My soul craved to be in the same physical space with her energy. Between the fear and agony, I was asking if I could travel to Martha's Vineyard.

I remained hopeful.

'Could I get on a train?'

"You would have to wear a bag," the doctor told me. "You are urinating blood clots."

'Yeah,' I told him. 'But I could, like, travel to Massachusetts, right?'

The doctor cast his eyes downward at me, "Sir, you have cancer."

Still, the universe was keeping us apart a little bit longer.

Depressed and devastated, I called Layne and told her I had bladder cancer. As she listened to the whole story and I apologized profusely, all she wanted to do was comfort me.

"Go within," Layne told me. "Talk to your body, meditate, and visualize your soul taking care of your well being."

Something within me awakened while I spoke with her. Each conversation drew me closer to her. Our connection was indescribable and an experience I wanted to explore. I was unsure what drew me to her almost instantaneously, but it was something.

My soul had an innate longing towards hers.

My soul needed to be understood, and she appeared to be the one who could translate the depths of my every waking thoughts.

I knew I had to heal, for I just had to get to her.

She sounded concerned, more than I figured she would be actually.

This is when Layne genuinely blew me away: she began to ask about the treatment options I had and started to look into holistic remedies for me.

I did not tell her the extent of my spirituality or how I was trying to find myself, as of yet, however she seemed to be so compatible with my views.

It was breathtakingly soothing.

Hours later I made it to my car to return to my mother's house.

Pensively, I sat glaring at the streaks on the windshield. Focusing on the glare only proves that you can look at something in front of you, something that is dirty and disgusting, and be blinded by fixating on it.

Yet, if you look beyond the mess, there is a whole world outside that window.

There are cars, trees, people, traffic lights, thoughts, hopes, emotions, and dreams. So much life exists at the edge of our fingertips, and so much light grows within us. Our light manifests itself within our soul, our skin, the little dip above our lips: the light shines in all of us... the question is, I asked myself, are you willing to focus on the dirt on the windshield, or the life behind it?

∞ ∞ ∞ ∞ ∞ ∞ ∞ ∞

I would say I was speechless, but there were so many words flooding through my mind, not even the alphabet could compose itself in an articulate manner.

I was torn between trying to expand my soul, pursue whatever insight Layne could provide, and manage the immense pain emulating from my bladder.

My eyes crept open on my mother's couch and stared at the brightly lit numbers that shined from my cell phone: 10:18 in the morning. I really overslept, but I knew I really deserved it. There were a few emails, but they primarily consisted of bill statements and spam messages.

Though I did not really tell anyone about my plight, no one was accustomed to checking in with me. No one was mindful of my well being minus my son, Morena, and this mysterious new individual in my life, Layne.

I worried so much about the feelings of others but it was easy to tell who cares about me. In the end though, I would always care about them, though in my heart I knew it was not always reciprocated.

I knew I honestly didn't have time to let things like that bother me at all. Life is way too short and I was getting a taste of that fear. I knew I was going to beat this diagnosis and probably become healthier than I had even been... as long as I focused. I could tell the universe was speaking to me; it was warning me about how it could be. If I didn't awaken my soul and appreciate the small blessings, such as the people who love me and go way above and beyond for me, then I could lose it all within seconds.

Instinctively, I found myself wandering to my car to get away from the emotional burden of being in my mother's house.

My car guided me to the Whitestone Bridge, where I would find some peace in Francis Lewis Park.

I got out of my car to stretch and feel the air caress my body. It was raining and the pellets on my skin felt like shots piercing my memories.

Each time it rained that heavily, something drastic happened in my life: my best friend Stacey's funeral, my grandfather's funeral, my aunt's funeral, Emma admitting that Greg wanted to propose, and Paul's death. I wondered what was next.

I could almost hear the angels surrounding me and saying:

"Do you get the lessons? Do you realize your potential? Are you hearing our messages? Keep going within. We are speaking. You must listen but even after you hear, it is your free will to adhere or fumble. Regardless we are always here to love you."

I think my story is really about love, but more specifically about the role of gratitude in loving ourselves, others, and any moment you find yourself in. Someone could be angry or ignoring you, but within that moment you have a choice: You can reciprocate that anger and lash out, which many people do, or you can breathe into the moment and say to yourself 'What do I love about this person? What am I grateful for? What can I learn from this? How can I make this moment an opportunity to be grateful?' Then whatever those answers are for you, you can love the feeling of knowing you rose above and made any situation special. That goes for family, partners, friendships, people you dislike in general, or random strangers, even the news.

This is higher consciousness. This is what matters to our souls. This is what we should be practicing. This is practicing "life." The same goes for any situation that isn't negative either, like sitting at the side of a lake and thinking about who you are. As you see the sunset on the horizon, breathe into its beauty, becoming mindful of just that moment.

There is beauty like that, and moments around us constantly to breathe into - to allow our souls to expand and gravitate towards... and what's great about this appreciation is the more you experience it from a state of awareness, the more beautiful opportunities like that will come to you. This is love. This is gratitude. This is higher consciousness. This is the message from God and the universe that I have been waiting for all along. This is my story.

I was almost certain that the pounding in my chest was a heartbeat, but at times I forgot it even existed…

My heart, that is.

Looking into the depths of a chunk filled bucket, I found peace knowing I woke up today. A chill crept up my spine, a reminder that I could feel whatever I please and react however I could.

The taste of stale antibiotics crept back up my esophagus again. It was going to be a long day, yet it would be as long of a day as I truly wanted.

It was all a matter of perception.

I knew I was sick, but with a smile and a soothing voice, I could conquer anything. Illness or not, I have a job to do… no, wait, forget I said that. It is a mission I need to fulfill. A dream I have to uphold. A vision I need to establish: a half-full bucket that needed to be emptied to make room for bigger and better things… chunk free.

The first doctor I was going to did not appear to bestow much tranquility upon my soul. Upon speaking about him with my boss and principal, Shirley, she referred me to another doctor who she highly recommended.

The new doctor, Dr. V, was considerate, compassionate, and seemed to have the same passion for medicine that I had for changing the world. Dr. V recommended that I have a second surgery, so that he could ensure that the cancer was truly decimated.

I was beyond nervous before my second surgery, but time was moving so rapidly that it became rather insignificant.

The potential for my dreams to collapse before they could even be built was more than I could bear. I could feel the possibility of embarking on some sort of collaboration with Layne though that was not fully clear yet, just a feeling. Morena and I were on the verge of developing strong leadership programs, and I was challenging youth to find their true voice at work.

How would any of these dreams be fulfilled if I were dying?

Why would I meet someone who I had such a fluid connection with just on the cusp of tragic news?

Would I ever witness the dawn of a brand-new day?

I wondered how life was ever going to be considered fair if everything would be built then taken away from me all at once.

Being in the same physical space to explore the connection I was strengthening with Layne was a priority.

Sleeping became irrelevant.

Work was filled with plenty of events to deter me from getting anxious about the cancer, but each day I would have to contend with my inner demons while leading youth. It was a crass juxtaposition that highlighted my need for balancing what I was passionate about and what my soul needed to attend to.

Remaining positive was on the forefront of my mind, but I was masking the panic stirring in my soul.

While meditating before the second surgery, I thought I could feel an angel trying to push through the permeable barrier between my soul and my mind, but the message was ensnared in my anxiety.

It gave me some peace of mind that they were encircling me.

I was hoping to awaken from the anesthetic and hear some amazing news from the doctor. The sharp pains in my stomach were forcing me into a fragile state of mind: my intestines, my bladder, my nerves, and a combination of all of the above were forcing me to spiral.

Going within to quell the voices in my body were ultimately necessary.

Adorned with a thin hospital gown and a crisp white bed sheet, I was wheeled into the operating room.

Before I felt the anesthesia consume my mind, Washington D.C. flashed before my eyes. Morena's notebook was on my mind, as well as the long talks and walks we engaged in by the bridge and at Alley Pond Park. Layne's text messages and phone conversations penetrated my soul quickly; they were a huge part of why I wanted to heal faster, for I knew I needed to see her.

I felt deeply sorry for any and all pain I caused others, as well as the wrongdoings I brought into my life and the lives of those I affected. My human ways were not always meticulous or righteous, though my intent was always considered to be for the good of others. I am far from truth and perfection, though I was learning and still am to this day.

Learning from the experiences I endured changed me forever. I asked the universe and God to allow me to heal completely and rise above.

I knew in my soul the blessings I had been a part of could make a difference. Everything has a purpose. Everything has-

My final thoughts before falling under the anesthesia drifted into another realm.

∞ ∞ ∞ ∞ ∞ ∞ ∞ ∞

Anesthesia can play tricks on your mind and body, though my soul was steadfast in acknowledging all that I deemed to be holy.

While under the anesthesia, I envisioned standing on The Great Lawn at the White House in Washington, D.C.; it was a mystical experience.

Under the condition I was in, thoughts of courage and leadership flurried around my brain. In my mind, I appeared to be wearing a carefully prepared suit with a bold, sky blue tie adorned around my neck.

My fist was resting upright on the podium as I spoke to a group of people:

'Our small moments and discussions carry so much weight in this country. Those who came before us carried the torch so that we could ignite the souls of this nation to pursue their dreams. The liberties we are accustomed to did not come without great sacrifices, and for those sacrifices I am truly grateful.'

Morena and Layne were standing side by side. Morena was in a black suit with her red blouse prominently displaying her presence on such a bright, sunny day. Layne was in a stunning black dress that featured her voluminous curves. Every inch of Layne's stance and appearance were genuine perfection.

It did not surprise me that either of them was with me, but the connection I felt with Layne was apparent even in my hallucinations.

My voice cut through the crowd: 'Where are our ideals? Where is our courage? What example do we set for one another and those who will be the future of our great nation?'

Layne wrapped her right hand around Morena's arm and rubbed Morena's shoulder with her left hand. They seemed to be close in their own right and respect.

Again, I continued to speak.

'The time to dig deep and find courage to move forward is now. We must create necessary change. It may be lonely at the top, as some say, and with bravery comes those who are critics. To face adversity and follow your own vision is vital. We must make our individualism and sense of community synthesize in order to grow as a cohesive country. We all have a voice. We all have the capacity to listen to one another. We all have the ability to lead. "Han" is a Korean word that has no literal English translation, however it is a state of mind. In actuality, it is a state of soul. It is a devout sadness so deep that no tears will come, and yet there is still a sense of hope. The state of our nation rests in the word "han." We all need to take a minute and measure the value of our own words.'

Everyone was glaring directly at me, staring in silence.

'What you say to someone today can impact their life tomorrow. It can impact all of our lives. We must be mindful of the words we feed our children and ourselves. For the youth are looking to us to learn how to lead. It is time for true respect for all.'

The audience began to clap as they dashed over to Morena and Layne.

"Everyone deserves a window of opportunity," Morena stated. "Every child, every soul, every being."

A man who appeared to be a reporter was writing down everything she was saying.

Layne was standing with a group of people who looked like dignitaries from other countries as she spoke.

"We have to create a system that emphasizes character building on all levels. It is about building passion and purpose within all of our souls, not just the few. It is about globalization. It is about growth. It is about humanity," Layne was being very professional and was clearly on a mission.

I found myself traveling to another part of Washington D.C. with Layne, Morena, and some other people I did not seem to recognize.

Upon standing on the steps of the Lincoln Memorial, gazing out at the reflection of the Washington Monument in the waters of the National Mall, I felt it.

I felt the sense that I was being watched. That it had taken me so long to get to DC because it just had to be the right moment. The right time. The manifestation of all of my experiences perching themselves atop the monument, and the overcast skies reminding me that I am, indeed, the light that could guide the way for millions.

It made sense. It all made sense: the trials, the triumphs, the days I wanted to crawl into a hole and never come out, the heartache, the pain. It was all to prepare me for a higher purpose.

Glaring into the stone eyes of President Abraham Lincoln, I knew just what I had to do...

Prepare to carry the torch.

The shadows crept along the wall with such fervor, as if they were pointing to something: My phone. I woke up from the anesthetic to a dimly lit room.

A sliver of light cut between the air and the still dust that lay suspended in time. The glow from the sun was a constant reminder that if it could rise, then I might as well try to.

It had been a while since I last heard from Layne, and I was beginning to think she, like all the others, had vanished into the ornate fabric of my life: caught between the threshold of when and how long. Trapped in the abysmal weaving of my complicated mind.

And I had hoped that in my absence, she would still remember I existed. For after all, she could never disappear from my memory... and I would never try to replace the feeling I get when I stare at her face: half excited, but half scared that she will never look at me the same way.

To all the angels, to all the powers that be in this universe, I pray she remembers me.

∞ ∞ ∞ ∞ ∞ ∞ ∞ ∞

The week consumed me with thoughts of trepidation and the possibility of spiritual enlightenment.

I kept the faith.

I had to.

The universe was on the verge of experiencing all that I had to offer, and something within me said to keep going.

The angels were on my side, Morena was whispering positivity and faith into my ears, and I was receiving soul-quelling insight from Layne.

Between the affirmations and meditation information she bestowed upon me, I was feeling incredibly grateful for her support.

Those who were promoting positivity and tranquility were helping me heal, and for them I will be forever thankful.

Everything within me hoped that all of this turmoil would soon be behind me.

The moment the phone rang I felt my heart palpitate within my chest: these next few moments would shift the balance within my soul forever. I knew deep down inside that no matter the diagnosis, I would fervently push forward and do what I had to do for the greater good of the universe, but just how difficult would my journey be?

I answered the phone and took a deep breath.

'Hello,' I am sure he could sense the nervousness in my voice.

"Hey Scott, it is Dr. V, how are you?" His voice seemed chipper.

'I don't know, how am I doc?' I let a smile seep from the edge of my mouth.

"Well," he said with a breathy chuckle, "good news, man."

I held my breath. The pause was what stung my soul. What was good? Why did this pause seem so painstakingly long?

"Scott," he began, with a tinge of hope in his voice.

"You are cancer free."

Silence blossomed in the air as I heaved a sigh of relief. His words drowned in the flood of emotions that filled my mind.

I was given another chance.

I was free.

Though I went through such a dramatic series of surgeries and moments, with more visits to the emergency room that no one will truly ever realize or fathom, I chose not to be a victim of circumstance. I chose to pursue my purpose with an even more devout sense of growth stirring within me.

It was a momentary resurgence of my faith manifesting into growth. It was proof that negative situations and refusing to listen to your inner voice could cause such horrid turmoil.

Though the cancer was not akin to literally hitting a concrete wall as I did decades ago, the cancer provided yet another metaphorical crash in order to guide me on my path.

Our experiences reveal the innate magic we contain within our souls.

Sometimes, we discover our gifts and growth on our own terms, other times the universe reminds us of what we can overcome.

To this day, I am not sure where the noise came from, but music was playing: Paul Simon's "You Can Call Me Al."

My aunt's memory and the last time we laughed and smiled flooded my soul.

∞ ∞ ∞ ∞ ∞ ∞ ∞ ∞

Morena was thrilled upon hearing that I got the all clear. She jovially hugged me when she saw me.

"What is your first order of business now that you are a *free* man?"

I looked over at her and made a promise: 'I'm going to truly live in the realm of a higher consciousness. I am going to eat healthy, feed my soul positivity, and keep moving forward.'

"I am proud of you," she grinned.

'I have to video call Layne, there is something I need to do.'

Upon pulling my phone from my pocket, my body shivered with excitement.

Layne answered immediately and was ecstatic. She appeared to want to see me just as much as I wanted to be in her presence.

If I could freeze a moment in time, I would have etched her genuine smile in my mind for the rest of eternity. I would infinitely drown in an ocean of my own emotions, if I knew that her love would be the life preserver waiting to catch me if I drifted too far or too deep.

Her inconsummate soul wrapped itself around me and poured itself into the shattered pieces of my deepest darkest dreams. Her heart and stamina were what sealed the pieces of my loneliness back together. If only the darkness inside her would conceal itself beneath the light she emulated regularly, she would then feel just how unequivocally blessed I am for her presence to be a constant gift in my life.

Without her glow as a persistent reminder of the light manifesting within me, I am not sure how my life would have been. It is just so poignant: two separate broken souls were almost able to fully mend each other, and simply by collaborating through trial and triumph; blood, sweat, and countless tears. Each drop an echoic memory of how far we have come...

And just how high we could fly with our souls intertwined and our hands interlocked, rising above the dust and crowds to proclaim, "Every child deserves a window of opportunity."

∞ ∞ ∞ ∞ ∞ ∞ ∞ ∞

That night, I had another weird dream:

Standing in the doorway, I could see a solitary white wolf inching closer and closer to where I was standing. It shifted its stern legs around a few times while maintaining eye contact with me.

We stood parallel for a little bit until it opened its mouth and formulated actual words. A deep voice inundated with soulfulness erupted from the animal.

"Do you know why you have been brought here?" Its pure fur shook in unison with its firm body.

I watched the white wolf in amazement. It spoke. The first time it spoke.

"You'll have time to rest later. Follow me," it spoke as it retreated from the light. "We have much to discuss."

As the wolf raced down the long corridor, I followed it with sheer curiosity.

'Why now? Why speak now?'

In the depths of my soul, I could feel something shifting. Something was not right. This was a warning of some kind. The earth below began to shake. The wolf caught my stunned expression.

"Are you waking up yet, peaceful warrior?" The wolf stopped in its tracks. It shifted its weight and moved closer and closer to me. I could feel the energy growing stronger between us.

It nudged its head for me to get closer to it. I leaned down, holding my body up by my bent knee and vicariously placed hand.

"It is time you woke up and faced the music. Run towards the light, my child," at once, the wolf leaned its head into my leg, and the energy shift was complete. A circle manifested itself above us as it morphed into an infinity sign. Lights flickered. Wind whisked around us and I held the wolf as if I were preserving it from the fierce wind.

"See you soon, my love," it started softly, "You know, in your soul, what you must do. Keep her safe."

I awoke in a darkened apartment. Sky blue walls cohesively circled beige furniture and a wooden coffee table. I did not recognize the room. A sole light crept between the doorframe and the neighboring wall: the entrance to a white bathroom.

'Where am I?' flew from my dehydrated lips.

I arose from the padded couch and headed towards the illuminated room. The door creaked slightly.

The wolf was sitting in the middle of the floor. It almost perfectly blended into the white tile floor, though its midnight eyes were a reminder that it was distinctly unique from its surroundings. It swung its head, motioning me closer once again.

Small whispers escaped its mouth, "Wake up."

Puzzled and very exhausted, I let a small sigh creep out: 'But I am awake.'

"Not yet," it peeped gently.

"Not yet. Give it time, Scott. You are almost there."

I jolted awake to find my phone buzzing with glee. Layne was calling to check up on me and ask when I would be returning to Martha's Vineyard. I checked my schedule and told her that I would be there this weekend.

"This weekend, really?" Her voice was illuminated with glee.

'Yes,' I replied instinctively. 'I am coming up there.'

"That is wonderful," she proclaimed. "But you do not have to come so soon after your surgery. You have to recover!"

'Telling me not to see you,' I began, 'is like telling the sun not to rise in the morning.'

I packed my bag and eagerly awaited the end of the week.

The calendar crept closer and closer to her presence becoming a devout reality in my life. I stood patiently at the edge of the curb, gazing up at the skyscrapers and wishing she were here.

We had so much to talk about. So much to catch up on and share. Pieces of a flourishing soul would collide to balance a universal shift. It was just a day away.

Sitting on the bench in the teacher's lot that Friday afternoon, I rolled my keys around in a circular motion - the jingling became music to my ears. Birds fluttered up above. Faint laughter from children and the murmurs of park goers swirled in the air: all poignant reminders of life diversifying the environment we have been so accustomed to. No one single conversation is the same.

My countdown from a day prior rang in my head: 17 hours, 52 minutes, and 36 seconds... 35 seconds... 34 seconds.

As I drove up to Massachusetts, anticipation mounted in the colorful kaleidoscope of memories that flooded my mind as her name and sweet nothings were on my lips.

The advantageous hope lingered in the placated pieces of my soul. Her aroma, though faint, was apparent. A gentle breeze ushered my longing to see her into clear view.

As I boarded the ferry to Martha's Vineyard and sailed closer and closer, time became irrelevant to the fact that she was coming nearer. Suddenly, the mundaneness of each fleeting moment became crass and almost turbulent.

The dock was nearing closer as the ferry rocked; it was a shift in the universe perhaps.

She arrived. Layne was here.

CHAPTER 42
Home

~

"Take me now. The world's such a crazy place. When the walls come down, you'll know I'm here to stay. There's nothing I would change. Knowing that together everything that's in our way. We're better than alright. Walking between the raindrops. Riding the aftershock beside you. Off into the sunset. Living like there's nothing left to lose. Chasing after gold mines. Crossing the fine lines we knew. Hold on and take a breath. I'll be here every step. Walking between the raindrops with you."

- Lifehouse, American Rock Band, Los Angeles, California

As she stood on the dock staring out at the ferry, it was almost as if she were a lighthouse. Her bright light appeared to beckon this tattered, worn soul to the shore: her soul was summoning me home.

I never knew what I wanted in life. In terms of love, professionalism, spirituality, I never knew. Yet something in her eyes told me that I was about to find out. I was about to dig myself into a deeper hole than I could have ever imagined...

And I just hoped that somewhere, deep within, she felt the passion burning between both of us.

She was captivating in the sense that she was driven by her heart. Layne's beauty was breathtaking, though it was her inner voice that made her spiritually enriching.

As I approached her on the dock, she was standing in a perfectly fitting trench coat that fanned out by her waist. The cotton black dress she wore hugged every curve of her body in a manner that summoned all eyes to adore her.

It is truly amazing how the universe works. Months ago, the two of us were physically strangers on this planet. Neither of us realized the other existed; yet the moment we met it was almost like our souls were destined to be together.

The light emulating from within us glowed just enough to illuminate the path before us. Both of us appeared to be on the same page when it came to energy and stamina, yet I was entranced by her passion.

Layne had a burning desire to pursue her dreams; she yearned to write a book to highlight the innate potential hiding deep within the world's souls.

Life grants you moments and situations that you never knew you needed. Speaking with her was an utter delight, as she harbored just the right amount of tenacity to inspire both herself and those who met her to move forward. I wondered if she was cognizant of just how empowering she was: in being such a strong icon of classic internal beauty, could she fathom the opportunities she could create within her own life?

Writing a book takes determination and stamina. I sensed she had the power within her, but I was not sure what was holding her back.

I wondered if she recognized the same diligence within herself that she appeared to discover in others.

Either way, I prayed that she would trust her heart to know what was true would come to fruition.

All beautiful things and dreams are worth the wait.

Fear of the future or pain from the past could ensnare you within a never-ending trap of "what ifs," "could," "should," and "would," though ultimately what matters is the passion in your heart, the strength within your mind, the words you feed to your body, and the voice that comes from deep within your soul.

At this point, it was clear to me that everything in this universe aligns at just the right moment: when things are supposed to happen, they will happen. When words are supposed to flow from deep within you, they will find a way to articulate themselves within the depths of your soul.

Everything has a purpose and nothing truly ever ceases to flow unless you make it so.

Above all, intuition may manifest itself when something seems to be blossoming. We must add water to the soil churning in our core, so that the flowers we develop can grow into whatever we hope our respective lives could become.

I was not sure what sort of connection Layne and I had, but I hoped to find out.

"Hi," her voice was like crushed velvet. It was pleasing to grace her presence.

'Hey,' I cheerfully replied. 'How are you?'

"I'm doing great," she pulled her hands from her pockets. "I'm doing great." She sounded excited, yet slightly anxious.

'I'm glad,' I smiled back at her.

The two of us stood in silence for a moment gazing out at the water.

"It's beautiful, right?"

'Yeah,' I turned to look at her admiring the waves. 'It really is.'

"There is a lot I want to show you," she began. "Martha's Vineyard is a gorgeous place, and I want to make sure you enjoy every moment of this island."

The two of us made our way out of the ferry terminal and onto the main road. The midnight blue sign above the terminal read "Oak Bluffs" in crisp white lettering.

'Oak Bluffs,' I pointed at the sign. 'I thought this was Martha's Vineyard.'

"It is silly, but there are different parts of the island. Most of the time it's a summer vacation spot for celebrities and rich people, but to the locals, it is just home."

'Just home,' lingered in my mouth as I repeated her.

She paused and looked up at me for a moment.

"Do not take this the wrong way, but your New York accent is so thick. The locals around here are going to know you are a visitor."

We laughed and a genuine grin grew across my face.

'I *do* take it the *wrong way*,' I replied sarcastically. 'I guess you'll just have to give me a full tour.'

"I guess so," she grabbed my hand and pulled me out towards the street. "This is Seaview Avenue."

'Seaview Avenue,' I murmured. 'How original.'

The two of us continued laughing as she pulled me towards her white sedan.

'I don't remember seeing too many cars last time I was here.'

"Oh," she remarked. "The island is not some quaint little vacation community. There is a lot of life on this beautiful treasure."

As the two of us got into her car, she began to list the places she wanted to take me to. While she gleefully spoke about introducing me to her version of the Vineyards, I gazed out the window at the picturesque houses that lined the streets.

I could only imagine what sort of higher conscious thinking she was manifesting on the island. It was the kind of place that you could only dream of. Every single building in town looked as if it would belong on a postcard. Every fiber within me wondered what was taking her so long to write, considering she had such a beautiful environment to manifest her creation.

Her voice trailed into my train of thought: "There's a gorgeous place called the Aquinnah Cliffs Overlook that is utterly breathtaking, and I guess the lighthouse there is a little small compared to the ones you would probably see in New York. I've heard about Long Island here and there..."

'I want to see everything,' I told her.

She gripped the steering wheel and looked over at me.

"Well, you are only here for less than two days, so I'll try jamming in as much as possible."

The intense energy between us was radiating off of our minds. It was such a joy to experience such a high vibrational conversation, and even though I felt like a tourist who was just sightseeing on the quaint little island, Layne made me feel like I was not a foreign entity.

In New York, I constantly felt like an outcast or someone terribly different, yet while wandering around with Layne, I felt a sense of peace.

The two of us drove to a place called Lighthouse Beach and she parked her car on one of the side streets. I was starting to lose my sense of direction, for she was glowing as she spoke about all of the different places I had to see.

"We are going to start with my favorite spot, but it isn't on this island."

'*This* island,' I was confused. 'I thought there was only one Martha's Vineyard.'

"Oh, there is," she grabbed my hand and started to dart down side streets. "But there's also Chappaquiddick Island."

'Chap of who?'

She giggled, "Chappaquiddick."

We continued to laugh as I repeatedly struggled, trying to pronounce Chappaquiddick properly.

A building adorned with faded shingles was eclipsed by an aquamarine and gold-lettered sign that read "Gallery."

'What's that?' I pointed to the building.

"That's the art gallery here. Sometimes I go there to get inspiration, but there are other beautiful places you need to see."

The two of us boarded another ferryboat. As it set sail, we could practically see the other island, as the sky was so incredibly pure.

'Aw,' I remarked. 'This is adorable. It is the Chappy Ferry!'

"What," she nudged me playfully. "They don't have cute names for things in New York?"

'I mean,' I stopped to think for a moment. 'There is a sign on the highway that says, "fuggedaboutit," which is kind of cool.'

"Huh," she started to laugh again. "Is that a town down there?"

'No, I think it is like a saying from one of the boroughs, either Brooklyn or Queens or the Bronx.'

"Oh, okay," she rubbed my shoulder with her open palm. "You need to teach me all about New York since I am telling you all about my home."

'Deal.' I shook her hand and before I could even blink, we were on Chappaquiddick Island.

The two of us rode these brightly colored scooters down the street. At first, I admit that I was nervous as I teetered on this oddly shaped vehicle, but Layne's reassuring nod reminded me that I could balance just about anything.

We drove down to a series of dirt roads and came across a pine-green sign adorned with bold white letters: "Welcome to Mytoi."

'What's this?' We parked and walked up to the sign.

"It is a Japanese-style garden that was manifested in the 1950s," Layne put her open hand on my shoulder.

'Did you get that from the sign?' I tilted my head diagonally towards her.

"No," she nudged me playfully once again. "I come here to think. This is one of my special writing spots."

'It-' I glanced at the ornate and stimulating greenery around us. Had I known where we were going, I think I would have prepared my thoughts in a more cohesive manner. In those moments upon seeing the natural beauty surrounding us, I felt a sincere sense of peace washing over my body. 'It's beautiful.'

"It's called the Mytoi Japanese Garden. I have always enjoyed being outdoors and walking through nature's most illustrious creations."

'It's breathtaking.'

"Come on," she grabbed my hand. "I'll show you around."

The two of us walked around gazing at the diverse colors wrapped in the leaves and flowers.

We paused in front of a small, thinly leafed tree that seemed like the centerpiece of the garden. Layne caressed the leaves with such purpose. Her fingers brushed through them so gently, as to not disturb their structural integrity.

"It's a Japanese Maple Tree," she glanced at it as if it were a young child. "I always wanted to have one of these in my own front yard, but I would be mortified if anything were to ever happen to it."

'Why do you say that?'

940

"I'm not exactly the best plant mother in the world. I used to forget to water the plants at the Italian restaurant."

'Nonsense,' I told her. 'I feel like I know you, though I don't know too much about you other than the fact that you exude naturalistic vibrations.'

"Vibrations," she responded matter-of-factly. "I like the sound of that."

We continued on through dirt paths and talked about our lives. Something compelled me to tell her about everything: my car accident, my aunt, and even my son. I was not afraid to be vulnerable with her, for she seemed like she was whispering, "I'm a safe person to talk to" with each and every tilt of her head.

The intense energy continued throughout the day as we traveled around Martha's Vineyard. It was quite thrilling to be a visitor on this heavenly island, almost to the point where I felt that Martha's Vineyard was a refreshing home away from home.

The two of us wandered for a while and found ourselves walking past a quaint church near the water.

She grabbed my hand and began dragging me towards the door.

"Come with me," Layne walked in and we were met with a flurry of faces drifting towards us. Formal services were not occurring, but there were many souls sitting on the pews with their eyes cast downward.

We approached a series of red candles resting dormant on a wooden table. Small glass jars were holding the candles in place, as if their presence was paramount in supporting the intentions behind the candles' purpose.

Layne brushed past me and reached for a long, solitary match.

As she whisked it towards a candle that was already lit, I could see the miniscule flame reflecting in her eyes. The glow from the match seemingly evaporated as the flame graced the candle.

"Since the moment you told me about your aunt," she spoke softly. "I have wanted to do something to honor her influence in your life."

I nodded silently, unsure of what to think next.

"I am lighting this candle in memory of your Aunt Barbara."

Layne waved the match in a zigzag pattern momentarily, until a trail of smoke leapt from the stick. The smoke drifted between us as we grinned at one another.

Her compassion and her unwavering dedication to honoring my aunt moved me in a way I never knew I could feel.

From then on, I knew that moment would cling to my soul for all eternity.

As night fell upon us, the two of us went back to the cozy bed and breakfast I was staying at and ate dinner on the porch.

There were ostentatious wooden rocking chairs situated at the far corner of the porch where we sat removed from the rest of the patrons staying there.

We felt comfort in knowing that the two of us were connecting so deeply and in such a breathtaking place.

"Seriously, between what you are working on and what I am working on," she eagerly rocked forward on her chair. "Something incredible is going to be born from all of this."

'I see how this can connect in a really powerful way to my larger vision of educational reform for the country and ultimately the world,' I replied.

"You talk a lot about education reform."

'It's a part of the very fabric of my life.'

We watched people walking down the street, their shadows growing taller as they disappeared towards the sunset.

"Us idealists have to stick together," she placed her hand over mine as we swayed in unison. The chairs were in perfect balance with the Earth's rotation.

'We will change this planet for the better in ways nobody can imagine at all.'

As the two of us were moving in tandem, it seemed like we were partners from another lifetime. I did not know how to label the sort of spiritual relationship we had, but it was riveting. While I thought about our sudden connection in more detail, she outright said what I was thinking:

"You know," she leaned over. "I think we are like twin flames."

'What's that?'

"There are different types of twin flames and spiritual relationships in this universe, but it feels like we have been working together for eternity."

'I guess we are the ones we have been waiting for,' I nudged her playfully.

"We are the ones the *world* has been waiting for."

The two of us continued to talk about the work we were creating. It was exciting to see how enthralled she was by the words coming out of my mouth.

"Thank you," she locked eyes with me and smiled.

'Why are you thanking me?' I leaned back in the chair and interlocked my fingers.

"I admire your tenacity for your vision. It makes me feel like my work matters, too."

'Why do you think your work wouldn't matter?'

She sighed and rested her elbow on the armrest. Her chin flopped into her hand.

"Who would ever listen to a waitress?"

'You are still a waitress?'

Layne sat up. "You sound disappointed."

'No,' I assured her. 'I just wonder why no one knows about your insight yet.'

"Family is incredibly important to me. The diner gives me a paycheck and the chance to meet fascinating characters. Writing is a hobby."

'Stuff that sets your soul on fire should not just be a hobby, Layne.'

"I know," she started. "I hear you."

'I hope that you truly do.'

"I share some of my ideas with the regular customers at this diner I work at, but that's about it." She smoothed out her pants. "The midnight crowd at the diner is relatively attentive... considering most of them are lonely or drunk."

The two of us laughed.

'One day you'll make it out of the diner, I get that sense.'

"It's not that I don't *want* to be a waitress. I am thankful for my job," she looked out at the people passing by again. "I just want more; more for this planet. I want my writing to inspire the world."

'I hear you,' I smiled at her. 'Have you ever heard of Paulo Coehlo?'

"Of course, the author of *The Alchemist*, who hasn't?"

'It took him years to get discovered. He writes masterpieces, but it was his second book that made his insight known globally.'

Layne caught my eye again and swallowed nervously.

"Anyway," she stood up. "I am sorry to do this to you, but I am going to have to call this an early night. I could not get off from work this weekend, and I am working the midnight shift."

'Oh,' I shuddered. I desperately wanted to spend more time with her. 'Do you want me to walk you to work?'

"That would be great, thanks."

We joined the patrons whose shadows were growing in the sunset. It was a short walk from my bed and breakfast to where she worked, which was refreshing. I had only been to Martha's Vineyard once before, and it would be easy to find my way back to where I was staying.

After I dropped her off, Layne darted into the diner and grabbed her apron. She seamlessly tied it around her waist as if she were preparing for a performance.

I wondered what she thought of me.

On my walk back to the bed and breakfast, I admired the stars more fondly. In New York City, there is usually so much light pollution that the sky is inundated with bright lights.

You can rarely see all of the bright stars shining up above.

I called Morena and the two of us started to talk about my thoughts. For some reason, I felt odd dropping Layne off at work and walking away from her.

"Why is that?" Morena asked when I told her about my feelings.

'It consumes me, not in an obsessive way, but in a manner like when you go to church and your spirits are uplifted.'

"What consumes you?"

'Layne's spirit... her energy,' I responded quickly. 'It is like sitting down and having tea with God. Not like I know what tea with God is really like... does that make sense?'

Morena chuckled, "With you, does anything ever make sense?"

Upon re-entering the bed and breakfast, I went straight into my room and started to wander around.

"You just need to go with the flow, Scott," Morena was trying to allay my nerves.

'I guess you are right, Mo.' I stood up and started to pace between the windows.

"I don't know," Morena said. "Maybe she is your missing puzzle piece."

'Do you think?' I threw myself onto the bed and heard the springs creak below me.

"The way you talk about her," she started. "It sounds like you are finally happy."

'*Finally*,' I scoffed. 'I don't know what happiness is anymore.'

"Give it time," she remarked. "You'll know when you know."

'I hope so,' I looked out the window at the night sky. 'I hope so.'

My voice trailed off and suddenly I felt more connected to whatever was out there in the universe. There was a sensation, some sort of feeling that for once everything would work out. Everything that was meant to be in this world would eventually be.

It was just a matter of time.

∞ ∞ ∞ ∞ ∞ ∞ ∞ ∞

As the sun rose and beamed through the windows, the light rested its energy just above the headboard of the bed. I rolled over and let the patterned quilt slip slightly off of my back. I folded my hands underneath my head and shut my eyes again.

A few moments later, and with a breathy sigh escaping my mouth; I threw the blanket off of me and leapt up. My toes curled over the hardwood floors below me.

Though my hair was askew and I was in need of a shower, I made it my duty to get ready in time to meet Layne at the diner. Something told me that I had to be the first person she saw in the morning after her long night at work.

I made my way down the street and pushed open the glass doors as fast as I could move my feet.

Layne had her hair tied neatly in a bun; her apron was covered in food stains that loosely resembled mashed potatoes and some form of cake. It looked like she had a really busy night.

"Scott," she looked up and appeared surprised. "Good morning!"

'Good morning, how are you doing?'

"Good, good," she wiped her hands on her apron. "Better now. You're up relatively early."

'I wanted to come see you.'

Layne tucked her notepad into her apron. "It's so nice of you. Are you hungry?"

'Starving, yeah.'

Layne grabbed two menus and plopped them on a table. The plastic clacked against the table as she motioned to the booth.

"Sit down, I'll treat you to breakfast."

She untied the apron and draped it over a nearby chair.

The two of us looked through the menus for a moment. I peeked over mine to see her squinting at the words.

'Are you okay with eating where you work?' I lowered the menu.

"Of course," she dropped the menu on the table. "I love it here. Who wouldn't want to sit on bright red foam with a cruddy plastic table in front of them?"

The two of us laughed again. Layne's laughter was infectious and uplifting.

Since I was leaving later that day, I wanted to make sure that the two of us could spend as much time together as possible. Our deep conversation took on new heights, as I continuously felt a weight being lifted from my soul as she spoke.

Without any trepidation, I pulled the makings of the educational reform framework that Morena and I were working on and slid it across the table.

"This Morena you work with, what is she like?" Layne started to flip through the pages of the binder.

'Honestly, I don't even know if she is real,' I chuckled.

Layne looked up and her face dropped. "Really? Then what is she?"

'If I said an angel, would you think I was crazy?'

We paused for a moment and I looked up at her. Layne's eyes seemed to be searching for something to say.

"No, because insanity means doing the same thing over and over again and expecting change," she reached across the table. "You are reinventing what it means to live."

'I am trying to come up with a holistic education system.'

She continued to read and flip through the pages. "Holistic," she paused. "I like that word a lot."

She pulled out a notebook that looked oddly similar to Morena's.

'What's that?'

"It's my journal," she replied as she scribbled furiously in the book. "I jot all of my ideas and words in here. Sometimes I doodle, but mainly it's for productive writings."

Before either of us realized it, over eight hours flew by. The two of us were consumed with asking questions about each other's plans and ideas. Layne yawned and I knew that my ferry would be leaving within the hour.

'I'm so sorry I need to leave now,' I swiveled the binder towards me.

"It's okay," she collected her papers. "I know we will be jamming together again soon."

'I sense *real* soon.'

Layne took the clip from her hair and shook out the bun. She placed a red baseball cap on her head and held the brim with her pointer finger and thumb before nodding in another waiter's direction.

We stepped out into the receding daylight and began to walk towards her car. Layne insisted that although she was up for over a day at this point, she just *had* to drive me to the ferry.

As I stepped out onto the street, I didn't even think to walk to the corner.

"Why am I not surprised," Layne laughed. "Of course, the New Yorker jaywalks."

'Jaywalking? That's what you think New Yorkers do.' I spun around to watch her run out into the street after me. 'We walk with *style*.'

I took the cap off of her and placed it backwards on her head. 'Live a little bit, Layne!'

She looked utterly ridiculous, but she had an adorable way about her.

"Real cute," she wrinkled her nose.

'Yes, you are.'

Layne nudged me playfully as she seemed to enjoy doing. It was one of those small actions that seem insignificant, but add such gravity to the soul-connecting relationships manifested in this universe.

When she dropped me back at the ferry terminal, the two of us peered into the darkness. I could hear the Atlantic Ocean calling me back to the mainland.

The two of us silently looked at one another as I pulled her closer for a hug. We embraced each other in a manner that spoke a thousand words without either of us opening our mouths.

As I released her from my hold, she gazed up at me. Her eyes appeared to be an olive color in the moonlight.

'Thank you,' I whispered.

"For what?"

'I admire your tenacity for your vision. It makes me feel like my work matters.'

"Hey," her smile took up her entire face. "You can't steal my lines."

'It's not stealing, I am just in awe of you.'

I saw her swallow hard. "I am also in awe of you."

There was another silence between us until the ferry's horn flooded the air.

'I'm sorry. I have to go.'

"I know," she held my hand for a moment. "I understand."

'I hope you do. I really, *really* hope that you do.'

As I turned to walk over to the ferry, her presence and aura sent a warm sensation throughout my body. Everything within me told me to turn and stay, but I did not listen to the voice within my soul.

While boarding the ferry I glanced on the dock to see her hair drifting in the wind. Layne waved slightly before she sauntered away and out of sight.

She seemed like the perfect woman in every way, and I could not help but realize that part of me was enamored by her. With my head resting against the window on the ferry, I watched the dock move further and further away.

My phone vibrated in my pocket and disrupted my train of thought: it was Layne.

'Hello?'

"Hey," I could tell that Layne was sobbing.

'What's wrong?'

"I am so sorry I am calling you, but I bumped the curb with my car and flattened my tire. I am just waiting for the repairman and I wanted to call you."

'Me,' I asked her. 'Why me?'

"Why not you?" She appeared to sound happier.

'I don't know. Are you safe?'

"Yeah," she replied. "Yeah, I-" she cleared her throat.

'Are you okay?'

"I was nervous and I wasn't paying attention, and I hit the curb."

'Well, you are also tired. Why were you nervous?'

Why do you ask so many questions?" Layne laughed.

'I am sorry, I am just curious.'

"You don't have to be sorry," she started. "I enjoy your curiosity."

We both paused for a bit too long.

"I enjoy your company."

The two of us talked about feeling a shift in the universe and how something major was building in the world and between us.

A horn honked in the background and she hurried to cover the phone for a moment.

"Scott," she sounded rushed. "I am sorry, the repairman is here."

'That's okay,' I assured her. 'I am just about at Woods Hole. Text me when you get home and get some rest.'

"Thanks, I am grateful for you."

'And I am grateful for you too.'

Staring out at the darkness beyond the window, I came to a startling epiphany: we were both looking up at the same sky; the same full moon… yet neither of us was whole without the other.

∞ ∞ ∞ ∞ ∞ ∞ ∞ ∞

As I drove back down to New York, I felt a distinct longing. I just met Layne not long ago, but her compassion and intelligence shook my core. Something deep within her made me want to learn more. Her thoughts and insight were reminiscent of a wise philosopher, though her cave was set in a diner and she was cognizant beyond Plato's wildest dreams.

When I finally made it back to the couch, a lot happened while I was dreaming. The imagery in my head bombarded my soul. The same words were chanted over and over again in my mind: chakras, energy, and flow.

My soul was trying desperately to translate what it meant.

The next morning, I realized that work felt mundane again. I wanted to be back in Martha's Vineyard with Layne.

Instinctively, I texted her to see how she was doing. Though I did not hear from her all day, Morena assured me that everything was going to be okay.

"Just breathe into the moment," Morena told me. "When the time is right, the connections in your life will fall into place. Unplug. Rest. Meditate."

'I wonder what she truly thinks of me,' my thoughts wandered into the abyss.

"You are too focused on what other people think of you and not what you should be. Breathe. You are tired and it is hard to communicate with you when you are like this."

'Like what?'

Her voice grew solemn, "You're disconnected."

I could not disagree with her. There was a shift happening deep within me and I could not fathom what it meant.

The path I once walked alone finally felt whole, and it was due to Layne's presence.

"Be brave," Morena spoke with the utmost confidence. "Be patient and be cognizant that you can choose whatever you wish to feel. Breathe positivity into your life."

At night, vivid dreams of Layne flooded my head. This time I was standing alone in a bar for a moment, I swished my finger around the rim of the cup while humming to the beat of a heartbeat that was not my own. I felt it reverberating through my core. A curious man cast his eyes down at a notebook; the green and gold pages peering back menacingly.

As I picked my hair up over my shoulder, I spoke to a shadow standing nearby, 'What are you writing, beautiful?'

Layne's voice faded "The next amazing spiritual masterpiece."

When I woke up, I realized I fell into a deep sleep.

It was a challenge to focus on anyone or anything else but Layne in those moments.

As I went to work begrudgingly, the smell of marijuana filled the streets. It is a smell that had my skin crawling, for it broke my concentration. In all honesty it is hypocritical for me to have that opinion due to my past. I think the term "opinion" was the operative word here.

I looked at acceptance in society.

No one bats an eye if there is a distinct marijuana smell lingering in the air. I was hopeful that if a society could accept the lingering scent, then people could accept higher consciousness as a genuine state of mind.

Who are any of us to truly judge?

We create our own versions of right and wrong and try to live by these standards. Society taught us that we must have rules; otherwise we are not inherently "good" people.

We manifest something to measure who we are in order for us to create value systems. Whether we consciously do it or not, the standards we put in place are developed by a somewhat forced ideology within our world.

What if we are all here to learn, evolve, and expand our souls?

What if this is just all experiential?

What if clearing the mind, as taught in meditation, clears the way to better communicate with your soul?

Burning questions ushered me into the next day of work. The questions continued to stand out in my mind as Layne's messages popped up on the screen.

She profusely apologized as she told me what she had been up to the past day or so.

Though Layne was constantly working at the diner, she used her free time to develop her ideas. Her insight was impeccable by any standard, and our conversations soon became a quintessential part of my day.

Each time I read anything that she wrote, I was blown away by the miraculous words that spilled onto her journal's pages.

As the two of us spoke, she seemed to shy away from any sweet comments I would make about her and her work.

It dawned on me that maybe I am not supposed to marry the greatest woman on the face of the planet. I thought that maybe the issue was that I kept finding amazing women who were slightly out of my reach.

The big dreams I had were always inundating my personal life. The love I had for the woman in my life matched my dreams, which tended to push them away.

I know that now.

Elyza helped plant the seeds that I was destined for bigger plans in this universe, though I developed a stronger sense of who I was upon being apart from Elyza.

My life has been filled with challenges, but is doused in quintessential blessings.

Each night, I continued to wake up at 3:14 in the morning. I looked up the implications the number has, and it apparently means that it is time to take action when it comes to your dreams. When I told Layne about this, she was stunned.

She explained to me that she kept seeing 315 wherever she went.

The two of us engaged in such a powerful conversation about spirituality. There is a war brewing within souls in this universe. We are all pawns in the game of ego versus ego, yet we are laced with manifestations of the deepest spirituality. We must be mindful of the voice within our respective souls.

We must rise above.

How do you guide righteousness and plant the seeds of faith and hope?

This is a leadership conundrum of the greatest kind. The stakes are only just building. Many factors play into this storyline and it leaves me concerned.

I wonder what lessons will play out in this world.

Even those who are viewed as the greatest leaders in society; there are deep wounds that bleed through.

Again, more questions flooded my mind about Layne. I was starting to feel deeply about her, and it became a reality that I needed to listen to the voice within me.

Do I play the game or push through the lesson from higher consciousness?

Do I be selfish or do I come from a place of self-love?

Who is the "self" in this scenario?

My heart remained heavy in not knowing the answers. These words remind me that there is so much beauty around that we don't recognize and that we are blinded by.

There is so much more than the little stories we allow to consume our lives.

This is all experiential, but we put so much pressure on ourselves to make this our all, and the answer to it all.

There is a bigger picture.

∞ ∞ ∞ ∞ ∞ ∞ ∞ ∞

I awoke in the morning before work, dreading another day not being by Layne's side. Something told me not to tempt fate and stop sweltering under the mounting pressure of my emotional selfishness.

Maybe I did not need to be near Layne.

Maybe I had to let go of any physical tethers that would conflict with my visions.

I wondered if divine love still mattered. My mind wanted to comprehend what my soul wanted, though I was wholeheartedly concerned with my future.

Layne seemed perfect, but I wondered if she was a distraction from the dreams I had.

The spiritual lessons I have received are to love unconditionally. It is not to let someone's actions or excitement for their perspective on success, inhibit personal truth and goals.

My emotions were selfish because I knew I desired this grander vision.

I knew I had so much I wanted to accomplish. Still, the resources handed to me through angelic stretches seemed to compete against or outdo the path before me.

I feared I would look like I was the follower.

There was a conscious feeling that slipped through my mind. A sense of knowing that something, somewhere was happening. A light and airy feeling perhaps, but one that I have yet to be able to put words to. A sign, a signal, a cardinal, a flash…

A flash of light that tells me something else is coming. A burning. A rising…

And the sensation that so many things in this universe and this planet are manifesting before our very eyes, whether we seek it or see it.

A soul, charred and damp, glaring blissfully out the window at the remnants of a broken restaurant. A shed of wood towering in the adorous distance.

An American flag. Waiting patiently. To represent a world and an entity so close to the spiritual world…

That the Earth's axis is placed back into its rightful, honorable location.

Spinning, waving… the crimson and blue shades wrapping rapidly in the air.

Only to wade and wave methodically as time spins over and over in the abysmal yard. Yet the flag is so much more than that. The whipping and whistling of the trees are calling.

Take the lantern, light the way, and answer the call.

It is ringing.

One moment, one step, one second, that's all it takes to make a change. That is all it takes to make a choice.

All the intricacies of the world: different systems, how they interconnect, how they can be improved, who makes those decisions, what team do I need, how do I comprehend history, how has it led to where we are, and how I have to steer the ship we call the United States of America was consuming my daily thoughts.

What do I want here on this planet?

What does my soul want to experience?

At that point I lived through a serious car accident, a bout with alcoholism, battled a drug addiction, dealt with unhealthy relationships, had cancer, and nursed a broken heart.

However, this is not a story of victimization. This is a journey of self-awareness, creation, and ultimate love in its different forms.

This is about living, experiencing, and expanding.

The words of this journey are inundated with spirituality and awakening.

Appearances are not what they seem, for our souls are a combination of energy and higher consciousness. It all comes down to our respective perceptions of reality. We are bigger than the nuances and drama of everyday life.

Everywhere I go, every step I take, and every person I see has a story behind the story. I hoped that I would be able to learn Layne's story behind the story.

I wondered what I could do to improve her life and the lives of others.

The decisions we make in our daily life, though some are crazy and irresponsible, are the fabric of our respective lives. Each of our quilts is composed of patchwork: squares of varying color and length but are the essence of humanity at large. We all have the ability to establish our patch on another's quilt, but our actions and words have the power to either keep others warm or leave them frigid.

On some level that may be a metaphorical perspective, but there is much more at stake here: the search for love.

We are on a continuous journey to find ourselves, and others in this lifetime. It is the natural human way. As we live our lives, we have the capacity to understand soulful love on a devout level.

If we could establish leadership roles that harness that desire for love, we have the potential to transform our planet. Sure, we would have our fair share of challenges, but we can make a drastic shift in the trivial negativity that plagues our lives.

When you think about it, it is clear that a higher love exists within our universe. It may be deep within the stars that cascade across the night sky, or locked away in a heart that beats in honor of the mantra, "The best is yet to come."

It is best we all look introspectively at ourselves in order to deter the pessimism that lurks in the shadows.

Fairness and light always win if we give power to those types of actions and words.

A higher love is present; it is just a matter of time before we unlock our souls to see what this world could become.

Acceptance and love are key goals, with the path to resolution being communication, respect, and listening. We should support one another, not fight each other, for often the battle within us is more consequential than the fighting around us.

Let's put down our fists.

Let's stop degrading one another due to the color of someone's skin or sexual orientation.

There is beauty in life.

Beauty exists within the connections we create, the communication between souls, and moments that take our breath away. Though sometimes they are few and far between, the blessings are apparent within our lives. Sometimes, it takes a moment of silence to comprehend what the voices within us are saying. Therefore, we must actively try to listen to our souls.

Though I was conflicted when it came to Layne, some sort of sensation was brewing deep within. My soul felt challenged by how devoted it was to speaking to and being in the presence of Layne.

I did not want my heart to be broken again, but then again, I did not know if what I was feeling for Layne was, indeed, love.

As our daily texts and insightful conversations continued, I was not sure exactly what direction we were going in. All I knew was that we were both moving towards something greater than ourselves.

I could feel it.

I chose to give into the voice within my soul and do what I felt was right: within weeks of finally seeing Layne, I decided I would go back to Martha's Vineyard to explore the connection between us.

For as long as I could remember, I was trying to save the souls on this planet. Many people blame human nature for their soul's detriment, but the truth is that humanity is not unkind.

It is learned behavior for when our souls are misunderstood.

We must make up our minds, for we have our whole lives to decide what is true. When we look up at the stars, we are not just wishing for love to blaze through our lives. Even when the night is over and it seems like our souls are drifting away from our true intentions.

I know I will still be here, stargazing.

∞ ∞ ∞ ∞ ∞ ∞ ∞ ∞

On the drive up to Massachusetts, I began gazing out at the lush trees that were in full bloom.

Morena and I spoke on the phone for a while to quell my nerves.

"I don't even know why you are nervous," She remarked.

'I don't know either,' I tapped on the steering wheel. 'I just have a feeling.'

"About what?"

I rubbed my neck with my open palm. 'I don't know, it's like... you know when you find something you have *really* been looking for? It's like that.'

"Okay, we are getting somewhere," she sounded relieved. "She is the one you have been looking for."

'Is that a question, Morena, or–'

"Oh," she sounded slightly startled. "Yeah, it was a question."

It was odd: Morena sounded like she knew what was going to happen regarding Layne. It was almost as if she had a premonition that life would be drastically different upon my arrival in Martha's Vineyard during this trip.

Her words were prophetic at times, and had I known what I would be walking into, I think I would have prepared myself a lot better.

At that point I had a challenging time being myself, for I was constantly evolving. I was still working through a lot, though I chose not to outwardly admit it to the world.

I was a transformative soul in progress and Layne's presence would soon be the tipping point.

When I parked at the terminal and boarded the ferry, I continued to remain in this weird reflective space. Now, don't get me wrong, it is not a negative place to be.

The universe just seemed to be speaking to me in a manner that was a lot stronger than usual.

For all intents and purposes, it seemed that the Circle of Angels was shining down upon me from the sunlight up above. The birds chirping and flying close to the boat were echoic of the messages from the Circle of Angels.

I closed my eyes and let the sea air inundate my body. Whispers to my community grew from deep within my soul. I was thankful for the courage bestowed upon me from the stars that are both seen and unseen. Before so many of the angels physically left this earth, they granted me so many life lessons.

Light carries on endlessly despite death.

The infinite remains despite the seemingly momentary presence each of my angels brought to my life.

It is so rare and beautiful to even exist within another soul's timeline; so much that in those moments I was grateful for Layne's impact on my life so far.

Upon reaching the dock, Layne cheerfully waved at the boat. I could see her beaming smile as we disembarked from the ferry.

"Hey," she rushed right over and threw her arms around me. "I missed you!"

The affection she granted me made it seem as if we had not been physically apart for a few weeks.

Layne and I chatted about my drive up from New York as we walked to her car. The white sedan had a small scuff on the passenger side, which was seemingly from the incident with her tire the last time I left town.

I was hoping she would not be nervous this time around.

As the two of us drove towards the bed and breakfast, it became clear that she had another side to her. In actuality she has several sides to her, but regardless of whatever side is present for the given moment, the two of us seem to connect and understand one another so well.

"I really hope you don't mind," she said as we got out of the car. "Tonight is my friend's birthday party and we were invited to the party."

'*We?*' I hoped I did not come off as uninterested.

"Yeah, is it okay with you that we go?"

I chuckled. 'Of course, I am just glad I am here with you. I am surprised I got an invitation, honestly.'

"Surprised," she touched my shoulder and her energy reverberated through my body. "My friends adore you."

'They don't even know me.'

"Don't worry, I told them everything there is to know."

'Oh,' I gulped. 'Great.'

"Don't worry! I explained how you are interested in education reform and they were all intrigued. Don't be surprised if you get asked a lot of questions tonight.'

'I am not worried,' I nudged her. 'I am with you.'

We gazed at each other until I came up with something to break the silence.

'Um,' I cleared my throat. 'Is your boyfriend or anyone else coming with us?'

She smiled endearingly. "I don't have a boyfriend *or anyone else.*"

'Oh,' I adjusted my collar. 'I didn't mean anything by that.'

"Okay." She walked past me and turned around. "I know."

Layne let out an exasperated sigh.

'What's wrong?'

"There-" she swallowed hard. "There is something you should know about me."

'Okay,' I leaned against the roof of the car for a moment. 'I am listening.'

Layne sighed again as she slammed the door. The two of us walked in silence to the front of the bed and breakfast. We took a seat on the rocking chairs on the porch.

She continued to explain to me why she did not have a boyfriend for quite some time. It appeared that years ago, she had a best friend who she did everything with. The two girls were practically inseparable.

Once Layne found a boyfriend, her best friend secretly grew jealous.

Through tears, she held my hand and let the words flow from her, "It got to the point where I left work early one day, and I came home and found both of them in bed together. I moved out of the house my boyfriend and I were living in that night."

'Layne, I am so sorry.'

"Don't be," she wiped her eyes. "I am thankful we didn't get married… and he said he loved me."

'Love is a special gift; he shouldn't have played with your heart like that'

"Thanks," she gripped my hand harder. "Thank you for saying that."

The two of us shifted to a more positive topic.

We spoke for hours about her plans and dreams. She hoped to do something powerful within this world, and she had such an abundance of ideas, but Layne claimed to need a catalyst to move forward.

I wondered what she meant by it, but I tried not to read into it.

As the night fell upon us, the two of us wandered into a rustic looking bar. Colored seashells and lights tucked into mason jars lined the wall. It appeared to be a secret paradise of sorts where her friends regularly convened.

Her friends greeted me jovially, and it was clear that they started to drink a lot earlier than expected. Layne worked the crowd with ease. She conversed with people she did not seem to know as if she belonged in their respective lives.

Still, the energy did not seem as strong as the connection the two of us had.

At one point as my lack of dancing skills consumed my body, a man cut in and tried to grab her hand. Though he was a stranger, she did not dismiss him in a nasty manner.

Layne gently took a step back.

"I am not interested, thank you though," she bowed out of respect and placed her hand back in mine.

As the man stepped away, the light bounced off of her eyes and cut directly into me. It was almost as if she was warning me: be careful with what you do.

Her friends were very cordial to me and did not leave me out of any conversation whatsoever. The whole situation reminded me that people are not always strangers. Upon having open and honest conversations, the universe continues to move in a symbiotic manner.

The next day, Layne was off from work and offered to show me another tour of Martha's Vineyard.

She took me to a place called the Aquinnah Cliffs Overlook, where the view of the ocean was utterly breathtaking. A quaint sepia-toned lighthouse sat precariously near the end of a long series of greenery.

The rushing water was the quintessential background noise to our discussion about changing the world.

With the sunlight beaming down upon her, the two of us started to move closer and closer to one another. I still did not have a clear read on her or her feelings towards me, but basking in her energy felt amazing.

Layne took me towards a secluded part of the overlook and motioned for me to sit. She took her place next to me and the energy between us took on the momentum of a firestone. With a single spark between us, we seemed to be able to light up the world.

It felt like I had known her for all eternity.

Her hair draped over my arm almost in an angelic manner as she fell into my arms. It was almost as if we were a majestic puzzle whose pieces were once scattered, yet now they were interconnected appropriately. My gentle kisses caressed her forehead in our everlasting symbiosis. Her cosmic energy mingled with every fiber of my heart's longing, yet we inherently knew that our conjoining would exacerbate a force to be reckoned with.

More than a shift, but a soulful awakening: a spiritual diaspora of the negativity we once harnessed melting into the infinite worlds we now expanded upon.

A cathartic sigh of "at last" in a once-concealed force field burdened by the scars of past pain that obscured all the goodness longing to be released into the world.

In that very moment, I felt unburdened by the shackles of expectations. I felt inner peace and frivolity for the first time in forever. I felt the weight of circumstance lift itself from my soul and ascend to its next mission: a means to establish my growth.

I had it within me all along. I had it. I knew I did. I just never realized that I could be the one to bring it out. I have a mind, body, and soul to nurture. I had a heart that still fervently beats as the band marches on.

It is transcendental. It is awe-inspiring. It is growth and freedom and an abundance of life.

It is a rebirth.

A solitary moment became lost in the fabric of time, simply because of the intertwining of two hands and two souls. Interlocking fingers signaling the conjunction of the timeline threading itself in our lives.

A soul connection could never be divided or severed. It could not be broken, though at times it could be bent in the cosmic whip that stands between the sky, the stars, and our human entities. The energy emitted into the air pollutes our minds, but without the negative connotation that comes with pollution existing in the atmosphere.

Love is intoxicating and love takes many forms. Love is its own monstrous being: merging with two respective souls within the blink of an eye or the erection of a smile.

Everything has reason and everything has purpose, it all just comes down to one question: how badly do you want the connection to strengthen?

Now find it within your own soul... then seek the goodness in other souls.

∞ ∞ ∞ ∞ ∞ ∞ ∞ ∞

I planted a gentle kiss on Layne's forehead before I left.

"Thank you for this weekend," she hugged me. "Your expressions and realness are a breath of fresh air. I appreciate you so much, beyond words."

A tinge of weirdness caused me to shudder at her touch.

'I am sorry,' I whispered to her.

"For what?"

'I just want us to stay in a state of symbiosis.'

"We always will be," she grinned majestically. "The universe has already determined it."

Notions of God, spirituality, and higher consciousness flooded my soul. I just knew I had to come back to her again as soon as possible. I was hoping that with the summer coming up, I would be able to make more trips up to Martha's Vineyard and hoped she might potentially visit New York soon enough.

New days were upon us to signify our advancement forward. We had to keep expanding, we had to keep growing; we had to continue to be grateful and inspirational.

Excitement was building with regard to all that was yet to be built. The journey forward was going to be of a soulful and more spiritual one.

It was a profound shift in the universe.

Before I boarded the ferry, she grasped my arms with her tender fingertips. I wanted to kiss her intensely, but I was not sure if the energy I was feeling towards her was truly mutual.

Again, I was fearful of making the same mistakes over and over.

The drive down to New York was filled with fond memories of dancing with her and holding her in my arms.

'What am I doing?' I wondered desperately.

There was a certain thickness in the energy that encircled me.

I felt alone though I should have been so elated after coming back from such an intense and magical weekend. Still, I felt scared and alone.

The cars were parked the same on my mother's street.

My daily routine was still the same.

The damp New York drizzle stemming from the trees ushered in its casual emotions.

My heart was on the verge of sensing a huge lesson here. I felt immersed in a movie scene; wherein the main character was about to have a spiritual awakening that arrives at a pivotal moment.

After everything I experienced, I wondered if I could, yet again, be at the crux of another earth-shattering moment.

I did not think that words could materialize on my lips, yet the letters were able to flow freely from my pen.

This was an atypical combination of energy and vibration that the universe seemed to orchestrate. I figured that above all, Layne needed to breathe into this new role we were both stepping into.

Much uncertainty lingered in what all of this meant and who we were to each other, but I was sure that we would soon find out.

I made it my mission to go back up to see her again.

To my soul, it was an inconsequential longing to be next to her. A bigger picture was forming before us, and we seemed like the ones who would be stepping into the light together.

I was still in the process of emotionally healing from the cancer and past wounds, but the scars were beginning to fade away rapidly.

It appeared that I found my way to Martha's Vineyard for one reason and one reason alone: Layne.

At the time, I wondered what that even meant.

Thinking about it in such complex terms left me somewhat paralyzed, yet I was struck by the numb sensation of feeling her fingers wrapped between mine.

It was not a pestilent numbness, but rather it was a sensation that my frozen soul was beginning to thaw.

As the New York clouds cleared, I realized that I really was not the same anymore. This time however, I could truly feel it.

"You are the best I have ever come across, Scott, I am so sold on you it's not even funny," Layne assured me as we spoke on the phone before I walked into work.

'You truly are the light on the darkest of days,' I assured her.

A breathy laugh trailed into a sigh, which left me slightly confused.

Her thoughts must have been running rampant.

As I walked throughout the building, nothing fazed me, not even Emma.

Standing in the eye of the storm, I felt a sudden rush of peace pass over my body. Her ghosts no longer haunted me. Her aroma did not linger on the forefront of my memory; rather she was an image of a past life.

Caught betwixt the balance of the swirling winds and torrential rain, I realized I had become a byproduct of all of the chaos and calamity that I had endured; yet I was not the chaos. I was not the turmoil. I was me. I was every fundamental aspect of growth and frivolity that had been masked by circumstance. In the eye, I was myself again.

The clarity gave me a rejuvenating feeling. The clarity wholeheartedly renewed and restored my faith. I was underneath the rubble all along.

The desolate destruction could no longer bear the weight of my soul.

Like a phoenix, I rise from the ashes and unburden myself from the stinging sensation of pain.

I rise.

And as I rise above... I realized something utterly earth shattering: I am not in the eye of the storm.

I am not in the eye of the storm... because the storm has passed...

And here I am. A bold new soul standing at the edge of the rocks... glaring out at the new opportunities ahead in the water. A green light holds steady on the buoy in the water: a reminder that I too could live.

I too can shine.

This old soul may have been down, but it is not out. I was buried; then I was planted...

Now it is time to grow.

∞ ∞ ∞ ∞ ∞ ∞ ∞ ∞

I became consumed and lost in the summer nights. Layne's crystalline eyes left me utterly speechless. Despite the darkness that once existed in my soul, I realized that nothing else mattered but her presence.

As I drove up to Martha's Vineyard for the third time in less than a few weeks, it dawned upon me: I would never let her go.

Exhausted and slightly fragmented, I fell onto the seat on the ferry.

There are so many souls in pain on the planet, yet despite the seeming agony we manage to make other souls happy.

It's priceless.

We are the ones who create our own reality. We attract what we desire in order to learn the lessons that excavate the broken bits of our respective souls.

The people we surround ourselves with are a testament to the ambitions we pursue in life. If we inherently want to go the distance, leaders must remember who stands beside them even when all seems chaotic and unclear.

Morena stood beside me for so long.

Best friend is a label that would slight her wholeheartedly; angel seems more fitting of a label for her, but definitely not a human angel. She is someone from some sort of different universe or realm.

Layne seemed to be the next person who I wanted on my team. The energy she emitted from her soul is genuine and spiritually enlightening. Everything within me screamed, "Whatever happens, don't screw this one up. She is the real deal."

In the past, I was too demanding, too pressuring, and attempted to fit people into a storyline that just did not add up. I was forcing love, rather than giving it the space to breathe.

I instilled fear in those I loved, which forced them to run.

Now I found myself in the midst of another test: was the love I felt for Layne real or one-sided?

A resounding thud followed by the boat lurching forward slightly meant that I was back at Martha's Vineyard. Layne was happy to see me once again, and even took off from work so we could spend the entire weekend flushing out ideas.

The overcast Friday afternoon did not put a damper on Layne's spirits, for rather she lit up the sky with the sunlight beaming from her soul.

The moment I got there, I could feel the energy burning through her skin. It almost grasped me and shook me to my core, but I had to reserve my emotions for a few moments.

Did she feel the same about me as I did for her?

The two of us walked down the street for a while until we came to a luscious gathering of trees.

"Scott, come on, I want you to see something," Layne grasped my hand and pulled me off of the concrete path. We whisked through trees and shrubs that were scattered for what looked like miles around. We were inherently alone together, an event that I longed for from the moment she grasped my hand that fateful day. From our first touch, I knew that my search had to be over: she was my destiny.

We pushed through the branches together, stumbling comically through the woods as if we were on a mission to dance in the solitude of the lush greenery forever: just the two of us. It felt as if we were creating our new home far away from civilization, yet we would develop our own society. Our souls would speak to each other in a manner only we knew and our hearts would open up a realm of their own. Just one kiss... and the connection would forever be bound together.

"This is my other spot. I come here to think and write. I wanted to share it with you." A smile crept up her cheeks as she pulled me towards the dirt.

We sat on the ground against a log with a stream rippling in front of us: it was a picturesque scene that would never leave my mind for as long as I live. We were immersed in nature where we both felt an instant connection to the universe. Outside this beautiful hidden cove was a concrete jungle... but hidden in here was just me and her. It was a safe spot to delve into this love story that seems like years in the making. Though in some juxtaposed, elaborate trepidation, we were a romance that blossomed centuries before our time. Our souls were intertwined long before our fingers met in this very moment.

As our bodies wrapped around one another in that fateful moment, Layne's face was merely an inch from my lips. She closed her eyes ambitiously, yet something was preventing us from sealing our combined fates in that moment.

"This scares me," Layne blurted out in a lucid whisper.

'Me too,' I responded.

"If we were together, we would get nothing accomplished because we would be doing…" Layne paused and collected some courage from within, "other things all the time."

I leaned in towards her and our mouths were mere seconds from each other.

Layne paused and placed her fingers on my lips. "Wait."

'What's wrong?'

"Before anything happens, I need you to know that I am afraid."

'Okay, let's talk about this,' I paused. 'I mean, if you would like to.'

"Honestly, I am still working through repairing my emotions. Nothing really replaced the love I felt for my boyfriend."

I placed my hand on top of hers. 'F. Scott Fitzgerald wrote, *"There are all kinds of love in this world, but never the same love twice."'*

She grinned and locked eyes with me. "Scott, I just don't trust myself."

'I promise I won't do anything you do not feel you are ready for.'

"Thanks."

We went back and forth, playing with the danger of what the universe provided us. Both of us fully knowing and admitting to each other that this love we felt for one another was real, but it couldn't go any further. Neither of us wanted to entirely admit it just yet, for we were immersed in the habitual beauty of the moment.

An "I Love NY" keychain dangled in between my fingertips, glowing in the great presence of her unfathomable eloquence. It took 15 hours to get to her after a five-hour drive to Massachusetts turned into a traffic nightmare. It took all of the strength within me from breaking down and melting into an abysmal depression due to what seemed like the universe pulling us apart. I explained to her that she needed to have the keychain, for I always keep an "I Love Martha's Vineyard" keychain in my pocket. Though it took all the energy I had to get to her, it was worth it. Gazing into her eyes that day, I knew it was worth every second of agony I dealt with.

As she gazed at me longingly, I pulled ants off of her shoulder as they crept along our bodies. Neither of us was phased in the moment. As she spoke about her hopes and dreams in more detail, I pulled blades of grass from near the log. Our arms were wrapped tighter around one another and I drew her closer to my chest to rub a yellow powdery substance from her nose. The sunlight shone brighter on her face as she glared into my eyes. If she were not there to hold onto, I would have melted in that very moment.

My eyes adored every inch of her supple skin pressed against mine. Her mouth was busy forming words that angels whisper to lovers in the night. Layne inhaled deeply and shot daggers through my soul: "Today can't go further than this... I need to feel safe..."

'What,' flowed out of my mouth in absolute shock. We were just getting comfortable holding one another, even in innocence.

"I don't trust myself.... this is a love on a higher level I don't quite comprehend..." Layne continued to speak, but I was deafened by the pain emulating from deep within me.

Each word slammed into me with the intensity of an atomic bomb. My soul was desolated between each breath she took. Our love rotted and morphed into a cataclysmic event: a war between the heart, mind, and soul: how could I just release this beautiful energy between us back into the world without savoring one more moment of her tender grasp? I was just getting accustomed to feeling like someone she loved.

It all came crashing down in minutes.

She pushed against my chest in a seeming fit of silent rage, "I need you to protect me Scott. I need to feel safe." Her voice shattered just as my soul was crackling at that very moment, "I need you to make sure this doesn't go further because I do not trust myself around you." I nodded rhythmically.

I sat in silence, glaring down at the river metaphorically rinsing my pain away.

'Layne, I-' as I began to speak, I could see her mounting another one-sided argument against my soul. I continued processing.

"This isn't good because you bring me so much joy. You confuse me. You blur the lines and I'm scared." My heart felt heavy and guilty. I wanted to grab her face tenderly, kiss her lips passionately, and tell her that my love for her was unyielding and unwavering. I wanted her to realize that I was the one. Me. I was her true soulmate and hers. All of me. Every last piece of my once shattered existence was hers to adore.

She needed to be loved. She needed to be seen and felt in ways that only exist in a state of higher consciousness... and that is exactly what this relationship had to be: higher consciousness. Nothing more; nothing far less than that.

'Layne, listen for a moment,' I adjusted my body so we were now face to face. I placed her shaking hands in mine and held them tightly.

'I will never hurt you. I promise that no matter what happens, I will love you to fill the cracks that permeate your gentle soul. We never have to have a physical connection between us. It is an honor and ultimately a blessing that you are who you are.'

She sat in devout silence and believed my words, though everything in the universe was restraining me from kissing her passionately and never turning back. My role was to love her how she needed to be loved. If that is not higher consciousness... then I do not know what is. To love someone deeply, yet always be at an arm's length, is one of the most soulfully challenging moments to endure. In a blink of an eye, she was mine and the universe's in one fatal swoop.

Layne fell into my arms and cuddled into my chest. I planted a solitary, slow kiss on her forehead and ran my fingers through her peaceful hair.

"I have wanted to touch you from the moment you arrived," Layne whispered. Our meeting in the midst of this universal shift was mind boggling, and in a matter of a few hours I would be back in another world again.

We sat there in the silence of each other's company as the universe filled our hearts with memories distinctly found in other lifetimes and other universes. I now know what a twin flame and true soulmate are. Those are exquisite lines that are reserved for her: the true light of my life and devout beauty eternally trapped in my mind.

"I never knew you would show up," Layne glared at me in a reaction laced with exquisite horror and fascination.

I chuckled for a moment. Emma spoke those very soul-shattering words just a few years ago. And now here we are again. Full circle. Yet this was so different. Layne was the real deal, while Emma had so much potential brewing in her bones. One day Emma will get there, hopefully soon, and I hope she has the courage to tell me how far she has come and how much she has grown. Layne however is already there. Layne is the energetic heartline that illuminates a true soul-to-soul connection. This is why things never worked with Emma: Layne was looking for our profound connection to materialize before our very eyes, but somehow our love was lost in translation.

We were both deeply in love with one another, Layne and I, and said it in the most alluring way imaginable. Being with Layne heightened my soul, for she is the perfect melody that exists between my drastic sense of who I was and who I started becoming. I needed her and she needed me…

But being together in such a spiritual sense of the term "together" always comes with its challenges.

"Scott," she looked up at the raindrops caressing her face from up above, "We should get going." As the rain kissed her skin in places I could now only dream of, neither of us moved from that spot. We longed to savor that memory. We were present to the moment we defined our very spiritual love.

As the rain washed over our bodies, I sensed we would always be intertwined… maybe not in the physical sense, but always in the spiritual sense.

'We can overcome anything together, Layne,' were the last words I whispered in her ear before we emerged into the seascape jungle once again. Our moment of intermingled solitude would never dissipate.

So much weight clenched the heartstrings I was desperately trying to keep elevated. I did not want to start ranting about hopeful messages of love, for this was not what this was about.

Honestly, I didn't know what this was about.

I just had to let go and merely go with the flow.

I believed Layne was here to stay and so much uncertainty lingered with regards to what that meant to the whole vision.

However, all I knew was that her creations and soul were remarkable.

That night, I dreamt that Morena, Layne, and I were hosting some sort of conference together. It was a retreat of sorts with global leaders from such diverse countries.

It felt very real.

It felt very different.

It felt like a memory.

We were hosting, we were not the ones attending the conference. We had global attention that previously felt unprecedented.

It was coming.

It was *all* coming.

∞ ∞ ∞ ∞ ∞ ∞ ∞ ∞

Leaving her utterly broke me. Sitting on a small ferry that's taking me back to the mainland left me with a heavy heart, yet I upheld this heavy heart that had never been happier. The phrases we uttered to one another in distinct silence lingered throughout my head.

Standing at the edge of two worlds, I felt the pressure mounting at the base of my skull. A flood of emotion rushed throughout my body as the gravity of the situation hit me... hard: the answer was finally before me. Layne was the answer to every hardship I endured. Layne was the final chapter. Layne was the missing puzzle piece that my heart finally found. My twin flame was standing before me, just an arm's length away, yet we would never be able to burn together. Still, neither of us was willing to face that fact yet. We both stood with our souls barely touching one another, hoping that the other person would tip the balance of the universe so we could crash into each other passionately. Our love was the manifestation of something that would be in a perfect movie scene: boy meets girl, girl loves boy, boy loves girl.

How do I return to what I once was after the sensation has already crept through my veins? How do I step back from the edge when I was always meant to jump and freefall into her arms?

Being on the ferry felt absolutely heavenly. The atmosphere around the boat was similar to the air we breathed into each other's souls that day. I was with Layne for only eight hours, but it felt like fifteen minutes.

When I look back though, it took fifteen hours to drive to her. Layne was utterly blown away.

This was the most incredibly loving hurt I had ever experienced in my life. It hurt, but I couldn't let it be painful. I had to feel the magnitude of the blessing and role I was upholding in her life. I don't know how to explain that day eloquently.

Yet as words fell short and my mind wandered to our intimate meeting, the ferry approached Woods Hole. I should leave what happened at the stream, at the rocks that are simply atoms moving so rapidly that it appears to feel solid and stationary, but our love permeates this universe with enough power to illuminate billions of souls. How could we hide our love? How could we resist the temptations that exist between us? No, we must. I must.

'We can overcome anything,' I whispered in her ear. 'Let me be the one who provides you the emotional strength,' I said.

Layne responded, "Please do." Her laughter is contagious. We connected on an entirely different level. I could't believe what had happened since the moment I laid eyes on that beautiful, powerful soul.

The boat slammed against the metal dock. That was fast.

Supposedly, and technically, I am going "home"...but I just left home at the water that reverently rippled through the rocks. Layne resting against my chest and embracing my lightened frame, a moment that made time as us humans know it stand still, was the true embodiment of home.

That's my home: her arms… our bodies cuddled as one. I finally found it.

I came to the stark realization that was already brewing within… I am homeless again.

While exiting the ferry it hit me, and it hit me hard: I think the reason I went through all this pain and anguish with Emma was to learn a lesson. "She has a purpose" echoed through my mind. The real reason I lost Emma was because I played my cards wrong. I was too demanding, too pressuring, and tried to get her to fit into the storyline I wanted. Emma needed to grow spiritually before we would be on the same level: our souls were disconnected the moment we met. I was forcing it and not giving her the space to figure things out and breathe. I scared her and she ran. I now found myself in a similar complicated storyline with someone I care about and could not make the same mistake. I must learn from past experiences and had to make sure I swim "in this delicious ice cream", as Layne put so eloquently, and not destroy our relationship. I needed to just enjoy the moments and let it be.

∞ ∞ ∞ ∞ ∞ ∞ ∞ ∞

Being apart from her felt awkward, though being with her meant trying to mask how deeply in love I was with her.

During the work week, I was a patron of Lincoln Memorial High School's atmosphere. Though I enjoyed my job and working with the teachers and the students, being with Layne made my soul sing.

Our regular phone conversations continued nightly to the tune of our hearts beating in tandem.

It became increasingly difficult to catch my breath.

I wondered why the universe was trying to keep me away from her. It was a simple reminder that I waited a lifetime to reconnect with Layne, so that we could finally fulfill our soul contract.

Another few hours before speaking to her on the phone again after each workday seemed like nothing.

I knew nothing would keep me away from her.

Anticipation flowed through my veins: she felt like home. It amazed me that a person could truly carry the sentiments of my heart, my soul, and my every thought.

God built us to love. We can love more than one person. We can be attracted to different things.

Society teaches that there are limitations to love, but that doesn't make sense. Love is the process of the soul expanding. Love is an abundance of appreciation. Love is everything and exists in everything.

Love is in these moments and in the pages of this book.

Love is in the connections, the alignments, the smiles, and in the tears. Fear is the manifestation of not loving your true self. Fear is not stepping into who you truly are. Fear is being asleep, not being awake.

We are all one and the one is split into an infinite amount of souls. Our limitations see this as separate entities, but in reality, we are not truly apart.

This was all making sense.

Our souls are genuinely infinite so that we may learn to develop our oneness. Separation and trepidation are mere illusions.

My heart became inundated with tears of joy.

I came to the conclusion that I was not falling in love; it was rather the opposite. Falling implies losing control, entering dangerous territory, and spiraling in a downward motion. I sense that this phrase came from a metaphorical notion that falling represented freedom and replicated an exciting rush.

However, those are fantastical fallacies we tell ourselves to make sense of the confusion we might be feeling.

Being in love with Layne provided me with an elevated state of mind and being. Love was lifting me up.

The sensation of love was empowering me to discover who I truly was. Any reality and experience I could think of had the potential to become a part of my timeline.

When you truly connect to the energy of love, souls are attracted to one another because we are one in the same.

Our souls desired to connect.

"I want to come see you," Layne whispered into the night.

'So, come to New York.'

"But if I do" she started, "Then I want to drive around and see things and talk about your Framework and our vision on the open road."

'Well, you are welcome to drive my car.'

"Really," she sounded stunned. "You would let me do that?"

'Yeah,' I replied matter-of-factly. 'Why wouldn't I?'

"Aren't guys really protective over their cars?"

'You'll be safe,' I assured her. 'I know you.'

I could hear her grin through the phone.

The two of us agreed that she would take a combination of buses to get to a certain point in Manhattan, and that I would pick her up from wherever the last bus would stop.

Layne was thrilled and by the following weekend, she was roaming the streets of New York City with me.

The two of us strolled in unison, our hands linked together perfectly. It was almost as if our fingers were created to fit between one another's.

With her coming to New York, it was a date marked in the infamy of our worlds colliding for a second. Our gravitational forces were compelled to crash into one another wholeheartedly and without remorse, yet there was something forcing us apart. Though the universe brought us together in a rather cataclysmic way in a matter of moments, it pulled us apart with such fury, as if it were beckoning the words, "No, you can't have her. She is not yours to keep." She is to be idolized and revered, like the statues placed on pedestals in museums. She is to be kept pristine and unmarked by the tainted words that shatter upon her skin upon their fateful release. She is to be regarded to the highest standard and with the most respect and sincerity.

She is to be admired by all, feared in her sense of power, and in accordance with the contract she signed with the universe long, long ago...

And she would be mine, regardless of what the universe said.

For her, I would twist the balance of fate and destiny... for she was what I yearned for all along.

And she would not escape my purview. I did not trek this path to not be in her presence, and as the universe as my witness, nothing physical or emotional would stop me from having her in my arms.

The two of us stopped for ice cream at some quaint shop in the city. As the two of us sauntered down the street, arm in arm, eating ice cream, something told me that this was how life was meant to be: innocent and simplistic.

As Layne walked ahead of me, I snapped a picture of her so I could savor the moment forever.

She shouted back to me: "Why do you do that?"

'Do what?'

"You take pictures of me sometimes when you think I don't notice. I notice."

We laughed for a moment and she seemed to drop the subject.

Little did she know, the faded pictures in my phone were frozen in the ripples of time. Each face she made consisted of smiling and laughing; she was forgetting for one moment that anything else was happening. Each expression's demeanor whittled away pain and accepted a snapshot of "Yes, my life is great," even for a split second between flashes.

The expressions faded once the camera marked its territory, but the photograph acts as a stark reminder that someone cared enough to clasp the moment and preserve it forever.

Photographs are windows to the soul. Pictures are persistent reminders that we were all once frozen in a different state of mind.

We develop, we bend, we break, we shape each other, we mold, and we transfer our energy into different avenues as the passing wind chimes reverberate. The leaves pick up and lift all of us onto another realm. We rise. We look at our pictures and smile at our reflections.

We gaze at ourselves and see our past, present, and future in one swoop. All at once, we are the whole parts of what we have left behind and what we intend to create.

And the beauty of it all? It is frozen in time, captured in a photograph… a treasured keepsake we hold dear forever.

The two of us meandered towards Bryant Park. Layne glared up at the two stone lions that guarded the New York Public Library; she seemed to be in amazement of their permanent beauty.

The lions, like the photographs, were perfectly frozen in time.

We found a quiet spot on the steps of the library where no one seemed to notice that two people were embarking on a spiritual journey of a symbiotic nature.

"I just want to make one thing very clear," Layne said.

'You have cleared up a lot in my life, but go ahead.'

"I would never cheat on you," she gripped my hands. "I don't want to hurt you, ever."

'Cheating implies secrecy,' I assured her. I gazed out at the faces of people passing by. 'We don't have that type of love.'

I spoke as if I knew this truth was coming from deep within my soul. There was no fear about losing her or any potential for her to cheat.

This was an eternal bond of a much deeper than human experience.

It wasn't about fear or loss; it was about a pure love that exceeded the humanistic way of life.

Layne was proof that the universe welcomes love openly, it is just a matter of finding your soul's voice.

Her exquisite soul's beauty, intellect, and poise were worth every single moment I endured throughout my lifetime.

I would live everything over again if I knew that I would find her again. She is worth it.

Layne was what humanity secretly prayed for. She is what I almost gave up searching for.

We both found our home and we had so much to learn before we could accept that fact. One thing was for certain though: we would travel this road together.

As the night fell upon us in Manhattan, Layne asked if we could head back towards Queens. I happily obliged and the two of us listened to music in my Dodge Charger as we sat in traffic on the Long Island Expressway.

The green road signs lined with white borders reflected in the sunroof of my car. The sunset was in the not-so-distant past, but it felt like we had been together for days at this point.

It was a refreshingly satisfying feeling.

As we pulled up to the hotel she was staying at, she asked if I would wait downstairs for a few moments while she freshened up.

Happily, I told her to take her time, for I knew that I could call Morena and fill her in on everything happening.

After about fifteen minutes of talking to her, I exhaled a sigh of relief.

"You really love, Layne, don't you?" Morena said.

'Yeah,' I tilted my head up to the stars above. 'Yes, I do.'

"I am glad your soul recognized her love."

'She is truly amazing,' I assured her.

"You don't have to tell me twice."

Our conversation ended as Layne jumped back in the car. She was wearing a tight black dress that hugged every single one of her curves. We agreed that we were going to go to a bar in Queens, so that she could experience New York's nightlife scene.

She watched my eyes drag along every inch of her body, "Are you okay?"

'Always.'

"Oh, the dress," she smoothed it out with her fingertips. "Sorry, I just figured this is what typical New Yorkers wear on a night out. I wanted you to see this side of me."

Layne fiddled with the radio for a moment until Eric Clapton's "Wonderful Tonight" materialized on the radio:

> *"I feel wonderful because I see*
> *The love light in your eyes*
> *And the wonder of it all*
> *Is that you just don't realize how much I love you."*

We glanced at one another and she placed her head on my shoulder.

"Thank you for all that you do," Layne grabbed my hand as I started to sing the lyrics to her.

We drove out of the lot as she asked if we could go to a place in Astoria, which was about twenty minutes from where she was staying in Bayside, Queens.

Although I am a native New Yorker, her directions were confusing me.

My eyes darted towards the passenger seat as I still tried to focus on the road.

'Are you just giving me random directions?'

"No," the glow from her phone screen illuminated her fingers. "Just drive."

At this point, it looked like we went south instead of west towards Astoria. The two of us pulled onto a dark street in what appeared to be a ritzy neighborhood.

I parked the car and tried to reach for her phone to see the map.

Layne shut the screen off on her phone, changed the radio station again, and pushed the seat back.

> *"We don't need no education*
> *We don't need no thought control*
> *No dark sarcasm in the classroom*
> *Teachers leave them kids alone*
> *Hey, teachers, leave them kids alone*
> *All in all it's just another brick in the wall*
> *All in all you're just another brick in the wall."*

The background noise of Pink Floyd's "Another Brick in the Wall" made it seem like we were in a dramatic movie scene.

Layne sat up and leaned on her left elbow for a moment.

"I'm dangerous, Scott," she moved closer to me and ran her fingers through my hair.

Unsure of what else to do, I ran my fingers through her chestnut-brown hair. As my fingers reached the bottom, her hair fell back to her shoulders with such grace.

As she leaned into me, seemingly in slow motion, my heart began to race.

My hands instinctively brushed against her shoulders as I swayed towards her neck. My lips searched out her neck and moved gently towards her ear.

Layne's soft moans grew slightly louder.

I whispered in her ear, 'Are you okay with this?'

"Yes."

'What are you thinking?'

She locked eyes with me for a moment, "Nothing."

'That's good.'

I continued to kiss her delicately until our mouths moved closer and closer.

Layne pulled away slightly and I stopped.

Her eyelids shut in such a sultry manner before drifting open once again. The two of us gazed at one another as the streetlight and moonlight beckoned down upon us.

I let my hand explore her outer leg for a few minutes. Her pupils dilated as she moved her right hand up the side of my face. I could sense her brushing the stubble growing on my face as I shut my eyes.

My fingers dropped between her thighs as I realized how wet she was getting. As my mind made a desperate attempt to comprehend what was happening, our lips collided.

Layne's teeth gripped my bottom lip as I let out a breathy grunt.

We kissed without remorse as I hoisted her on top of my lap. With her legs straddled around me as I sat in the driver's seat, her thigh rode up and down across my lap.

Our furious kisses grew more passionate as she wrapped her hands around the base of my neck.

My hands were all over her body, leaving a trail of my fingerprints in a fervid path along her skin.

I thought that I was dreaming.

As I felt her reaching such a deep level of passionate intensity, she stopped and began to tear up.

'Don't go inside your head,' I whispered to her.

She tossed her head back and pushed it forward again.

Layne left a solitary kiss on my cheek and moved back into the passenger seat.

"This can't happen."

My chest was throbbing as my heart crashed in the pit of my core.

Unsure of what to do, I decided to keep driving into the night. We sat in silence and let the static of the radio fill the empty space between us.

When the two of us finally reached a random bar, she got out of the car and glanced up at me.

"I'm sorry."

I shut the door and walked to her side of the car, 'Why are you sorry?'

"I wanted to know what it was like to be with you."

'Were you disappointed?'

"No," she gripped my fingers. "Not at all. I crave the way you touch me, but I don't want to get hurt again."

'Okay,' I dropped my hands as she released my grasp.

The two of us walked into the bar and did not talk about what had just happened. My anxiety kicked in, but I tried not to make it obvious.

She was likely processing what just happened, but masked her emotions in the alcohol she was putting in her body.

After about an hour, I brought her back to her hotel and told her to have a great night. She flashed a smile at me and shut the car door.

Layne did not text me that night, although I thought she might.

I wondered if she was feeling guilty or if she just drifted off to sleep.

As I wallowed in my own emotions, I realized that I was petrified for whatever tomorrow could bring.

I desperately did not want to hurt her, yet I thought I might have destroyed her. My usual line of questions infiltrated my head:

How could I betray her trust?

Did she actually want to be with me?

What did I do?

I let the slew of questions usher me to sleep for the night as I passed out on my mother's couch, unsure of what tomorrow would consist of.

To my surprise, when I awoke in the morning to her phone call, she did not seem upset at all.

"Are you ready to find some special writing places today?" Her voice sounded chipper and overjoyed.

I assumed that it would be just another day, but I was very, very wrong.

∞ ∞ ∞ ∞ ∞ ∞ ∞ ∞

When my aunt passed away, we buried her in the pouring rain. Each time someone died in my life, it rained, whether it was my grandfather, Paul, or Stacey. Rain had become synonymous with pain and fear for years.

That all changed with Layne.

Because of her, rain became a sign of healing and a symbol of spiritual growth.

The rain spoke to me in a way that is truly indescribable. I wondered if I misheard the original messages from the rain: Be sad now, but bliss is coming. Just have faith, and you will be protected.

Layne and I drove to Francis Lewis Park so I could show her where I went to connect to my soul.

As we walked down towards the Whitestone Bridge, the two of us were clearly basking in the sound of the water's ebb and flow.

Though we were laughing and talking about our respective projects, I could not help but think about the night before.

Layne's profound words burst my train of thought: "You don't have to go anywhere to teach me the courage of stars, that light carries on endlessly, how infinity works, and how rare and beautiful it is to exist. All of that I'm learning through your life. Your life holds the pathway of my education, Scott. And it will for all of eternity."

I glanced over at her as the wind picked up her hair and swirled it around.

'You have no idea how much that means to me,' I smiled.

She looked me in the eyes and grinned, "I love you too. So much."

Layne's illustrious words crept into my soul:

"My heart is glowing, Scott. The way you reach inside my soul with the beauty of your expression is truly a blessed and divine experience. Every cell within me has bonded to every cell within you. Thank you for sharing your light. I honor you for just… being. I don't want to see a world without you in it."

It struck me that her love was wholeheartedly present, though her past was obscuring her physical expression of that love...

And I was totally okay with that.

Just having her in my life was a beautiful experience.

The overcast weather hinted that we should go inside and work at a coffee shop, so we did.

Hours upon hours later, it looked like her journal was filled with such beautiful writings. She would not let me read it, but she would occasionally shoot me a coy look from over the edges of the journal.

As the night fell upon us once again, we noticed the downpour pushing at car windshields and billowing umbrellas.

"Come on," she picked up her journal and tucked it into her bag. I followed suit with my papers. "Let's go."

As we dashed out onto the sidewalk, the rain began to drip impatiently from the overhanging trees. The pristine beauty of the damp leaves drew us further away from the music of the coffee shop. Our ears were becoming less enchanted by the melody of the repetitive conversations, and more engrossed in the distilled silence that hung between our bodies in the brisk nightfall around us.

As droplets of rain began caressing her face, I snatched her hand and tried pulling her down the winding roads and to the car. Her soul was caught in the balance of the light from the streetlights above and the lingering sensation that grew more passionate from within her.

Every fiber of her being longed for a night like this: to be exquisitely free.

She yearned to be woken from the frail imbalances within her, which startled her once she was finally immersed in the delicious taste of the drizzle cascading down her now moistened lips.

The grin on her face became more sincere and apparent.

Anyone walking down the street could feel her positive energy bursting forth from once deep within her soul.

Her fingers linked firmly between mine as we started to frolic in the manifesting rainstorm. Our thoughts melted away, and in those innocent, exquisite moments, our once youthful existence sprung forth. Our hair was drenched, but we were not drowning in the mediocre day-to-day troubles that wore us down once before.

Our souls were in a state of infinite youthfulness.

She released her hand from mine and darted into the gutter: she took a running jump and collided with a puddle, which sent water every which way.

Though she was totally engulfed in water from head to toe now, her sweet demeanor said the words she could not materialize just yet.

In those childlike moments, we knew we were far from toy trucks and dolls, for this was far from what our imaginations could develop regardless of how mature we were.

This was paradise and this was solace, for we both knew we took a rainstorm and created a playground of our own.

As she leapt back onto the sidewalk and we trotted down the street giggling, something was brewing inside me. In that moment, with the rain rolling down our skin and the stars disappearing behind the clouds, her face glowed far brighter than the moon ever could.

The picturesque scene evaporated into a quaint, pleasant moment between our two bodies.

In one swift motion, I swung Layne around and swiveled her body so the two of us were swaying peacefully in the torrential downpour. Her head rested on my chest as if it was always a part of me, and we succumbed to the rhythmic motions of the Earth's gravitational pull.

Our hearts synced and beat in time to the harmonious whispers that vibrated from somewhere within my chest: I was genuinely happy.

Our joyous adventure in the rain took precedence over any classic cinematic moment, for it was an experience that surpassed all human expectations: its elegance and beauty were unmatched in the most wholesome of ways... as the outline of our dancing bodies became etched in the stars.

I glared into her eyes and said the first thing that came to mind, 'Layne... I-'

She stopped me mid-sentence, wrapped her arm around mine, and whispered, "I know, Scott. I know."

Layne leaned into my chest and I held her tight. The street was getting dark as the skies opened up.

The Spider-Man poster from my office at my first high school came to mind. The word "Sacrifice" flashed in front of my eyes.

It reminded me to never give up and to do what I could to find answers in life.

The answer was dancing with me slowly in the rain.

Our movements quickly turned into a soft, elongated kiss that whispered passion into our souls.

She wanted me to protect her from herself, yet this was the only way I knew how: to let her go to the spaces where she was conflicted in order to comprehend her soul's wishes.

The rain shattered upon the sidewalk and I sensed people drifting by, but nothing affected us: this was our moment in time.

Rain, pedestrians, our respective pasts, nothing would stop us.

Sometimes when you try to find the right words to tell a specific story, it would taint the purity or meaning of those moments.

It was a moment that was not supposed to happen, though as I tried pulling away from her to respect her space, she kept wrapping her fingers around my neck and drawing me closer.

We inched towards the car and leapt in.

Droplets of water fell along the leather seats as the two of us continued to kiss.

As the two of us undressed one another and let the wet clothes plop on the floor of the car, our hands sought comfort along each other's skin.

The windows began to fog up as our lips crashed upon one another's.

Rain cascaded along the windows as the two of us brushed along the surface of each other's souls. The careful whispers and gentle strokes we placed upon our skin were reflective of the devout connection we had with one another.

"Please don't stop," Layne begged impetuously.

After Bryan, I always used a condom and always had the willpower to stop what I was doing. I would never not use a condom unless I was sure of two things: I was definitely, truly, and deeply in love and I wanted to be a parent with that person. I knew that they would be both incredibly rare to find and if I was ever in that scenario, I knew it would have to be the ultimate, truthful love.

I knew I would just feel it.

When it came to Layne, I finally felt it.

I was sure of it. I was sure of everything.

The two of us continued our passionate twists and turns until a shadow appeared at the edge of my windshield.

A police officer was writing a parking ticket for a long-expired parking slip.

We remained still, slightly panicked that he would see us through the fogged and tinted windows.

It was the most peaceful sensation I had ever felt despite almost getting caught.

After the officer walked away, Layne readjusted herself so we were cuddled into one another. She fit perfectly in my arms and life was perfect.

There were no other words to say.

As the two of us went back to her hotel room for the night, she embraced me in the doorway.

"I never thought I would find a love like yours," she kissed me on the lips and wrapped her fingers around my collar.

As Layne dragged me into the room, I sensed the night was far from over. I texted my sister and asked if she would be okay with me staying out late.

Without hesitation, she agreed, and my night with Layne continued into the effervescent dawn.

There is an indescribable feeling of peace that washes over me while watching Layne sleep against my shoulder.

I felt that the world stopped spinning on its axis for the time being, just so I could embrace the tenderness of her touch against my slightly rising chest. Layne's body moves gently to the ebb and flow of her soul.

For a moment in time, between her heart's synchronous beats, there was such a remarkable stillness that hung in the air.

It was the entanglement of our fingers that drew me into her beauty the most.

The essence of her soul lingered deep within me. It had since the moment I met her, but this was different.

I looked down at the photo of her that I snapped on my phone.

The way she looked at me and genuinely saw me was breathtaking.

Her glance was a key that unlocked my heart. For years, I did not realize it was in a cage. Layne's presence clung to my skin in a manner that rivaled moisture from last night's rain.

We were interconnected and in a state of synthesis.

It was as if I could somehow hear the thoughts of her soul.

Our bodies had become one. Our energy ensnared our souls onto a level of higher frequency.

I must have fallen asleep at some point, for when my eyes fluttered open and I saw her silhouette moving in tandem with my heartbeat, every fiber of my soul sighed peacefully.

As I watched her resting eloquently on the bed, I dashed out to grab some breakfast for her. I wanted to make sure that when she woke up, Layne would have everything she needed: food, love, and my shoulder to rest her head upon.

Just as I softly shut the door behind me and brought our breakfast in, Layne stretched and I could hear her nails tap against the headboard.

Her eyes lit up when she gazed over at me.

"Hey," her sultry voice touched my soul.

'Hey.' I smiled at her as she sat up in bed.

"What's that?"

I held up the bag, 'Breakfast.'

The two of us cuddled up to one another between the sheets.

As she ate breakfast and caressed my arm with her tender fingerprints, I watched her expression turn sour.

'What's wrong babe?'

"It's nothing," she shrugged.

'Something is wrong.'

"I don't know," she started. "Last night, this whole trip, you." Layne moved her hand towards my chest.

'What about it?'

"It has been nothing but magical. Scott, this is so hard. I know what my heart and soul are saying about you."

My fingers searched for her skin. As my hand ran up and down her back, she shifted her head towards mine and planted a gentle kiss on my lips.

Gazing deep into my eyes, she whispered, "I wanted to experience you. I wanted to have last night. I want all of this, but I am scared."

She gulped and I held her tight.

"I don't know what to do. I think..." she moved away from me. "I know this cannot go on. We have to stop and just keep this as a beautiful memory."

'I hear you,' I began to tear up. The wave of powerful, spiritual emotions washed over me. 'I want what is best for you.'

"I don't want to hurt you. You don't deserve to carry my pain with you."

'You could never hurt me,' my pointer finger brushed along the side of her head.

"I am scared, but I love you so much." She paused. "Please promise me this will not be painful."

Without hesitation, I assured her that I would not be hurt by her.

"I want you to stay in my life. I want to explore the book I'm writing and the framework, but sleeping together and connecting on such a high level clouds everything."

We both paused for a moment.

'Layne, I love you, I honor you, I respect you... and I understand.'

"Promise me you will not be in pain."

I forced the tears to remain within my eyes. 'I promise.'

She swallowed. "Thank you."

An impatient silence hung between us.

"We are here," she began. "And I don't want this fleeting moment to disappear forever."

'I'll never let this moment go, Layne.'

She placed our food on the table beside her and pressed her body against mine. As she inched closer and closer onto my chest, our lips crashed into each other's in such a passionate manner.

I felt each sway of her body rock against me sensually.

Her reflection from the mirror was erotic beyond my wildest imagination. My eyes wandered to the daylight creeping through the windows and back to the mirror where I caught the shadow of her body thrusting against mine.

I was lost in her ecstasy.

The two of us were fully immersed in what seemed like our last moment together. Our fingers intertwined as she kissed my neck softly.

I craved her soul.

The next few moments faded into the recesses of my mind as I etched our experience into my memory forever.

I barely remember taking her back to the bus terminal, for my body was so exhausted from our spiritual rendezvous.

"I love you," escaped her lips as she kissed me.

'I love you, too.'

"We will figure this out."

Layne held me tight before releasing my soul from her gentle grasp. As she walked away and boarded the bus, a trail of her spirit lingered with me.

When she left New York, I still felt her throughout the day: a soul connection like ours feels like home.

As I returned to my mother's house and shut my eyes, I felt her heartbeat. I could taste her sultry lips and sense her breathing. It was not just a replay of the intense, physical love we shared.

It was something I never felt before.

This was a new magnitude of spirituality shaking my core.

A sensation woke from within me and I did not even know it was there. Every fiber of my being wanted to get back to her instantly.

I did not want to just stay with her; I wanted to swim in the beautiful flow of what we created.

Part of me knew she could feel our mutual energy simmering within our souls.

If the concept of twin flames does exist, we surely found one another in this lifetime, and for eternity we would find each other again and again.

∞ ∞ ∞ ∞ ∞ ∞ ∞ ∞

After Layne went back up to Martha's Vineyard, the air in New York was stale and unforgiving. Morena sat complacently in my car, dangling a bag of food before me as I leapt into the driver's seat.

Recounting all of this seemed to be somewhat cathartic, but nothing could detract from the longing I had to hold Layne in my arms again. Morena was in deep thought and rather silent. The only time she spoke was thirty minutes into our car ride as I approached a red light. She glared into my eyes and spoke chilling words that I never thought were humanely conceivable or possible: "Scott, you have a phone call."

I glanced down at my black phone screen for a moment. Nothing. Then almost instantaneously Layne's name appeared on my screen.

"Scott, are you okay?" Layne seemed eager to hear my voice.

I paused for a moment, looking into Morena's eyes searching for what to say. She motioned towards the phone and mouthed something like, "Speak to her."

'Hey,' I paused, retraining from letting the tears cascade down my face, 'Hey Layne.'

"Scott, why do you sound so sad?"

'Nothing. Nothing, it...' I choked back tears, 'It was a long day.'

"You promised, Scott!" Her voice boomed through the phone.

'What are you talking about?' I began to panic as Morena gripped my hand tightly.

Morena mouthed me the words "Go within."

"You promised you were not in pain!" Layne's voice cracked.

'Layne, I-" She cut me off and began to berate me with her unfiltered passion.

"You told me you loved me, and you told me that you were okay with how you would love me, yet I hear it. I hear it in your voice, Scott. You love me more than you realize. You crave me, you crave me in a devastatingly drastic way that drowns your soul in an ocean of our everlasting love..." Her tears and heaving were more apparent as she went on. "And I crave you too, Scott. I really, wholeheartedly desire you. I can't explain it; I just really can't find the words to express how I feel right now. I am struggling with processing our love, because I know it is real, but I don't want to be the cause of your hurt. Scott, I just need time."

Morena and I gazed up at each other and back down at the phone.

Layne and I had a higher consciousness love that could never shatter the physical boundaries on this earthly realm. She seemed to agree with me, and her anxiety dissipated. We spoke amicably for a few moments and she thanked me profusely for doing what no other person ever did for her.

As our call ended, Morena looked up at me. She seemed distant and I was worried about her. Maybe she really isn't real. People are not usually too spiritually connected, so when there is even a tinge of low vibration in the world or low frequency conversations, she disappears.

That needs to be rectified.

Angels are not supposed to get hurt, but I suppose they do.

My head started spinning and Morena gazed up at me with shallow eyes.

"Don't even think about going low vibrational, Scott." I could feel the energy building from her soul.

Once the conversation ended and the phone clicked, it hit me: I was in love with Layne and when the time came, I would not know how to say goodbye. I knew at that very moment... this will break me, AND I refused to leave her.

I drove over to the Throgs Neck Bridge and parked the car as close to the rocks as possible. I desperately needed a change of scenery.

After walking around aimlessly for an hour, I was about to call it a night when Layne called.

I was deep in thought.

Everyone has their own lives and I can't expect everything to stop because of me. Still, I embarked on this walk hoping to hear a certain someone's voice, to share, to bounce things off of, yet when I saw the flag waving in the sunset, I knew she would call.

I wondered if there would ever come a time when I don't have to be alone with my thoughts.

Layne's exquisite wisdom rang through my soul. She understands people and she just understands me. I understand her, the real her, not just the waitress who busts her butt at a diner day in and day out.

The two of us found ourselves in the midst of a deep conversation about life, the soul, and existing in general.

We spoke about how "I think I will live today" are the most painstaking words that are ever spoken. After a certain point, when it gets incredibly difficult to move forward or see the bright side of a situation, the difficulty of managing a mass of negativity, or however you chose to describe it, it burns. It burns in an unfathomable way. It burns so deeply that only those privy to the burden genuinely sense it.

When it seems as if every ounce of hope is overshadowed by the plague of darkness, cling.

Hold on.

I tried to think of the goodness from deep within. I tried to extend the light within to those around me. Yet the definition of "goodness" was askew in the public eye. Though good means helpful, honest, fair, unbiased, impartial, appropriate, professional, compassionate, caring, considerate, and being an overall caring person in one respect, the whole world does not always speak your language.

My perspective and my insight into the word "good" are just that… mine. Not everyone is willing to open their hearts to the world. Not everyone is understanding of the higher vibrations and sincere intentions of others.

Though this may seem judgmental, there is no ill will in these words.

I wish everyone in the world could see themselves through pristine, unfiltered eyes. I wish everyone could feel they are wanted, loved, and needed in this universe. When the burden of judgment presses too heavily on your chest, remember to breathe.

It can be hard to breathe. It can be hard to stand up once you feel you have been buried. Change the narrative. Rewrite the script. Do not give into the clutches of hatred that may seem to pull you down.

Keep going.

I stood with my feet in the sand, firmly planted in the belief that I could move forward. I repeatedly affirmed, "I can. I can. I can." You may ask: "Why do I feel ensnared in a trap, desperately trying to claw my way out of the depths of purgatory? Why do I feel the sins of foul words ripping apart the fundamental pieces of my soul?"

Seek for the epiphany within your soul: see the sign that is your soul being uplifted.

You are your own energy source. Dig deep, deep within… allow the wave of acceptance to flood your intricate soul. Turn your pain into power. Turn the misunderstood parts of you into higher consciousness.

Pray deeply and honestly for the lost and lonely. Pray for a better moment. Pray for the weak and the struggling for there are moments where we are all there: in the balance of what to do and how to do it.

The challenges we face may be mounting and tough, but we will face them head on. We will face them and we will survive.

"We will do more than just survive, my dear, we will overcome," Layne's words cemented into my soul.

So, after it all: the sharp words that sting so effervescently, the shock of having to swim while you conceive the notion that your feet may be sinking, the phrases and monikers gifted to you by those who misunderstand…

They will be heard but they will not hurt. They are apparitions of projections underdeveloped souls feel so rooted in their bones. They will grow, as will you, and pray for them. Pray they will awaken to a better tomorrow and a brighter path. Pray they see their innate beauty.

Tomorrow is unknown in the present moment, but live for today. Continue to live. Continue to shine and grow. Fill the emptiness with the angelic wisdom that shines from above and beyond.

Then mutter those words that sever the confusion in your soul: "I think I will live today."

For even angels need to learn how to fly.

We yearn for what we cannot materialize. We grasp at the chances that roll before us, while we mingle exquisitely in the factions that exist before us. We are spirituality and soul wrapped in flesh entities. We are inherently guided by a moral compass that can become askew depending on what we individually recognize as due north. We hastily give in to our human emotions, for we fall short enough from perfection that we tend to fall into realms that materialize in the form of desires. We look not into the light before us. We look not into the areas of growth that lay between the colors painted on the horizon.

We are angelic, though we do not uphold halos. We are spiritual, yet we do not always obtain the lens to visualize all we can become. We manifest a sense that we must comply with the rules of society, for we assume that these are the standards that must dictate our lives.

What about us?

What about soul?

What about divine love and sincere connections?

Why do we tend to trip off of the path while running for our futures? We could speculate for years and get caught up in the horror that is delving into the whys and longing questions of the human world, yet we fall short in the sense that we ruminate too long on the logic. Give in to the spirit. Give in to patience and understanding. Forgive. Forgive others for they are still developing. Forgive yourself for you are still growing.

Wish genuine sincerity upon those still finding their light, for we are all harmonizing on different levels and with different frequencies. It is about time we try diligently to vibrate higher.

Challenge the status quo and remind yourself you were crafted in the hands of the legacies that existed far before your human form was a conceptual thought.

Live and believe in the sense that you can overcome challenges and grow... for life may seem like a dark room, but you, too, can develop from the negatives and illustrate a glorious landscape that is your soul's growth and divine intentions.

∞ ∞ ∞ ∞ ∞ ∞ ∞ ∞

Like magnets, Layne and I found our way back to each other within a weekend.

I travelled up to Martha's Vineyard again, so that she did not have to take off of work. Although she loved the sights and sounds of New York, and she said it inspired her to write, Layne did need to stay close to her father and sister in Massachusetts.

Layne helped me realize that I learned the value of truly savoring little moments, for it is the little moments that string together so eloquently to manifest a genuine sensation that just cannot be disrupted.

Once you begin to place value on those little moments, time becomes insignificant. Time becomes just a social construct that fades into the background, but those moments stay on the forefront of our hearts, minds, and spirits forever.

We have an innate power beholden in our souls: we can choose where to place our energy. We decide who owns our passion, for we are the ones who signed a contract with the universe years ago.

Our respective destinies were aligned to fit a purpose, and we had to extend our souls onto a level of higher consciousness in order to discover this prophecy developed in our honor long ago.

On our respective journeys, we may sometimes feel like an outsider.

We may sometimes think we are consumed by the cataclysmic culture of hate and negativity that is around us... yet we must remember to look in each other's eyes.

Look into the eyes of those around you.

What do you see?

You can see a story behind the story.

You can see the patterned specks of stardust lingering in their eyes.

You can feel the emotion reverberating through their bodies and transmitting messages out for the world to see.

It is when we stop and look into the eyes of another that we find their souls and we see ourselves.

Layne's eyes held such a beautiful experience that etched into my soul with just a touch of the experience that is her.

This double intensity ferments a growing need within us: we yearn to be understood and we yearn to be in another's arms, but it is rather difficult to find a place to call home as you try to find yourself.

Yet we as human beings make it happen: we find our home in the arms of another, and not just in the explicit definition of four walls and a roof.

We find our way through the consummation of ideas and the thorough processing of information. We create our own realities and we develop on a vertical continuum: we seek out our purpose and redefine who we are once we unlock key pieces of our own puzzles. Integration and togetherness then becomes a key.

Just let your soul flower into something bigger or brighter than you could ever imagine.

Embrace the moments as you would embrace another, seep compassion into this world through your positivity and your light, and uncover bits of your path through the proceeding moments before you.

It does not matter who you are in this world, your experience is part of a greater and overarching cohesive whole: our society. We create the fabric of society through the moments we weave together in the cosmic essence of space and this universe.

As the moments melt into the fabric of our lives, I can't help but smile knowing that I am a part of so many little moments in this universe.

My only wish for each soul on this earth is that they realize how fundamental they are to who I have become. Souls grow into their own because of the pleasantries bestowed upon them from other beautiful souls. Shine your light upon another's soul, and see just how magical this world can become.

We may live in juxtaposed worlds or different mandates in society, but at the end of the day, if we all take a moment to gaze up at the stars, odds are we are glaring into another soul's journey... and we will always be able to see a clearer picture of the hearts and minds of those near and dear to us.

Distance is just a matter of being moments away, for we always have the little moments and memories to usher us into the next chapter.

We always have the rose-colored images of our kindled flames plastered in the walls of our memory... and all in all we are not just another brick in another person's wall... we are souls etched in the prophetical tapestries of each other's paths... and that is how it always shall be.

Always.

Layne recognized that and welcomed me with open arms the moment I stepped off of the ferry.

Her soul is a wild, yet reserved and exquisite life force.

Layne tries so hard to restrain herself, but when she sets her mind on something, she will stop at nothing until she gets what she yearns for.

Our pasts paralleled one another: we had both been afflicted by love, but we did not let love of a clearly higher power, hinder our present.

The past became the past.

My love for her stemmed from a place of purity and soul.

Within moments of getting to Martha's Vineyard, we were kissing passionately in her white sedan. The engine revved when she accidentally stepped on the gas pedal, though fortunately we were still in park.

After a short ride to the bed and breakfast, we found ourselves tangled in the sheets together.

Our love stemmed from a place of purity, innocence, and insanity in the most wholesome of ways.

I brushed Layne's hair behind her ear as she cuddled into my chest. My fingers rubbed her shoulder as she wrapped her hand around my torso.

"I love you Scott. My heart has never felt so full," she whispered.

I kissed her forehead tenderly.

'My soul craves yours.'

Both of us laughed gently as she picked up her head.

Layne's eyes pierced my soul as we managed to communicate without uttering a single word. Our lips met again in another spiritually uplifting exchange.

"You are very dangerous, Scott," as the words left her lips, each syllable wrapped itself around my skin.

'Why?'

"If you were here all of the time, you would end up having all of me."

'Then I should move here,' I grinned.

Layne did not respond. There was no doubt that we loved one another.

'I love you.' The way those three words hung off of my lips as I softly kissed her made me never want to leave her side.

Our souls were tethered to one another in a way that whispered, "I know you."

The two of us rose and agreed to physically part from one another for a few hours. I promised that I would take Layne on a date and she agreed. My mind raced as I tried to figure out how to make her happy without overwhelming her.

I didn't want to take a shower simply because I aspired to swim in her scent.

The acceptance and comprehension of two souls can be a complicated process, especially when the energy exchange is heightened past the limits of human normalcy.

This place, each passing second, and this experience are all parts of where I have never been before. It is not a bad thing, but I had to process what this all meant to me.

Life's moments are precious gifts from the universe that are always to be treasured. Everything is a beautiful message or lesson.

It is a blessing for me to stand witness to a soul's full expansion and expression. Layne's passionate experiences are a gift from heaven, from the physical to the emotional aspects of her being.

The universe manifested Layne and created our love.

Layne picked me up as the two of us drove to the Manuel F. Correllus State Forest.

As we got out of the car, I managed to wrestle a picnic basket from the backseat of the sedan.

"What are you doing?" She giggled.

'I wanted to take you on a romantic date that you deserve.' I picked up the basket. 'It is a good thing there was a general store within walking distance of the bed and breakfast.'

We basked in another oasis of hers. I soaked in the moments that danced in my soul; at a point in time, she walked the paths of this land by her lonesome. Odds are, she was processing the emotional pain she harbored from her ex-boyfriend and ex-best friend.

The possibilities of her life were endless.

While walking in her space, I injected myself into her aura, her safety, and her sanctuary.

I disturbed it and filled it with my energy.

Together, our presence elevated the space to an entirely new level.

As we got to an open field in the forest, I dropped the picnic basket on the grass. The weather was more perfect than I had ever felt.

While she unravelled the contents of the basket, something compelled me to put on music. "Blaze of Glory" by Bon Jovi was the first thing to play from my phone.

> *"You ask about my conscience*
> *And I offer you my soul*
> *You ask if I'll grow to be a wise man*
> *Well I ask if I'll grow old."*

I do not know why I chose that song, but something told me I needed to expose Layne to the music of my soul.

The notes, the rhythm, and the lyrics were delicately moving throughout the air in a way I never felt them before. It was akin to a musical high.

In moments when we delve deeper into our soul's layers, we understand how deeply and devoutly the universe speaks to us. Our words materialize as a means of finding who we truly are, and as a way to touch other souls that are on their respective paths.

We intersect, even for a split second, and succumb to the sensations and emotions that can be perceived as overwhelming, but on another level could be the most beautiful incredible experience of your eternal existence.

Fight the fear; expel the darkness and confusion.

Light the way knowing full and well that we are encountering a new level of growth that was previously unfathomable and thought unattainable.

In these moments the universe is providing a magical gift that is an infinite blessing.

We are not at the top of the mountain yet, we have merely reached the plateau, and are about to continue our ascent... in due time. There is no rush when you have these eternal reunions and realizations. There is no doubt about it, that as the universe speaks to us in ways that are beyond incredible, and if you truly listen, she will shake you to your core.

Do not give up because times seem confusing or tough. The clouds clear. The universe speaks truth.

Breathe deeply and inhale the positivity that is all around you, for the universe is so powerful.

When you position your soul to be open to receive truth it will align the most beautiful gifts for you. Everything will be okay. The feelings and energy can be heightened to a level never felt before. It can be awesome and scary all at once, but it will be okay.

The universe looks kindly on those with pure hearts, and Layne had one of the purest hearts I had ever encountered.

As I closed my eyes to process these emotions, I knew I was surrounded and shrouded with those who are sent to protect me.

The universe cheers us on.

In our metamorphic process, we can transform from a solemn, enclosed entity to something greater and larger than we ever could imagine. Our wings are hidden and unfathomable, then one day we discover we can fly.

One day, after all this soul work, you will see energy, sometimes colliding in a way you never thought possible, and the future will look more clearer to you than ever before... and yes, that's scary because we were never prepared for that type of realization. Being in this type of a moment is so exciting and at the same time incredibly scary.

We discovered we could run.

We can soar.

We can push forth as far as we so wish to go.

We are invincible in the eyes of the universe, yet we are trained to be limited by societal norms and our human conditions.

We are fluttering in the sky and flickering in the beckoning wind.

We are drawn to the elements from which our souls once stemmed from, and we feel peace and solace in knowing how close we are to the earth and the water, yet we inject our human emotions into every situation.

If only we stepped back for a moment. If only we thought soulfully from a place of love consciousness instead of in such a human fear-based emotionally driven way, which words would hold more value?

Which words would seep into our soul and seek out the light from within?

Which words would draw upon our inner voice and true purpose?

Would we then realize the weight of the world was just a matter of soul over heart over mind, rather than the other way around?

How do we internalize happiness and genuine love or genuine truth?

Is it all "too good to be true," or if we quiet the mind do you hear the clear and coherent whisper in our souls?

In living in a world of "if only," "should," "could," "would," and any other doubt-fueled words, are we merely hindering our souls from their devout possibilities?

The universe loves us and has our backs and it's important to let go and trust, but these questions plague my soul in a deeper way than I have ever gone.

I am listening. I am trusting. I am scared at times... fleeting moments but there is fear there.

Hope, but fear.

On the other hand, I truly do believe.

I feel.

I know.

I live in between the breaths of words Layne spoke into existence.... for our words are manifesting a true shift on this planet that will last more than seven generations.

For only when words of partially unrequited love are spoken to the universe, will you realize that what you tell yourself, and what you choose to hear, will be your words of wisdom.

Hear clearer.

Hear your kindness.

Speak your passion and let your heart soar; know you are protected by the highest of angels and the entire universe.

Most of all continue to follow your beautiful passionate soul as you speak unto others as you always should speak to yourself.

Choose light over darkness and decide upon your voice... then allow it to manifest.

As my mind wandered to all of these different places, I looked up at Layne who was nibbling on some fruit.

My thoughts quieted long enough to say: 'You are amazing beyond words.'

She moved closer to me and kissed my cheek. "I love you, and I am going to tell you ten more times so that you never forget."

As she recited, "I love you" in my ear very slowly, tears streamed down my face.

It was the making of a true love story.

Layne moved backwards and glanced at me. The sunlight reflected in her eyes and were literally windows to the soul. I see the whole universe when I look into them.

I see Source.

I see divine love.

As the sunlight caressed her pristine face, I could not help but feel a sense of innate peace emulating from my core. Her presence was like no other. We could sit in resolute silence for hours, yet her words would still seep into my soul with the passion and pressure of the Hoover Dam. I felt that I had to hold back, but I knew, deep down within me, that I needed her.

I longed for her.

I yearned to be woven into the fabric of her life in every possible way.

That is what true love is. That is what a soul connection is: wanting to be a consummate part of another's whole being, while inspiring that person to flourish and reach another level of higher consciousness. Her physical absence was painstaking. It weighed my soul down in unfathomable language.

She is due north, my magnetic pole that I base all soulful, spiritual connections upon. Am I being too crass in saying how tethered I am to her every twist and turn? This I do not know.

Am I assuming too much in hanging on her every word and action? Again, I am unsure.

How do you verbalize a soul connection?

How do you comprehend the most beautiful mind you have ever laid eyes upon?

How do you actualize a relationship forged in the particles of stardust that never appeared before?

Layne is perfection, without a doubt. When you formulate a love as deep as ours, you make room in your soul for the fibers of their being. Your individual broken pieces may be sharp and jagged, but together those pieces appear smooth and connective.

You cannot describe, in words or in actions, the value someone grants to your soul. You cannot, in a concrete shape, align a form to something so beautiful and exquisite.

In searching for myself, I found someone who was lost on her own path.

Then somehow, whether it be divine intervention from the universe or just chance, our souls looked upon one another and said, "I know."

Looking at a stranger and recognizing their soul is refreshing.

In an instant, you just know. You realize why everything did not work out all along. You discover your light is brighter than it seems. You configure how this world could be so cruel and so calming in one swoop; Layne was my reason why.

You recognize your reflection in the eyes of another… and when you truly love someone with all of your heart, mind, body, and soul… you make room.

Priorities and excuses juxtapose themselves more transparently, for you finally realize that the holes in your soul stemmed from the universe in order for both of you to merge spiritually when the time is right.

…And that is the beautiful thing: our love was in the universe's hands now.

The two of us packed up our picnic basket and walked along the trails. As we spoke, she would stop periodically to write down what we were talking about.

Our conversation consisted of the notion that we should all become the source of energy that ignites passion in another's soul.

Yearn to create the fundamental parts that will be integrated into society for years to come. Communicate with respect and dignity to those who are embarking on their respective journeys through their purpose.

When you meet someone who generates unfiltered and unfettered happiness in your soul, hold onto him or her tightly. It is like no other feeling to look into the eyes of another soul who just understands you, and to forge a bond that exists in spiritual and humanistic terms.

To watch someone process a soul connection is riveting.

To see someone speak higher consciousness into existence and translate their own soul into a language we can understand and internalize is passion.

The combination of soulful energies and passions coming together is overwhelming, but beautiful. Individuals who are powerful enough to light their own fire in order to shift themselves are exhilarating.

Those who can collaborate and combine their spiritual energies to shift the world will strengthen the universe for generations to come. If you think you have a soul connection with someone, cherish it.

A soul connection's worth is far more valuable than anything else this world may offer you. Show gratitude to the universe for sending you blessings, and pay attention to what the world does. For when you least expect it, miracles can happen.

The balance of the universe could majestically shift and you will enter a realm of new opportunities. Listen closely to what happens around you, for you never know what will happen... and when those miracles display themselves in your presence, never let that person go.

As we continued on through the town, she would grab my arm and kiss me passionately.

I could feel her heartbeat as she curled into my arms.

The two of us strolled down a sidestreet and she pressed her body firmly against mine. Layne caressed my arm slowly and let her nails run up and down my skin.

Her sensual touch made me melt.

The two of us went back to my room at the bed and breakfast before she had to go to work for the night. While she sat and wrote in her journal, I watched her in utter amazement. Part of me could not believe that the first day we met one another was not too long ago.

Though Layne was clearly reserved in some ways, she loved me wholeheartedly in the words and actions she committed to the universe.

I had visions of holding her in my arms at the Brooklyn Bridge. My dream was to bring her there and kiss her with the landscape of Manhattan behind us. This picturesque scene would be a quintessential moment in my life, for it would mark our respective souls' journey coming full circle.

Between her dreams and writing, and my knowledge and vision, we were a force to be reckoned with.

Layne fell sound asleep on the bed with her journal in hand. She looked like a heavenly human being wrapped in beauty and brilliance.

It made me wonder:

How did I win her love?

How did I turn her angel eyes my way?

Why was my soul so special that it was permitted to be a part of her life?

I feel so alive with her and relish in the sensation that I am the strongest man in the world with her by my side. Her eyes fluttered open for a moment before sealing shut again.

When she looks at me I know she's swimming inside my soul.

Soft music from my phone murmured Bon Jovi's "Save the World,"

"It comes down to this
I wouldn't exist
Without you it ain't worth the grind
I'd fight for one kiss
On a night like this
You make me feel I could fly, like
I could save the world
Since the night your love saved me
Maybe I can't save the world
But as long as you believe
Maybe I could save the world."

The song was always on an infinitesimal loop within my mind, but with Layne in my life the words finally had a meaning.

They had a purpose.

They had a voice.

They had a devout reason.

Everything in the universe seemed possible, for she was the angelic light guiding the way.

Her eyes fluttered open and she watched me gaze at her for a few moments.

"I want you to read this," she pushed her open journal towards me.

I shifted the book towards me to take a peek at what she was creating. Her writing was of a higher love:

"My thoughts on Scott:

I want to thank you from the deepest crevices of my soul for being by my side through all of this. Your words speak to me in such a beautiful manner. My gratitude just cannot fully express how much you move me. Thank you. A zillion times. Thank you.

I wish for you to know that today is a beautiful blessing to every soul on this planet because of the breaths you take. Your breaths endlessly expand the universe and even if it's underneath every person on this planet's awareness - they will have a better day because you are here, existing.

The power of your heart and soul is the rarest gift to all of us, and we get to see our light, because you are the beacon guiding us to see it.

Without you this world would be in darkness. Unaware that we have the strength, power and illumination inside of us to truly go after our destinies in life. Thank you for constantly being my shining light that guides my path and unveils the curtains so I can really see myself.

I see myself in the way you see me... and the way you see me is unlike the way anyone has seen me before.

I want you to know that you can only possibly see me in this way because it is so similar to you. I am your mirror, and I am so proud, honoured and humbled, to be your reflection.

Thank you - a zillion times for existing so that this could be my reality.

You make life an undeniably glorious experience. I'm so proud that you are doing the work and paving the path for so many to come after you.

Following your footsteps. I am so proud that you are finishing your framework and completing the first chapter of getting your soul out in its full expression with all of that glory.

Great things are ahead and the energy of this rifle wave we are creating is shattering souls at their core in this moment - even if they have no clue what's coming. When your words reach their ears and what you are creating reaches their eyes - they will know.

Hearts will open, as will eyes and ears.

Chapter two will be started soon - and I am the world's luckiest human to be beside you when the world starts picking up on who you are, what you're about, and what you're here to do.

I love you, Scott Matheson."

Layne stirred and woke softly.

"Are you enjoying my great American novel?" Her groggy voice was obscured by her smile.

'Yes,' I placed it back on the bed. 'You are truly my soul's desire.'

She grinned. "Then come here and kiss this soul."

We leaned closer for a passionate kiss and embrace. Layne propped herself up and brushed her fingers through my blonde hair.

"I need to go to work soon, but there is somewhere I *need* to go with you before I go to work."

The two of us hopped in her car and drove towards an industrial part of town. The stars still glistened with such awe through her windshield.

We lowered the seats and started to kiss again as she caressed my back.

Instinctively, I pulled my shirt down to hide my stomach. Layne placed her hands over mine.

"Babe," she whispered. "You don't have to be afraid. I love you. I love all of you. I love every single part of your body."

Layne moved downwards and began to plant sweet kisses on my skin.

The two of us held one another as the night fully fell upon us.

Within moments, it was so difficult to say goodbye to her for the night as the moon crept over us. As she wandered off to work, I had a sinking feeling emerge in the pit of my stomach.

I wished that I could have slept next to her in the quaint bed and breakfast. It would be our little oasis from the world.

I set my alarm for very early in the morning, so when she got off of work I would be the first loving face she would see.

When my eyes shot open as the sunlight crept in the window, I dashed into the shower and got ready in record timing. Though she was the woman of my dreams, I needed to see her in real life to quench my thirst for her everlasting spirit.

As she looked up while untying her apron for the day, the smile she shot in my direction was a breathtaking way to begin my day.

"Come on," she rushed up to me and grabbed my hand. "We're going on an adventure."

'An adventure?' I was startled. 'But you need to get some rest.'

"I'll rest later. It's time to live, Scott!"

'Okay,' I gleefully followed Layne to her white sedan.

The next few hours were filled with driving through cute towns and winding roads. WIth the windows rolled down and her hair blowing in the wind, I found even more ways to love her. We were blasting music and relishing in the togetherness we shared.

It seemed like the whole world was ours.

Song after song came on over the radio, and with each new tune, Layne's entire body took on a different persona. You could see a shift rising over her soul as she started to sway to the music. Layne felt each vibration in the song as her hands would rise and fall.

Her eyes were on the road, but her heart was transfixed by the rhythm of the music.

Layne's entire soul was alluring, for each and every aspect of her was genuinely beautiful.

It does not matter whether you are within an arm's reach of someone or if you are thousands of miles apart. True compassion and a spiritual connection will always strengthen the soul without the need for a hand to hold or gazing into a person's eyes.

High vibration and acknowledging that there are individuals out there who genuinely care about your well being and personal growth are what matters.

You can be an ocean apart from someone, yet they can still swim through your mind.

Their essence becomes their presence, and that is something that could never be replaced.

A bond between two souls cannot be severed.

There are souls on this planet that remind you to be more than a bird, more than a plane, more than some pretty face beside the train. Superman always looked out for the best interests of Lois Lane, but she was not beside him when he was doing his heroic deeds, nor he beside her when she was putting the puzzle pieces of the world together and inspiring others for a better tomorrow.

We are connected and parallel in the spiritual sense.

At times, we must cherish the souls of those who are closest to us deep in our hearts. We must honor those who we care about by traveling on a journey that may take us far from them for some time, yet we harbor the memory of them in our souls and beckon them to our shores. In rough seas or on the darkest nights, the ones we truly care about are our lighthouses, ushering us home. We may sail far and wide, but the compass will always point due north towards them. We must remember that for ourselves too.

We must remember to call upon the energy emitted from other souls when we need reassurance of who we are. We must conquer fear, trepidation, and doubt with the love, sincerity, and compassion that our connections bestow upon us.

We should honor our Superman, honor our Lois Lane, and honor the souls of those who are our everyday heroes.

We must honor the hearts and minds of those who progress with us and grow with us despite their distance.

Live in the glorious now that is your own progressive existence, go forth and flourish, fly, and float. Still, in the brightest day or in the blackest night, do not let those who vibrate low hinder your vision or sight.

Everything will be okay even if you think you are alone, for in the souls of those you love, you will always be home.

In those moments in the car, as we sat by the Aquinnah Cliffs on Martha's Vineyard, and in the writings she bestowed upon my soul, it became clearer and clearer that Layne was my home.

The two of us sat in her car for a few moments, overlooking parts of the water.

'Can I play you a song?' I reached for my phone.

"Yes, of course," Layne leaned her shoulder against the driver's seat. "You always talk about how music is the window to your soul. I want to see everything in your world."

I fiddled with my phone for a bit until the song started to play. As we hit the chorus of the song, she looked up at me.

> *"They don't know how long it takes*
> *Waiting for a love like this*
> *Every time we say goodbye*
> *I wish we had one more kiss*
> *I'll wait for you I promise you, I will*
> *I'm lucky I'm in love with my best friend*
> *Lucky to have been where I have been*
> *Lucky to be coming home again."*

"What's this," Layne asked.

'The song is called "Lucky," it's by Jason Mraz,' I responded.

"Who is that?"

'Did you *just* ask me who Jason Mraz was?'

She giggled for a moment, "Yeah, why is that weird."

'A little bit, yeah.'

We both laughed as she nudged me.

"Don't make fun of me," she smiled. "Teach me."

The two of us continued to talk about the impact music creates on our respective lives. As we listened to songs and walked up to the cliffs, I told her all about Bon Jovi and the soul connection that each of his songs manifested within my life.

How rare and beautiful is it to exist in the mere presence of a genuine soul. I could not help but ask for more eloquent memories to grace my mind with each passing day.

For her to express the words she says over and over again would be an exquisite masterpiece.

Layne looked up at me as we spoke and said, "I would try to write down all of the brilliance that flows forth from your lips, but just one pen could not fathom the amount of ink it would cost to express your worth to this world. I would give anything to hear you speak your wisdom each and every day."

'Well,' I replied. 'There would not be enough songs on this planet to express to you my unwavering sense of awe that springs forth from your very essence. Your soul is a universe that was made to be experienced by so many, and is a genuine gift in my eyes.'

"Oh wow," she placed her hand over her chest. "How poetic."

With shortness of breath, I would explain the infinite: how rare and beautiful it truly is that we exist in this very time, in this very epoch, within the crystalline drops of magic and stardust swirling down to these very moments. We are the faceted elements of pristine reality that lay as gemstones of a higher consciousness relationship. We are the equation that all adds up to peace and coexistence in another realm.

Neverland is on a plane that we do not dance upon, for the tinges of always and the glory that is the billowing shrubs at the cliffs, sway in our hearts... just as devoutly as the clouds clear and the sun rises.

We are a flame, short of a fire; in need of intertwining light... we touch and we inspire the changes in this world tonight.

In those moments, I whispered to the universe to pick me up, take me higher, for I realized that there is a war not far from here, doused in the pain and tragedy that plagued both of our lives before these nights together. It made me see that we can dance in desire upon the rings of Saturn, or we could burn in love tonight.

"Scott," Layne wrapped her body in between my arms.

'What is it, love?'

"I know that one day we will make it big, we will go further than these cliffs, but I never want to lose these moments. Promise me that we will come back here together."

She looked up at me with purpose in her eyes.

'I promise.'

The wind picked up our hair and swirled it across our respective faces.

We brought lunch with us to the cliffs and began to eat together. Our conversation trailed to painful stories from our separate pasts. She told me all about her ex-best friend and her ex-boyfriend, and what they did to betray her trust.

I shared about how Emma hurt me deeply.

"They are blessings in disguise," she murmured. "They showed us how we could become better versions of ourselves."

She was right. Layne was wholeheartedly right.

I became a better person due to how I healed.

"You know," she stood up and motioned for us to start walking. "Our true love will be the foundation to our global success."

She is everything I ever hoped for and dreamed of.

When I was wishing upon those stars on lonely nights, I was truly wishing for her to walk into my life.

"Even though I push you away sometimes, you still show up for me constantly." We walked on opposite sides of the car and hopped inside. "I honor your soul."

She leaned over and kissed me.

"Come on," she wiped a tear from her eye. "There is more I want to show you."

We drove off to the tune of a playlist we were building together.

As "Never Say Goodbye" from Bon Jovi played over the radio, my tears could not fight gravity much longer. I felt every single emotion burst from my eyes realizing that things would never be the same again.

"Are you okay?" She placed her hand in mine.

'Yes, I am' I locked eyes with her for a split second. 'I am, because of you.'

Isn't it great when the universe nudges you?

The universe does not always send the messages loud and clear like fireworks that illuminate the sky, rather, the messages could appear in between the silent pangs of your heartbeat.

Tune into your own frequency and hear the language of love manifest peacefully in your soul. The signs may appear miniscule and subtle, though the messages are bountiful and often rather generous.

In tranquility and silence, there is clarity.

We cannot ignore the signs that are downloaded and injected into the roots of who we are and what we are growing into.

Relationships, like the one that Layne and I manifested, stem from this soul and spirit connection. As a result of these revelations, it is clear that a lot of work may need to be done between two souls in order to construct a stable house built upon the foundation of love.

Often, rather than not, relationships will be built upon the premise of unconditional love.

However, unconditional love comes with one condition: an unconditional bond must come with understanding. This understanding means that communication lines must be open, clear, and unabashed: being honest is difficult, but unconditional love means that you and the other person involved will talk things through and openly process each other's emotions.

The universe is with you through every twist and turn of your tongue: the words you emit into this world stem from the precedents you set forth. The precedent could be laced with positivity and higher consciousness: if it is not, what you speak into existence may not be fully realized. What you speak into existence becomes your reality, so live it.

Live your words and stand by what you say.

Being honest with yourself and another person could fill you with fear, for fear manifests out of manners of uncertainty and the conditioned sense that we are not enough. Yet, in saying that you may not be "enough," what are we saying to our souls?

I allowed myself to live in pain for far too long.

Layne made me realize that.

She taught me that we must cherish and preserve the infinite potential within us, and we must display the same kindness to ourselves that we wish to transcend to other souls. When you connect on a deeper level and choose to evolve naturally, you attract who you are in your truest and highest form.

You attract what you need... even if you didn't realize that's what you were asking the universe for.

Your past experiences signify how much growth and beauty you have placed in this universe.

Even a solitary drop in the ocean creates a ripple effect, as do you with your consciousness and existence.

You are able to find more of what you are looking for, as opposed to what you are searching for, once you speak with much poise and sincerity to this universe. No words may even need to be said, for your thoughts can be acknowledged and felt. Your prayers and beliefs can be answered. Honor your existence and honor your soul.

When you release and trust in the process, the universe guides you to an incredible truth. It is so elevated that if you do not trust it fully, it can consume you with fear. The polarity of life has to be navigated carefully and there is such intricate beauty laced within that navigation. The destination is a heightened love that's never been created: the highest version of the expansion of love and its possibilities flow freely in the universe... in your soul and in souls you encounter.

Sometimes your heart knows the truth and it just takes time to admit the epiphanies within you. When there is truth, there is no rush. Time and patience are endless and on a continuum. Love is truly unconditional, and self-love is of a divine consciousness. Listen to your soul and your heart, for your mind will shortly follow. Embrace uncertainty, for in those moments, support may not always be seen or heard.

It lingers in between the pangs of your heartbeat.

Beat on and walk on, for there is a present in the gifts you transcend into this universe's timeline, and one hundred percent of your inhibitions will melt away the moment you choose what you want and head in that direction. Still, your path will be intertwined with other aspects of sense and sensibility: let your mind guide you to the messages this universe bestows upon you, and never forget to play with the ideas that may bewilder you or stun your spirit: there is always a story behind the story and a lighthouse beckoning you home to the shore: wade in the waters and always anchor yourself to those who make you see your own value.

Always.

As our drive came to a halt, I realized that we were sitting outside of a pristine olive-colored house with mint-colored gutters that outlined the building.

'This is such a cute place,' I remarked.

"Thank you," she waved at a young girl in the window. "This is my home."

We got out of the car and a large, burly man opened the front door. A petite girl who looked like Layne popped out from behind the man.

I began to hyperventilate slightly as the moment consumed me. Her father and sister stood before us grinning sweetly.

"I've heard good things," her father extended his hand. "My name is Raymond."

'I'm Scott,' I grasped his hand as he welcomed me into the house.

The young girl walked over and sat on the couch next to me.

"Hi, I'm Marissa. Layne told me not to embarrass her in front of you."

Layne stood up and yelled, "Marissa!"

Her father laughed and placed his hand on his knee.

The three of them leaned into one another on the cornflower blue sofa. It was blatantly obvious that they were incredibly close and a tight-knit trio. Layne definitely surprised me by coming here.

The three of us spoke for a while about Layne's childhood and their journey to Martha's Vineyard. Raymond explained that the family once lived close to the Grand Canyon in Arizona, where Layne and Marissa would hike with their father.

"I have always been drawn to beautiful places," Layne glanced over at me and flashed a smile.

Her father's eyes grew more nostalgic and peaceful.

"Scott, Layne has told me you have big plans for this world." Raymond leaned towards me.

'I mean, I do-' I looked over at Layne who was beaming with excitement.

"He's being modest, dad. Tell them what you told me, Scott."

'No, I-' I chuckled nervously.

"Come on," Marissa encouraged me. "It's okay. Tell us!"

They were literally sitting at the edge of their seats.

'Okay,' I swallowed. 'My vision is that the world becomes one healthy community through higher consciousness education. Education should promote healthy communication to encourage trust-based relationships, support acceptance of each other and reduce fear, and create an expressed open society. This leads to people connecting to and expanding their souls through a higher love consciousness that helps people live optimal lives and supports others to do so as well. I am building the world's first and most comprehensive education system for raising 21st Century leaders and engineering a society that is going to support them.'

They sat in silence for a moment as Layne rubbed my arm.

"Wow," Raymond said. "You have really thought about this."

'I try to think about what this universe deserves, and I just-'

Layne cut me off, "Create it."

'Precisely.'

The four of us continued to talk for a while until Layne began to yawn.

"Looks like you've been up all day again, Layne," Marissa said.

"Yeah," Layne replied. "But I am still focused."

Layne suggested we go to the next few places she wanted to take me, but she asked if I could drive. Naturally, I obliged.

"Take care of her heart," Raymond said as we both walked out the door.

'I will. I promise, sir.'

We embraced each other for a moment as Marissa tried to hug both of us at the same time. Her family was pure and so incredibly sweet.

The two of us hopped in the car and she instinctively reached for the radio. "Never Tear Us Apart" from INXS blared over the speakers:

"I told you
That we could fly

'Cause we all have wings
But some of us don't know why
I was standing
You were there
Two worlds collided
And they could never ever tear us apart."

We travelled back towards my bed and breakfast as I realized our time together was coming to a close. My ferry would be leaving within a few hours, and I would be thrown back into New York's concrete jungle without Layne by my side.

I was praying and wishing that she would come back to New York again, because I wanted another dose of her. Layne is an elixir of the most ravishing kind.

All I knew at that moment was that she was an addiction of mine.

'Where are we going?' I looked over at her.

"I just wanted to cuddle up next to you, can we go back to your place?"

My place. I had a place on Martha's Vineyard.

As we arrived at the bed and breakfast, she asked if we could just rest for a little while together. I wanted nothing more than to hold her in my arms.

We curled up in the bed next to each other as she slept.

I was laying there with a heaviness in my soul. It was not a tragic heaviness, but it was a consuming one. I didn't want to leave her.

I could not leave her.

Yet, I had to temporarily.

The enriching scent of her hair lingered just below my nose.

As I shut my eyes, I heard the lyrics to Bon Jovi's "Always" reverberate throughout my mind:

"Yeah I, will love you, baby
Always and I'll be there
Forever and a day, always
I'll be there, till the stars don't shine
'Til the heavens burst and the words don't rhyme
I know when I die you'll be on my mind
And I'll love you, always."

Layne's voice cut through the melody playing in my head, "Scott, wake up, you'll miss the ferry!"

My eyes jolted open to see her watching over me in an angelic manner. I leapt out of the bed and started to grab my things. I felt refreshed lying next to her, but I felt incredibly sad knowing that we would need to be physically apart from each other again.

There's a difference between sleeping with someone and sleeping with someone whose soul awakens yours. Even just from laying next to her, I felt our hearts soaring above us.

I glanced up at her and murmured, 'I love you.'

She did not reply, but I could see her starting to tear up. Layne's pain was seeping back into her mind.

We made it to the ferry with some time to spare, so Layne suggested we listen to one last song before I made my trip back to New York.

I knew she was still somewhat reserved with her love for me, so I played her "What Ifs" by Kane Brown and Lauren Alaina:

> *"You say what if I hurt you, what if I leave you*
> *What if I find somebody else and I don't need you*
> *What if this goes south, what if I mess you up*
> *You say what if I break your heart in two then what*
> *Well I hear you girl, I feel you girl but not so fast*
> *Before you make your mind up I gotta ask*
> *What if I was made for you and you were made for me*
> *What if this is it, what if it's meant to be*
> *What if I ain't one of them fools just playin' some game*
> *What if I just pulled you close, what if I leaned in*
> *And the stars line up and it's our last first kiss*
> *What if one of these days baby I'd go and change your name*
> *What if I loved all these what ifs away."*

Layne instantly started to cry.

I put my hand on her shoulder, 'What's wrong?'

"Our souls," she wiped her tears. "They are integrated. They are bonded by the positive vibrations we express."

Her words were beautiful.

"I don't want you to go," she whimpered. "I just don't want to hurt you. I am healing."

'I know,' I reached for her hands, but she pulled away.

"Please. I need time."

'I'm sorry.'

"Here," she reached into her pocket and pulled out a rock. "I want you to have this. It's an aquamarine stone. Whenever you feel like you need me close to you, hold it in the palm of your hand."

As I took it from her, it seemed like the universe was whispering something to me. I was not sure what it was, but I figured I would trust the process.

She loved me; it was clear she loved me.

I boarded the ferry and watched her slowly pivot away from the dock. Something told me I would not hear from her for a while, but thankfully I was wholeheartedly wrong.

Upon docking at Woods Hole and getting back to my car, I put some music on to quell my anxiety. I missed Layne, I needed Layne, I wanted her to be with me forever, and not just in spirit.

The song "Feels Like Home" by Matt Johnson ushered me onto the highway:

"If you knew how lonely my life has been
And how long I've been so alone
If you knew how I wanted someone to come along
And change my life the way you've done
It feels like home to me."

The tears streaming down my cheeks resembled the fluid love Layne and I have been experiencing.

I felt that our souls should never truly be apart.

As I reached my mother's driveway, I pulled the stone from my pocket. I spoke to it with the same passion and reverence that reminded me of Layne.

'I love you,' I said to the stone. I followed it up with nine more expressions of my adoration for her.

Ten 'I love yous' in total filled the air.

When I opened my eyes, it was 3:15 in the morning.

∞ ∞ ∞ ∞ ∞ ∞ ∞ ∞

I only remember myself getting just a few hours of sleep. My skin seemed to congeal to the sofa in the oppressive summer humidity.

I could not help but feel her absence creep up each dip and groove of my spine. The sinking feeling in my chest was only contrasted by the weight of where her hand once was pulling me closer to wherever she was off to.

I was eternally her compass, and she would forever be my own personal due north. In due time, we would find our way back to one another, for she gave my life direction. She, for all intents and purposes, embodies every ounce of spiritual meaning that her aura bestows upon this universe: faith.

Layne called and said that being apart from me was harder than expected. She respected that we had to take care of our responsibilities at home and work, but she could not help the yearning she had for our souls to be together again.

"I've been writing still," Layne said with a tinge of hope in her voice.

'I am sure of it,' I replied. 'I would love to hear what you have been up to.'

She giggled. Her infectious laughter made me melt yet again.

"You are amazing, Scott." Layne's voice started to crack. "I miss you in every way."

Our conversation was short. My heart sank the moment I heard the silent pause when she hung up.

As I took a deep breath, I called Morena and asked her for advice. After explaining the magical moments I had with Layne, Morena's jubilance could be felt through the phone.

"Give her time, Scott," she continued assuring me. "Give her time."

As the Fourth of July rolled around, I realized it should not be enough to just eat hot dogs and barbeque. The day was always synonymous with freedom, but I can't just wave the flag and watch the parade go by.

Yes, I love all of the camaraderie the holiday brings, but I did think about my father who was still ill because of a war in the 60s and 70s. My grandfather who fought in WWII and my great grandfather who fought for England in WWI crossed my mind. I think of all my family members and our forefathers who fought for a higher ideal on our planet.

The Fourth of July was bigger than just a day off from work.

I was present for all of the day's events, but I was surely thinking about more than where it's best to see the fireworks. More so than usual, we need to remember and honor the values our nation celebrates.

The world is at a crossroads, for the values we cherish today should be welcome to all of humanity.

It is easy to wear red, white, and blue, attend a parade, eat apple pie, watch a baseball game with friends, and wave a flag, but after centuries of war and unrest, our entire planet is at risk of dying on so many levels.

This is not a political statement; rather it is a call to awareness, to action, and to love.

The United States of America was built on faith, and we all need an ounce of faith at this time.

We must have ideals that are built on human rights and unconditional love for all.

We celebrate a nation that has these precious concepts built into the Constitution and a Bill of Rights, but we must go beyond physical documents.

It is imperative to discover peace, love, happiness, and oneness, and not just within our country, but within our world, and especially within ourselves.

There are so many souls who I tend to see panicking about their daily lives, but we have the ability to introduce tranquility in our world.

The fundamental human rights live within us along with how we care for others, and ourselves.

We hold these truths to be self-evident: the United States of America is bigger than these times. Truth, courage, love, and respect that we need for humanity are within our souls.

We can stand for and represent our country, and we should stand and represent our souls as well.

Later that night, Layne called me and read me a new entry from her journal. She told me that she thought of our soul connection and began to write:

"This is a roller coaster.
Never in my wildest dreams did I think I would be here: doing this, feeling this, being this.

Some days I am eternally grateful for the best and biggest blessing the universe has ever bestowed on me. I feel like for the first time, I know what true friendship, love, spiritual mutualism and support feels like in a healthy way, and all at the same time from one more than incredible person.

I have hit the jackpot.

Who even needs another person when they have a Scott?

Still, I am pained by my past. My soul was gutted and crushed by those who were close to me.

I am not strong enough yet to act upon our connection.

This would be the ultimate betrayal to my soul's healing process.

This won't go away. This feeling in my chest, my stomach, my being. Knowing that we can go deeper and deeper means that at no point is this going to be a surface game again.

Managing this seems pointless now.

My logical brain succumbs to my heart in each instant and I don't know what my heart can possibly do to keep me safe.

When all it wants are things that spell danger to the souls of others.

At some point something needs to give. The rubber band breaks.

Deep breath... Why would the Universe send me something that is so perfect to my soul while I am still healing?

In a time that is so fragile, you are my ultimate test.

I hate to reduce what we have to that word, but it truly feels like every moment with you is a soul-enriching moment.

Every word that comes out of your mouth.

Every text.

Every phone call.

Every moment.

So it's either you're a test, or a huge sign.

What do you want me to do with this? Give me something.

I fear that no matter what that something is, loss is the flip side to that coin: either my soul connects to your soul and I never heal, or you are gone forever.

I need some time to process. I know I don't want to lose you.

I can't lose you.

I love you."

I sat there for a few moments, utterly speechless.

How was it possible that someone could be so self-reflective and spiritually connected to my soul?

We spoke for a while longer about our soul connection and what our respective growth would look like.

Layne's voice cracked, "How do we make this work, Scott?"

I did not know what to say.

I thought about how I soothed my soul in the past, and what methods helped me.

'Meditation,' I replied stoically.

"What do you recommend we do with meditation?"

'Each day, let's take some time to meditate together. We can talk about what that will look like and where it will take place.'

"So," Layne said inquisitively. "We go within."

'We go within,' I confirmed.

The two of us kept firm with our respective commitments to our souls.

On the first night we meditated together, I took her to the bridge and video called her. Layne was in the middle of getting ready for work. She was putting her earrings in as she spoke to me.

'This is where I usually go to connect to my soul: the Whitestone Bridge.'

She glanced at the screen. "It's beautiful at night."

'There is something so attractive about the bridge.'

I recalled looking through my father's station wagon windows at the bridge as we crossed over from the Bronx to Queens when we moved decades ago.

It was a connection to a new light.

It was symbolic of a new hope.

It would become a metaphor for my entire life's journey.

This particular bridge would prove as a means of comfort for my soul throughout my life. When I was abused as a child, I rode my bicycle to the bridge to find peace and happiness.

I try to process the difficult questions in my life on the pine green benches in front of the sandy beach.

'I could go on and on about bridge stories,' I smiled as the waves crashed close to my feet.

"Thank you," Layne said.

'Why are you thanking me?'

"For being you," she smiled.

We continued on about all of the wonderful places where our respective souls have grown and will continue to flourish.

After a few days of this meditative process, we decided that I should travel to Martha's Vineyard to see her again.

As I drove into Massachusetts, my anxiety seeped in.

Every trip prior has become progressively more intense for us.

If the intensity continued, would we reach our pinnacle? Could we reach our breaking point?

The ferry ride was painstaking as my nerves got the best of me. More tourists were on the boat with me: young children smacking tiny plastic shovels against their empty pails.

The sand in their buckets had yet to arrive, but I feared that mine and Layne's bucket might overflow.

As the boat approached the dock, Layne stood there in a flowing turquoise dress. Her baby pink nail polish and hot white heels were glorious accessories to her beaming smile.

Her entire aura was perfect.

'Hello, my love,' I walked over to her and kissed her cheek.

She coyly responded, "Hi."

Layne adorned a tart expression on her face.

'What's wrong?'

"Um," she cleared her throat. "Could you not say that word?"

'Which word?'

"Love. I'd rather we pick out a different word to say."

'What other word encompasses the peace-inducing soul connection we have?'

She looked down towards her feet for a moment, as she appeared to collect her thoughts. Layne locked eyes with me as the word flew from her mouth, "Namaste."

'I namaste you,' I replied.

"No," she laughed. "Just namaste."

We got in the car and drove towards a marina on the island. There were sailboats floating about the water without a care in the world.

We went back to the Mytoi Japanese Garden and continued to walk the different paths there. Our conversations grew more intense as the night fell upon us.

Two vibrant souls were glowing in the starlight descending on Martha's Vineyard.

As the two of us found our way back to the main part of the island, we both managed to start crying almost in unison.

Layne laughed, "Why are you crying?"

I wiped my eyes. My soul was aching for I sensed that she was about to end our relationship. I was fearful that she was going to walk out of my life forever, and that the soulful connection between us would be severed.

'You are just so beautiful,' was all I could come up with. I could not tell her the truth. I thought she might run.

Her tears flowed more rapidly. "Can you stop being so perfect?"

Layne leaned over and kissed me passionately. She began caressing my arm and chest so sensually, but that is where we paused for the time being.

'I can't do this to you.'

"What?"

'I don't want to hurt you, I don't want to add more pain to your soul.'

She wiped small tears from the edges of her eyes, "I namaste you."

'Why did you pick namaste, Layne?'

"Namaste means that my soul recognizes your soul."

I couldn't help myself. My lips were instinctively drawn to hers as we kissed once again.

Part of me thought that I had to leave, but all of me wanted to fight for her. I had to hold the space for her so she could figure things out.

Layne's soul was integrated with my soul. It was obvious that our energies were intertwined. We truly could not get enough of each other.

The number of days that Earth revolves around the sun does not satisfy the flavor of our souls. The recipe for our love was crafted as a cosmic part of this universe, and our love appeared to have the tenacity of an infinitesimal amount of revolutions around the sun.

This is a love story from another plane.

It may be non-existent in humanistic terms, but it is a realm that all souls should be privy to.

How many people can say they truly met their twin flame?

Just because we cannot see something within our current line of sight, it does not mean that nothing else exists.

Everything and anything beyond our purview is just something we have yet to discover.

Upon discovering Layne, I knew my life would never be the same.

She loves me in a humbling way that eclipses any and all pain. Layne knew that her soul was still healing, but chose to welcome me into her light.

Together, we shine brighter than the darkness embodying the depths of our respective pasts.

As the end of our experience came to a halt, for she had to go to work, I stood outside of the diner and looked up at the neon lettering:

"Twilight Diner."

I never realized how fitting it was.

As the sun set, so did my adventures with Layne.

It reminded me of Don Henley's song by a similar name:

> *"You see a lot more meanness in the city*
> *It's the kind that eats you up inside*
> *Hard to come away with anything that feels like dignity*
> *Hard to get home with any pride*
> *These days a man makes you somethin'*
> *And you never see his face*
> *But there is no hiding place.*
> *Respectable little murders pay*
> *They get more respectable every day*
> *Don't worry girl, I'm gonna stick by you*
> *And someday soon we're gonna get in that car and get outta here."*

I yearned to bring Layne away from here. I hoped her writings would be worldwide. I prayed her family would be safe, well, and financially stable when she became a writer.

The lyrics echoed through the catacombs of my mind.

I am here, in her world, watching her life manifest her soul's intentions.

The stained glass orange chandeliers reflected against the windows. I could see Layne's tied back hair flourishing about.

Universe, this is all in your hands, I realized.

You brought her to me, you gave me her, she is the answer to everything.

Why would you introduce her to me only to pull her away?

While Layne was at work overnight, my mother's condition began to deteriorate and I had to return to New York. I ran to see her at the diner before leaving, and she tucked a note into my pocket:

"So much to say...but first...thank you for being and for all of the things that you project on my soul. I recognize and know your sweetness, kindness, loveness, connectedness, openness, intenseness, understanding and aligned soul.

There are no words to articulate the pressure in my own heart and know this: everything you feel, I feel.

Thank you for being the blessing and gift that you are in this life, and to this planet. Standing on the outside of what you have created and have been creating your entire life is breathtaking. I am in awe of who you are, and how you express yourself in this world. I truly have also never met anyone in my life like you. You are powerful beyond measure.

I know that you are the answer as well. Your heart will save this world. I know that, because your heart has saved mine.

There will never be enough to say to you. My story for you is never ending. You open my senses in ways I've never experienced nor expressed. There are no words for what you have given me, done for me, or created within me.

I know you. Deeply. That I AM SURE of.

That's all I can say for now as well. Namaste."

I held the crinkled note in my hand as the ocean breeze blew through my hair.

I loved her, and it was that simple. The polarities of the universe turned the situation into "a this and a that" conversation, but the truth remained between us.

How could we have both scenarios so that I get to spend eternity with her and her soul heals?

Layne loves in so many languages and her intellect is beyond anyone's wildest imagination.

I could take a moment and bring up her writing or ask a philosophical question, and her mind expands and flows with the most impeccable perspective. Whatever her soul is made of is the same material needed to save our planet, I was sure of it.

Our souls combined, mingling in the universe, were beyond magic.

As I touched my forearm, I felt her fingers caressing my soul. I held her aquamarine stone in my hand before planting a gentle kiss on its surface.

I was hoping that wherever Layne was, she would feel my love.

We fit perfectly in every way, shape, and form, including spiritually, mentally, emotionally, soulfully, and physically.

My chest grew tight with trepidation. Again, I was worried I would lose her.

∞ ∞ ∞ ∞ ∞ ∞ ∞ ∞

When I got home, my sister and my mother were sound asleep on the couch. I took a wrinkled magazine off of the brown recliner chair and let my mind wander.

In my dreamlike state, I imagined that Layne and I were getting married.

She was standing before me in a crisp, luxurious white gown that wrapped around her perfectly.

I felt myself tearing up at the sight of her beauty.

When it was time to give my vow to her, I knew exactly what to say:

From day one, I knew you were it. Every second, every moment, every experience: it was you. All of my life's questions were unanswered. I was roaming and rambling through what I thought was a lifetime of confusion, then you answered my prayers. The second I looked at you, all of my worries and issues faded to black, and you were the light. You were a beacon of hope that beckoned me to live. You reminded me to keep the faith and genuinely refuse to sink under the weight of this world.

With your hands intertwined in mine, I know for a fact that every weight, every hardship, every agonizing tear, was shed knowing that you would be waiting for me at the end of the storm.

And when I was at my breaking point, you picked me up and held my hand. You looked into my eyes and spoke the words I never knew I would need to hear.

You are the best thing I never knew I needed. You are the response to every call I made that echoed through the darkness. You are my destiny, my empowering heart, and the divine love that encompasses the phrase, "seize the day."

You are my brand-new day.

I owe my soul to your undying, exquisite beauty. I owe my love to the woman who recognized the twin flame standing across from her. Our love burns brighter than that of a classic love story, because we live our lives beyond the boundaries of society standards, and with this ring, I pledge my loyalty to our bond, our growth, and our coexistence together.

It is a brand-new day, and we are going to live it together. We will live it time after time in each other's arms and with passion. For you are one-hundred percent of the reason why my soul is floating high above the clouds, and I know, for sure, that our love story embodies the notion that the best is yet to come.

All my life, I wanted an ocean view somewhere. As long as I am next to you, I do not care. I want to live our life in an infinite realm of possibilities, for you, my darling, you are truly my home.

Before she could say anything, a beam of light brushed against my face. I could feel the ghost of where her fingers were just a few hours ago. I hoped her touch was not just a dream, I had hoped that last night really happened and that she would long to hold me in her arms once again. She was an angel who was thrust into my life for no apparent reason, though months later I understood that she flew in to show me that there is a fire within me.

And now all I want to do is let it burn.

∞ ∞ ∞ ∞ ∞ ∞ ∞ ∞

When it came to trying to figure out how to love Layne without causing her any unintentional pain, I reverted to my pen to dig deeper into my soul. I wrote for hours in what should have been my framework notes to comprehend what to do with my mind's discontent.

Layne was the one person that could communicate with me and connect with me on a level that I never experienced before.

I promised Layne I would not hurt her, yet I feared that I was pushing too hard against the firm walls she constructed to protect her soul.

Every fiber of my being loved her with all I manifested to that point, but how could I express myself fully while honoring her? I felt the sun setting on my soul, yet she said I was supposed to see the sunrise at those moments.

I convinced myself I had to be stronger and remember the vision.

I knew what I saw in her eyes, I knew what I heard in the timbre of her voice. Her connection to souls and the way our hearts beat in tandem were not misaligned or misguided.

Her mind and soul lit the flame deep within me. Once you've seen something magical, it is not like you can just reset your brain. There are some things that awaken you in a way that reveal the positive vibrations deep within you. As a result, you can't deny what your soul truly desires.

You cannot unseen what you have seen.

When I look in her eyes, tears may be falling from mine, but I see happiness and feel happiness because I see her energy.

Anything can change in a moment. Within the blink of an eye she walked into my life, and I must cherish that.

She managed to resist me quite well, but like I had noticed before, when she caves into her desires, she crashes wholeheartedly. Within the parameters of this human experience, I loved her with all of my heart and soul and I knew she loved me.

I wondered, 'Why does this relationship seem to challenge me so much?'

What were two souls, that love one another and stand for a higher consciousness connection, supposed to do?

I wept openly over my book as Morena came into the room.

She placed a cup of tea on the table next to me, "What is wrong, sunshine?"

'Nothing,' I wiped my eyes and gazed up at her. 'Just nothing.'

"You miss her," Morena sat next to me and folded her hands over each other.

'Yeah,' I picked up the tea and sipped it gently.

"How could you not miss someone so crucial to your soul?"

I looked over at her again. 'You get it.'

"Heh," she laughed. "I see more than you realize. I heard a quote somewhere that said, *'Let the waves of the universe rise and fall as they will. You have nothing to gain or lose. You are the ocean.'*"

'How wise.'

"It is from the Ashtavakra Gita."

'It's like something Layne would know.'

"Maybe she does know it, maybe she just needs to unlock that part of her soul."

'I think it's just time to hand everything to the universe.'

"Stop saying it over and over again, unless you are truly going to start believing it."

'Is that judgment I hear, Morena?'

"Judgment is not my cup of tea, rather," she cleared her throat. "Sometimes you just need to let go of fear."

'Oh,' I coughed for a moment. 'Is that what I am feeling?'

"Maybe," Morena stood up. "Maybe you just need to listen to the voice in your soul."

'I am listening to the voice.'

She smoothed out the creases on her blue dress. "Listen closer."

Morena walked out of the living room and I called after her as I stood up, 'Morena, I-'

When I looked into the kitchen, she was gone. It figures.

I was convinced she was, indeed, an angel of sorts.

As the summer was speeding before me, I went to a conference in Baltimore with Morena to present about the framework. Though I was in my element talking about education, I missed Layne standing beside me.

Baltimore was not far from Washington, D.C., so I chose to go there to surprise Morena. As the signs on the highway flashed by, I watched Morena's eyes light up when the sign for the Arlington Memorial Bridge appeared on the road.

The possibility of real change existed in the streets I was about to enter, with the desire to change the world burned deep inside.

As we walked down the streets of D.C. at night, I envisioned what it must have been like for the presidents who passed through these roads in their motorcades.

Real systemic change was being conjured within my soul, but I feared I was being too histrionic and grandiose for my own good.

The streets were empty and I thought: If New York is the city that never sleeps, why did it appear like D.C. was taking a nap?

Morena turned her eyes to the Washington Monument as we stood on the steps of the Lincoln Memorial. Standing up there gazing out at the Reflecting Pool was majestic.

It solidified my dreams and put it all into perspective. It gave me a path of hope. As I took in every step, I felt the universe guiding me and welcoming me to the next stage.

The White House, much smaller than I thought, felt like home.

It seemed so doable, almost as if I had lived there before.

There was a homeless veteran out at the front of the gates, I wondered if any President spoke with him.

I was told he's been there forever.

Can we invite him into dinner and hear him out? Why is he there? What does his soul search for?

World peace has to be a possibility.

The game has to change.

Standing on the steps of the Lincoln Memorial made me feel as if I was looking up at the gates of heaven. Lincoln and I have a long spiritual relationship, and I have always been amazed by his story.

There is something about a man who brought this country back together while struggling with his own physical illness, depression, and a difficult family is phenomenal.

He struggled with who he was but cared about all others.

He fought a war based on civil rights: the right to be human, to love yourself for who you are, and to have faith.

How is that different from the social emotional work we do daily?

He was a man of heart and true character.

When I think about my relationship with the heavens, I always feel pulled in by the story of Lincoln, just as I felt invited up the stairs of the monument. I felt invited by him tonight as if the angels lined this moment up for me.

I took each step consciously and mindfully felt my feet touch each stone, raising me slowly to the message I was about to hear.

Walking into the temple was as if the universe and angels were calling me into a realization about what my life is all about.

On some spiritual level you can see the words of God and the angels intertwined in the words of his speeches.

We need to go back to that time of conviction, of making this world better for a higher purpose.

We must search our souls and we must become one.

There is still a civil war going on, not just in our country between Democrats and Republicans, but in the world and in our individual souls.

We must bridge the gap, we must soul-search, and we must have peace on earth. It's as if the closer we got to accepting love of same sex marriages, the older child known as civil rights resurfaces in the form of gun violence, systemic racism, wrongful deaths, and police shootings. Like raising a family, we must love and nurture all our children.

If society's issues are our children, we must navigate and communicate in a way we can understand the roots of souls better.

At the end of the day, we can love one another and love thy neighbor.

We must bring the world to gather as one, UNIFIED, as Abraham Lincoln wanted. Staring up into his eyes, I felt like he was passing the torch to me, but he was also with me, putting his hand on my shoulder as I sat in his temple and meditated.

I prayed for guidance and I felt the puzzle pieces come together.

It took me a long time to realize I love my life, I love the world we live in, I love the anticipation of hopes and dreams, and that look in Layne's eyes.

Maybe some things are not meant to be no matter how you look at them, but that night, as I stared into Lincoln's eyes and felt his presence, I knew anything was possible.

Later on in the evening as my legs grew weary I stopped at McDonald's for a Happy Meal. I walked with Morena to the Capitol building at two in the morning enjoying my chicken and my All-American meal.

'Whether Layne is by my side or not,' I told Morena. 'I am moving ahead on this journey as I now realize no matter what path you take, it will lead to the same place.'

"The place you are meant to be," she responded.

Morena and I walked the streets of Washington, D.C. until the sun started to rise. We began to talk about love in its most pure form.

As a kid, there was nothing more romantic than creating a mixtape for a girl you liked. It was the utmost expression of love and just showed creativity. I always believed music was the language of the soul, and going all the way back to the days of being with Robin, I knew the melodies and harmonies created a vibration to lift our consciousness to a new level.

Yet with modern technology, mixtapes have been escalated to playlists of sometimes hundreds of songs.

Layne texted me here and there since my last trip at Martha's Vineyard, but we did not seem to harbor the same soul connection as we did during the first few times we were physically occupying the same space. I wondered if our mutual melody hit its final verse.

Our first kiss, our first physical encounter, the way the vibrations from music make her body sway, it was clear that when love can't be expressed in terms of words, music fills the space between us.

"Sometimes it's about words and music," Morena replied.

'You can't have one without the other most of the time.'

Layne's aural melody was exquisite.

I only wished that love could stand the test of time, just like the music notes that graced my mixtapes and playlists over the years. However, the greatest concierto by far was not one written by Mozart or Beethoven, rather it was composed by Layne's connection to my soul and the way my heartbeat fluttered when she looked at me.

Love is truly the greatest music of all.

∞ ∞ ∞ ∞ ∞ ∞ ∞ ∞

As Morena and I got back to New York, a taxicab was pulling up to my mother's house. Confused and slightly concerned, I got out of the car and placed my right elbow on the roof of the Dodge Charger.

"Surprise," Layne exclaimed so loudly that she almost dropped her suitcase from her hand.

'Layne?'

She rushed over and threw her arms around me.

'How did you get here?'

"I can navigate a bus map, but this city is surely something else," Layne grinned and glared at me lovingly.

We lingered in the moment, waiting for each other to say what we both longed to hear.

'Oh,' I turned. 'Layne there is someone I want you to meet.'

When I went to the passenger side of the car, I noticed that Morena was gone.

"Who, Scott?"

'My,' I hesitated for a moment. 'My mother. Come inside!'

The two of us walked into the house as Layne explained she had to see me after my short stint in Baltimore. We chatted for a few moments until my mother emerged from the living room.

"The men are working on the plumbing again," she muttered.

Layne looked at me quite confused, "What?"

I pointed to my head and Layne got the hint.

'Mom, this is my friend Layne. Layne, this is my mom.'

Layne extended her hand, "Nice to meet you, Ms. Matheson."

"Oh," my mother seemed startled. "Hello dear, it's nice to see you again."

Layne and I moved into the living room and spoke with my mother for a while. As she recounted stories of her teaching days, Layne looked on in amazement. When we left the house later on, I realized why.

The two of us took a walk in Alley Pond Park and spoke about past pain.

"It is fascinating how the human brain works," Layne looked over at me. "Your mother doesn't remember anything she did to you when you were younger?"

'No, not at all.'

"Fascinating," she looked ahead on the trail. We waited there a little too long again, which made it seem like we were going to ease into another passionate kiss.

Somehow, Layne managed to contain her soul's desire.

As we walked further into the park, she fell into my arms crying hysterically.

'Layne?' I rubbed her shoulder.

"I just didn't realize how hard this was going to be." Her tears pooled on my t-shirt.

'I am here for you no matter what,' my voice softened. 'I am not going anywhere and you call the shots.'

"Thank you," she nestled into my chest.

'I will be whatever you need me to be, even if it means I need to disappear forever in order to soothe your soul.'

"I never want you to disappear," she whipped her head up towards my face. "You are always in my soul."

We walked the park for a little bit longer, until she said she wanted to go back to her hotel to rest. As we drove back, she sat in relative silence while I kept my eyes on the road.

As my car drove into the underground parking lot, static filled the radio. The two of us locked eyes for a moment before we opened the doors.

When the two of us made our way towards the elevator, a whole barrage of rats scurried past our feet. We ran quickly and started to slam the buttons on the elevator. The two of us darted away from the rats and rushed into the stairwell.

While giggling over the sheer chaos that just occurred, I looked over at her.

'They never do this,' I assured her. 'Yeah, I mean, there is that rat who stole a whole slice of pizza, but... that was in the subway.'

"You're adorable," she grabbed her bag from my hand as we walked up the steps. We laughed and made our way up to her room.

It was clear we were ensnared in a cycle of struggle and passion, with hope for the future.

The moment the door shut behind us, she put on some music. The way her body moved to the lyrics was exhilarating, though I had to restrain myself from moving towards her.

I stood there in the doorway as she swayed her hips in the shape of an infinity sign. Layne extended her hand, "Dance with me."

The lyrics called me in.

Ed Sheeran's words to "I See Fire" were perfect in that moment:

"Oh, misty eye of the mountain below
Keep careful watch of my brothers' souls
And should the sky be filled with fire and smoke
Keep watching over Durin's sons
If this is to end in fire
Then we should all burn together
Watch the flames climb high into the night."

When the song ended, she flopped on the bed and curled into the sheets. I saw her sigh heavily as she gazed out at the city's skyline. From Queens, she had the perfect view of Manhattan.

Not lying next to her felt like I was missing something.

My soul felt empty and I could not catch my breath.

"You can lay next to me," Layne motioned for me to sit on the bed. I left space between us so that she did not feel pressured.

'You came all the way to New York, after you relax for a bit, I want to take you to a few places.'

She flipped over in the bed so she was facing me. "Okay."

A smile crept up both of our faces.

'Okay.'

A few hours later, the two of us were walking along the Brooklyn Bridge Promenade. We strolled arm in arm glaring out at the Freedom Tower.

'The Twin Towers once stood there,' I pointed out towards the southern part of Manhattan.

Layne shut her eyes and seemed to feel the energy from my aunt's soul. A few deep breaths later, she opened her eyes and we continued to walk.

I took her to eat at a blues bar in Manhattan. She loved the music, the decor, and the food they had.

"We don't really have anything like this on Martha's Vineyard," she pulled out her journal and started writing.

As the stars rose in the sky, I took her on a driving tour of New York City. The two of us listened to music throughout the entire ride, with her body ebbing and flowing with each elegant note.

"So Alive" from the Goo Goo Dolls appeared to reflect her soul's intentions at those moments:

> *"Open up my heart like a shotgun*
> *Blinded by the light of a new sun*
> *Get up, get up, get out and get done*
> *For the first time I feel like someone*
> *Breaking down the walls in my own mind*
> *Keeping my faith for the bad times*
> *Get up, get up, stand like a champion*
> *Take it to the world*
> *Gonna sing it like an anthem."*

So many people take New York City for granted, especially since the hustle and bustle of commuters regularly fills the atmosphere. Watching Layne breathe in every single element of Manhattan was breathtaking.

After driving uptown, downtown, and across midtown for quite some time, we found ourselves gazing out at the bridge in Astoria Park.

"You have such beautiful bridges in New York," Layne watched the lights twinkle atop Hellgate Bridge.

The water has a certain calming presence over my soul, which has captivated me ever since I was a young boy. Even at the tender age of eight years old, I sensed that I had a higher purpose and a story that transcended even my deepest insecurities.

That was why it was water, her tears that streamed down her alabaster face, which awoke me from the trance-like slumber my heart was in. Though in the midst of facing some of my darkest moments, I couldn't help but hear her tears as an echoic reverberative melody inside of my soul.

The love that emulated from her heart was beyond real. It was powerful. It was magical on an entirely different level.

Coexisting with her is a type of fire that I didn't mind getting burned by, though it is more than that.

Her love and her spirit were cosmically intoxicating.

Her essence was a solitary flame that sparked my inferno. On nights like those, I tended to walk through the cool, crisp night trying to gain my thoughts; I usually caught myself glancing at the stars.

Part of me hoped that wherever in the universe her soul truly was, she was not in pain.

The universe has become brighter since the moment she walked into my life. There was a light coming from her that shined so bright, no shadow could come close to touching her glowing nature. In the moments she whispered to me that she loved me, she missed me, or when she simply grabbed my hand or cuddled into my chest, all of the internal storms brewing within fell to a complete silence.

Her energy crept inside of me in a way that repaired every torn crevice of my soul. She taught me that when we allow ourselves to open our hearts, and in expressing and exploring this higher love consciousness, love will open your mind to new dimensions.

It would expand your soul to the furthest corners of the universe.

Loving her, and receiving her love, is the igniting of potential which unfurls an unimaginable force across the universe. It lifts our spirits vibrationally, and that of every soul in, and not of, this universe. Walking through these streets, looking at these stars, and remembering all of our magical moments uplifts me and blesses me with the ability to see a brighter tomorrow.

There is a silence here.

There is a silence that carries your name in my heart throughout every second of the day, every moment of the week, and every season of the year.

I love Layne this way because my soul knows no other way.

I leaned over to her and whispered: 'You are the path to my dreams, and each cobblestone represents the little moments that led me to your effervescent beauty. It made me see that once you realize the dreams of your heart, anything you face is manageable. Your life takes on an entirely new meaning... and I mean anything I have tried to run away from: my heart, from my truth, and beyond that. The only thing I have discovered is that it is impossible to escape from my heart, no matter how hard I try. Instead, I have now stopped trying to run as fear cascades through me. I sit and listen.'

Layne looked over at me and smiled.

'I listen to my heart and it screams at me passionately. It has much to say. Much of it makes my soul sing. I'm coming to the end of this starry night, and this cool brisk air creeps inside me sending a chill down my spine. It is almost as powerful as the memory of your kisses, your smooth skin, your electrifying touch, and the kindness that emanates off your soul, leaving my soul trembling. Though my mind is racing with questions, the only word that surfaces on my lips is the one that you gave meaning to: "Namaste." And suddenly, the world does not seem like it is succumbing to the dawn and dispersing the illustrious stars above.'

"Rather," Layne spoke. "We are creating an infinite, spiraling path into the sun, and actualizing just what it means to be immersed in the essence of two words that describe our everlasting growth: twin flames. We are twin flames who will burn forever, and no matter what, forever will always be ours to cherish eternally."

We glanced at each other as the next song played over the speakers.

Layne shut her eyes as Amy Lee's voice seeped into the car. Evanescence's "My Immortal" seemed to touch yet another exquisite part of her soul.

I watched the music move through her as she closed her eyes and sang in such an angelic manner:

> *"I'm so tired of being here*
> *Suppressed by all my childish fears*
> *And if you have to leave*
> *I wish that you would just leave*
> *'Cause your presence still lingers here*
> *And it won't leave me alone*
> *These wounds won't seem to heal; this pain is just too real*
> *There's just too much that time cannot erase*
> *When you cried, I'd wipe away all of your tears*
> *When you'd scream, I'd fight away all of your fears*
> *And I held your hand through all of these years..."*

I watched the next few words spring from her mouth with such illustrious purpose. It was almost as if her soul was guiding her lips:

> *"But you still have..."*

She paused for a moment along with the song. I honed in on the energy she emitted while singing the next few words:

"All of me."

Layne opened her eyes and saw my tears rolling down the edges of my eyes. I could not help but cry at the sound of her illustrious beauty, both internal and external.

The two of us sat in silence when the song ended until she asked if I could drop her off at the hotel.

When I walked her up to her room for the night, she kissed me gently on the cheek. The metal door opened as she slid inside. As it slammed shut, I walked down the hall hoping to hear the door open again.

The elevator arrived and the only sound I could hear was the ding reminding me that my soul was in a current state of solitude.

Layne only came in for the weekend, so I had to make Sunday count as best as possible. The two of us had breakfast after I picked her up, and we sat in Francis Lewis Park talking about our relationship.

"We are beyond the 3D aspects of our world," Layne spoke softly.

'What do you mean?' I adjusted my body so I was directly facing her.

"As human beings, we live in a perpetual state of physical consciousness. Our world has concrete, black and white realities: we are born, we are here," she motioned towards both of us. "We die."

I nodded my head and leaned towards her.

"The 3D view mandates relationships have a lower vibrational frequency and are integrated with a lot of fear. Sometimes even that fear is so strong that it constricts us from growing spiritually. Our souls are not respected as a higher power."

'So, it's like a non-spiritual way of being.'

"We are 5D," she said matter-of-factly.

'5D?'

"It is the elevated sense of love. It is the highest and most challenging state of consciousness, yet we live it each day."

Layne stood up and walked over to the iron fence in front of us. She spoke as if she was educating the water before us; I felt the wind tearing through my soul.

"Everything is spiritual, of a higher power, and focuses on the foundation of love in a 5D relationship."

'Love is the life force.'

"Yes," she turned towards me and her hair got caught in the wind. "The heart, the mind, and the soul each have a different language."

'Feelings are more intense and expanded upon.'

"Love is not love, connection is not connection, integration is not integration," her entire face illuminated as if she suddenly became enlightened. Layne ripped her journal from her bag and started to write furiously.

'You live authentically and as a universal, spiritual being.'

"Yes, yes!" She dropped onto the bench and continued writing.

'When you live from your heart and soul, there is an instant connection.'

"And in this 3D world, life is challenging because we struggle to balance the 3D and 5D aspects of our lives."

'It's the vibrations in our soul that make us who we are.'

Her scribbling was more audible, "Vibrations."

'It's unconditional love without any asterisks, without what ifs, and without buts.'

"Yes," Layne slammed the journal shut and smiled at me. "It's an instant connection."

Her eyes began to wander around the park. She glanced over at the bridge, the grass, the children playing on the swings.

The rest of the day flew by, but she seemed to have a renewed sense of who she was. It was almost as if something finally clicked in her brain.

When I dropped her off at the bus stop in Manhattan, she seemed happier than usual.

'Thank you,' I held her tight for a moment.

"I am glad I got to see you, Scott."

We did not let go. It seemed like that was our final goodbye, though I knew that something was shifting within both of us.

It was more of a "hello" situation. We were finally meeting each other without filtered hearts.

Still, as she boarded the bus and it drove off, my heart sank in my chest once again. I needed her desperately and I missed her so much, even though she had just left.

When I returned to my mother's house, I was clearly sulking as I got out of the car.

"What are you doing?" Morena appeared in the shadows as she usually did.

'Nothing,' I wiped the tears from my eyes.

Morena flew in front of me as her dress swooshed past my leg.

"Don't let yourself get like this. She is what you prayed for and you wanted for the longest time. The universe presented you with her."

I tried walking away from her, but she appeared in front of me again.

"You wanted to love yourself, holistically and without remorse, and she brings out that side of you. She is the epitome of happiness and all that genuinely stands for the term holy."

'Morena, I-'

Her voice cut through my thoughts: "She is your happiness and light serendipity, you must understand this on a spiritual level."

The two of us walked into my mother's house and started to review the latest ideas I had about the framework. Every time I paused to turn the page I envisioned Layne sitting across from me, scribbling something down in her journal as she wrote the greatest novel known to humankind.

I shut my eyes for a moment and allowed the breeze from the fan to usher me into a tranquil state of rest.

∞ ∞ ∞ ∞ ∞ ∞ ∞ ∞

As I woke, a smile crept over my face. The image of her faded deep into the recesses of my mind, as I sat up hopeful I would see her again in my dreams tonight.

Something swimming around in my subconscious anchors her to my soul. My undying love for her exists within multiple universes, and it blatantly shows through how she manifests while I sleep. Though she is not really next to me, I find comfort waking up in the morning and seeing her image be projected in the empty space next to me.

Hearts may break, but nothing will break my unwavering dedication to what we once were. I will cherish her memory in my mind, soul, and heart until every ounce of life is drained from me.

Even in whatever afterlife exists, I will still make it my mission to reconnect with her soul. If not in this universe, I will find her in the next.

That is how strong our connection is.

And it always will be. Even if sometimes a little bit of me strays from her light, I know that her shadow stands tall. The remnants of our shadows lay somewhere intertwined, if not in the light, then in the recesses of all visibility where souls have the privilege to connect.

Layne was pushing me away as if doing so would fix everything.

I wondered if she was wrong.

I wondered if pushing me away would be the biggest mistake she would ever make.

What if we don't get the chance to live out the blessing we were handed?

I did not want to do anything without Layne by my side. Everything felt wrong without her there.

Our love may not have a stronger word than love, but it is what we have. It's from somewhere else and we both acknowledged that. We both felt the energy between us.

I knew we had to follow through with this feeling.

Since the second our eyes met, I knew that my life had meaning because of her.

'Please don't leave me' escaped my lips. 'Look in my eyes and tell me you love me.'

As I turned the aquamarine stone over between my fingertips, there was no answer from the universe.

My soul was screaming out to hers, but a dull silence filled the air.

When I stood up, the stuffing from the couch appeared to follow me. Even the internal filling of the couch wanted to rise above, how metaphoric.

Days were flying by and before I knew it, I would be counting down the final days of summer. I wanted to make one last-ditch effort to confess my love to Layne, although she was fully aware we were in love.

The two of us did not have labels, but when it all comes down to the inherent truth, we were each other's twin flame.

Her texts and calls were coming few and far between each sweltering day, and I wanted more than anything to run right up to Martha's Vineyard and whisk her into my arms.

Layne's pain seemed to be overbearing and her soul was still on its path to recovery, and I wanted more than anything to be her hero.

I had the potential to be her savior; every fiber of my soul assumed my love would rescue her from the internal hurt that haunted her each day.

As my march towards going back to work was starting to take place, Layne called me one day in a fit of excitement.

"I'm doing it," she exclaimed.

'Doing what?'

"I am going to head back towards the Grand Canyon where my father, Marissa, and I used to visit."

'That's awesome,' I assured her. 'Why now?'

"I think my book needs that final scene where the Grand Canyon acts as the backdrop. It was the most illustrious place where I used to write as a child, and I need to go there and breathe in the scenery."

'That's cool,' I swallowed hard for a second. 'Do you mind if I come with you?'

She paused for a moment and sighed, "Of course."

Layne was taking a flight from Boston and I was taking one from LaGuardia Airport in New York.

We met at Jackpot Airport at the very top of the state of Nevada. She was able to convince some of her old friends to drive up and pick us up, but my flight somehow managed to come in a bit earlier than hers.

Since she was ensnared in a layover in Chicago, I found myself wandering around all alone.

I was looking at a screen with incoming flights, and was curious about the airport's code: KPT.

My inquisitive mind compelled me to ask a flight attendant why the code was KPT. She shrugged and continued walking by. Sometimes people are so busy, I wonder if they ever stop to notice the little things in life like airport codes.

When Layne finally arrived, her friends and I jumped in a pine green Jeep and headed south towards the Canyon.

We had a great conversation about Layne's book and she began to read some entries to us. I was in awe of how much her writing grew over the past few months.

She nudged me and replied, "I have you to thank."

Her smile was wider and she appeared to be more in tune with my soul's vibrations. I lingered on her compliment for the rest of the car ride.

The sun was setting as the two of us got all the way to the south rim of the Grand Canyon.

"The south rim arguably has the best view," Layne said.

"Oh yeah," her friend remarked. "Hands down."

Layne's friend dropped us off and said she would come pick us up when it started to get really dark.

As we walked closer to the Canyon, I saw the setting sun touch each rock with a pristine softness. The vivid colors drenched the Canyon in a rare vibrancy that I never even knew existed.

'It's,' I took a breath for a moment. 'Beautiful.'

Layne looked over her shoulder at me and extended her hand. "Let's keep walking."

I took her hand and began to follow her through the path. There were multiple places that were not fenced off too well, and a sudden fear of heights seemed to seep into my mind.

Looking down at the huge drop, I must have worn my fear on my face.

"We'll make it, I swear," she laughed and pulled me towards the path again.

I watched Layne sit and write underneath a partially rotten tree for a while. My own mind wandered to a state of peace, for the sounds of the Grand Canyon compel the soul to go deep within the cavernous elements of your own being.

When the sun completed its dissent, we got a ride back to a hotel in town. At the front desk, they revealed that only one room was booked instead of two, so I naturally offered for Layne to stay in my room.

She accepted with a petite grin.

We sat in the hotel room on the sole queen-size bed debriefing what we saw out at the Canyon.

'How long are you staying here?'

"Just a few days, I want to make sure that I get all of the scenery just right."

Layne began to flip through her journal, which appeared to be almost full.

'Wow, you have written a lot.'

"Mhm," she nodded. "Since my last trip to New York, I had a sudden burst of energy. Everything seems to make sense in my soul."

'Everything?'

"Yes," she replied. "Including our relationship."

I swallowed hard, 'Oh?'

"Our love is real, it's intense, and I have so many choices to make."

'Like what?'

"Are you everything I ever wanted? Yes. Are you more than perfect? Yes."

'Do you love me?'

"Is that even a question?"

'Sorry,' I propped my head up against the headboard. 'Continue.'

"Is all of this enough?" She paused. "No."

'No?'

"No, Scott."

We sat in silence for a few moments before lying parallel to one another.

"Higher love consciousness is extremely rare. To lie together and love one another, and speak about why we can't be a couple is beyond rare, but I need to grow. You need to grow."

As tears slowly cascaded from my eyes, I murmured, 'But you need to grow?'

"And you do, too," she extended her hand and touched my forearm.

I sat in desolate silence.

"Based on my life choices, I know I need more time to heal before I fully commit myself to anything or anyone else. I have my book. I have my writing. Who knows where it will go?"

'But what about us?'

"I love you," she began to cry. "I namaste you."

We sat in silence a little while longer, while Layne continued to search for the words stemming from the voice in her soul.

"I can't continue expressing to you what is in my soul, for I know I am still healing." She placed her hand over my heart. "You are still healing."

'I know,' I teared up a bit more.

"I am still healing."

I saw the tattered wallpaper in my peripheral vision. The terra cotta pots sitting on the night table were still and rustic, almost echoic of the way my soul seemed to shrivel up inside.

The rest of the night into the morning consisted of a long, emotional talk about our respective pain and our individualistic journeys.

"We made it here, because we are the souls the world has been waiting for."

Her words struck my soul with the truth. How could I deny I was still relishing in my past pain?

My love for her seemed to consume my soul at times, and I was rejecting any sort of healing energy I could manifest.

All of my energy was going into our relationship, not who I could become.

I needed to step into my own power, as did she, no matter how much it hurt our souls for the time being.

If it were meant to be, then it would be.

Before we fell asleep, the two of us decided we would dance to one last song together.

Layne snatched my phone and started to scroll up and down with her finger. As she squinted at the screen, the faint light from my phone illuminated her eyes.

As the song started playing, she looked at me and said, "I am thankful for you, and I hope you know that this song reminds me so much of your soul."

The melody and lyrics to Vanessa Williams' "Save the Best for Last" echoed throughout the room:

> *"Sometimes the snow comes down in June*
> *Sometimes the sun goes 'round the moon*
> *I see the passion in your eyes*
> *Sometimes it's all a big surprise*
> *'Cause there was a time when all I did was wish*
> *You'd tell me this was love*
> *It's not the way I hoped or how I planned*
> *But somehow it's enough*
> *And now we're standing face to face*
> *Isn't this world a crazy place?*
> *Just when I thought our chance had passed*
> *You go and save the best for last."*

I doubt that either of us remembered falling asleep.

An hour later, I looked over at the clock and panicked. It was four in the morning. I had to run and catch my flight, since I was only there for less than a day. There was no time to shower or waste a moment.

I kneeled down next to her and tousled her hair between my fingers. I planted a solitary kiss on her forehead and whispered into her ear just how much she meant to me.

And I loved her.

I couldn't leave her.

I knew once I did, I could be penning our final goodbye in our chapter.

Layne's eyes crept open in the darkness. The dim light from the bathroom shined bright enough for me to see the outline of her pure facial features.

Her groggy voice lurked out into the dusk: "Are you going?"

'I don't want to, Layne.'

She shifted her body so she could hold me.

"I know."

'I have been trying to leave for ten minutes.'

I could feel her smile as she held me close. Her heart was beating in tandem with mine once again. Our bodies fit perfectly together.

"Don't miss your flight."

'Yes, my love.' I held back the tears.

"Have a good day, Scott."

'I will, babe,' I whispered back.

Neither one of us moved, as there was clearly a deeper message in this embrace.

After what seemed like an hour, we slowly pulled apart. My lips were just as close as they were on that first day we kissed, except this time I honored her request and did not give into what I so passionately wanted to do.

My lips were right there.

I felt her about to cave as well.

For a moment, I ran my fingers through her hair and held her forehead against mine.

'I love you Layne,' I inhaled and exhaled deeply. 'I always will.'

She was silent for a moment and whispered, "Namaste."

I softly kissed her forehead and pressed my ear against her chest for a moment. Her beating heart was the last sound I wanted to hear before I fully said goodbye.

As I pulled away, she whispered, "Text me when you land."

'Of course, Layne.'

I wasn't sure if I would.

She rolled over and was consumed by the darkness.

With my heart racing to the tune of what would normally be tears, I glanced over at the pad and pen on the night table.

I lifted the pen with such purpose, and wrote her a quick note:

Layne,

I will love you forever. You are perfect, your story is perfect, you have made my existence perfect, and the world needs you. Don't ever forget that.

Always,
Scott

As the door shut behind me, I took one last look at her fast asleep under the blankets. She looked like an angel.

My angel.

My love.

The door closed behind me as two long, slow teardrops fell from each eye.

I remember that day, for the world shifted back to a sadness I had not experienced in almost a year.

I got to the terminal and through security in what seemed like record time.

KPT is an airport code I will never forget.

It is an airport I will never return to.

It is a memory I never want to revisit, though in usual fashion, even a final goodbye with Layne is extremely breathtaking.

I wondered if she would be sitting in this same airport in a few days' time feeling the stale air of this universe, which I clearly felt at that moment.

Nothing will ever be the same again.

I looked around.

Maybe Morena's essence would guide me through this. I could have used that angelic wisdom at that moment.

I was alone.

Upon arriving in New York, the souls in the airport seemed to have an emptiness to their energy: I could not connect to anyone.

Layne and I talked last night about how we are no different than the other souls on this planet, and how our ability to connect is a responsibility to the planet.

We could feel one another miles away, and we can connect to other souls and show them their possibilities. Just because we see the light doesn't make us better. It's a gift we must pay forward.

We deep dived for hours, just the two of us.

A hotel room, two hearts, two souls, and one vision.

Our conversation was insightful, stoic, and exponentially deep... it had global implications. Her vision, her energy, and her writing could connect souls to their inner power, and ignite their healing process so that they can work to improve our planet. It sounds like a very valuable reason to sacrifice the greatest love story never told.

Her soul was leaps and bounds ahead of our time, and knowing that she would still be out there in the world gave my soul a tranquil feeling.

The darkness behind the large terminal windows mirrored the darkness in my soul. I had to mirror her wisdom and also try to make a change on this planet in a devout manner.

However, my numbness didn't feel like I could do so.

Last night we spoke about how Layne and I need to take the final step into owning our respective power, yet my hypocritical heart didn't believe I could do the same.

There will never be another Layne and Scott. There is never the same love twice; she is proof of this.

Goodbye Layne. Namaste times an eternal infinity.

Your soul will always be my home.

The automatic doors opened and I stepped out into the bustling cityscape once again.

Morena picked me up at the airport. The sun was shining brightly in New York, which was an utter juxtaposition to what my soul was feeling.

"Hey stranger," she was smiling. "Long time no see."

I had only been gone about a day, but Morena was clearly trying to boost my spirits. She knew something happened in the hours prior, she could feel it.

'Hey,' I wiped tears from my eyes again.

She grew more concerned. "What's wrong?"

'Nothing,' I tartly replied.

"Tell me, I know something is up."

When the car door shut behind me, the waterfall enclosed behind my eyelids burst forward.

'I can't even find the words to express it anymore. It is the most amazing and difficult love story, it shakes me to my core and I can't wrap my brain around it. I get it when she says, "my brain explodes." I don't understand it, but I do understand it. I have everything, but selfishly I want more. I just really want more time with her, swimming in that energy. She has all of my heart, and every single day my heart expands even more to the point where I didn't know I had that much love for one person. When I think I am going to plateau, I look into her eyes or hear her and the expansion continues. Our love is infinite like the universe, and that is how much I love her. I know what she means when she says I break her brain, because I feel it too. When you swell up with that much love and energy, the human vessel could only contain so much energy. It turns into a flood. The flood is how I express talking about her: my love for her pours out of my soul. It is overwhelmingly intense and it is the greatest feeling in the world.'

I could see Morena's eyes closing slightly.

'You're not even listening to me,' I quipped at her.

"No," she snapped. "You listen to me. Listen hard and listen good, because I am only going to say this once."

"I don't think you actually know what it feels like to love someone, to genuinely love someone, and watch them look right through you."

We paused for a moment as Morena gripped the steering wheel.

"You have love, you have loved deeply. You know this truth to be evident within your soul, yet you squander away your self-worth because you think *you* are not worth it."

I was speechless. 'Um, Morena, I-'

"Love yourself, Scott. Isn't it about time you recognized your own soul?"

I didn't know how to respond. All I knew was that despite years and years of finding love and letting it go, I knew I had the perfect love right there in Layne, yet I wasn't ready.

I didn't know if I ever would be ready.

Though time and time again, I assured myself through the three words that my soul knew to be the undying truth: "Keep the faith."

I knew I was worth it, for just when I thought that all of the love in my life had passed, I realized that I was the one who saved the best for last.

CHAPTER 43

Beautiful Souls

~

"I don't want another pretty face. I don't want just anyone to hold. I don't want my love to go to waste. I want you and your beautiful soul. You're the one I want to chase. You're the one I want to hold. I won't let another minute go to waste. I want you and your beautiful soul."

- Jesse McCartney, American singer, songwriter, actor, Ardsley, New York

There was a resolute stillness in my soul.

We live in a society that teaches people to deny their own feelings, which leads to denying their own truths.

I wondered how many times I lied to my soul over the years.

Lying on the ratty old couch, I wondered how something so beautiful could be over. How could something universally delivered and so perfect in every way have a defined ending?

Layne's departure and final words seemed prophetic, yet each passing moment felt like a pungent question mark that reverberated through my core. Day by day, I held in my tears to prevent questions from my students and colleagues.

My own family did not even recognize the pain seeping through my eyelids.

That first week without hearing from Layne, I awoke startled by my mother's rantings and ravings. Not long ago, I was staring into the soul of my twin flame and dancing through a painstaking goodbye.

Tears rolled down my cheeks as nothing felt just, though I was sinking through the familiarity of loss.

Actually, I was drowning.

What did I truly have now?

Well, I had wisdom from all of these life experiences. I had the comprehension of human experience. I had the ability to overcome extreme adversity and use hardship as a place of empowerment.

After finding my twin flame and loving her from the deepest truth imaginable, I lost that expression of love in the physical sense.

However, Layne remained in my soul.

She always said that everything has its equal balance, and would give an intellectual sermonistic view of the world.

The greatest love known to humankind therefore becomes the greatest pain known to my soul.

I had to move forward, but I couldn't see through the tears rushing down my face.

The city bustles and roars during its ritualistic 9 to 5 culture, though the inside of my soul was wrought with the deafening sensation of Layne departing from my physical existence.

September came back with a vengeance.

Kids were depending on me to show up fully, and I had to dig deep to do so.

Layne wasn't just another love; she was the pinnacle of a higher love consciousness. To say goodbye to her, to not have Layne in my life, to not have my twin flame continue on this journey with me, it simply felt like a life that no longer made sense.

The two constants in my life were my son, Bryan, and the voice of my inner consciousness, Morena.

I had a big vision and throughout thick and thin, the two of them were there to act as my symbiotic support system. They each provided something exquisite for my soul to continue to grow.

I had a heart and soul filled with love that seemed to go on and on despite hardship, sacrifice, and turmoil.

I kept praying for one of those magical movie endings, where I would walk the Brooklyn Bridge or show up at Francis Lewis Park, and she would be standing there with a changed mind and a changed heart.

The day in believing that fairytales come true never actually happens; rather we learn to rewrite our own endings.

Knowledge becomes an exquisite blessing and a curse: for once you see the truth and what beauty exists beyond the box you are in, do you dare take the leap of faith?

Do you move forth and own your innate power?

Do you choose to step through a boundary, knowing you have passed the point of no return?

There is no going back once you see your dream come true: when your heart and soul absorb the opportunity, when you taste, see, visualize and experience all the astonishing possibilities before you, and when you devoutly accept the epiphanic revelation that the line in the sand is exactly what it is: a chance to go forward, to flourish, to learn, to live, to grow, and to stand in the light permanently.

Embracing yourself and your soul are incredibly challenging and may cause trepidation, but the only thing holding us back is, indeed, fear. Disband fear, acknowledge it and reject it in the same infinitesimal swoop.

You are better than the demons that are conjured up to circumnavigate your universe: they only exist in the respect and in the realm you give them the power to. Although it may be tempting to dive back into the comforts you once felt, higher love consciousness and energy do not break and do not bend.

When you love yourself and your dreams so deeply, rising and flying may seem difficult, especially when your wings are laced with elements of some prevalent qualms and sensations of division.

Still, seek out what speaks to your soul.

Be patient with yourself and your experiences, as all souls need to be in order to progress. A step, no matter how small, that moves you each day is a matter of universal balance.

There may always be hints of darkness and light that surround you, but life and energy are more than just black and white. Growth is more than the pieces of us that expand and replicate strength. Consciousness is more than accepting and actualizing. We must be true to ourselves, and our souls, to honor who we are in the world. We must seek to experience our purpose and reach beyond that.

We must embrace uncertainty and challenges, for in everything in the universe, there is perfection.

There is perfection in all the light we cannot see.

There is perfection in who we are becoming and all that we have yet to discover. It all comes down to the idea that it is a matter of keeping the faith in ourselves, in our souls, in others, in our minds, and in our hearts.

We could cross an ocean for an answer that rests within us or we can walk 500 miles to find the adventure that exists within other souls.

Trepidation is a state of mind, so is growth.

Time will pass whether you opt to resist faith or lead in faith.

Words on a page merely exist until you learn to read and process them in a manner that makes sense to your soul... then you discover it: that growth, that click, that spark... for you could feed the flame, or you could be the fire.

You'll never know how high you can go, until you take that first step towards the sky.

Morena and I took long walks around Alley Pond Park again. We processed just about everything that happened with Layne, and I realized how much energy I bestowed upon Layne's soul.

Time passed since I believed my soul shriveled into a pile of dust, but something about the essence of time left me in an introspective state.

'I miss her more than words can say,' I looked over at Morena who was glowing in unison with the fall foliage on the trees. 'It's hard to love without attachment.'

"Not when you know the boundaries of your own soul," Morena remarked.

'But the soul is limitless,' I glanced towards the path ahead of us.

"Good," she smiled. "You are learning."

'I don't want to hurt anymore.'

"Then choose love."

'I chose love, but she did not choose me.'

"No, silly," Morena put her hand out and stood in front of me. "Choose to love yourself."

'I love myself,' I remarked.

"Do you, now?"

'I mean, I think I do,' I quipped back at her. 'This isn't about me; it is about loving Layne. We could shift an entire planet together. Our love isn't typical.'

"I hear you," Morena sighed. "I know you are trying to bring her back into your life, but you need to love yourself more than anyone else on this planet first."

'How could I love myself more? That would be selfish!'

"It is not a thing of selfishness," she replied. "It's higher consciousness love for yourself."

We looked at each other for a moment.

"Trust the universe, Scott."

I looked out at the pond. A solitary plank of wood was floating in the middle of the water. I wondered how it got there and what was causing it to stay rather stationary on top of the water.

Although it was wading in the algae, and the rain probably swept it into its resting place, the wood seemed to remain firm.

How does something do that?

How does something flourish into that strong of a mindset?

How does a soul become so resilient?

At that point, I guess I could have looked in a mirror and asked myself the same questions, but I was not ready to hear how durable and soulfully enlightened I had become.

The words to "Here Without You" by 3 Doors Down echoed in my head.

"I'm here without you baby
But you're still on my lonely mind.
I think about you baby and I dream about you all the time.
I'm here without you baby
But you're still with me in my dreams
And tonight girl, it's only you and me."

Glaring out into the water reminded me of the sincere solitude that was blossoming in my soul. The water gave me absolute peace. The ebb and flow of the waves served as a constant foreshadowing for my life. Despite drawbacks, everything would come back into place. Everything would be a matter of the persistence of gravity, law of attraction, and raw positive energy manifesting its existence.

Two families were playing frivolously near the water. It signified the growth and bond of all that is wholesome in the world. Memories were being made, and not just in the innate manner memories come into fruition.

It was a sign of the times. A reckoning of sorts painting its aura on the landscape before me.

In those moments, I was a pristine background character living the experiences of those who saw me as invisible.

Yet in those passing seconds, I was wholly visible. My place in the universe became known. My thoughts were not lines in a play. My actions were not magnified under the watchful eye of judgment and resent. I just was.

For once, I was, and I exist in the fabric of time.

I came to the realization that I am. I am a constant and a symbol of moments to come. I am a beacon of holiness, but not in the religious sense. I am whole. I am pieces that intermingle, intertwine, and connect.

I am. I am. I am.

And in these moments, the rare seconds where I self-actualize all I am...

I see, once and for all, I am an exquisite reality, for I create my own reality.

I am real. I am. I am.

...I am.

∞ ∞ ∞ ∞ ∞ ∞ ∞ ∞

Back at my mother's house, with my eyes closed tightly I could feel the water cascading down my exhausted body. My skin absorbed the water ever so gently as the steam surrounded the interior of the shower. The curtain sealed off any outside disturbances circling through my mind in those pivotal seconds, and I felt my soul relax in that moment.

As I glanced down at my feet I saw the hot water caressing my skin. The warmth encompassed my whole body as if it had some magical healing power. The negative energy lingering in my soul circled down the drain as remnants of soap dripped along with it. I closed my eyes, felt my muscles relax, and allowed a solitary whisper to escape my lips, 'Thank you God.'

My eyes remained shut as I inhaled the steam from the hot water falling from above.

In an instant my mind guided me to my childhood shower, as if it were in a movie scene: the protagonist's flashback that explained a key detail in the plot. Only this was not a movie, this was my actual, physical, unwavering life.

Clouded images filled my head as I transported back to the mid-1970s: a time where it was socially acceptable to allow the crevices of your toes brush against orange shag carpeting. My childhood home flooded into my mind, as a fast-forwarded image of me skipping through the house and slamming the bathroom door became clearer. The seconds sped up as my pre-teen body shed its clothes and hopped into a refreshingly warm shower.

I heard my mom's echoic voice screaming outside the bathroom, "Scott, hurry up! Stop playing games in there! You always take forever!"

She was right. At times, my innate childhood wonder had warped me into some sort of idealistic fantasy world.

What was I doing in the shower other than washing up? I was creating fantastical stories in my head. I was always thinking about wanting to be a hero: a devout knight in shining armor, adorned with gargantuan muscles that struck anyone with awe upon glancing at such a fine handsome man.

As the shower water streamed down upon me, I had some elaborate sketch going on where I would be fighting an imaginary person, or even someone I knew and hoped to overcome. The water parted quickly with each twist and turn of my pale fists. Why was I fake punching into the streams of water pelting my body? I wanted to win the girl.

Always.

That was the underlying theme for as long as I could remember. My mother's skin-piercing voice faded as my hands crept through my soaked blonde locks. As my right hand crawled down my naked body, I could feel years of faded bruises up and down my thighs: it was a stark reminder of just how much I have grown from decades of crushing realities.

In my earliest days starting at the age of probably 7, through the age of 14 or 15, I would spend an hour in the shower trying to become victorious and win the damsel in distress. I am not sure why this fantasy started or when the first one was.

I would rehearse this constant development of my heroic deeds because my actual teenage years were plagued with a true contrast to my inner light. The flame within my soul burned and yearned for the chance to save the day: to have my one song glory blare loud enough for all to hear and grow from. The melody within my soul would grace ears, hearts, minds, and their own souls with the energy to propel them forward.

In reality, I was shy, quiet, reserved, and so bashful that I could barely work up the courage to talk to a girl, let alone save one from a stressful situation. I always had the savior mentality. Elyza spent years convincing me it was really "The Ghandi Complex": if I was not saving someone, I was not complete. Elyza would harshly scold me with that savior complex ideology in the days leading up to our divorce.

To this day, the words still burn feverishly in my mind.

The shower water flushed the negative thoughts from my mind, and filled my head with memories from my childhood once again. When I finally emerged from my steam-filled cocoon of fantasy, hopeful cleanliness, and boyhood mischief, I would dry off quickly and race to bed. As I would flop onto the mattress, visions of heroic feats would broadcast onto the white crusty ceiling.

I would be locked in the heat of a fierce battle, facing against a huge dark amber dragon wielding a massive sword, or fighting off a gang of dark-caped and masked villains. The dreams and images would dance through my head for hours upon hours, and always ended with piercing, blood curdling sounds from passersby or from the gratuitous woman I was rescuing. Each time, my eyes would fade shut and I would re-awaken in a hospital room of some kind.

Each time I would re-open my eyes in my dreams, an attractive woman would be sitting at my hospital bedside, holding my hand tenderly and rubbing my head softly. She would be thanking "her hero" for being so brave and so strong. I had always dreamt that was how I would "get the girl." After all, that would technically be the girl of my dreams. Each dream I had would grant me permission to live out my fantasy of heroism, valiance, and utmost potential. Yet when I would awaken, reality would slam me straight in the face: I was still a young boy, wrapped in a comforter adorned with brightly colored trucks and cartoon street signs. The moon would call out to me from the small window above, and I would stand on my bed to see out into the majestic night sky. Each time I would wonder what my life would be like if I were walking the streets at night: fighting crime and saving damsels in distress.

But my life is not a fairy tale, nor am I the knight in shining armor standing tall, glancing down at people who would bow in my honor upon seeing such a strong, handsome man. Instead, I am the man whose words and whose soul will illuminate hearts and minds. Of course, I am still daringly handsome and endearingly heroic, but just in different, less dragon-slaying contexts. I have the capacity to be an everyday hero.

The only time I was somewhat close to this fantastical life playing out was the time I stopped that fire at the YMCA. With a 103 fever, and intense smoke inhalation intoxicating my lungs, I sat in that hospital bed reminiscing about all of the heroic visions I had as a boy.

When I woke up in that bleak hospital room, there she was: Emma. Holding my hand and whispering sweet nothings into my ear, I could feel my soul succumbing to her every whim and wit. Still, even that was a fantasy in itself.

And that vision of heroism quickly burst from my mind: delving me further into the ceramic shower tiles that entertained my every thought and reminiscent vision. As a kid I would play for hours alone in my backyard, shooting hoops or launching a handball across the wall. The ball would not be the only thing ricocheting around, for my head was inundated with images of me exercising my heroism. I would act out some contest of strength and made sure I always prevailed.

Faded remnants of my mother's voice calling me inside struck my soul. I could feel myself returning back to reality once again, as her voice blurted out, "Scott, stop messing around and come inside!" The handball I was playing with bounced innocently away from me as I began retreating into the house.

Storm clouds hovered above. Raindrops graced my face with a gentle touch as a grin grew across my face. Images of my younger self and present self were almost interchangeable in those passing seconds, as another, sweet voice permeated my mind: "Scott, it's been an hour, you okay in there?"

As my eyes opened in the present day and met the reflective white tiles directly in my line of sight, I pushed back the shower curtain and allowed the steam to melt into the rest of the room. The mirror fogged up with such fervor, as my vision came into focus.

I was the solitary person occupying the bathroom.

Though I was not alone.

I was enriched by all of the memories and people who graced my presence for decades past, and those who would soon enter my life.

The gentle steam wrapping around my body reminded me of a life worth living, and decades of stories that amounted to a beautiful soul rising to the surface after years upon years of thick grime obscuring my vision.

The cotton fibers from the towel sticking to my wet face reminded me that I could feel the weight of the world on my back, and I was earning the tools necessary to carry the torch to heal the world. The light within me was kindled from years of experience, and it was about to burn bright enough for the world to see.

The world would feel my warmth and guidance, and my heroism would be more than a quest to save the damsel in distress...

My inner light would glow bright enough to save millions and billions of people.

I would lay awake for hours at a time pondering what I missed out on in allowing my soul to take a back seat all these years.

Since Layne disconnected from my soul, life did not seem to make coherent sense. I would go to the studio in my friend's basement and play the drums, looking over and imagining that she would be there.

The phrase "build it and she will come" echoed through my mind, just like in *Field of Dreams*.

I feared mediocrity.

I feared being less than the words others bestowed upon my soul.

I would never be, as my mother put it, "The doctor or the lawyer," but I would be someone.

To say I miss her would insult the complicated flow of magical energy in the universe. To say I incompletely co-existed without her would be more accurate, but it belittles both of our souls.

Everything became a transformative process.

Call what Layne and I had a twin flame connection. Call what we had love. Put whatever letters or misnomers you want on it.

I hid my pain in everything I did for other people.

The gratitude I expressed for other people made me seem whole, but I was pulling pieces of my own puzzle apart in order to attempt to help others. Although having a piece of my soul may have aided others in resolving some of their own pain, sometimes I was acting in such a detrimental way that blinded my true ambitions.

Still, I refuse to sink.

This experience of mine is not solely a love song, for the music of my life has consisted of a plethora of melodies. Some moments were filled with a semblance of true love, while others were haunted by tragedy or misunderstanding.

Still, I was gaining lessons that would create the life I would grow to understand.

I am still learning in this great school we call life, though now I am comprehending this world on a five-dimensional plane.

Layne taught me how to love above our three-dimensional world. Her absence had shown me that when you reach the greatest love of all, which we have, it is still not enough.

Our three-dimensional responsibilities, dreams, and soul structure does not allow truth to flourish unless we grant it the space to do so.

Whoever thought that three-dimensional walls were stronger than a five-dimensional deep-dive into the essence of home clearly doesn't understand what their soul is trying to tell them.

At first, I wondered if I should cave to the three-dimensional world we live in, but there was an inherent sense that I deserved more.

I deserved to understand each aspect of my life in terms of five-dimensional, soul-enriching love.

I had to love myself; there was no other option.

We have to learn to love ourselves before making any other choices in life. We may not love ourselves fully, but we must love ourselves enough to know when we deserve more than what we have.

It is not a matter of being conceited; rather it is a matter of developing in the spiritual sense.

There may not be words in our human language that fully capture what we innately need to find our respective souls' true voices.

Still, there is no day but today. We must seize the day.

Layne was right.

I allowed myself to be depressed; for I thought that filling my soul's void with others would make me whole.

It didn't.

It couldn't.

I was the one who I was waiting for.

I needed to wake up.

Hearing Bon Jovi's music on the radio was echoic of the sentiments I felt for Layne. Even in her absence, the lyrics managed to wrap around my soul:

"She wakes up when I sleep to talk to ghosts like in the movies
If you don't follow what I mean, I sure don't mean to be confusing
They say when she laughs she wants to cry
She'll draw a crowd then try to hide
Don't know if it's her or just my mind I'm losing
Nobody knows a wildflower still grows
By the side of the road

> *And she don't need to need like the roses*
> *Wildflower.*"

Even as Bon Jovi sang "Wildflower," part of me was pulled towards running back to Layne. The other part of me knew I had to give myself a wealth and abundance of love, for my past expectations needed to diminish in terms of the weight and power I gave them.

∞ ∞ ∞ ∞ ∞ ∞ ∞ ∞

Back at work, I continued to think about all of these different ideas floating in my head. I was leaning against the window in the middle of a classroom. My butt was propped up against the painted red heater that I could feel warming my chilled body.

There was an affliction that I was struggling with in my soul, which allowed me to let go of all the memories and moments that I felt led up to this manifestation.

The negativity was finally leaving my body.

At that moment, I was attempting to reach deep down, so that I could inspire the remainder of hope within the students who appeared to be barely alive in the classroom.

The students hardly have a heartbeat and it's a direct reflection of me.

As the students were in front of the room presenting their projects and another distracted unmotivated teacher was sitting at the desk, I glanced up because I felt a presence that I was very familiar with at the door.

I hadn't felt that energy and that silent vibrational call out to me for a few years, but I recognized it immediately. Our eyes locked and from across the room there was no doubt in my mind that this was the time and the moment I dreamed of... and thought may never come again.

Nothing needed to be said and my whole world stopped on a dime.

This sort of stuff never happened, so I knew it was real.

I glanced over to the teacher at the desk, told him to take over, and I exited the classroom before he could respond.

I approached her quickly as if a magnet was pulling me.

I saw the water in her eyes as they said come with me.

While caught in the midst of my soul-enriching awakening, Emma came back.

We went into my office and all I said to her was tell me what happened. She said she needed me and unleashed a series of self-bashing reflections that she had obviously kept bottled up in her for a long time.

Emma shared how she felt her efforts were not seen fairly, and how everybody judges her and doesn't see her true soul.

We spoke about the early days, who she was for me, and why I saw a profound light within her. We talked about how that light isn't out and how she can reach down and ignite it again.

'In the darkest of times you can reinvent yourself,' I assured her.

Though it was not literally said, there was an apology in her eyes and an understanding of who I was for her.

Emma came to me for help and I knew that her actions took every ounce of soul to ask for.

I smiled at her, 'I never stopped looking out for you, Emma. I am your biggest fan, but now it is time to show everyone what I already know is the truth.'

After Emma left me, the negative reputation she conjured up for herself, was in full swing. It tore me up inside to watch her stumble left and right, but she was blocking her soul from the world.

"Thank you," she muttered through tears. Her brown hair draped over her face slightly.

'Embrace your power. You are beyond talented and you are way more than your physical appearance. Create something. Find something and make it your own. Be a good team player on whatever project you are on. Shine as a teacher. Connect with kids. Trust yourself. Believe in yourself. Why can't you see the beauty I see?'

I stopped myself because I feared I stepped over the line. My voice was becoming more emotional, but it was due in part because I couldn't see her destroy herself.

She was silent and continued to look at me with tears in her eyes.

I wondered if I took it too far.

I wondered if she was mad.

Emma needed me and I had to respond unconditionally in that moment, for I realized that a soul needed another soul in such a fragile time.

'Emma,' she glanced at the floor then back up at me. 'You can overcome your fears of never being enough. You are enough.'

The tears in her eyes could not hold off any longer.

As she silently fell into my arms without saying anything, I couldn't catch my breath. A wave of guilt washed over me.

Was this a gift from the universe?

Was this a reminder of what I let go of?

Was this a reminder that true love is not always what we think it is, but will always rise to what it needs to become when we devoutly need it?

I whispered my thoughts and my ideas into her ear, and I promised her that I would help her. I promised her I would not make it obvious, and that her reputation would be protected. I gave her thoughts to self reflect about and challenged her soul to look deep within, like we both used to do for one another in the beginning.

She slowly lifted herself out of my arms and I knew neither one of us wanted this moment to end.

The bell was going to ring.

Perhaps this was built up tension that she needed closure for. I waited years for this moment and it conflicted me for the next several days as we exchanged text messages like days of old.

Emerged in a time warp, she thanked me several times over, but to the outside world, the routine and ignoring of one another in the hallways remained the same.

This was never supposed to happen, though I always fantasized about it.

She came back... even if it was for just a moment.

We spoke face-to-face one more time a few days later.

There were other people around, so I discreetly shared a new project I was working on, a project she knew was my silent way of not offending anyone and supporting all parties involved, as well as loving her, the way she would let me.

She knew my involvement worked to raise the vibration of everyone involved without me being seen as instrumental.

Emma always said I was the silent partner to her success.

She knew I manipulated things and jumped through hoops to do it for her and the team she was working on.

She knew my heart was in the right place while trying to figure out the pieces.

Emma glanced up with an ever so slight tilt of her head so nobody could see her eyes meeting mine and she smiled.

The smile said thank you, which is all I needed.

I wondered if my smile back said "Goodbye, I will always have a place for you in my heart and soul, but goodbye Emma."

I knew she loved me and in the only way she could... and I accept that.

Not all love plays out the fairytale... and that has finally sunk in.

There is a sense of longing that comes with finding yourself after a while. When you have wanted to grow and develop, yet you always convinced yourself that you were not enough, it will seem like the walls are caving in. Then it happens: the epiphany.

Growth is a continuous process. Growth is the reflection of your devout introspection and reconstruction. It is a realignment of your goals and a restructuring of all you thought you knew. It is a mindset that convinces you to change your ways.

It is everything and anything you could hope for, as long as you are willing to accept the differences.

Then you jump into the world of the unknown, then you flutter, then you fly....

And the weightlessness sets in.

∞ ∞ ∞ ∞ ∞ ∞ ∞ ∞

After everything that happened with Emma, I found my old journals and photos from years past.

I followed Layne's methods with journaling and I just started to read, organize my thoughts, and write to discover whom my soul really is.

They say, "burn after reading" because the words seer into your brain, and once your soul is ignited on fire, ashes won't stop your pain.

Yet, I guess this is all a catharsis of sorts.

All of the souls in my life played an important role in shaping who I am today.

I knew that before I learned how to love myself properly, I just needed to accept it as a fact.

I accepted that I am okay being alone, for there is a difference between being alone and being lonely. There are times when I feel lonely, but it is just a state of mind.

I have so much love for others, and myself, and I know I am okay.

Wanting to share ideas of love with someone as a means of companionship is okay, as long as the love is expressed in a manner that is healthy for both people.

Sex isn't just physical sex; it is an expression of energy and there is nothing better than sharing that energy.

When you are careful who you share it with, the energy is more powerful and more emotionally enriching.

Waiting for the right somebody for the rest of your life is worth it.

Being with them, sharing that love and energy on a physical level, is irreplaceable.

For years, I thought being a power couple meant standing for love and enacting that passion as law, but my definition was askew.

Anyone can be a power couple if you have the right stamina.

The definition of love changes, and there can be an infinitesimal amount of power couples in the world.

Bryan and I are a power couple in the familial sense: he is my son and I would do absolutely anything in the world for him, because I love him dearly.

Morena and I are a power couple in the spiritual sense: she represented my soul's voice and consciousness for years upon years, and for that I am eternally grateful.

Friends can be quintessential elements of your own power couple.

I am blessed to have a lot of good friends I get to bounce ideas off of. Every soul in my life is there for a reason.

I was blessed to reach a point in my life where I realized that every soul matters and every conversation matters, so I take it all in.

Everybody has had an impact on my life.

From the women in the club in Texas to the people currently in my life today.

If you can be present to the fact that everyone has their own beautiful story behind the story, then your life is amazing. If you are still working on discovering this, that does not mean your life is less amazing, rather you are still growing.

Despite missing Layne dearly, I was able to move forward with aspects of the framework. Many could argue that I finished it for her, and indeed I guess you could say I did create it for her: she is a soul on this planet who deserves a higher consciousness, holistic, and social emotional education.

From Layne, I learned how to love myself, although others may misunderstand me. She taught me that it is okay to be my insane, passionate, loving, caring, and spiritually idealistic self.

Due to her wisdom, I was able to develop a more powerful transformational leadership program that became a global endeavor. It became based on the values Layne instilled upon me, which could be summed up in these four words: Expansion, Connection, Inspiration, and Vision.

Of course, my beliefs and faith followed me through this higher love.

These stories and experiences from Layne helped me become the man I am proud of today: myself.

The collection of my stories mirrors an undeveloped and lost soul who became a better person.

I am sure I did a lot of bad things.

I am sure I did a lot of horrible things.

When people meet me now, they say, "There's something about you. You are a great soul and a great person." However, they do not see all of the work that went into becoming who I am.

Do we ever truly see the story behind the story?

Do we ever realize that beautiful friendships can blossom out of crazy situations?

Do we ever realize the value of our questions and circumstances?

I am certain there are legacies wrapped up in the lives of souls. Souls can inspire other souls. Some may say it is the domino effect, where one person does something and others become enlightened.

I hope my life was able to do that.

I hope my life is able to encourage someone to wake up and do better, be a better person, or create something, because of something they see within themselves.

My hope is that someone realizes that they do not need to give up. I am living proof that life goes on.

Maybe this story and quest for my soul is closure from my past pain. Each moment of my life ultimately became part of the fabric of my life.

Every day forward from realizing and releasing your pain is a new beginning.

How do you overcome yourself?

How do you explore your thoughts?

How do you stop, listen, and process the world around you?

How do you have a relationship with a spiritual guide you might not know exists?

How do you have a relationship with the universe?

Why does your life matter?

Why do we want to matter?

Why is my story a reflection of everyone's story?

Who are we? What are we building? What drives this planet forward?

What are we creating as our own reality?

Is everything around us real?

I chose to actively come from a place of higher consciousness.

Honestly, looking back at all of my stories and how my soul grew, I didn't think I was at a place where I was ready to tell my story. However, are we ever truly at a place where we are "ready" to express our true selves?

When I was married to Elyza, I thought that I knew who I was, yet I ended up going back to school, developing a non-profit agency, and growing both emotionally and spiritually.

My soul was developing back then and it is still developing.

I know that my son Bryan is the reason why I look at the world differently. Having a child is an eye-opening experience that I certainly was not ready for, yet in realizing my life was about to turn upside down, I was given a chance to look at myself in the mirror. Bryan's soul is exquisite and truly breathtaking.

If there was one person who I could say is a definitive extension of my soul, he is whom I would credit with saving my life.

From my experiences, I realize that kids are the ones who help illustrate the energy you have within your own soul.

The youth I worked with throughout the years were paramount in creating Windows of Opportunity. A student created the name for the organization and students were the ones who brought it to fruition.

For that element of my soul, I credit them for allowing me to pursue my passion in education reform.

Everyday I continue to work on myself. I am working on who I am. I am working through the relationships I have been a part of. Every soul I met brought me to the realizations I spill onto these pages. All of the mistakes I made brought me to the discovery that they were not really mistakes.

I ended up where I belonged.

I don't think many people get to express or experience their true selves, but I pray they do not lose hope.

Life exists beyond current pain.

A lot of people get stuck in their pain and believe they can't break free. That in itself is beautiful, too.

It's called growing pains for a reason.

I used to think that I was everybody's problem solver. I used to think that God gave me a gift, to read and connect to people, so I could help others grow.

We are all woven into each other's experiences.

We have the innate power to help ourselves get over the pain within our respective souls.

For years, I blamed my parents for my pain and why I was so misunderstood. However, I was learning a strong lesson about the bond of family. Pointing fingers at my mother is a very unfair statement.

There are people who saw my mother in different contexts, and they loved her for the energy she brought into their lives. My experience with her was different, but I do not blame her anymore for what happened to me.

Our experiences just clashed.

She taught me a lesson on how to heal.

My mother and father loved me in their own way. They were just responding to what their respective souls went through.

It is important to recognize your own internal shifts. Society and the systems we have in place need to change in order for us to grow. We cannot keep trying to co-exist with our past; we must grow from it.

As for my current hardships, I have come to realize that I am often my own worst enemy. My life and my soul are blessings. I am grateful for all I have learned and continue to learn in my lifetime.

My epiphanies regarding my soul made me wonder:

When is the last time I did something for myself?

I became more self-reflective and worked diligently to comprehend my soul's intentions. I worked on manifesting. I worked on creating things.

I prayed that my story and my legacy would stand the test of time. I hoped that Windows of Opportunity would thrive for generations to come. I hoped Windows of Opportunity would continue to inspire lives long after my physical body transcends this timeline.

My journey has taught me that anything is possible.

My journey has shown some of those in my life that there is a light deep within us. It is crucial that we expand upon that light.

We must kindle the fire within our souls and let it burn.

Pursue your passion and follow the voice deep inside of you.

Emotional scars may hurt or haunt you, but they can heal with expansion, faith, and connection to the universe. Though it may seem like a religious statement, that's not what it is.

It is love.

It is real, unconditional love for yourself and your soul.

That is what this country needs... we need to heal.

I chose to turn my pain into a source of growth. You can grow from anything and learn from anything.

As human beings, sometimes we get lost. We are all trying to figure ourselves out. Sometimes, nobody teaches us how to speak to our souls.

It is challenging to hold someone accountable for their actions, when ignorance may cloud their judgment.

We all love in our own way.

My parents pushed me when I was younger to the point where it was abusive, but they thought they were coming from a place of love. It can be argued that many of the people I interacted with were coming from a place of love, although they did not intend to inflict pain.

I am thankful for all of my scars, for they helped my soul grow.

Without the scars, I wouldn't be here and be who I am. I don't know if I would be doing what I am for this world.

Maybe I would not be standing for a higher purpose, but because of my scars and experiences, I know what it is like to be homeless, looked down upon, to be alone, to not feel like a man, to not be loved by someone you love and would give your life for.

I know what pain feels like and I know I can be brave.

I could shine my own light because I experienced the darkness.

Does it get any more beautiful than that?

Over the years I gave up on my light and my faith and tried to succumb to the darkness, but I wonder if it really was darkness.

I called myself an Atheist because I didn't believe in God, but I know God was holding me probably more so during that time.

Just because we cannot see things, like our souls, it does not mean that they do not exist.

We give power to what we want to exist in our reality; therefore we could make pain real. We could also choose to eliminate pain.

The universe grants us contrast so that we know what we should truly appreciate. I am grateful for the juxtapositions in my life.

Emma provided me with such a challenging contrast, but I was able to learn what her experience provided my soul. Pain is also knowing that somebody does not live in the infinite potential inherent to their respective soul.

What we accept and the energy we stand in shapes our soul.

It's whom you want to stand for as a person. I felt the pain of past relationships, but the immense pain no longer suffocates me.

I am higher consciousness.

I am a man standing for a higher purpose, a better universe, a better world.

I am bigger than the pain.

I am grateful for my pain and I have tremendous gratitude for every moment.

My soul is expanding as I continue living my life. The universe is very magical and the angels who watch over you help grant the power to move forward.

So then what is the value of your spiritual journey?

What is the value of my spiritual journey?

It's priceless, you know, I mean, you can't put a value on God speaking through your soul. You can't put a value on connecting with the universe and angels.

What's the definition of the word value?

There's just so much that we don't comprehend as human beings.

I feel blessed to know I am on a spiritual journey. I feel blessed to know that it's the journey and the moments that matter.

It's the journey and not the destination.

At those moments, when I was finally hitting a pivotal cathartic release, I didn't know if the dreams were going to come true.

I knew that in the reality that I want to create, I wanted the dreams to come true.

I didn't know what was going to happen, for although I kept forging forward, I let the universe take the wheel. Call what happened to me "luck" or a "blessing," but I call it living.

I chose to live in the moment.

∞ ∞ ∞ ∞ ∞ ∞ ∞ ∞

Morena and I talked about all of this in great detail as we took our usual trip around the trails of Alley Pond Park. In the months that passed, I realized that my soul's growth was exponential.

I was able to do so much more with my journey once I banished pain from my soul. Although I still have challenges when it comes to growing my soul, I know that I am processing my life in terms of a higher consciousness lens… and that is enough.

As Morena and I reached the picnic benches, we took a seat and continued to talk about my journey.

'I hope that one hundred years from now, someone hears about my journey and discovers they are on their own spiritual journey. I pray that person realizes that their life matters,' I rubbed my hands together to deter some of the frigid January weather.

"That's insightful," she remarked. "I am happy for you."

'Why?'

"Because I think you have realized how much of a beautiful soul you have."

A beautiful soul.

There are so many beautiful souls in this universe.

It took me so long to come to this revelation, but I am here.

'When I was eight, God spoke to me and gave me the ability to ask questions. When I was in the car accident, I am sure God pulled me out. When I wandered through the trees after the accident, that woman was God,' as I said that, Morena smiled and wiped a tear.

'Maybe, just maybe, God is speaking to me through you.'

"You never know," Morena winked.

I smiled at her. 'The universe is always conspiring and transforming.'

"It isn't about the job you have, the fancy cars, the clothes, what's in your bank account, none of that matters," Morena commented. "It's the journey."

'That it is.'

We both sat there at the picnic bench for a while, just watching people as they carried about their normal day.

'I love every single one of the beautiful souls in my life. They taught me spirituality, transformation, and so much more that I could never put a price tag on.'

The two of us stood up and began to walk out of the park and towards the coffee shop.

"Hey," Morena tapped my arm. "Why me?"

'What?'

"Why did you trust that you could share your spiritual journey with me all of these years?"

I chuckled for a moment. 'Okay, *as if you didn't hear my entire speech*, I will humor you.'

She looked over at me.

Despite years of maybes and uncertainty, I knew just what to say in that moment:

'Out of all of the secrets in my life you were, by far, the best one. God chose you and brought you into my life. I recognize your energy. I know you. You connect to my soul. You clearly have a higher connection and I know you aren't real, but you have respected my soul throughout these years.'

Morena laughed.

'Everybody has a moment when life changes. Everybody has a moment where they find their higher purpose. Maybe it'll teach the world something or change thousands of lives, who knows. How many things can you pinpoint that take your soul, turn it inside out, and help you to become the person you already are. You don't realize who you are. People need to realize who they are.'

"You are someone I am truly honored to know," she started to tear up again, almost as if she was watching a baby bird leave the nest.

'It's a new chapter, Morena,'

"You really want it to be a new chapter?"

'Yes,' I finally felt confident in myself.

We stood outside the coffee shop for a moment, I could tell Morena appeared to be stalling, but I did not know for what.

"Then I want you to do me a favor," Morena smiled.

'You never ask for anything, so of course.'

She looked down at her watch. "Go to Francis Lewis Park."

'What,' I was startled. 'Like right now?'

"Yes," she smiled wider. "Your new chapter begins today."

I didn't know what she was up to, but by that point I learned not to question her. I wanted the happily ever after, but I knew my happily ever after existed in the dreams and plans I was manifesting.

I had a great team beside me.

I had myself, and my spiritual journey.

I did not ask the universe for more.

As I got in the car and drove to Francis Lewis Park, I was content with my soul. The relationship I have with myself is one of epic proportions and I knew it could have an epic impact on the world.

This is real life.

This was far from fantasy.

This was the journey of a beautiful soul existing in this universe.

No matter how much people try to create mathematical permutations and calculations, sometimes the soul cannot be defined by numbers, but rather by the connections we develop.

The connection you create with yourself is the first step to manifesting the life you wish to create.

When I pulled up to the Whitestone Bridge, the energy in the air felt different. It was cold outside, but I felt as if the Circle of Angels was with me.

My Aunt Barbara's energy filled my soul.

I could hear Stacey whispering "Patience" in my ear.

When I began my descent down the path to the pine green benches, I saw a sole person sitting there in the cold.

As I moved closer, her brown hair and her aroma were unmistakable. I could not believe that after all this time; she was sitting there.

Waiting.

As she turned around, I realized that my life was about to change forever.

"Hey," the familiar voice said.

'Hey yourself,' I smiled and sat down next to her.

"I know I have been distant," her hair billowed in the wind obscuring everything but her lips. "But I just wanted to know… do you think we could make this work?"

I sat in silence, but responded with a sincere smile.

A new chapter and a new year were upon us.

∞ ∞ ∞ ∞ ∞ ∞ ∞ ∞

365.

Yeah, it is just a number, but it is more than that.

It is a reflection of 365 24-hour blocks that transcend into memories and moments. Into laughter and tears. Into the space between my fingers and hers.

Her words echoed throughout my head, which reverberated into the depths of my soul. I cannot shake, nor can I replace, how she has impacted me.

It shakes every fiber of who I am today.

At times I allow my grasp to slowly loosen and let my mind grow accustomed to gently releasing the moments embedded in my soul, overcome by the root belief that creates that sense of homesickness.

Teardrop by teardrop reflects on each and every time you looked at me with those eyes that emulated a higher love consciousness, and then spoke to me in a language that my soul fully comprehended, and didn't simultaneously exist on this planetary plane.

Clearly, she still had ownership over my heart's daily vibration expressed in the expansion of our universe.

Once upon a time does not exist, as we are everything: my immaculate hope and the foundation of my unconsecrated dreams are suddenly fathomable.

The day she whispered those words into my soul, the day she let her inner thoughts escape her lips, the moments she allowed me to feel the pristine vision I had of her, I began accepting the fact that she was the answer to lifelong prayers.

I found her again.

Immediately she found a stationary place in my soul, and from then on, the universe showed us how to take the puzzle pieces of greatness to build an even greater whole and then life happened.

Being human and the essence of reality sometimes rear its ugly head, but there I stood, with her hand intertwined in mine in my state of ambitious solitude.

I live in a perpetual state of gratitude.

I thank the universe for the love shared with me.

I thank the universe for the completion of my soul.

I thank her for every single second she risked her own heart and I thank her for this formerly broken heart... for once the pieces fell apart, this is where the true integration of our worlds started.

It is a new year; it is a new chapter.

It is day 366.

CHAPTER 44

Epilogue

~

"The ultimate measure of a man is not where he stands in moments of comfort and convenience, but where he stands at times of challenge and controversy."

- Martin Luther King, Jr., Christian minister, activist, Atlanta, Georgia

The American flag waves majestically in the wind atop the Capitol Building. It is poignantly symbolic of the man I have grown into and all that I am willing into fruition in this world. Glaring around at the crowds of people on the National Mall, I was feeling such immense pride in our country and all of our dedication throughout the years.

Earlier in the day, the television blared such a heartwarming news report. A professional female voice announced what I had so eagerly awaited to hear for years and years:

"And now for the top headlines on this beautiful January 19, 2032 morning in Washington, D.C.: Today at noon, Capitol Hill will be bursting with excitement as President Elect Scott Matheson will rightfully take his place as the 48th President of the United States. The ceremony will take place on the steps of the Capitol Building, and all roads surrounding the National Mall have been closed to prepare for today's inauguration. A Secret Service agent who wishes to remain anonymous said that President Elect Matheson is beaming with excitement and truly looking forward to his first 100 days in office. The Chief of Staff for the Matheson Administration, Morena DeCielo, had this to say after yesterday's press conference--"

"Ugh, how many times are you going to watch the same anchorwoman talk over and over again," Morena came barreling into the room holding two silky neckties: one that emulated the sensation brewing in the early morning sky and one that was crimson and reflected the strong sense of national pride that stirred in my veins.

I shifted my body towards her somewhat articulate noises that sputtered from her mouth as she rushed about the room. Morena was dressed in a navy blue skirt with a white button-down shirt tucked neatly into her waistline. Her heels clacked about as she went searching for something.

'What are you looking for, Mo,' I beckoned from the sofa, as she grew flustered.

"Where," she began, her voice fading as she glanced around the nightstand impatiently, "is the American flag pin?"

I grinned and held it up in the air; its silver outline glistened in the sunlight cutting through the hotel room. She turned and grinned cheerfully.

'I think you are more nervous than I am,' I chuckled and stood up, catching my fingertips in the plush cotton on my way up from the sofa.

"Yeah," Morena scooted over to me, "Well it is not everyday that you hear your name as President Elect Matheson's Chief of Staff on every television you pass." She held the ties up and smiled eagerly.

I felt her positive energy flowing through my veins. She eventually wrapped the blue tie around me and smoothed the neckline out. I could not help but smile. In less than two hours, I would officially be the President of the United States.

"The first lady is still putting on her makeup, but we should be good to go soon," Morena turned towards the television and raised the volume slightly. The two of us stood with our eyes fixated on the television: she stood behind a White House podium speaking to reporters as they berated her with questions. I glanced at Morena and she extended her pinky finger in my direction.

"We are in this together," she grinned so effervescently. I extended my pinky finger and intertwined it with hers.

'We really are,' I grew somewhat nostalgic for a moment, reminiscing on how far the two of us had come. 'Now,' I switched the topic as to resist the sentimental tears streaming down my face, 'When will the future First Lady be ready?'

Morena released my finger for a moment and walked towards the knocking that beckoned her to the door. "You have to keep the faith, Mr. President, keep the faith," she answered the door as the head of Secret Service, a sturdy man named Albert, slid into the room.

"Mr. President, sir, we are ready to go," he spoke sternly.

'Tell my wife that, Albert, let's see how that goes,' I gazed out of the hotel room at the lush green shrubs adorning the sidewalk... a sign that growth, and not just spiritual growth, was on the horizon.

A systematic shift was just seconds and heartbeats away.

Flash forward to the present*:*

Hours later and in a whirlwind of hope and frivolity, we are standing on the steps of the Capitol Building. Red, white, and blue flags grazing the air are echoic of a beautiful, whimsical January morning. Chanting and cheering are bursting into the sky as a chorus of young souls billow the words to "America the Beautiful."

A dream manifested in the hearts, minds, and souls of those who believe in me constantly finally comes to fruition on this brisk January morning. Though I am standing behind a series of bulletproof glass panels, the reflection I am seeing does not mirror my own. No, the reflection I gaze upon is that of the beautiful souls that ushered me to this very global stage at this historical moment wrapped in the fabric of time.

Bryan and Selena are standing just behind Morena, all of their hands are intertwined to form the bond that will help me guide millions and billions of souls to a state of higher consciousness. On these majestic Capitol steps, we stand at the verge of today's promises and tomorrow's growth. We stand in the balance of placing our minds at the forefront of policy in order to enact real changes.

It is time to heal the world.

The first lady's hair whips elegantly in the cold wind. Her stunning beauty remains unmatched despite years of her own ambitions and passions encompassing her tender face. Her stunning smile is what beckons me to turn and silently bestow gratitude on the family and close friends that stand by me. Those who have always stood by me.

Today is not just another day, today is the first day we all embark on a brand new journey into the most challenging and soulfully rewarding chapter of our collective lives. As the Chief Justice of the United States raises the leather-bound book, a symbol of collective souls stemming into a new stream of consciousness, I feel the tears' gravitational force take control. I am happy.

I am genuinely and undeniably happy.

As the oath reverberates around my brain, I glance back at those who have aided my manifestation in this very spot…

The Chief Justice's voice snaps me into the very reality that rests before me: the Presidential Oath. His smile could not be more welcoming or sincere. In breaking tradition and in juxtaposition of the crowds chanting and cheering my name, I look into his eyes and ask him a simple question: 'Could my friends and family join me at this very spot?'

His face softens and his voice assumes a compassionate nature, "Of course, Mr. President… I mean… yes, yes of course sir."

A solitary motion beckons Bryan, Selena, my most treasured friends and family, Morena, and the First Lady to my side. They all stand firmly, each of their hands resting on my back as they intertwine their free hands with one another, and in that moment I know we are the team that will bring immense light to our nation.

From the corner of my eye, I see Morena and the First Lady wrap their fingers together, silently praying and beckoning the circle of angels to join us in spirit.

The Chief Justice recommends I follow his words, and of course I wistfully comply:

"I, Scott Zachariah Matheson…"
'I Scott Zachariah Matheson.'
"Do solemnly swear…"
'Do solemnly swear…'
"That I will faithfully execute…"
'That I will faithfully execute…'

I can feel the fingertips of my family and friends tenderly grasping my shoulders and back. Their love and affection can be felt in the hearts, minds, and souls of the spectators as well.

"The Office of the President of the United States…"
'The Office of the President of the United States…'

Cheers are beginning to erupt from the audience.

"And will to the best of my ability…."
'And will to the best of my ability…'
"Preserve"
'Preserve'

My wife's grip becomes more passionate.

"Protect"
'Protect'

Morena's hand presses onto my shoulder.

"And defend"
'And defend'

I can hear Bryan's blissful tears begin to cascade down his cheeks.

"The Constitution of the United States..."
'The Constitution of the United States...'
"I will, so help me God."

Silence fills the air. An overwhelming feeling that the circle of angels surrounds me flows with absolute certainty that this is the destiny I manifested decades ago. This is the dream. This is the beginning of a journey that traverses time. This is the key to unburdening so many souls caught in the delicate balance we so often lay dormant to.

'I will, so help me God.'
"By the power vested in me as the Chief Justice of the United States, I present to you, the 48th President of our great nation, President..."

A flood of memories rushes through my soul. My aunt's face appears before me in a sudden lapse in time. The words spoken by the Chief Justice fade as cheering commences.

"Scott Zachariah Matheson."

An eruption of bliss leaks into my mind. My aunt's pristine words, "I am proud of you," bleed through the crowd and shower me with love from up above.

Epilogue

The day blurs itself into the landscape upon us. The Washington monument stands as a stark contrast to everything going on around us. Confetti and pieces of paper twist and turn into my line of sight as The Lincoln Memorial stands firmly in the distance.

∞ ∞ ∞ ∞ ∞ ∞ ∞ ∞

As the night beckons us through the streets of Washington, D.C. and we find ourselves in the corridors of the White House, I finally reach an epiphany. It has taken me so long to get to D.C. because it just had to be the right moment. The right time. The manifestation of all of my experiences perching themselves atop a solid monument, and the clear skies reminding me that I am, indeed, the light that will guide the way for millions. It makes sense. It all makes sense: the trials, the triumphs, the days I wanted to crawl into a hole and never come out, the heartache, the pain. It was all to prepare me for a higher purpose.

Glaring into the painted eyes of President Abraham Lincoln that beckon from his portrait, I know what I have to do: carry the torch.

Morena appears beside me in the majestic, elusive way she usually does. She somehow managed to shed her business attire for an illustrious beige and black lace gown, which whips around the floor as she moves.

I rest my head on hers as she tilts towards me, "the circle is pleased with you Scott, I mean…" she collects her words hurriedly, "Mr. President."

I chuckle and she turns smiling right into my soul. "Wha," she says curiously.

'Hey, Morena, thank you,' I looked over at her and I could see small tears welling in her eyes.

"For what," she leads me out the door and down the hallway. We pass portraits of great men who served before me. Their eyes look gentle and reminiscent of their days in office. I, too, hope I can serve as a warm and gentle face for those who follow in my footsteps.

'For making me a better man,' we stop behind two large doors and embrace for a moment.

In her genuine hold, she whispers something inaudible into my chest. As she lifts her head up, she grins and seems to continue to speak: "Your dance partner is waiting for you."

We walk into the huge banquet area as the doors shut firmly behind us, almost reflective of the last chapter sealing itself deeply in our collective pasts.

Cheers erupt in the room. Bryan emerges with Selena in his arms, "Dad, dad, dad!" He releases Selena as Morena and her move about the dance floor. Selena's sequin dress glistens for miles around.

"Dad," Bryan rests his head on my shoulder, "I am beyond proud of the man you are."

Choking back tears, at my own inauguration ball nonetheless, I feel a flood of pride and honor. Here I stand, with my son in my arms, wistfully dancing into our future.

'And I am so proud of you Bryan,' I am beyond proud of him, and I hope he knows it deep within his soul.

"Pop, I knew you could do it," he says gleefully.

'I knew you would help me grow into who I am today.'

"You are my role model and you are my hero, I hope you know that."

'I know son, I know.'

"Dad," a fervent pause rests between us, "It did not take you becoming president to make me say that."

'I-' with tears streaming down my face, I mutter everything he truly means to me whittled down to four words: 'I love you, Bryan.'

"I love you too, dad."

Embracing him is the most natural feeling in the world. Seeing a room filled with those I love dearly is a breathtaking emotion.

As she walks up to me, I sense her poise and grace succumbing to my touch. I feel her body rocking slowly against mine. I feel every gentle kiss she planted on my heart. Her beautiful presence causes a cathartic wave of serenity and longing in my soul.

Bryan parts from my grasp and whispers in my ear, "Dad, I am glad she came back."

'Me too,' I give him a kiss on the cheek, 'Me too, son.'

"Care to dance, Mr. President?" She extends her hand.

Without a word fluttering into the air, I pull her into my chest. She fits to my soul like the connection of two cosmic puzzle pieces. The two of us whisk around the room in a flurry of cheers and well wishes. As we dance, I recall the fond days leading up to this very moment.

It is the faith within me that restored our bond. It was the will of the universe that drew us into one another. Such strong gravitational force could never keep two beautiful souls apart. We are infinite. We are the beacons of light. We are the existential glue that will spark the growth of every life we encounter.

We are the start of something universe shifting and earth-shattering. We…

In the midst of the monologue that rushes through my head, she gazes up at me: those eyes intertwining with my heightened soul.

I dip her sensuous body closer to the floor as I open us up to the heavens that guide us. Our center of gravity remains constant as floods of "oohs" and "ahs" fill the room. Applause rings out as she wraps her hands closer to my body.

A passionate kiss bursts from my lips as the attention in the room dissipates from our intimate moment.

Brushing her hair behind her ear, she whispers the words I long to hear each and every day: "Do you love me?"

'Always.'

Every soul is as beautiful as we feel, for each passing moment is a chance for us to heal…

∞

About the Author

~

Hal Eisenberg is the founder and CEO of Windows of Opportunity, Inc. – The Eisenberg Learning and Leadership Academy, a non-profit agency that is essentially a series of community outreach initiatives built for youth by youth. WOO partners with kids, teens, and young adults ages 6 through 24 to develop in-school and after school programs, workshops, conferences, and curriculums for themselves and their peers. These programs form partnerships with local school districts, universities, and community social service agencies. Windows of Opportunity's goal is to assist and empower our at-risk youth in designing, executing, and participating in positive leadership roles through social emotional learning initiatives, innovative programs, workshops, and curriculums that address all the compartments of their life, while building their self-esteem. With a strong knowledge in creating innovative programs for over 20 years, Hal has been credited with implementing and coordinating events, and raising over half a million dollars for various charities. He has also created programs for young people interested in developing their own self-expression through music, fashion, and film. Hal has authored several age-appropriate leadership curriculums that range from K-6, 7-12, and higher education platforms, with social emotional learning activities that provide students with an expansive understanding of our ever-changing society. He is extremely involved in community service projects, with a commitment to make a difference for all around him. He has recently coordinated youth leadership programs in Haiti, Nigeria, Guyana, Kenya, the UK, and Canada. Hal holds a Master's Degree in Social Work from Adelphi University and is a Licensed Master Social Worker in New York State. In 2021 Hal will complete his 2nd Master's Degree in School Leadership and will hold a licenses in School Building Leadership and School District Leadership. He is certified by the New York State Department of Education to provide violence prevention training to professionals under Project Save (Safe Schools Against Violence in Education) and was awarded both the Evelyn Pliego Social Work Student of the Year Award presented by the Borough of Queens President Claire Schulman, and a City Council Citation, awarded by Councilman Sheldon Leffler. Hal also earned training in Therapeutic Crisis Intervention for Schools (TCIS) designed by Cornell University. In 2018, he was awarded the NYCDOE School Social Worker of the Year Award for his tireless efforts in one of the largest school districts in the world. Hal is currently exploring doctorate programs in educational reform.

About Windows
of Opportunity

~

Windows of Opportunity, Inc. – The Eisenberg Learning and Leadership Academy, is a non-profit agency that is essentially a series of community outreach initiatives built for youth by youth. The organization shifts the current educational model from a disempowering system to one that includes leadership, empowerment training, and values identification, with a focus on increasing self-esteem. Windows of Opportunity, (WOO for short), uses media, entertainment, and education to inspire awareness, build excitement, and create partnerships that support our youth in being the leaders of today. WOO sources the power of youth to allow them to have a voice in understanding who they are, what they value, and how that translates into the world. WOO manifests classrooms that are free from harassment, violence, and bullying, and focuses on acceptance and diversity. The team at WOO is dedicated to revitalizing all aspects of education reform, and created an educational framework to match all of the strong core values promoted in the various optimization programs developed by Windows of Opportunity, Inc. - The Eisenberg Learning and Leadership Academy, and all of those who collaborate with the organization. Windows of Opportunity is currently collaborating extensively with The Passion Centre out of Toronto, Canada, on building the world's first and most comprehensive education system for raising 21st Century leaders and engineering a society that is going to support them. It is their combined vision that the world becomes one healthy community through higher consciousness education. In addition, this vision intends to promote healthy communication to encourage trust-based relationships that support acceptance of each other, reduce fear, and create an expressive, open society. This school of thought will lead people to connecting to and expanding their souls through a higher love consciousness, which helps people live their lives in an optimal manner, and will support others to do so as well. For more information contact Hal S. Eisenberg at Hal@wooinc.org today!

About The Passion Centre

~

The Passion Centre is a collective of amazing people finding and activating people's passions, building dreams, and creating optimized humans. The Passion Centre acts like a Passion Incubator; we help people from all walks and stages in life understand their PASSION and turn it into ACTION to move the world forward in a positive way. At The Passion Centre, we know that following your Passions and building your dreams aren't easy, but they are ENTIRELY worth every effort you put into it. What The Passion Centre has learned over the years of working with hundreds of people is that Passion is **NOT** an elusive abstract concept that is hard to understand, or one that is based on 'pie-in-the-sky' emotional luxury thinking. It is a very real component of whom we are, how we operate as humans, and if properly understood is a tool to help us live out our most optimal life. The Passion Centre has gathered research from areas in Neuroscience, Psychology, Design Thinking, Orientation and Navigation Training, to Business and more, to reveal the world's most comprehensive way of understanding peoples PASSIONS and identifying ways to put it to good use. The Passion Centre is fundamentally guided by the notion that people's passions are their most sacred value to the world around them. Our Passion to see a better world drives our inspiration and motivation to provide you with a unique opportunity to get the guidance you are looking for to move into the life you were made for. The Passion Centre's programs have been designed to help you answer two of life's most BURNING questions: ***What do I REALLY desire?*** AND ***Where should I be spending my time to get there?*** The Passion Centre has built the world's most comprehensive system that will teach you everything you need to know in order to find your passion and make decisions around stepping into your dream and bringing it to the world. You will learn from leading experts who have done exactly what you are thinking of doing, or thinking of thinking of doing, so that you can be given the best formula for success possible. The Passion Centre's proprietary methodology allows all participants to go from absolute confusion, to clarity in just a matter of weeks. And from that point of clarity we take them further into a structured system that step-by-step allows them to unveil the direction that is sure to create excitement! The Passion Centre's method has won the hearts of our clients who have taken our system and have created entirely new Passion Ventures. Passion Ventures are projects that align to their Passions and GIFTs. We have helped people start net new business ventures, foundations, not-for-profits, entirely new careers, post retirement passion projects, books such as the one you just read, and a host more! The Passion Centre caters to those of you who want to experience a live community to work alongside, those that would prefer to experience the program from the comfort of their own home via our webinar trainings, and those that prefer one on one coaching. No matter your goal, objective, or style of learning, The Passion Centre caters to you. As long as you have a deep desire to find that dream that you know is in your heart somewhere, we can take it from there! For more information contact Kira Day at kira.day@thepassioncentre.com today!

Jeslee Martinez — Illustrator bio

~

Throughout high school, Jeslee was the type of young woman who was genuine, sweet, considerate, and all-around kind. Though she was proficient in connecting to other students and school staff members about spirituality and wisdom beyond her years, Jeslee struggled when it came to her academics. Oftentimes, she would be seen drawing elaborate and intricate pieces of art in her notebooks or within a sketchpad. Jeslee was convinced that her hobby was just that, though I strongly recommended she continue to pursue her passion for drawing, painting, and just about anything artistic. At the Dream Out Loud leadership conference we held annually through the high school, Jeslee would single-handedly design and construct a mural and posters for the event. I empowered her and encouraged her to see that each and every single one of her designs were masterpieces of her soul, which solidified the idea that her remarkable talent was something that had to be admired by many. In creating *Beautiful Souls*, I knew that the only masterpiece I wanted representing the cover of my book would be one she designed and painted by hand. In bridging the story of *Beautiful Souls* to the universe, it was only natural that Jeslee's artwork becomes a bridge to the world's heart and soul.

Jeslee, I thank you from the bottom of my heart for the masterpiece you bestowed upon *Beautiful Souls*.